Advanced Intelligent Control in Robots

Advanced Intelligent Control in Robots

Editors

Luige Vladareanu
Hongnian Yu
Hongbo Wang
Yongfei Feng

MDPI • Basel • Beijing • Wuhan • Barcelona • Belgrade • Manchester • Tokyo • Cluj • Tianjin

Editors
Luige Vladareanu
Institute of Solid Mechanics of the Romanian Academy
Bucharest, Romania

Hongnian Yu
Edinburgh Napier University
Edinburgh, UK

Hongbo Wang
Fudan University
Shanghai, China

Yongfei Feng
Ningbo University
Ningbo, China

Editorial Office
MDPI
St. Alban-Anlage 66
4052 Basel, Switzerland

This is a reprint of articles from the Special Issue published online in the open access journal *Sensors* (ISSN 1424-8220) (available at: https://www.mdpi.com/journal/sensors/special_issues/Control_Robots).

For citation purposes, cite each article independently as indicated on the article page online and as indicated below:

LastName, A.A.; LastName, B.B.; LastName, C.C. Article Title. *Journal Name* **Year**, *Volume Number*, Page Range.

ISBN 978-3-0365-8148-4 (Hbk)
ISBN 978-3-0365-8149-1 (PDF)

Contents

About the Editors . . . . **vii**

Luige Vladareanu, Hongnian Yu, Hongbo Wang and Yongfei Feng
Advanced Intelligent Control in Robots
Reprinted from: *Sensors* **2023**, *23*, 5699, doi:10.3390/s23125699 . . . . **1**

Ching-Chang Wong, Chong-Jia Chen, Kai-Yi Wong and Hsuan-Ming Feng
Implementation of a Real-Time Object Pick-and-Place System Based on a Changing Strategy for Rapidly-Exploring Random Tree
Reprinted from: *Sensors* **2023**, *23*, 4814, doi:10.3390/s23104814 . . . . **7**

Bassant M. Elbagoury, Luige Vladareanu, Victor Vlădăreanu, Abdel Badeeh Salem, Ana-Maria Travediu and Mohamed Ismail Roushdy
A Hybrid Stacked CNN and Residual Feedback GMDH-LSTM Deep Learning Model for Stroke Prediction Applied on Mobile AI Smart Hospital Platform
Reprinted from: *Sensors* **2023**, *23*, 3500, doi:10.3390/s23073500 . . . . **25**

Mihai-Alin Stamate, Cristina Pupăză, Florin-Adrian Nicolescu and Cristian-Emil Moldoveanu
Improvement of Hexacopter UAVs Attitude Parameters Employing Control and Decision Support Systems
Reprinted from: *Sensors* **2023**, *23*, 1446, doi:10.3390/s23031446 . . . . **61**

Marian Marcel Abagiu, Dorian Cojocaru, Florin Manta and Alexandru Mariniuc
Detecting Machining Defects inside Engine Piston Chamber with Computer Vision and Machine Learning
Reprinted from: *Sensors* **2023**, *23*, 785, doi:10.3390/s23020785 . . . . **101**

Konrad Wojtowicz and Przemysław Wojciechowski
Synchronous Control of a Group of Flying Robots Following a Leader UAV in an Unfamiliar Environment
Reprinted from: *Sensors* **2023**, *23*, 740, doi:10.3390/s23020740 . . . . **117**

Marcello Chiurazzi, Joan Ortega Alcaide, Alessandro Diodato, Arianna Menciassi and Gastone Ciuti
Spherical Wrist Manipulator Local Planner for Redundant Tasks in Collaborative Environments
Reprinted from: *Sensors* **2023**, *23*, 677, doi:10.3390/s23020677 . . . . **135**

Di Wu, Zhi Yu, Alimasi Adili and Fanchen Zhao
A Self-Collision Detection Algorithm of a Dual-Manipulator System Based on GJK and Deep Learning
Reprinted from: *Sensors* **2023**, *23*, 523, doi:10.3390/s23010523 . . . . **151**

Meng Ning, Jun Yang, Ziqiang Zhang, Jun Li, Zhi Wang, Longxing Wei and et al.
Method of Changing Running Direction of Cheetah-Inspired Quadruped Robot
Reprinted from: *Sensors* **2022**, *22*, 9601, doi:10.3390/s22249601 . . . . **173**

Min Seop So, Gi Jeong Seo, Duck Bong Kim and Jong-Ho Shin
Prediction of Metal Additively Manufactured Surface Roughness Using Deep Neural Network
Reprinted from: *Sensors* **2022**, *22*, 7955, doi:10.3390/s22207955 . . . . **195**

Junjie Tian, Hongbo Wang, Siyuan Zheng, Yuansheng Ning, Xingchao Zhang, Jianye Niu and et al.
sEMG-Based Gain-Tuned Compliance Control for the Lower Limb Rehabilitation Robot during Passive Training
Reprinted from: *Sensors* **2022**, *22*, 7890, doi:10.3390/s22207890 . . . . **209**

Musong Lin, Hongbo Wang, Congliang Yang, Wenjie Liu, Jianye Niu and Luige Vladareanu
Human–Robot Cooperative Strength Training Based on Robust Admittance Control Strategy
Reprinted from: *Sensors* **2022**, *22*, 7746, doi:10.3390/s22207746 . . . . **229**

Taehyeon Kim, Myunghyun Kim, Sungwoo Yang and Donghan Kim
Navigation Path Based Universal Mobile Manipulator Integrated Controller (NUMMIC)
Reprinted from: *Sensors* **2022**, *22*, 7369, doi:10.3390/s22197369 . . . . **245**

Yongfei Feng, Mingwei Zhong and Fangyan Dong
Research on Monocular-Vision-Based Finger-Joint-Angle-Measurement System
Reprinted from: *Sensors* **2022**, *22*, 7276, doi:10.3390/s22197276 . . . . **269**

Qiongqiong Li, Yiqi Xu, Shengqiang Bu and Jiafu Yang
Smart Vehicle Path Planning Based on Modified PRM Algorithm
Reprinted from: *Sensors* **2022**, *22*, 6581, doi:10.3390/s22176581 . . . . **285**

Jun He, Yanlong Sun, Limin Yang and Feng Gao
Model Predictive Control of a Novel Wheeled–Legged Planetary Rover for Trajectory Tracking
Reprinted from: *Sensors* **2022**, *22*, 4164, doi:10.3390/s22114164 . . . . **299**

Ionel-Alexandru Gal, Alexandra-Cătălina Ciocîrlan and Luige Vlădăreanu
The Hybrid Position/Force Walking Robot Control Using Extenics Theory and Neutrosophic Logic Decision
Reprinted from: *Sensors* **2022**, *22*, 3663, doi:10.3390/s22103663 . . . . **321**

Maryam Munir, Qudrat Khan, Safeer Ullah, Tayyaba Maryam Syeda and Abdullah A. Algethami
Control Design for Uncertain Higher-Order Networked Nonlinear Systems via an Arbitrary Order Finite-Time Sliding Mode Control Law
Reprinted from: *Sensors* **2022**, *22*, 2748, doi:10.3390/s22072748 . . . . **349**

Nauman Qadeer, Jamal Hussain Shah, Muhammad Sharif, Muhammad Attique Khan, Ghulam Muhammad and Yu-Dong Zhang
Intelligent Tracking of Mechanically Thrown Objects by Industrial Catching Robot for Automated In-Plant Logistics 4.0
Reprinted from: *Sensors* **2022**, *22*, 2113, doi:10.3390/s22062113 . . . . **365**

Fawaz W. Alsaade, Qijia Yao, Mohammed S. Al-zahrani, Ali S. Alzahrani and Hadi Jahanshahi
Indirect-Neural-Approximation-Based Fault-Tolerant Integrated Attitude and Position Control of Spacecraft Proximity Operations
Reprinted from: *Sensors* **2022**, *22*, 1726, doi:10.3390/s22051726 . . . . **387**

Xinkai Zhang and Justin Bradley
Rethinking Sampled-Data Control for Unmanned Aircraft Systems
Reprinted from: *Sensors* **2022**, *22*, 1525, doi:10.3390/s22041525 . . . . **403**

Mingcong Deng, Shotaro Kubota and Yuanhong Xu
Nonlinear Intelligent Control of Two Link Robot Arm by Considering Human Voluntary Components
Reprinted from: *Sensors* **2022**, *22*, 1424, doi:10.3390/s22041424 . . . . **421**

About the Editors

Vladareanu Luige

Vladareanu Luige is the Coordinator of the Robotics and Mechatronics Department of the Institute of Solid Mechanics, Romanian Academy, and Director of the Technologic Transfer Center on Robotics and Advanced Technologies (ROBTA). His scientific work is focused on real-time control in solid mechanics, AI in robotics, multi-microprocessor systems, semi-active control of magnetorheological dissipater systems, complex industrial automation in distributed and decentralized structures, etc. He has published over 50 books and book chapters, 30 edited books, and over 300 papers in journals, proceedings, and conferences in these areas. He is the author of the virtual projection method known as the Vladareanu–Munteanu method, and the robot neutrosophic control (RNC) method known as the Vladareanu–Smarandache method. He is the winner of two awards, has achieved gold medals for Excellence in Research, SIR 2000, from the Romanian Government, and has received over twenty awards from the World Exhibition of Inventions from Geneva, Brussels, Barcelona, etc. He received the "TraianVuia" Award from the Romanian Academy, Romania's highest scientific research forum. He is a Corresponding Member of the American Romanian Academy and a member of the International Institute of Acoustics and Vibration (IIAV), Auburn University, USA, and is on ABI's Research Board of Advisors, American Biographical Institute etc. He is a PhD advisor in the field of mechanical engineering and robotics at the Romanian Academy. He has served as the organizer of numerous international conferences, is the General Chair of Congress, CANWEST, 2023, Madrid, and of four WSEAS International Conferences, and gives Chair and Plenary lectures at Houston, Harvard, Boston, Penang, Malaysia, Paris, Florence, etc.

Hongnian Yu

Hongnian Yu is a Professor in the School of Computing, Engineering and the Built Environment, Edinburgh Napier University. His research covers two main areas: 1) robotics with applications in rescue and recovery operations and healthcare and 2) ICT-enabled healthcare including assistive technologies in supporting the elderly and people with dementia, and activity recognition of elderly people. He has published over 200 journal and conference research papers. He is a member of the Engineering and Physical Sciences Research Council Peer Review College, Fellow of the Institution of Engineering and Technology and Fellow of the Royal Society of Arts.

Hongbo Wang

Hongbo Wang is a professor and doctoral supervisor at Fudan University, an expert on the Expert Committee on Transformation of Scientific and Technological Achievements of the China Association of Industry–University–Research Cooperation, the Chairman of the Hebei Robotics Industry Innovation Alliance, and a member of the Standing Committee of the Rehabilitation Engineering and Industrialization Promotion of the Chinese Society of Rehabilitation Medicine. He received his BS and MS degrees from the Institute of Northeast Heavy Machinery, Qiqihar, China, in 1982 and 1986. He received his PhD from Nagasaki University, Nagasaki, Japan 1997. He studied as a Visiting Scholar at the Institute of Robotics of the Swiss Federal Institute of Technology (ETH Zuerich), Switzerland, and at Nagasaki University as a researcher. From 1998, he worked at DAIHEN Corporation as a Deputy Manager, Osaka, Japan. From 2009, he worked at Yanshan University, Qinhuangdao, China, as a Professor. Since 2021, he has worked as a Professor at Fudan University, Shanghai, China. He has been involved in rehabilitation and nursing robotics research for more than 30 years. He has published more than 150 papers in international and national journals and has presented them at international academic conferences. He has been granted more than 60 national invention patents as the first inventor. He has presided over and undertaken 13 national projects and 10 provincial and ministerial projects. He has won two first-class awards from the Ministry of Education, one second-class award and one third-class award from Hebei Province, China, the Industry–University–Research Cooperation Innovation Award (Individual), the China Productivity Award (Service Elite), one gold award, and two other awards from the Geneva International Invention Exhibition. His current research interests are surgery robots, rehabilitation robots, and assistance robots for the disabled and the elderly.

Yongfei Feng

Yongfei Feng is currently an Associate Professor and Graduate Supervisor at Ningbo University, as well as a member of the Special Committee for Rehabilitation Engineering in Ningbo. He received his Ph.D. degree in Mechanical Engineering from Yanshan University, Qinhuangdao, China, in 2018. From 2016 to 2017, he was part of a joint Ph.D. program at the Institute of Solid Mechanics within the Romanian Academy of Sciences. He has served as the Principal Investigator for projects funded by the Zhejiang Provincial Natural Science Foundation, the Zhejiang Provincial Education Department Research Program, the Ningbo Municipal Natural Science Foundation, and the Ningbo Municipal Major Science and Technology Project (as a Sub-Project Lead). In addition, he has contributed to three national- and provincial-level projects, including the National International Cooperation Special Project and the European Union Seventh Framework Program. He has published over 20 technical papers in peer-reviewed journals and prestigious conference proceedings. He has also filed over 20 invention patents, with 15 of them being granted. As a mentor, he has guided students to achieve multiple national-level discipline competition awards. His honors include the 2017 Mechanical Industry Outstanding Scientific and Technological Achievement Project Award, the 2015 Geneva International Invention Exhibition Gold Award, and the Chinese Delegation Honor Award. His research interests include mechanical and control engineering theory, with applications in nursing robots, rehabilitation robots, and industrial robots.

sensors

Editorial

Advanced Intelligent Control in Robots

Luige Vladareanu [1,*], Hongnian Yu [2], Hongbo Wang [3] and Yongfei Feng [4]

1 Institute of Solid Mechanics of the Romanian Academy, 010141 Bucharest, Romania
2 The School of Computing, Engineering and the Built Environment, Edinburgh Napier University, Edinburgh EH11 4BN, UK; h.yu@napier.ac.uk
3 Academy for Engineering and Technology, Fudan University, Shanghai 200433, China; wanghongbo@fudan.edu.cn
4 Faculty of Mechanical Engineering & Mechanics, Ningbo University, Ningbo 315211, China; fengyongfei@nbu.edu.cn
* Correspondence: luige.vladareanu@vipro.edu.ro

Citation: Vladareanu, L.; Yu, H.; Wang, H.; Feng, Y. Advanced Intelligent Control in Robots. *Sensors* **2023**, *23*, 5699. https://doi.org/10.3390/s23125699

Received: 24 May 2023
Accepted: 13 June 2023
Published: 19 June 2023

1. Introduction

Advanced intelligent control (AIC) is a rapidly evolving and complex field that poses significant challenges. It is a practically important field and has potential applications. In this context, this Special Issue aims to foster advancements in science and technology by addressing the theoretical and practical aspects of intelligent control techniques and their applications using advanced intelligent control in robots. The main purpose of this Special Issue is to gather in-depth research and explore new trends in the design, control and applications of the real-time control of intelligent sensor systems. These trends include the use of advanced intelligent control methods and techniques, as well as the integration of innovative multi-sensor fusion techniques into robots. These advancements are combined with various technologies such as computer vision; virtual and augmented reality (VR&AR); and intelligent communication including remote control, adaptive sensor networks, human–robot (H2R) interaction systems and machine-to-machine (M2M) interfaces.

This Special Issue highlights intelligent decision support systems (IDSS), including remote sensing and its integration with DSS, GA-based DSS, fuzzy set DSS, rough set-based DSS, intelligent-agent-assisted DSS, process mining integration in decision support, adaptive DSS; computer-vision-based DSS and sensory and robotic DSS in AIC in robots. This Special Issue is an extension of the previously published successful Special Issue entitled "Advanced Intelligent Control" and the book entitled "AIC through VIPRO Platforms".

Special attention is paid to the utilization of new and emerging technologies with AIC that apply complex robotic systems, such as enhanced IoT technologies and applications in the 5G densification era; bio-inspired techniques for future manufacturing enterprise control; a cyber-physical systems approach to the cognitive enterprise; the development of the IT Industry 4.0 concept; industrial systems in the digital age; cloud computing; robotics; and automation. This Special Issue addresses applications such as human aid mechatronics, military applications, rescue robots, firefighting robots, rehabilitation robots, robot-assisted surgery, and domestic robots.

2. Review of the Contributions in This Special Issue

AIC in robots is an interdisciplinary field which combines and extends theories and methods from control theory, computer science, and operations research areas with the aim of developing controllers which are highly adaptable to significant unanticipated changes. In line with this goal, in this Special Issue, 21 papers have been carefully selected through a rigorous review process.

The first paper, entitled "Nonlinear Intelligent Control of Two Link Robot Arm by Considering Human Voluntary Components" [1], investigates a nonlinear intelligent control system of a two-link robot arm by considering the human voluntary components and the feed-forward characteristics of a human multi-joint arm. The proposed feedback controller uses the multi-joint viscoelasticity of the human arm, while the feed-forward controller is based on a support vector machine (SVR), and the stabilization controller is based on operator theory. The viscoelastic properties of the multi-joint arm are measured and analyzed through experiments. To reduce the influence and uncertainty caused by interference inside the controlled object, the control system is designed based on the operator theory. The experimental results of using a feed-forward controller based on a mechanical model are compared with those using a feed-forward controller based on an SVR.

"Rethinking Sampled-Data Control for Unmanned Aircraft Systems" [2] explores the recent advancements and challenges at the intersection of real-time computing and control and develops innovative reconsidered sampling strategies that can improve performance and resource utilization. The proposed design framework can efficiently integrate the computational and physical characteristics of the system, increase robust performance and avoid the pitfalls of event-triggered sampling strategies. The paper focuses on comparing the control performance of a multicopter Unmanned Aircraft System (UAS) using different sampling strategies varying in terms of the "co-design" of computing resources (sampling rate) and the holistic system performance. The unique benefits of the proposed co-regulation strategy on control performance, computational efficiency and system robustness in comparison to the traditional fixed-periodic, event-triggered and self-triggered controllers are highlighted. A co-regulation strategy is implemented to provide insight into how to design co-regulated systems for control engineers. The pitfalls of event-triggered and self-triggered sampling strategies on UASs are discussed. Quantitative evaluations of all of these strategies are conducted based on evaluation metrics that could reflect both control performance and computing costs.

"Indirect-Neural-Approximation-Based Fault-Tolerant Integrated Attitude and Position Control of Spacecraft Proximity Operations" [3] investigates Fault-Tolerant Integrated Attitude and Position Control of Spacecraft Proximity Operations in the presence of unknown parameters, disturbances and actuator faults. The authors propose a controller which combines a relative attitude control law and a relative position control law, which are designed by adopting neural networks (NNs) to approximate the upper bound of the lumped unknowns. The indirect neural approximation is used to approximate the upper bound of the lumped unknowns. A simulation study on a 6-DOF spacecraft is conducted, and the results indicate that the proposed neural adaptive fault-tolerant controller can achieve superior performance and good uncertainty rejection capability, which guarantees the successful implementation of the spacecraft proximity operation.

"Intelligent Tracking of Mechanically Thrown Objects by Industrial Catching Robot for Automated In-Plant Logistics 4.0" [4] aims to accelerate the transportation process and increase productivity through the optimized utilization of in-plant facilities. The authors develop a 3D simulated environment which enables users to throw objects with any mass, diameter or surface air friction properties in a controlled internal logistics environment. To observe trajectories more accurately, they create an enormous dataset of thrown object trajectories to train an encoder–decoder bidirectional Long Short-Term Memory network (LSTM) deep NN using multi-view geometry among simulated cameras. This research contributes an enhanced intelligent tracking algorithm that can predict the remaining 3D interception positions of a thrown object by observing its initial flight trajectory. To demonstrate the proposed method, the training and testing results obtained via the encoder–decoder bidirectional LSTM deep NN, trained through 1000/3000 throws with 50/100/300 epochs and 100/200 neurons, are analyzed.

"Control Design for Uncertain Higher-Order Networked Nonlinear Systems via an Arbitrary Order Finite-Time Sliding Mode Control Law" [5] proposes a novel Sliding Mode Control Law by considering uncertainties including parametric variations and matched bounded disturbances. The topology of the system network of one leader and four followers sharing information under the action of the distributed control protocols is illustrated. The consensuses in the positions, velocities and accelerations among the followers and leader are displayed, with the corresponding convergences of position errors, velocities error and acceleration errors. The simulation results confirm that the newly designed law is an interesting candidate for higher-order uncertain systems.

"The Hybrid Position/Force Walking Robot Control Using Extenics Theory and Neutrosophic Logic Decision" [6] investigates Hybrid Position/Force Walking Robot Control by applying the method to a hexapod walking robot. The authors apply the Extenics theory and Extension set to obtain clear separation of the properties and specific characteristics of the control methods required by the hexapod robot. The result is then used with Neutrosophic logic and DSmT (Dezert Smarandache Theory) to create a decision algorithm between kinematic and dynamic regulators for each leg of the hexapod robot during its walking phases. A control probability graph and equations are used to create the decision algorithm. A Matlab Simulink simulation study is conducted to demonstrate the proposed hybrid control algorithm.

"Model Predictive Control of a Novel Wheeled–Legged Planetary Rover for Trajectory Tracking" [7] develops an innovative Wheeled–Legged Planetary Rover for Trajectory Tracking, and a hybrid serial–parallel topology is utilized to realize a rigid–flexible coupling mechanism. The control strategy for the wheeled–legged rover includes a trajectory tracking module based on model predictive control, the steering strategy and the wheel speed allocation algorithm. A cosimulation model is established in both NX/Motion and Simulink software to verify the control strategy.

Smart Vehicle Path Planning Based on Modified PRM Algorithm [8] proposes a pseudo-random sampling strategy with the main spatial axis as the reference axis, optimizing the generation of sampling points, removing redundant sampling points, setting the distance threshold between road points, adopting a two-way incremental method for collision detections and optimizing the number of collision detection calls to improve the construction efficiency of the roadmap. The proposed PRM is verified and analyzed using a ROS-based test platform. Compared with the basic PRM algorithm, the modified PRM algorithm has advantages in terms of the speed with which the roadmap is constructed, path planning and path length.

"Human–Robot Cooperative Strength Training Based on Robust Admittance Control Strategy" [9] designs a stiffness adjusting law of the admittance model based on the biomechanics of knee joints. The designed control law can guide the user to use force correctly and reduce the stress on the joint soft tissue. It not only avoids excessive compressive force on the joint soft tissue, but also enhances the stimulation of quadriceps femoris muscles. A novel sitting and lying lower limb rehabilitation robot (LLR-II) is developed. To verify the function, feasibility and effectiveness of the proposed lower limb flexion and extension strength training, eight stroke survivors were selected to participate in the test experiment using the LLR-II robot. The experiment results show that the designed controller can effectively reduce the possibility of joint soft tissue injury and enhance the stimulation of the quadriceps, and this active training method is effective for exercising the quadriceps.

"sEMG-Based Gain-Tuned Compliance Control for the Lower Limb Rehabilitation Robot during Passive Training" [10] develops a surface-electromyography-based gain-tuned compliance control (EGCC) strategy for a lower limb rehabilitation robot based on the mapping function relationship between the normalized surface electromyography (sEMG) signal and the gain parameter. The experimental results demonstrate that the adoption of the EGCC strategy could significantly enhance the compliance of the robot end-effector by detecting the sEMG signal and improving the safety of the robot in different training modes. This indicates that the EGCC strategy has good application prospects in the rehabilitation robot field.

"Research on Monocular-Vision-Based Finger-Joint-Angle-Measurement" [11] considers an industrial monocular-vision-based knuckle-joint-activity-measurement system, with a short measurement time and the simultaneous measurement of multiple joints, applied to an existing computer-vision detection system. An Experimental Platform is designed to acquire high-quality multi-angle light-source-irradiated multivariate images. Through the PC image-processing algorithm, the images can be processed to segment finger-joint identifiers for the subsequent calculation of the finger-joint angle and length. Nine healthy male volunteers were recruited for the experiment, and three different finger-joint angles were detected using TS–HOMLDM to verify the monocular-vision-based finger-joint-angle measurement system. The experimental results show that the average angular deviation in the flexion/extension of the knuckle is a minimum of 0.43° and a maximum of 0.59°, and the average angular deviation in the adduction/abduction of the knuckle is a minimum of 0.30° and a maximum of 0.81°, which are all less than 1°.

"Navigation Path Based Universal Mobile Manipulator Integrated Controller" [12] proposes a versatile integrated controller which is able to execute motion planning in a stable manner in various environments with simultaneous control, leading to great benefits with regard to the execution time compared to the traditional sequential control method. To validate the proposed method, an experiment for motion planning towards the given target coordinates using the mobile manipulator robot in a simulation environment is conducted.

"Prediction of Metal Additively Manufactured Surface Roughness Using Deep Neural Network" [13] considers robotized product manufacturing technology by introducing 3D printing into the manufacturing process based on a prediction of Metal Additively Manufactured Surface Roughness using a deep neural network (DNN). It proposes a methodology to improve the quality of AM products based on data analysis through various analysis methods such as data pre-processing and DNN combined with sensor data used to predict surface roughness in the proposed methodology. The usefulness and feasibility of the proposed methodology are proved by the experimental data collected from the gas metal arc welding (GMAW)-WAAM system applied to a robotized product manufacturing technology.

"Method of Changing Running Direction of Cheetah-Inspired Quadruped Robot" [14] establishes a dynamic model of a quadruped robot and a two-level stability index system, including a minimum index system and a range index system. A two-level stability index system, including a minimum index and range index, is developed based on the dynamic model of the robot, and the optimization variables, including leg landing points, trunk movement trajectory and posture change rule, are determined.

"A Self-Collision Detection Algorithm of a Dual-Manipulator System Based on GJK and Deep Learning" [15] introduces AI technology into a control system based on the Gilbert–Johnson–Keerthi (GJK) algorithm. A dataset and trained deep neural network (DLNet) are generated to improve the detection efficiency. By combining DLNet and the GJK algorithm, a two-level self-collision detection algorithm (DLGJK) is developed to solve real-time self-collision detection problems in a dual-manipulator system with fast-continuous and high-precision properties. The experimental results show that compared to that with the global use of the GJK, the DLGJK significantly increases the detection efficiency in both single detection and working-path detection.

"Spherical Wrist Manipulator Local Planner for Redundant Tasks in Collaborative Environments" [16] proposes a path planner for manipulators to execute tasks with a redundant number of joints executing redundant tasks in workspaces shared with dynamic obstacles such as humans. An intuitive parameterization of the end-effector (EE) angular motion, which decouples the rotation of the third joint of the wrist from the rest of the angular motions, is presented. The path planner is developed by considering that the rotation of the third wrist joint must be decoupled from the rest of the EE angular motion, the resulting EE manipulator dynamics should behave as a linear dynamical system, the collision avoidance strategy must consider the entire surface of the manipulator and all the local planner parameters must have a physical meaning. The approach enables industrial and medical applications, in which robot stiffness and dexterity can greatly improve task efficiency.

"Detecting Machining Defects inside Engine Piston Chamber with Computer Vision and Machine Learning" [17] develops robotic industrial applications for automotive manufacturing with the main goal of replacing the visual inspection performed by a human operator with a computer vision application. A machine leaning algorithm which has conventional processing and a prediction method that uses a machine learning model is established. The results demonstrate that the robustness of image processing applications from the field of manufacturing can be considerably improved by replacing the classic method with the machine learning algorithm, which ensures greater flexibility in developing the backbone of the application, mainly consisting of PLC communication, socket services and a human–machine interface.

"Synchronous Control of a Group of Flying Robots Following a Leader UAV in an Unfamiliar Environment" [18] investigates a quadrotor drone group which follows an automatically flying leader with drones equipped with low-end cameras. This provides a considerable number of resources necessary to help people trapped in dangerous environments without risking the health or lives of rescuers. The main innovation is the structure of the multi-agent group of UAVs, with inexpensive followers without data exchange between actors and computational power requirements. The obtained results suggest that the organization of such tasks in an automatic system is realistic and, most importantly, effective.

"Improvement of Hexacopter UAVs Attitude Parameters Employing Control and Decision Support Systems" [19] conducts tests on Hexacopter Unmanned Aerial Vehicles to verify their operational parameters, hover flight, drone stability and reliability, including the aerodynamics and robustness at different wind speeds. The flight parameters extracted from the sensor systems, comprising accelerometers, gyroscopes, magnetometers, barometers, GPS antenna and EO/IR cameras, are analyzed. An innovative hexacopter platform architecture in two variants, equipped with avionic components and sensors, is developed. The results of the tests carried out both in the laboratory and in situ during the start–stop maneuvers of the hexacopter engines are described and discussed.

"A Hybrid Stacked CNN and Residual Feedback GMDH-LSTM Deep Learning Model for Stroke Prediction Applied on Mobile AI Smart Hospital Platform" [20] develops a stroke prediction model by combining AI techniques with the existing Internet of Medical Things (IoMT) on a Mobile AI Smart Hospital Platform to improve the quality of medical care that patients receive remotely at home. A mobile AI engine that implements AI-based cloud computing complexities, especially in real-time environments of AI technologies, is presented. A Hybrid LSTM with a Dense-Layer Deep Learning Model for Stroke Prediction is proposed. The algorithm is lightweight for the proposed mobile AI engine and facilitates continuous diagnostics and accurate GMDH–LSTM-based EEG signal prediction for IoMT-simulated inputs. The innovative AI mHealth app achieves high accuracy determined by a stacked CNN which reaches 98% for stroke diagnosis. The GMDH neural network proves to be a good technique for monitoring EMG signals, with an average accuracy of 98.60% and an average of 96.68% for signal prediction, and by extending the GMDH model and a hybrid LSTM with a dense-layer deep learning model, the accuracy can reach an average of 99%.

"Implementation of a Real-Time Object Pick-and-Place System Based on a Changing Strategy for Rapidly-Exploring Random Tree" [21] implements a six-degree-of-freedom (DOF) robot with an external camera and a two-finger gripper through an ROS-based real-time Pick-and-Place System and an improved Rapidly Exploring Random Tree (RRT) algorithm, named the Changing Strategy RRT (CS-RRT) algorithm. By implementing the proposed CS-RRT algorithm in the Open Motion Planning Library and according to the imported URDF file, MoveIt can perform motion planning for different robot manipulators; thus, the proposed method can be easily applied to other six-degree-of-freedom (DOF) robots using the ROS-based real-time Pick-and-Place System.

Acknowledgments: The authors gratefully acknowledge the support of the Romanian Academy, the Robotics and Mechatronics Department, Institute of Solid Mechanics of the Romanian Academy, RO, the Edinburgh Napier University, the School of Computing, Engineering and the Built Environment, UK, the Fudan University, the Academy for Engineering and Technology, Shanghai, China and the Ningbo University, the Faculty of Mechanical Engineering & Mechanics, China.

Conflicts of Interest: The authors declare no conflict of interest.

References

1. Deng, M.; Kubota, S.; Xu, Y. Nonlinear Intelligent Control of Two Link Robot Arm by Considering Human Voluntary Components. *Sensors* **2022**, *22*, 1424. [CrossRef] [PubMed]
2. Zhang, X.; Bradley, J. Rethinking Sampled-Data Control for Unmanned Aircraft Systems. *Sensors* **2022**, *22*, 1525. [CrossRef]
3. Alsaade, F.W.; Yao, Q.; Al-zahrani, M.S.; Alzahrani, A.S.; Jahanshahi, H. Indirect-Neural-Approximation-Based Fault-Tolerant Integrated Attitude and Position Control of Spacecraft Proximity Operations. *Sensors* **2022**, *22*, 1726. [CrossRef] [PubMed]
4. Qadeer, N.; Shah, J.H.; Sharif, M.; Khan, M.A.; Muhammad, G.; Zhang, Y.-D. Intelligent Tracking of Mechanically Thrown Objects by Industrial Catching Robot for Automated In-Plant Logistics 4.0. *Sensors* **2022**, *22*, 2113. [CrossRef]
5. Munir, M.; Khan, Q.; Ullah, S.; Syeda, T.M.; Algethami, A.A. Control Design for Uncertain Higher-Order Networked Nonlinear Systems via an Arbitrary Order Finite-Time Sliding Mode Control Law. *Sensors* **2022**, *22*, 2748. [CrossRef] [PubMed]
6. Gal, I.-A.; Ciocîrlan, A.-C.; Vlădăreanu, L. The Hybrid Position/Force Walking Robot Control Using Extenics Theory and Neutrosophic Logic Decision. *Sensors* **2022**, *22*, 3663. [CrossRef] [PubMed]
7. He, J.; Sun, Y.; Yang, L.; Gao, F. Model Predictive Control of a Novel Wheeled–Legged Planetary Rover for Trajectory Tracking. *Sensors* **2022**, *22*, 4164. [CrossRef]
8. Li, Q.; Xu, Y.; Bu, S.; Yang, J. Smart Vehicle Path Planning Based on Modified PRM Algorithm. *Sensors* **2022**, *22*, 6581. [CrossRef]
9. Lin, M.; Wang, H.; Yang, C.; Liu, W.; Niu, J.; Vladareanu, L. Human–Robot Cooperative Strength Training Based on Robust Admittance Control Strategy. *Sensors* **2022**, *22*, 7746. [CrossRef]
10. Tian, J.; Wang, H.; Zheng, S.; Ning, Y.; Zhang, X.; Niu, J.; Vladareanu, L. sEMG-Based Gain-Tuned Compliance Control for the Lower Limb Rehabilitation Robot during Passive Training. *Sensors* **2022**, *22*, 7890. [CrossRef]
11. Feng, Y.; Zhong, M.; Dong, F. Research on Monocular-Vision-Based Finger-Joint-Angle-Measurement System. *Sensors* **2022**, *22*, 7276. [CrossRef] [PubMed]
12. Kim, T.; Kim, M.; Yang, S.; Kim, D. Navigation Path Based Universal Mobile Manipulator Integrated Controller (NUMMIC). *Sensors* **2022**, *22*, 7369. [CrossRef] [PubMed]
13. So, M.S.; Seo, G.J.; Kim, D.B.; Shin, J.-H. Prediction of Metal Additively Manufactured Surface Roughness Using Deep Neural Network. *Sensors* **2022**, *22*, 7955. [CrossRef]
14. Ning, M.; Yang, J.; Zhang, Z.; Li, J.; Wang, Z.; Wei, L.; Feng, P. Method of Changing Running Direction of Cheetah-Inspired Quadruped Robot. *Sensors* **2022**, *22*, 9601. [CrossRef] [PubMed]
15. Wu, D.; Yu, Z.; Adili, A.; Zhao, F. A Self-Collision Detection Algorithm of a Dual-Manipulator System Based on GJK and Deep Learning. *Sensors* **2023**, *23*, 523. [CrossRef]
16. Chiurazzi, M.; Alcaide, J.O.; Diodato, A.; Menciassi, A.; Ciuti, G. Spherical Wrist Manipulator Local Planner for Redundant Tasks in Collaborative Environments. *Sensors* **2023**, *23*, 677. [CrossRef]
17. Abagiu, M.M.; Cojocaru, D.; Manta, F.; Mariniuc, A. Detecting Machining Defects inside Engine Piston Chamber with Computer Vision and Machine Learning. *Sensors* **2023**, *23*, 785. [CrossRef]
18. Wojtowicz, K.; Wojciechowski, P. Synchronous Control of a Group of Flying Robots Following a Leader UAV in an Unfamiliar Environment. *Sensors* **2023**, *23*, 740. [CrossRef]
19. Stamate, M.-A.; Pupăză, C.; Nicolescu, F.-A.; Moldoveanu, C.-E. Improvement of Hexacopter UAVs Attitude Parameters Employing Control and Decision Support Systems. *Sensors* **2023**, *23*, 1446. [CrossRef]
20. Elbagoury, B.M.; Vladareanu, L.; Vlădăreanu, V.; Salem, A.B.; Travediu, A.-M.; Roushdy, M.I. A Hybrid Stacked CNN and Residual Feedback GMDH-LSTM Deep Learning Model for Stroke Prediction Applied on Mobile AI Smart Hospital Platform. *Sensors* **2023**, *23*, 3500. [CrossRef]
21. Wong, C.-C.; Chen, C.-J.; Wong, K.-Y.; Feng, H.-M. Implementation of a Real-Time Object Pick-and-Place System Based on a Changing Strategy for Rapidly-Exploring Random Tree. *Sensors* **2023**, *23*, 4814. [CrossRef]

sensors

MDPI

Article

Implementation of a Real-Time Object Pick-and-Place System Based on a Changing Strategy for Rapidly-Exploring Random Tree

Ching-Chang Wong [1], Chong-Jia Chen [1], Kai-Yi Wong [2,*] and Hsuan-Ming Feng [3]

[1] Department of Electrical and Computer Engineering, Tamkang University, New Taipei City 25137, Taiwan; wong@ee.tku.edu.tw (C.-C.W.)
[2] Department of Electrical Engineering, Chung Yuan Christian University, Taoyuan City 32023, Taiwan
[3] Department of Computer Science and Information Engineering, National Quemoy University, Kinmen County 892, Taiwan; hmfeng@nqu.edu.tw
* Correspondence: kywong@cycu.edu.tw

Abstract: An object pick-and-place system with a camera, a six-degree-of-freedom (DOF) robot manipulator, and a two-finger gripper is implemented based on the robot operating system (ROS) in this paper. A collision-free path planning method is one of the most fundamental problems that has to be solved before the robot manipulator can autonomously pick-and-place objects in complex environments. In the implementation of the real-time pick-and-place system, the success rate and computing time of path planning by a six-DOF robot manipulator are two essential key factors. Therefore, an improved rapidly-exploring random tree (RRT) algorithm, named changing strategy RRT (CS-RRT), is proposed. Based on the method of gradually changing the sampling area based on RRT (CSA-RRT), two mechanisms are used in the proposed CS-RRT to improve the success rate and computing time. The proposed CS-RRT algorithm adopts a sampling-radius limitation mechanism, which enables the random tree to approach the goal area more efficiently each time the environment is explored. It can avoid spending a lot of time looking for valid points when it is close to the goal point, thus reducing the computing time of the improved RRT algorithm. In addition, the CS-RRT algorithm adopts a node counting mechanism, which enables the algorithm to switch to an appropriate sampling method in complex environments. It can avoid the search path being trapped in some constrained areas due to excessive exploration in the direction of the goal point, thus improving the adaptability of the proposed algorithm to various environments and increasing the success rate. Finally, an environment with four object pick-and-place tasks is established, and four simulation results are given to illustrate that the proposed CS-RRT-based collision-free path planning method has the best performance compared with the other two RRT algorithms. A practical experiment is also provided to verify that the robot manipulator can indeed complete the specified four object pick-and-place tasks successfully and effectively.

Keywords: rapidly-exploring random tree (RRT); path planning; robot manipulator; object pick-and-place; collision-free; robot operating system (ROS)

Citation: Wong, C.-C.; Chen, C.-J.; Wong, K.-Y.; Feng, H.-M. Implementation of a Real-Time Object Pick-and-Place System Based on a Changing Strategy for Rapidly-Exploring Random Tree. *Sensors* **2023**, *23*, 4814. https://doi.org/10.3390/s23104814

Academic Editors: Luige Vladareanu, Hongnian Yu, Hongbo Wang and Yongfei Feng

Received: 1 March 2023
Revised: 3 May 2023
Accepted: 12 May 2023
Published: 16 May 2023

1. Introduction

Due to the presence of various objects in the working environment, path planning for robots is one of the most important topics in robotics research and is widely discussed [1–4]. If the robot does not have a good path planning method to choose a collision-free path, various collision situations may occur. Once a collision occurs, unpredictable or large losses may be caused. Therefore, many researchers devote themselves to the field of collision-free path planning. Based on differential search methods, path planning algorithms are divided into three categories: search-based, heuristic-based, and sampling-based. The A* algorithm proposed by Hart et al. is a search-based path planning algorithm [5]. It first models the environment and then determines objective node information to avoid ineffective exploration of the environment and find a better solution efficiently. However, when exploring high-dimensional spaces or wide environments, the computing time of the A* algorithm increases significantly. The ant colony system proposed by Dorigo et al. is a heuristic-based path planning algorithm [6]. It finds a better solution through a function, iteration by iteration, in each exploration of the environment. However, the convergence speed of the heuristic-based algorithm cannot be guaranteed. Due to the long computing times of search-based and heuristic-based path planning algorithms, they are not suitable for real-time system applications. The probabilistic roadmap algorithm proposed by Kavraki et al. is a sampling-based path planning algorithm [7]. The advantage of the sampling-based algorithm is that it reduces the burden of modeling the environment by using sampling points to scatter the entire space into a partial area of the environment. This makes it easy to represent all the features of the environment. It can handle the path planning of robots in high-dimensional spaces. However, the search efficiency and success rate of the probabilistic roadmap will decrease when there are dense obstacles in space. The rapidly-exploring random tree (RRT) proposed by LaValle is also a sampling-based path planning algorithm [8]. It combines the advantages of sampling and searching abilities in the environment. Random trees will randomly expand new nodes in the environment. This algorithm not only inherits the advantages of the fast search speed of the probabilistic roadmap algorithm but can also perform a wide range of exploration in the environment, which is more powerful to deal with the online path planning of high-dimensional spaces.

Although the basic RRT algorithm can find a better path in the search space relatively quickly, it still has some problems that need to be improved, such as spending a lot of time exploring some invalid areas. Therefore, there have been many studies aimed at improving the basic RRT algorithm. For example, Wang et al. proposed an RRT algorithm based on a node control mechanism [9]. Based on this mechanism, the node expansion of the random tree is constrained by defined conditions, which reduces the generation of invalid nodes and thus finds a better solution more efficiently than most RRT algorithms, especially in narrow areas of the search space. Kang et al. proposed an RRT algorithm based on a goal-oriented mechanism [10]. It improves the search efficiency by increasing the sampling probability of the search point that is near the target. In addition, the sampling strategy is appropriately switched through the node counting mechanism to adapt to the complex environment. In addition, sometimes the RRT algorithm will overfocus on the goal area, which makes it difficult to find a path when encountering a complex environment. On the other hand, if the algorithm only focuses on improving its adaptability, it will not be fast enough to find a path to the goal in simple environments. Therefore, there are still many ways to improve the path planning for robot applications. In order to improve the computing time and environmental adaptability of the existing RRT algorithm, an improved RRT algorithm is proposed in this paper.

Path planning is important for any robot. In addition, we can find a wide range of industrial applications for robot pick-and-place operations on robot manipulators [11–13]. This research includes the discussion of path planning, object picking and placing, collision avoidance, and control of the robot manipulator. Many improved RRT algorithms have been used in robot manipulators to achieve good results. However, most of them only established a simulated environment to present simulation results. In order to illustrate the proposed RRT algorithm, let a real robot manipulator perform object pick-and-place tasks in real time. The robot operating system (ROS) is used to design and integrate the hardware and software of an object pick-and-place system. Since ROS can transmit or receive different types of data at the same time through "messages" and "services", it is one of the most popular platforms for research in robotics. Moreover, MoveIt, which is open-source motion planning software, has been widely used in industry and research. It is easy to integrate with ROS to set up new robots, and it is already available for more than 150 robots. Therefore, in the design of motion planning, MoveIt is used to complete the required motion of the robot manipulator.

There are six sections in this paper. In Section 1, the background is introduced. In Section 2, an implemented object pick-and-place system based on ROS is described. In Section 3, three sampling strategies used in the RRT algorithms are described. In Section 4, a basic RRT algorithm and an improved RRT algorithm based on an existing RRT algorithm are described. In Section 5, an experimental environment with four pick-and-place tasks is setup, and some simulation and actual experimental results are presented to illustrate that the implemented object pick-and-place system using the proposed RRT algorithm can allow a robot manipulator to pick and place objects in real time. Finally, conclusions and future work are described in Section 6.

2. ROS-Based Object Pick-and-Place System

The system architecture diagram of the implemented ROS-based object pick-and-place system is shown in Figure 1. The input of this system is the RGB image captured by Microsoft Azure Kinect DK (a RGB-D camera), and the outputs are the control commands of Universal Robots UR5 (six-degree-of-freedom (DOF) robot manipulator) and Robotiq 2F-85 (a two-finger parallel gripper). Azure Kinect DK has the features of a wide field of view and easy installation; it is directly installed on a bracket to capture images on the table. UR5 has some features, such as a light weight, a user-friendly interface, and collision detection capability. The related unified robot description format (URDF) files for the specific MoveIt applications are also provided. These features make experiments easy to perform and avoid collisions between the robot manipulator and surrounding objects during the experiment. Robotiq 2F-85 is easily integrated into robot manipulators. It has the feature that it can avoid damage to the gripper itself and prevent the robot manipulator from injuring the object during the grasping task.

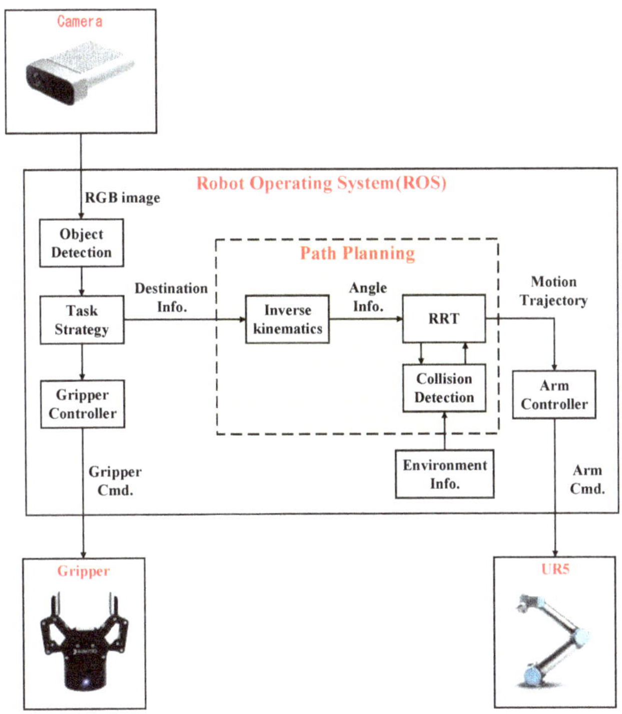

Figure 1. System diagram of the proposed ROS-based object pick-and-place system.

The object detection module is implemented by the you only look once (YOLO) algorithm [14] to obtain the position information of the object on the table from the captured RGB image. The task strategy module is used to decide the destination of the robot manipulator when a pick-and-place task is given. The path planning module is implemented by the improved RRT algorithm, which can quickly select a collision-free path so that the robot manipulator and the two-finger gripper can successfully complete the given tasks in real-time.

In the system integration of the proposed pick-and-place system, ROS is used to handle the communication between each module. The robot motion information is calculated by MoveIt through ROS. The version of ROS Melodic with Ubuntu 18.04 is used. MoveIt is an open-source motion planning software that is a state-of-the-art implementation of robot motion and path planning. Thus, it is used for the motion planning of the robot manipulator. MoveIt provides a variety of functional packages for users to choose from and integrates various functional plugins such as kinematics, collision detection, and motion planning so that it can provide the desired motion planning for various robots. Moreover, MoveIt is a package of ROS, and it is highly integrated with ROS so that the results of motion planning by MoveIt can be easily transmitted to the robot manipulator through ROS. Users can use the 3D visualization tool RViz to visually present the motion planning results in the ROS. For MoveIt, the unified robot description format (URDF) and semantic robot description format (SRDF) are used to describe robots. The proposed RRT algorithm is designed for the robot manipulator UR5 in this paper, but it can be used for the other six DOF robot manipulators. MoveIt imports the URDF file to set the parameters of the robot and the simulated environment, then sends a request to the default library, the open motion planning library (OMPL), to design a suitable motion trajectory. After calculating a path, MoveIt will divide this path into the same distances and add information such as speed, acceleration, and the consumed time of the robot at each piece of the path. In addition, OMPL is the main library of sampling-based planning algorithms, which includes many modules of common RRT algorithms. Because of its modular program design, it is easy for users to add custom motion planning algorithms. Therefore, MoveIt is adopted as the motion planning software for the robot manipulator in this paper.

As shown in Figure 1, the image information is sent by the object detection module, and the motion information is calculated by MoveIt through ROS. Since ROS can transmit or receive different data through messages and services, the proposed system integrated through ROS can be applied to various input and output devices, so it has good applicability. In the communication mode between the object detection module, task strategy module, MoveIt, and UR5, there are mainly three two-way communication services in the implemented pick-and-place system, which are, respectively, named Service1, Service2, and Service3.

In order to ensure that the task strategy module can indeed receive the object position information from the object detection module, Service1 is used to make the control command of the task strategy module for the robot manipulator to move only after it has received the object position information. The nodes of the server and client of Service1 are the task strategy module and the object detection module, respectively. The request sent by the task strategy module to the server has a status value of 0 (false) or 1 (true) while the control command is received. The response is given by the object detection module as the client after it receives the request for the object coordinates (x, y) on the table. The nodes of the server and client of Service2 are the task strategy module and MoveIt, respectively. The request sent by the task strategy module as the server is the target position (x, y, z) of the end effector and the quaternion of the robot manipulator pose (w, x, y, z). The response given by MoveIt as the client after receiving the request is the result of forward and inverse kinematics and the motion trajectory obtained by RRT. The nodes of the server and client of Service3 are MoveIt and UR5, respectively. The request sent by MoveIt as the server is the joint motion trajectory of the robot manipulator. The response given by UR5 as the client after receiving the request is a status value of 0 (false) or 1 (true), depending on whether UR5 is busy or not.

3. Sampling Strategy

Random sampling is the sampling strategy used by the basic RRT algorithm. The algorithm randomly samples the entire space to determine sampling points. The simulation result of 1000 random samplings in a 200 × 200 two-dimensional space is shown in Figure 2, where the black point is the goal point. It can be seen that the sampling points randomly fall throughout the entire space. For the RRT algorithms, random sampling can fully explore the environment, find a path from the start point to the goal point, and avoid obstacles in the environment. However, due to its randomness, it spends a lot of time exploring invalid areas in most environments. Therefore, many improved sampling strategies were proposed to reduce computing time.

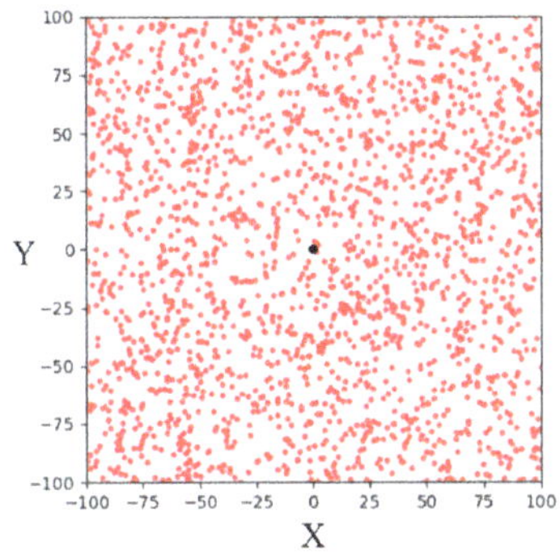

Figure 2. Schematic illustration of random sampling in a two-dimensional space.

Goal-biased sampling is an improved sampling strategy over random sampling. By adding a random variable *rand* and set: if *rand* is less than the specified probability p, then the point will be selected as a sampling point. Otherwise, use the original random sampling method to randomly sample the space. This sampling strategy causes the random tree of the RRT algorithm to take the goal point to sample with a certain probability. In this case, random trees can approach the goal area faster and reduce computing time while maintaining random sampling to fully explore the environment. The simulation result of 1000 goal-biased sampling points in a 200 × 200 two-dimensional space is shown in Figure 3. It can be seen that more sampling points fall within the goal area.

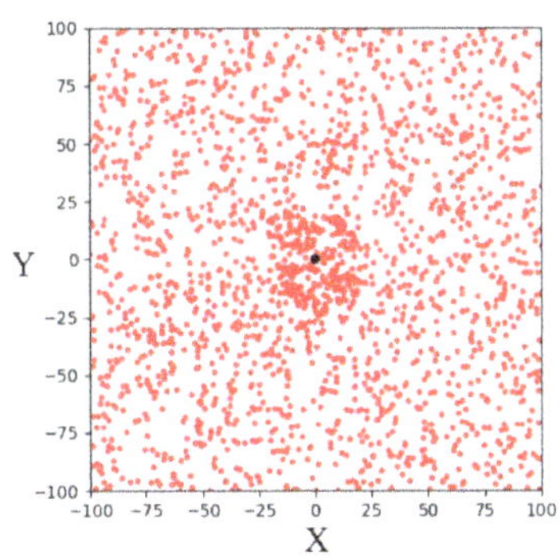

Figure 3. Schematic illustration of goal-biased sampling in a two-dimensional space.

Bounded sampling is a sampling strategy to limit the sampling area to a radius from the goal point and let the random tree explore toward the goal area. The simulation result of 1000 bounded sampling in a 200 × 200 two-dimensional space is shown in Figure 4. It can be seen that the sampling points are limited within a radial space centered on the goal point. Compared with the RRT algorithm using a goal-biased sampling strategy, the RRT algorithm using bounded sampling can make the random tree explore the goal area stably. By gradually reducing the sampling radius, this algorithm can find a path to the goal point. However, since such bounded sampling may be overly focused on exploring towards the goal area, random trees can easily get trapped in some complex environments.

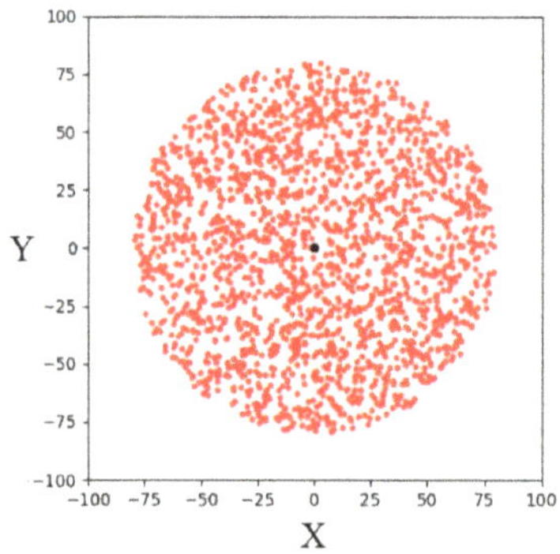

Figure 4. Schematic illustration of bounded sampling in a two-dimensional space.

4. Changing Strategy RRT Algorithm

In the design of the sampling-based path planning method, two items, such as computing time and path length, are usually considered. For offline path planning, the path length is usually the main consideration. On the other hand, for online path planning, computing time is the priority consideration. Real-time object picking and placing tasks require online path planning, so we mainly focus on how to reduce the computing time of the improved RRT algorithm.

The basic RRT algorithm, as a sampling-based path planning method, is mainly designed to perform random sampling in the configuration space [15]. A schematic illustration of the basic RRT algorithm for finding a path from a starting point (S) to a goal point (G) in a two-dimensional space is shown in Figure 5. It can be seen that the random tree fully explores the environment. The advantage of this method is that it does not require modeling the entire environment. Such path planning algorithms can explore two-dimensional spaces faster than other path planning algorithms. Therefore, it is suitable for solving the path planning problem in complex or constrained environments.

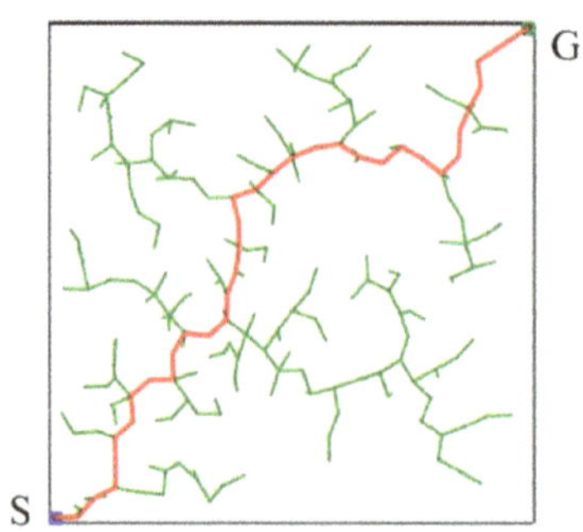

Figure 5. Schematic illustration of the basic RRT algorithm for finding a solution in a two-dimensional space.

The proposed algorithm is named changing strategy RRT (CS-RRT), which is improved on the basis of the method of gradually changing the sampling area based on RRT (CSA-RRT) [9]. The pseudocode of the CSA-RRT algorithm is shown in Algorithm 1. It needs to calculate the distance D_{max} between the two nodes q_{far} and q_{goal}, where q_{far} is the node farthest from the goal point q_{goal}. Since the tree only has the initial node q_{start} at the beginning, the algorithm will initially use q_{start} as q_{far} to calculate D_{max}, which is the initial sampling radius R of bounded sampling. When the dimension of the space is s, the maximum distance D_{max} is calculated by:

$$D_{max} = \sqrt{(q_{goal(1)} - q_{far(1)})^2 + \ldots + (q_{goal(s)} - q_{far(s)})^2} \quad (1)$$

The CSA-RRT algorithm uses the random sampling method to randomly select a sampling point q_{rand} in the space. The distance D_{rand} between q_{rand} and q_{goal} is calculated by:

$$D_{rand} = \sqrt{(q_{goal(1)} - q_{rand(1)})^2 + \ldots + (q_{goal(s)} - q_{rand(s)})^2} \quad (2)$$

Compare the distance between D_{rand} and R to make sure that the sampling point q_{rand} is inside R. If D_{rand} is less than R, then q_{rand} is considered a valid sampling point. Conversely, if D_{rand} is greater than R, it means that q_{rand} is outside R, and the algorithm will resample until q_{rand} is inside R. If a new node q_{new} is successfully added to the random tree in an iteration, it means that there is no obstacle between q_{new} and the nearest node q_{near}. When the new point q_{new} is closer to the goal point q_{goal}, it becomes the nearest node. At this time, the value of R is changed to the distance from the new nearest node q_{new} to the goal point q_{goal}. Conversely, it means that an obstacle is encountered during the expansion process. At this time, a step size ε of k times is added to R, which means that the sampling area is expanded so that the random tree can avoid nearby obstacles. The value of k is a positive integer for adjusting the sampling radius, which needs to be manually adjusted according to the complexity of the environment. This allows the algorithm to explore the direction of q_{goal} as much as possible while having the ability to randomly explore the environment. The comparison results of the CSA-RRT algorithm and the 10% goal-biased RRT algorithm are shown in Figure 6. It can be seen that the CSA-RRT algorithm can reduce the generation of invalid nodes more than the goal-biased RRT algorithm.

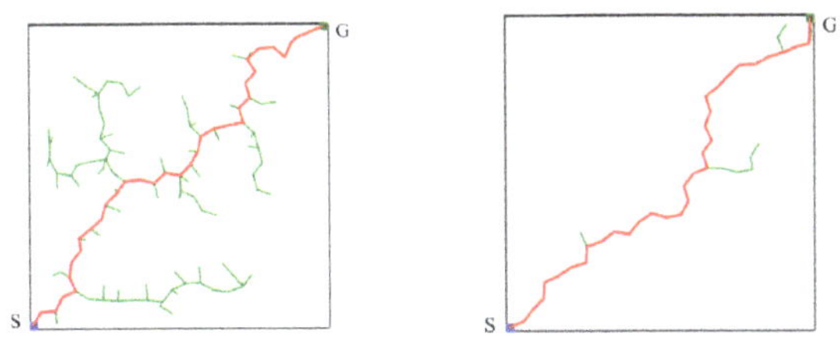

(a) **(b)**

Figure 6. Schematic illustration of the comparison results of the two RRT algorithms. (**a**) 10% goal-biased RRT algorithm. (**b**) CSA-RRT algorithm.

The CSA-RRT algorithm has the advantage that the invalid nodes of the CSA-RRT algorithm are much lower than those of the goal-biased RRT algorithm. However, the computing time of the CSA-RRT algorithm is not much faster than that of the goal-biased RRT algorithm. After observation, we found that although the sampling radius R will gradually shrink as q_{new} gets closer to the goal area, thereby reducing the generation of invalid points. However, on the other hand, because of the reduction in R, q_{rand} selected by random sampling becomes more and more difficult to fall within R. As shown in Figure 7, when the new point q_{new} is close to the goal point q_{goal}, R will become smaller and smaller.

This results in a very small chance that the sampling point q_{rand} will fall within R. As a result, the CSA-RRT algorithm spends a lot of time doing computation at certain stages. Therefore, the CSA-RRT algorithm has the advantage of generating fewer invalid nodes, but it still cannot significantly reduce the computing time of path planning. This becomes more apparent when sampling in larger environments.

Algorithm 1: CSA-RRT algorithm

```
T ← InitTree(q_start);
R ← D_max;
for i = 1 to n do
  q_rand ← RandomSample();
  if Distance(q_rand, q_goal) > R then
    continue;
  end if
  q_near ← NearestNeighbor(q_rand, T);
  q_new ← Extend(q_rand, q_near, ε);
  if CollisionFree(q_near, q_new) then
    AddNewNode(T, q_new);
    R ← Distance(q_new, q_goal);
  else
    R ← R + k × ε;
    continue;
  end if
  if Distance(q_new, q_goal) < ρ_min then
    return T;
  end if
end for
return Failed;
```

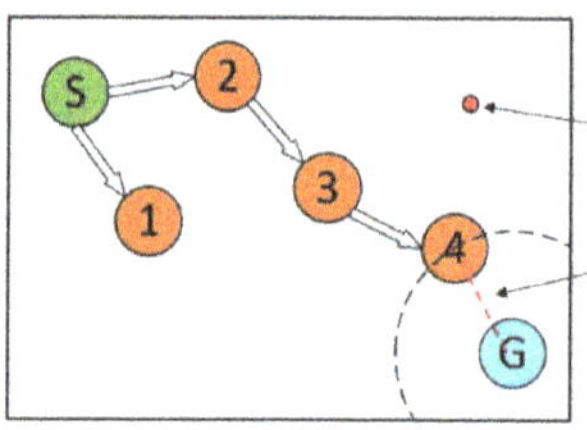

Figure 7. Schematic illustration of the sampling point. It is difficult to fall within the sampling radius R when the new point is close to the goal point.

A sampling-radius limitation mechanism is adopted to solve this problem that q_{rand} is difficult to fall into R when q_{new} is close to q_{goal}. An additional statement is used to determine whether the random tree is approaching q_{goal}. Whenever q_{new} is added to the random tree, R and D_{max} are compared before the next sampling. If R is greater than one-fifth of D_{max}, it means that the random tree is still far away from q_{goal}. Thus, it continues to use the random sampling of the CSA-RRT algorithm to select q_{rand}. On the other hand, if R is smaller than one-fifth of D_{max}, it means that the random tree is close to q_{goal}. At this time, a sampling-radius limitation mechanism based on bounded sampling is adopted to limit the sampling area within the radius R from the goal point. In this way, the problem that q_{rand} cannot successfully fall within R when it is close to the goal point can be solved. This makes the proposed CS-RRT algorithm not only quickly find valid nodes but also reduce the computing time of path planning. In the case of two-dimensional simulations, the CS-RRT algorithm improves by about 0.5 times compared with the CSA-RRT algorithm.

In addition, the CSA-RRT algorithm has the advantage that it can quickly find an initial path to the goal area. However, as shown in Figure 8, if the CSA-RRT algorithm is performed in a complex environment and the value of k is not adjusted properly, the tree may be trapped due to focusing too much on the goal point. As a result, the random tree keeps expanding in the same area but cannot find an escape path until the number of node expansions of the algorithm reaches the maximum limit of expansions and fails. In order to solve this problem, a node counting mechanism is adopted to appropriately switch the sampling strategy to an appropriate sampling method in complex environments. It can avoid the search path being trapped in some constrained areas and improve the adaptability of the proposed CS-RRT algorithm to various environments.

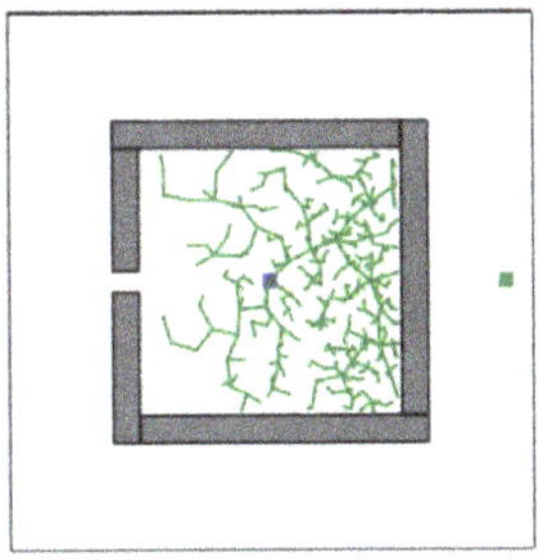

Figure 8. Schematic illustration of CSA-RRT algorithm trapped in a complex environment with a restricted region.

The CSA-RRT algorithm with the node counting mechanism will calculate the distance D_{min} from the node q_{min} that is closest to the goal point q_{goal} and set the node count variable *nodecnt* to zero during initialization. As shown in Algorithm 2, in the sampling stage, the algorithm will choose which sampling method to use according to the value of *nodecnt*. If *nodecnt* is less than the set threshold, the sampling method of CSA-RRT is used to make the random tree quickly extend to the goal point. Otherwise, the random sampling method, which fully explores the environment, is used.

Algorithm 2: SelectSample($nodecnt, q_{goal}, R$);

if *nodecnt* < 20 **then**
    $q_{rand} \leftarrow$ RandomSample();
    if Distance(q_{rand}, q_{goal}) > R **then**
        continue;
    end if
else
    $q_{rand} \leftarrow$ RandomSample();
end if
return q_{rand};

After completing the collision detection stage in each iteration, the algorithm calculates the Euclidean distance D_{new} from q_{new} to q_{goal}, no matter if q_{new} is successfully added to the random tree. After this, compare D_{new} with D_{min} in the CheckEnvironment() function. The pseudocode of the CheckEnvironment() function is shown in Algorithm 3. If D_{new} is smaller than D_{min}, then *nodecnt* is set to zero. At this time, q_{new} is closer to q_{goal}, which means that the tree is approaching the goal area, so there is no need to change the sampling strategy. After that, change q_{new} into q_{min} as the basis for the next check of the expansion status. On the other hand, if D_{new} is greater than D_{min}, it means that q_{new} is not closer to q_{goal}. At this time, *nodecnt*+1. If D_{new} continues to be greater than D_{min} for the next few times, it is considered that the random tree is trapped in the current area. Then the algorithm will switch the sampling method to random sampling in the SelectSample() function to try to escape the current area until D_{new} is smaller than D_{min}. In addition, an upper limit is set to avoid the algorithm wasting too much time using random sampling to explore the space. Therefore, when *nodecnt* reaches the set upper limit, it will reset to zero immediately. A schematic illustration of node count adjustment is shown in Figure 9.

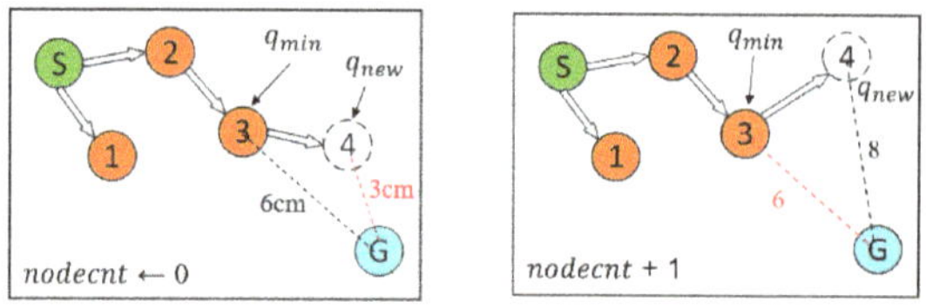

(a) (b)

Figure 9. Schematic illustration of two different node number adjustments. (**a**) The new node is close to the goal point. (**b**) The new node is far from the goal point.

Algorithm 3: CheckEnvironment(D_{new}, D_{min}, *nodecnt*)

if $D_{new} < D_{min}$ **then**
  $D_{min} \leftarrow D_{new}$;
  nodecnt ← 0;
else
  nodecnt ← *nodecnt* + 1;
end if
if *nodecnt* > 100 **then**
  nodecnt ← 0
end if

In short, the proposed CS-RRT algorithm is based on the CSA-RRT algorithm and uses the sampling-radius limitation mechanism and the node counting mechanism to solve the problems existing in the CSA-RRT algorithm. The sampling-radius limitation mechanism allows the random tree to finish the sampling stage more quickly when it is close to the goal area, so that the proposed CS-RRT algorithm can further reduce the computing time. The node counting mechanism makes the algorithm avoid overfocusing on the goal area, so the proposed CS-RRT algorithm also has good adaptability to the environment. The results of the proposed CS-RRT algorithm performed in two different environments are shown in Figure 10. When encountering simple environments, as shown in Figure 10a, the proposed CS-RRT algorithm can quickly find a path. When encountering complex environments, as shown in Figure 10b, the proposed CS-RRT algorithm can also prevent trapping by switching sampling strategies. Comparing the results shown in Figure 8, we can see that the CSA-RRT algorithm is trapped in this environment. With these improvements, the proposed CS-RRT algorithm indeed not only reduces computing time but also improves environmental adaptability.

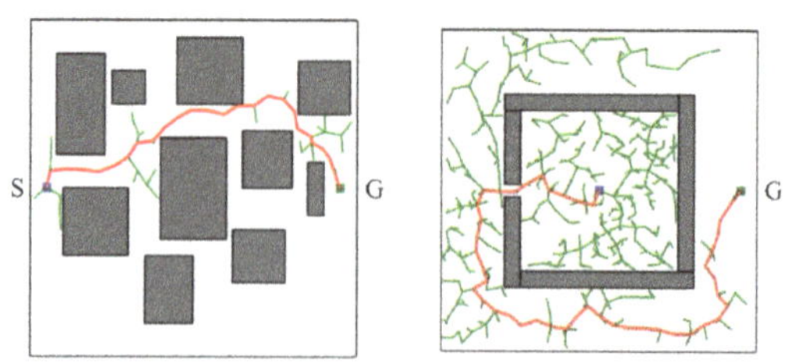

(a) (b)

Figure 10. Schematic illustration of the performance of CS-RRT algorithm in two different environments. (**a**) A simple environment with many obstacles. (**b**) A complex environment with a restricted region.

5. Simulation Results and Experimental Results

5.1. Simulation Results of Robot Manipulator

The simulation setup of the robot manipulator and experimental environment is shown in Figure 11. In order to demonstrate the performance of the motion planning of the robot manipulator based on the proposed CS-RRT algorithm, a series of tasks (Task 1~Task 4) is designed, and then the success rates and average computing time after 50 experiments of each algorithm, the proposed CS-RRT, CSA-RRT, and the 10% goal-bias RRT algorithm, provided by the open motion planning library (OMPL), are compared. The tasks are described as follows:

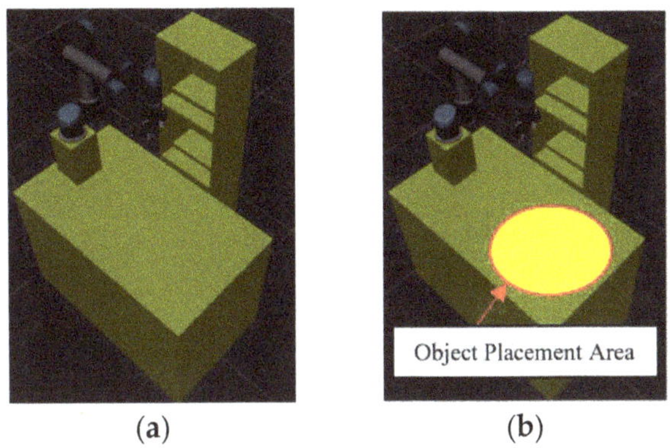

Figure 11. Schematic illustration of experimental environment. (**a**) The robot manipulator and experimental environment. (**b**) An object will be randomly placed inside the red circle.

Task 1: The implemented pick-and-place system uses the YOLOv4 algorithm to obtain the position of Object A on the table and then commands the robot manipulator to grasp the Object A. This task verifies the motion planning performance of algorithms in an open space without obstacles.

Task 2: The implemented pick-and-place system commands the robot manipulator to place the grasped object at a certain location on the upper layer of the cabinet. The sides of the cabinet can be considered obstacles for the movement of the robot manipulator. This task verifies the motion planning performance of algorithms from open space to restricted space.

Task 3: The implemented pick-and-place system commands the robot manipulator to move from the upper layer of the cabinet to the lower layer and grasp the Object B that was placed on the lower layer of the cabinet. This task verifies the motion planning performance of algorithms in two restricted spaces.

Task 4: The implemented pick-and-place system commands the robot manipulator to move from the lower layer of the cabinet to the grasping position in Task 1 and to place the grasped object. This task verifies the motion planning performance of algorithms from a restricted space to an open space.

Figure 12 illustrates the motion flow from Task 1 to Task 4. Note that the gray and orange robot manipulators indicate the initial and finish positions of each task, respectively. Four simulation results for each task are illustrated as follows:

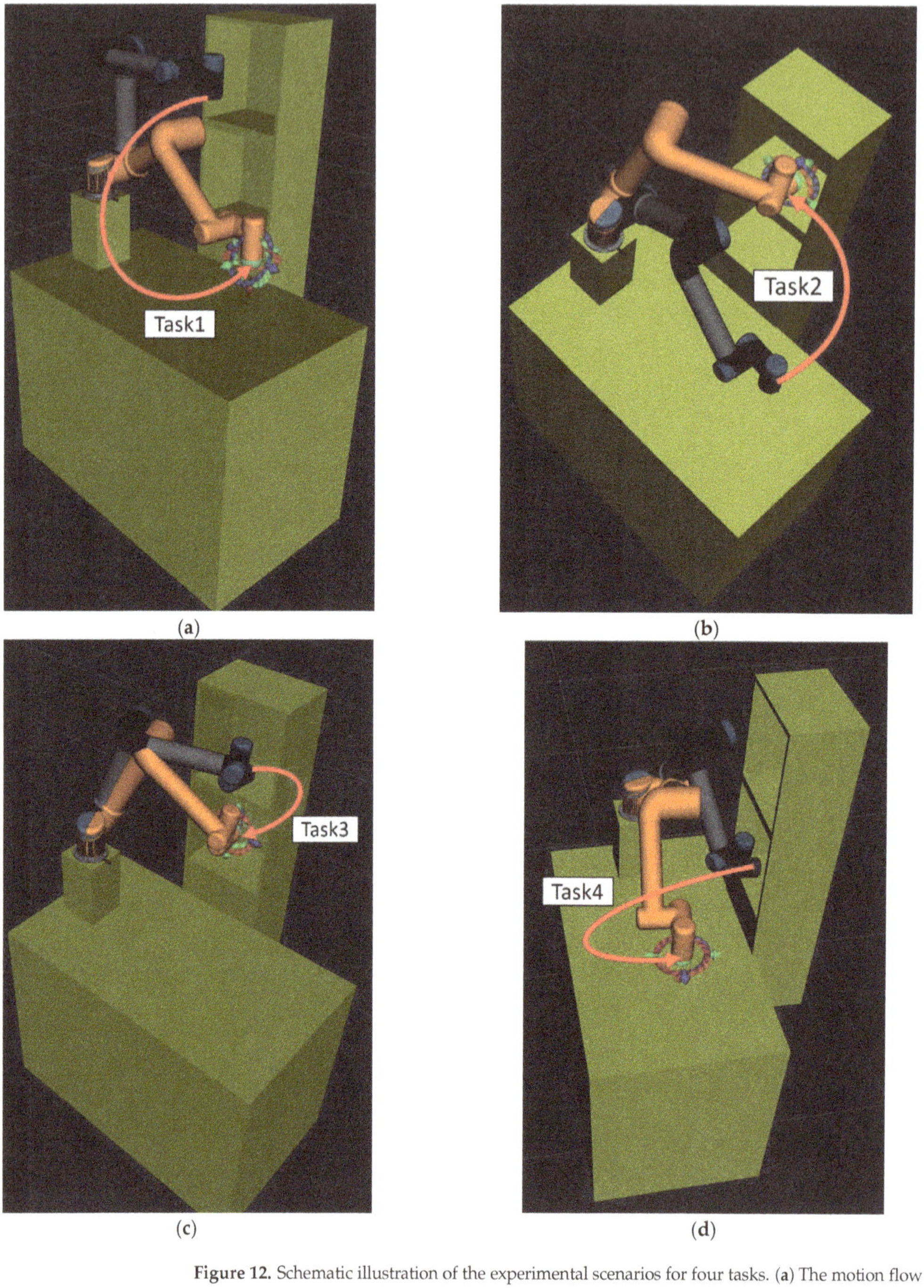

Figure 12. Schematic illustration of the experimental scenarios for four tasks. (**a**) The motion flow of the manipulator in Task 1. (**b**) The motion flow of the manipulator in Task 2. (**c**) The motion flow of the manipulator in Task 3. (**d**) The motion flow of the manipulator in Task 4.

In the experimental scenarios of Task 1, as shown in Figure 12a, the robot manipulator is commanded to move from its initial position to grasp the object on the table. Figure 13a,b are bar graphs of the success rate and the average computing time of the three algorithms executed 50 times in Task 1, respectively. From the results in Figure 13, it can be seen that the success rate and the average computing time of the proposed CS-RRT and the 10% goal-biased RRT are the same. We infer that the proposed CS-RRT needs to compute the sampling radius at each iteration. Therefore, searching in an open space without obstacles, does not have the advantage of taking less computing time. In addition, CSA-RRT makes it difficult for the sampling points to fall within the sampling radius when they are close to the goal area. Therefore, the computing time of the CSA-RRT is higher than that of the proposed CS-RRT.

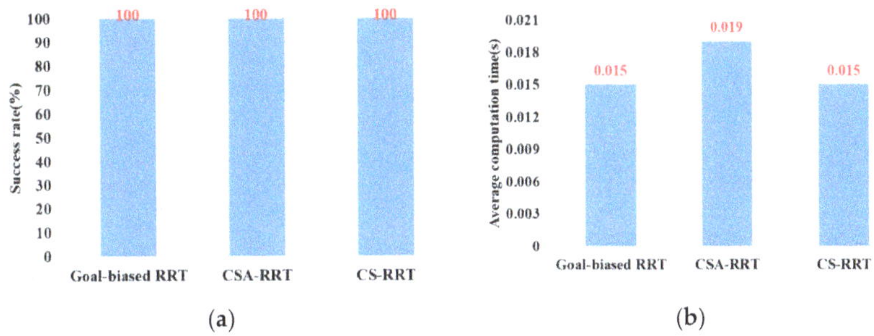

Figure 13. Experimental results of three algorithms in the scenarios of Task 1. (**a**) Success rate. (**b**) Average computing time.

Remark: The experiment sets the maximum path planning time to 1 second because it is basically not regarded as real-time motion planning after more than 1 second. In addition, the robot manipulator may rotate a full circle and cause damage to surrounding objects due to the randomness of the RRT algorithms. Thus, we restrict each axis of the robot manipulator to rotating between plus and minus 180 degrees.

In the experimental scenarios of Task 2, as shown in Figure 12b, the robot manipulator is commanded to move from the finished position of Task 1 to a specific position on the upper layer of the cabinet to place the grasped object. Although moving in a straight line is the fastest way to reach the destination, it will collide with the sides of the cabinet. Therefore, for the robot manipulator to reach its destination safely, it needs a collision-free path to avoid collisions with the sides of the cabinet. Task 2 tests the motion planning performance of algorithms from an open space to a restricted space. From the results shown in Figure 14, it can be seen that the proposed CS-RRT has the highest success rate and the shortest average computing time. Therefore, the proposed CS-RRT has better performance than the other two algorithms when planning a motion in a restricted environment.

In the experimental scenarios of Task 3, as shown in Figure 12c, the robot manipulator is commanded to move from the upper layer of the cabinet to a specific position on the lower layer of the cabinet. Since the robot manipulator has entered the upper cabinet, the environment of the two restricted areas in Task 3 is more complex than that in Task 1 and Task 2. In this experiment, we found that the default step size ε using OMPL is too small. As a result, the random tree of the three algorithms grows slowly, and the motion planning cannot be completed within the specified time. Therefore, the step size ε is increased by three times in Task 3. In other words, the expansion distance of each iteration of the random tree is increased. From the results shown in Figure 15, we can see that the proposed CS-RRT has the highest success rate and the shortest average computing time too. Therefore, the proposed CS-RRT has better performance than the 10% goal-biased RRT algorithm and CSA-RRT when planning in a complex environment.

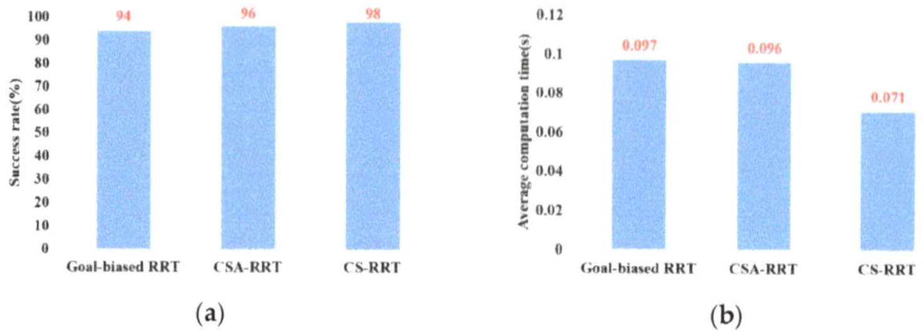

Figure 14. Experimental results of three algorithms in the scenarios of Task 2. (**a**) Success rate. (**b**) Average computing time.

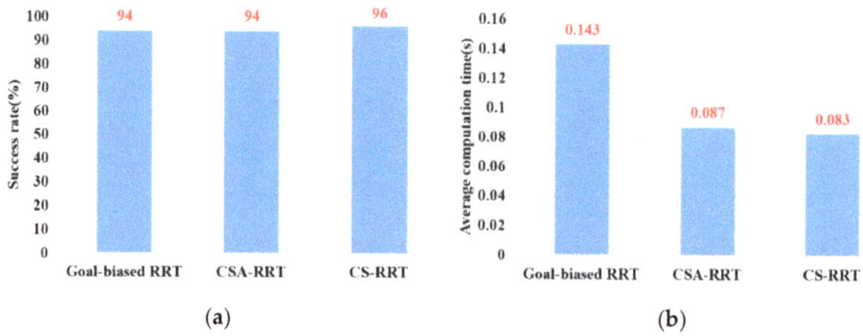

Figure 15. Experimental results of three algorithms in the scenarios of Task 3. (**a**) Success rate. (**b**) Average computing time.

In the experimental scenarios of Task 4, as shown in Figure 12d, the robot manipulator is commanded to move from the lower layer of the cabinet to the top of the table. This task verifies the motion planning performance of algorithms from a restricted space to an open space. From the results shown in Figure 16, we can see that the success rate and the average computing time of the proposed CS-RRT and 10% goal-biased RRT are the same. However, the average computing time of CSA-RRT under Task 4 is still longer than that of CS-RRT and 10% goal-biased RRT. Judging from the fact that the success rate of all three algorithms is 100 percent, we infer that once the robot manipulator comes out of the cabinet, there are multiple ways to move to the destination. Since the restricted area is near the initial point in Task 4, once the robot manipulator leaves the restricted area, all three algorithms can easily find a collision-free path to the destination in an open space with only a few explorations.

Based on these results shown in Figures 13–16, the simulation results of three algorithms in the four scenarios of Tasks 1~4 are summarized in Table 1. Compared with goal-biased RRT and CSA-RRT, the implemented pick-and-place system based on the proposed CS-RRT algorithm has a higher success rate and requires less computing time. We can see that the results of CS-RRT are similar to those of the 10% goal-biased RRT when planning is performed in non-complex environments, such as Task 1 and Task 4. However, the advantages of the proposed CS-RRT in terms of success rate and computing time can be seen when planning is performed in complex environments with space restrictions, such as Task 2 and Task 3.

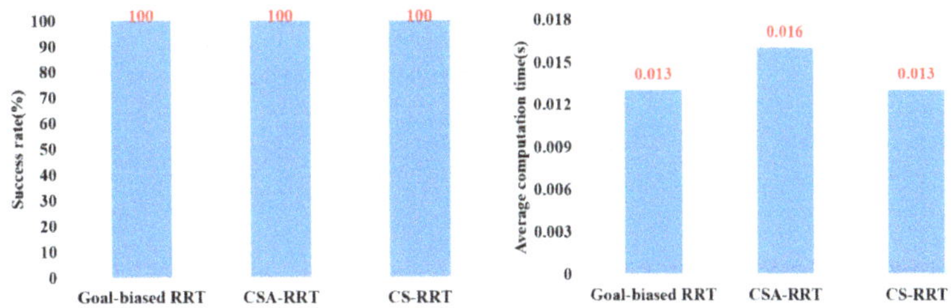

(a) (b)

Figure 16. Experimental results of three algorithms in the scenarios of Task 4. (**a**) Success rate. (**b**) Average computing time.

Table 1. Simulation results of three algorithms in the four scenarios of Tasks 1~4.

	Success Rate (%)			Average Computing Time (Second)		
Task	**Goal-Biased RRT**	**CSA-RRT**	**CS-RRT**	**Goal-Biased RRT**	**CSA-RRT**	**CS-RRT**
Task 1	100	100	100	0.015	0.019	0.015
Task 2	94	96	98	0.097	0.096	0.071
Task 3	94	94	96	0.143	0.087	0.083
Task 4	100	100	100	0.013	0.016	0.013
Average	97	97.5	98.5	0.067	0.0545	0.0455

5.2. Experimental Results of Real Robot Manipulator

In the practical experimental demonstration, a real pick-and-place system with a depth camera (Microsoft Azure Kinect DK), a six DOF robot manipulator (UR5), and a two-finger parallel gripper (Robotiq 2F-85) is presented to illustrate the efficiency of the proposed CS-RRT algorithm applied in the pick-and-place system. The camera is installed above the table and the YOLOv4 algorithm is used to obtain the position coordinates of Object A, which is randomly placed on the table. Code runs on the robot with ROS implemented in Python. The communication method of ROS Services is used to ensure that the task strategy module actually receives the coordinate information and MoveIt is used to execute the motion planning results of the proposed CS-RRT algorithm to complete the four pick-and-place tasks described in the previous section. The video of the demonstration of the real pick-and-place task can be viewed on this website: https://youtu.be/lcdy2byIG_g (accessed on 20 January 2023). The snapshots of the real robot manipulator performing Task 1, Task 2, Task 3, and Task 4 are, respectively, shown in Figures 17–20. The procedure can be described as follows:

Step 1: Obtain the position coordinates of object A randomly placed on the table through the camera installed above the table and the YOLOv4 algorithm.
Step 2: Move to the top of Object A.
Step 3: Move downward to grasp Object A.
Step 4: Move upward from the table.
Step 5: Move to the outside of the upper layer of the cabinet.
Step 6: Move into the upper interior of the upper layer of the cabinet.
Step 7: Move downward to place Object A.
Step 8: Move to the outside of the upper layer of the cabinet.
Step 9: Move to the outside of the lower layer of the cabinet.
Step 10: Move to the top of Object B in the lower layer of the cabinet.
Step 11: Move downward to grasp Object B.
Step 12: Move to the outside of the lower layer of the cabinet.
Step 13: Move to the top of the initial position of Object A, where it was originally placed on the table.

Step 14: Move downward to place Object B on the table.
Step 15: Move to the top of the object placed on the table.
Step 16: Return to the initial position of the robot manipulator.

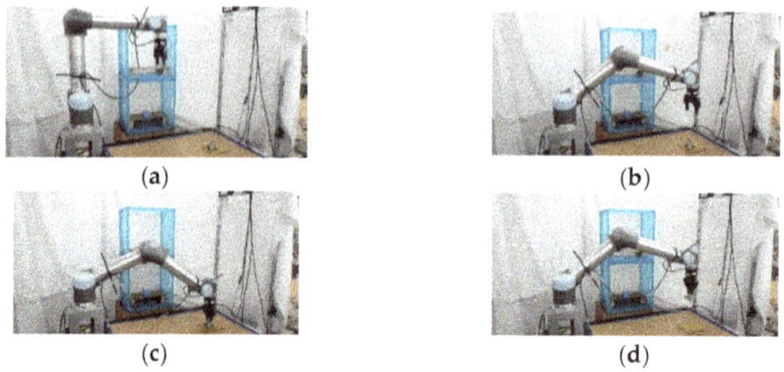

Figure 17. Snapshot of the robot manipulator during the object pick-and-place in Task 1. (**a**) Initial position. (**b**) Move to the top of Object A. (**c**) Move downward to grasp Object A. (**d**) Move upward to the top of the table.

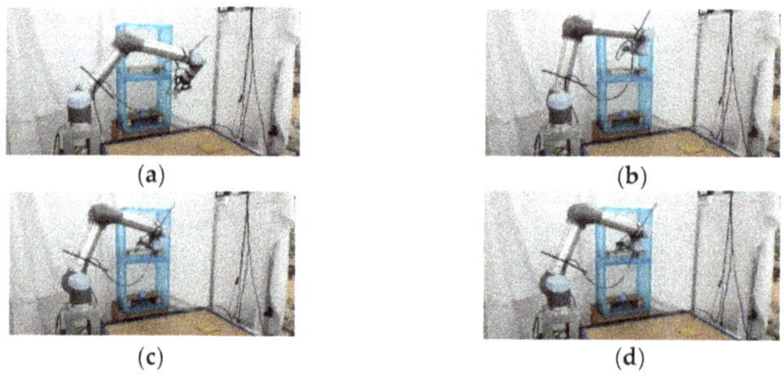

Figure 18. Snapshot of the robot manipulator during the object pick-and-place in Task 2. (**a**) Move to the upper layer of the cabinet. (**b**) Reach the outside of upper layer of the cabinet. (**c**) Move into the upper interior of the cabinet. (**d**) Move downward to place Object A.

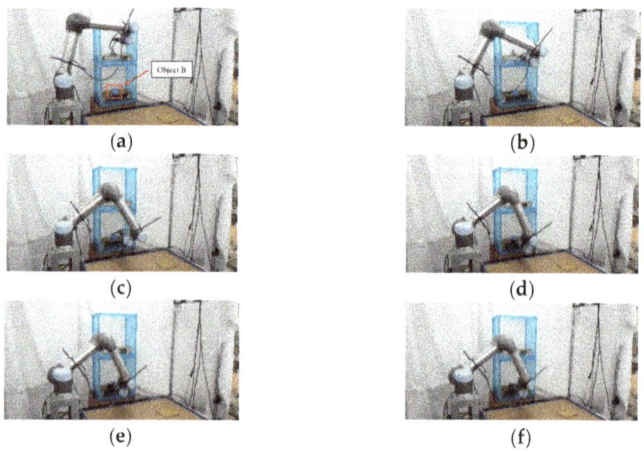

Figure 19. Snapshot of the robot manipulator during the object pick-and-place in Task 3. (**a**) Move back to the outside of the upper layer of the cabinet. (**b**) Move to the outside of the upper layer of the cabinet. (**c**) Move to the outside of the lower layer of the cabinet. (**d**) Reach the outside of the lower layer of the cabinet. (**e**) Move to the top of Object B, placed in the lower layer of the cabinet. (**f**) Move downward to grasp Object B.

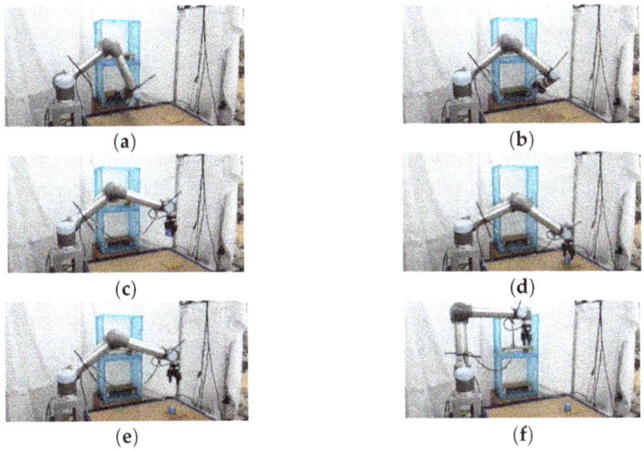

Figure 20. Snapshot of the robot manipulator during the object pick-and-place in Task 4. (**a**) Move back to the outside of the lower layer of the cabinet. (**b**) Move to the outside of the lower layer of the cabinet. (**c**) Reach the top of the initial position of Object A where it was originally placed on the table. (**d**) Move downward to place Object B on the table. (**e**) Move to the top of the object placed on the table. (**f**) Return to the initial position of the robot manipulator.

6. Conclusions and Future Work

An ROS-based object pick-and-place system is implemented, and a CS-RRT algorithm is proposed so that the robot manipulator can efficiently pick-and-place objects in real time. There are three main contributions in this paper. (1) Path planning for robots is one of the most important topics in robotics research. In the research on robot manipulators for picking and placing objects in a constrained environment, most of the research only completed simulation results to verify the effectiveness of their path planning methods. Many improved RRT algorithms have been proposed, but they are rarely applied to actual robot manipulators for object pick-and-place tasks in real time. Both simulation and actual experiments are used to demonstrate that the proposed CS-RRT algorithm and the implemented system can allow the robot manipulator to effectively avoid obstacles and pick-and-place objects in real time. (2) Some disadvantages of existing RRT algorithms are addressed, and two mechanisms of sampling radius counting, and node counting are adopted in the proposed CS-RRT algorithm. The sampling-radius limitation mechanism, by limiting the sampling radius, can make the random tree finish the sampling stage faster when the tree is close to the goal point. It can reduce the computing time of the proposed CS-RRT algorithm. The node counting mechanism allows the algorithm to switch to an appropriate sampling method in a complex environment. It can avoid excessive exploration in the direction of the goal point so that the random tree does not trap itself in constrained areas. It can make the proposed CS-RRT algorithm have better environmental adaptability. In addition, an experimental environment with four object picking and placement tasks has been established. Experimental results show that the object pick-and-place system based on the proposed CS-RRT algorithm has a higher success rate and lower computing time compared with the other two path planning algorithms. (3) The robot operating system (ROS) is used to implement the object pick-and-place system. By implementing the proposed CS-RRT algorithm in the open motion planning library (OMPL), MoveIt can be used to plan the motion of the robot manipulator. According to the imported URDF file, MoveIt can also perform motion planning for different robot manipulators, so the proposed method can be easily applied to different robot manipulators.

There are two parts to the future work: (1) In the part of switching strategy and step size adjustment, switching sampling strategy can improve the adaptability of the proposed algorithm to the environment, but its own parameters need to be manually designed according to the environment. In addition, the step size also needs to be chosen according to the environment. Therefore, some optimization methods can be used in the future to select appropriate parameters for the switching strategy and step size according to the environment. (2) In the part of the sampling method where the distance needs to be calculated. In the path planning of the six-dimensional joint space of the robot manipulator, more parameters are needed to calculate the distance, which increases the computing time of the proposed algorithm. Therefore, the number of calculation distances can be reduced in the future to reduce the computing time needed to meet the system requirements.

Author Contributions: Conceptualization, C.-C.W., K.-Y.W. and H.-M.F.; methodology, C.-C.W. and C.-J.C.; software, C.-J.C.; validation, C.-C.W., K.-Y.W. and H.-M.F.; formal analysis, K.-Y.W.; investigation, H.-M.F.; resources, C.-C.W.; data curation, C.-J.C.; writing—original draft preparation, C.-J.C.; writing—review and editing, C.-C.W., K.-Y.W. and H.-M.F.; visualization, K.-Y.W.; supervision, C.-C.W.; project administration, C.-C.W.; funding acquisition, C.-C.W. All authors have read and agreed to the published version of the manuscript.

Funding: This research was partly funded by the Ministry of Science and Technology (MOST) of the Republic of China, under grant numbers MOST 110-2221-E-032-046 and MOST 111-2221-E-032-030.

Institutional Review Board Statement: Not applicable.

Informed Consent Statement: Not applicable.

Data Availability Statement: Not applicable.

Conflicts of Interest: The authors declare no conflict of interest.

References

1. Wang, W.; Zuo, L.; Xu, X. A Learning-based Multi-RRT Approach for Robot Path Planning in Narrow Passages. *J. Intell. Robot. Syst.* **2018**, *90*, 81–100. [CrossRef]
2. Mashayekhi, R.; Idris, M.Y.I.; Anisi, M.H.; Ahmedy, I. Hybrid RRT: A Semi-Dual-Tree RRT-based Motion Planner. *IEEE Access* **2020**, *8*, 18658–18668. [CrossRef]
3. Yuan, Q.; Yi, J.; Sun, R.; Bai, H. Path Planning of a Mechanical Arm Based on an Improved Artificial Potential Field and a Rapid Expansion Random Tree Hybrid Algorithm. *Algorithms* **2021**, *14*, 321. [CrossRef]
4. Wen, S.; Jiang, Y.; Cui, B.; Gao, K.; Wang, F.A. Hierarchical Path Planning Approach with Multi-SARSA Based on Topological Map. *Sensors* **2022**, *22*, 2367. [CrossRef] [PubMed]
5. Hart, P.E.; Nilsson, N.J.; Raphael, B. A Formal Basis for the Heuristic Determination of Minimum Cost Paths. *IEEE Trans. Syst. Sci. Cybern.* **1968**, *4*, 100–107. [CrossRef]
6. Dorigo, M.; Maniezzo, V.; Colorni, A. Ant System: Optimization by A Colony of Cooperating Agents. *IEEE Trans. Syst. Man Cybern. Part B (Cybern.)* **1996**, *26*, 29–41. [CrossRef] [PubMed]
7. Kavraki, L.E.; Svestka, P.; Latombe, J.C.; Overmars, M.H. Probabilistic Roadmaps for Path Planning in High-dimensional Configuration Spaces. *IEEE Trans. Robot. Autom.* **1996**, *12*, 566–580. [CrossRef]
8. LaValle, S.M. Rapidly-Exploring Random Trees: A New Tool for Path Planning. The Annual Research Report. 1998, 1–4. Available online: http://msl.cs.illinois.edu/~lavalle/papers/Lav98c.pdf (accessed on 20 January 2023).
9. Wang, X.; Luo, X.; Han, B.; Chen, Y.; Liang, G.; Zheng, K. Collision-Free Path Planning Method for Robots Based on an Improved Rapidly-Exploring Random Tree Algorithm. *Appl. Sci.* **2020**, *10*, 1381. [CrossRef]
10. Kang, G.; Kim, Y.B.; Lee, Y.H.; Oh, H.S.; You, W.S.; Choi, H.R. Sampling-Based Motion Planning of Manipulator with Goal-oriented Sampling. *Intell. Serv. Robot.* **2019**, *12*, 265–273. [CrossRef]
11. Han, S.D.; Feng, S.W.; Yu, J. Toward Fast and Optimal Robotic Pick-and-Place on a Moving Conveyor. *IEEE Robot. Autom. Lett.* **2020**, *5*, 446–453. [CrossRef]
12. Wong, C.C.; Yeh, L.Y.; Liu, C.C.; Tsai, C.Y.; Aoyama, H. Manipulation Planning for Object Re-Orientation Based on Semantic Segmentation Keypoint Detection. *Sensors* **2021**, *21*, 2280. [CrossRef] [PubMed]
13. Wong, C.C.; Tsai, C.C.; Chen, R.J.; Chien, S.Y.; Yang, Y.H.; Wong, S.W.; Yeh, C.A. Generic Development of Bin Pick-and-Place System Based on Robot Operating System. *IEEE Access* **2022**, *10*, 65257–65270. [CrossRef]
14. Bochkovskiy, A.; Wang, C.Y.; Liao, H.Y.M. Yolov4: Optimal Speed and Accuracy of Object Detection. *arXiv* **2020**, arXiv:2004.10934.
15. Yu, X.; Tang, X.; Ye, B.; Song, B.; Zhou, X. Obstacle Space Modeling and Moving-window RRT for Manipulator Motion Planning. In Proceedings of the IEEE International Conference on Information and Automation (ICIA), Ningbo, China, 1–3 August 2016.

sensors

MDPI

Article

A Hybrid Stacked CNN and Residual Feedback GMDH-LSTM Deep Learning Model for Stroke Prediction Applied on Mobile AI Smart Hospital Platform

Bassant M. Elbagoury [1], Luige Vladareanu [2,*], Victor Vlădăreanu [2], Abdel Badeeh Salem [1], Ana-Maria Travediu [2] and Mohamed Ismail Roushdy [3]

[1] Faculty of Computer and Information Sciences, Ain Shams University, Cairo 11566, Egypt
[2] Institute of Solid Mechanics of the Romanian Academy, 010141 Bucharest, Romania
[3] Faculty of Computers and Information Technology, Future University in Egypt, New Cairo 11835, Egypt
* Correspondence: luige.vladareanu@vipro.edu.ro

Abstract: Artificial intelligence (AI) techniques for intelligent mobile computing in healthcare has opened up new opportunities in healthcare systems. Combining AI techniques with the existing Internet of Medical Things (IoMT) will enhance the quality of care that patients receive at home remotely and the successful establishment of smart living environments. Building a real AI for mobile AI in an integrated smart hospital environment is a challenging problem due to the complexities of receiving IoT medical sensors data, data analysis, and deep learning algorithm complexity programming for mobile AI engine implementation AI-based cloud computing complexities, especially when we tackle real-time environments of AI technologies. In this paper, we propose a new mobile AI smart hospital platform architecture for stroke prediction and emergencies. In addition, this research is focused on developing and testing different modules of integrated AI software based on XAI architecture, this is for the mobile health app as an independent expert system or as connected with a simulated environment of an AI-cloud-based solution. The novelty is in the integrated architecture and results obtained in our previous works and this extended research on hybrid GMDH and LSTM deep learning models for the proposed artificial intelligence and IoMT engine for mobile health edge computing technology. Its main goal is to predict heart–stroke disease. Current research is still missing a mobile AI system for heart/brain stroke prediction during patient emergency cases. This research work implements AI algorithms for stroke prediction and diagnosis. The hybrid AI in connected health is based on a stacked CNN and group handling method (GMDH) predictive analytics model, enhanced with an LSTM deep learning module for biomedical signals prediction. The techniques developed depend on the dataset of electromyography (EMG) signals, which provides a significant source of information for the identification of normal and abnormal motions in a stroke scenario. The resulting artificial intelligence mHealth app is an innovation beyond the state of the art and the proposed techniques achieve high accuracy as stacked CNN reaches almost 98% for stroke diagnosis. The GMDH neural network proves to be a good technique for monitoring the EMG signal of the same patient case with an average accuracy of 98.60% to an average of 96.68% of the signal prediction. Moreover, extending the GMDH model and a hybrid LSTM with dense layers deep learning model has improved significantly the prediction results that reach an average of 99%.

Keywords: artificial intelligence; mobile health; stroke monitoring; iomt-stacked convolutional neural networks; GMDH neural networks; Deep LSTM; biomedical EMG signal processing

Citation: Elbagoury, B.M.; Vladareanu, L.; Vlădăreanu, V.; Salem, A.B.; Travediu, A.-M.; Roushdy, M.I. A Hybrid Stacked CNN and Residual Feedback GMDH-LSTM Deep Learning Model for Stroke Prediction Applied on Mobile AI Smart Hospital Platform. *Sensors* **2023**, *23*, 3500. https://doi.org/10.3390/s23073500

Academic Editor: Joanna Kolodziej

Received: 28 December 2022
Revised: 15 February 2023
Accepted: 7 March 2023
Published: 27 March 2023

1. Introduction

The proposed architecture aims to develop, analyze and incorporate artificial intelligence and deep learning technology and extend our previous research on mobile AI telemedicine platforms [1] to harness the findings of research and development in the fields of biomedical signal processing (ECG, EMG/ECG). In the sense of emergency, artificial intelligence, and tracking in a healthcare setting, this article is intended to create adaptive, collaborative, and creative artificial intelligence and intelligence technologies for patients.

Artificial intelligence (AI) technologies in Smart health living hospitals for connected and mobile health AI edge computing integrated with telemedicine systems have opened up new opportunities in healthcare systems and complex diseases. Predictive analytics [1–4] and intelligent mobile edge computing in healthcare [5–9] help patients manage their treatments, especially for stroke monitoring and predictive analytics [5,9], which is a complex problem due to real-time detection of patient cases and real-time biomedical sensor signal streaming of each person independently. The intelligent mobile health application aims to help stroke patients record their episode once it occurs based on EMG signals. However, classifying real-time EMG signals [10–12] is a complex task, especially due to problems with patient muscle signal feedback. This research paper introduces a new predictive analytics model for stroke prediction using technologies of mobile health, and artificial intelligence algorithms such as stacked CNN, GMDH, and LSTM models [13–22]. A new prototype of a mobile AI health system has also been developed with high-accuracy results, which are going to be discussed in this paper. The main motivation is automating classification and intelligent emergency assistance for patients who suffer strokes.

Deep learning (multiple layer neural networks) enables end-to-end learning, where higher dimensional features (e.g., the correlation between multi-bio signal measurement datasets) are input directly to the neural network. IoMT devices such as ECG, and EMG send information directly so that signals can be analyzed and used as input for mobile devices and intelligent telemedicine platforms.

In addition, stroke prediction research is still missing a real-time AI-based heart diagnosis and stroke prediction system to be developed as an AI-based platform to be used, especially in the new era of smart hospitals and artificial intelligent technologies in European hospitals [23–31].

The experiments presented in this paper discuss the measurements of the EMG dataset and signal prediction results. The focus is on using IoMT implemented within the framework of a novel deep learning telemedicine platform for an AI smart hospital setting that can deliver care to stroke patients. This platform can be used as a portable patient/person assistive emergency tool and as a telemedicine hospital support system as well as an inter-hospital support system for larger hospital associations due to the flexible system model. Several deep learning models have been introduced in research [32–40], targeting cardiovascular and stroke diseases.

The experiments presented in this paper discuss the measurements of the EMG dataset and signal prediction results. We are focused to use IoMT implemented within a framework of novel deep learning telemedicine platform for AI smart hospital settings that can deliver care to stroke patients and people in a smart health environment. This work proposed the following artificial intelligence platform and deep learning techniques applied for stroke patients' emergencies:

1. An innovative automated proposed biomedical deep learning cloud platform for stroke patients' emergencies and remote using stacked convolutional neural networks the proposed solution offers complete intelligent healthcare services inside homes, for elderlies, families, and emergency care services. The main goal is heart stroke prediction, monitoring, and diagnosis. The AI-connected health platform includes deep learning models to the cloud and a mHealth module to send alerts.
2. The innovative artificial intelligence telemedicine platform for stroke prediction and emergency situations. That depends on statistical methods for EMG signal tracking and prediction such as group handling methods (GMDH) neural network [8,9] for patient stroke real-time prediction. The GMDH deep learning model is further enhanced with LSTM deep learning module [18,19].
3. A new real-time CNN-stroke and heart and BAN-IOT: a deep learning model for signal deep feature extraction and classification within big data streaming environment

4. A new mobile AI engine prototype has been developed and tested for the proposed AI techniques.

The paper consists of four sections as follows: the introduction consists of background and related work. Section 2 presents related works, Section 3 discusses materials and methods used, explains EMG signal processing features extraction, explains the stacked CNN deep learning technique, and presents the usage of GMDH neural networks for stroke prediction, along with extended LSTM prediction results. Section 4 presents experimental results and the simulated AI mobile app and Section 5 discusses conclusions and future work.

2. Related Works

AI has been in development for decades, but only recently become good enough for people to notice, mostly due to advances in other industries besides health care. The rise of intelligent machines is approaching, and the world, especially the healthcare industry, is far from prepared for what is to come. Mobile health [19,24] applications are receiving increased attention largely due to the global penetration of mobile technologies. It is estimated that over 85% of the world's population is now covered by a commercial wireless signal, with over 5 billion mobile phone subscriptions [11]. Tarik Taleb et al. [12] present a study on MEC (mobile edge computing) [9,19,24,33] that discusses the major enabling technologies in this domain. It explores MEC deployment considering both the perspectives of individual services as well as a network of MEC platforms supporting mobility. It also delves into an analysis of a MEC. reference architecture and its main deployment scenarios that can offer multitenancy support for application developers. R. Yongbo Li et al. [14] have developed MobiQoR: for Pushing the Envelope of Mobile [9,19,20,24,33] Edge Computing Via Quality-of-Result Optimization. Fang, S.H. et al. [16] proposes a deep learning mechanism to identify the transportation modes of smartphone users. The proposed mechanism is evaluated on a database that contains more than one thousand hours of accelerometer, magnetometer, and gyroscope measurements from five transportation modes including still, walking, running, bike, and vehicle.

Oguz Karan [5], presented an ANN model applied to smartphones to diagnose diabetes. In this study, a three-layered multilayer perceptron (MLP) feedforward neural network architecture was used and trained with the error backpropagation algorithm. Peter Pes [6], developed a smartphone-based decision support system (DSS) for the management of type 1 diabetes in order to improve quality of life. Jieun Kim [16], proposed a case-based reasoning [19,24,41–48] approach to matching the user needs and existing services, identifying unmet opportunistic user needs, and retrieving similar services with opportunities based on Apple smartphones. Swapna et al. [38] have worked on EEG signal generation and heart rate in cardiac diseases, however, they did not address stroke prediction issues. Complications of acute ischemic stroke from a medical perspective, but without addressing prediction issues were addressed. Park et al. [39] have developed an intelligent stroke monitoring system during sleeping cases only but not for outdoor multi-event systems. Aminova et al. [40] have developed a single-channel EEG predictor for cognitive function after stroke and not using EMG as a pre-stroke prediction system. Z. Yang [41] proposed a model of an IoT-cloud [42,45] based wearable ECG monitoring system for smart healthcare. Satija et al. [48] presented continuous cardiac health monitoring with signal quality-aware IoT-enabled [42,43,47,48] ECG telemetry system. Ihsanto et al. [7] proposed depthwise separable convolutional (DSC) NNs for the cardiac arrhythmia categorization. The MIT-BIH arrhythmia database was utilized for the assessment of the proposed ensemble CNNs' performance. The proposed algorithm could classify the data into sixteen classes. In addition to that, the sensitivity was 99.03%, specificity was 99.94%, positive predictive was 99.03%, and accuracy was 99.88%. Predictive analytics in healthcare decision-making [3,47,48] deals with information retrieval to predict an unknown event of interest, typically a future event. Using technology that learns from data to predict these unknown events could drive better decisions.

3. Materials and Methods

The architecture of the proposed intelligent hospital for the connected health modules is presented in Figure 1. It consists of a wearable sensors module that sends signal streams for signal processing modules and mobile AI health for stroke prediction. It can be connected to the cloud, as seen in the following figure, in order to accomplish effectively the aims of the research. The smart hospital stroke system, which integrates recent advances in artificial intelligence and predictive computing with telemedicine applications, is a continuously growing field in telemedicine. A stroke can cause sudden death and is a matter of urgency. It is one of America's leading causes of death. Heart/brain stroke, for these reasons, is an emergency and must be treated promptly before any complications occur. Recent research shows that a smart hospital heart/stroke system is at the forefront of current research, especially in the field of chronic diseases and emergency conditions such as heart attacks. Today, however, an intelligent patient control screening device is lacking. In addition, such a system needs smart algorithms for patient stroke prediction and emergencies to warn better diagnostic decisions and fast patient care response in the process. In this paper, a modern intelligent hybrid architecture is proposed. The most important activities and actions in this innovative architecture for smart hospital-connected health approach are concentrated around the individual person/patient.

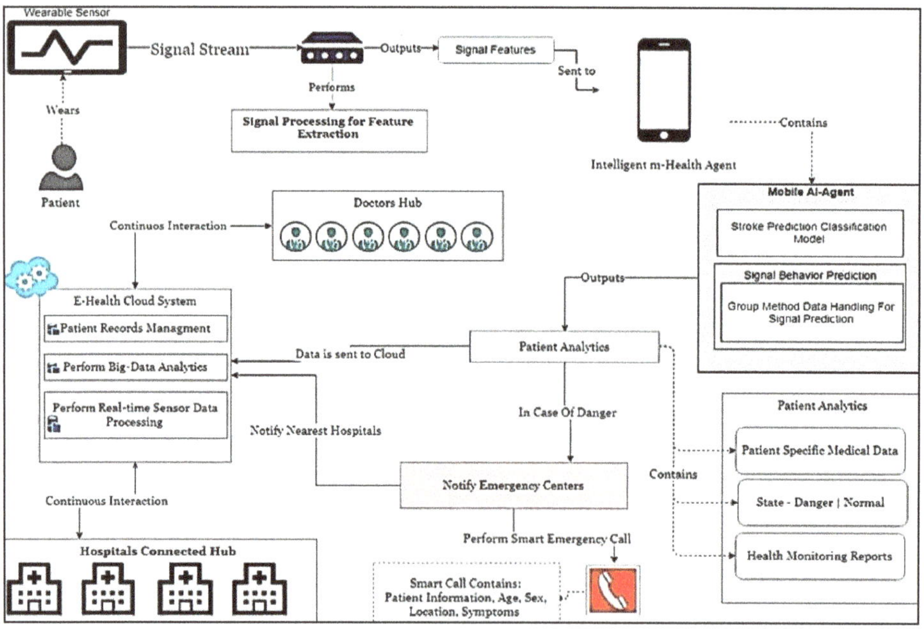

Figure 1. The artificial intelligence architecture for smart hospital connected health.

The proposed Mobile AI Health Agent receives all necessary inputs from medical sensors, and sensors operating on EMG, as will be explained in this article, but it can be extended to other biomedical sensors for stroke and heart diseases [24]. On the other hand, after the sensors' data and information are processed and results are obtained, they are delivered to the individual under tracking.

The proposed architecture of Figure 1 is also integrated with set of DSS tools for explainable artificial intelligence (XAI)-based human-centric (HC) applications, as shown in Figure 2, where a medical decision support system (MDSS) is proposed. It is directed to cover concrete individualized needs of the patient under treatment, medication, or social care, as well as on-hand competence of concrete sub-division in a medical institution taking care of this personal case. Here, the block of comparatively static diagnostics contains a personalized toolset dedicated to primary diagnosis, predictive state classification, assignments, and individual recommendations (A), based on a set of DSS tools built on the basis of XAI.

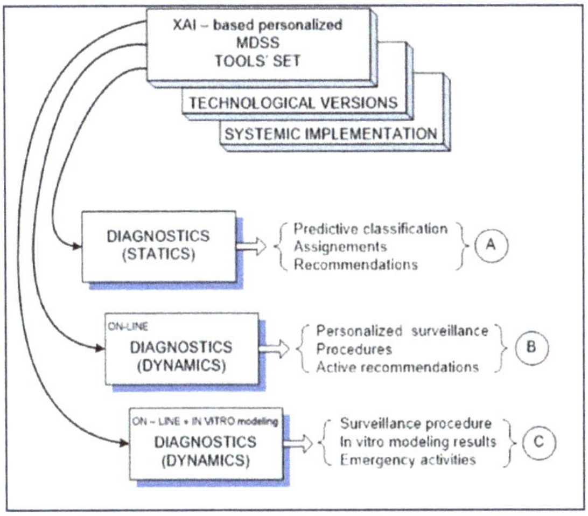

Figure 2. Concept of the XAI-based HC tools for MDSS. Blocks A, B and C are described in details in the related paragraphs in this section.

The next block of dynamic diagnostics online is dedicated to individualized observation of the individual under permanent healthcare service and is responsible for personalized surveillance, all prescribed procedures, and active recommendations (B) for both actors: the patient, and health professionals as well.

The third block is similar to the second, but it is equipped with additional tools for offline modeling of proposed procedures in case any uncertainty appears. So, the output of this block (C) contains all recommended procedures of surveillance, results of the in vitro modeling, and recommendations concerning all possible emergency activities.

Figure 3 illustrates the relation between the XAI tools concept and it is integrated into our mobile AI smart hospital platform, where all digital data and evaluations are ready to be analyzed and pre-processed using deep learning [4,11,13–15] and feature extraction methods [28] for both Artificial intelligence telemedicine for smart ai hospital heart/stroke health units and IoT-edge cloud AI biomedical sensors processing [23–25,28]. On the other hand, after the sensors' data and information are processed and results are obtained, they are delivered to the individual under tracking (A), this is where this paper presents most of the research article. The next block of XAI architecture dynamic diagnostics online is dedicated to individualized observation of the individual under permanent health care service and is responsible for personalized surveillance, all prescribed procedures, and active recommendations (B) for both actors: a patient, and health professionals as well.

The main and most important activities and actions in this human-centric approach are concentrated around the individual on TIER 1 (on the left side of Figure 3). Here, DSS receives all necessary inputs from ordinary body sensors, sensors operating on information based on individual's location (location-based sensors) and for the first time involved Soft sensors dealing with information about environment. TIER 2 consists of fuzzy logic modules, which are not yet implemented in this paper. It will be considered for future work.

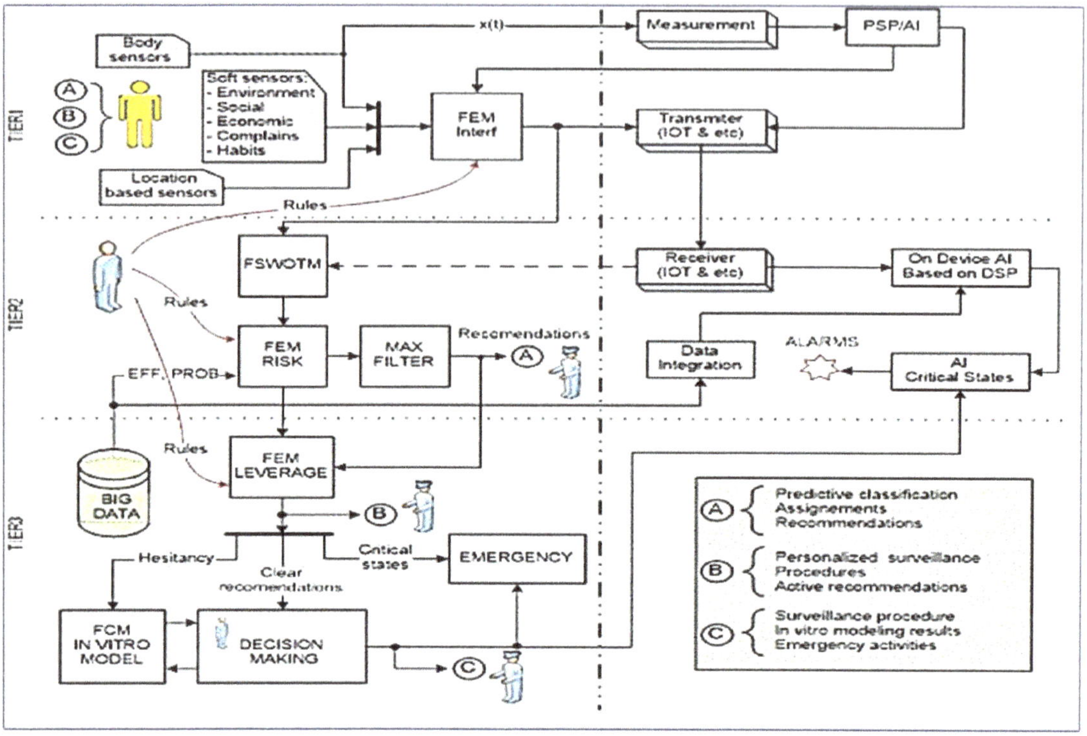

Figure 3. XAI general architecture consists of TIER1, TIER2, and TIER3. TIER 1 has been implemented as AI software modules for the proposed mobile AI smart hospital system.

3.1. Mobile AI Smart Hospital Platform: Artificial Intelligence Materials and Methods for Stroke Prediction at Home Care Emergencies Scenarios

An innovative automated biomedical deep learning cloud platform for stroke patients' emergencies and remote monitoring is presented in this section. Figure 4 illustrates the possible implementation of the system for home care stroke emergencies. Personalized early risk detection and intervention solutions for prevention and treatments based on early risk detection are paramount for people facing increased health and social risks. As shown in Figure 3, the proposed solution offers complete intelligent healthcare services inside homes, for the elderly, families, and emergency care services. The main goal is for heart/brain stroke prediction, monitoring, and diagnosis. The platform [24] includes deep learning models and a mHealth module to send alerts. Two important techniques, stacked convolutional and pooling layers for biomedical sensors signal correlations are presented in this section.

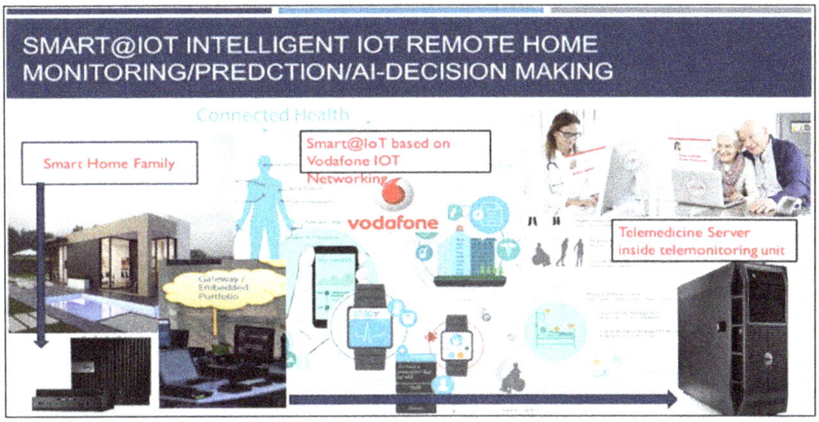

Figure 4. Ubiquitous intelligent IOT smart health/brain stroke deep learning platform.

3.2. Stacked Convolutional and Pooling Layers for Biomedical Sensors Signal Correlations

This section exploits the usage of convolutional layers, as shown in Figure 5 and their ability to extract several activation maps per signal, thus enabling us to deeply extract the correlated signal features.

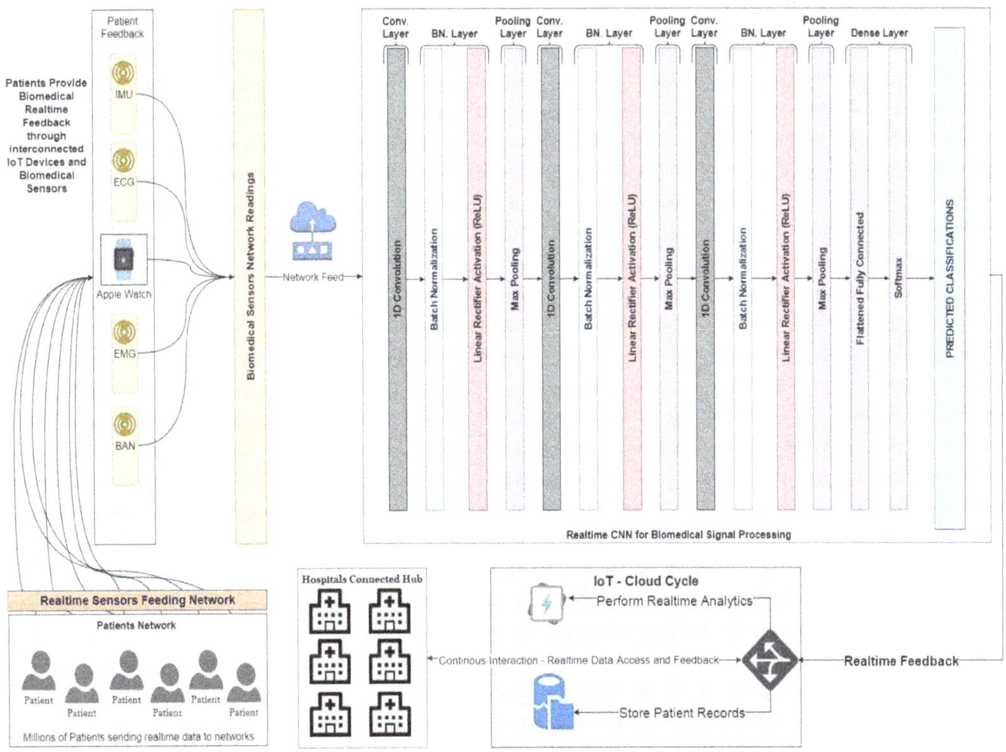

Figure 5. Proposed deep learning architecture: stacked convolutional and pooling layers for biomedical sensors signal correlations.

Thus, the usage of stacked convolutional and pooling layers has been introduced that act as deep convolutional networks for extracting hidden signal features. A Softmax layer is then added to evaluate the model's ability to classify input signals. The extracted features can later be used as input to another learning model that will act directly on the constructed feature vectors. Figure 5 illustrates the architecture of the tested CNN deep learning model.

The model has been tested in a scenario with a significant number of patients, sending biomedical real-time feedback through interconnected IoT devices and biomedical sensors, such as EMG, ECG, BAN, and IMU signals. The CNN model architecture is given as follows:

Convolutional Layer: It aims to extract deep features of the input signal through several activation filters. The network extracts deep features by applying 1-D filters through the input signal and then outputs a different shape of the input signal. Pooling Layer: It aims to lower the dimensionality of the big data streamed to the convolutional layer and its output, reduces computation time, and helps the network converge. Max pooling has been used along with batch normalization. Fully Connected Layer: It flattens the output from higher dimensions down through a fully connected network of neurons, and then reduces its dimension. Multiple fully connected layers are used to feed the Softmax experimental classifier. The proposed stacked CNN network time measurements are shown in Table 1.

Table 1. Network time measurements.

Operation	Time Cost (Seconds)
Feedforward during training	0.152 s
Total Training for 500 Epochs	240 s (4 min)
Sample Extraction and Prediction	0.025 s
10 million Samples on 8 Nodes	25 s per Node

Datasets Used

Dataset Name: EMG Lower Limb Dataset

The EMG Lower Limb dataset includes different 24 patients, performing three different actions, each patient is classified as binary normal, and abnormal.

Dataset Characteristics:

Signal Type	Time Series
Number of Instances per Channel	~12,000 Sample
Number of Channels	5 Channels

Dataset Name: mHealth Dataset

The mHealth dataset includes 10 different subjects performing 12 different actions, it also includes different measurements of subject kinematic information.

Dataset Characteristics:

Signal Type	Time Series
Number of Instances per Channel	~160,000 Sample
Number of Channels	24 Channels

EMG Physical Action dataset [48]

EMG dataset contains

4 subjects

2 main binary classes normal and aggressive

10 human activities

Aggressive: elbowing, front kicking, hammering, heading, kneeing, pulling, punching, pushing, side kicking, slapping

Normal: bowing, clapping, handshaking, hugging, jumping, running, seating, standing, walking, waving

Almost 10,000 samples for each activity

Number of features: 8 muscles

R-Bic, R-Tri, L-Bic, L-Tri, R-Thi, R-Ham, L-Thi, L-Ham

3.3. *Stroke Prediction Using GMDH-Type Neural Network Enhanced with LSTM Module*

This section describes the use of group method data handling (GMDH) to predict the value of the signal time series. For this, a multi-layered parametric iteration GMDH algorithm with polynomial reference functions is implemented.

It is a sorting out of gradually complex models generated from Kolmogorov–Gabor polynomial (Figures 6 and 7).

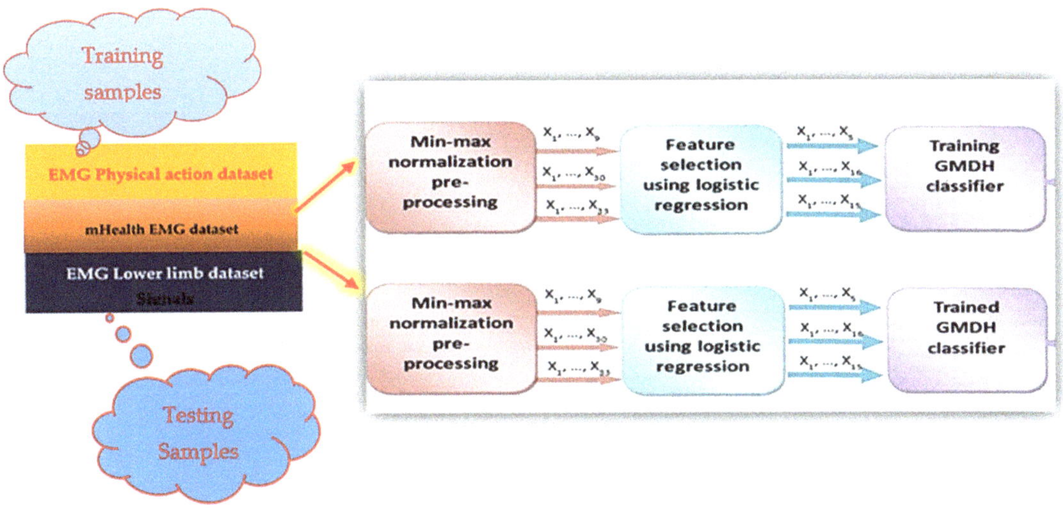

Figure 6. GMDH training preprocessing.

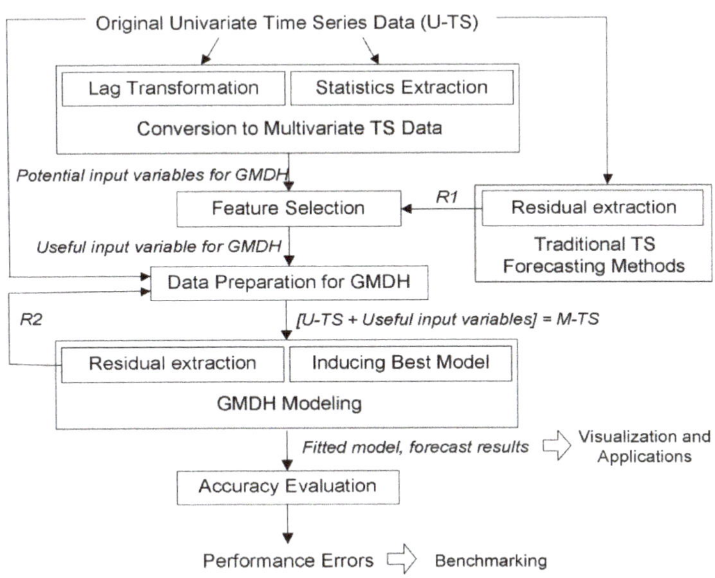

Figure 7. GMDH data preprocessing.

We transform the input signal into a supervised problem, therefore making the GMDH able to predict its behavior. The graph below (Figure 8) shows a sample signal that will be later transformed into a supervised problem to feed the neural network.

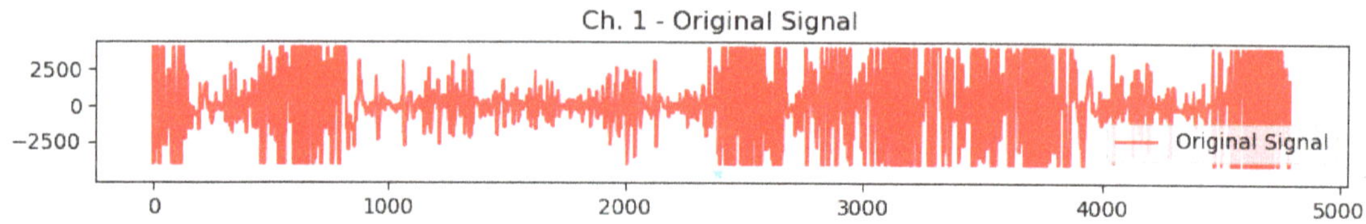

Figure 8. Sample of the original EMG signal.

The best model is chosen by the minimum of a specified external criterion characteristic, thus making it equivalent to an artificial neural network with polynomial activation functions for neurons.

The values of the previously shown signal are then transformed into a supervised problem as follows:

$$[x_{i-1}, x_i] \rightarrow [y] \mid where\ y = x_{i+1}$$

We then feed the resulting feature matrices and their corresponding labels to the neural network to start the training process. The developed GMDH deep learning model [30] is built based on the reference function, then during the training process based on the selected external criterion the neurons are eliminated during the training process and the best model is created.

A selection criterion exists to perform the neurons dropout at each layer thus performing the select-and-drop training process. Selection criteria are: validation score, bias, validation score, and bias. As seen in the graph, specific neurons are selected based on the criterion and are dropped out in the next layer training process.

The training process of the neural network is stopped based on two criteria: error is not decreasing anymore, or the neural network has reached its maximum number of layers.

Least mean squared error (LMSE) is used as a loss function. The maximum number of layers for the network is defined externally before the training process.

The resulting feature matrices and their corresponding labels are then fed to the neural network to start the training process. Several transfer functions are available for the polynomial neural network; the transfer function is used as an activation function for regression problems using GMDH-type neural network. A GMDH can formulate an optimization of the structure based on the current transfer function, each transfer function is also adaptively created by another self-organizing process.

3.4. *A Proposed Hybrid LSTM with Dense Layers Deep Learning Model for Stroke Prediction*

LSTM is a special kind of RNN [15,22], which shows outstanding performance on a large variety of problems. It maintains state (memory) across very long sequences, basic architecture is shown in Figure 9, because LSTM is very sensitive to the data ranges we applied data normalization and scaling in the input and output. We used standard scaling for the input. It can be solved using linear activation in the output layer.

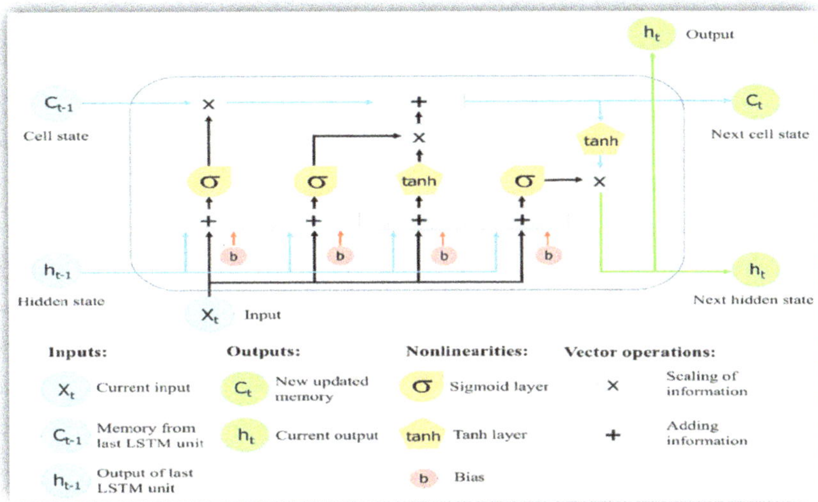

Figure 9. Basic LSTM deep learning gates [15,22].

A novel Stroke prediction algorithm is proposed based on EMG signals prediction. The proposed solution employs a novel architecture consisting of multiple LSTM recurrent dense networks as shown in Figure 10. Experimental evaluations show superior EMG prediction performance compared to previous works. Measurements with different deep learning methods such as combining CNN with LSTM show that the proposed algorithm meets performance requirements for continuous and real-time execution on IoMT devices. In contrast to many GMDH deep learning-based approaches, the proposed algorithm is lightweight for the proposed mobile AI engine, and therefore, brings continuous diagnosis and prediction with accurate GMDH–LSTM-based EMG signal prediction to IoMT simulated inputs.

The first part chooses whether the information coming from the previous timestamp is to be remembered or is irrelevant and can be forgotten. In the second part, the cell tries to learn new information from the input to this cell. At last, in the third part, the cell passes the updated information from the current timestamp to the next timestamp.

In this article, we have built a hybrid LSTM model concatenated with dense layers. The LSTM modules are based on the basic parts of LSTM gates, each of which consists of three parts, the first part is called forget gate, the second part is known as the input gate and the last one is the output gate [15,22].

The detailed hybrid model LSTM/dense deep learning model is shown in Figure 10. For more illustrations as shown below. Its input_output takes all the EMG 8 channels of the EMG physical action dataset [47,48]. Our input features shape is (1, 256) for each 8-muscle signal.

lstm_input	input:	[(None, 1, 256)]	[(None, 1, 256)]
InputLayer	output:		

In addition, output classes are one-shot encode vectors with shape (None, 20).

dense_11	input:	(None, 32)	(None, 20)
Dense	output:		

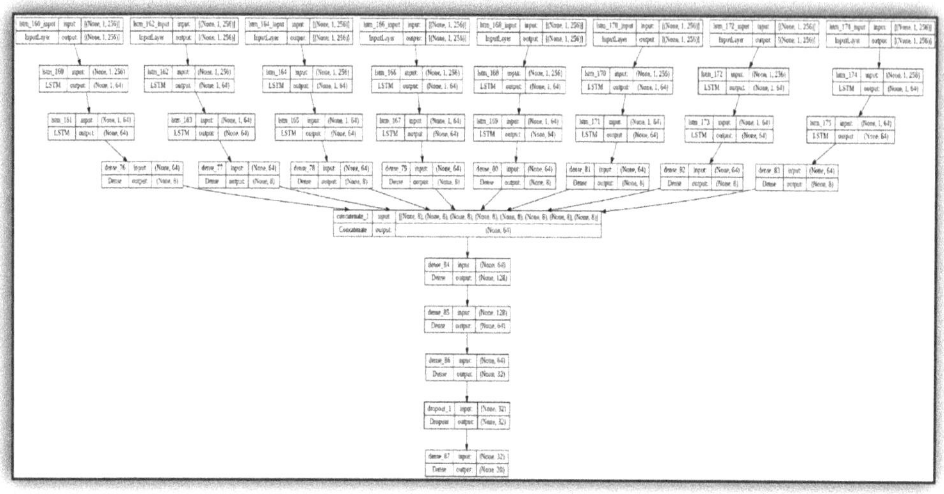

Figure 10. Hybrid LSTM and dense deep learning layers for EMG signals with 8 channels input.

LSTM Training Results:

- Hyperparameters
    - Batch size = 256
    - Epochs = 100
    - Starting learning rate = 0.0001
- After 100 epochs from the 50
    - Training loss: 0.1890
    - Training accuracy: 0.9365
    - Validation loss: 0.2364
    - Validation accuracy: 0.9238
- End learning rate: 1.0000×10^{-9}

3.5. Data Preprocessing

Two methods have been used to preprocess the data

The first one is called feature scaling, these methods do not aim to extract new information from the data, it changes the scale of it only.

The user's biofeedback signal is extracted on a server that is monitoring human health conditions based on emerging wireless mobile technologies with wireless body sensors. Different datasets have been used for the experiments. The first contains EMG signals with two target classes: normal and aggressive. This task is considered a time series data classification problem.

Table 2 shows the EMG physical action dataset includes 4 different patients, performing 10 different actions, each patient is classified as binary normal or abnormal.

Table 2. EMG physical action dataset specifications.

Signal Type	**Time Series**
Number of Instances per Channel	~10,000 Sample
Number of Channels	8 Channels
Number of patients	4 patients

The second method produces new features from the data such as RMS. We tested the two methods with different models and this section needs more investigation.

- Feature Scaling:
- Standard Scaling:

Standardize features by removing the mean and scaling to unit variance.

This is a 2D vis. For the effect standard scaling at 8 channels of Subject 1 at normal state while handshaking.

- Robust Scaling

Scale features using statistics that are robust to outliers.

- Min–Max Scaling

It essentially shrinks the range such that the range is now between 0 and 1 (or −1 to 1 if there are negative values).

- Normalizer

The normalizer scales each value by dividing each value by its magnitude in n-dimensional space for n number of features (Figure 11). This is a 3D vis. For the effect normalization at 3 channels of Subject 1 at normal state while handshaking.

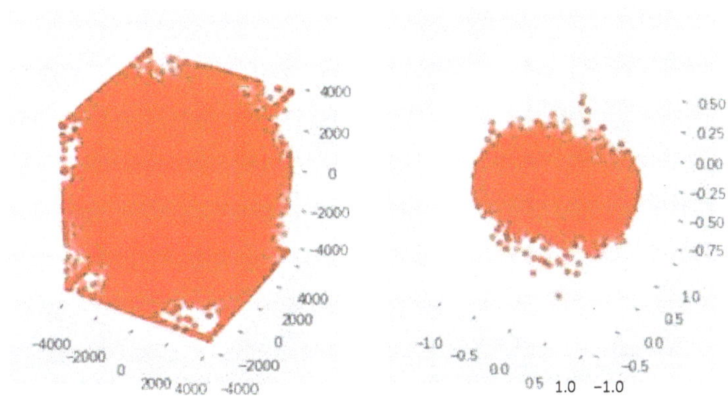

Figure 11. This is a 3D vis. For the effect normalization at 3 channels of Subject 1 at normal state while handshaking. The aim of this figure is to picture the way the data are pre-processed by representing three dimensions out of eight.

Wavelet transforms are some of the more efficient techniques for processing nonstationary signals such as biomedical signals (e.g., EMG). Wavelet transforms the signal into its time–frequency domains. There are two types of wavelet analysis, discrete wavelet transform (DWT) and continuous wavelet transform (CWT). Figure 11. The subfigure on the left corresponds to feature scaling process while the subfigure on the right corresponds to standard scaling. Standardize features by removing the mean and scaling to unit variance in order to process the signals easier.

Both of them consume little time for signal processing. CWT is more consistent, but DWT has proven efficiency in analyzing nonstationary signals, although it yields a high-dimensional feature vector. In our research, discrete wavelet transform (DWT) is used for analyzing the EMG signal and extracting significant features which are very useful in identification of healthy, myopathic, and neuropathic subjects.

Seven features of the EMG signal are taken into consideration in this research. Root mean square (RMS), mean absolute value (MAV), zero crossing (ZC), slope sign change (SSC), and standard deviation (SD). Each one of these features is used as input to the classification process which is the next phase after the feature extraction process. The EMG MAV feature window size and values sample are presented in Figure 12.

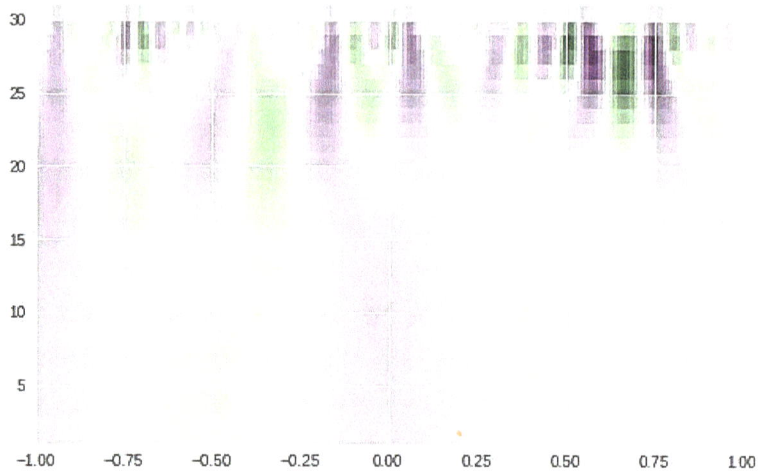

Figure 12. EMG MAV feature window size and values sample.

A Daubechies wavelet function [34] of degree four (db4) was applied on each frame of the EMG signals in training and testing data so that the next step is to extract time and time–frequency features from the resulting processed signal (Figure 13).

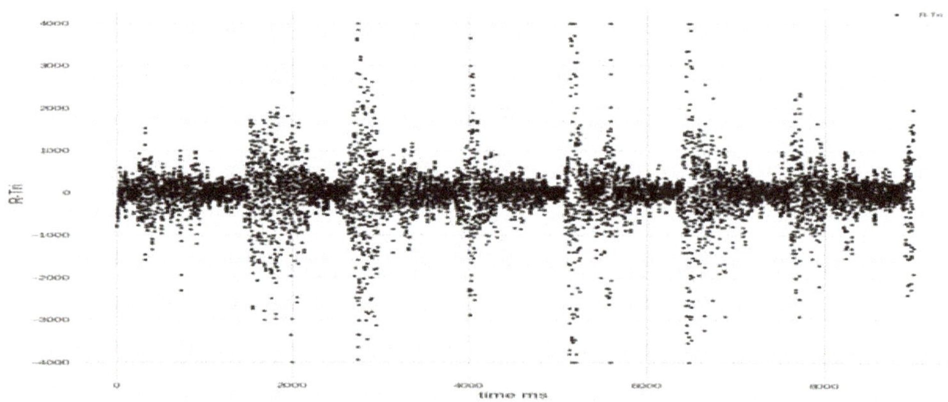

Figure 13. Real-time EMG muscle sample raw data in time ms [14–16].

This will be the main expert system engine for suggested initial diagnosis and emergency calls to the nearest hospitals for overall patient management and safety. It will depend on neural networks and case-based reasoning technologies.

The first step in our system is the sensor collects data. Mobile sensing process is shown in Figure 14, where mobile device evaluates data. Then, mobile device sends aggregated data to the telemedicine server. Then, telemedicine server evaluates data and informs physicians about our upcoming developments in artificial intelligence expert system.

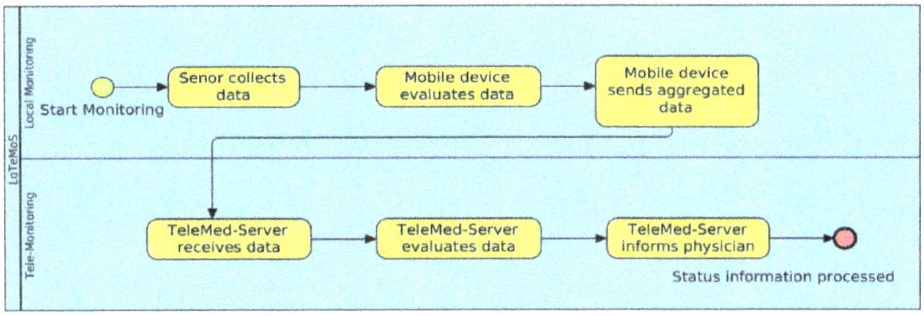

Figure 14. Mobile sensing, sensor collects data, mobile device, and telemedicine server.

In this research, analyzing data of stroke based on EMG sensors, as shown in Figure 15 of muscle readings to enable extracting best features. Then, significant features for efficient classification are selected since it determines the success of the pattern classification system. However, it is quite problematic to extract the best feature parameters from the EMG signals that can reflect the unique feature of the signal to the motion command perfectly. Hence, multiple feature sets are used as inputs to the EMG signal classification process. Some of the features are classified as time domain, frequency domain, time–frequency domain, and time-scale domain; these feature types are successfully employed for EMG signal classification. The next step is the signal classification phase.

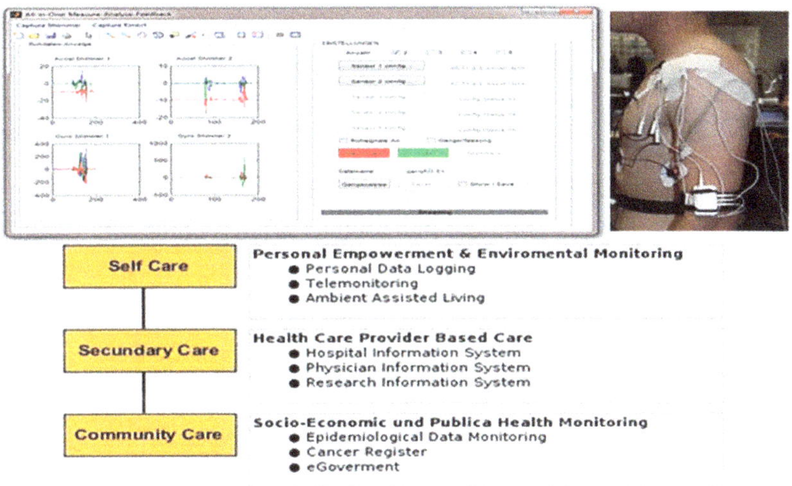

Figure 15. Real-time patient EMG data acquisition process by shimmer sensor [14–16].

The data acquisition process (Figure 15) consists of both real-time methodology as experiments conducted by German researchers at the Brandenburg University [14–16], and comparison to the offline dataset of the UCI and the Ain Shams University researchers [3] for different EMG signals channels samples, different colors, at different scaling.

The EMG signals are known for their uniqueness in every subject. An EMG sample consists of five channels:

(1) RF: Rectus Femoral
(2) BF: Biceps Femoral
(3) VM: Vastus Medial
(4) ST: Semitendinosus
(5) FX: Knee Flexion

Several feature combinations have been tested for obtaining the optimal signal results, which total 128 features. The number of classes of motions is 20, which consists of 10 normal and 10 aggressive physical actions.

The following are normal: bowing, clapping, handshaking, hugging, jumping, running, seating, standing, walking, and waving. the following are aggressive: elbowing, front-kicking, hammering, heading, kneeing, pulling, punching, pushing, side-kicking, and slapping.

Figure 16 shows a sample of normal and abnormal EMG signals [14–16]. Seven features have been selected to obtain optimal results in signal classification. A sample of extracted features with the final selected features is shown in Table 3.

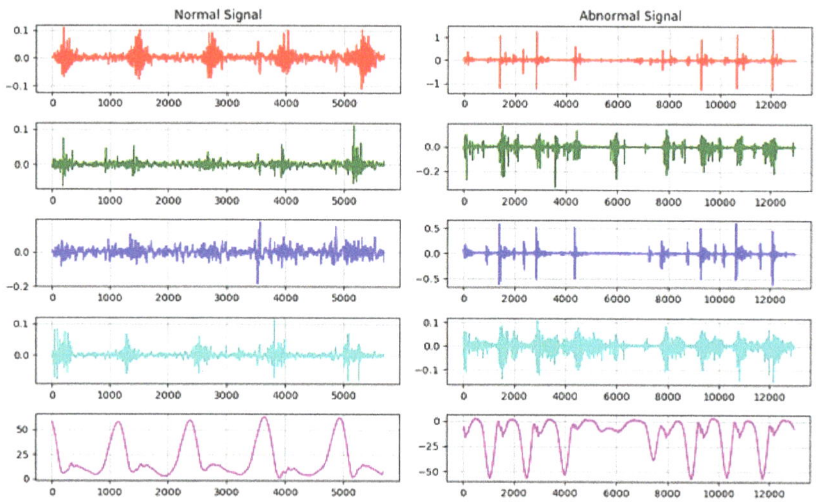

Figure 16. Real-time EMG signals sample histogram of normal and abnormal signals for different EMG signals channels samples at different scaling.

Table 3. Final selected features.

Abv.	Name of Feature	Definition
IEMG	Integrated EMG	$IEMG = \sum_{i=1}^{N} \lvert X_i \rvert$
MAV1	Modified mean absolute value type 1	$MAV1 = \frac{1}{N}\sum_{i=1}^{N} w_t \lvert X_i \rvert, \quad w_t = \begin{cases} 1 \text{ } if \text{ } 0.25N \leq i \leq 0.75N \\ 0.5, otherwise \end{cases}$
RMS	Root Mean Square	$RMS = \sqrt{\frac{1}{N}\sum_{i=1}^{N} X_i^2}$
AAC	Average Amplitude Change	$AAC = \frac{1}{N}\sum_{i=1}^{N-1} \lvert X_{i+1} - X_i \rvert$
ZC	Zero Crossing	$ZC = \sum_{i=1}^{N-1} [\mathrm{sgn}(X_i \times X_{i+1}) \cap \lvert X_i - X_{i+1} \rvert \geq treshold]$
WAMP	Willison Amplitude	$WAMP = \sum_{i=1}^{N-1} [f(\lvert X_n - X_{n+1} \rvert)]$
WL	Waveform length	$WL = \sum_{i=1}^{N-1} \lvert X_{i+1} - X_i \rvert$

Integrated EMG	IEM
Modified Mean Absolute Value 1	MAV1
Root Mean Square	RMS
Average amplitude change	AAC
Zero crossing	ZC
Willison amplitude	WAMP
Waveform length	WL

The following datasets were used:

Dataset Name: EMG lower limb dataset

The EMG lower limb dataset includes different 24 patients, performing three different actions, each patient is classified as binary normal, and abnormal.

Dataset Name: mHealth dataset

The mHealth dataset includes different 10 subjects performing different 12 actions, it also includes different measurements of subject kinematic information.

Both of the datasets are being used in the experiment for evaluating the model speed and accuracy in handling case-by-case. One patient sends two signal channels per time: the EMG signals reading and the ECG signals reading.

So, each patient has a multi-dimensional vector describing his input X = [EMG Signal Samples, ECG Signal Samples].

4. Results

Accuracy reached 85% with the following characteristics: A learning rate of $L = 0.0001$ Binary Cross Entropy Loss (BCE) function for loss measurement. The accuracy increased to 92% by using each supplied signal feature as a CNN input. The total test time was 5 s for 4 test subjects and there were a total of 24.576 test signal samples.

There are two approaches for distributing deep learning models on the cloud, as shown below.

1. Model Parallelism:

In this paradigm, there is only one model distributed on different machines or different GPUs. For example, different layers may be assigned to different machines. This paradigm is useful for big models.

2. Data Parallelism:

In this paradigm, the model is copied between more than one machine. Each model runs on a different subset of the data.

Figure 17 shows a graphical explanation of the two paradigms. All computations are completed based on model parallelism.

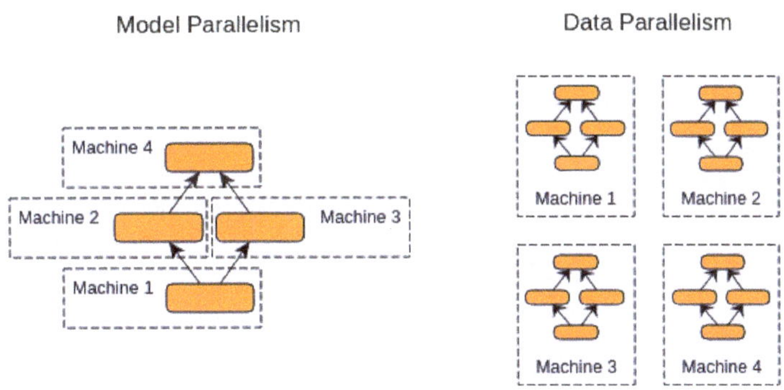

Figure 17. Model and data parallelism.

The following properties of the GMDH-type polynomial network have been used during the test:

Activation Function	Linear
Selection Criterion	Validate and Bias
Epsilon Training Error	0.001

The proposed mobile AI smart hospital platform consists of two main parts, the first one uses the stack CNN as AI cloud-based and the other GMDH and LSTM modules are used for the mobile AI app. For the first one, its main objective is presented as a new real-time CNN-stroke and Stroke and BAN-IOT: a deep learning model for signal deep feature extraction and classification within a cloud streaming environment. First, the use of stacked CNN is for handling the big data streaming of several signals sent from wearable sensors and body area networks (BAN) that include a variety of signals that do not correlate with each other on a shallow feature level. Scenario: Table 4 shows a sample of the EMG 8 channels.

Table 4. Shows a sample of the EMG 8 channels data included in the dataset [48].

Channel 1	Channel 2	Channel 3	Channel 4	Channel 5	Channel 6	Channel 7	Channel 8
−8.3532	2.5062	−2.406	−1.821	−1.1889	0.39931	−9.4774	−2.199
−7.073	2.1373	−2.6182	−2.0345	−1.3689	1.0842	−8.8761	−1.4746
−7.6434	2.3723	−2.4497	−2.2773	−1.4443	2.2408	−9.8723	−1.0962
−8.0995	2.4517	−2.7688	−2.4155	−1.4903	1.8016	−9.8628	−1.1314
−8.3307	2.3913	−3.0164	−2.1852	−1.394	0.44444	−9.9628	−1.2333
−8.7935	2.8082	−2.7473	−1.9383	−1.3229	1.0435	−9.7058	−1.2769
−8.9454	2.8268	−2.7351	−1.6787	−1.1889	1.8488	−9.6066	−1.2535
−9.4027	2.9628	−2.6491	−1.4568	−1.0424	1.6883	−9.5739	−0.95139
−8.9815	3.116	−2.4038	−1.4401	−1.0382	1.2073	−10.205	−0.69609
−9.1775	2.8138	−2.6836	−1.4903	−1.0173	1.1904	−10.231	−0.37467
−8.64	2.7076	−2.63	−1.4819	−0.90424	1.2918	−9.992	−0.19502
−8.7625	3.7808	−3.0071	−1.0717	−0.55259	1.8689	−9.5166	−0.17589
−8.5805	3.7717	−2.9237	−0.7619	−0.40607	1.9708	−9.4467	−0.1193
−8.6582	3.6193	−2.9164	−0.51073	−0.20513	1.7172	−9.9153	−0.43692
−8.6379	3.6099	−2.9593	−0.29304	−0.029304	1.2985	−9.9256	−0.4833
−8.4253	3.5899	−2.7716	−0.15489	0.066981	1.0929	−9.9872	−0.69676

- EMG Signal
- ECG Signal
- BAN Signal
- IMU Signal

Case Characteristics:
One patient sends two signal channels per time: 1—EMG signals reading
2—ECG signals reading
So, each patient has multi-dimensional vector describing his input

$$X = [\text{EMG Signal Samples, ECG Signal Samples}]$$

This model has been tested on mHealth [ref.] dataset, and on the EMG lower limb dataset.

Accuracy increased to reach 92% by using each supplied signal feature as a CNN input.

$$\text{Total test time} = 5\text{ s for 4 test subjects}$$

Total test signal samples = 24.576 signal samples

Concerning the processing time of GMDH it has taken nearly 30 min for the training.

(2) The evaluation method has tested different modules for the overall new smart hospital platform, as AI-based software implementation only.

Performance and results on cloud platform (GCP): Table 5 shows the performance and validation accuracy that has been achieved in our experiments, when implementing the stacked CNN, using two Nvidia GPUs. The use of AI-based cloud simulating the smart hospital platform.

Table 5. The performance and validation accuracy for the stacked CNN-cloud-based experiments.

Framework	Time to Train	Inference Time	Achieved Validation Accuracy	Number of GPUs	Scaling Efficiency
Keras	2 min	40 µs	98%	1	-
Keras + Tensoflow	2.3 min	45 µs	97.96%	2	88.88%

Tests have been conducted on 10 different physical action signals, the test samples have been divided almost evenly, 5k samples for training and ~5k samples for testing the prediction.

Table 6, below, shows the characteristics and scores for a selected subject, where 10 aggressive different actions are predicted using the GMDH-type neural network.

On average, among the selected subjects the model is able to predict accurately 96.02% of the signal in low time.

The table below shows the characteristics and scores for the previously selected subject, 10 normal different actions are predicted using the GMDH-type neural network.

As shown in Table 6, different experiments have been conducted by training the GMDH deep learning model on different input sizes of EMG channels. As illustrated different layers have different accuracies, according to input sizes of EMG 4 channels, EMG 8 channels, and EMG of mHealth dataset. On average, the selected subject's model is able to predict accurately 96.85% of the signal in low time.

Table 6. Model average prediction accuracy on the selected subjects was 96.85%.

Channels	Layers	RMSE	NRMSE	R-Squared	Train Time (s)	Test Time (s)
EMG 4 channels	7	355.257	0.039	98.60%	0.08924	0.000844717
EMG 8 channels	7	96.517	0.013	97.61%	0.08548	0.000657558
EMG m health channels	7	134.699	0.015	97.47%	0.07976	0.000873566
EMG 4 channels	3	29.893	0.007	97.23%	0.04030	0.000925303
	2	14.610	0.009	96.78%	0.01175	0.000540018
EMG 8 channels	3	61.059	0.011	96.41%	0.02851	0.000662088
	2	2.203	0.032	96.15%	0.01576	0.000739336
EMG m health channels	3	233.189	0.025	96.13%	0.03011	0.000577211
	2	27.089	0.026	96.08%	0.01697	0.000613451
	50	148.183	0.014	95.99%	0.59829	0.000548363
	Averages	110.27012	0.0191853	96.85%	0.09962	0.000698161

The following plots demonstrate two selected actions from the previously conducted test experiments, 1 normal action, and 1 aggressive action.

As shown in Table 7, different experiments have been conducted by training the GMDH deep learning model on different input sizes of EMG channels. As illustrated different layers have different accuracies, according to input sizes of EMG 4 channels, EMG 8 channels, and EMG of mHealth dataset.

Table 7. On average, among the selected subjects the model is able to predict accurately 96.02% of the signal in low time.

Channels	Layers	RMSE	NRMSE	R-Squared	Train Time (s)	Test Time (s)
EMG 4 channels	7	232.583	0.028	97.12%	0.07720	0.00047
	2	171.787	0.018	96.98%	0.01279	0.00055
EMG 8 channels	7	220.009	0.024	96.96%	0.08461	0.00090
EMG m health channels	7	204.746	0.025	96.85%	0.10477	0.00059
	3	191.501	0.020	96.68%	0.02523	0.00074
	2	213.642	0.021	96.06%	0.01341	0.00082
EMG 4 channels	3	265.888	0.027	95.94%	0.02851	0.00083
	7	304.756	0.031	95.43%	0.09501	0.00066
EMG 8 channels	3	262.885	0.027	95.34%	0.03835	0.00100
EMG m health channels	3	347.536	0.032	92.82%	0.03151	0.00095
	Averages	241.53331	0.0252804	96.02%	0.05113833	0.000750542

The graphs from Figure 16 show the following: original signal in red, read from the EMG sensor; predicted signal in orange, using the GMDH-type neural network; overlapped signals, to show prediction visual accuracy, in both blue and green, and finally, the cross-correlation between the two signals. It can be clearly seen how visually both signals (predicted and original) are almost equal.

The graphs from Figure 18 show the following: original signal in red, read from the EMG sensor; predicted signal in orange, using the GMDH-type neural network; overlapped signals, to show prediction visual accuracy, in both blue and green, and finally, the cross-correlation between the two signals. It can be clearly seen how visually both signals (predicted and original) are almost equal.

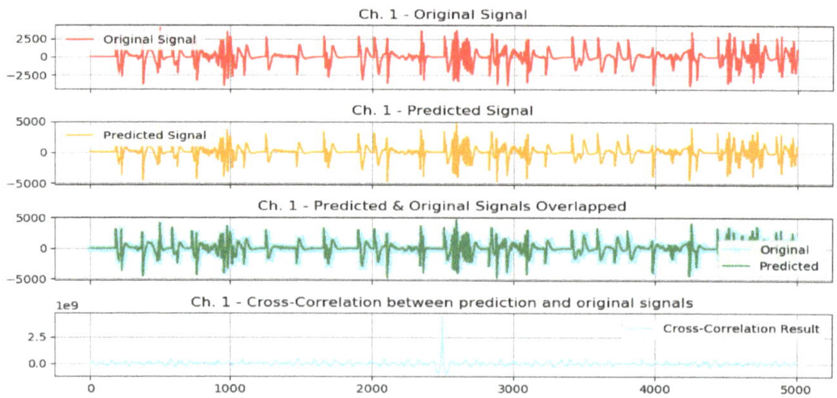

Figure 18. Plot of aggressive action for selected subject.

We show the same graph but for a normal action below (Figure 19).

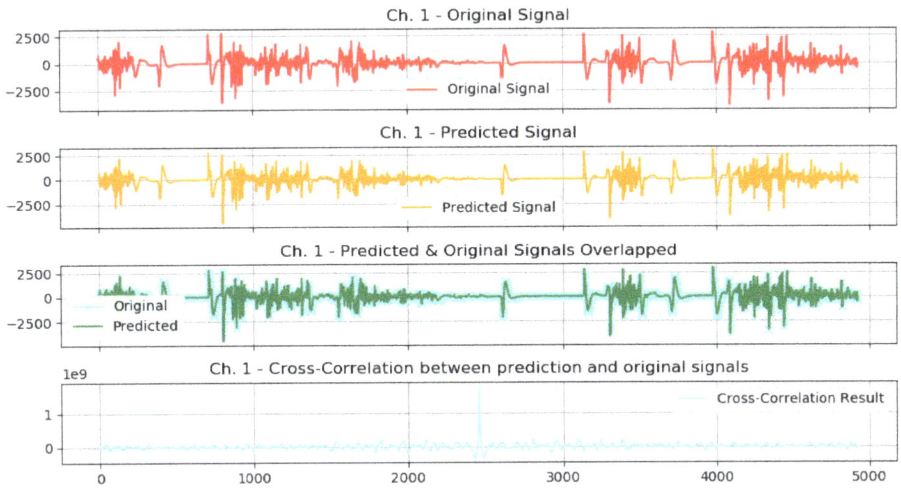

Figure 19. Plot of normal action for selected subject.

In addition, based on the previous plot it can be clearly seen how visually both signals (predicted and original) are almost equal.

The previous graph shows a prediction sample of an aggressive action (Figure 20), and the following graph shows a closer look at the signal prediction details (Figure 21).

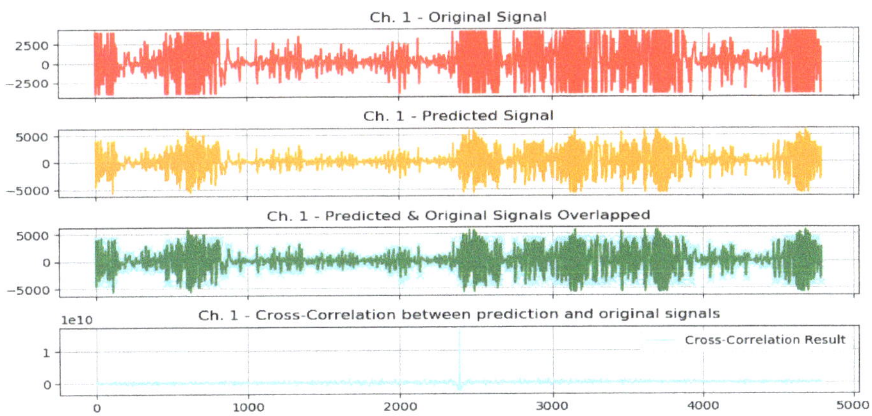

Figure 20. Signal prediction closer results: sample aggressive action prediction.

It can be clearly seen how the signal-predicted values are close to the original values, most of the values differ by a small value that will not change the behavior of the signal when analyzed, thus preserving the information needed for further analysis and classifications.

Next, we will show each subject test scores and then show a generalized average score for the model with training statistics.

The aggressive action/normal action test scores for Subject 1/Subject 2 are shown in Tables 8–11.

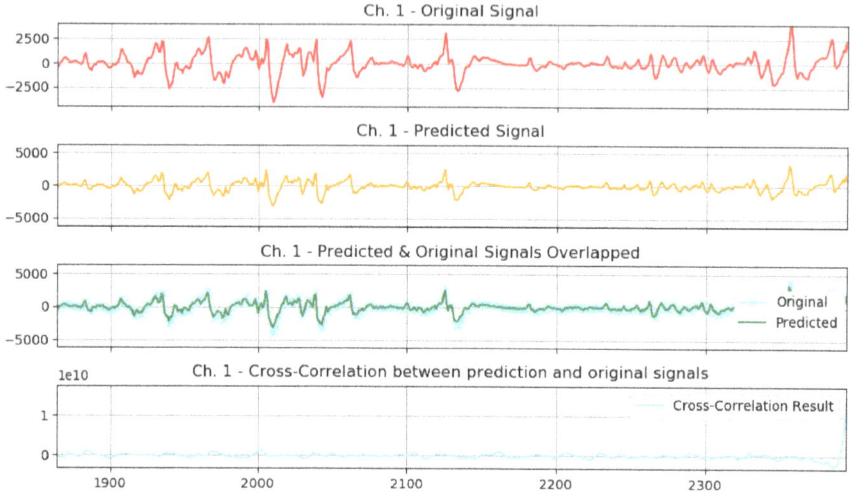

Figure 21. A closer look at the signal prediction details.

Table 8. Aggressive action test scores for Subject 1, the overall average reaches 90.01%, after training of adjusting different layers with different EMG signals channels as used before in Table 4 and Table 5, respectively.

Subject 1					
Layers	**RMSE**	**NRMSE**	**R-Squared**	**Train Time (s)**	**Test Time (s)**
3	522.285	0.043	86.46%	0.03084	0.00056
2	148.729	0.024	90.79%	0.01768	0.00083
2	552.910	0.036	90.79%	0.01298	0.00066
2	48.896	0.027	91.09%	0.01208	0.00059
7	234.463	0.027	90.15%	0.08429	0.00067
2	621.693	0.040	92.03%	0.01433	0.00072
7	491.597	0.038	89.49%	0.09936	0.00037
3	424.720	0.036	89.46%	0.04247	0.00083
3	209.147	0.023	87.80%	0.02835	0.00093
2	370.014	0.030	92.07%	0.02202	0.00114
Averages	362.4453	0.0324189	90.01%	0.03644128	0.000729

Table 9. Normal action test scores for Subject 1, the overall average reaches 81.43%, after training of adjusting different layers with different EMG signals channels as used before in Table 4 and Table 5, respectively.

Subject 1					
Layers	**RMSE**	**NRMSE**	**R-Squared**	**Train Time (s)**	**Test Time (s)**
3	7.683	0.019	95.33%	0.03059	0.00088
7	110.723	0.024	90.46%	0.09436	0.00065
3	205.429	0.022	89.36%	0.02513	0.00083
2	84.455	0.029	89.12%	0.01444	0.00089
7	85.226	0.020	87.21%	0.10529	0.00076
3	193.760	0.036	86.41%	0.03894	0.00092
2	99.943	0.051	74.39%	0.01358	0.00158
2	22.388	0.112	68.79%	0.01468	0.00144
3	7.941	0.196	66.66%	0.02479	0.00083
2	7.983	0.171	66.57%	0.02555	0.00075
Averages	82.55306	0.067997	81.43%	0.03873329	0.0009532

Table 10. Aggressive action test scores for Subject 2, the overall average reaches 96.2%, after training of adjusting different layers with different EMG signals channels as used before in Table 4 and Table 5, respectively.

Subject 2					
Layers	RMSE	NRMSE	R-Squared	Train Time (s)	Test Time (s)
3	262.885	0.027	95.34%	0.03835	0.00100
7	232.583	0.028	97.12%	0.07720	0.00047
7	304.756	0.031	95.43%	0.09501	0.00066
2	171.787	0.018	96.98%	0.01279	0.00055
7	220.009	0.024	96.96%	0.08461	0.00090
3	191.501	0.020	96.68%	0.02523	0.00074
3	347.536	0.032	92.82%	0.03151	0.00095
7	204.746	0.025	96.85%	0.10477	0.00059
3	265.888	0.027	95.94%	0.02851	0.00083
2	213.642	0.021	96.06%	0.01341	0.00082
Averages	241.53	0.0252804	96.02%	0.05113833	0.00075054

Table 11. Normal action test scores for Subject 2, the overall average reaches 96.68%, after training of adjusting different layers with different EMG signals channels as used before in Table 4 and Table 5, respectively.

Subject 2					
Layers	RMSE	NRMSE	R-Squared	Train Time (s)	Test Time (s)
7	355.257	0.039	98.60%	0.08924	0.00084
7	96.517	0.013	97.61%	0.08548	0.00066
7	134.699	0.015	97.47%	0.07976	0.00087
3	29.893	0.007	97.23%	0.04030	0.00093
3	61.059	0.011	96.41%	0.02851	0.00066
2	2.203	0.032	96.15%	0.01576	0.00074
3	233.189	0.025	96.13%	0.03011	0.00058
2	27.089	0.026	96.08%	0.01697	0.00061
50	148.183	0.014	95.99%	0.59829	0.00055
7	252.557	0.028	95.10%	0.08081	0.00075
Averages	134.06	0.0210994	96.68%	0.10652237	0.00071871

The confusion matrix of the GMDH model is shown in Figure 22 is generated. Different metrics generated by the neural network of results are shown in Figure 23. This is to show for classification of whether the action is aggressive or normal a combination of results between normal action test scores and aggressive action test scores in order to more clearly see the results from these two cases. Additionally, the classification report represented below helps us to better understand the metrics taken into consideration for this example (Table 12).

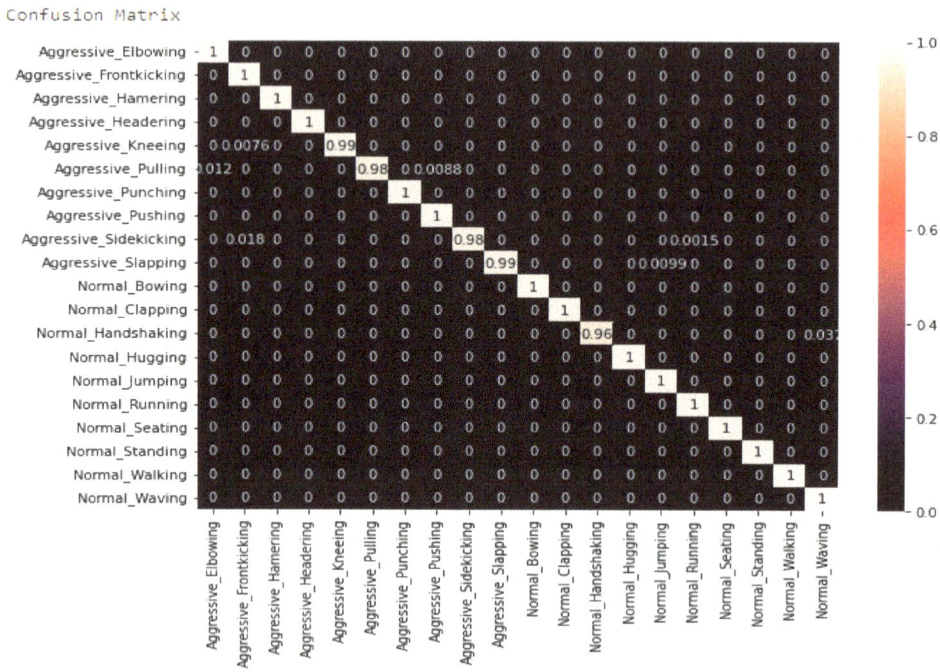

Figure 22. The confusion matrix generated.

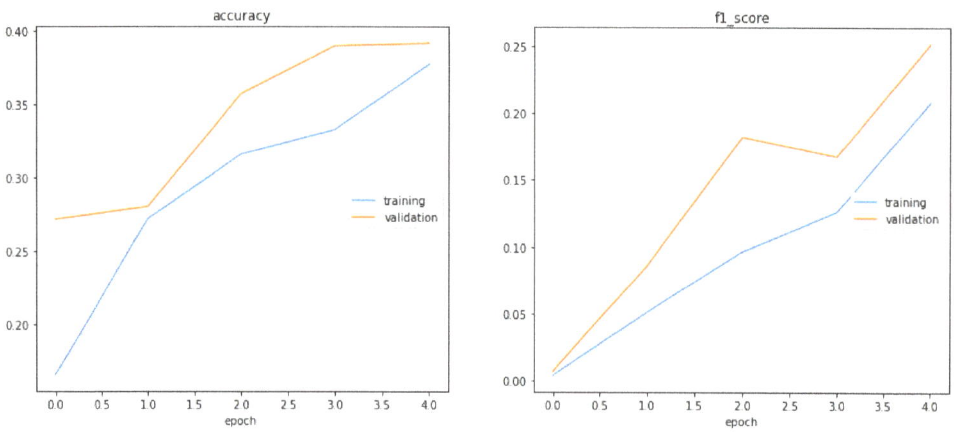

(a) (b)

Figure 23. The accuracy evaluation (**a**) and f1 score over epochs (**b**).

Table 12. The classification report.

Action	Precision	Recall	F1-Score	Support
Aggressive_Elbowing	0.99	1.00	0.99	1881
Aggressive_Frontkicking	0.97	1.00	0.99	1861
Aggressive_Hamering	1.00	1.00	1.00	1949
Aggressive_Headering	1.00	1.00	1.00	1949
Aggressive_Kneeing	1.00	0.99	1.00	1964
Aggressive_Pulling	1.00	0.98	0.99	1921
Aggressive_Punching	0.99	1.00	1.00	1876
Aggressive_Pushing	1.00	1.00	1.00	1867
Aggressive_Sidekicking	1.00	0.98	0.99	1953
Aggressive_Slapping	1.00	0.99	1.00	1926
Normal_Bowing	1.00	1.00	1.00	1915
Normal_Clapping	1.00	1.00	1.00	1949
Normal_Handshaking	1.00	0.96	0.98	1943
Normal_Hugging	1.00	1.00	1.00	1900
Normal_Jumping	0.99	1.00	1.00	1930
Normal_Running	1.00	1.00	1.00	1939
Normal_Seating	1.00	1.00	1.00	1949
Normal_Standing	1.00	1.00	1.00	1894
Normal_Walking	1.00	1.00	1.00	1949
Normal_Waving	0.96	1.00	0.98	1877
accuracy			1.00	38,392
macro avg	1.00	1.00	1.00	38,392
weighted	1.00	1.00	1.00	38,392

In Figure 23, section (a) presents the accuracy evaluation and (b) presents f1 score

$$F = 2 \cdot \frac{precision \cdot recall}{precision + recall}$$

$$Accuracy = \frac{tp + tn}{tp + tn + fp + fn}$$

In Figure 24, section (a) the loss function is represented while in section (b) the learning rate is represented. We can see that the learning rate is constant and equal to 10^{-3}.

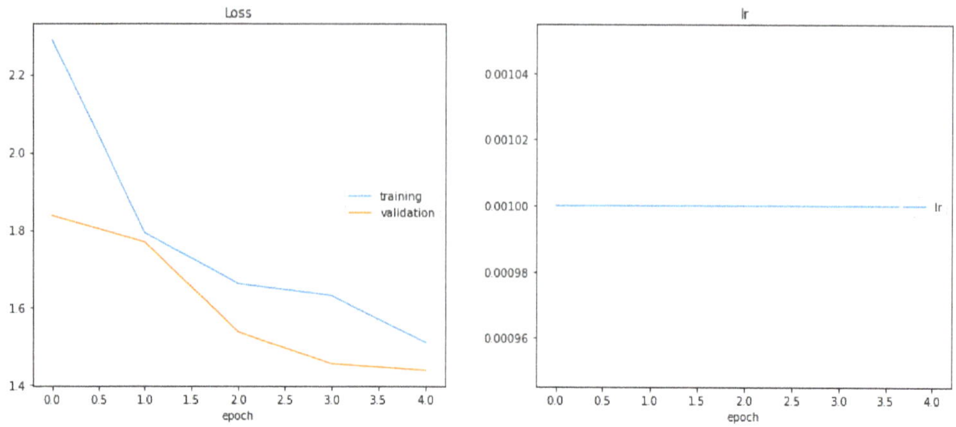

(a) (b)

Figure 24. The loss function (**a**) and the learning rate (**b**).

In Figure 25, the precision is represented regarding epochs (a) and in section (b) the recall is presented also regarding epochs.

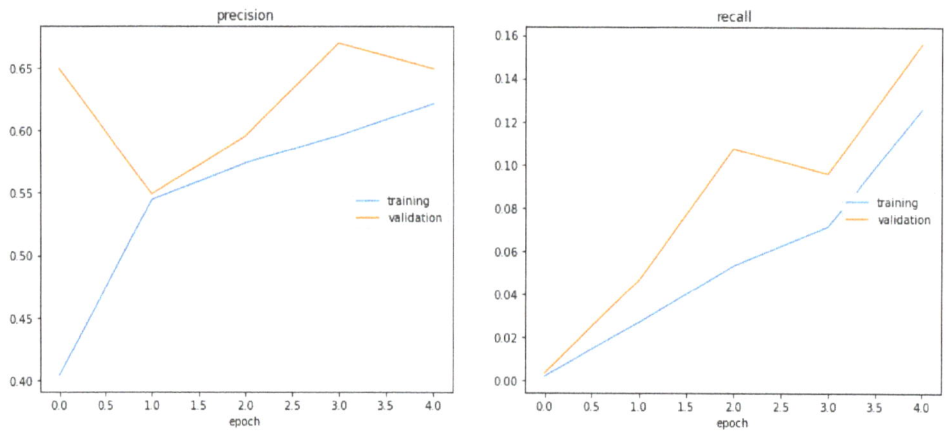

(a) (b)

Figure 25. The precision (**a**) and the recall (**b**) represented by epochs.

$$Precision = \frac{tp}{tp + fp}$$

$Recall = \frac{tp}{tp+fn}$, where tp = true positive, tn = true negative, fp = false positive, fn = false negative

In contrast to many GMDH deep learning-based approaches, the proposed algorithm is lightweight for the proposed Mobile AI Engine, and therefore, brings continuous diagnosis and prediction with accurate GMDH-LSTM-based EMG signal prediction to IoMT simulated inputs. The highest precision of parallel LSTM achieves 99.9% and the average reaches 93.65%. Figure 26a shows LSTM Model training visualization, while Figure 26b shows LSTM accuracy curves and Figure 26c shows the overall hybrid LSMT model results. The main advantage of the parallel LSTM model is that it is more stable than the GMDH deep learning model, as it has been trained on the 8 EMG channels directly. In addition, the parallel LSTM model is more suitable for the implementation of the mobile health app. However, the GMDH deep learning is good as a standalone predictive model for mathematical modeling EMG signal predictions. In contrast to many GMDH deep learning-based approaches, the proposed algorithm is lightweight for the proposed mobile AI engine, and therefore, brings continuous diagnosis and prediction with accurate GMDH–LSTM-based EMG signal prediction to IoMT simulated inputs. The highest precision of parallel LSTM achieves 99.9% and the average reaches 93.65%. The main advantage of the parallel LSTM model is that it is more stable than the GMDH deep learning model, as it has been trained on the 8 EMG channels directly. Additionally, the parallel LSTM model is more suitable for the implementation of the mobile health app. However, the GMDH deep learning is good as a standalone predictive model for mathematical modeling EMG signal predictions. The GMDH could predict most of the signals tested accurately with a high R^2 score, below is a table of the general prediction scores tested on both normal and aggressive action signals.

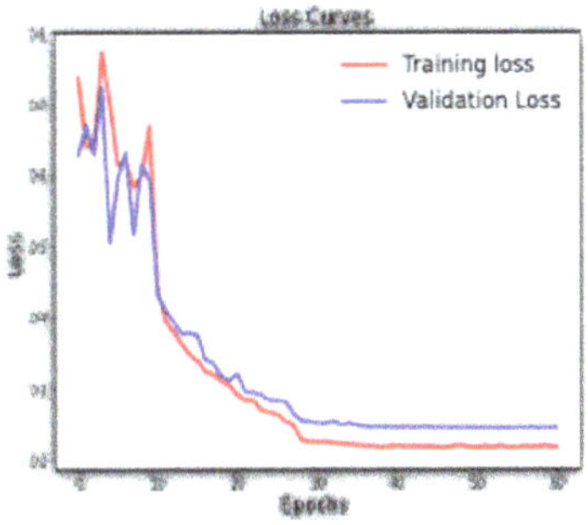

(a): LSTM Model training visualization

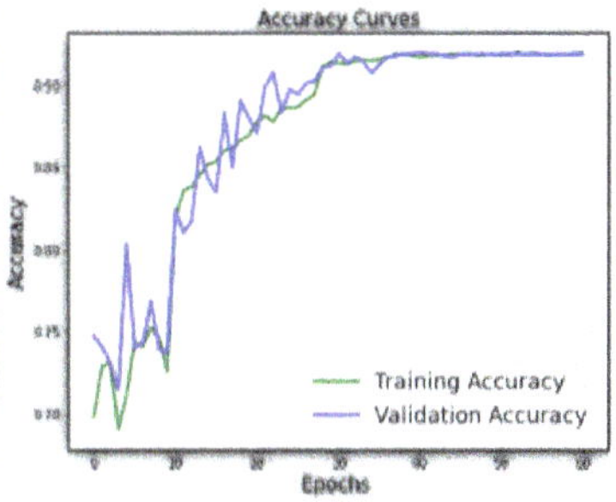

(b): LSTM Accuracy Curves

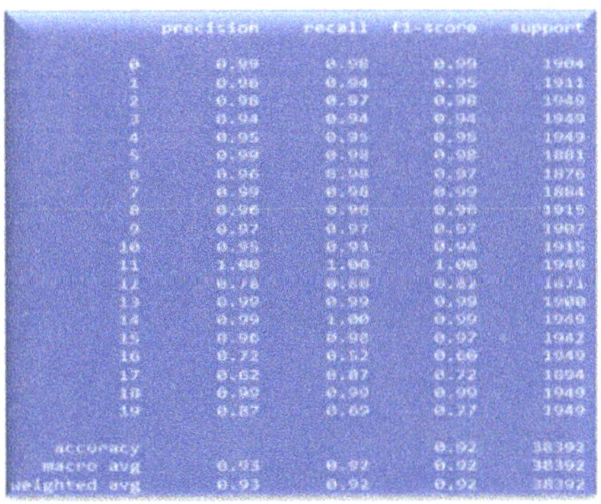

	precision	recall	f1-score	support
0	0.99	0.98	0.99	1904
1	0.96	0.94	0.95	1911
2	0.98	0.97	0.98	1949
3	0.94	0.94	0.94	1949
4	0.95	0.95	0.95	1949
5	0.99	0.98	0.98	1881
6	0.96	0.98	0.97	1876
7	0.99	0.98	0.99	1884
8	0.96	0.96	0.96	1915
9	0.97	0.97	0.97	1907
10	0.95	0.93	0.94	1915
11	1.00	1.00	1.00	1949
12	0.78	0.88	0.82	1871
13	0.99	0.99	0.99	1900
14	0.99	1.00	0.99	1949
15	0.96	0.98	0.97	1942
16	0.72	0.52	0.60	1949
17	0.62	0.87	0.72	1894
18	0.99	0.99	0.99	1949
19	0.87	0.69	0.77	1949
accuracy			0.92	38392
macro avg	0.93	0.92	0.92	38392
weighted avg	0.93	0.92	0.92	38392

(c): Hybrid LSTM Precision results

Figure 26. The parallel LSTM method (**a**) visualization of LSTM model training, (**b**) LSTM accuracy curves, (**c**) Overall results of LSMT hybrid model.

It can be seen that the ability of the GMDH to predict more event-based signals with more peaks and more aggressive spectrum, is higher than normal signals with lower peaks and less aggressive spectrum.

The main disadvantages of the GMDH model are that: the peaks of the signal for the GMDH predictive model vary from channel to channel of the EMG signal. In addition, the GMDH training algorithm takes a lot of memory for training and may crash, it crashes at using memory above 13 GB and it is not suitable for real industry applications of the mobile

AI health app. GMDH is a self-organizing approach by which gradually complicated models are generated based on the evaluation of their performances on a set of multi-input–single-output data. However, it is good for modeling the predictive analytics modeling of the stroke prediction system. It can be tested in the future for cloud computing or AI high-performance computing side. However, the hybrid parallel LSTM model is suitable for the mobile AI app implementation in python.

5. Discussion

The GMDH could predict most of the signals tested accurately with a high R^2 score, and below is a table of the general prediction scores tested on both normal and aggressive action signals (Table 13).

Table 13. Prediction scores.

Score/Action Set	Normal Actions	Aggressive Actions
RMSE	141.3881606	391.8395819
NRMSE	0.039652622	0.033451407
R-Squared	88.02%	90.54%

It can be seen that the ability of the GMDH to predict more event-based signals with more peaks and more aggressive spectrum is higher than normal signals with lower peaks and less-aggressive spectrum. Below are two different plots for a normal signal and an aggressive signal (Figures 27 and 28).

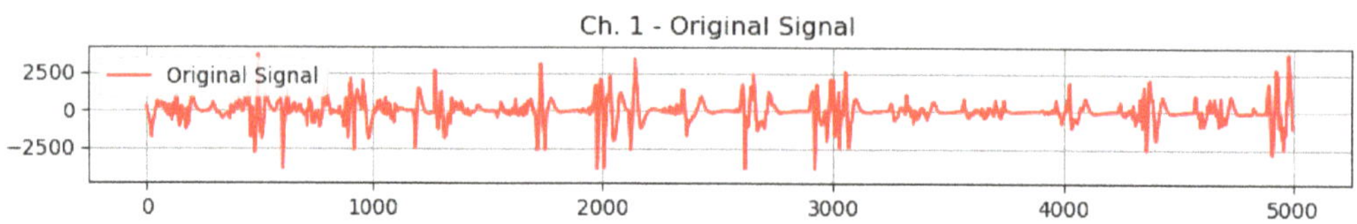

Figure 27. Normal action signal sample.

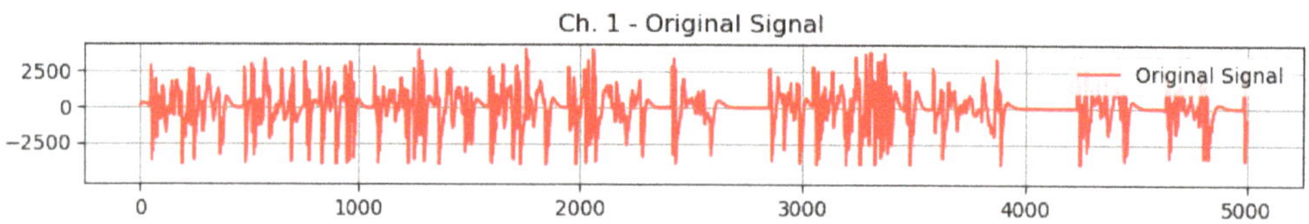

Figure 28. Aggressive action signal sample.

Concerning the mobile GMDH algorithms analysis and time series data forecasting:

As we know time series data are a sequence of data taken in multiple time stamps. There are two main goals of processing time series data. The first task is to try to classify the data into predefined subcategories. The second task is to predict the future of the input data using the current data. There are multiple algorithms to process and forecast time series data (parametric and nonparametric algorithms). These include:

- Univariate time series forecasting
- Multivariate time series forecasting multi-step time series forecasting
- Deep networks based on the group method of data handling

GMDH networks are the first feedforward deep learning neural network (since 1969). It consists of a family of inductive algorithms that use automatically generated architecture and parametric optimization methods.

Given a training set, layers are incrementally growing by regression analysis, then pruned with help of a validation set. The number of layers and units can be learned in a problem-dependent fashion. When the architecture consists of a multilayer procedure, it becomes equivalent to the artificial neural network with a polynomial activation function of neurons.

GMDH only: We tried to follow the same conditions described in the previous report for training and testing but we faced some problems due to missing information in the report so we tried our best to reproduce the previous results which takes a lot of time and effort. We depended on the python implementation "GmdhPy".

There are multiple ways we can define our inputs and our outputs given that we have four people. Every person has 20 actions given by 8 channels. At the same time, we have extracted 39 features from this data as described in previous reports. This gives us a huge space for experiments. We did not test all the possibilities, we only focused on the most obvious ones. We framed the problem as univariate time series forecasting. So the input is one channel for one subject. For example, we took the fourth subject with his first channel (RBic) and tried to predict the future of this channel as shown in Figure 29.

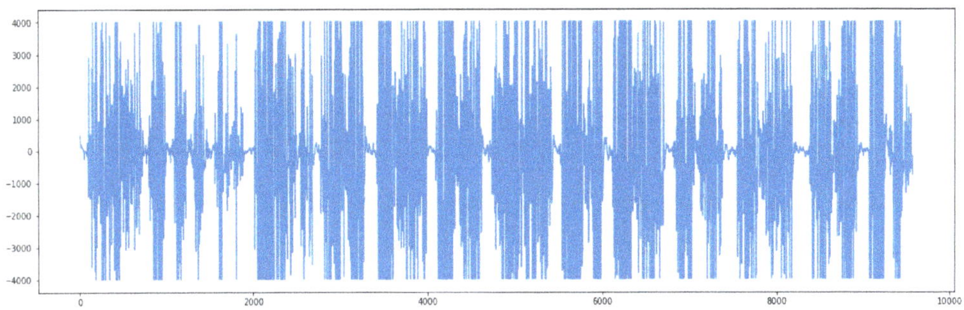

Figure 29. GMDH mobile AI signal sample prediction.

There are multiple hyper-parameters that should be studied in the future such as how many readings from the past should we depend on and the hyperparameters of the GMDH.

We took 10 readings from the past and tries to predict the next one in the future.

As our scope was to develop a fast and stable model for the deployment we considered these settings:

ref_functions = ('linear_cov'),
criterion_type = 'validate',
criterion_minimum_width = 5,
stop_train_epsilon_condition = 0.001,
layer_err_criterion = 'top',
l2 = 0.5,
manual_best_neurons_selection = True,
min_best_neurons_count = 30,

Calculating the root mean square error in time series data forecasting is very critical. So, we considered the time shift that happened in the data generation. So, GMDH achieved a train score of 1103.42 RMSE and a test score of 968.80 RMS

We see that the predicted signal has higher peaks than the original signal as shown in Figure 30. The problem with the GMDH-only setup is that the network did not keep the previous information from the previous time steps or residual connections. As described in this paper, when GMDH is combined with some information from the previous time steps it can give better performance with residual connections results as shown in Figure 31.

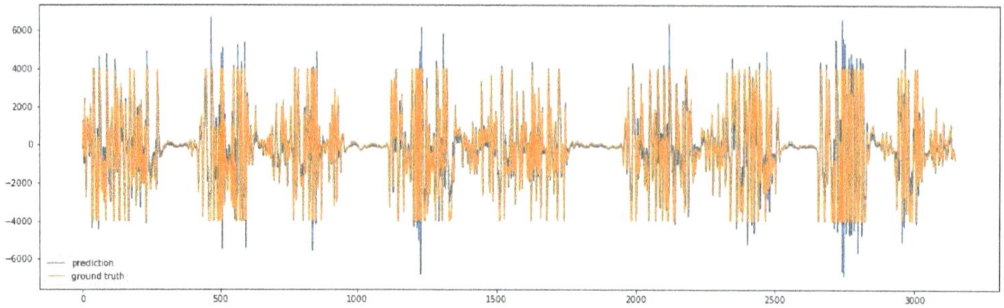

Figure 30. GMDH with predicted signal of higher peaks than the original signal when no residual connections or previous time steps are included.

Training and testing:

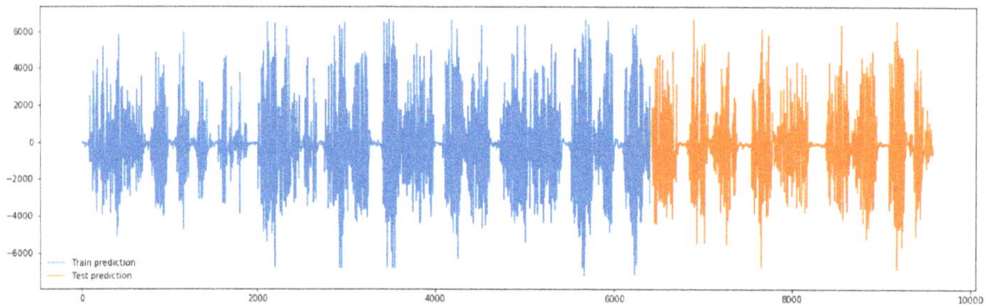

Figure 31. GMDH with predicted signal of better results of predicted signal with residual connections or previous time steps are included.

The number of subjects samples is four subjects, three male and one female. Three of them are because Subject 2 has noisy data.

We found that there is a pattern between the action and the aggressiveness, for example, when you are running this state is classified as normal. The upper body returns normal signals but the lower body returns high peak signals. Although in the aggressive class, for example, the lower and upper body return relatively high peak signals, as illustrated in Figure 32.

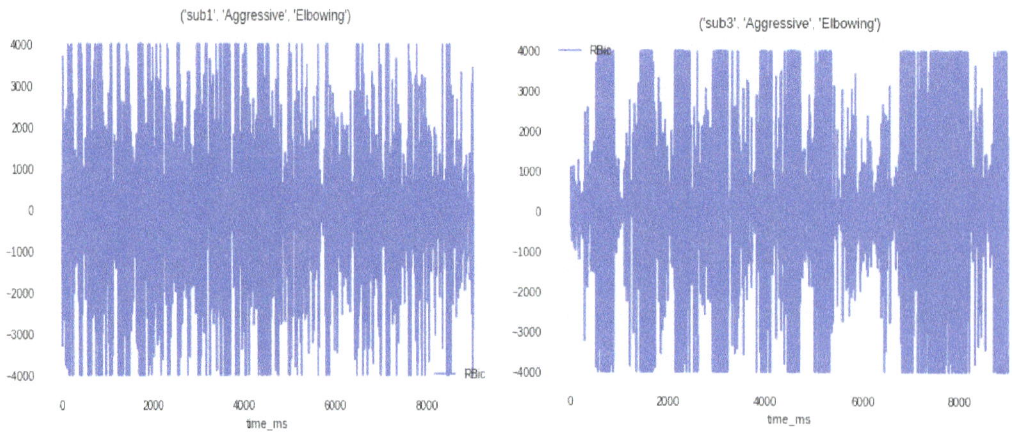

Figure 32. EMG signals aggressive class gives high peaks during analysis.

In Figure 33, the subject is in an aggressive move, he is doing an elbowing move. We found that all eight channels have the same pattern of highly distributed points in all the graphs with some concentration in the middle.

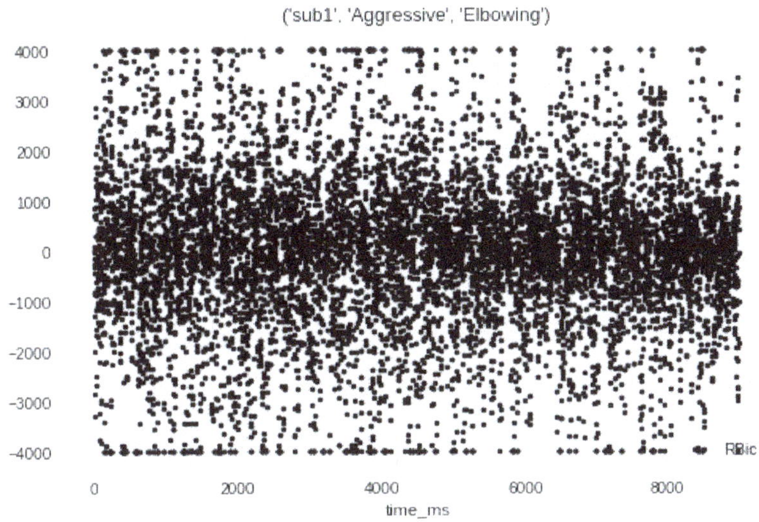

Figure 33. EMG signals of all 8 channels have the same pattern of highly distributed points during elbowing motion examples.

Long Short-Term Memory Network (LSTM):

Maintain state (memory) across very long sequences. Temporal information was used because LSTM is very sensitive to the data ranges we applied. Data normalization and scaling were used in the input and output. We used standard scaling for the input. It can be solved using linear activation in the output layer.

A novel stroke prediction algorithm is proposed based on EMG signals prediction. The proposed solution employs 612 a novel architecture consisting of a group method of data handling and multiple LSTM recurrent neural networks. Results: Experimental evaluations show superior EMG prediction performance compared to previous works. Measurements with different deep learning methods as combining CNN with LSTM show that the proposed algorithm meets performance requirements for continuous and real-time execution on IoMT devices. Conclusion: In 616 contrast to many compute-intensive deep learning-based approaches, the proposed algorithm is lightweight for the proposed mobile AI engine, and therefore, brings continuous diagnosis and prediction with accurate GMDH–LSTM-based EMG signal prediction to IoMT simulated inputs.

Mobile open architecture. We adopted an open architecture to make it easy for any researcher. They will be able to add their own model to the mobile in an easy way. Most mobile apps are currently closed systems, meaning that the researcher cannot add his/her model without many changes. Any model can be added instead of our trained models.

Findings: The first idea about the data, it has a huge variance and the data are not zero, meaning there are two levels of classification. The first level is normal or aggressive. This level depends on the activities which the subjects are doing to differentiate between the two classes. In the second level, for every state from level 1 (normal or aggressive), the subject was doing 10 activities for normal and 10 activities for aggressive.

To conclude, the signal for both classes normal and aggressive was processed and there were observed differences that helped us extract characteristics such as integrated EMG, modified mean absolute value 1, root mean square, average amplitude change, zero crossing, Willison amplitude, and waveform length. Great results were obtained by using a deep learning model, the new GMDP deep learning model.

Bearing all these things in mind, a model that can detect these two sides of behavior may help people that suffered a stroke to communicate easier and interact more with the environment. Even though this study was intended to help patients of a hospital, there may be applications in the security domain field in order to predict aggressive behavior.

In addition, a new hybrid LSTM/dense deep learning architecture has been added with detailed experimental results for EMG stroke prediction and as compared to GMDH, it is better as a parallel model that takes as input all the EMG 8 channels with high results; however, the GMDH algorithm can be easily deployed as mobile AI app with high accuracies. More results need to be tested in future work for parallel inputs to the GMDH algorithm. However, both models achieve high stroke prediction accuracies. Additionally, a single LSTM module has been integrated into the GMDH algorithm for enhancing the mobile AI implementation for stroke prediction.

6. Conclusions and Future Work

Artificial intelligence (AI) technologies in smart health patients' safety and care for connected health and intelligent diagnostics and predictive health ai edge computing integrated within smart hospital environments, have opened up new opportunities in healthcare systems and complex disease predictions and early detection for issues such as heart and stroke diseases. Smart hospital technologies [21–27] are a steadily growing field in artificial intelligence (AI), biomedical big data analytics [44–47] Internet of Medical Things (IoMT). Heart diagnosis and stroke prediction have urgent patient cases that may cause problems such as cardiovascular diseases [28–31], heart attacks, and brain strokes. It may also cause sudden death. These are the leading cause of death in the Middle East, Europe, and the United States. For these reasons, heart and stroke diseases are considered emergency cases. In the recent research of artificial intelligence technologies in the healthcare domain, what we witness is high competition and new revolution [1–3]. However, today's AI research and development of technologies in the fields of heart diseases diagnosis [16–20] and stroke prediction research are still missing a real-time AI-based heart diagnosis and stroke prediction system to be developed as AI-based platform R&D to be used in the industry and the new era of smart hospital developments [21–27]. This research paper innovation introduces a new AI system design that consists of an integrated real-time IOT-AI smart heart/stroke platform to be in the future inside hospitals as a new IoMT-AI-based heart/stroke platform and as an independent mobile AI telemedicine system for stroke prediction. Artificial intelligent IOT hospital edge-connected health diagnostic and predictive systems integrated with telemedicine services for both elder patients with chronic and brain stroke cases aim to help heart/brain stroke patients to discover their disease once it occurs based on EEG/ECG/EMG signals. However, classifying real-time ECG/EMG signals [14,15] is a complex task, especially for patient muscle signal feedback problems. This proposal introduces an integrated artificial intelligence telemedicine platform including AI software for heart disease diagnosis, and AI software for brain stroke diagnosis and prediction. The highest precision of parallel LSTM achieves 99.9% and the average reaches 93.65%. AI/DL telemedicine services could be useful for the nearest hospital and patients' telemonitoring at-home care services. In this research paper, we have only presented some innovative research results for the full mobile AI system cycle, and some real implementations in simulated tests. Our solution is more innovative than previous research on stroke prediction using only single deep learning or some sample stroke cases such as during sleeping, as discussed previously in the paper in Section 2.

This research article also presents an overall state-of-the-art artificial intelligence mobile health system architecture for stroke that can be implemented by AI and IoT companies such as Dell technologies for real-life scientific implementations. The main focus is on predictive analytics and edge computing solutions in healthcare and emergency situations.

Predictive analytics deals with information retrieval to predict an unknown event of interest, typically a future event. Using technology that learns from data to predict these unknown events could drive better decisions. This research paper utilizes the concepts of deep learning (GMDH) for signal predictions for mobile edge computing future implementations of complete solutions in a smart health home living scenario.

This research paper has successfully presented several steps in the predictive analytics process: identification of the problem and a determination of the outcomes and objectives is a crucial first step. The first data of the model used EMG from both real-time and offline datasets.

Future work may include different ways to process the signal, and data processing time concerning the processing time of GMDH it has taken nearly 30 min for the training, but the networking connections are out of the scope of this article and we are honored to present them in the future work of next phase of app implementation. Additionally, other deep learning model architectures will be presented in order to achieve better precision in classification. In addition, for the XAI decision-based tools, extended parts of TIER 2 and TIER 3 of fuzzy logic and surveillance-based systems will be considered for future works. Additionally, future work may include different ways to process the signal, and other deep learning model architectures in order to achieve better precision in classification.

Author Contributions: Conceptualization, B.M.E., L.V., V.V., A.B.S. and A.-M.T.; Methodology, B.M.E. and L.V.; Software, B.M.E., V.V. and A.-M.T.; Validation, B.M.E., L.V., V.V., A.B.S., A.-M.T. and M.I.R.; Formal analysis, B.M.E., L.V., V.V., A.-M.T. and M.I.R.; Investigation, B.M.E., L.V., V.V. and A.-M.T.; Resources, B.M.E., V.V. and M.I.R.; Data curation, B.M.E.; Writing—original draft, B.M.E. and L.V.; Writing—review & editing, B.M.E., L.V., V.V., A.B.S., A.-M.T. and M.I.R.; Visualization, B.M.E., L.V., V.V., A.B.S., A.-M.T. and M.I.R.; Supervision, B.M.E., L.V., V.V., A.B.S., A.-M.T. and M.I.R.; Project administration, B.M.E. and L.V.; Funding acquisition, B.M.E., L.V., A.B.S. and M.I.R. All authors have read and agreed to the published version of the manuscript.

Funding: This research received no external funding.

Institutional Review Board Statement: Not require ethical approval.

Informed Consent Statement: Not applicable.

Data Availability Statement: Not applicable.

Conflicts of Interest: The funders had no role in the design of the study; in the collection, analyses, or interpretation of data; in the writing of the manuscript, or in the decision to publish the results.

References

1. Elbagoury, B.M.; Zaghow, M.; Salem, A.-B.M.; Schrader, T. Mobile AI Stroke Health App: A Novel Mobile Intelligent Edge Computing Engine based on Deep Learning models for Stroke Prediction—Research and Industry. In Proceedings of the 2021 IEEE 20th ICCI*CC, Banff, AB, Canada, 29–31 October 2021; pp. 39–52. [CrossRef]
2. Mohan, S.; Thirumalai, C.; Srivastava, G. Effective heart disease prediction using hybrid machine learning techniques. *IEEE Access* **2019**, *7*, 81542–81554. [CrossRef]
3. Janke, A.T.; Overbeek, D.L.; Kocher, K.E.; Levy, P.D. Exploring the Potential of Predictive Analytics and Big Data in Emergency Care. *Ann. Emerg. Med.* **2016**, *67*, 227–236. [CrossRef]
4. Chantamit, P.; Goyal, M. Long short-term memory recurrent neural network for stroke prediction. In Proceedings of the International Conference on Machine Learning and Data Mining in Pattern Recognition (MLDM 2018), New York, NY, USA, 15–19 July 2018; pp. 312–323.
5. Wang, X.; Han, Y.; Leung, V.C.M.; Niyato, D.; Yan, X.; Chen, X. Convergence of edge computing and deep learning: A comprehensive survey. *IEEE Commun. Surv. Tutor.* **2020**, *22*, 869–904. [CrossRef]
6. Yousefpour, A.; Fung, C.; Nguyen, T.; Kadiyala, K.; Jalali, F.; Niakanlahiji, A.; Kong, J.; Jue, J.P. All one needs to know about fog computing and related edge computing paradigms: A complete survey. *J. Syst. Archit.* **2019**, *98*, 289–330. [CrossRef]
7. Ahmed, E.; Rehmani, M.H. Mobile edge computing: Opportunities, solutions, and challenges. *Future Gener. Comput. Syst.* **2017**, *70*, 59–63. [CrossRef]
8. BCC Research. Mobile Health (mHealth) Technologies and Global Markets. 14 March 2014. Available online: www.bccresearch.com/market-research/healthcare/mobile-health-hlc162a.html (accessed on 27 December 2022).
9. Amin, S.U.; Hossain, M.S. Edge intelligence and internet of things in healthcare: A survey. *IEEE Access* **2021**, *9*, 45–59. [CrossRef]

10. Farid, N.; Elbagoury, B.M.; Roushdy, M.; Salem, A.-B.M. A Comparative Analysis for Support Vector Machines for Stroke Patients. In Proceedings of the 7th WSEAS European Computing Conference. (ECC'13), Dubrovnik, Croatia, 25–27 June 2013.
11. Khan, M.U.; Aziz, S.; Bilal, M.; Aamir, M.B. Classification of EMG signals for assessment of neuromuscular disorder using empirical mode decomposition and logistic regression. In Proceedings of the 2019 International Conference on Applied and Engineering Mathematics (ICAEM), Taxila, Pakistan, 27–29 August 2019; pp. 237–243.
12. Rouillard, J.; Duprès, A.; Cabestaing, F.; Leclercq, S.; Bekaert, M.H.; Piau, C.; Vannobel, J.M.; Lecocq, C. Hybrid BCI Coupling EEG and EMG for Severe Motor Disabilities. *Procedia Manuf.* **2015**, *3*, 29–36. [CrossRef]
13. Chin, C.-L.; Lin, B.-J.; Wu, G.-R.; Weng, T.-C.; Yang, C.-S.; Su, R.-C.; Pan, Y.-J. An automated early ischemic stroke detection system using CNN deep learning algorithm. In Proceedings of the 2017 IEEE 8th International Conference on Awareness Science and Technology (iCAST), Taichung, Taiwan, 8–10 November 2017; pp. 368–372.
14. Liu, L.; Chen, S.; Zhang, F.; Wu, F.-X.; Pan, Y.; Wang, J. Deep convolutional neural network for automatically segmenting acute ischemic stroke lesion in multi-modality MRI. *Neural Comput. Appl.* **2019**, *32*, 6545–6558. [CrossRef]
15. Zhang, S.; Zheng, D.; Hu, X.; Yang, M. Bidirectional long short-term memory networks for relation classification. In Proceedings of the 29th Pacific Asia Conference on Language, Information and Computation, Shanghai, China, 30 October–1 November 2015; pp. 73–78.
16. Jeong, J.H.; Shim, K.H.; Kim, D.J.; Lee, S.W. Brain-controlled robotic arm system based on multi-directional CNN-BiLSTM network using EEG signals. *IEEE Trans. Neural Syst. Rehabil. Eng.* **2020**, *28*, 1226–1238. [CrossRef]
17. Guntari, E.W.; Djamal, E.C.; Nugraha, F.; Liem, S.L.L. Classification of Post-Stroke EEG Signal Using Genetic Algorithm and Recurrent Neural Networks. In Proceedings of the 2020 7th International Conference on Electrical Engineering, Computer Sciences and Informatics (EECSI), Yogyakarta, Indonesia, 1–2 October 2020; IEEE: Piscataway, NJ, USA, 2020; pp. 156–161.
18. Schuster, M.; Paliwal, K. Bidirectional recurrent neural networks. *IEEE Trans. Signal. Process.* **1997**, *45*, 2673–2681. [CrossRef]
19. Shin, S. Myoelectric Human Computer Interaction Using Reliable Temporal Sequence-based Myoelec-tric Classification for Dynamic Hand Gestures. Doctoral Dissertation, Texas A M University, Commerce, TX, USA, 2016. Available online: https://hdl.handle.net/1969.1/174271 (accessed on 27 December 2022).
20. Semwal, V.B.; Gupta, A.; Lalwani, P. An optimized hybrid deep learning model using ensemble learning approach for human walking activities recognition. *J. Supercomput.* **2021**, *77*, 12256–12279. [CrossRef]
21. Yu, Y.; Si, X.; Hu, C.; Zhang, J. A Review of Recurrent Neural Networks: LSTM Cells and Network Architectures. *Neural Comput.* **2019**, *31*, 1235–1270. [CrossRef]
22. Amiri, M.; Soleimani, S. ML-based group method of data handling: An improvement on the conventional GMDH. *Complex Intell. Syst.* **2021**, *7*, 2949–2960. [CrossRef]
23. Zhang, H.; Li, J.; Wen, B.; Xun, Y.; Liu, J. Connecting intelligent things in smart hospitals using NB-IoT. *IEEE Internet Things J.* **2018**, *5*, 1550–1560. [CrossRef]
24. Gopal, G.; Suter-Crazzolara, C.; Toldo, L.; Eberhardt, W. Digital transformation in healthcare—Architectures of present and future information technologies. *Clin. Chem. Lab. Med.* **2019**, *57*, 328–335. [CrossRef]
25. Sun, T.Q.; Medaglia, R. Mapping the challenges of Artificial Intelligence in the public sector: Evidence from public healthcare. *Gov. Inf. Q.* **2019**, *3*, 368–383. [CrossRef]
26. Tsopra, R.; Fernandez, X.; Luchinat, C.; Alberghina, L.; Lehrach, H.; Vanoni, M.; Dreher, F.; Sezerman, O.; Cuggia, M.; de Tayrac, M.; et al. A framework for validating AI in precision medicine: Considerations from the European ITFoC consortium. *BMC Med. Inform. Decis. Mak.* **2021**, *21*, 274. [CrossRef]
27. McKee, M.; Merkus, S.; Edwards, N.; Nolte, E. *The Changing Role of the Hospital in European Health Systems*; Cambridge University Press: Cambridge, UK, 2020.
28. Artificial Intelligence in Medical Technology: Delive, Ring on the Promise of Better Healthcare in Europe. Available online: https://www.medtecheurope.org/wp-content/uploads/2019/11/MTE_Nov19_AI-in-MedTech-Delivering-on-the-Promise-of-Better-Healthcare-in-Europe.pdf (accessed on 17 December 2020).
29. Haluza, D.; Jungwirth, D. ICT and the future of health care: Aspects of health promotion. *Int. J. Med. Inform.* **2015**, *84*, 48–57. [CrossRef]
30. Manas, M.; Sinha, A.; Sharma, S.; Mahboob, M.R. A novel approach for IoT based wearable health monitoring and messaging system. *J. Ambient. Intell. Humaniz. Comput.* **2019**, *10*, 2817–2828. [CrossRef]
31. Parthiban, G.; Srivatsa, S. Applying machine learning methods in diagnosing heart disease for diabetic patients. *Int. J. Appl. Inf. Syst.* **2012**, *3*, 25–30. [CrossRef]
32. Chapman, B.; DeVore, A.D.; Mentz, R.J.; Metra, M. Clinical profiles in acute heart failure: An urgent need for a new approach. *ESC Heart Fail.* **2019**, *6*, 464–474. [CrossRef]
33. Ansarullah, S.I.; Kumar, P. A Systematic Literature Review on Cardiovascular Disorder Identification using Knowledge Mining and Machine Learning Method. *Int. J. Recent Technol. Eng.* **2019**, *7*, 1009–1015.
34. Shah, D.; Patel, S.; Bharti, S.K. Heart Disease Prediction using Machine Learning Techniques. *SN Comput. Sci.* **2020**, *1*, 345. [CrossRef]
35. Geweid, G.G.; Abdallah, M.A. A New Automatic Identification Method of Heart Failure Using Improved Support Vector Machine Based on Duality Optimization Technique. *IEEE Access* **2019**, *7*, 149595–149611. [CrossRef]

36. Dudchenko, A.; Ganzinger, M.; Kopanitsa, G. Machine Learning Algorithms in Cardiology Domain: A Systematic Review. *Open Bioinform. J.* **2020**, *13*, 25–40. [CrossRef]
37. Zhang, X.; Gu, K.; Miao, S.; Zhang, X.; Yin, Y.; Wan, C.; Yu, Y.; Hu, J.; Wang, Z.; Shan, T.; et al. Automated detection of cardiovascular disease by electrocardiogram signal analysis: A deep learning system. *Cardiovasc. Diagn. Ther.* **2020**, *10*, 227–235. [CrossRef] [PubMed]
38. Swapna, G.; Ghista, D.N.; Martis, R.J.; Ang, A.P.C.; Sree, S.V. ECG Signal generation and heart rate variability signal extraction: Signal processing, features detection, and their correlation with cardiac diseases. *J. Mech. Med. Biol.* **2012**, *12*, 12. [CrossRef]
39. Park, S.; Hong, S.; Kim, D.; Yu, J.; Hussain, I.; Park, H.; Benjamin, H. Development of Intelligent Stroke Monitoring System for the Elderly during Sleeping. *Sleep Med.* **2019**, *64*, S294. [CrossRef]
40. Aminov, A.; Rogers, J.M.; Johnstone, S.J.; Middleton, S.; Wilson, P.H. Acute single channel EEG predictors of cognitive function after stroke. *PLoS ONE* **2017**, *12*, e0185841. [CrossRef]
41. Yang, Z.; Zhou, Q.; Lei, L.; Zheng, K.; Xiang, W. An IoT-cloud based wearable ECG monitoring system for smart healthcare. *J. Med. Syst.* **2016**, *40*, 286. [CrossRef]
42. Hu, S.; Wei, H.; Chen, Y.; Tan, J. A Real-Time Cardiac Arrhythmia Classification System with Wearable Sensor Networks. *Sensors* **2012**, *12*, 12844–12869. [CrossRef]
43. Hogan, N.; Mann, R.W. Myoelectric Signal Processing: Optimal Estimation Applied to Electromyography—Part I: Derivation of the Optimal Myoprocessor. *IEEE Trans. Biomed. Eng. BME* **1980**, *27*, 382–395. [CrossRef]
44. Bruballa, E.; Wong, A.; Epelde, F.; Rexachs, D.; Luque, E. A model to predict length of stay in a hospital emergency department and enable planning for non-critical patients' admission. *Int. J. Integr. Care* **2016**, *16*, 24. [CrossRef]
45. Dinov, I.D. Methodological challenges and analytic opportunities for modeling and interpreting Big Healthcare Data. *Gigascience* **2016**, *5*, 12. [CrossRef] [PubMed]
46. Bates, D.W.; Saria, S.; Ohno-Machado, L.; Shah, A.; Escobar, G. Big data in health care: Using analytics to identify and manage high-risk and high-cost patients. *Health Aff.* **2014**, *33*, 1123–1131. [CrossRef] [PubMed]
47. EMG Lower-Limb Dataset. Available online: http://archive.ics.uci.edu/ml/datasets/emg+dataset+in+lower+limb (accessed on 27 December 2022).
48. EMG Physical Action Dataset. Available online: https://archive.ics.uci.edu/ml/datasets/EMG+Physical+Action+Data+Set (accessed on 27 December 2022).

sensors

MDPI

Article

Improvement of Hexacopter UAVs Attitude Parameters Employing Control and Decision Support Systems

Mihai-Alin Stamate [1], Cristina Pupăză [1,*], Florin-Adrian Nicolescu [1] and Cristian-Emil Moldoveanu [2]

[1] Faculty of Industrial Engineering and Robotics, University Politehnica of Bucharest, 060042 Bucharest, Romania
[2] Faculty of Integrated Weapon Systems, Military Technical Academy "Ferdinand I", 050141 Bucharest, Romania
* Correspondence: cristina.pupaza@upb.ro

Abstract: Today, there is a conspicuous upward trend for the development of unmanned aerial vehicles (UAVs), especially in the field of multirotor drones. Their advantages over fixed-wing aircrafts are that they can hover, which allows their usage in a wide range of remote surveillance applications: industrial, strategic, governmental, public and homeland security. Moreover, because the component market for this type of vehicles is in continuous growth, new concepts have emerged to improve the stability and reliability of the multicopters, but efficient solutions with reduced costs are still expected. This work is focused on hexacopter UAV tests carried out on an original platform both within laboratory and on unrestricted open areas during the start–stop manoeuvres of the motors to verify the operational parameters, hover flight, the drone stability and reliability, as well as the aerodynamics and robustness at different wind speeds. The flight parameters extracted from the sensor systems' comprising accelerometers, gyroscopes, magnetometers, barometers, GPS antenna and EO/IR cameras were analysed, and adjustments were performed accordingly, when needed. An FEM simulation approach allowed an additional decision support platform that expanded the experiments in the virtual environment. Finally, practical conclusions were drawn to enhance the hexacopter UAV stability, reliability and manoeuvrability.

Keywords: sensor systems; remote control and communication; UAV; simulation

Citation: Stamate, M.-A.; Pupăză, C.; Nicolescu, F.-A.; Moldoveanu, C.-E. Improvement of Hexacopter UAVs Attitude Parameters Employing Control and Decision Support Systems. *Sensors* **2023**, *23*, 1446. https://doi.org/10.3390/s23031446

Academic Editor: Luige Vladareanu

Received: 26 December 2022
Revised: 21 January 2023
Accepted: 25 January 2023
Published: 28 January 2023

1. Introduction

DRONE is a generic name for a whole family of aerial, land, water, and underwater platforms. The term DRONE is an English acronym, one of the definitions being Dynamic Remotely Operated Navigation Equipment. The following main categories of vehicles belong to the DRONE family are as follows: UAV—unmanned aerial vehicle, UGV—unmanned ground vehicle and UUV—unmanned underwater vehicle.

Aerial drones are also found under other names: UAV—unmanned aerial vehicle, UAS—unmanned aerial system, RPAS—remotely piloted aircraft system and ROAV—remotely operated air vehicle.

UAVs fall into two main categories: fixed wing (airplane) and rotorcraft (single rotor—helicopter, or at least two rotors—multicopters). Recently (2020–2022), a third category of UAVs has seen rapid development: fixed-wing UAVs with vertical takeoff and landing (VTOL) capabilities [1–3], which combine the capabilities of an aircraft with those of a multirotor UAV, with either electric or combined propulsion [4–6] (electric with internal combustion engine) to extend flight range and develop superior flight performance, with the aim of being able to carry large payloads over long distances.

The main purpose for which UAVs were originally developed was their use in military applications and special operations. Subsequently, they have been widely developed and employed in an increasing number of civilian applications: law enforcement surveillance missions, firefighting assistance, securing borders, strategic and governmental targets, detecting illegal hunting, measuring landslides, monitoring incidents involving crowds of people, inspecting large industrial facilities, large buildings and constructions, oil and gas pipelines, inspection of continuous-flow machinery in quarries (to monitor temperatures in the area of high-friction pits using thermal imaging cameras), inspection of petrochemical installations (to detect cracks, fissures and leaks in pressure vessels using thermal imaging cameras) and, more recently, (2020–2022) home parcel delivery [7,8], warehouse stock management [9,10] using specialized software, passenger transport, air travel, etc.

Multirotor drones have seen continuous development over the past ten years as the need for this type of platform has grown continuously, and they are employed in a wide range of activities and fields such as inspection of large industrial installations [11,12], large buildings and constructions, oil and gas pipelines [13,14], inspection of continuous-flow machinery in quarries (to monitor temperatures in the area of high-friction pits using thermal imaging cameras), inspection of petrochemical installations (to detect cracks, fissures and leaks that may occur in pressure vessels using thermal imaging cameras [15,16]), etc. They can be equipped with a wide range of electromagnetic spectrum sensors [17,18], gamma ray sensors [19], biological sensors [20–22] and chemical sensors [23,24], which provide remote sensing functions.

Electromagnetic sensors include visual spectrum, infrared or near-infrared cameras and radar systems. Some other electromagnetic wave detectors such as microwave and ultraviolet spectrum sensors are less used. Biological sensors can detect the presence of various microorganisms and other biological factors in the air. Chemical sensors employ laser spectroscopy to analyse the concentration of each element in the air.

A UAV possesses almost all the characteristic strengths of a manned aircraft, in addition to surmounting the physical limitations of the pilots and thus preventing the human error. The absence of the pilot from the cockpit allows drones to be operated at their performance limit, thus increasing endurance, payload, altitude ceiling and manoeuvrability.

Likewise, current advances in microelectronics and proximity/optical sensors [25,26], coupled with the availability of detailed geographic information systems mapping [27–29], contributed to the development of micro-UAVs [30] that can be operated autonomously at very low altitudes within dense urban locations and provide accurate intelligence data.

This paper aims to treat the category of multicopters UAVs, specifically the category of hexacopter drones. Given the upward trend in the aviation industry in the field of unmanned aerial vehicles (UAVs), especially in the field of multirotor drones [31–34], whose advantage over fixed-wing aircraft (airplanes) is that they can hover at a fixed point, which obviously allows their use in remote surveillance applications of different types of targets, the use of UAVs in the field of surveillance is also a key issue, and, at the same time, taking into account that the market for components for this type of vehicle is constantly growing and developing, with increasingly lower costs. Due to their cost efficiency and numerous possibilities for use in a wide range of civil, commercial and industrial applications (inspection of power lines, inspection of road infrastructure, bridges, inspection of oil pipelines, inspection of industrial facilities of strategic interest, e.g., oil refineries, nuclear power plants, inspection of disaster areas), multirotor UAVs have already been the subject of study for more than a decade. Since then, numerous research studies have been carried out on the modelling [33–35] and design of actuation, command and control systems [36] and the development of various design solutions [37,38]. Despite the abundance of the scientific literature, the topicality of the subject remains high, due to the subtle balance between the sensor features and involved outlays.

This paper is structured as follows: Section 2 encompasses a synthetic and critical overview of the latest developments in hexacopter drones design, sensors equipment and experimental procedures but also regarding numerical evaluation of the drone stability and reliability. Section 3 depicts a novel hexacopter platform architecture in two variants, equipped with avionic components and sensors. In Section 4, the results of the carried-out tests, both in the laboratory and in situ, during the start–stop manoeuvres of the hexacopter engines are described and discussed, and it also discusses the necessary corrective measures that were taken accordingly to check and assure the reliability of the hexacopter. Section 5 encompasses an extended FEM decision support study to investigate if resonances of the structural components interfere with the operational frequencies in order to avoid flight instabilities. The structural integrity of the hexacopter in case of a drop event was assessed, and the influence of the air pressure at different wind speeds was also investigated in respect to the hexacopter flight path accuracy. The accomplishments are summarized in Section 6, where conclusions are drawn and perspectives for the future work are highlighted.

The novelty of the work consists of a new perspective of comparative analyses of the performance of the hexacopter drone in different equipment variants in terms of battery, propellers, avionics components and engines employed by carrying out simulations using devoted simulation platforms. These studies also allowed us to establish the appropriate criteria for choosing the best combination of the propulsion system, consisting of a battery, such as an electronic speed controller (ESC), or a brushless DC motor (BLDC)—propeller—depending on the size of the drone frame, in order to achieve maximum efficiency (range vs. maximum carried payload).

Another original viewpoint covered in the article is the extended CFD study of the behaviour of the hexacopter drone during stationary flight at a fixed point (hover), which deals with several aspects, namely, ensuring the stability of the hexacopter drone during stationary flight manoeuvres at hover, development of a complete and complex simulation model for all types of CAE analysis, validation of the FEM (finite element model) computation model, synchronization of the results obtained analytically, experimentally and numerically and the use of the results obtained from the FEM study to improve flight parameters such as rotor speeds.

2. Related Work

2.1. Latest Developments in Hexacopter Drones Design

Darvishpoor et al. [39] present in a complex review many different configurations, flight mechanisms and applications in which drones are currently employed. The UAVs are categorized, and their characteristics, advantages and drawbacks are discussed. This study also presents vertical takeoff and landing (VTOL) hexacopter drones in a flat configuration, used by the last mile delivery drone, the HexH2O seaplane drone, an antidrone hexacopter, which uses a net to capture rogue drones; power tower cleaning hexacopters; and agriculture, inspection, survey and mapping hexacopters.

Delbecq et al. [40] presents a generic methodology that analyses the sizing aspect of the multicopter drones with electric propulsion, which allows configuration optimization for different applications. The study starts from a set of algebraic equations based on scaling laws and models that have resemblances. In the next phase, the optimization of the drone sizing is analysed through a proposed methodology. The obtained results are validated by comparing the characteristics of existing multirotors and performance predictions of these configurations which were performed taking into account different flight types and payload variants.

In the case of the classic hexacopter, studies have been carried out on mounting the rotors under certain tilt angles, this modification allowing the hexacopter to be fully actuated in the sense that all six degrees of freedom associated with the three translational and three rotational movements become independently controllable. These types of platforms are still the subject of study, making it difficult to explain which type of structure is suitable for a particular type of application. One of the proposed approaches to obtain a structure close to the one already mentioned is to develop a scheme to optimize the construction design of the drone. Aspects related to the design and optimization of hexacopter drones can be found in several variants proposed by Gupta et al. [41], Suprapto et al. [42], Setiono et al. [43], Verbeke et al. [44], Abarca et al. [45] and Arellano-Quintana et al. [46].

Work performed by Ferrarese et al. [47], Ryll et al. [48] and Tadokoro et al. [49], respectively, present an analytical characterization of the relationships between the dynamic properties of the drone, the arrangement of the rotors and their pitch angles. The results obtained are then taken into account when formulating the design aspects of the hexacopter and the manoeuvrability of the fully powered drone is analysed after the rotors are placed under a certain tilt angle. The following aspects are addressed: the effect of the rotor placement is analysed using the dynamic model of the hexacopter and the dynamic manipulability measure (DMM)—an index measuring the omnidirectional acceleration. An adapted version of the DMM suitable for a hexacopter is introduced. The DMM evaluates the input–output relationship between the thrust developed by the rotors and the acceleration of the vehicle and the introduction of a new type of structure, namely, symmetric coplanar tilted rotor (SCTR). The DMM method applied to the hexacopter in the new SCTR structure is considered suitable for the evaluation of the integral drive property of the multirotor structure. Finally, issues of optimizing the hexacopter construction design are considered by Rajappa et al. [50].

Köse et al. [51] presented an interesting approach that combines modelling and simulation for different drone configurations, employing an original software combination between Solidworks–PID Simulink and SPSA (Simultaneous Perturbation Stochastic Approximation) to develop an algorithm for optimizing flight parameters and studying different flight regimes for a certain fixed length of the motor support arms.

Mehmood et al. [52] depict the manoeuvrability of a fully powered hexacopter over all six degrees of freedom by installing all the propellers under the same pitch angle. In order to evaluate the manoeuvrability, a biaxial propeller tilt was considered to allow for two possible study situations, i.e., inward and/or lateral propeller tilt. Over a wide range of tilt angles, it was discovered, for all six degrees of freedom, that inward tilt of the propellers either results in decreased drone manoeuvrability or provides less optimal gains at a low cost of efficiency of the propulsion system.

Budinger et al. [53] present several models to estimate the performances of the main components of multirotor drones with electric propulsion. The mathematical models described in the paper facilitate the employment of design and optimisation tools. Using the current available technologies, these models can be employed for the preliminary design of new sensor systems. Alternate developing methods were utilized to find an analytical model built on datasheet records (propellers) and on FEM simulations records (landing gear). Thus, the dimensional assessment simplifies the selection of the primary individual parameters and increases the assessment of the models.

The present paper comprises an original design and deployment of the hexacopter, the extended experimental study, the choice and integration of avionics components, command and control, video acquisition, telemetry data and the explanations regarding the future development of an equipment variant for the command and control of the hexacopter out of direct line of sight (BVLOS).

2.2. Sensors Equipment

In addition to the propulsion system, the sensors with which the drone is equipped play a critical role in terms of manoeuvrability, stability, command and control of the drone. The sensors also capture information from the surrounding environment (images, video, GPS location, photogrammetry, LIDAR), depending on the specific missions or activities that the drone is meant to perform.

Hussein and Nouacer [54] provide a source design pattern for building new drone systems, which includes blocks of the drones and relations between them that are distributed into four main groups: flight navigation, flight control, flight management and mission supervision.

Cao et al. [55] treat the examination of low power transmission lines using multicopter drones, in terms of making the right decision, cantered on data fusion acquired from a multisensor system. The information fused refers to the main aspects affecting the UAV parameters (flight speed), wind velocity, errors of the navigation positioning and size of the drone frame. A method called MFD-LPTL (multisensor fusion data analysis for low power transmission lines) is presented. This method's main purpose is to conceive a model for secure distance prediction between the drone and the power lines. Based on the multisensor data fusion, combining data from various sensors including radars, LIDAR and camera models, a statistical model which uses the autonomous avoidance navigation of the problems was applied.

Severin and Soffker [56] treat the problem of optimization of the sensors used for altitude estimation mounted on multicopter drones employed for spraying the vineyards. The study makes a comparison between a variety of low-cost sensors for measuring the distance between the drone and ground level, sensors which are most appropriate for vineyard-spraying drones. The signals were acquired from ultrasound, radar and Doppler sensors and were filtered using a Kalman filter. The study describes a variety of measures employed to improve the assessed altitude of the drone and to enhance the trustworthiness regarding the relative altitude approximation of the multicopter drone.

In Pena et al.'s [57] WILD HOPPER UAV study, a 600 *L* platform designed for forest firefighting is presented. The paper reveals a multilayer steadiness system for enhanced stability of the drone during the flight in severe conditions. WILD HOPPER is equipped with a range of sensors which include thermal cameras, geolocalization and navigation systems: satellite navigation and a new technology based on visual attitude estimation methods.

The study presented by Ravin et al. [58] explains the extraction and analysis of GPS data from three different drone manufacturers, followed by analysis and representation of the positioning data as flight paths. GPS-related data from any drone's flight is of vital importance as it helps in establishing a legal framework for operating a drone in a country's airspace. In terms of sensors, all these data are obtained from the GPS antenna/antennae mounted on the drone.

To be able to fly, a multicopter drone needs a flight controller, which is the brain of the drone. In terms of sensors, this flight controller consists of an AHRS (attitude and heading reference system) IMU (inertial measurement unit), which is a device that integrates multiaxes accelerometers, gyroscopes and magnetometers to provide estimation of the drone's orientation in space, providing measurements of pitch, roll and yaw. When the drone flies in an environment where GPS signal can be acquired, to ensure the reliability and highest performance, a sensor that includes an AHRS, as well as a GNSS receiver, which utilizes the GPS, GLONASS, BeiDou and Galileo satellite constellations, provide the best navigation system.

If the drone needs to be flown BVLOS (beyond visual line-of-sight) without being reliant on GPS, it is mandatory to have mounted on the drone a fully calibrated and temperature compensated AHRS IMU sensor under all dynamic conditions. In order to compensate for the three-axis movement of the drone based on user's input, the flight controller needs PID (proportional-integral-derivative) controllers or combinations of these (PI, PD and so on).

The study performed by Sree Ezhil et al. [59] concentrates on the efficacy of PID controllers in maintaining the stability of a multicopter drone. The results showed that by altering the gain values based on the different conditions of the disturbances, one can achieve a stabile drone. During further testing, it was observed that by adjusting PID gain values, the stability of the drone can be achieved within a specific fixed measure of time for a changing number of disturbances, even in tough conditions, which include wind speed and change in direction.

Madokoro et al. [60] illustrate in a comprehensive study a drone with advanced mobility on which four prototype brackets were developed. These prototypes include optimized sensors, devices and a camera, which work together as an integrated system platform. The sensors and communication system were employed as a new platform for atmospheric measurements at in situ locations, including the development of a wireless communication system for long distances and also a system for monitoring and visualizing in real-time the in situ local area measurements. The study was focused on gathering data regarding atmospheric phenomena and related environmental information, especially particulate matter (PM), as a major cause of air pollution. The obtained results were satisfactory, though, as a forthcoming design, based on regular flight measurements, and it is necessary to validate the resilience of the suggested system and its stability for long-term operation.

The novelty of the present study, from the sensors point of view, is the relatively economical and largely accessible equipment of the hexacopter, in two versions, in terms of avionics equipment, respectively photo/video acquisition components and telemetry data transmission and reception.

2.3. Experimental Procedures

Megayanti et al. [61] describe the mathematical modelling and implementation of a command-and-control system for a hexacopter employed to monitor radioactive–chemical–nuclear contamination using fuzzy logic. For accurate tracking of a trajectory, the hexacopter requires a high-performance altitude and attitude controller for its in-flight movement, since in conditions of external disturbances it introduces wind. In the first step, the dynamic equation of the hexacopter is developed using Newton–Euler equations, and in the second step, a solution consisting of a PID controller combined with fuzzy logic is proposed in order to include correction signals to eliminate positioning errors of the hexacopter when moving. Before implementation on the drone, the effectiveness of the proposed method was verified using a software-in-the-loop (SITL) robotic operating system (ROS) simulation environment together with the Matlab matrix calculation utility. Based on the numerical simulation and experimental results and using the fuzzy–PID intervention algorithm, the following parameters were improved: faster transient response hexacopter trajectory tracking performance, smaller errors in maintaining the steady state of the system, faster settling times to transient changes and better and more robust static and dynamic performance under disturbances introduced by different wind speeds.

Sharipov et al. [62] implemented a mathematical model of a hexacopter control system. Employing the Matlab/Simulink environment, it was possible to mathematically simulate the dynamics of the forces acting on the hexacopter rotors by inserting external disturbances: wind forces alongside one of the hexacopter axis. The block for estimating the model parameters is programmable and performs the computations using the theoretical formulae developed previously. Other aspects also treated in the paper were the problems associated with the selection of the optimal control for the hexacopter when flying along the path in the occurrence of wind. The attitude of the hexacopter in flight is adjusted using PID controllers because stabilization must be provided on all the axes of the drone during flight. Thus, four PID controllers must be implemented: one controller for roll motion stabilization, the second controller for pitch motion stabilization, the third controller for yaw motion stabilization and the fourth controller for hexacopter altitude stabilization. The stabilization of the hexacopter at a certain altitude was considered by Toledo et al. [63]. The Ziegler–Nichols method is employed to adjust the parameters of the PID controllers.

Wen Fu-Hsuan et al. [64] present an analysis and management strategy for hexacopters during fixed-point hovering manoeuvres in the event of one or more engine failures. The study suggests keeping the deviation between input and output values unchanged by reallocating the thrust forces to the rotors. Simulations are performed on a hexacopter in different fixed-point flight modes [65]. Linear dynamics problems of the hexacopter are analysed and subsequently numerically validated for the unique nonlinear dynamics. If failure of one of the hexacopter motors occurs, the study proposes an allocation matrix to reallocate the lift forces to the functional motors. The study takes into account seven cases of engine failure; the conclusions derived from analytical analysis show that reduced control for emergency landing is achievable in four scenarios at the linear level, and for the other three scenarios, the drone is completely uncontrollable. To demonstrate the validity of the recommended algorithm, the paper also presents numerical simulations.

Derawi et al. [66,67], Poksawat et al. [68] and Zheng et al. [69] present the mathematical modelling, estimation, attitude (drone position) control and altitude control of a hexacopter. Their works present the following contributions: First, mathematical modelling is performed, based on which the equations of the hexacopter model are obtained.

Again, the problem of rigid solid dynamics is pointed out by the study being performed on a hexacopter with an "X" configuration. The modelling is carried out employing the homogeneous transformation matrix, the Euler angles (ϕ—roll, θ—pitch, ψ—yaw) and the two reference systems, one associated to the drone frame and one inertial, grounded. It also introduces certain notions about the aerodynamic forces and moments that act on the drone frame. The dynamic model of the hexacopter illustrates the translational and rotational motions in response to the thrust generated by each rotor. A new approach for real-time drone attitude estimation is proposed by Benzemrane et al. [70] and Benzerrouk et al. [71] using a complementary nonlinear observer based on a special orthogonal group of rotation matrix SO (3)—special orthogonal—compared to the conventional extended Kalman filter (EKF). The works propose an attitude controller based on a PI and PID inner–outer loop structure, aiming to lead to faster response and improved strength at transitory response, while the altitude controller proposed in the paper is based on a standard closed-loop PID control system. The hexacopter employed in the tests is equipped with low-cost sensors (an inertial measurement unit (IMU) sensor modelled by Neumann and Bartholmai [72], and Sushchenko and Beliavtsev [73] and a barometric pressure sensor). Finally, through the experiments performed (flight manoeuvres inside a building and flight manoeuvres performed in outdoor free space, also taking into account the effects of disturbing factors, in particular, wind), Heise et al. [74], Dong et al. [75] and Lee et al. [76] demonstrate the efficacy of the suggested attitude of the observer, and Seah et al. [77] determine the attitude controller and altitude controller in real flight conditions, both in indoor and outdoor environment.

All the analysed papers present theoretical and laboratory-performed tests. In order to demonstrate the full functionality of the proposed hexacopter, the present work addresses a compound laboratory and in situ test procedure, comprising both ground and flight tests in a new perspective.

2.4. Multirotor Drones Stability Assessment Based on FEM Approach

When discussing the hexacopter stability [78–82], aspects related to the structural components of a hexacopter platform have to be considered. In the case of FEM analysis, this frequently focuses on structural stiffness and stability and requires a detailed assessment of the hexacopter model in a synergic connection between the virtual CAD model and FEM codes. The results matter not only in the decision-making process regarding the design of the hexacopter structure but also to the flight stability and the position control on the trajectory.

Reducing the drag force remains one of the main challenges in UAV aerodynamics research, as battery consumption can be significantly reduced if the drag decreases. Felismina et al. [83] analyse the aerodynamic behaviour of a quadcopter equipped with a seeding device in order to determine the appropriate bank angles (0°, 15° and 30°) for take-off and drone flight evolution during the seeding operation. Moreover, the work aims to define a suitable flight plan to increase the battery range. Aerodynamic results demonstrate that for take-off, the 30° tilt represents the most favourable aerodynamic position, due to the lower drag force that occurs during climb. In terms of the drone's behaviour during seeding, the 0° tilt is the one that creates a lower frontal drag and a lower drag force coefficient, respectively.

Lei et al. [84] discuss the aerodynamic performance of a hexacopter with different rotor spacings. The hovering flight efficiency of the drone is analysed by performing experimental tests and numerical simulations. A number of indices characterising the aerodynamic performance of the hexacopter are analysed theoretically, followed by tests and simulations on a hexacopter drone with different rotor-spacing ratios in relation to propeller size (i = 0.50, 0.56, 0.63, 0.71, 0.83). Using a custom-conceived test platform, the thrust, power load and hover flight efficiency of the hexacopter were obtained. Finally, CFD simulations were performed to obtain the fluid flow, pressure and velocity contour distributions of the hexacopter. The results show that the aerodynamic performance of the hexacopter drone varies by changing the rotor spacing. It was also observed that the thrust force increased by 5.61% and the overall efficiency increased by about 8.37% at i = 0.63 for the working mode (2200 RPM), indicating that the rotor spacing ratio at i = 0.63 achieved the best aerodynamic performance.

The design and development of a hexacopter capable of lifting a high payload has been investigated by Suprapto et al. [42] to ensure a stable attitude in flight. The evaluation focusses on the frame displacement and stress analysis to ensure the expected payload. In [85], experimental and CFD simulation tests for a small size UAV model to test wind influences at low speeds were reported. The study is comprehensive, but the prototype geometry as well as the flow regimes were found to be below the common level of UAV applications.

The flow regimes of air streams from the upper to the lower surface at different fixed-point flight altitudes were simulated and analysed by Zheng et al. [86] for plant protection applications. Although the study is substantial, the results are particular to the field of agricultural engineering.

In conclusion, many FEM simulation attempts have been reported on hexacopters, but the most interesting results for this type of platform have been achieved by software developers to demonstrate the capabilities of the solvers, as simulation in this case is still considered a challenge. In the case of the six rotors, the rotational domains of the propellers are so close to each other that the narrow space induces even more modelling and computational difficulties. From this point of view, the current research aims to bring a new perspective to the scientific literature.

3. Hexacopter Platform Architecture

The proposed hexacopter is presented in two equipment variants (v1 and v2), with two different sets of avionics equipment. Variant 1 (v1) (Figure 1) illustrates the Tarot ZYX-M avionics kit composed of the following: Tarot ZYX-M flight controller (AP—autopilot), 5V/12V voltage distribution module, GPS antenna sensor, status LED and radio receiver Turnigy 9X 8C v2 sensor on eight channels, frequency 2.4 GHz. A Turnigy Multistar 4-cell LiPo battery in 4S1P configuration with a capacity of 6600 mAh was employed as the drone power source. The radio control is model Turnigy TGY 9X, mode 2 with nine transmission channels, which is paired with the Turnigy 9X 8C v2 radio receiver mounted on the drone. For this variant, no data transmission–reception equipment was endowed for telemetry and video signals from drone to the operator. This variant is employed only for the preliminary testing of the normal operational parameters, on the ground and during the flight of the hexacopter, without a detailed analysis of the flight outputs.

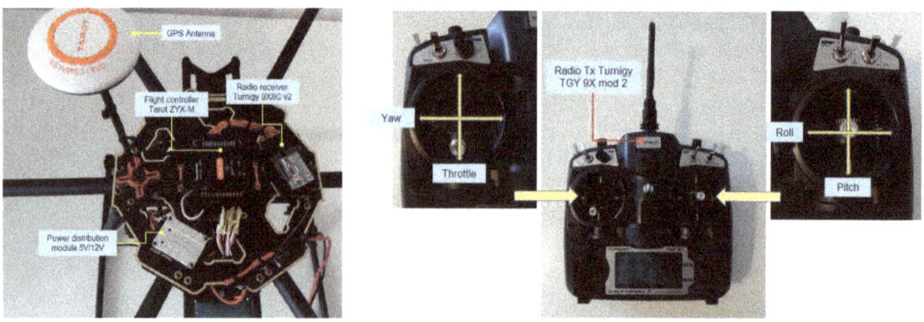

(a) (b)

Figure 1. Variant v1 of the hexacopter. (**a**) Equipment; (**b**) Radio control.

Figure 2 depicts the second version of the hexacopter, composed of the flight controller AP Pixhawk 2.4.8 sensor, a PPM protocol encoder sensor that allows the encoding of eight signals using the pulse width modulation (PWM) protocol in a single signal employing the pulse position modulation (PPM) procedure; loudspeaker, for AP status beeps; fail-safe on/off switch for protection against accidental starting of the motors; data transmitter telemetry transmitter YRRC at the 433 MHz frequency and 1000 mW power for the transmission of telemetry data on the ground, paired with the signals telemetry on the ground receiver, model YRCC, which transmits the video signal on 32 channels at a 5.8 GHz frequency; 600 mW power, for video signal transmission from the GoPro Hero 4 model camera mounted on the three-axis rotation gimbal, Tarot T4-3D model; a 12-channel RadioLink R12DS radio receiver; 2.4 GHz frequency for radio command reception from the transmitter built into the control box at the ground operator; GPS signal reception antenna; and the ReadytoSky model.

Figure 2. Variant v2 of the hexacopter.

Both variants were mounted on the same hexacopter frame structure, made of carbon fibre and consisting of two central plates of the frame between which six supported arms are fixed. At the arm ends, the motors and electronic speed controllers are mounted on six special supports. The landing gear is composed of two tubular structures mounted in the form of the letter T at a specific angle to the end plate of the frame. At the bottom of the lower plate, a bracket is mounted for fixing the battery. In the v1 variant, an additional support is mounted on the right arm of the landing gear for fixing the video transmitter. The carbon fibre provides the drone frame with elasticity, i.e., increased resistance to deformations, stresses, bending and a reduced structural mass of the platform. However, a drawback arises from the fact that carbon fibre attenuates the strength of the transmitted/received radio signal. That is why it is necessary to carefully choose the location of the radio/video signal transmission–reception equipment on the hexacopter or its proximity by mounting spacers.

Figures 3–5 depict the described design details both focused on components and on the entire equipment assembly for variants v1 and v2 (with 4S1P LiPo battery, 14.8 v, 12,000 mAh).

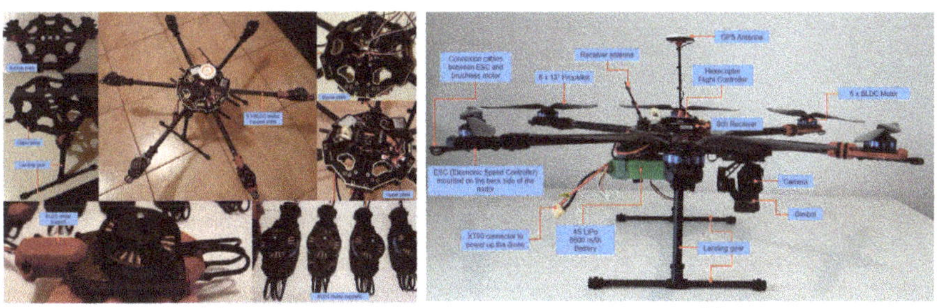

(**a**) (**b**)

Figure 3. Hexacopter variant v1. (**a**) Components; (**b**) Assembly.

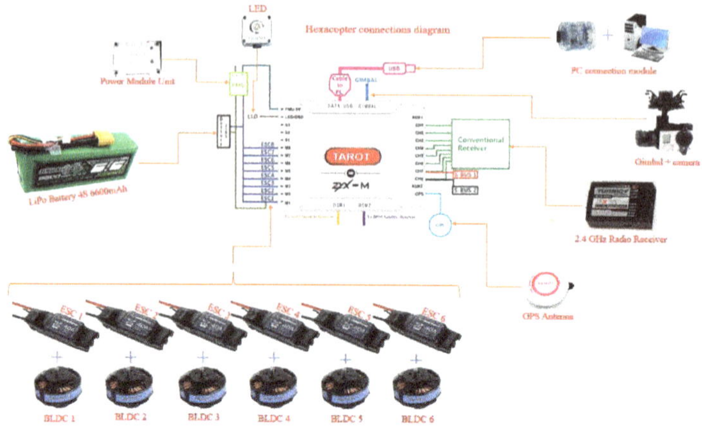

Figure 4. Connections diagram for hexacopter variant v1.

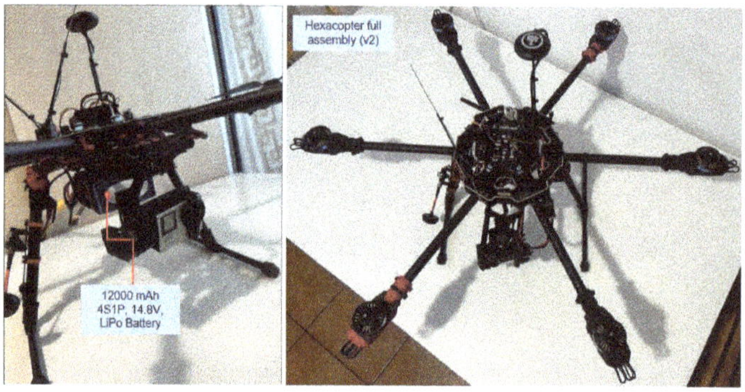

Figure 5. Hexacopter assembly for variant v2.

The block diagram of the hexacopter platform architecture is presented in Figure 6 illustrating the main components of the hexacopter, respectively the command-and-control ground station and the relationships between them. Hexacopter telemetry data are transmitted via a YRCC transmitter equipped with an antenna operating at 433 MHz. On the ground, an YRCC receiver is equipped with an antenna paired with the one placed on the hexacopter and at the same operating frequency. The receiver can be connected to a mobile device (tablet or smartphone) or a laptop, on which a GCS (ground control station) platform is installed.

The two components of the telemetry kit are illustrated in Figure 7: the transmitter mounted on the drone and the receiver in two connection options (Samsung tablet and HP Omen laptop), on which the Mission Planner GCS was installed.

The video signal from the hexacopter is either stored on the GoPro camera's internal microSD card (when it has to operate in record mode) or transmitted in real time to the ground by means of the following chain: the GoPro camera is connected to the Tarot T4-3D gimbal via a special dedicated connector; the video signal is then transmitted to a 32-channel antenna operating in the 5645–5945 MHz frequency range. This communicates with a dual receiver (two built-in antennas for better signal reception) on 32 channels, on the same frequency of 5.8 GHz, and the image is displayed on a 7″ HD monitor. Following laboratory tests, for optimal operation of the transceiver chain, the transmitter was set to channel 4 (5645 MHz), and the receiver was set to channel 5 (5885 MHz), according to the frequency matrices in the specifications of each component. Figure 8 illustrates the composition and location of the video transceiver system from the hexacopter to the operator. The HD video monitor with the built-in receiver is shown in the tripod-mounted version, but it can also be mounted on the operator's radio remote control for easy observation of real-time images and gimbal control to obtain the desired frame during the surveillance, reconnaissance, investigation and shooting missions.

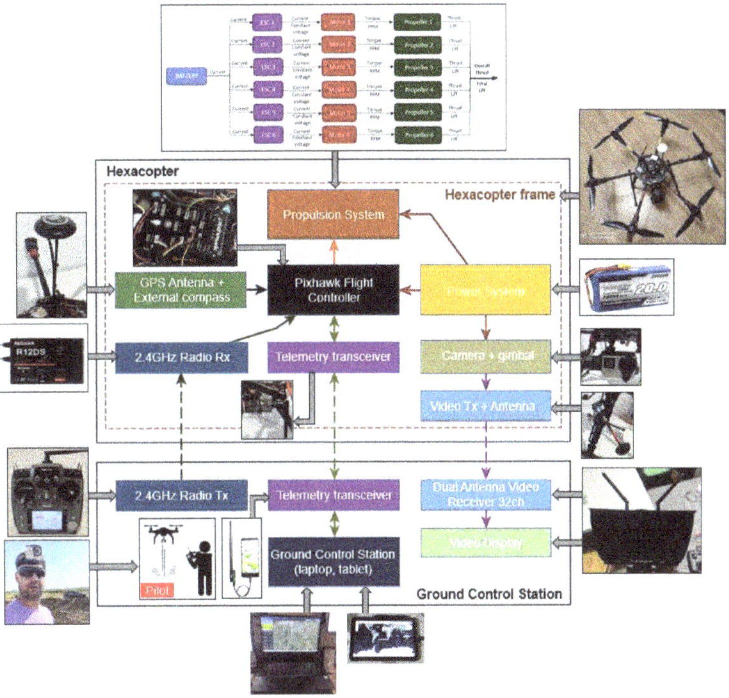

Figure 6. Blocd diagram of hexacopter platform.

Figure 7. Arrangement of the telemetry kit on the drone and on the ground.

The Pixhawk 2.4.8 flight controller (FMUv2) installed on the hexacopter v2 version, with the interfaces to various peripheral equipment, are illustrated in Figure 9.

The flight controller hardware components are the following:

- System-on-Chip STMicroelectronics STM32F427 Cortex-M4F 32-bit main microcontroller, operating frequency 180 MHz, RAM: 256 KB SRAM (L1), 2 MB Flash memory for writing instructions.
- System-on-Chip STMicroelectronics STM32F100 Cortex-M3 32-bit, 24 MHz operating frequency, 8 KB SRAM (L1), 64 KB Flash memory for writing instructions.

- Embedded sensors on the motherboard: • a 3-axis STMicroelectronics L3GD20H 16-bit gyroscope sensor; • a 14-bit STMicroelectronics LSM303D accelerometer/magnetometer sensor; • an Invensense MPU-6000 3-axis accelerometer/gyroscope sensor; • a TE Connectivity MEAS MS5611 barometer sensor.

Figure 8. Video signal transmission–reception chain from hexacopter to the operator.

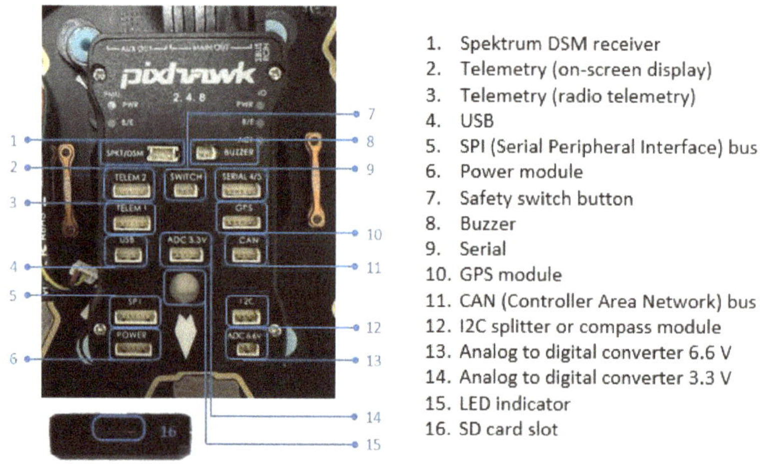

Figure 9. Pixhawk 2.4.8 flight controller and the peripheral connection interfaces.

Also connected to the flight controller is an external GPS antenna/bus module consisting of a Ublox M8N GPS receiver sensor and a Honeywell HMC5883L digital compass sensor.

For the subsequent analysis of the flight parameters both on the ground and in flight an ArduCopter firmware, version v4.x, was employed and installed on the Pixhawk 2.4.8 AP motherboard. A laptop and a tablet were utilized for the ground control station on which the mission planner platform was installed and employed. In the v2 version, the drone powering was achieved with three Turnigy batteries, LiPo type with four cells, in 4S1P and 4S2P configurations, maximum supported current 12-24C, with capacities 12,000 mAh, 16,000 mAh and 20,000 mAh.

The hexacopter presented in the two variants, equipped with avionics components and sensors, can be employed in a wide range of civil applications, as well as in the field of homeland and national security. The solutions developed represent a relatively economic option in terms of the component acquisition costs and integration.

4. Laboratory and In Situ Measurement Results and Discussion

Tests were carried out, both those on specialized online platforms specifically tailored for the multirotor drone segment as well as extended laboratory, ground and flight tests to confirm the optimal real-world operation of the hexacopter, in accordance with the original design; practical realization of the hexacopter; and choice and integration of avionics components, command and control, video acquisition and telemetry data, taking into account a future development of a variant of equipment for command and control of the hexacopter out of direct line of sight (BVLOS).

4.1. Laboratory Tests

To ensure that all the components were correctly chosen and the hexacopter will perform as expected, preliminary laboratory tests were conducted using dedicated built test stands and testing equipment.

Aside from the mentioned sensors, the electronic speed controller (ESC) sensor must be considered due to its major importance when discussing motors functionality. The basic function of an ESC is to control the motor speed based on the PWM (pulse width modulation) signal that the AP sends to the motor, which is too weak to drive the brushless DC motor directly (Figure 10). This is achieved by the pilot operating the speed stick in the range 0–100%, and the ESC will send the power commanded by the pilot to the motor. In addition, some ESCs also perform other functions: dynamic braking, battery short-circuit protection, motor start protection and power supply (battery disposal circuit) for the radio receiver or servo motors. Unlike a general ESC, the ESC for brushless motors can act as an inverter, converting the direct current received from the battery into three-phase alternating current (AC), which is then applied to the motor. The ESC also determines the direction of rotation of the motor.

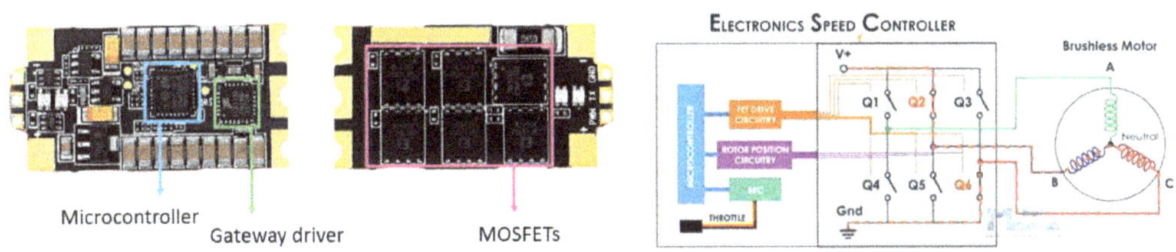

(a) (b)

Figure 10. The ESC architecture and simplified diagram of ESC operation. (**a**) ESC general architecture; (**b**) Simplified diagram of ESC operation.

The simplified diagram of ESC, depicted in Figure 10b, employs real-time operation. The main features and parameters of the ESC mounted on the hexacopter are as follows: it is equipped with specially optimized firmware for disc-type motors and a special core program for rapid throttle response, and the refresh rate of the throttle signal supported is up to 621 Hz, making the ESC perfectly compatible with various flight controllers (if the refresh rate is higher than 500 Hz, then the ESC control signal is the nonstandard throttle signal); it is equipped with driving efficiency technology (DEO), which effectively reduces the ESC operating temperature by about 20%, improves the flight time and brings a better throttle linearity and good stability—thus the operating efficiency improves by maximum 10%. In addition, its MOSFETs have extra-low resistance, offering high performance and great current endurance, with a continuous output current of 40 A and a burst of 60 A up to 10 s.

The most important components of the ESC, as presented in Figure 11, are the microcontroller, the driver for the gateway between the autopilot (AP) and the MOSFETs and the MOSFETs, respectively. As illustrated previously, the hexacopter is equipped with six Hobbywing XRotor 40A Opto ESCs sensors, each of these being connected to each of the six BLDC motors.

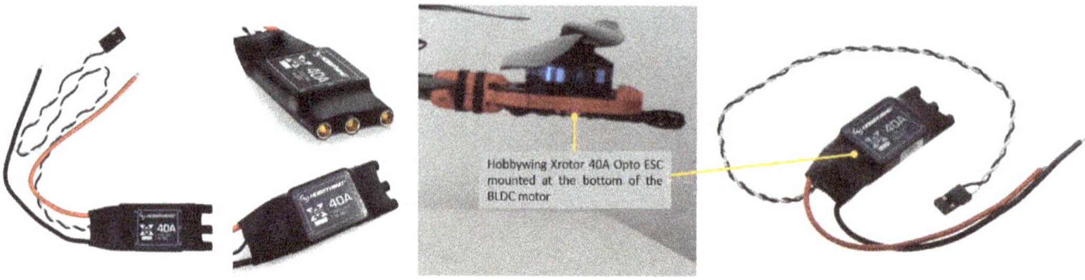

Figure 11. Hobbywing XRotor 40A Opto ESC.

To determine the thrust force, and therefore the efficiency of the propulsion system, laboratory tests were carried out using the Mayatech MT10PRO 10KG test stand. A Turnigy LiPo battery, 20,000 mAh capacity, 4 cells in 4S1P configuration, voltage 14.8 V, was employed to power the ESC–motor–propeller assembly. The Tx–Rx chain was provided by a 2.4 GHz radio remote control, model RadioLink AT10II, and a 12-channel receiver, model RadioLink R12DS. The test configuration is shown in Figure 12.

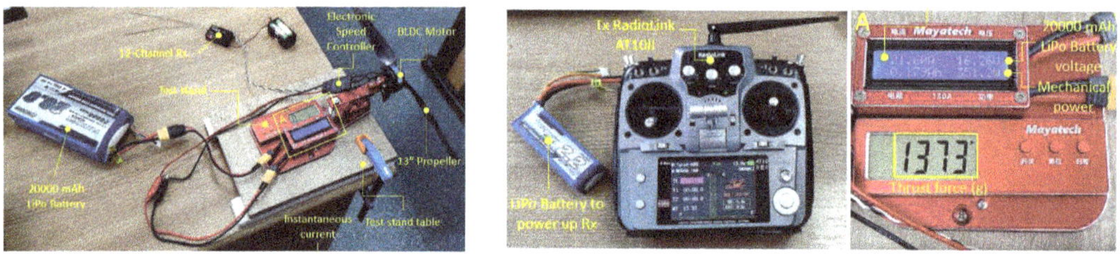

Figure 12. Propulsion system efficiency test stand configurations.

Using a tachometer, in the same test configuration, the maximum speed of the rotor assembly was determined, obtaining a maximum value of 13418 RPM (Figure 13).

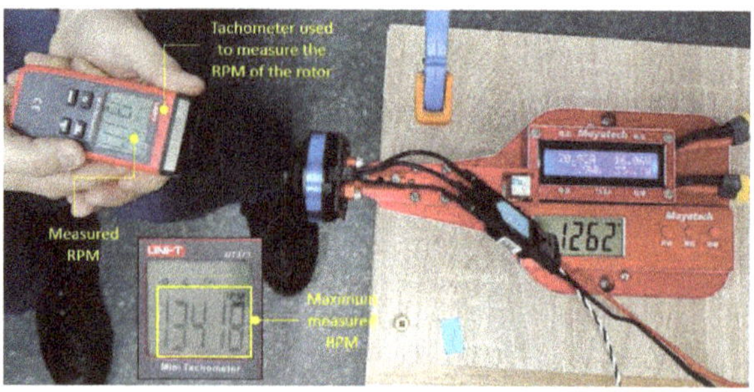

Figure 13. Measurement of the rotor assembly maximum RPM.

The thrust force, current consumption, battery voltage and mechanical power were measured using the test stand (Figure 12), and the rotational speed using the tachometer (Figure 13). The results are plot in the graphs presented in Figure 14.

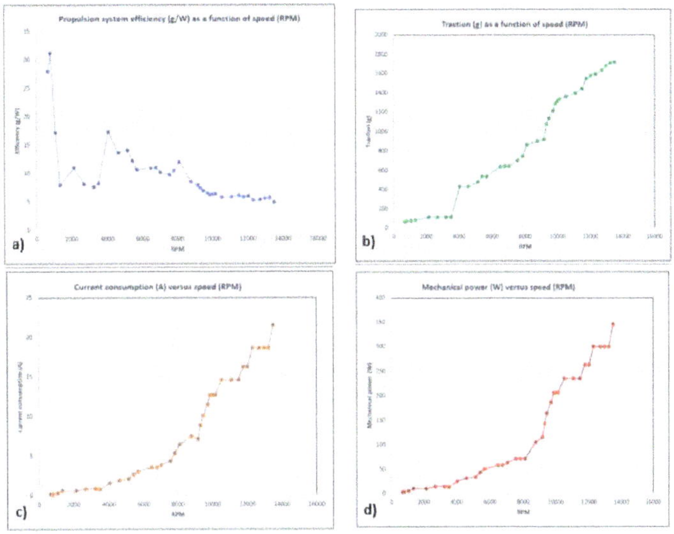

Figure 14. Propulsion system tests results. (**a**) Propulsion system efficiency; (**b**) Traction force as a function of RPM; (**c**) Current consumption based on RPM; (**d**) Mechanical power versus RPM.

Therefore, the results obtained were as follows:

- The maximum thrust force produced by the rotor assembly, measured on the stand, was approximately 1.718 Kgf $\approx$ 16.84 N.
- Maximum speed measured by the tachometer—13418 rpm.
- The efficiency of the propulsion system decreases with increasing rpm. In the idling zone, at 30–40% rpm, the efficiency reaches a value of 13–14 g/W ($\geq$6 g/W—high-efficiency drone). In the 50–75% rpm range, which is equivalent to operating the drone in hover and light horizontal manoeuvres, the efficiency decreases to a value of 6.49 g/W ($\geq$6 g/W—high-efficiency drone). In the speed range of 85–100%, the efficiency further decreases to a minimum value of 4.96 g/W (4 $\div$ 6 g/W—low-efficiency drone).
- With increasing speed, the current consumption increases proportionally, reaching a measured current value at 100% speed of 21.6 Ah.
- The mechanical power produced also increases to a value of 346.2 W at 100% speed.

The optimum operating temperature of the BLDC motors is of critical importance as high temperatures can lead to premature engine damage and failure. Thus, it is necessary to test the operating temperatures at idle, midthrottle and maximum throttle to determine the RPM ranges where their performances are at best. During the tests on the test stand, motors temperatures at different RPM ranges were measured employing a FLIR E86 thermal imaging camera (Figure 15).

By analysing the results, the following points of interest were found:

- At idle, with the throttle stick at 30%, for a 3–5-min interval, the motor temperature reached 40 °C.
- At idle, with the throttle stick at 50% for 3–5 min, the motor temperature reached 60 °C.
- In maximum mode, with the throttle stick at 100%, for 3–5 min, the temperature reached over 200 °C, which means that it is only desirable to operate the drone in maximum mode for very short periods, around 10–15 s, to avoid these temperature increases in the motor windings, which can eventually lead to burn-out and thus their permanent damage.

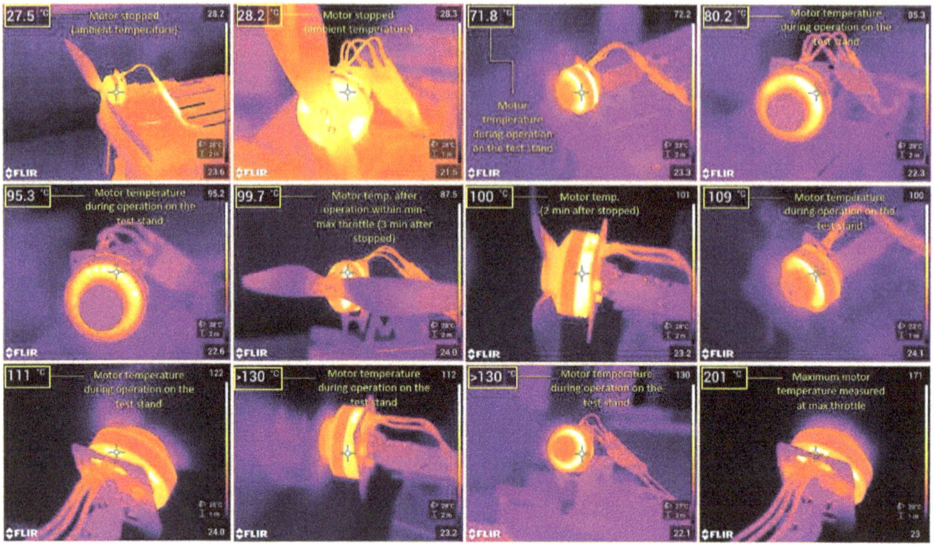

Figure 15. Measurement of motor temperature during operation on the test stand, within 5–100% throttle range.

4.2. Online Testing Platforms Results

In order to find the best configuration to ensure a stable flight with the best range within safe flight conditions, several variants of equipment, including sensors, propellers and batteries, were tested using online platforms specialized in the multirotor drone segment. This section presents the best results for the proposed hexacopter in terms of stability and flight range employing the *xcopterCalc* simulation platform, one of the most popular tools in terms of configuration simulations for multirotor drones.

Similar results for the hexacopter were obtained for both variants, were two different flight controllers and avionics components were employed, Tarot ZYX-M and Pixhawk 1, respectively, as presented above. Figure 16 illustrates the results obtained in variant 1 of the hexacopter, where Tarot ZYX-M flight controller and subsequent avionics components were utilized. The configuration used was as follows:

- Frame size is 695 mm and is made of carbon fibre epoxy resin with a total mass of only 833 g, while providing increased shock and vibration resistance.
- The propellers were 13″ with 5.5″ pitch—the size of the drone frame limits the mounting of propellers with a maximum diameter of 13″.
- Four-cell LiPo battery capacity—16 Ah, in 4S2P configuration with 12-24C C-rating, 14.8 V nominal voltage.
- Flight testing of the HDT was simulated at an altitude of about 85 m above sea level (Bucharest altitude), at a temperature of 22 °C and at an atmospheric pressure of 1010 hPa (757.5 mmHg).
- Electronic speed controllers (ESC) can withstand a maximum current of 40A and have an internal resistance of approximately 0.0006 Ohm and a mass of 26 g each.
- The hexacopter has a three-axis rotating and stabilizing gimbal; it has a mass of 178 g and consumes approximately 0.05 A.
- Tarot 4006/620KV BLDC motors produce 620 rpm/V and have an internal resistance of 0.126 Ohm and a mass of 82 g each.

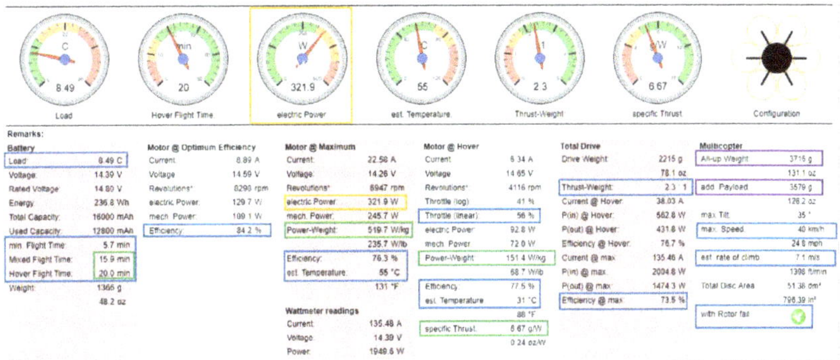

Figure 16. Results obtained after running the simulation using *xcoperCalc* platform.

After running the simulation, the following results were obtained, as illustrated in Figure 16.

The following conclusions were drawn:

- Load on the battery (load) is 8.49C (which means a continuous load below 12C A of the battery, i.e., 8.49 × 16A ≈ 136A < 12 × 16 ≈ 192A).
- A considerable increase in flight time to 15.1 min for combined flight and 20 min for hover flight, compared to lower capacity batteries used in previous tests.
- For optimum motor performance, a slight increase in efficiency from 84.1% to 84.2% is obtained; for fixed-point flight, a speed of 4116 rpm is obtained. The motor speed increases from 48% to 56% of capacity (which is a good result), a power-to-mass ratio of 151.4 W/kg, an efficiency of 77.5% and a temperature of only 31 °C. However, as an element to be taken into account, an increase in power (at engine input) to 321.9 W (but only at maximum engine speed) is noted.
- The thrust-to-mass ratio in this case is 2.3:1 (>1.8—very good value).
- The specific thrust of the propellers is 6.67 g/W, so high efficiency.
- Additional equipment with a mass of about 3.6 kg can be attached.

Figure 17 depicts two graphs (a) and (b), obtained after running the simulations, showing data regarding flight distance, speed and engine characteristics at maximum speed.

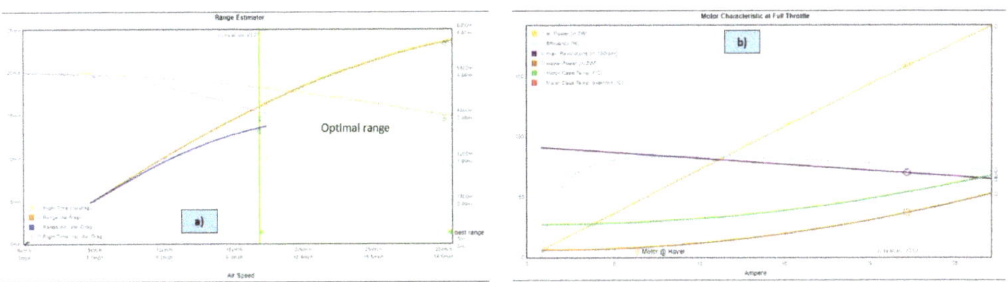

Figure 17. Online tests. (**a**) Range estimator; (**b**) Motor characteristics at full throttle.

The following conclusions were summarized:

- The maximum speed is 40 km/h, and the ascent rate of 7.1 m/s;
- The maximum flight time (without drag) is about 20 min;
- Maximum flight time (with drag) decreases to 15.1 min;
- The maximum flight distance (without drag) is approximately 7600 m;
- The maximum flight distance (with drag) is approximately 4400 m;

- The best performance for the hexacopter is achieved within the speed range 17 ÷ 31 km/h;
- From Figure 16, it can be observed that the engines succeeded to operate in all speed ranges at an acceptable temperature of maximum 55 °C, which is very good for flight stability and proper functioning of the avionics and airborne sensors.

4.3. In situ Ground and In-Flight Experiments

The results presented in this section were attained from tests carried out for the hexacopter v2 configuration, equipped with the Turnigy 12000 mAh 12-24C LiPo 4S1P battery.

4.3.1. Hover Flight

The purpose of these tests is to ensure, verify and prove the appropriate functioning of the hexacopter in the proposed configuration, both in terms of the structural design and the avionics components, especially the employed flight controller. These tests are divided into two main categories: ground and flight tests. The purpose of the ground test is to ensure that the drone's structure and avionics systems comply with the requirements so that the hexacopter will perform the flight as expected.

Ground Test

This test consists of:

- Inspection of the structural integrity of the drone. Each joint of the structural elements is checked and must be well secured to ensure its rigidity.
- Checks of the weight and the drone equilibrium. These checks provide information on the location of the actual centre of gravity in respect to all three axes X, Y and Z. The centre of gravity location affects the performance and stability of the drone in flight.
- Examination of the avionic systems operation: controller, navigation, power supply, video system, telemetry data transmission system and wiring. All data concerning the operating limits of the equipment must be memorized in order to avoid undesirable events such as maximum drone range, maximum operating range of the radio controls, battery capacity, power consumption of the various electronic components, maximum authorized flight altitude and legislative aspects concerning the operation of the drone in certain areas, depending on the geographical layout. In the case of autonomous flight following a preprogrammed route, the flight controller has programmed the flight scenario, the flight parameters and the failsafe measures required in the event of emergencies such as the loss of radio link between the drone and the operator, battery voltage falling close to the critical value and a motor shutdown.
- Test of the motor's operation by simple on/off commands to ensure the rated static performance based on throttle stick position, increasing the speed incrementally up to 10–15% and checking their operation, oscillations, noises, proper propeller rotation directions.
- Telemetry data link tests between the drone and the mission planner ground control station. This ensures the stability of the radio link between the drone and the operator. With the help of the control station, the operator can either plan autonomous flights on preprogrammed routes or intervene in the control of the hexacopter in emergency conditions if the radio control is not used.
- Weather condition checks: wind speed, temperature, precipitation and atmospheric pressure. This is an extremely important step in planning a flight, as there are limitations to operating the hexacopter.

For the GCS, the mission planner platform was employed, whose main interface is illustrated in Figure 18a, which also shows the map of the test location. Figure 18b depicts the HUD window, which provides valuable data for the operator during flight stage and also during ground operations.

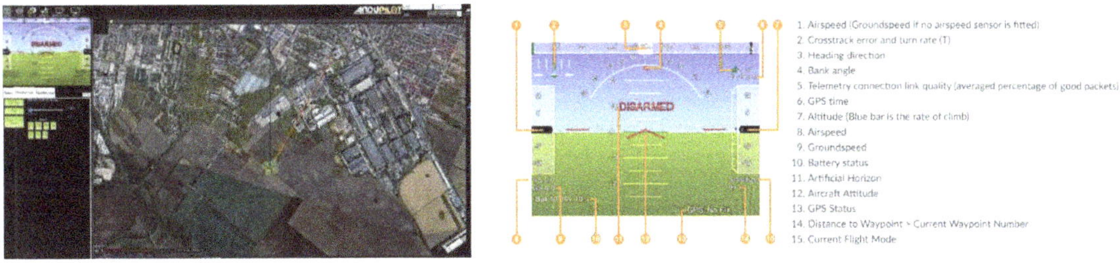

(a) (b)

Figure 18. Mission planner ground control station. (**a**) Main window; (**b**) HUD window.

Figure 19 pictures the test stands, the ground control station and the test location, while Figure 20 encompasses details during the execution of the hexacopter manoeuvres: take-off, climb, hover, descent and landing.

Figure 19. Employed open area test rigs.

Figure 20. Hexacopter in stationary flight at a fixed point—flight stages.

Images of the drone on the ground and in flight received from the GoPro Hero 4 camera mounted on the hexacopter are illustrated in Figure 21, while Figure 22 represents the mission planner interface with the layout of the hexacopter on the test location map and the video received from the GoPro camera on the built-in dual receiver monitor.

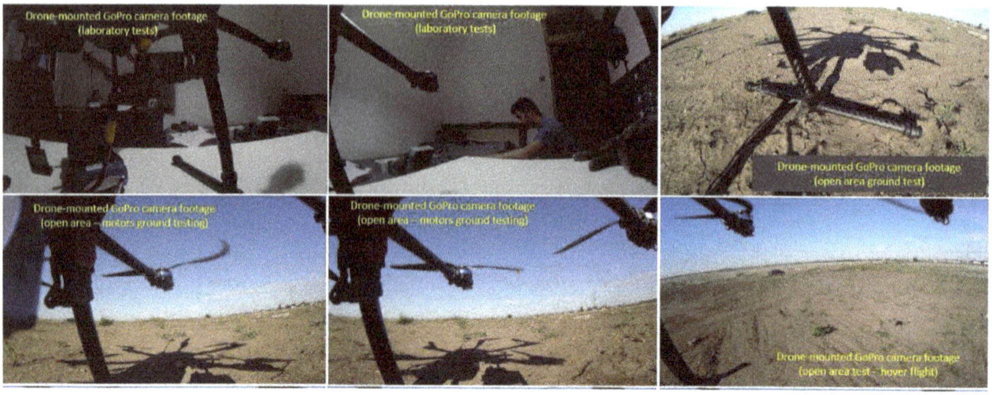

Figure 21. Drone-mounted GoPro camera footage, on the ground and in flight.

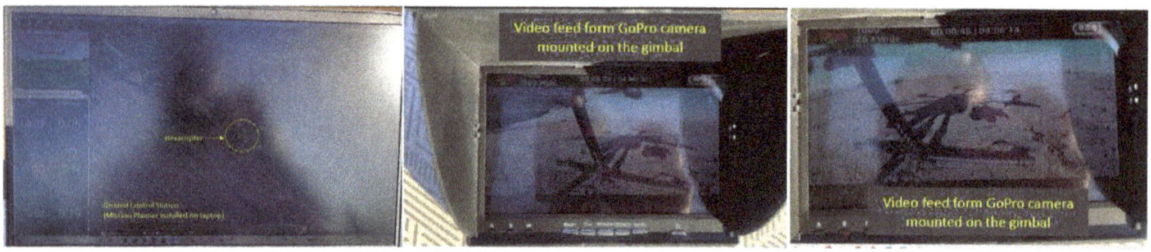

Figure 22. Mission planner interface. Images acquired by GoPro camera mounted on the hexacopter.

Hover Flight Tests

After the completion of the ground experiment, the hexacopter was tested in stationary flight. The tests were carried out in a plain area without obstacles around, within a radius of 5 km, in order to avoid the occurrence of unpleasant events such as drone crash, property destruction or person injuries. Regarding the wind speed at the test site, days with low wind speed of 1–2 m/s were chosen, measured with an anemometer (Figure 23).

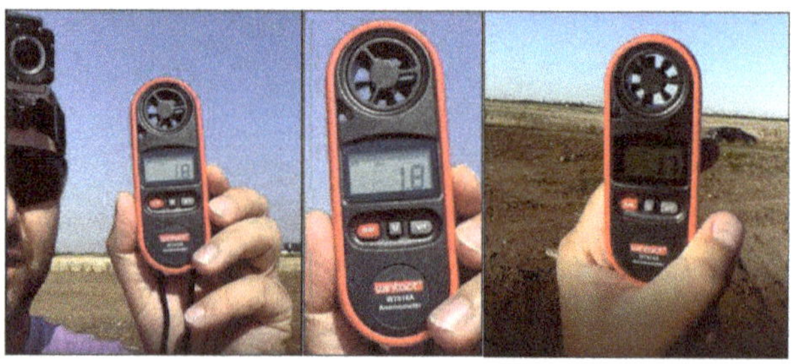

Figure 23. Wind speed measurement with anemometer.

In this manoeuvre, after the operator has given the command to increase the engine speed, the speed stick is kept in the 50–75% rpm range (for the hexacopter configuration), and the lift force required to lift the drone off the ground and keep it stationary is obtained. The lift force is created by the rotation of the six rotors, which revolve at the same rpm during the vertical climb, while the hexacopter tries to stabilize its attitude. During the vertical lift, until the altitude set by the operator is reached and in respect to the command given by the operator, the hexacopter attitude PIDs apply corrections to maintain the position of the drone within the values of the commanded parameters. When stabilizing the hexacopter at a given altitude, the operator keeps the speed stick in the appropriate speed range, and the PID altitude controller applies the necessary corrections to the thrust of the engines to maintain the drone at the desired altitude.

The general architecture of the closed-loop PID controller is depicted in Figure 24.

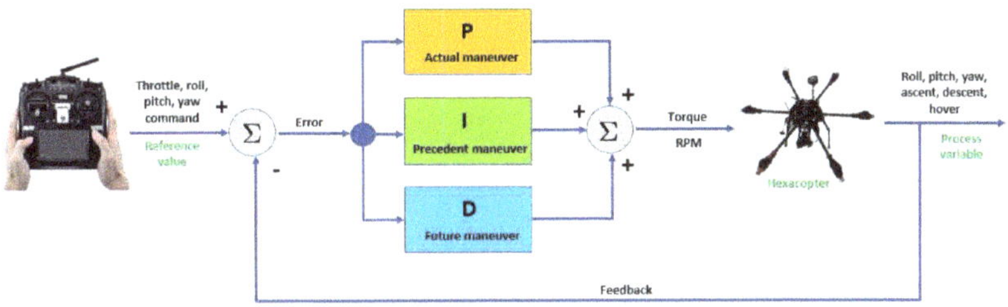

Figure 24. Closed-loop PID scheme—general approach.

In the case of the physically designed hexacopter equipped with a three-axis gimbal and a photo/video camera, the drone must be able to maintain its position at a fixed point in order to carry out surveillance, reconnaissance and photography missions. For this purpose, when using the manual radio control by the ground operator, it is recommended to operate it in the following modes: stabilize, in which the PID controllers automatically adjust pitch and roll; alt hold, in which the PID controllers automatically adjust pitch and roll and maintain drone altitude; and RTL (return to land) for emergency cases. Loiter can also be employed (semiautonomous flight—the PID controllers automatically adjust the drone's altitude and position; the hexacopter uses GPS for movement), PosHold (similar to loiter mode, but when the roll and pitch sticks are not centred, the operator controls the two movements) and land (the hexacopter descends and lands directly, without returning to the take-off point). Auto mode is utilized for autonomous movement along a predefined flight path. For PID controller tuning procedures, AUTOTUNE mode is employed after sensor calibration procedures (accelerometers, gyroscopes, magnetometers) and initial tuning.

In the case of fixed-point tests, take-off was performed in stabilize mode, which was then switched to alt hold mode and subsequently to RTL mode.

4.3.2. Hexacopter Flight Parameters Extracted from Sensors during Hover Flight

The drone was raised up to an altitude of 8.5 m. The EKF subsystem is responsible for generating attitude, velocity, position and altitude estimates for the drone so that the navigation and control systems can operate correctly. EKF takes the inputs from IMU, GPS and BARO sensors and integrates them to provide these assessments, one of which is the estimated altitude. This is then passed to the vehicle's altitude control system, which attempts to align to the target altitude in altitude-controlled flight modes. Figure 25 plots the altitude reached by the drone in blue, the commanded altitude in red and the altitude measured by the barometer in green. It can be noticed that there are no significant differences between the three values. The maximum recorded difference between programmed and measured values is less than 1 m, representing less than 10% of the real value.

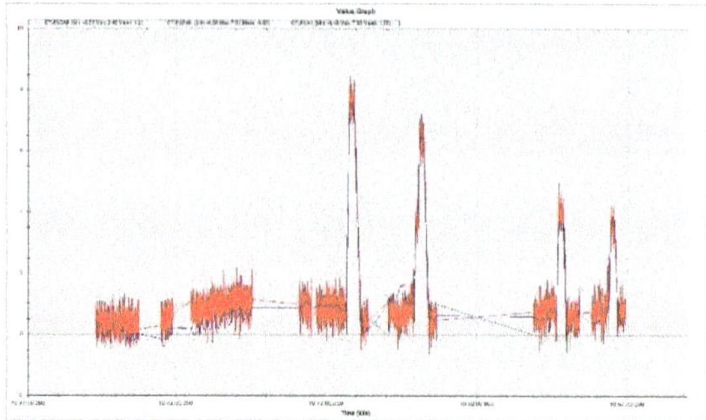

Figure 25. Hexacopter programmed and recorded altitude.

The graph extracted from the MAVExplorer platform (Figure 26a) depicts the altitude at which the drone was lifted and the ambient temperature at the test site in Fahrenheit degrees. The graph presented in Figure 26b shows the in situ atmospheric pressure (Pa) extracted from the data measured by the barometer with which the drone AP is equipped.

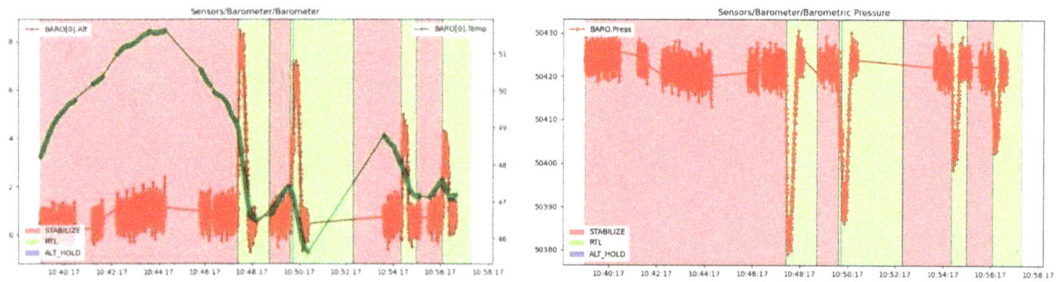

(**a**) (**b**)

Figure 26. Hexacopter measured parameters. (**a**) Altitude and ambient temperature; (**b**) Ambient atmospheric pressure.

For optimal operation of the hexacopter, radio control calibration was initially performed using the GCS mission planner. The minimum maximum PWM signal duration limits for the employed channels by the RadioLink AT10II radio control, mode 2 (motor stick is located on the left side), operate within the range 1000–2000 μs. The channels are assigned as follows: Channel 1 (CH1)—roll, Channel 2 (CH2)—pitch, Channel 3 (CH3)—throttle, Channel 4 (CH4)—yaw, Channel 5 (CH5)—flight modes (stabilize, alt hold and RTL), Channel 6 (CH6)—engine kill switch mode.

The PWM signal is utilized to control the pulse width modulation signal for each electronic speed controller that is connected to each of the six motors. The PWM signal is a periodic square wave signal with a period of 20 ms, which means it has a refresh rate of 50 Hz. Each cycle of the PWM signal lasts for 1–2 ms high level (1000–2000 μs), which is the control value of that channel. In the case of speed, 1000–1100 μs corresponds to 0 speed of the hexacopter, and 1900–2000 μs corresponds to maximum speed.

Prior to ground and flight manoeuvres, laboratory tests were performed on the motors without propellers to verify their operation within parameters. Figure 27a illustrates the command given by the operator from the radio control, in the range 1083–1916 μs, as it was previously calibrated, and Figure 27b shows the response of the ESC-controlled motors in respect to the operator's command to increase speed. It can be noted that the engines operate within the appropriate parameters, with values between 1000–1950 μs, and respond directly to the command given by the operator.

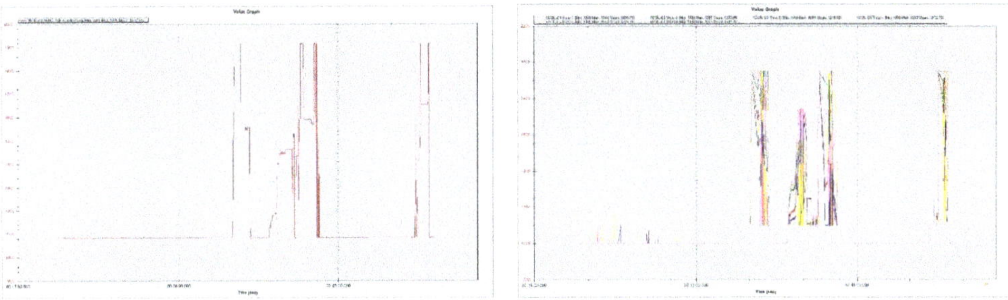

(a) (b)

Figure 27. Tests performed on the motors without propellers. (**a**) Speed command given by the operator; (**b**) Engine response to the operator command.

Figure 28a depicts the altitude of the test site, which is 79–80 m above sea level (mean sea level). The peaks of the graph represent the altitudes to which the hexacopter was lifted during the manoeuvres. In Figure 28b, the geographic coordinates of the location (maximum altitude of the hexacopter stationary at the fixed point—8.5 m) are illustrated.

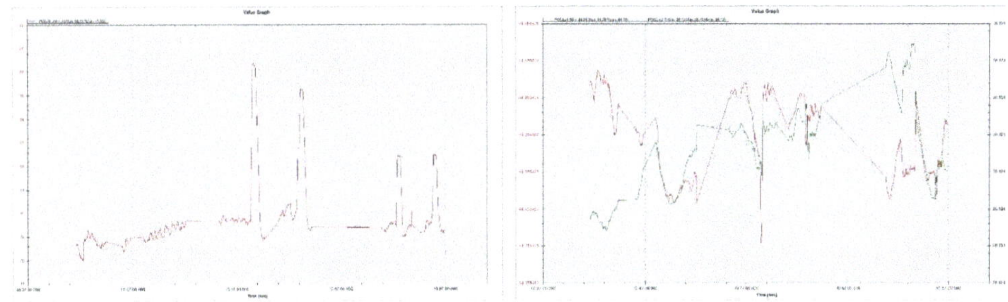

(a) (b)

Figure 28. The altitude of the test site. (**a**) Operating altitude of the in situ location; (**b**) Test location.

The results were processed with the mission planner and MAVExplorer platforms. Figure 29a depicts the command given by the ESCs to the drives in response to the operator moving the speed stick in the 50–75% range. The motor increases the rotational speed to a value at which the hexacopter becomes detached from the ground and begins to lift until the operator clamps the stick at a certain percentage of the speed. The operation of the motors is observed in the range 1000–1725 μs, as the rotational speed range does not reach 100%, leaving room for additional manoeuvring if needed. It is noticed that there are small delays in response times between 100 and 200 μs, representing less than 10%, possibly due to the natural frequencies of the motors or the structural elements on which they are mounted. High vibrations can cause wrong accelerometer altitude and horizontal position estimations, leading to problems in maintaining altitude. The hexacopter may start an uncontrolled lift manoeuvre without the operator being able to intervene. Position control problems in flight modes such as loiter, PosHold and auto may also occur. Vibrations are best visualized by plotting the VibeX, VibeY and VibeZ values in the VIBE menu. These represent the raw vibration values before being filtered by the accelerometers. Vibration levels below 30 m/s^2 are normally acceptable. Levels above 30 m/s^2 can cause problems, and levels above 60 m/s^2 nearly always cause position or altitude maintenance problems. The graph in Figure 29b shows acceptable vibration levels that are consistently below 30 m/s^2 and around 13 m/s^2.

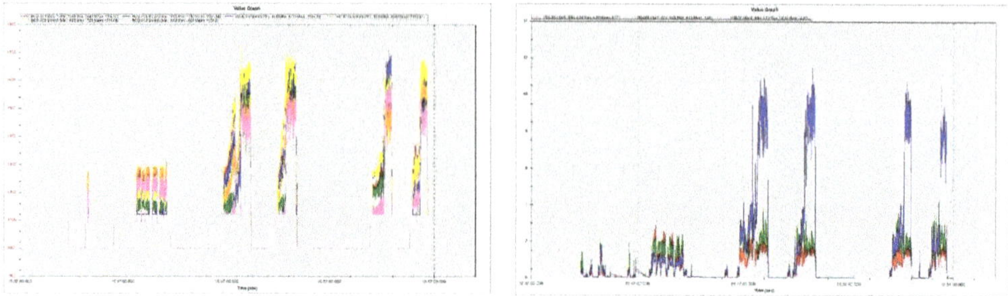

(**a**) (**b**)

Figure 29. Results processed with the online platforms. (**a**) Engines response to the lift command; (**b**) Accelerometer (0) vibration recordings.

Similar results in terms of accelerometer vibrations (0) were found when performing another flight under similar conditions with the hexacopter, as shown in Figure 30a.

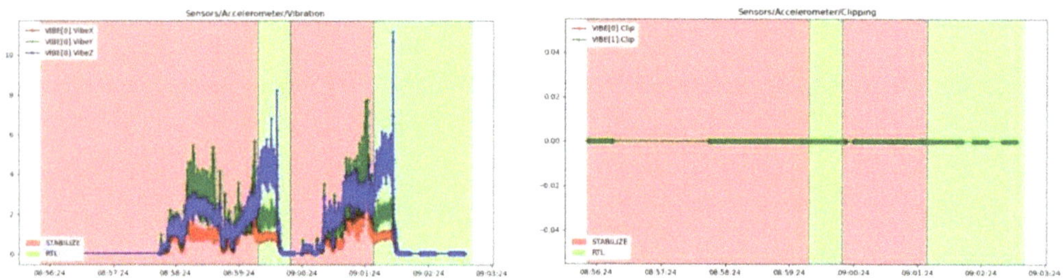

(**a**) (**b**)

Figure 30. Vibration and clipping. (**a**) Accelerometer (0); (**b**) Clipping.

The phenomenon of accelerometer clipping, which means that the accelerometers have been exposed to a level of vibration that exceeds their full measurement range, is illustrated in Figure 30b. These are feedback signals to the control loop; therefore, if they are not operating in optimal parameters, the attitude control cannot be maintained. This phenomenon usually occurs when the drone collides with a hard object, such as crashing or landing on a hard surface. If the value increases during the flight, it is recommended to rebuild the damping system by fitting double adhesive strips or soft rubber mounts to allow the three-axis movement and avoid inducing vibration in the flight controller housing, which is then transmitted to the on-board sensors. In the case of the studied hexacopter platform, it was observed to have a value of 0.

To illustrate the operation of gyroscopes, in Figure 31a, the measured raw values of the rotational speeds in rad/s of the gyroscopes are represented. Very low values are recorded because the hexacopter does not pitch, roll or yaw during the ascent to the fixed-point hover altitude, but only compensates in very small increments the constant attitude. Because the controller has two IMUs, namely (0) and (1), both graphs are plotted comprising data from both subsystems. As expected, the measured values of both IMUs gyroscopes are identical, indicating the appropriate operation of these sensors. In the case of the GPS signal received by the GPS antenna, which has the Ublox M8N GPS built-in receiver, in Figure 31b, the accuracy of the received GPS signal is presented. HAcc indicates a horizontal positioning accuracy of 0.5–1.2 m, VAcc indicates a vertical positioning accuracy of 0.55–1.45 m and SAcc indicates a velocity measurement accuracy of up to 0.2–0.4 m/s. NSats indicates the number of satellites received, up to a maximum of 15.

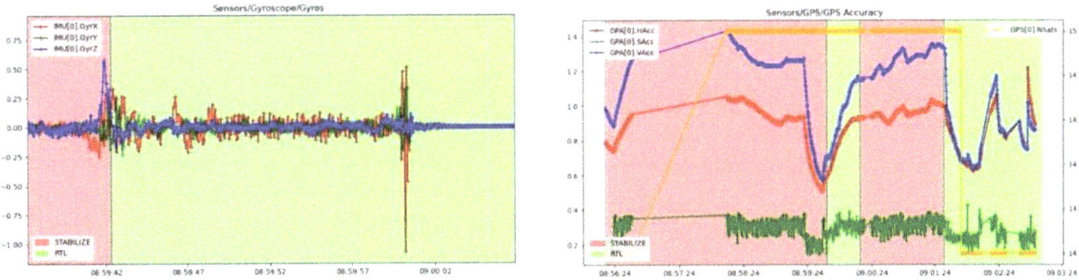

(**a**) (**b**)

Figure 31. Gyro rotational speeds and accuracy of data received from GPS satellites. (**a**) Gyro rotational speeds in rad/s for IMU (0) and (1); (**b**) Accuracy of data received from GPS satellites.

While operating in one of the autonomous modes (loiter, RTL, auto, etc.), GPS position errors can cause the hexacopter to "feel" that it is in a different location than the correct one, which can lead to the drone flying aggressively to correct its perceived erroneous location information. These "errors" appear in both tlogs and dataflash logs as a decrease in the number of visible satellites and an increase in the horizontal HDop accuracy value.

Hdop values less than 1.5 are very good, and values above 2 could indicate that the GPS positions are not correct. Decreasing the number of satellites below 12 leads to erroneous measurements of the hexacopter position and speed relative to the ground. A significant change in these two values often accompanies a change in GPS position. Figure 32 proves that the number of received satellites is 15 and the horizontal position accuracy is 0.65–0.71 m, so both values correspond to a parameterized operation of the GPS signal receiving equipment from satellites.

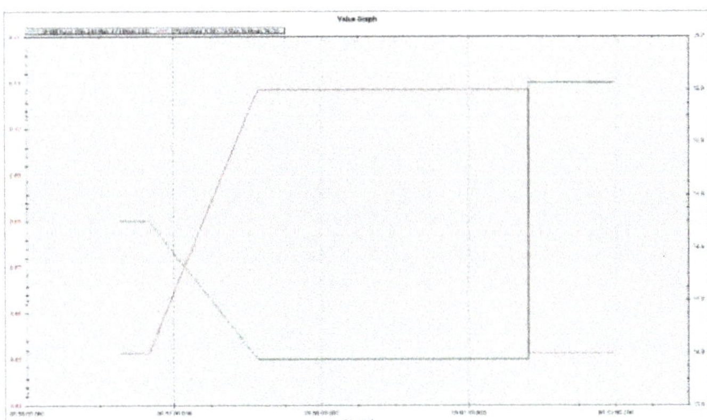

Figure 32. Accuracy of HDop positioning data received from GPS satellites.

Figure 33 shows a graph recording the relative speed of the hexacopter to the ground, based on the information received from the GPS. Given that the UAV performs the ascent and hover manoeuvre at a fixed point with small position adjustments, it can be seen that the value of this velocity is generally close to 0 m/s.

Mission planner, via the IMU batch sampler menu, has the option to record high-frequency data from IMU sensors to the flash data log on the flight controller. These data can be analysed after the flight to diagnose vibration-related problems using graphs created employing fast Fourier transforms (FFTs). A common feature of these plots is a peak at the "propeller blade crossing frequency", that is, the frequency at which the blade passes over the arms and causes an acceleration in the frame. In the graphs presented in Figure 34 with data collected from accelerometers and gyroscopes, there are, however, certain noises corresponding to the eigenfrequencies of the motors. The accelerometer and gyroscope data show on the vertical axis the amplitude and on the horizontal axis the natural rotational frequency of the motors. The amplitude is not scaled to a useful value, so we cannot tell whether the levels of these values are high or low, which means that the graph is only useful for determining the frequency of vibrations. Vibrations at frequencies higher than 300 Hz can lead to attitude or position control problems. In this case, peak frequencies are observed at 40 Hz/2400 rpm, 47 Hz/2820 rpm, 95 Hz/5700 rpm, 130 Hz/7800 rpm and 153 Hz/9180 rpm.

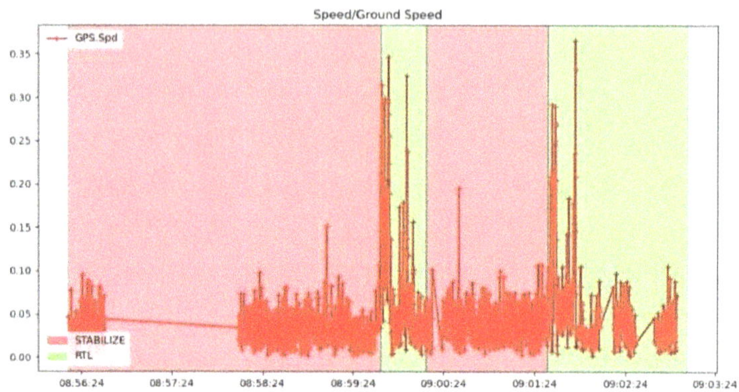

Figure 33. Relative speed of the drone to the ground.

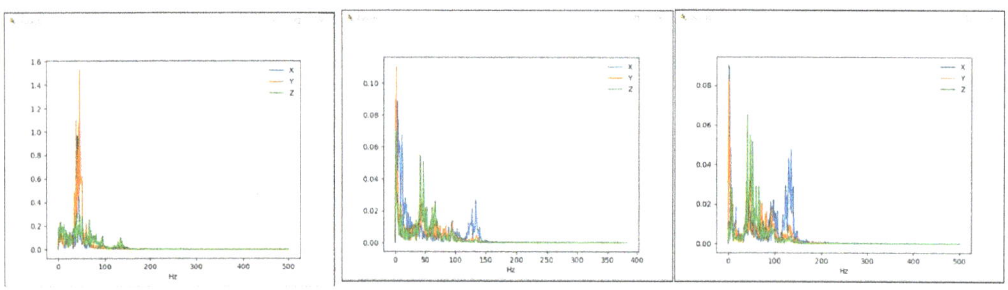

Figure 34. Vibration frequencies induced by motors rotation.

It is possible to filter out these noises in order to increase the hexacopter performance and to allow a better parameter tuning by activating the harmonic notch filter(s). The harmonic notch filter is designed to match the frequency of the noise introduced by the engine rotation. Its value changes as the motor rotates by means of interpreting the value of the engine acceleration. The frequency is scaled up from the hover frequency and will never drop below this frequency. However, during a dynamic flight, it is quite common to reach low motor operating frequencies during propeller rotation. To address this, it is possible to modify the reference value in order to scale the filter to a lower frequency.

For the operation of the hexacopter beyond visual line of sight (BVLOS), the necessary components for implementation on the drone have been acquired. Ground and flight tests can be carried out to demonstrate their ability to control the hexacopter via 3G/4G LTE mobile networks. These include the Raspberry Pi 3B board, IR camera + EO camera and 4G LTE modem. Other hexacopter flights in different flight regimes, both manual and autonomous, can be carried out to test the drone limits. This research focused on the behaviour of the drone in stationary flight at a fixed point.

5. FEM Decision Support

The hexacopter was conceived to provide a robust structure for transporting large payloads. The aim of this approach is to ensure the stability of the hexacopter during stationary flight manoeuvres, to set out a composite simulation model for different analysis types and to validate the computational model in order to synchronize analytical, experimental and numerical results. FEM model reduction, efficiently tuning the discretization parameters with the available computational resources, was also a computational goal.

The problem in the case of six propellers is that the rotating domains are close to each other, and the narrow space causes modelling and computational convergence issues. The results obtained from the FEM study were employed to optimize flight parameters, such as the rotor speed. Another important target of CFD simulations is the power requirements and the evaluation of the lift and drag forces.

Hover flight is one of the most important flight regimes of the hexacopter, when the UAV requires maximum stability. In package delivery tasks, the fixed-point turbulences are essential, as they may act in the close proximity to buildings or even to the ground, especially in urban areas. This was considered when creating the flow domain around the hexacopter. The air pressure under the hexacopter is higher the closer the hexacopter is to the ground. It is therefore important to know the air pressure values so that the hexacopter remains stable. On the hexacopter frame, the pressure increases correspondingly as it approaches the ground or a target. Some of the turbulences are redirected on the drone components and on the rotors. The hexacopter can work in areas with dust, sand and even snow, which can then interact with the vehicle. This is another reason why the CFD study is essential to ensure the stability and safe operation of the hexacopter.

5.1. CFD Approach

The proposed study consists of three main steps: geometry modelling and defeaturing, followed by the CFD computations to extract the lift and drag forces on each propeller and then the evaluation of the displacements on the mechanical structure of the hexacopter for the worst-case scenario. The results were compared with the analytical ones. The workflow is represented in Figure 35a, encompassing the five environmental settings: lateral wind speed of 0 m/s, 4 m/s, 10 m/s, 15 m/s and 20 m/s (Figure 36a) and the CFD enclosure (Figure 35b). For all cases, the maximum rotational velocity of the propellers of 6500 rpm was considered. The final step is the fluid–structure interaction to evaluate the effect of the air fillets on the hexacopter structure.

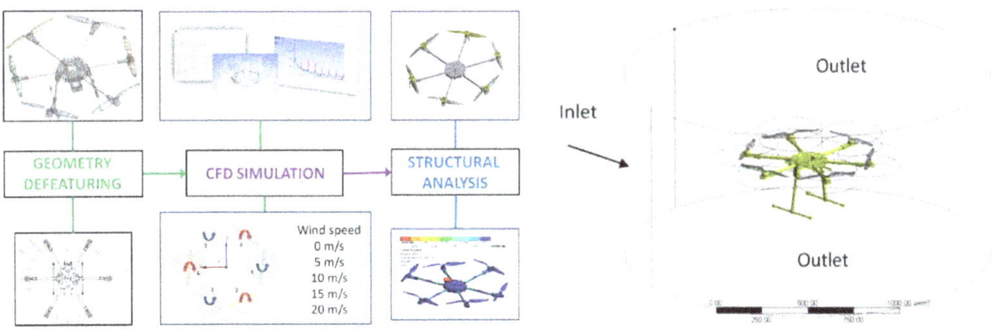

(a) (b)

Figure 35. Fluid dynamics simulation. (**a**) CFD approach; (**b**) Enclosure.

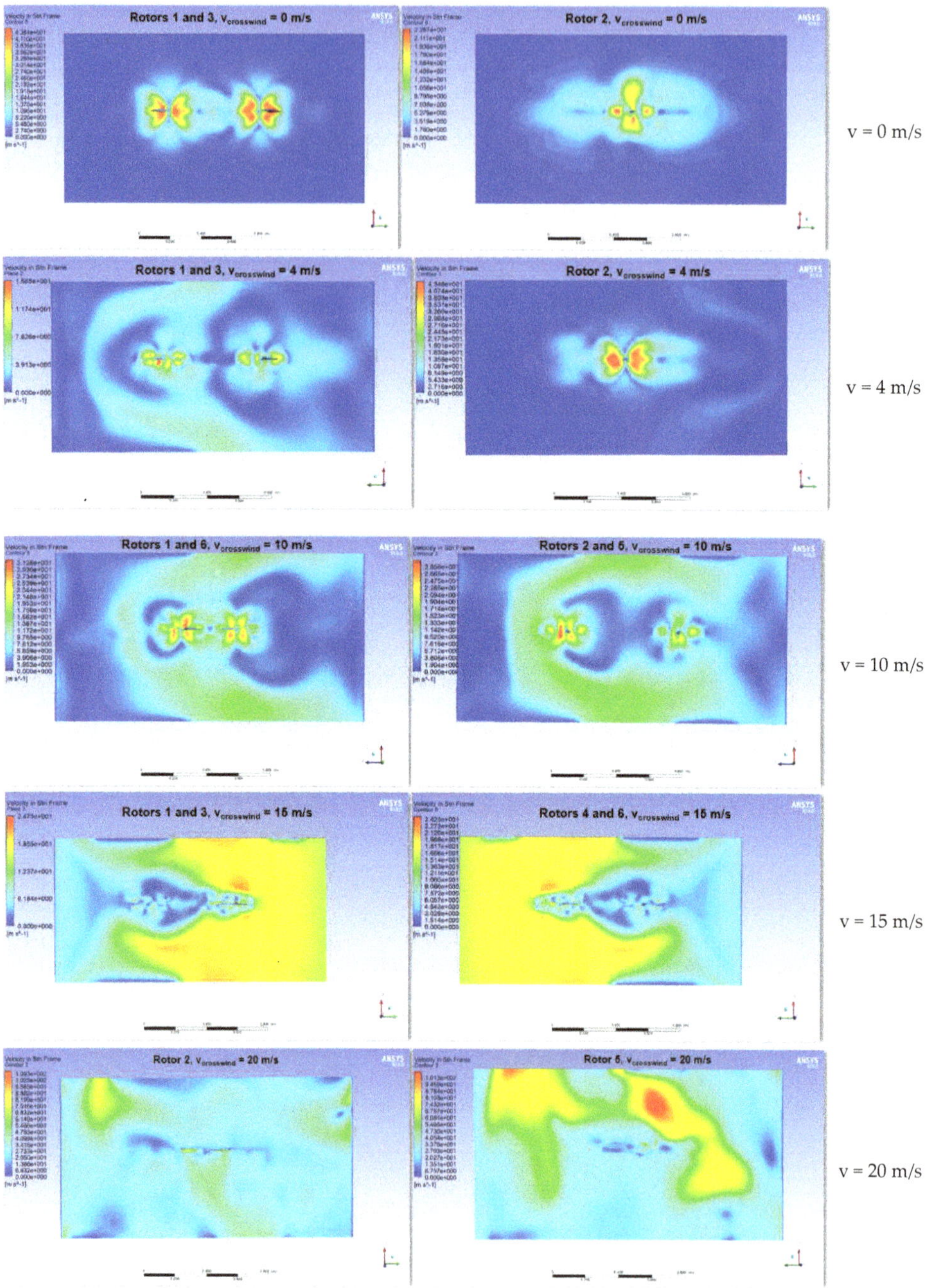

Figure 36. Velocity profile and dissipated turbulences for no wind and lateral wind scenarios.

The CFD simulation model explored a transient regime, and a corresponding mesh size was determined considering the Curant number. To avoid the numerical instability, this number must be 1 [87].

$$Co = v_{max} \cdot \frac{dt}{dx} = 1 \tag{1}$$

where v_{max} is the maximum velocity in the flow domain, dt is the time increment and dx is the finite element size.

The CFD model comprises nearly 2,900,000 elements with controlled inflation layers, named selections and multiple sizing options. The quality of the mesh was controlled, taking into account the skewness criterion, and the flow regime was based on the realizable k- ε flow model, employing advanced scalable wall functions and near-wall treatment interfaces.

In Figure 36, the contours of the velocities and pressures in the vertical plane are plotted, and the streamlines at rotor level for all the turbulent flows are processed. The influence of the wind on the fluid flow of the propellers occurring in the vertical plane can be observed, and the dissipation of the central turbulence is significant. The turbulence is deflected by the crosswind progressively for the cases v = 4 m/s, v = 10 m/s, v = 15 m/s and v = 20 m/s, respectively. The reaction thrust forces of the six propellers were between 0 and 38 N in absolute values. The lift forces were exported in a static analysis, and the spatial orientation of the hexacopter structure was evaluated as a function of the air pressure caused by the created turbulences, the rotational speed of the six rotors and the acceleration of the hexacopter.

The velocity streamlines were processed in Figure 37, as well as the contour plot of the air pressure on the six drone rotors for the case of 10 m/s side wind speed. The maximum air pressure of 383 Pa on the rotors is low, but the influence on the hover flight attitude is further investigated in this paper in a fluid–structure interaction approach. The vortices and joint interferences at the small rotor spaces are compressed by the side wind, increasing the power consumption. The wind produces the movement of the coupled turbulences in the same direction, and this may cause the vibration of the rotors. The consequence is that a power increase and changes of the attack angle are necessary in order to maintain the desired hover flight. The aerodynamic efficiency is also ensured by high trust forces and small power consumption. These parameters were also reported by the CFD analysis.

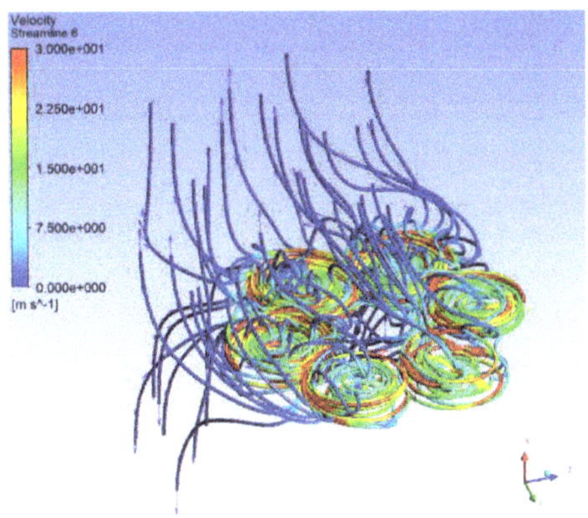

Figure 37. Streamlines and pressure contours on the rotors.

Figure 38 depicts the graph of the drag force on propeller 1 (0.552486 N) computed in the CFD simulation and the same force calculated analytically (0.5605 N). The difference is lower than 1.5%. The same comparison is performed for the lift force on propeller 3 (29.6611 N) as the output of the CFD simulation and by means of hand calculations

(29.1486 N) employing the same analytical model. The difference remains low, of approximately 1.72% between the two methods. This validates the CFD computational model and the accuracy of the simulation results. The advantage of the results obtained in the virtual model is that they give access to information difficult to acquire by experiments in the entire CFD domain.

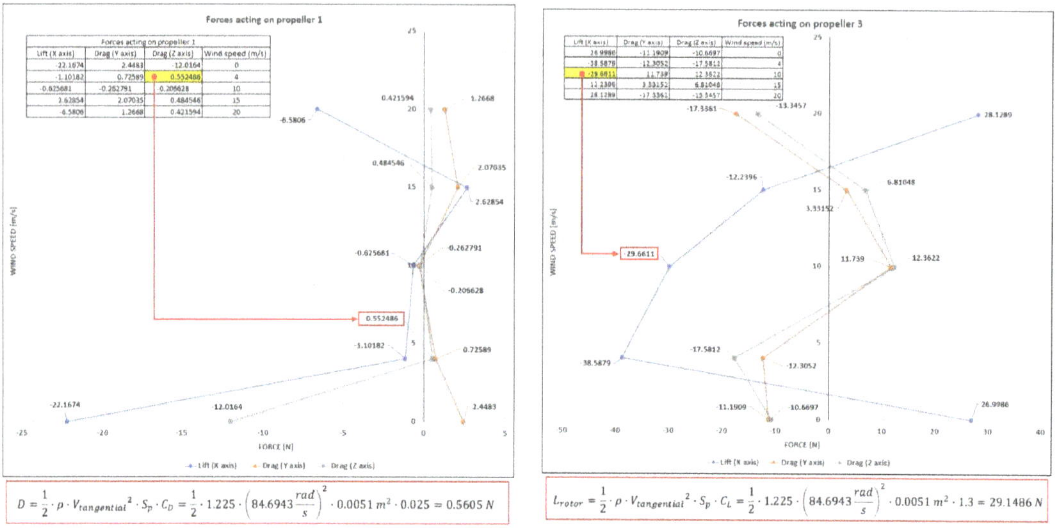

Figure 38. Drag and lift forces -numerical vs. analytic computation.

Finally, a static analysis was completed, and the maximum displacement of the rotors and the frame have been processed in Figure 39. The static analysis on the hexacopter structural elements revealed that the directional deformation in the YZ plane caused by pressure distribution and the thrust forces resulting from the transient CFD computation at t = 0.25s in case of 10 m/s lateral wind is 0.51 mm. From this perspective, the structure is robust and does not influence the stability and the manoeuvrability of the hexacopter during hover.

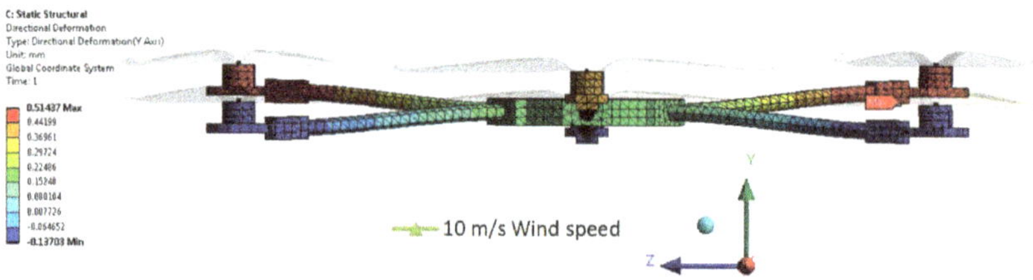

Figure 39. Maximum displacements on Y axis after 0.25s hover flight time.

Optimization of flight control parameters can be performed in respect to the CFD simulation results, namely, to the lift forces on the rotors (Z-axis), as well as the forces in the Z and Y directions, during hover.

5.2. Dynamic Analysis and Hover Stability

The dynamic analysis focused on both the modal analysis and a drop test simulation to verify the stability and the structural integrity of the hexacopter at impact, as detailed in Figure 40.

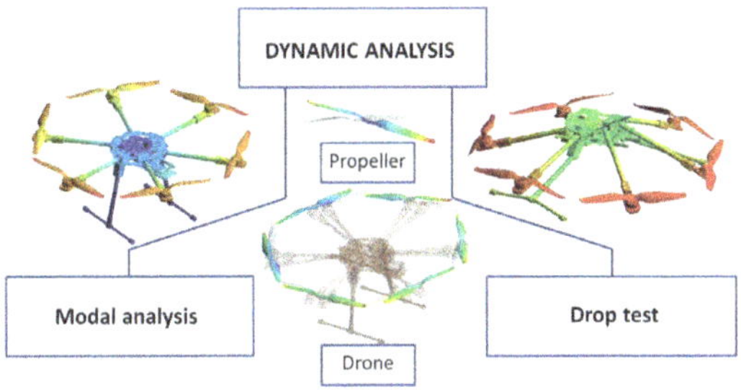

Figure 40. Hexacopter dynamic analysis using FEM.

The purpose of the modal analysis is to determine the eigenvalues for the drone's structural elements and the propeller in order to design the hexacopter control system accordingly, to ensure the structural stability of the drone for the operational rotational speed of the propellers in surveillance, photography or recording operations. An orthotropic elastic epoxy carbon woven (230 GPa) prepreg material (Tsai-Wu) was employed for the hexacopter structural elements and the rotors. For reaching a realistic behaviour of the system, the mass of the assemblies and individual components of the hexacopter were carefully checked as recorded in Table 1.

Table 1. Mass of the hexacopter components.

Hexacopter Component	Mass (kg)
Frame	0.833
Brushless electric motor	0.082
Electronic speed controller	0.026
13″ Propeller	0.014
Avionics and accessories	0.763
12 Ah Battery 12 Ah	1.080

Figure 41 illustrates an efficient model in terms of computational time and mesh quality, based on shells and beams processed in the ANSA preprocessing system in order to combine different advanced discretization strategies.

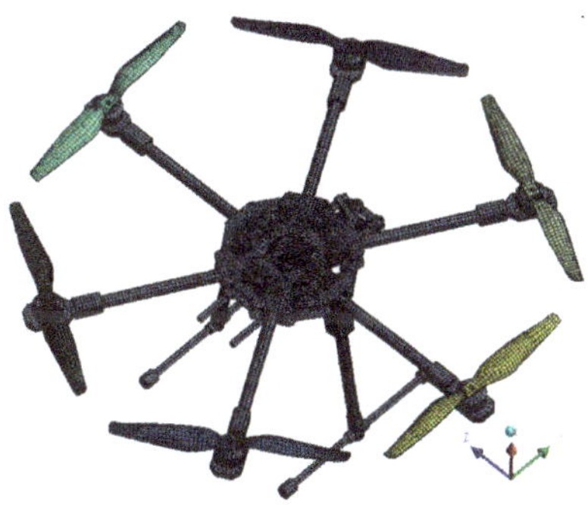

Figure 41. FEM model.

The structure has two symmetry planes, and this is underlined in the modal response. In Figure 42, only relevant eigenvalues have been processed. Thus, the first mode shapes are bending modes in the vertical plane, followed by bending modes in the vertical plane combined with torsion in the horizontal plane. Participation factors were analysed to select the dominant vibration modes. For this purpose, ten mode shapes were calculated, with the normalization of the eigenvectors in respect to unity. The modal analysis of the hexacopter main structural components proves that there are no eigenfrequencies in the operational range; therefore, no problems arise from this point of view for controlling the attitude or position of the drone.

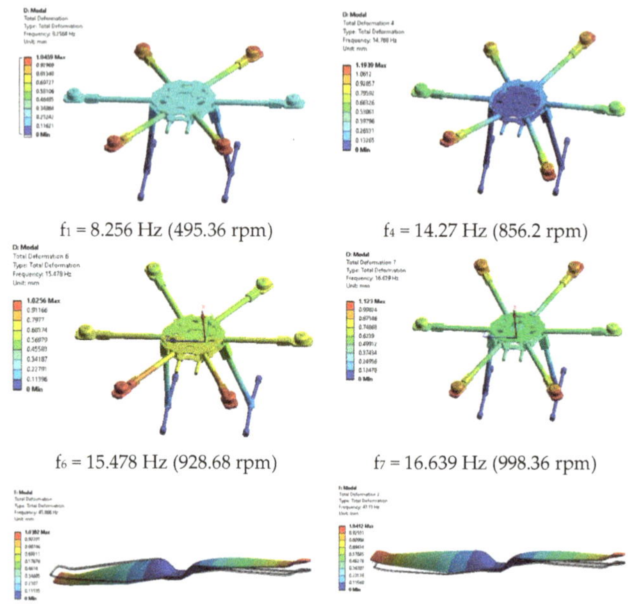

f_1 = 8.256 Hz (495.36 rpm) f_4 = 14.27 Hz (856.2 rpm)

f_6 = 15.478 Hz (928.68 rpm) f_7 = 16.639 Hz (998.36 rpm)

f_1 = 45.866 Hz (2751.96 rpm) f_2 = 47Hz (2820 rpm)

Figure 42. Mode shapes of the structural components and of the propeller.

The study also confirms that the amplitude peak at 47 Hz (Figure 34, Section 5) corresponding to 2820 rpm is caused by the natural frequency of the propellers that are overlapping the manoeuvring frequency. This can lead to high stresses at the propeller hub and may cause them to exceed the material yield strength or simply reduces the fatigue strength of the rotors. Considering that the manoeuvring speed range [58.34 Hz/3500 rpm—66.67 Hz/4000 rpm] is at least 24% higher than the rotor eigenvalues, it can be assumed that no resonances can occur for the manoeuvring regime of the hexacopter, but only for the fixed-point stationary regime. The maximum rotor speeds for different flight conditions in the range [6500–8000 rpm] should be mindfully chosen, as resonances may occur on the third and fourth rotor eigenvalues, but the amplitudes are expected to be low.

The resonant rotational speeds have to be avoided and can be taken into account when monitoring the hover flight parameters. High-order frequencies may interfere with the flight parameters in manoeuvring mode, but this was not observed during the experiments.

The hexacopter performance can also be improved by removing the resonances induced by the drives rotation from the operational range using dynamic harmonic notch filters.

5.3. Hexacopter Drop Test

The aim of this test in a virtual environment was to assess the possible damage of the hexacopter frame in the occurrence of a crash or an accidental landing on a stiff plate from a height of 20 m. All contacts between the components were considered rigid to avoid the mitigation effects. Because of the computationally intensive procedure, the simulation was stopped after the impact, before the complete kinetic energy consumption. Figure 43 depicts large displacements after the impact, but the stresses are not high due to the robust design.

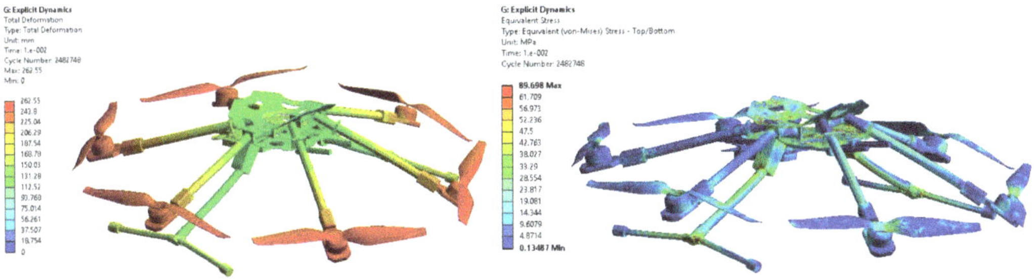

Figure 43. Drop test results at 0.1s after the impact.

The fact that the postimpact stresses remain acceptable were reflected during the experiments, when the drone dropped somehow similarly. The hexacopter deforms strongly, but the original shape of the hexacopter can be recovered, even if large displacements can be observed. Experiments upheld the conclusions of the simulation test results when the hexacopter dropped from a lower height but on a less rigid soil (Figure 44).

Figure 44. Hexacopter impact during field tests.

Impact simulations confirmed that when the hexacopter accidentally falls from a height of 20 m, the drone's structure undergoes significant deformations, but no failure occurs. Maximum deformations arise on the vertical and horizontal struts in the joint areas. Due to the fact that the maximum strains are not high, the hexacopter structure can be recovered, as observed during field experiments. In this study, the hexacopter rigging was not considered; only the behaviour of the structural elements was taken into account. It was also observed that the rotors are much stiffer than in the solutions reported in the literature, confirming the robust design of the structural elements of the drone.

6. Conclusions and Future Work

This study was conducted employing two hexacopter variants in which the sensor system was analysed and synchronized so that the drone's performance in stationary fixed-point flight was continuously improved. The flight parameters extracted from the tests were analysed, and the necessary corrective measures were taken accordingly to verify if the platform operates at optimal parameters, but also for stationary flight manoeuvres at hover, in average atmospheric conditions: temperature of 10–30°, 1–2 m/s wind and no precipitation.

The peculiarity of this work lies in the combination of experiments (both in the laboratory and in situ) with the FEM analysis in an original approach. The study also involved the development of a mathematical model for analytical calculation, not included in the paper, to determine the aerodynamic performance, as well as the verification of the solution of the hexacopter platform architecture. Only excerpts from the analytical computation were included in the discussion of the CFD simulation results for comparison purposes. Test outcomes were assessed, and conclusions regarding the numerical results were synchronized with the experimental ones.

Regarding the hexacopter frame, it may be concluded that having a smaller distance between the rotors can improve the aerodynamic performances of the hexacopter by increasing the interference between the propellers. Similarly, the effects of interference between propellers are progressively reduced with the increase in rotor positioning. Thus, the homogeneity of the distribution of the airfoils and the shape and symmetry of the vortex are essential conditions for the hexacopter to generate better lift forces. These must be deeply understood in the sense that the simulation required to create flow domains may result in values slightly lower than the experimental, real values.

FEM simulations are essential for achieving the aerodynamic stability and ensuring low power consumption and stable flight behaviour at high wind speeds, as well as achieving the ability of the vehicle to carry high payloads and increased operational areas of the hexacopter. These are mandatory requirements when launching a new, powerful hexacopter on the market. The simulation study can be continued by considering the hexacopter speed during manoeuvres and adjusting the rotational speeds of the propellers according to the experimental data.

The experiments completed employing the online platforms revealed a major drawback regarding the accuracy of the provided data. The deviation margin in respect to the real values was around ±15%; thus, when making the configurations and integrating the components, this error margin must be considered by choosing high-quality components and sensor systems to compensate this value.

The data extracted from sensors mounted on the drone illustrated good results in terms of altitude, attitude, GPS, vibrations, response of the motors, temperature, atmospheric pressure and ESC readings, respectively. The hexacopter parameters acquired during hover flight allowed the remark regarding the accelerometers' behaviour that they are not significantly affected by vibration during operation. Further adjustments to the current hexacopter-mounted sensors are underway to achieve even better results in terms of altitude and attitude estimation, positioning error compensation, engine control and command, telemetry data transmission, video signal transmission and radio interference compensation. Work regarding adding other sensors such as anemometers, LIDAR, acoustics and IR cameras is also in progress. Today, BVLOS is of major importance; thus, a variant of the BVLOS sensors kit is currently under development and will be mounted and tested on the hexacopter.

Author Contributions: Conceptualization, M.-A.S. and C.P.; Data curation, C.-E.M.; Formal analysis, F.-A.N.; Funding acquisition, M.-A.S.; Investigation, M.-A.S. and C.P.; Methodology, M.-A.S.; Project administration, F.-A.N.; Resources, M.-A.S.; Software, M.-A.S. and C.P.; Supervision, C.P.; Validation, M.-A.S., C.P., F.-A.N. and C.-E.M.; Visualization, C.-E.M.; Writing—original draft, M.-A.S.; Writing—review and editing, C.P. All authors have read and agreed to the published version of the manuscript.

Funding: This research was funded by the Sectorial Operational Program Human Capital 2014–2020, European Fund, Contract no. 51680/09.07.2019—SMIS code: 124539.

Institutional Review Board Statement: Not applicable.

Informed Consent Statement: Not applicable.

Data Availability Statement: Data described as result of this study are available on request to the corresponding author.

Conflicts of Interest: The authors declare that they have no conflict of interest. The funders had no role in the design of the study; in the collection, analysis or interpretation of the data; in the writing of the manuscript; or in the decision to publish the results.

Abbreviations

The following abbreviations are used in this manuscript:

AHRS	Attitude and heading reference system
AP	Autopilot
BLDC	Brushless DC electric motor
BVLOS	Beyond visual line-of-sight
CAD	Computer-aided design
CFD	Computational fluid dynamics
DRONE	Dynamic remotely operated navigation equipment
EKF	Extended Kalman filter
EO/IR	Electro-optical/infra-red
ESC	Electronic speed controller
FEM	Finite element method
FFT	Fast Fourier transforms
GIS	Geographic information system
GNSS	Global navigation satellite system
GPS	Global Positioning System
IMU	Inertial measurement unit
LIDAR	Light detection and ranging
MFD-LPTL	Multisensor fusion data analysis for low-power transmission lines
MOSFET	Metal–oxide–semiconductor field-effect transistor
PID	Proportional–integral–derivative
PPM	Pulse position modulation
PWM	Pulse width modulation
ROAV	Remotely operated air vehicle
ROS	Robotic operating system
RPAS	Remotely piloted aircraft system
SITL	Software-in-the-loop
SPSA	Simultaneous perturbation stochastic approximation
UAS	Unmanned aerial system
UAV	Unmanned aerial vehicle
UGV	Unmanned ground vehicle
UUV	Unmanned underwater vehicle
VTOL	Vertical takeoff and landing

References

1. Chu, P.H.; Huang, Y.T.; Pi, C.H.; Cheng, S. Autonomous Landing System of a VTOL UAV on an Upward Docking Station Using Visual Servoing. *IFAC-PapersOnLine* **2022**, *55*, 108–113. [CrossRef]
2. Sethi, N.; Ahlawat, S. Low-fidelity design optimization and development of a VTOL swarm UAV with an open-source framework. *Array* **2022**, *14*, 100183. [CrossRef]
3. Patel, T.; Kumar, M.; Abdallah, S. Control of Hybrid Transitioning Morphing-wing VTOL UAV. *IFAC-PapersOnLine* **2022**, *55*, 554–559. [CrossRef]
4. Bahari, M.; Rostami, M.; Entezari, A.; Ghahremani, S.; Etminan, M. A comparative analysis and optimization of two supersonic hybrid SOFC and turbine-less jet engine propulsion system for UAV. *Fuel* **2022**, *319*, 123796. [CrossRef]
5. Bahari, M.; Rostami, M.; Entezari, A.; Ghahremani, S.; Etminan, M. Performance evaluation and multi-objective optimization of a novel UAV propulsion system based on PEM fuel cell. *Fuel* **2022**, *311*, 122554. [CrossRef]
6. Zhou, K.; Liu, Z.; Zhang, X.; Liu, H.; Meng, N.; Huang, J.; Qi, M.; Song, X.; Yan, X. A kW-level integrated propulsion system for UAV powered by PEMFC with inclined cathode flow structure design. *Appl. Energy* **2022**, *328*, 120222. [CrossRef]

7. Lu, S.H.; Kuo, R.J.; Ho, Y.T.; Nguyen, A.T. Improving the efficiency of last-mile delivery with the flexible drones traveling salesman problem. *Expert Syst. Appl.* **2022**, *209*, 118351. [CrossRef]
8. Jung, H.; Kim, J. Drone scheduling model for delivering small parcels to remote islands considering wind direction and speed. *Comput. Ind. Eng.* **2022**, *163*, 107784. [CrossRef]
9. Jeong, H.Y.; Song, B.D.; Lee, S. Optimal scheduling and quantitative analysis for multi-flying warehouse scheduling problem: Amazon airborne fulfillment center. *Transp. Res. Part C Emerg. Technol.* **2022**, *143*, 103831. [CrossRef]
10. Zhai, D.; Wang, C.; Cao, H.; Garg, S.; Hassan, M.M.; Al Qahtani, S.A. Deep neural network-based UAV deployment and dynamic power control for 6G-Envisioned intelligent warehouse logistics system. *Future Gener. Comput. Syst.* **2022**, *137*, 164–172. [CrossRef]
11. Mourtzis, D.; Angelopoulos, J.; Panopoulos, N. UAVs for Industrial Applications: Identifying Challenges and Opportunities from the Implementation Point of View. *Procedia Manuf.* **2021**, *55*, 183–190. [CrossRef]
12. Yuan, C.S.; Cheng, W.H.; Su, S.Y.; Chen, W.H. Field measurement of spatiotemporal distributions of ambient concentrations of volatile organic compounds around a high-tech industrial park using a drone. *Atmos. Pollut. Res.* **2021**, *12*, 101187. [CrossRef]
13. Wang, Y.; Li, Y.; Yin, F.; Wang, W.; Sun, H.; Li, J.; Zhang, K. An intelligent UAV path planning optimization method for monitoring the risk of unattended offshore oil platforms. *Process Saf. Environ. Prot.* **2022**, *160*, 13–24. [CrossRef]
14. Cho, J.; Lim, G.; Biobaku, T.; Kim, S.; Parsaei, H. Safety and Security Management with Unmanned Aerial Vehicle (UAV) in Oil and Gas Industry. *Procedia Manuf.* **2015**, *3*, 1343–1349. [CrossRef]
15. Garcia-Vasquez, A.C.; Mokari, E.; Samani, Z.; Fernald, A. Using UAV-thermal imaging to calculate crop water use and irrigation efficiency in a flood-irrigated pecan orchard. *Agric. Water Manag.* **2022**, *272*, 107824. [CrossRef]
16. Cheng, K.H.; Jiao, J.J.; Luo, X.; Yu, S. Effective coastal Escherichia coli monitoring by unmanned aerial vehicles (UAV) thermal infrared images. *Water Res.* **2022**, *222*, 118900. [CrossRef] [PubMed]
17. Qin, G.; Xu, Y.; Li, F.; Zhou, W.; Li, W.; Zhao, G. Calibration of an airborne γ-ray spectrometer based on an unmanned aerial vehicle using a point source. *Ann. Nucl. Energy* **2022**, *178*, 109349. [CrossRef]
18. Lipovský, P.; Novotnák, J.; Blažek, J. Possible Utilization of Low Frequency Magnetic Fields in Short Range Multirotor UAV Detection System. *Transp. Res. Procedia* **2022**, *65*, 106–115. [CrossRef]
19. Amodu, O.A.; Busari, S.A.; Othman, M. Physical layer aspects of terahertz-enabled UAV communications: Challenges and opportunities. *Veh. Commun.* **2022**, *38*, 100540. [CrossRef]
20. Xie, C.; Yang, C. A review on plant high-throughput phenotyping traits using UAV-based sensors. *Comput. Electron. Agric.* **2020**, *178*, 105731. [CrossRef]
21. Da Silva, S.D.P.; Eugenio, F.C.; Fantinel, R.A.; Amaral, L.D.P.; dos Santos, A.R.; Mallmann, C.L.; dos Santos, F.D.; Pereira, R.S.; Ruoso, R. Modeling and detection of invasive trees using UAV image and machine learning in a subtropical forest in Brazil. *Ecol. Inform.* **2023**, *74*, 101989. [CrossRef]
22. Amarasingam, N.; Ashan Salgadoe, A.S.; Powell, K.; Gonzalez, L.F.; Natarajan, S. A review of UAV platforms, sensors, and applications for monitoring of sugarcane crops. *Remote Sens. Appl. Soc. Environ.* **2022**, *26*, 100712. [CrossRef]
23. Hao, Z.; Li, M.; Yang, W.; Li, X. Evaluation of UAV spraying quality based on 1D-CNN model and wireless multi-sensors system. *Inf. Process. Agric.* 2022; *in press*. [CrossRef]
24. Lin, B.; Xu, J.; Yin, C.; Chen, L.; You, Y.; Hu, L. An ultralight dual-wavelength and dual-beam chemical sensor on small UAV for in-situ determination of phosphate and nitrite in surface water. *Sens. Actuators B Chem.* **2022**, *368*, 132235. [CrossRef]
25. Mumuni, F.; Mumuni, A.; Amuzuvi, C.K. Deep learning of monocular depth, optical flow and ego-motion with geometric guidance for UAV navigation in dynamic environments. *Mach. Learn. Appl.* **2022**, *10*, 100416. [CrossRef]
26. Bauer, P.; Kun, S. Optical flow-based angular rate sensor fault detection on UAVs. *IFAC-PapersOnLine* **2022**, *55*, 46–51. [CrossRef]
27. Stöcker, C.; Bennett, R.; Koeva, M.; Nex, F.; Zevenbergen, J. Scaling up UAVs for land administration: Towards the plateau of productivity. *Land Use Policy* **2022**, *114*, 105930. [CrossRef]
28. Wang, T.; Mei, X.; Alex Thomasson, J.; Yang, C.; Han, X.; Yadav, P.K.; Shi, Y. GIS-based volunteer cotton habitat prediction and plant-level detection with UAV remote sensing. *Comput. Electron. Agric.* **2022**, *193*, 106629. [CrossRef]
29. Tan, Y.; Li, G.; Cai, R.; Ma, J.; Wang, M. Mapping and modelling defect data from UAV captured images to BIM for building external wall inspection. *Autom. Constr.* **2022**, *139*, 104284. [CrossRef]
30. Yap, Y.L.; Toh, W.; Giam, A.; Yong, F.R.; Chan, K.I.; Tay, J.W.S.; Teong, S.S.; Lin, R.; Ng, T.Y. Topology optimization and 3D printing of micro-drone: Numerical design with experimental testing. *Int. J. Mech. Sci.* **2023**, *237*, 107771. [CrossRef]
31. Tolba, M.; Shirinzadeh, B. Generic modeling and control of unbalanced multirotor UAVs. *Aerosp. Sci. Technol.* **2022**, *121*, 107394. [CrossRef]
32. Lee, S.; Chung, W.; Son, H. Online parameter identification framework for a multirotor UAV: Application to an arm stretchable morphing multirotor. *Mech. Syst. Signal Process.* **2022**, *166*, 108468. [CrossRef]
33. Michel, N.; Wei, P.; Kong, Z.; Sinha, A.K.; Lin, X. Modeling and validation of electric multirotor unmanned aerial vehicle system energy dynamics. *eTransportation* **2022**, *12*, 100173. [CrossRef]
34. Lim, D.; Kim, H.; Yee, K. Uncertainty propagation in flight performance of multirotor with parametric and model uncertainties. *Aerosp. Sci. Technol.* **2022**, *122*, 107398. [CrossRef]
35. Zhang, H.; Qi, L.; Wan, J.; Musiu, E.M.; Zhou, J.; Lu, Z.; Wang, P. Numerical simulation of downwash airflow distribution inside tree canopies of an apple orchard from a multirotor unmanned aerial vehicle (UAV) sprayer. *Comput. Electron. Agric.* **2022**, *195*, 106817. [CrossRef]

36. Liu, Z.; Zhang, Y.; Chen, H.; Zhang, Z. Incremental control system design and flight tests of a micro-coaxial rotor UAV. *Aerosp. Sci. Technol.* **2022**, *131*, 107979. [CrossRef]
37. Mishra, A.; Pal, S.; Singh, P. Design and analysis of an Eight Rotor Co-Axial UAV using carbon fiber composites. *Mater. Today: Proc.* **2022**, *68*, 1011–1015. [CrossRef]
38. Liscouët, J.; Pollet, F.; Jézégou, J.; Budinger, M.; Delbecq, S.; Moschetta, J.M. A methodology to integrate reliability into the conceptual design of safety-critical multirotor unmanned aerial vehicles. *Aerosp. Sci. Technol.* **2022**, *127*, 107681. [CrossRef]
39. Darvishpoor, S.; Roshanian, J.; Raissi, A.; Hassanalian, M. Configurations, flight mechanisms, and applications of unmanned aerial systems: A review. *Prog. Aerosp. Sci.* **2022**, *121*, 100694. [CrossRef]
40. Delbecq, S.; Budinger, M.; Ochotorena, A.; Reysset, A.; Defay, F. Efficient Sizing and Optimization of Multirotor Drones Based on Scaling Laws and Similarity Models. *Aerosp. Sci. Technol.* **2020**, *102*, 105873. [CrossRef]
41. Gupta, A.K.; Jha, V.; Gupta, V.K. Design and Development of Remote Controlled Autonomous Synchronic Hexarotor Aerial (ASHA) Robot. *Procedia Technol.* **2014**, *14*, 51–58. [CrossRef]
42. Suprapto, B.Y.; Heryanto, A.; Suprijono, H.; Muliadi, J.; Kusumoputro, B. Design and Development of Heavy-lift Hexacopter for Heavy Payload. In Proceedings of the International Seminar on Application for Technology of Information and Communication (iSemantic), Semarang, Indonesia, 7–8 October 2017; pp. 242–247. [CrossRef]
43. Setiono, F.Y.; Candrasaputra, A.; Prasetyo, T.B.; Santoso, K.L.B. Designing and Implementation of Autonomous Hexacopter as Unmanned Aerial Vehicle. In Proceedings of the 8th International Conference on Information Technology and Electrical Engineering (ICITEE), Yogyakarta, Indonesia, 5–6 October 2016; pp. 1–5. [CrossRef]
44. Verbeke, J.; Hulens, D.; Ramon, H.; Goedemé, T.; de Schutter, J. The Design and Construction of a High Endurance Hexacopter suited for Narrow Corridors. In Proceedings of the International Conference on Unmanned Aircraft Systems (ICUAS), Orlando, FL, USA, 27–30 May 2014; pp. 543–551.
45. Abarca, M.; Saito, C.; Angulo, A.; Paredes, J.A.; Cuellar, F. Design and Development of an Hexacopter for Air Quality Monitoring at High Altitudes. In Proceedings of the 13th IEEE Conference on Automation Science and Engineering (CASE), Xi'an, China, 20–23 August 2017; pp. 1457–1462.
46. Arellano-Quintana, V.M.; Portilla-Flores, E.A.; Merchan-Cruz, E.A.; Nino-Suarez, P.A. Multirotor Design Optimization Using a Genetic Algorithm. In Proceedings of the International Conference on Unmanned Aircraft Systems (ICUAS), Arlington, VA, USA, 7–10 June 2016; pp. 1313–1318.
47. Ferrarese, G.; Giulietti, F.; Avanzini, G. Modeling and Simulation of a Quad-Tilt Rotor Aircraft. *IFAC Proc. Vol.* **2013**, *46*, 64–70. [CrossRef]
48. Ryll, M.; Bicego, D.; Franchi, A. Modeling and Control of FAST-Hex: A Fully–Actuated by Synchronized–Tilting Hexacopter. In Proceedings of the IEEE/RSJ International Conference on Intelligent Robots and Systems (IROS), Daejeon, Republic of Korea, 9–14 October 2016; pp. 1689–1694.
49. Tadokoro, Y.; Ibuki, T.; Sampei, M. Maneuverability Analysis of a Fully-Actuated Hexrotor UAV Considering Tilt Angles and Arrangement of Rotors. *IFAC PapersOnLine* **2017**, *50*, 8981–8986. [CrossRef]
50. Rajappa, S.; Ryll, M.; Bulthoff, H.H.; Franchi, A. Modeling, Control and Design Optimization for a Fully actuated Hexacopter Aerial Vehicle. In Proceedings of the IEEE International Conference on Robotics and Automation (ICRA), Seattle, WA, USA, 26–30 May 2015. [CrossRef]
51. Köse, O.; Oktay, T. Hexarotor Yaw Flight Control with SPSA PID Algorithm and Morphing. *Int. J. Intell. Syst. Appl. Eng.* **2022**, *10*, 216–221.
52. Mehmood, H.; Nakamura, T.; Johnson, E.N. A Maneuverability Analysis of a Novel Hexacopter UAV Concept. In Proceedings of the International Conference on Unmanned Aircraft Systems (ICUAS), Arlington, VA, USA, 7–10 June 2016. [CrossRef]
53. Budinger, M.; Reysset, A.; Ochotorena, A.; Delbecq, S. Scaling laws and similarity models for the preliminary design of multirotor drones. *Aerosp. Sci. Technol.* **2020**, *98*, 105658. [CrossRef]
54. Hussein, M.; Nouacer, R. Reference architecture specification for drone systems. *Microprocess. Microsyst.* **2022**, *95*, 104705. [CrossRef]
55. Cao, S.; Fan, Q.; Yu, W.J.; Wang, L.T.; Ni, S.; Chen, J. Multi-Sensor fusion and data analysis for operating conditions of low power transmission lines. *Measurement* **2022**, *190*, 110586. [CrossRef]
56. Severin, T.; Soffker, D. Sensor optimization for altitude estimation of spraying drones in vineyards. *IFAC-PapersOnLine* **2022**, *55*, 107–112. [CrossRef]
57. Pena, P.F.; Ragab, A.R.; Luna, M.A.; Isaac, M.S.A.; Campoy, P. WILD HOPPER: A heavy-duty UAV for day and night firefighting operations. *Heliyon* **2022**, *8*, e09588. [CrossRef]
58. Ravin, K.; Agrawal, A.K. Drone GPS data analysis for flight path reconstruction: A study on DJI, Parrot & Yuneec make drones. *Forensic Sci. Int. Digit. Investig.* **2021**, *38*, 301182. [CrossRef]
59. Sree Ezhil, V.R.; Rangesh Sriram, B.S.; Christopher Vijay, R.; Yeshwant, S.; Sabareesh, R.K.; Dakkshesh, G.; Raffik, R. Investigation on PID controller usage on Unmanned Aerial Vehicle for stability control. *Mater. Today: Proc.* **2022**, *66 Pt 3*, 1313–1318. [CrossRef]
60. Madokoro, H.; Kiguchi, O.; Nagayoshi, T.; Chiba, T.; Inoue, M.; Chiyonobu, S.; Nix, S.; Woo, H.; Sato, K. Development of Drone-Mounted Multiple Sensing System with Advanced Mobility for In Situ Atmospheric Measurement: A Case Study Focusing on PM2.5. *Local Distribution, Sensors* **2021**, *21*, 4881. [CrossRef]

61. Megayanti, M.; Nugraha, Y.P.; Sary, I.P.; Hidayat, E.; Trilaksono, B.R. Modeling and Implementation of Hexacopter Guidance System Using Fuzzy Logic Control Under Wind Disturbance. In Proceedings of the IEEE 8th International Conference on System Engineering and Technology (ICSET), Bandung, Indonesia, 15–16 October 2018; pp. 12–17. [CrossRef]
62. Sharipov, D.; Abdullaev, Z.; Tazhiev, Z.; Khafizov, O. Implementation of a mathematical model of a hexacopter control system. In Proceedings of the International Conference on Information Science and Communications Technologies (ICISCT), Tashkent, Uzbekistan, 4–6 November 2019; pp. 1–5. [CrossRef]
63. Toledo, J.; Acosta, L.; Perea, D.; Morales, N. Stability and performance analysis of unmanned aerial vehicles: Quadcopter against Hexrotor. *IET Control Theory Appl.* **2015**, *9*, 1190–1196. [CrossRef]
64. Wen, F.-H.; Hsiao, F.-Y.; Shiau, J.-K. Analysis and Management of Motor Failures of Hexacopter in Hover. *Actuators* **2021**, *10*, 48. [CrossRef]
65. Leishman, R.; Macdonald, J.; McLain, T.; Beard, R. Relative Navigation and Control of a Hexacopter. In Proceedings of the IEEE International Conference on Robotics and Automation, St Paul, MI, USA, 14–18 May 2012; pp. 4937–4942.
66. Derawi, D.; Salim, N.D.; Azizi, M.; Rahman, A.; Mazlan, S.A.; Zamzuri, H. Modeling, Attitude Estimation, and Control of Hexacopter Micro Aerial Vehicle (MAV). In Proceedings of the IEEE International Conference on Industrial Technology (ICIT), Busan, Republic of Korea, 26 February–1 March 2014; pp. 55–60.
67. Derawi, D.; Salim, N.D.; Zamzuri, H.; Liu, H.; Azizi, M.; Rahman, A.; Mazlan, S.A. Robust Attitude Controler for Uncertain Hexacopter Micro Aerial Vehicles (MAVs). In Proceedings of the IEEE/RSJ International Conference on Intelligent Robots and Systems (IROS), Chicago, IL, USA, 14–18 September 2014; pp. 4776–4781.
68. Poksawat, P.; Wang, L. Automatic Tuning of Hexacopter Attitude Control Systems with Experimental Validation. In Proceedings of the 21st International Conference on System Theory, Control and Computing (ICSTCC), Sinaia, Romania, 19–21 October 2017; pp. 753–758. [CrossRef]
69. Zheng, Y.; Dong, L.; Wang, Q. Multi-Rotor UAV Attitude Calculation Based on Extended Kalman Filter. In Proceedings of the 30th Chinese Control and Decision Conference (CCDC), Shenyang, China, 9–11 June 2018; pp. 478–483.
70. Benzemrane, K.; Damm, G.; Santosuosso, G.L. Adaptive Observer and Kalman Filtering. In Proceedings of the 17th World Congress, The International Federation of Automatic Control, Seoul, Korea, 6–11 July 2008; pp. 3865–3870.
71. Benzerrouk, H.; Nebylov, A.; Salhi, H. Quadcopter UAV state estimation based on High-Degree Cubature Kalman filter. *IFAC-PapersOnLine* **2016**, *49*, 349–354. [CrossRef]
72. Neumann, P.P.; Bartholmai, M. Real-time wind estimation on a micro unmanned aerial vehicle using its inertial measurement unit. *Sens. Actuators* **2015**, *235*, 300–310. [CrossRef]
73. Sushchenko, O.A.; Beliavtsev, Y.V. Modelling of Inertial Sensors in UAV Systems. In Proceedings of the IEEE 4th International Conference Actual Problems of Unmanned Aerial Vehicles Developments (APUAVD), Kiev, Ukraine, 17–19 October 2017; pp. 130–133. [CrossRef]
74. Heise, C.D.; Falconi, G.P.; Holzapfel, F. Hexacopter Outdoor Flight Test Results of an Extended State Observer based Controller. In Proceedings of the IEEE International Conference on Aerospace Electronics and Remote Sensing Technology (ICARES), Yogyakarta, Indonesia, 13–14 November 2014; pp. 26–33.
75. Dong, W.; Gu, G.Y.; Zhu, X.; Ding, H. High-performance trajectory tracking control of a quadcopter with disturbance observer. *Sens. Actuators* **2014**, *211*, 67–77. [CrossRef]
76. Lee, S.J.; Kim, S.; Johansson, K.H.; Kim, H.J. Robust Acceleration Control of a Hexacopter UAV with a Disturbance Observer. In Proceedings of the IEEE 55th Conference on Decision and Control (CDC), Las Vegas, NV, USA, 12–14 December 2016; pp. 4166–4171.
77. Seah, C.H.; Inyang, I.J.; Whidborne, J.F. Bilinear Modelling and Attitude Control of a quadcopter. *IFAC PapersOnLine* **2017**, *50*, 193–198. [CrossRef]
78. Herrada, F.J.; García-Martínez, J.; Fraile, A.; Hermanns, L.K.H.; Montáns, F.J. A method for performing efficient parametric dynamic analyses in large finite element models undergoing structural modifications. *Eng. Struct.* **2017**, *131*, 625–638. [CrossRef]
79. Karthik Vinayaga, K.; Vasanthanathan, A.; Nagaraj, P. Finite element modeling of smart piezoelectric beam using ANSYS. *Mater. Today Proc.* **2018**, *5*, 7078–7085. [CrossRef]
80. Ryzhakov, P.; Rossi, R.; Viña, A.; Oñate, E. Modelling and simulation of the sea-landing of aerial vehicles using the Particle Finite Element Method. *Ocean. Eng.* **2013**, *66*, 92–100. [CrossRef]
81. Jiapeng, T.; Ping, X.; Baoyuan, Z.; Bifu, H. A finite element parametric modeling technique of aircraft wing structures. *Chin. J. Aeronaut.* **2013**, *26*, 1202–1210.
82. Papa, U.; Russo, S.; Lamboglia, A.; Del Core, G.; Iannuzzo, G. Health structure monitoring for the design of an innovative UAS fixed wing through inverse finite element method (iFEM). *Aerosp. Sci. Technol.* **2017**, *69*, 439–448. [CrossRef]
83. Felismina, R.; Silva, M.; Mateus, A.; Malça, C. Study on the aerodynamic behavior of a UAV with an applied seeder for agricultural practices. *AIP Conf. Proc.* **2017**, *1836*, 020049. [CrossRef]
84. Lei, Y.; Cheng, M. Aerodynamic performance of a Hex-rotor unmanned aerial vehicle with different rotor spacing. *Meas. Control.* **2020**, *53*, 711–718. [CrossRef]

85. Lei, Y.; Cheng, M. Aerodynamic Performance of Hex-Rotor UAV Considering the Horizontal Airflow. *Appl. Sci.* **2019**, *9*, 4797. [CrossRef]
86. Zheng, Y.; Yang, S.; Liu, X.; Wang, J.; Norton, T.; Chen, J.; Tan, Y. The computational fluid dynamic modeling of downwash flow field for a six-rotor UAV. *Front. Agric. Sci. Eng.* **2018**, *5*, 159–167. [CrossRef]
87. Courant, R.; Friedrichs, K.; Lewy, H. On the partial difference equations of mathematical physics. *IBM J. Res. Dev.* **1967**, *11*, 215–234. [CrossRef]

sensors

MDPI

Article

Detecting Machining Defects inside Engine Piston Chamber with Computer Vision and Machine Learning

Marian Marcel Abagiu, Dorian Cojocaru *, Florin Manta and Alexandru Mariniuc

Faculty of Automation, Computers and Electronics, University of Craiova, 200585 Craiova, Romania
* Correspondence: dorian.cojocaru@edu.ucv.ro

Abstract: This paper describes the implementation of a solution for detecting the machining defects from an engine block, in the piston chamber. The solution was developed for an automotive manufacturer and the main goal of the implementation is the replacement of the visual inspection performed by a human operator with a computer vision application. We started by exploring different machine vision applications used in the manufacturing environment for several types of operations, and how machine learning is being used in robotic industrial applications. The solution implementation is re-using hardware that is already available at the manufacturing plant and decommissioned from another system. The re-used components are the cameras, the IO (Input/Output) Ethernet module, sensors, cables, and other accessories. The hardware will be used in the acquisition of the images, and for processing, a new system will be implemented with a human–machine interface, user controls, and communication with the main production line. Main results and conclusions highlight the efficiency of the CCD (charged-coupled device) sensors in the manufacturing environment and the robustness of the machine learning algorithms (convolutional neural networks) implemented in computer vision applications (thresholding and regions of interest).

Keywords: computer vision; sensors; machine learning; industry; manufacturing; robotics

Citation: Abagiu, M.M.; Cojocaru, D.; Manta, F.; Mariniuc, A. Detecting Machining Defects inside Engine Piston Chamber with Computer Vision and Machine Learning. *Sensors* **2023**, *23*, 785. https://doi.org/10.3390/s23020785

Academic Editor: Xinyu Li

Received: 30 November 2022
Revised: 24 December 2022
Accepted: 29 December 2022
Published: 10 January 2023

1. Introduction

Computer vision applications are being used intensively in the public area for tedious tasks, e.g., surveillance and license plate detection and reading, as well as in robotics applications for tasks, e.g., object detection, quality inspection, and human machine cooperation [1–3].

In the initial stages of development, implementing a computer vision application (machine vision or robotic vision versions) was considered an exceedingly challenging task. With the increase of the processing power, new hardware development, and new, efficient, and performant image sensors, the development of such applications was made significantly easier [4,5].

A huge boost in popularity for the image processing and computer vision application was achieved with the increase in popularity of Python programming language and the implementation of various image processing frameworks such as OpenCV (for C++ initially and Python afterwards) and the development of machine learning and deep learning frameworks [6,7].

Solutions implemented in the robotic manufacturing environment are based on cameras using CCD sensors and industrial systems, which consider the computer vision application as a black box providing a status. This approach proved to be robust and efficient. The needs of industry are now growing different and becoming more complex. The control systems also need to integrate with computer vision applications to provide full control for the production process [8,9].

The current global and geopolitical context from the last years, the tendency for accelerated car electrification, and recent innovation from Industry 4.0 have encouraged car manufacturers to integrate more computer vision applications in the production process. Applications are mostly used for counting parts and ensuring traceability, e.g., barcode readings, QR code readings, OCR, and defect detection in distinct stages of the manufacturing process, e.g., painting, assembly, and machining. In this environment more complex applications can be found, e.g., high precision measurement tools based on computer vision, complex scanning, and applications based on artificial intelligence (machine learning) [10].

The solution presented in this paper is based on the integration of a CCD sensor camera with a robotic control system that is also able to provide all the information needed in the robotic manufacturing environment for traceability and planning while detecting complex defects in real time. Two algorithms are used for detecting a class of defects inside the cylinder chamber of an engine block. The main role of the computer vision algorithms is the reducing the number of input features for the convolutional neural network by isolating the region of interest (walls of the cylinder chamber). The convolutional neural network scope is to process the newly generated image for providing a decision.

The future actions of the entire robotic system that manipulates these mechanical parts depends on the results provided by the visual inspection system. Moreover, based on the global results obtained on the entire visual inspection process, reprogramming or even reconfiguration of the robotic systems involved in the manufacturing process of mechanical parts will take place [11].

In order to implement this solution, the goal was to develop a computer vison system that is able to detect machining defects from the cylinder chamber of the engine block. This was achieved by developing the following steps:

- The system with reused parts.
- A new system architecture based on the available parts.
- A new software architecture to match the industrial standards.
- A new user interface for the software application.
- Integrating and updating the software development kits of the camera and input/output ethernet module.
- An algorithm to isolate the region of interest in the acquired image.
- A machine learning algorithm able to receive an input in the format generated by the previous computer vision algorithm.

2. Related Work

Defect detection technologies are used in the manufacturing industry for identifying the surfaces (spots, pits, scratches, and color differences) and internal parts (defects holes, cracks, and other flaws) of the products having problems. Computer vision defect detection applications must be fast, non-destructive, and accurate, and they have become widely used in the recent years. Zhou et al. [12] developed an artificial imaging system for the detection of discrete surface defects on vehicle bodies using a three-level scale detection method for extracting the defects that might appear on the vehicle surface. The method distinguishes the defect location, comparing the features of the background from the defect images, which allows for detection in concave areas or areas with abrupt changes in the surface style lines, edges, and corners. It extracts defects that are hardly perceived by the human eyes.

In various computer vision industrial applications, the basic setups for image acquisition are similar. For example, in the automotive manufacturing industry, a basic computer vision application is needed a light source alongside a camera and a computer powerful enough to process the acquired image. As light sources, LEDs are mostly used. LED light sources offer high efficiency and versatility when it comes to triggers and dimming control. Infrared light sources used with monochrome industrial cameras (or as infrared panels) as well as multiple light sources are frequently used. For settings and environment closer to the laboratory, in the majority of the computer vision application, cameras and light sources are placed in a light absorbing room where the lighting can be controlled. A special application, e.g., an assembly robot, may require a special camera. In this case, the light source and the camera will be attached to an actuator (servomotor, robotic arm, etc.). Industrial cameras contain CCD (charge-coupled device) or CMOS (complementary metal-oxide semiconductor) sensors and the lenses are chosen having in focus the environment and the vision application. Trying to achieve real time processing, the software algorithms must be executed on powerful machines. Algorithms are developed by customizing to each particular application and each hardware configuration (camera and lighting). For detecting different defects of a car after the painting process, a four-camera setup can be used to achieve stable light and multiple cameras (e.g., five cameras) to acquire the same affected area from multiple angles (light conditions different). In the acquired images, the region on interest will be isolated, several specific filters for noise reduction will be also applied, in addition to a feature extraction algorithm (specific to the vision application) for isolating the different defects detected [11].

When a certain amount of data can be acquired and used, then a deep learning model training supervised learning is adopted instead of a conventional recognition based on feature descriptors. A classification module, an integrated attention module with an image segmentation module, is used for weekly supervised learning. The classification module extracts the defect features from the image. The integrated module has as a purpose the detection of different irregular defects (e.g., for metal pieces) which can appear after casting or shaping processes. The segmentation module is used to determine if a pixel from the image is associated to a defect area [13].

Other common defect detection methods are ultrasonic testing, osmosis testing, and X-ray testing [14]. The ultrasonic methods are used in the detection of defects in the internal structure of the product under test (like X-ray testing). These methods are based on filtering for feature extraction and the ability to describe the identified defect.

Alongside common methods, in recent years, deep-learning defect detection methods have been used in various applications. Some of these algorithms are based on the use of a deep neural network, e.g., a convolutional neural network, residual networks, or recurrent neural networks. Computer vision defect detection applications have shown good accuracy in binary defect detection [15].

In their paper, Zhonghe et al. [16] address the state of the art in defect detection-based machine vision, presenting an effective method to reduce the adverse impact of product defects. They claim that artificial visual inspection is limited in the field of applications with possible dangerous consequences in the case of a failure because of the low sampling rate, slow real-time performance, and the relatively poor detection confidence.

The replacement of artificial visual inspection is machine vision, which can cover the whole electromagnetic spectrum, from gamma rays to radio waves. Machine vision has a great ability to work in harsh environments for a long time and greatly improves the real time control and response. Therefore, it can improve many robotic manufacturing processes to support industrial activities. In this paper, the proposal for an industrial visual inspection module consists of three modules: optical illumination, image acquisition, and the image processing and defect detection module. It is stated that an optical illumination platform should be designed. Then, CCD cameras or other acquisition hardware should be use in such a way that the information carried by them to the computer should have an extremely high quality. Finally, either classical image processing algorithms or better, deep learning algorithms should be used, which are able to extract the features and perform the classification, localization, segmentation, and other image operations, image processing being the key technology in machine vision. In industry, this architecture can be used as a guideline for designing a visual inspection system. It is given as an example in the paper for inspecting surface characteristics in designing a highly reflective metal surface.

Wang Liqun et al. [17] focused on the idea of detecting defects using deep learning. They also based their research on convolutional neural networks for training and learning big sets of image acquisition data and they claim that it can effectively extract the features and classify them accurately and efficiently. They use PatMax software, which can recognize twenty-five different filter shapes, and determines the location of the filter while being 99% accurate. The process first collects the information from the camera, reads the image preprocessed result and trains on the processed images, then establishes a complete information model and obtains the target image. A diffuse bright led backlight illumination is used. Light sensitive components were used for image acquisition, and a wavelet smoothing was used for image preprocessing, after which Otsu threshold was used to segment the image. In the end, the support vector machine classifier was designed for defect classification. The goals should be high precision, high efficiency, and strong robustness. Therefore, the system needs an excellent coordination of the three modules. The features are afterwards matched with the template, and the quality of the assembly process is judge according to the matching result. Difficulties remain in detecting component defects due to the variety of vehicle parts which have different shapes, and due to the fact, the defects are very diversified. Moreover, the image structure of the parts is more complex, incorporating irrelevant factors around the image and a lot of noise, which makes feature extraction difficult. The authors managed to improve the VGG16 network model structure by adding the inceptionv3 module, increasing the width of the model based on depth. Their resulted accuracy was improved from 94.36% up to 95.29%, which is almost 1% more accurate than previously.

Zehelein et al. [18] presented in their paper a way of inspecting the suspension dampers on the autonomous driving vehicles between inspections. Their theory claims that in a normal vehicle, the driver always monitors the health state and reliability of a vehicle, and that it could be dangerous for an autonomous driving vehicle to not be monitored between inspections. To solve this problem, they discussed one of the problems in defect diagnosis while driving, namely the robustness of such a system concerning the vehicle's configuration. The main problems are the variable factors, such as tire characteristics, mass variation, or varying road conditions. They decided to combine a data driven approach with a signal-based approach, which led to a machine learning algorithm which can incorporate the variations in different vehicle configurations and usage scenarios. In their paper, it is stated that they used a support vector machine for classifying signal features, and they also needed features that can distinguish between different health states of the vehicle. Convolutional neural networks can deal with multidimensional data and demonstrate good feature extraction, which makes them perfect for the job. They used the driving data of the longitudinal and lateral acceleration as well as the yaw rate and wheel speeds. Using FFT (fast Fourier transform), input data were shown to give the best results regarding classification performance.

The authors were not able to check the real time implementation of the system because there is not a specific value for the computing power of an automotive ECU (electronic control unit). Therefore, the algorithm might not run optimally for every vehicle on the market [19]. They also propose the feature extraction method and divide the defects into three categories (pseudo-defects, dents, and scratches) using the linear SVM (scan velocity modulation) classifier. Their detection results were close to the accuracy of 95.6% for dents and 97.1% for scratches, while maintaining a speed of detection of 1 min and 50 s per vehicle. They state that their system could be improved using deflectometry techniques for image defect contrast enhancement, or by improving the intelligence of the method, but the latter could slow down the detection speed. Moreover, if they could use parallel computing techniques on graphic processing units, the speed of detection could be further improved.

A conventional computer vision approach is implementing the following algorithm [20,21]:

- Image acquisition
- Circle and point edge detection
- Length and radius measurements
- Feature collection
- Matching features
- Generate the verdict and store it in a database

A drawback of this approach would be the high processing time of the high-resolution input image and the volatile environment from where the image is acquired, which will lead to a repeatability issue in the image due to dynamic shapes and contrast of the emulsion marks [22].

In this paper, a description of a combination between a conventional approach and a machine learning approach is given.

3. Solution Overview

3.1. Process and Issue Description

The purpose of the inspection machine is to detect a certain class of defects, to sort the engine blocks on the production line, and to wash the bottom part of the block using a special system for removing dirt, dust, and other mechanical process impurities. When a defect is detected, the engine block is removed trough a conveyor from the production line. In the washing process, some special solvents and emulsions are used.

The CCD sensor camera was configured to match a high range of environment conditions with a fixed exposure, fixed gain, and a special set of lenses. The specification of the lens used are further described in Figure 1. The implementation completes the already installed inspection machine by adding a new station with the purpose to automate the visual inspection performed until now by the operator. The complete layout of the process can be observed in Figure 2.

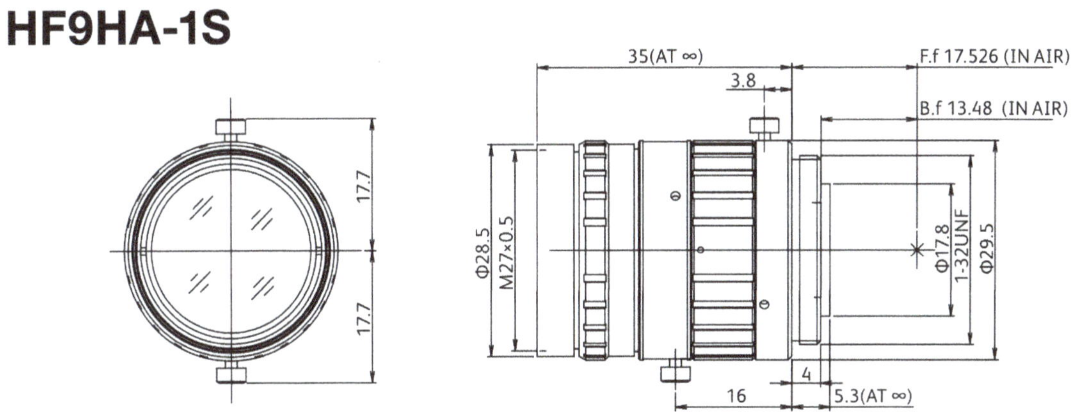

Figure 1. Fujinon lens dimensions.

The next step after washing will be the drying and cleaning of the block with an airflow through the bottom part and the cylinder chambers. The drying process leaves behind dried cleaning emulsion, which will make the automated inspection more difficult. In Figure 3a,b, the traces of dried emulsion can be observed on a flawless cylinder chamber. Figure 4a,b describes the defect to be automatically detected from the cylinder chamber alongside dried emulsion.

The engine block is made from cast iron with green sand insertions. In the process of filling the mold with liquid metal, some environment factors can interact with the product in an unwanted way. The damaged sand core can generate inclusions inside or at the surface of the part. Another defect is generated by the impossibility of removing all the gases from the mold when the liquid metal takes contact with the surface of the mold. This process involves generating blowholes.

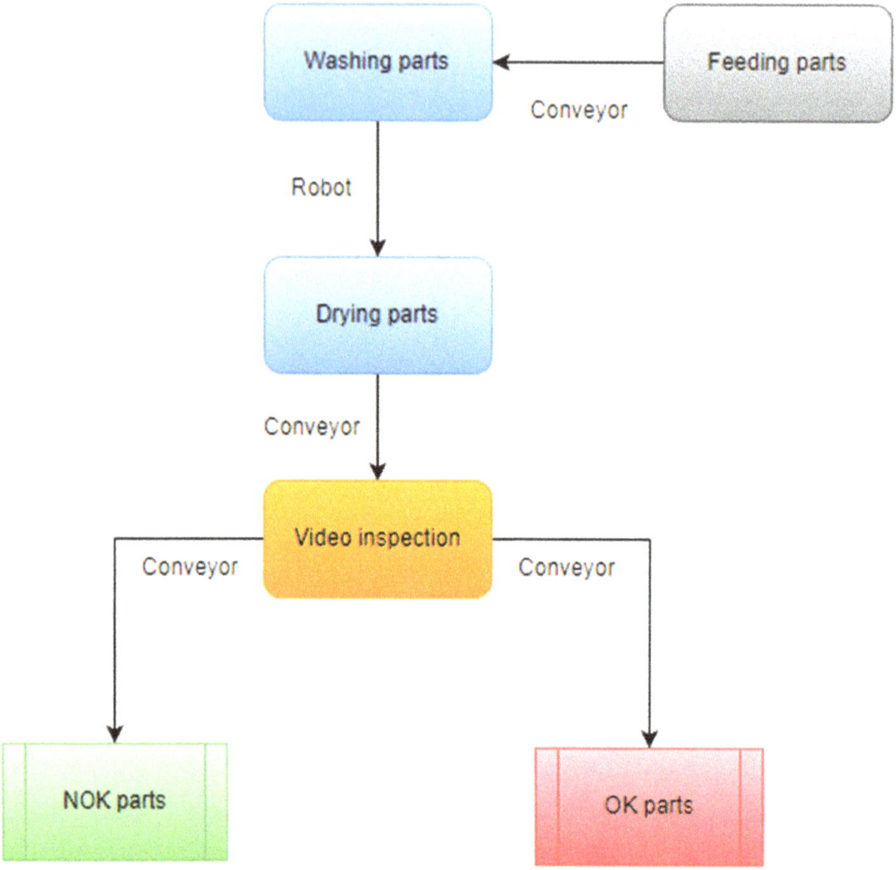

Figure 2. Architecture of the washing and sorting machine on the production line.

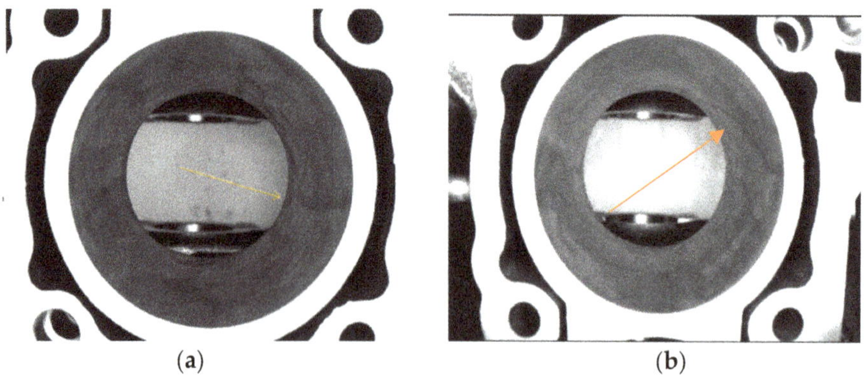

Figure 3. No defects in the cylinder chamber. In (**a**,**b**) can be observed a part with no defects and dried emulsion marks indicated by the arrows.

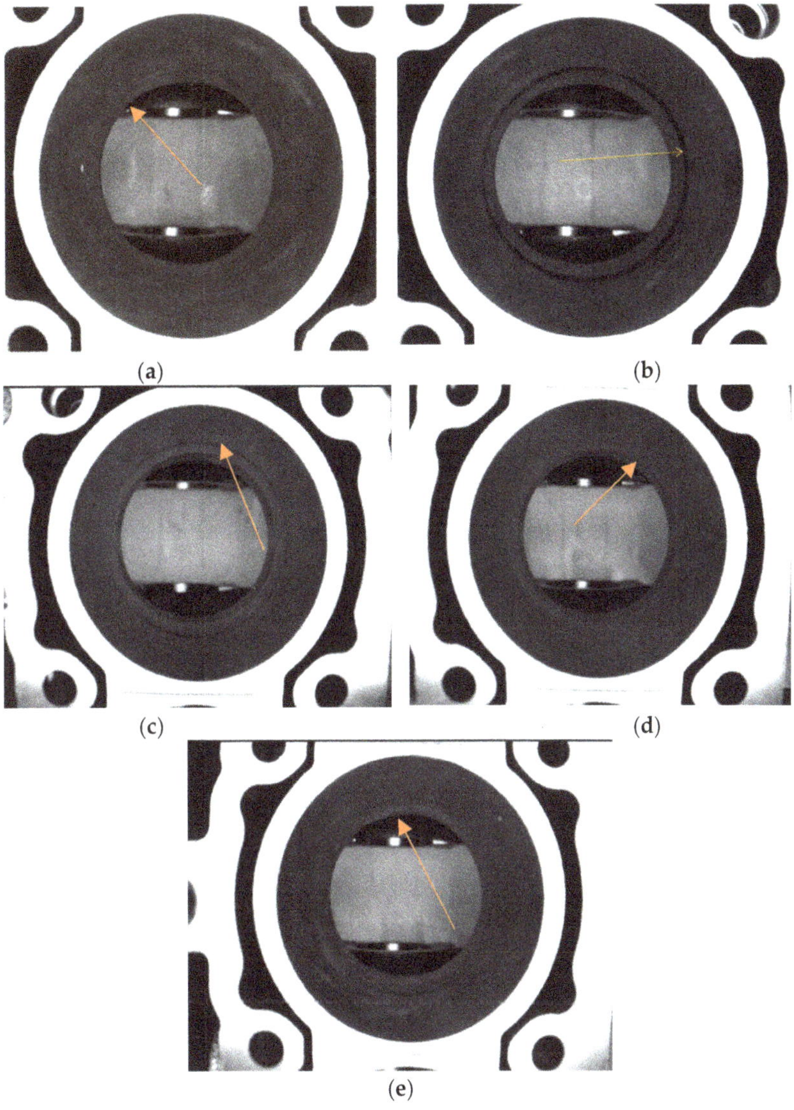

Figure 4. Defects in the cylinder chamber. In (a–e) parts with machining defects can be observed. (a) presents a barely observable defect and (b–e) presents a more prominent one.

3.2. Architecture Description

Figure 5 describes the system architecture including the sensor. The solution was implemented using a single camera capturing an image of the area that needs to be inspected. For moving the camera, a PLC that is controlled directly by the main inspection machine was used. When the PLC receives the trigger, a stepper motor is actuated. The camera is hovered over each of the cylinders for acquisition and is connected to the stepper motor with a coupling in order to create a linear movement. When the camera is in position, the acquisition and processing system is triggered.

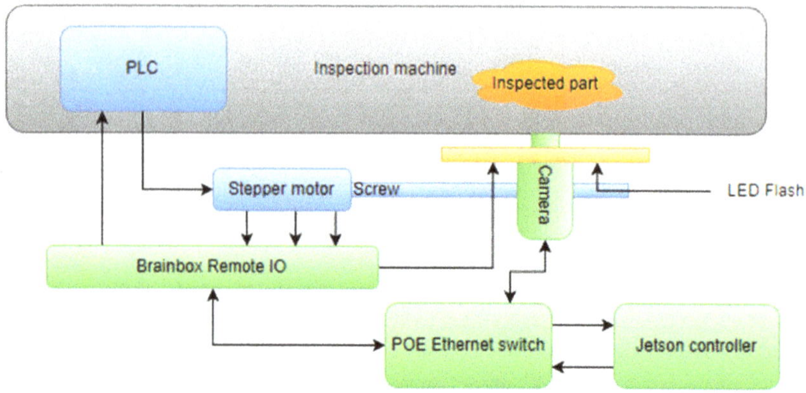

Figure 5. System architecture of the video inspection operation.

For ensuring a more increased degree of repeatability in the image acquisition, an infrared LED flash is used. The LED is controlled by the acquisition system. The main controller used for acquisition and processing is represented by a Jetson Nano development kit, which has a high computing power, especially in artificial intelligence applications. The Jetson interacts with the PLC trough an industrial remote I/O module from Brainbox by controlling it over ethernet. The Brainbox module also triggers the LED flash. The control of the CCD camera is also implemented over Ethernet, in this case POE (power over Ethernet) because the camera is also powered by the ethernet switch.

3.3. Hardware Description

For implementing the computer vision solution, the following hardware components were used:

- Nvidia Jetson Nano controller with 4 GB RAM memory, 128 core GPU, an ARM Cortex A57 Quad-Core CPU
- The Imaging Source DMK 33GX290e Monochrome Camera
- ED-008 Ethernet to Digital I/O Brainboxes module
- EffiLux LED Infrared Light flash EFFI-FD
- Industrial compliant POE Ethernet Switch

The Jetson controller is connected to the Ethernet switch alongside the camera with a CCD sensor and remote I/O module. The LED Flash is connected with a pull-up resistor (24 V) to the remote I/O module and is controlled via ethernet requests by the Jetson controller.

3.4. Software Description

The application was implemented using Python programming language. All the used hardware components integrate Python software development kits provided by the manufacturer. Therefore, the choice of programming language for implementation came naturally. The human–machine interface was implemented using the PyQt framework (PyQt5-Qt5 version 5.15.2, developed by Riverbank Computing, open-source), which is a Python wrapper of the open-source framework Qt developed by the Qt company. Software was designed to cover all of the manufacturing necessities, e.g., logging, user management, process handling, and so on [21–30]. In Figure 6, a complete sequence diagram of the process can be observed.

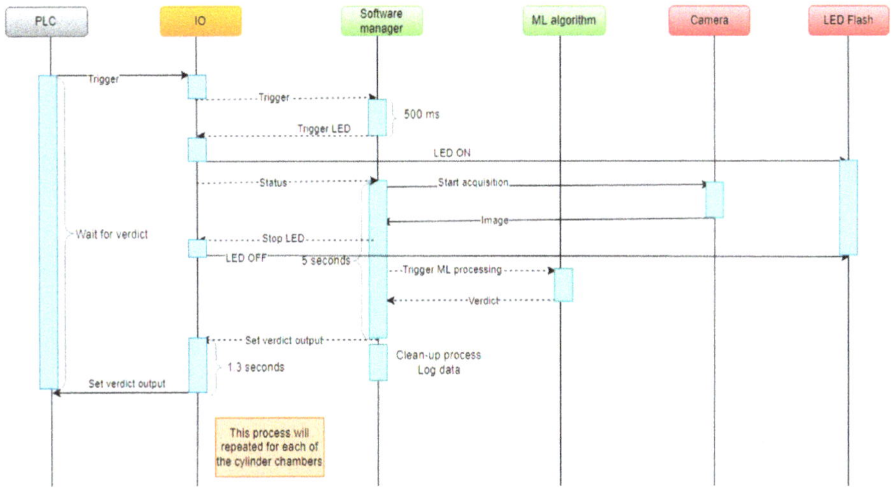

Figure 6. Process sequence diagram.

3.5. Processing Algorithm Description

The processing algorithm has two main parts: the conventional processing and the prediction using a machine learning model. As input, the algorithm takes a grayscale image with a resolution of 1920 × 1200. In the conventional processing, the ROI of the inner chamber of the cylinder is extracted by the algorithm, normalized, and a gaussian filter is applied. After applying the filter, an adaptive thresholding is also performed by the algorithm because the defects have a lower grayscale level and can be isolated this way. When the defects are isolated by the thresholding, they are marked with a contour function. This function returns the area of the detected contours (each contour detected represents a possible defect).

The area can be evaluated for establishing a verdict. The conventional processing works verry well when there are no significant traces of cleaning emulsion on the cylinder. When the emulsion becomes mixed with dust, traces become increasingly noticeable and with a lower grayscale level. Because of that, the thresholding is no longer able to distinguish between traces of emulsion and actual defects [22–30].

The second part of the processing algorithm is the convolutional neural network implemented using the PyTorch framework. The first layer takes as input the three RGB channels of the image and splits it in eight features for the next layer. The second layer is a max pooling layer with a kernel size of 3 × 3 and with padding enabled for looping through the entire image. Third layer is another convolutional layer, similar to the first layer, followed by a fully connected layer [31–33].

The spatial size of the output is obtained:

$$\frac{W - K + 2P}{S} \tag{1}$$

where W is the volume input size, K is the kernel size of the convolutional layer neurons, S represents the stride, and P is the amount of zero padding at the borders of the neural network [20].

A typical pooling layer is calculated with the following formula:

$$f(x,y) = \max_{a,b=0}^{1} S_{2x+a,\, 2y+b} \tag{2}$$

The activation functions for the convolutional layers are ReLu (rectified linear unit), applying the following non-saturating activation function for removing the negative values from the activation map by setting them to zero [20].

$$f(x) = \max(0, x) \tag{3}$$

In Figure 7, an architecture of the neural network is proposed [19–30].

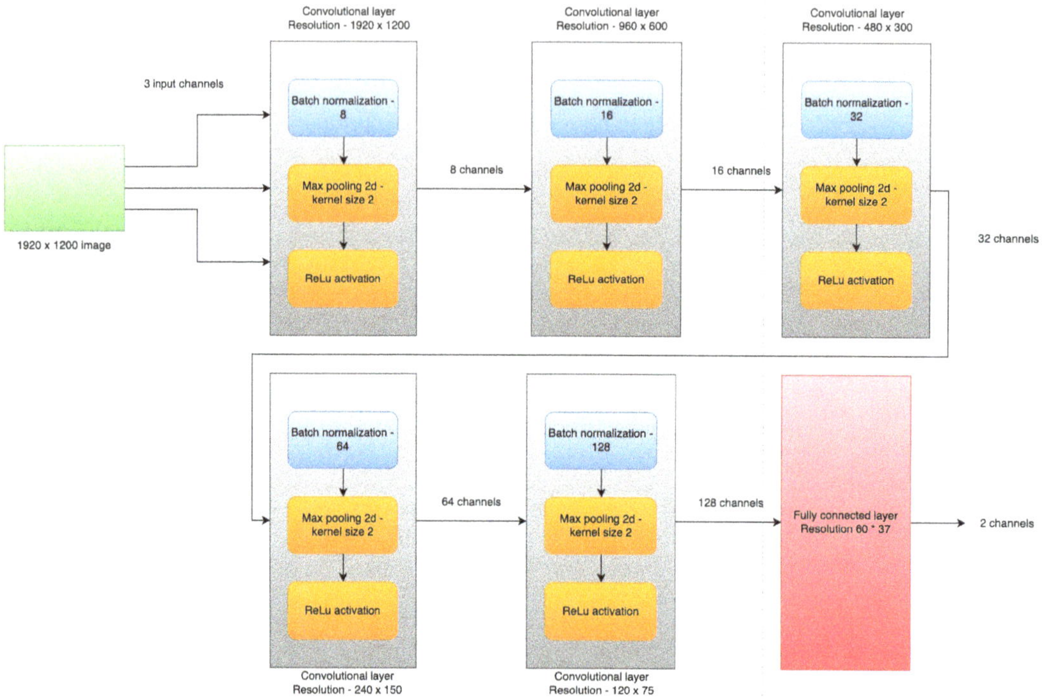

Figure 7. Convolutional network architecture.

Hyper-parameters:

- Input channels—3
- Convolutional layers—5
- Fully connected layer—1
- Batch size—8
- Epochs—30
- Output channels—2

4. Results

The model was trained using old defective engine blocks as well as on fixed periods of time with new batches of images evaluated by the model as defects. The false defects were labeled as no defects in the dataset and the actual defects were added in the dataset. The model did not perform very well, as can be observed in the results, due to the high number of features that needed to be extracted and processed before setting a verdict.

The architecture presented in Figure 7 has five convolutional layers with max pooling and a fully connected layer. The end image now has a resolution of 60 × 37 with 128 unique features. In Figure 8, we can see that the loss function generated during training with the new model has better performance and is able to detect the defects much faster.

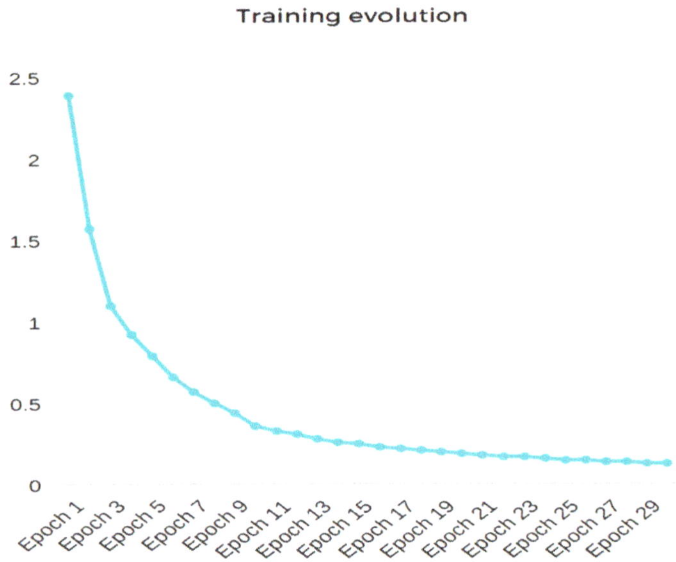

Figure 8. Training progress of the convolutional neural network. The X-axis describes the loss function value can be observed. The Y-axis shows the corresponding epoch.

Below, the training results can be observed:

- Accuracy on training set: 100%
- Accuracy on test set: 100%
- Loss at the end of the training: 0.13

The main indicators tracked during commissioning was the number of the false detections reported by the neural network and the rate of detection for real defects. The number of false detections was initially high due to emulsion marks and system calibrations (refer to Figure 9). After the dataset was established and the system calibrated, the indicator decreased substantially, below a desired threshold such that we can consider that the algorithm is reliable enough.

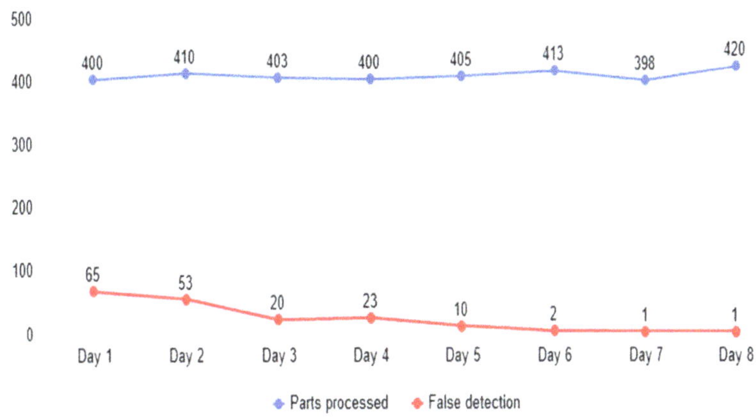

Figure 9. Evolution of false detections.

It was observed that after including images with prominent marks of emulsion and with small imperfections generated by improper lighting (camera stabilization), the number of false detections decreased considerably (refer to Figures 10 and 11).

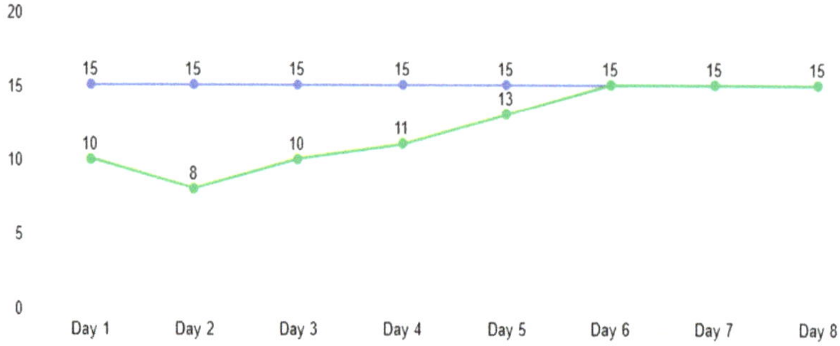

Figure 10. Evolution of detections. Blue line represents the real number of defects provided to algorithm and the green line represents the defects detected by the algorithm over 8 days.

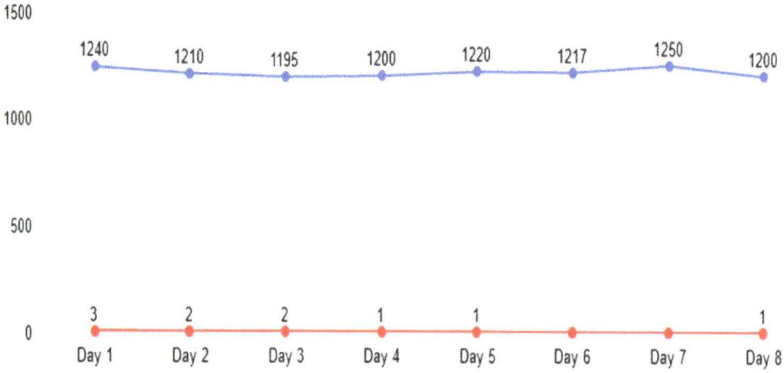

Figure 11. False detection evolution after final training.

Table 1 also shows the type of defects detected during operation in relation to false detections and real defects. It can be observed that the highlight is still on the emulsion marks resulting from the washing and drying process in the presence of the dust or other impurities, this being the main false detection generator.

Table 1. This table shows the evolution of detections.

Number of Parts	False Detections	Actual Defects	Error Type	Defect Type	Remarks
1200	100	10	Emulsion marks	Machining defect	Tests performed
1160	50	0	Emulsion marks	N/A	N/A
1193	52	0	Emulsion marks	N/A	N/A
1203	37	0	Emulsion marks and lighting issues	N/A	N/A
1210	10	0	Highly intense emulsion marks	N/A	N/A
1205	1	1	Highly intense emulsion marks	Machining defect	Tests performed

There is a lot of research being conducted on how different algorithms are responding to already established datasets. The main approach used involves software pre-processing, the use of a convolutional neural network for feature extraction, and in some cases another network for classification [34–42].

This solution is uses only hardware pre-processing (camera as sensors and environment related) and one convolutional neural network for feature extraction and classification. The setup proved to be sufficient and robust for the needed classification.

5. Conclusions

From the point of view of robotics applications developed in the automotive industry, the robustness of image processing applications from the manufacturing area can be increased considerably by using a machine learning algorithm to replace the classic method of processing with filters, hardware, complicated optics, and complex software algorithms. The machine learning algorithm can replace the classic approach and thereby ensure greater flexibility in developing the backbone of the application, e.g., PLC communication, socket services, and human–machine interface, so indispensable in this environment.

The weak point of this implementation remains the dependency on a sufficient and a correct dataset. By ensuring that we have the correct data to work with, we can develop and train a robust application for use in the manufacturing environment.

The advantage of using such an approach is that other implementations, e.g., communication, HMI, logging, and others, can be abstracted and reused in new implementations. The training of the algorithm can also be abstracted and reused. The flexible part needs to remain the architecture of the neural network and the dataset used.

Based on the work presented in this paper, a new application is already in development. The scope of the new implementation is to detect the presence of a safety pin inside the piston locking mechanism. This operation will be performed using three cameras which are triggered simultaneously for acquisition, a new architecture for the neural network, and different hardware to support a more complex application.

Author Contributions: Conceptualization, D.C.; Methodology, F.M.; Software, M.M.A.; Validation, M.M.A., D.C. and A.M.; Formal analysis, D.C. and F.M.; Investigation, A.M.; Data curation, M.M.A. and A.M.; Writing—original draft, M.M.A. and A.M.; Writing—review & editing, M.M.A. and A.M.; Visualization, M.M.A. and A.M.; Supervision, D.C. and F.M. All authors have read and agreed to the published version of the manuscript.

Funding: This research received no external funding. Authors are researcher in the frame of University of Craiova.

Institutional Review Board Statement: Not applicable.

Informed Consent Statement: Not applicable.

Data Availability Statement: Our dataset is not publicly available.

Conflicts of Interest: The authors declare that they are not aware of any conflict of interest.

References

1. Cob-Parro, A.C.; Losada-Gutiérrez, C.; Marrón-Romera, M.; Gardel-Vicente, A.; Bravo-Muñoz, I. Smart Video Surveillance System Based on Edge Computing. *Sensors* **2021**, *21*, 2958. [CrossRef]
2. Han, B.-G.; Lee, J.T.; Lim, K.-T.; Choi, D.-H. License Plate Image Generation using Generative Adversarial Networks for End-To-End License Plate Character Recognition from a Small Set of Real Images. *Appl. Sci.* **2020**, *10*, 2780. [CrossRef]
3. Park, M.; Jeong, J. Design and Implementation of Machine Vision-Based Quality Inspection System in Mask Manufacturing Process. *Sustainability* **2022**, *14*, 6009. [CrossRef]
4. Smith, M.L.; Smith, L.N.; Hansen, M.F. The quiet revolution in machine vision—A state-of-the-art survey paper, including historical review, perspectives, and future directions. *Comput. Ind.* **2021**, *130*, 103472. [CrossRef]
5. Chai, J.; Zeng, H.; Li, A.; Ngai, E.W. Deep learning in computer vision: A critical review of emerging techniques and application scenarios. *Mach. Learn. Appl.* **2021**, *6*, 100134. [CrossRef]
6. Zhang, W.; Liu, D.; Wang, C.; Liu, R.; Wang, D.; Yu, L.; Wen, S. An Improved Python-Based Image Processing Algorithm for Flotation Foam Analysis. *Minerals* **2022**, *12*, 1126. [CrossRef]

7. Sánchez-Jiménez, D.; Buchón-Moragues, F.; Escutia-Muñoz, B.; Botella-Estrada, R. Development of Computer Vision Applications to Automate the Measurement of the Dimensions of Skin Wounds. *Proceedings* **2019**, *19*, 18. [CrossRef]
8. Pérez, L.; Rodríguez, Í.; Rodríguez, N.; Usamentiaga, R.; García, D.F. Robot Guidance Using Machine Vision Techniques in Industrial Environments: A Comparative Review. *Sensors* **2016**, *16*, 335. [CrossRef]
9. Kostal, P.; Prajova, V.; Vaclav, S.; Stan, S.-D. An Overview of the Practical Use of the CCTV System in a Simple Assembly in a Flexible Manufacturing System. *Appl. Syst. Innov.* **2022**, *5*, 52. [CrossRef]
10. Nguyen, T.T.H.; Jatowt, A.; Coustaty, M.; Nguyen, N.V.; Doucet, A. Deep Statistical Analysis of OCR Errors for Effective Post-OCR Processing. In Proceedings of the 2019 ACM/IEEE Joint Conference on Digital Libraries (JCDL), Champaign, IL, USA, 2–6 June 2019; pp. 29–38. [CrossRef]
11. Ye, M.; Zhang, W.; Cui, G.; Wang, X. Surface Defects Inspection of Cylindrical Metal Workpieces Based on Weakly Supervised Learning. *Int. J. Adv. Manuf. Technol.* **2022**, *119*, 1933–1949. [CrossRef]
12. Nguyen, H.; La, H. Review of Deep Reinforcement Learning for Robot Manipulation. In Proceedings of the 2019 Third IEEE International Conference on Robotic Computing (IRC), Naples, Italy, 25–27 February 2019; pp. 590–595. [CrossRef]
13. Yang, H.; Yu, L. Feature extraction of wood-hole defects using wavelet-based ultrasonic testing. *J. For. Res.* **2016**, *28*, 395–402. [CrossRef]
14. Gholizadeh, S.; Leman, Z.; Baharudin, B. A review of the application of acoustic emission technique in engineering. *Struct. Eng. Mech.* **2015**, *54*, 1075–1095. [CrossRef]
15. Du Plessis, A.; le Roux, S.G. Standardized X-ray tomography testing of additively manufactured parts: A round robin test. *Addit. Manuf.* **2018**, *24*, 125–136. [CrossRef]
16. Ren, Z.; Fang, F.; Yan, N.; Wu, Y. State of the Art in Defect Detection Based on Machine Vision. *Int. J. Precis. Eng. Manuf.-Green Technol.* **2022**, *9*, 661–691. [CrossRef]
17. Liqun, W.; Jiansheng, W.; Dingjin, W. Research on Vehicle Parts Defect Detection Based on Deep Learning. *J. Phys. Conf. Ser.* **2020**, *1437*, 012004. [CrossRef]
18. Zehelein, T.; Hemmert-Pottmann, T.; Lienkamp, M. Diagnosing Automotive Damper Defects Using Convolutional Neural Networks and Electronic Stability Control Sensor Signals. *J. Sens. Actuator Netw.* **2020**, *9*, 8. [CrossRef]
19. Boaretto, N.; Centeno, T.M. Automated detection of welding defects in pipelines from radiographic images. *Mater. Sci.* **2017**, *86*, 7–13. [CrossRef]
20. Convolutional Neural Networks. Available online: https://en.wikipedia.org/wiki/Convolutional_neural_network (accessed on 22 April 2022).
21. Kiruba Shankar, R.; Indra, J.; Oviya, R.; Heeraj, A.; Ragunathan, R. Machine Vision based quality inspection for automotive parts using edge detection technique. *IOP Conf. Ser. Mater. Sci. Eng.* **2020**, *1055*, 012029. [CrossRef]
22. Berwo, M.A.; Fang, Y.; Mahmood, J.; Yang, N.; Liu, Z.; Li, Y. FAECCD-CNet: Fast Automotive Engine Components Crack Detection and Classification Using ConvNet on Images. *Appl. Sci.* **2022**, *12*, 9713. [CrossRef]
23. Riba, J.-R. Application of Image Sensors to Detect and Locate Electrical Discharges: A Review. *Sensors* **2022**, *22*, 5886. [CrossRef]
24. Tao, X.; Zhang, D.; Ma, W.; Liu, X.; Xu, D. Automatic Metallic Surface Defect Detection and Recognition with Convolutional Neural Networks. *Appl. Sci.* **2018**, *8*, 1575. [CrossRef]
25. He, Y.; Song, K.; Meng, Q.; Yan, Y. An End-to-End Steel Surface Defect Detection Approach via Fusing Multiple Hierarchical Features. *IEEE Trans. Instrum. Meas.* **2020**, *69*, 1493–1504. [CrossRef]
26. Li, Y.; Huang, H.; Xie, Q.; Yao, L.; Chen, Q. Research on a Surface Defect Detection Algorithm Based on MobileNet-SSD. *Appl. Sci.* **2018**, *8*, 1678. [CrossRef]
27. Kang, G.; Gao, S.; Yu, L.; Zhang, D. Deep Architecture for High-Speed Railway Insulator Surface Defect Detection: Denoising Autoencoder With Multitask Learning. *IEEE Trans. Instrum. Meas.* **2019**, *68*, 2679–2690. [CrossRef]
28. Cheon, S.; Lee, H.; Kim, C.O.; Lee, S.H. Convolutional Neural Network for Wafer Surface Defect Classification and the Detection of Unknown Defect Class. *IEEE Trans. Semicond. Manuf.* **2019**, *32*, 163–170. [CrossRef]
29. Li, J.; Su, Z.; Geng, J.; Yin, Y. Real-time Detection of Steel Strip Surface Defects Based on Improved YOLO Detection Network. *IFAC-Pap.* **2018**, *51*, 76–81. [CrossRef]
30. Shang, L.; Yang, Q.; Wang, J.; Li, S.; Lei, W. Detection of rail surface defects based on CNN image recognition and classification. In Proceedings of the 2018 20th International Conference on Advanced Communication Technology (ICACT), Chuncheon, Republic of Korea, 11–14 February 2018; pp. 45–51. [CrossRef]
31. Czimmermann, T.; Ciuti, G.; Milazzo, M.; Chiurazzi, M.; Roccella, S.; Oddo, C.M.; Dario, P. Visual-Based Defect Detection and Classification Approaches for Industrial Applications—A SURVEY. *Sensors* **2020**, *20*, 1459. [CrossRef]
32. Chandan, G.; Jain, A.; Jain, H.; Mohana. Real Time Object Detection and Tracking Using Deep Learning and OpenCV. In Proceedings of the 2018 International Conference on Inventive Research in Computing Applications (ICIRCA), Coimbatore, India, 11–12 July 2018; pp. 1305–1308. [CrossRef]
33. Fernández-Sáez, A.M.; Chaudron, M.R.V.; Genero, M. An industrial case study on the use of UML in software maintenance and its perceived benefits and hurdles. *Empir. Softw. Eng.* **2018**, *23*, 3281–3345. [CrossRef]
34. Hynninen, T.; Kasurinen, J.; Knutas, A.; Taipale, O. Software testing: Survey of the industry practices. In Proceedings of the 2018 41st International Convention on Information and Communication Technology, Electronics and Microelectronics (MIPRO), Coimbatore, India, 11–12 July 2018; pp. 1449–1454. [CrossRef]

35. Motta, R.C.; de Oliveira, K.M.; Travassos, G.H. On challenges in engineering IoT software systems. In Proceedings of the XXXII Brazilian Symposium on Software Engineering (SBES '18), Sao Carlos, Brazil, 17–21 September 2018; Association for Computing Machinery: New York, NY, USA, 2018; pp. 42–51. [CrossRef]
36. Garousi, V.; Giray, G.; Tuzun, E.; Catal, C.; Felderer, M. Closing the Gap Between Software Engineering Education and Industrial Needs. *IEEE Softw.* **2020**, *37*, 68–77. [CrossRef]
37. Oztemel, E.; Gursev, S. Literature review of Industry 4.0 and related technologies. *J. Intell. Manuf.* **2020**, *31*, 127–182. [CrossRef]
38. Ungurean, I.; Gaitan, N.C. A Software Architecture for the Industrial Internet of Things—A Conceptual Model. *Sensors* **2020**, *20*, 5603. [CrossRef] [PubMed]
39. Hoda, R.; Salleh, N.; Grundy, J. The Rise and Evolution of Agile Software Development. *IEEE Softw.* **2018**, *35*, 58–63. [CrossRef]
40. Coda, F.A.; Salles, R.M.; Junqueira, F.; Filho, D.J.S.; Silva, J.R.; Miyagi, P.E. Big data systems requirements for Industry 4.0. In Proceedings of the 2018 13th IEEE International Conference on Industry Applications (INDUSCON), Paulo, Brazil, 12–14 November 2018; pp. 1230–1236. [CrossRef]
41. Hanga, K.M.; Kovalchuk, Y. Machine learning and multi-agent systems in oil and gas industry applications: A survey. *Comput. Sci. Rev.* **2019**, *34*, 100191. [CrossRef]
42. Kannengiesser, U.; Müller, H. Towards viewpoint-oriented engineering for Industry 4.0: A standards-based approach. In Proceedings of the 2018 IEEE Industrial Cyber-Physical Systems (ICPS), St. Petersburg, Russia, 15–18 May 2018; pp. 51–56. [CrossRef]

sensors

MDPI

Article

Synchronous Control of a Group of Flying Robots Following a Leader UAV in an Unfamiliar Environment

Konrad Wojtowicz *and Przemysław Wojciechowski

Faculty of Mechatronics, Armament, and Aerospace, Military University of Technology, 00-908 Warsaw, Poland
* Correspondence: konrad.wojtowicz@wat.edu.pl; Tel.: +48-261-837-529

Abstract: An increasing number of professional drone flights require situational awareness of aerial vehicles. Vehicles in a group of drones must be aware of their surroundings and the other group members. The amount of data to be exchanged and the total cost are skyrocketing. This paper presents an implementation and assessment of an organized drone group comprising a fully aware leader and much less expensive followers. The solution achieved a significant cost reduction by decreasing the number of sensors onboard followers and improving the organization and manageability of the group in the system. In this project, a group of quadrotor drones was evaluated. An automatically flying leader was followed by drones equipped with low-end cameras only. The followers were tasked with following ArUco markers mounted on a preceding drone. Several test tasks were designed and conducted. Finally, the presented system proved appropriate for slowly moving groups of drones.

Keywords: drone; UAV; multi-agent; ArUco; markers; group of drones; machine vision

Citation: Wojtowicz, K.; Wojciechowski, P. Synchronous Control of a Group of Flying Robots Following a Leader UAV in an Unfamiliar Environment. *Sensors* **2023**, *23*, 740. https://doi.org/10.3390/s23020740

Academic Editors: Luige Vladareanu, Hongnian Yu, Hongbo Wang and Yongfei Feng

Received: 5 December 2022
Revised: 29 December 2022
Accepted: 4 January 2023
Published: 9 January 2023

1. Introduction

Due to global technological development and commercial opportunities, vast growth in the unmanned aerial vehicle market has been observed. Software, control systems, structures, and methods of analyzing the environment with drones are developing. There are high hopes for using drones for rescue and medical purposes. Thanks to the commercialization of the drone market, emergency services receive professional tools that make their work faster, easier, and safer. Often, after a fire, earthquake, or collapse, it is difficult or even impossible to assess the level of damage and determine the necessary action based on external observations. Using drones equipped with multispectral observation heads is recommended to monitor the situation inside buildings. Unmanned aerial vehicles, transmitting live, high-definition images, e.g., from a collapsed building or mining collapse, minimize the risk and do not expose rescuers to unnecessary danger while simultaneously offering first aid.

In rescue operations, particular attention is paid to the time needed to provide help. Drones searching for injured persons often cannot carry additional cargo in the form of essential materials such as bandages, medications, or even water. This paper presents a system of underequipped "follower" drones tracking a "leader" drone. The leader is equipped with systems enabling the identification and avoidance of obstacles and the location of the injured, in order to immediately provide the necessary means of survival for the victims of disasters (Figure 1). An example application of a group of drones is a mobile crop-monitoring system employing several drones in a group carrying optical sensors [1]. A comprehensive review listing other multi-agent system applications was presented in [2].

The project aimed to investigate whether it is possible to send several drones into unknown surroundings and control them via UAV "leader" tracking using ArUco tags. This seems to be the simplest and least expensive method, providing a considerable number of resources necessary for survival to people trapped in hard-to-reach or dangerous environments without risking the health or lives of rescuers. The main innovation is the structure of the multi-agent group of UAVs, wherein raising the number of inexpensive followers increases neither the data exchange between actors nor the computational power requirements.

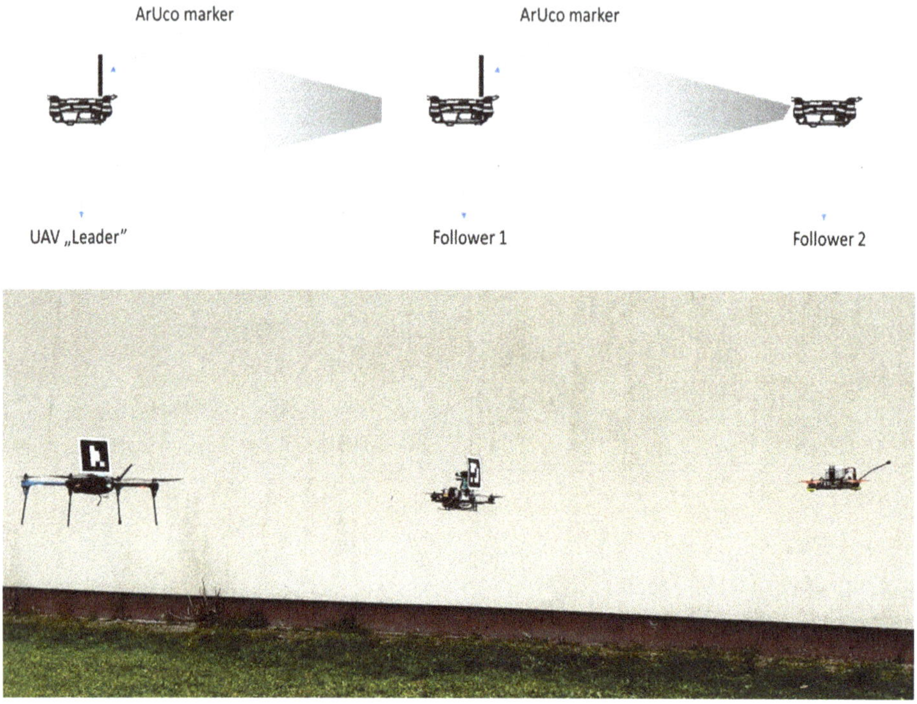

Figure 1. Assumptions of the designed system.

2. Related Works

Regarding autonomous flights, the research can be divided into two areas. The first typically focuses on improving and increasing the efficiency of control algorithms. The second deals with teaching UAVs that have previously been operated in manual mode to "learn by heart", recreating the required trajectory with corrections from external threat monitoring systems. Of course, there are many commercial structures wherein it is possible to use GPS. However, we are more interested in scenarios wherein the environment and surroundings through which one is to move are unknown, and it is impossible to estimate the position based on GNSS systems. Many works have indicated that solutions involving laser scanners, RGB-D sensors, or ultrasonic sensors mounted on the UAV board are fundamental and most effective. There are also solutions employing a synthetic aperture radar in addition to optical sensors [3].

It should be noted, however, that such solutions take up much space on the supporting structure of the drone, and their weight makes it impossible to take on additional cargo. Another approach is the simultaneous monitoring and remote control of each vehicle in the group [4]. Theoretically, it is possible to plan a trajectory for multiple drones in a constraint area [5]. However, in a natural environment, flights are only collision-free for a short time, because of unexpected disturbances. In the case we tested, i.e., small drones that can carry a small load, each gram of equipment is essential. According to many research results, the best solution is to track another UAV leader [6–11]. A multifunctional group of drones can be achieved by providing situational awareness by mounting sensors on the leader drone only [12] and a variety of mission sensors onboard group-member vehicles [13], e.g., to deliver enhanced scanning capabilities to infrastructure inspection systems [14] or build models of ancient sites [15].

A group of UAVs can be controlled by one of multiple formation strategies and techniques [16]; for rescue missions within disaster management systems, these include: virtual structure [17,18], consistency algorithm [19], behavior-based control [20], and leader–follower techniques. There are many advantages of using biological models, behavior-based formation control, and tracking, which give custom roles to particular agents [21–23]. However, these models can be adapted to swarms of vehicles and require constant agent-to-agent or agent-to-ground communication. In our case, we needed to bring a group of drones to a destination without putting additional tasks in their way. In the leader–follower formation, the followers can stay passive without any communication link. Various proposals exist for keeping the group together and moving forward in a leader–follower formation [24–27]. Many have introduced novel methods, algorithms, and ideas for controlling agents and the group. One of these, a linear consistency algorithm based on the leader–follower technique, was presented in [28]. It comprised a method of tracking the leader's position, heading, and speed. In [29], a virtual piloting leader algorithm was designed. It successfully coped with a leader failure but required high computational power onboard all the agents. Further, a distributed UAV formation control method was designed in [30]. However, the applied higher-order consistency theory required a preorganized communication topology.

A summary of the simulations and applications of the leader–follower technique highlights a significant disadvantage: a high dependence on the leader. Any failure of the leader affects the mission. Another problem is the substantial computational power requirement when the number of agents rises. In this work, we addressed the second issue as this project's main innovation, since the structure of the leader and followers does not change according to the number of agents in the group.

Visual passive markers are commonly used in every area of life. The visual pattern was first proposed in 1948 by two students, Bernard Silver and Norman Joseph Woodland. Due to the lack of appropriate technology, it was almost 30 years later that the barcode was used commercially and automatically.

Currently, markers are commonly used to mark goods, position machines in production, or read the position and orientation of medical devices during minimally invasive treatment, primarily due to their low production cost (Figure 2).

Figure 2. Eight existing marker systems. Top, from left to right: ARToolKit, Circular Data Matrix, RuneTag, ARToolKit Plus. Bottom, from left to right: QR code, barcode, ArUco, Cantag.

One of the best-known passive markers is a QR code [31]. A large amount of information can be stored under one tag, making it suitable for data transfer. In addition, they are resistant to damage, which means that depending on the percentage of damage to the entire code, it is possible to read at least part of the data contained in it.

Another type of tag is one used to track objects. ARTag and Artoolkit are characterized by the speed of detection and easy tracking, but they are not immune to changes in lighting. The ArUco marker was designed with similar technology. Its advantage is that it generates a small percentage of false-positive recognition, while the method of its encoding increases the effective recognition distance and the number of bit conversions. Some works indicate that these are the most effective candidates for use in AR [32,33]. ArUco markers proved to be solid reference points for mobile test beds [34] and stationary test benches [35]. The markers provided a reliable reference for position and attitude determination, which could be enhanced by setting the markers in three-dimensional patterns [36]. The accurate positioning of the markers allows their application as characteristic points to support simultaneous localization and mapping systems [37]. We applied ArUco markers as reference points in our previous research on a drone automatic landing system [38].

Researchers from the University of Michigan built a square-shaped AprilTag with a barcode, similar to QR codes and ArUco. A significant problem with their use seems to be the low recognition speed. Olson et al. proposed an updated version of AprilTag called AprilTag2, which resulted in increased detection speed [39]. Another modification was a circular ring marker that was tested for efficiency but lacked feature recognition [40].

The CircularTag, WhyCon, RUNE-Tag, and TRIP tags present a different approach. These round tags allow for high positioning accuracy but involve a complex, system-intensive detection algorithm [41–45].

3. Materials and Automatic Control Algorithm

3.1. Test System Design

A classic X-shaped quadrotor was used for the tests. A Raspberry Pi 4 minicomputer was used as the system for the implementation of the detection and tracking program. Due to the desire to reduce costs, a HAMA C400 in Full HD 1080p webcam with a 70° visual angle was responsible for recording the image. The design was based on our previous research experience with drone airframes and flight controllers [46].

In the initial part of the study, a test of the limit values of the system was carried out (Figure 3). The main parameters that were determined during the tests were the maximum effective detection distance of the marker (Tables 1 and 2), the maximum marker detection angle (change in marker position in the field of view of the camera), and the possibility of marker detection depending on its position in the camera's field of view at the horizontal level. The marker detection was checked 2 m from the camera, in order to represent a system working in limited space. The effective detection angle of the markers at the horizontal level was 38° (Figure 4).

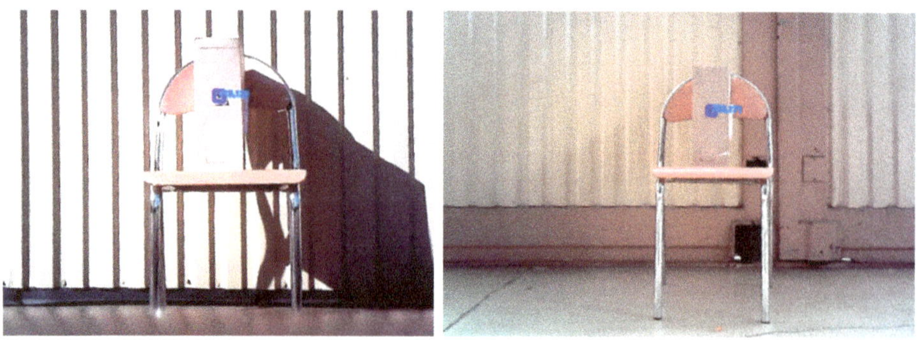

Figure 3. The marker identification rate versus distance.

Table 1. Measurement results at 770 lx light intensity.

Marker Size [cm]	Max Distance [cm]	Max Angle L [°]	Max Angle R [°]
3 × 3	174	38.5	30
6 × 6	320	45	43
12 × 12	586	50.5	56

Table 2. Measurement results at 63.7 klx light intensity.

Marker Size [cm]	Max Distance [cm]	Max Angle L [°]	Max Angle R [°]
3 × 3	132	40	30
6 × 6	257	46	44
12 × 12	574	52	57

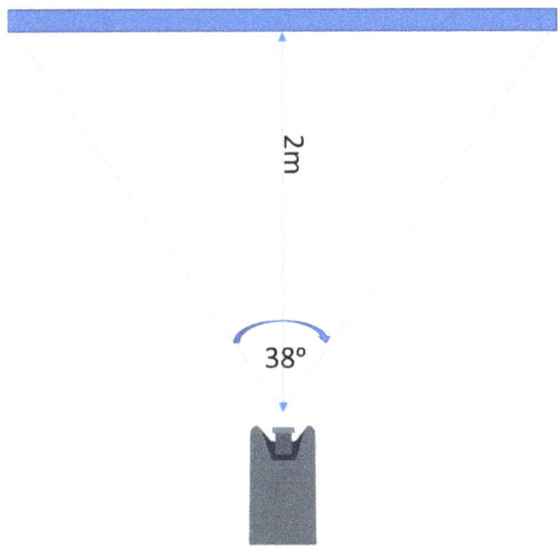

Figure 4. Effective camera field of view.

Three sizes of ArUco marker (3 cm × 3 cm, 6 cm × 6 cm, and 12 cm × 12 cm) were tested at different light intensities (770 lx and 63.7 klx).

Based on the obtained results, it was concluded that the attempts to track the markers in flight would be carried out only for markers with dimensions of 12 × 12 cm. This was due to the quick recognition of the marker and the ability to maintain tracking more easily at greater distances (maximum over 5.5 m) and with more pronounced changes in the leader's course (52 left and 57 right in clear weather conditions), allowing the drones to follow the leader on more complicated routes.

3.2. Marker Detection Algorithm

The primary purpose for which the Aruco markers were designed was to quickly determine the three-dimensional position of the camera relative to a single marker. Here, the Hamming coding algorithm was applied. The tag detection algorithm was optimized for a low false-detection rate. We could distinguish five stages of the detection process (Figure 5). After the entire algorithm is completed, the marker ID and the rotation and translation vectors are generated (to determine the position of the marker).

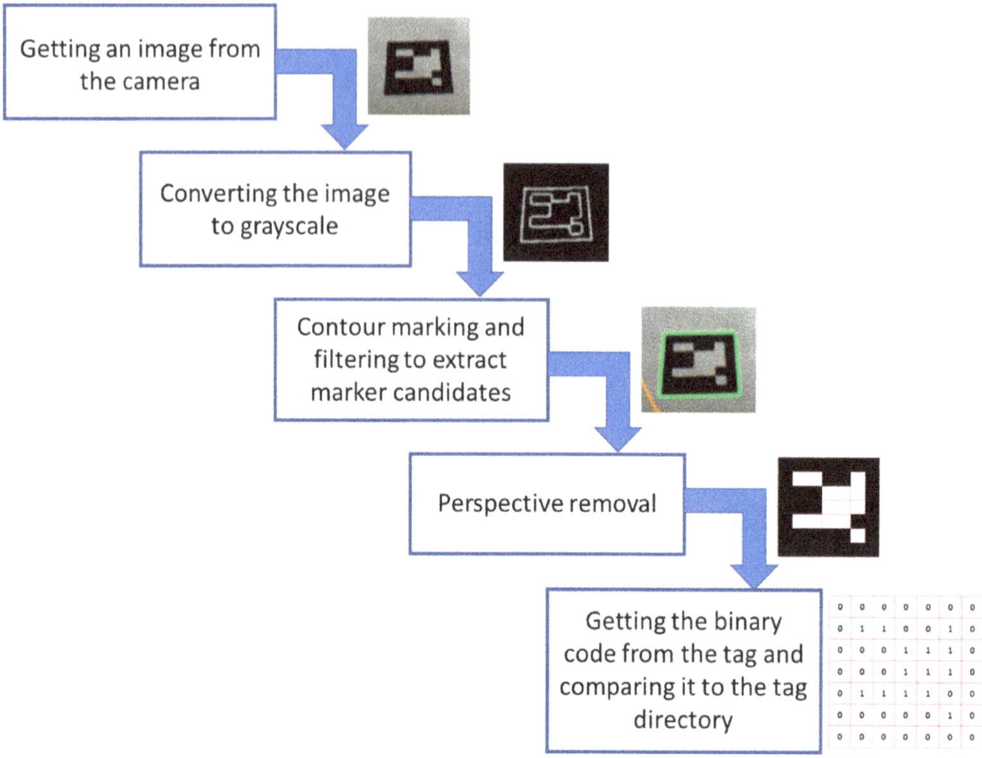

Figure 5. Marker detection process.

The Hamming encoding of the internal tag matrix provides one-bit error correction detection on each binary line. Unique tag identifiers are included in the directory, which can be placed in the ArUco module or created by the user. Once the tag ID is detected, the solvePnP (Perspective-n-Point) function is used for each corner of the tag. This function returns a list of all the possible solutions (a solution is a <rotation vector, translation vector> couple). Then, after solving the equation (Equation (1)), the 3D location of the point in is determined based on the 2D image.

$$s\begin{bmatrix} u \\ v \\ 1 \end{bmatrix} = \begin{pmatrix} f_x & \gamma & c_x \\ 0 & f_y & c_y \\ 0 & 0 & 1 \end{pmatrix} \begin{bmatrix} r_{11} & r_{12} & r_{13} & t_1 \\ r_{21} & r_{22} & r_{23} & t_2 \\ r_{31} & r_{32} & r_{33} & t_3 \end{bmatrix} \begin{bmatrix} X_G \\ Y_G \\ Z_G \\ 1 \end{bmatrix} \quad (1)$$

where the vector $\begin{bmatrix} u \\ v \\ 1 \end{bmatrix}$ describes the position of the point on the image (u, v); $\begin{pmatrix} f_x & \gamma & c_x \\ 0 & f_y & c_y \\ 0 & 0 & 1 \end{pmatrix}$ and $\begin{bmatrix} r_{11} & r_{12} & r_{13} & t_1 \\ r_{21} & r_{22} & r_{23} & t_2 \\ r_{31} & r_{32} & r_{33} & t_3 \end{bmatrix}$ stand for the optics parameters; and X_G, Y_G, and Z_G describe the point in space based on the camera reference system. After placing the plane over the four points, the algorithm determines rotation vectors and translation between the camera and marker planes.

3.3. Automatic Control Algorithm

The "leader" drone is tracked automatically. The algorithm applied works continuously in real time. By detecting the marker, the drone determines its center and locates it by taking into account the center of the field of view. On this basis, it determines the direction in which it must move and the speed it should maintain to avoid losing the marker from the field of view (Figure 6).

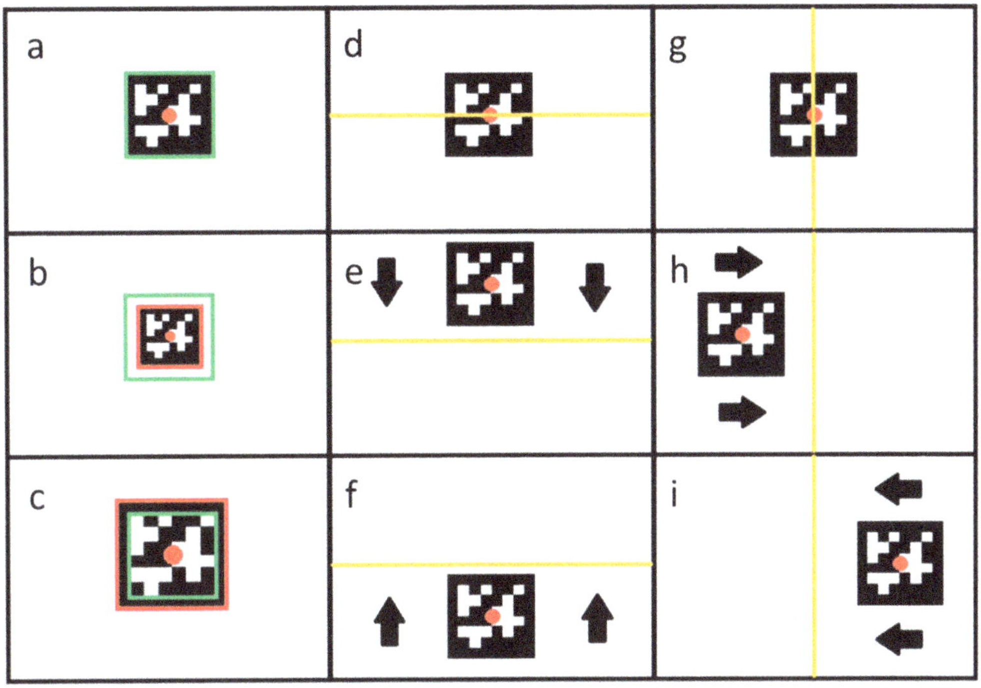

Figure 6. All conditions of the marker position. (**a**) desired distance—no action; (**b**) too far—move forward; (**c**) too close—move backward; (**d**) desired vertical position; (**e**) too low—move up; (**f**) too high—move down; (**g**) desired horizontal position; (**h**) too right—move left; (**i**) too left—move right.

The first column shows the drone's behavior in the case of forward and backward movement (movement along the *X*-axis). In this case, the determining factor for the drone's behavior is the detected marker (Figure 6a) size. If the detected marker covers a smaller area than the assumed area (Figure 6b), the drone receives the command "move forward", because the marker is too far away. Case (Figure 6c) describes a situation wherein the detected marker is too large, which means that the distance between the "leader" drone and the tracking drone is too small. Therefore, the drone receives the command to "move backward" and changes its position to obtain the optimal position.

The drone's behavior along the *Z*-axis is shown in the second column. The decisive factor for the command sent to the FC is the position of the indicator's center (Figure 6d). When the center of the marker is above the center of the field of view, the drone receives information that it is too high and must decrease the flight altitude (Figure 6e), while when the marker is below the center indicated in the image, the drone receives information that it is too low and must increase the flight altitude (Figure 6f).

The situation is similar for determining the required flight trajectory according to the *Y*-axis (Figure 6g). When the center of the marker is on the left side of the image center, the drone receives the command to "move to the right" (Figure 6h), while when the marker is on the right side of the image center, it receives the command "move to the left" (Figure 6i).

A PI controller was used to eliminate overshoots. The proportional and integral coefficients were determined and applied to the following algorithm:

In the first step, the difference between the marker area and the arithmetic average of the declared marker size range (*fberror*) in relation to close range (*Fbc*), away range (*Fba*), the declared max and min values of the distance between the drone and the marker (*fbrange*), and the marker area (Area) was calculated (Equation (2)).

In the second step, the difference between the marker area and the arithmetic average of the declared marker size range (*fberror*2) in relation to *Fb* back speed (*Fbb*), *Fb* forward speed (*Fbf*), and the declared maximum speed values (*fbspeedrange*) was calculated (Equation (3)).

Finally, a speed value (*Fbspeed*) in relation to the proportional term (*P*), the integral term (I), the previous loop error (*Pfberror*), *fberror*, and *fberror2* was calculated (Equation (4)).

In addition, to avoid exceeding the speed limits for the follower drone, we decided to protect it using a conditional statement (Equation (5)).

$$fberror = area - \frac{fbc + fba}{2} \tag{2}$$

$$fberror2 = \frac{(fberror - fbc) * (fbf - fbb)}{fba - fbc} + fbb \tag{3}$$

$$fbspeed = \frac{P * fberror2 + I * (fberror2 - pfberror)}{100} \tag{4}$$

$$fbspeed = \begin{cases} -2 & fbspeed < -2 \\ fbspeed & fbspeed \in [-2,\ 2] \\ 2 & fbspeed > 2 \end{cases} \tag{5}$$

The program code performing the controller function is shown in detail in Figure 7.

```
fbrange = [400,1600]

fbspeedrange = [– 200, 200]
    fberror = area – (fbrange[0] + fbrange[1]) // 2
    fberror2 = (fberror – fbrange[0]) / (fbrange[1] – fbrange[0]) * (fbspeedrange[1] –fbspeedrange[0]) + \
fbspeedrange[0]
    fbspeed = pid[0] * fberror2 + pid[1] * (fberror2 – pfbError)
    fbspeed = int(np.clip(fbspeed, fbspeedrange[0], fbspeedrange[1]))
    fbspeed = round(fbspeed/100,2)

    pfbError = fberror2
```

Figure 7. Programmatic implementation of the control algorithm.

4. Results

Due to the desire to use the reconnaissance drone tracking system in unfamiliar surroundings, we did not consider the speed of following the "leader" drone. The main element of the test was to determine the forward speeds at which the flight would be smooth without losing the marker. For this purpose, the ArUco marker was installed on an IRIS 3DR UAV. The IRIS 3DR could plan the mission's route and the speed of movement. The measurements were conducted for the three selected speeds using a 12 × 12 cm marker, which had the highest recognizability (Figure 8).

Figure 8. Flight in a straight line behind the leader. The bottom right image was taken by the camera, showing the detected marker.

The research was divided into two parts. The first study was designed to determine the minimum corridor necessary for a safe flight. The corridor was calculated by having the drones repeatedly follow the leader moving at a constant speed in a straight line. The speeds were selected based on the limitations of the data processing steps for routing and decision making by the leader drone.

The determined properties were superimposed on a single chart, while the initial position of the leader was compared to the location at which the tracking drones started the tracking process to facilitate the route analysis of the individual followers (Figure 9).

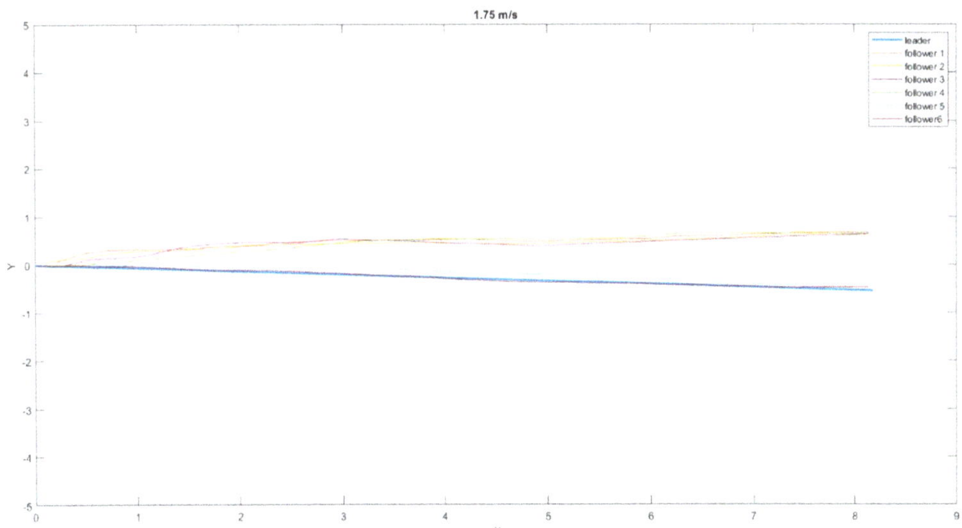

(**a**)

Figure 9. *Cont.*

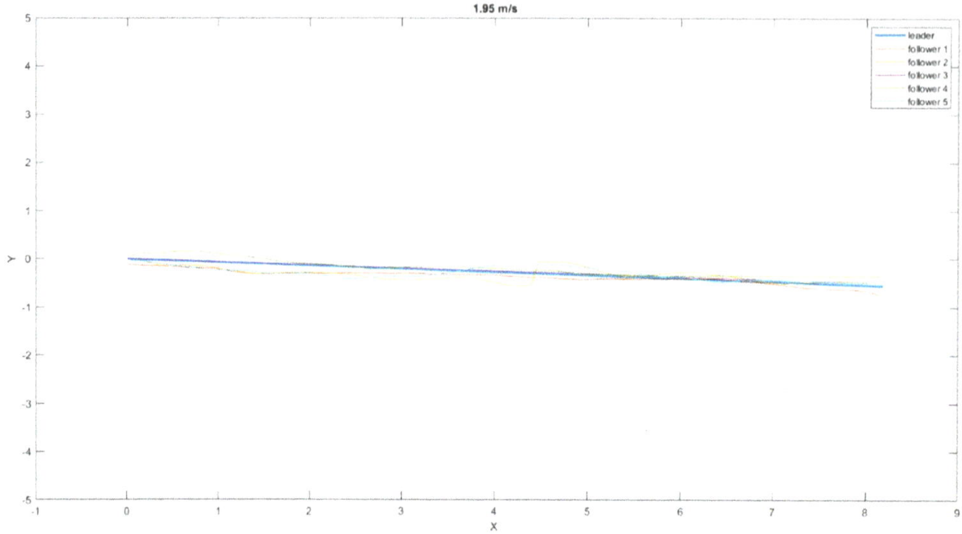

(b)

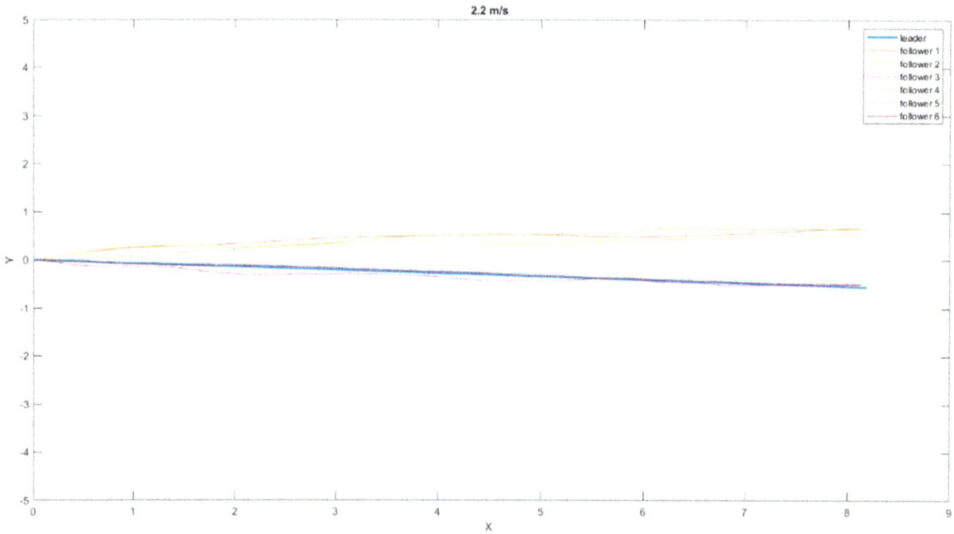

(c)

Figure 9. Position of the drones relative to the leader in the XY plane at different speeds: (**a**) 1.75 m/s; (**b**) 1.95 m/s; (**c**) 2.2 m/s.

The results were obtained by subtracting each axis's leader and follower route parameters. The data obtained this way were averaged using the arithmetic mean as the best approximation of the actual value. In contrast, to calculate the average "dispersion" of individual results around the mean value, the standard deviation from the mean was calculated with the following Equations (6)–(8).

$$\overline{X} = \frac{\sum_{i=1}^{k}\left(\left|x_{Li} - x_{F_i}\right|\right)}{k} \quad (6)$$

$$\overline{Y} = \frac{\sum_{i=1}^{k}(|y_{Li} - y_{F_i}|)}{k} \quad (7)$$

$$\sigma = \frac{\sum_{i=1}^{k}(x_i - \mu)^2}{N} \quad (8)$$

where $|x_{Li} - x_{F_i}|$ and $|y_{Li} - y_{F_i}|$ are the absolute values of the distance between the leader and the follower in a given plane.

At the specified speeds, no tracking loss of the ArUco tag was registered, and the leader's tracking was smooth. Table 3 shows values for the mean distance to the marker on the XY plane and the standard deviations at a speed of 1.75 m/s.

Table 3. The average distance and standard deviation between the follower and leader routes at a speed of 1.75 m/s.

	Follower 1	Follower 2	Follower 3	Follower 4	Follower 5	Follower 6
Arithmetic average (m)	0.7626	0.7181	0.7087	0.7243	0.1868	0.1341
Standard deviation (m)	0.2785	0.2907	0.2807	0.3680	0.0996	0.0776

Rejecting the last two measurements, which were much better than the others, and averaging the obtained results, the minimum safe corridor that would allow the drones to follow the leader had a diameter of 0.7284 m, with an SD of 0.3045 m.

In the case of measurements at 1.95 m/s, the average value of the safe corridor was lower and amounted to a surprising 0.1326 m, with an SD of 0.053 m. The distance values of the individual drones from the leader in the XY plane are presented in Table 4. Only five followers were included in this dataset, because the data from one flight were corrupted.

Table 4. The average distance and standard deviation between the follower and leader routes at a speed of 1.95 m/s.

	Follower 1	Follower 2	Follower 3	Follower 4	Follower 5
Arithmetic average (m)	0.1379	0.1369	0.0499	0.1896	0.1489
Standard deviation (m)	0.039	0.0696	0.0171	0.0798	0.0549

Comparable results to those obtained at 1.75 m/s can be seen in the third measurement at 2.2 m/s. The average safe corridor value was 0.7025 m, with an SD of 0.3044. The distance values of the individual drones from the leader in the XY plane are presented in Table 5.

Table 5. The average distance and standard deviation between the follower and leader routes at a speed of 2.2 m/s.

	Follower 1	Follower 2	Follower 3	Follower 4	Follower 5	Follower 6
Arithmetic average (m)	0.7223	0.6343	0.0837	0.7511	0.0675	0.1830
Standard deviation (m)	0.2929	0.2622	0.0452	0.3582	0.0283	0.2008

In the next step, we decided to examine how the tracking drones behaved when following the leader along the programmed route. A route in the form of a rectangle with sides of 4 m and 2.5 m was chosen. The leader's set speeds were 1.7 m/s, 2 m/s, and 2.75 m/s (Figure 10).

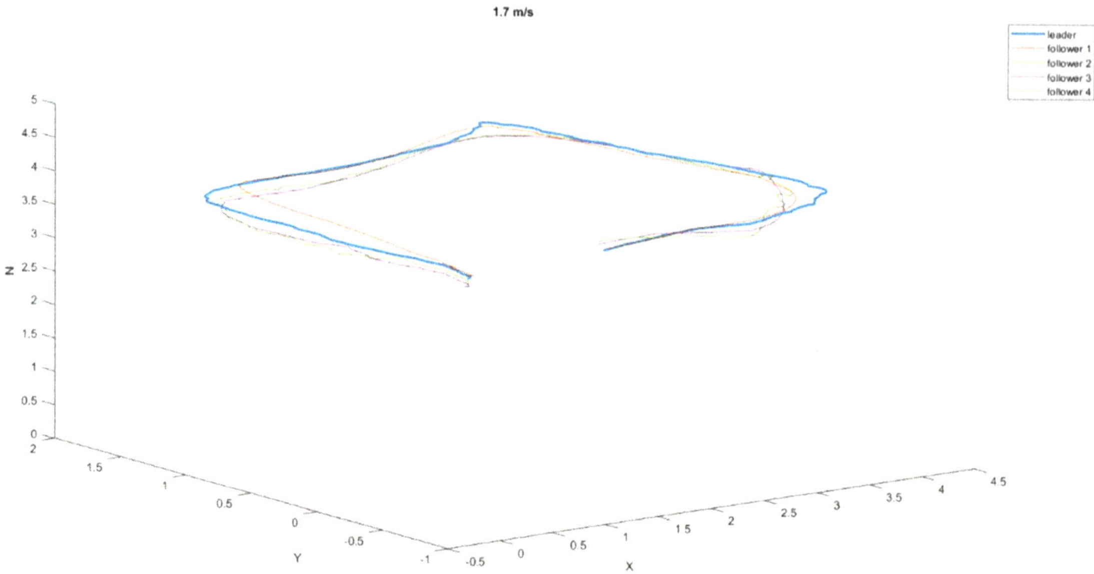

(**a**)

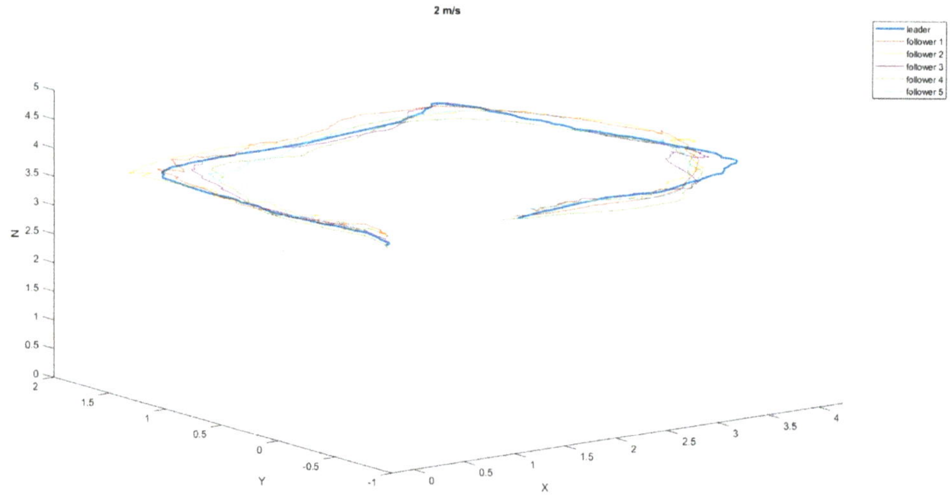

(**b**)

Figure 10. *Cont.*

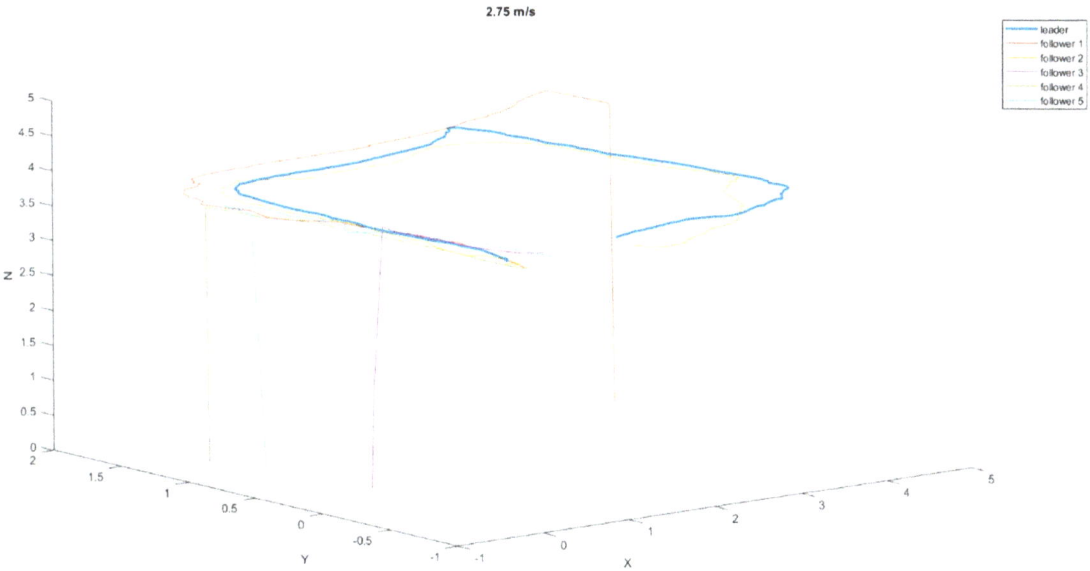

(c)

Figure 10. The 3D position of the drones relative to the leader at different speeds during flight around the perimeter of the rectangle: (**a**) 1.7 m/s; (**b**) 2 m/s; (**c**) 275 m/s.

It can be noticed in the attached graphs that at the speeds of 1.7 m/s and 2 m/s, the tracking drones did not lose the leader over the entire route, while at the speed of 2.75 m/s, four out of five tracking attempts ended the marker being lost from sight (Table 6).

Table 6. The average distance and standard deviation between the follower and leader routes at a speed of 1.7 m/s during flight around the perimeter of the rectangle.

	Follower 1	Follower 2	Follower 3	Follower 4
Arithmetic average [m]	0.1655	0.1982	0.1896	0.2312
Standard deviation [m]	0.1113	0.1160	0.1126	0.0934

In the case of flights at a speed of 1.7 m/s, the followers' routes were closest to the leader's route (average distance 0.1948 m, SD 0.1114 m). Satisfactory results were also achieved at a speed of 2 m/s. According to Table 7, all followers moved at similar distances from the leader's route. The value of the average safe corridor, in this case, was 0.2418 m, and the SD was 0.1475.

Table 7. The average distance and standard deviation between the follower and leader routes at a speed of 2 m/s in flight around the perimeter of the rectangle.

	Follower 1	Follower 2	Follower 3	Follower 4	Follower 5
Arithmetic average (m)	0.2334	0.2301	0.2276	0.2642	0.2537
Standard deviation (m)	0.1109	0.1129	0.1506	0.1827	0.1802

Figure 9c shows tracking blackouts for followers 1, 3, 4, and 5, which ended the mission early (for safety reasons, a landing procedure was established when the marker was lost). Due to only one drone completing the task, the mean values and standard deviations were not counted. In addition, it was recognized that the leader's flight speed of 2.75 m/s in open space disqualified the possibility of using such speeds in missions.

5. Discussion

Preliminary tests determined the boundary conditions at which the system operated satisfactorily. The best recognition results for ArUco markers in terms of the distance from the camera were obtained at the marker size of 12 × 12 cm (5.86 m), while for the sizes of 6 × 6 cm and 3 × 3 cm, detection was possible at distances of 3.2 m (45% less than the best result) and 1.74 m (70% less than the best result), respectively. In addition, the best angular recognition results were also achieved for the 12 × 12 cm marker. The achieved marker deflection angles, at which the marker was still detectable, of 50.5° left and 56° right exceeded the recognition capabilities of the system for the 6 × 6 cm and 3 × 3 cm markers by 11.5% and 22.8% (46° left and 44° right) and 23.1% and 47.4% (40° left and 30° right), respectively. The results of the tests carried out under the conditions of a sunny day (63.7 klx) did not differ significantly from those of the tests carried out under shaded conditions (770 lx). The only significant differences were observed in the marker recognition distance, which increased by an average of 15% with a lower light intensity. In addition, the maximum angle of view of the camera at which marker recognition was still possible was set at 38°.

Our major research task was to determine the flight parameters at which the tracking process would be continuous and smooth while maintaining the flight trajectory as close as possible to that set by the leader. Two scenarios were provided for in the research. The first, i.e., a straight flight behind the leader at a constant speed, was used to optimize the tracking system and determine the optimal speed of the leader. Six repetitions of the flight behind the leader were carried out for the first speed adopted for the tests—1.75 m/s. The fifth and sixth attempts achieved the best results, with an average distance of 0.1868 m and 0.1341 m, respectively, from the leader's flight trajectory on the 8 m planned route. The results from these two measurements were so favorable (78% lower than the rest of the average results obtained in this experiment) that we decided not to take them into account in the tests determining the average safe corridor that must be provided for the follower to complete the mission. Such a discrepancy in the results could have been due to the ideal weather conditions (windless day) in which these two flights were performed. The flights of the other four followers were similar to each other. The average distances from the leader's flight trajectory were 0.7626 m, 0.7181 m, 0.7087 m, and 0.7243 m, respectively. In the case of flights at a speed of 1.95 m/s, particularly satisfactory results were obtained, with an average distance from the leader's trajectory of 0.1326 m. The resulting distance was less than 3 cm in the consecutive tests with a leader flight speed of 2.2 m/s and 1.75 m/s.

In the second scenario, flights were carried out along a planned rectangular route. This test was performed in order to check the traceability of the tag in the proposed system. The leader's speeds were pre-determined for the tests, just as in the first part of the study. Thus, the leader was moving at speeds of 1.7 m/s, 2 m/s, and 2.75 m/s. In the case of the first two speeds, the average distances from the leader's trajectory were similar (0.1948 m for the speed of 1.7 m/s and 0.2418 m for 2 m/s), while the third speed turned out to be too high for the followers to keep up with the leader. Out of five attempts, only one was successful, and the follower reached the route's endpoint with an average distance from the leader's trajectory of 0.22 m.

According to the results of the conducted research, it can be assumed that rescue missions carried out based on the proposed system could be successful. The obtained results suggest that the organization of such tasks in an automatic system is realistic and, most importantly, effective. Of course, there are some limitations to the use of such a procedure. The main problem is the aerodynamic drag surface of the ArUco marker. Despite good tracking results, difficulties resulting from strong gusts of wind (which cannot be ruled out in open-air operations) substantially reduced the usefulness of the entire system. In closed rooms, the detection of all markers at no more than 150 cm from the "leader" UAV was achieved with 100% efficiency, while the detection of the same markers in an open space under windy weather conditions was occasionally unsuccessful, and a new procedure for finding the marker was required. In addition, it seems reasonable that a communication system should be created for the leader, connecting it to a tracking drone to avoid losing the marker. In such a case, the leader could receive information in the form of a "STOP" command, which would remain until the follower rediscovered the marker.

The great advantage of the system is that it can move freely in limited spaces where it is impossible to use GNSS navigation systems. The achieved tracking speeds corresponded to the movement of drones in an unknown space with the continuous analysis of the surrounding image. High speeds are not required in such situations, but high maneuverability is expected, which is ensured using a multi-rotor platform.

Another advantage of the proposed solution is the possibility of cascading drones depending on the amount and weight of the equipment needing to be transported. The only modification that would have to be made is that each tracking drone would have to be equipped with an ArUco marker and would become a "guide" for the next tracking drone.

The flight duration for this type of task is related to the battery used. If an extended flight time is required, a battery with a larger capacity must be used. However, it should be remembered that as the power reserve of batteries increases, their weight also increases, which is crucial considering the possibility of transporting equipment necessary to save lives and protect health.

In further studies on this project, we plan to replace the ArUco markers with infrared diodes. With such a modification, drones could track the leader even in conditions without lighting. In addition, it would eliminate problems resulting from the resistance to movement set by the marker. Another option to improve the system is to mount the camera on a gimbal placed on the drone. The proposed solution would reduce the probability of losing the tracked marker resulting from a sudden direction change by the leader.

Additionally, tests should be carried out in closed rooms, for which this system was also designed, to verify the system. In this way, we would limit the impact of external factors (such as gusts of wind, precipitation, or dust) on the entire system. Determining the characteristics of the follower and leader movement in closed rooms would contribute to creating a list of minimum requirements that must be met to use the system safely and effectively in rescue missions.

6. Conclusions

The proposed system could prove effective in the assumed scenarios of rescue missions. Our research found that its use in closed spaces and outdoors was possible and practical. The system had certain limitations, such as the impossibility of its use in intense winds or during missions conducted in complete darkness. The system's capabilities could be increased, and it could be used in the dark. Using such a system would substantially reduce the cost of multiple-vehicle drone operations, but the most significant advantage of this solution is its minimization of the threat to the lives and health of rescuers who would otherwise have to perform the mission independently. Its main benefit is the innovative way of organizing the group of robots within a leader–follower formation without active communication between agents in the group or between the agent and the ground control station. This results in a considerably lower cost of expanding the group with further agents, which we identified as one of the primary drawbacks of leader–follower formations. Moreover, the system can be used immediately, without prior preparation, saving the time usually needed to perform reconnaissance and decide on how to carry out a mission.

Author Contributions: Conceptualization, K.W. and P.W.; methodology, K.W. and P.W.; software, P.W.; validation, K.W. and P.W.; formal analysis, K.W. and P.W.; investigation, K.W. and P.W.; resources, P.W.; data curation, K.W.; writing—original draft preparation, K.W. and P.W.; writing—review and editing, K.W. and P.W.; visualization, P.W.; supervision, K.W.; project administration, K.W. All authors have read and agreed to the published version of the manuscript.

Funding: This research received no external funding.

Institutional Review Board Statement: Not applicable.

Informed Consent Statement: Not applicable.

Data Availability Statement: Not applicable.

Acknowledgments: The authors thank Adam Marut, Jakub Kochan, and Jakub Djabin for their assistance and contribution to developing the system described in this work.

Conflicts of Interest: The authors declare no conflict of interest.

References

1. Lee, H.-S.; Shin, B.-S.; Thomasson, J.A.; Wang, T.; Zhang, Z.; Han, X. Development of Multiple UAV Collaborative Driving Systems for Improving Field Phenotyping. *Sensors* **2022**, *22*, 1423. [CrossRef] [PubMed]
2. Rubio, F.; Valero, F.; Llopis-Albert, C. A review of mobile robots: Concepts, methods, theoretical framework, and applications. *Int. J. Adv. Robot. Syst.* **2019**, *16*, 172988141983959. [CrossRef]
3. Siemiatkowska, B.; Stecz, W. A Framework for Planning and Execution of Drone Swarm Missions in a Hostile Environment. *Sensors* **2021**, *21*, 4150. [CrossRef]
4. Flores Peña, P.; Luna, M.A.; Ale Isaac, M.S.; Ragab, A.R.; Elmenshawy, K.; Martín Gómez, D.; Campoy, P.; Molina, M. A Proposed System for Multi-UAVs in Remote Sensing Operations. *Sensors* **2022**, *22*, 9180. [CrossRef] [PubMed]
5. Sabetghadam, B.; Cunha, R.; Pascoal, A. A Distributed Algorithm for Real-Time Multi-Drone Collision-Free Trajectory Replanning. *Sensors* **2022**, *22*, 1855. [CrossRef]
6. Grzonka, S.; Grisetti, G.; Burgard, W. Towards a navigation system for autonomous indoor flying. In Proceedings of the IEEE International Conference on Robotics and Automation (ICRA), Kobe, Japan, 12–17 May 2009.
7. Huang, A.S.; Bachrach, A.; Henry, P.; Krainin, M.; Maturana, D.; Fox, D.; Roy, N. Visual odometry and mapping for autonomous flight using an RGB-D camera. In Proceedings of the IEEE International Symposium of Robotics Research (ISRR), Karon Beach, Thailand, 7–11 December 2011.
8. Bylow, E.; Sturm, J.; Kerl, C.; Kahl, F.; Cremers, D. Real-time camera tracking and 3D reconstruction using signed distance functions. In Proceedings of the Robotics: Science and Systems (RSS), Berlin, Germany, 24–28 June 2013.
9. Achtelik, M.; Bachrach, A.; He, R.; Prentice, S.; Roy, N. Stereo vision and laser odometry for autonomous helicopters in GPS-denied indoor environments. In Proceedings of the SPIE Unmanned Systems Technology XI, Orlando, FL, USA, 17–20 March 2009.
10. Schmid, K.; Ruess, F.; Suppa, M.; Burschka, D. State estimation for highly dynamic flying systems using key frame odometry with varying time delays. In Proceedings of the IEEE International Conference on Intelligent Robots and Systems, Vilamoura-Algarve, Portugal, 7–12 October 2012.
11. Grabe, V.; Bulthoff, H.H.; Giordano, P. R Robust optical flow based self-motion estimation for a quadrotor UAV. In Proceedings of the IEEE International Conference on Intelligent Robots and Systems, Vilamoura-Algarve, Portugal, 7–12 October 2012.
12. Balestrieri, E.; Daponte, P.; De Vito, L.; Picariello, F.; Tudosa, I. Sensors and Measurements for UAV Safety: An Overview. *Sensors* **2021**, *21*, 8253. [CrossRef]
13. Balestrieri, E.; Daponte, P.; De Vito, L.; Lamonaca, F. Sensors and Measurements for Unmanned Systems: An Overview. *Sensors* **2021**, *21*, 1518. [CrossRef]
14. Potenza, F.; Rinaldi, C.; Ottaviano, E.; Gattulli, V. A robotics and computer-aided procedure for defect evaluation in bridge inspection. *J. Civil Struct. Health Monit.* **2020**, *10*, 471–484. [CrossRef]
15. Balestrieri, E.; Daponte, P.; De Vito, L.; Picariello, F.; Tudosa, I. Guidelines for an Unmanned Aerial Vehicle-Based Measurement Instrument Design. *IEEE Instrum. Meas. Mag.* **2021**, *24*, 89–95. [CrossRef]
16. Khan, A.; Gupta, S.; Gupta, S.K. Cooperative Control between Multi-UAVs for Maximum Coverage in Disaster Management: Review and Proposed Model. In Proceedings of the 2022 2nd International Conference on Computing and Information Technology (ICCIT), Tabuk, Saudi Arabia, 25–27 January 2022; pp. 271–277.
17. Askari, A.; Mortazavi, M.; Talebi, H.A. UAV Formation Control via the Virtual Structure Approach. *J. Aerosp. Eng.* **2015**, *28*, 04014047. [CrossRef]
18. Wen, Y.J. Design and Optimization of Wing Structure for a Fixed-Wing Unmanned Aerial Vehicle (UAV). *Mod. Mech. Eng.* **2018**, *8*, 2164–2165.
19. Milena, R.; Yannis, D.; Anđelija, M. Identification of the factors affecting the consistency of DBS formation via experimental design and image processing methodology. *Microchem. J.* **2019**, *145*, 1003–1010.
20. Yang, J.; You, X.H.; Wu, G.X.; Mohammad, M.H.; Ahmad, A.J. Application of reinforcement learning in UAV cluster task scheduling. *Future Gener. Comput. Syst.* **2019**, *95*, 140–148.
21. Madden, J.D.; Arkin, R.C.; MacNulty, D.R. Multi-robot system based on model of wolf hunting behavior to emulate wolf and elk interactions. In Proceedings of the 2010 IEEE International Conference on Robotics and Biomimetics, Tianjin, China, 14–18 December 2010; IEEE: New York, NY, USA, 2010; pp. 1043–1050.
22. Xie, Y.; Han, L.; Dong, X.; Li, Q.; Ren, Z. Bio-inspired adaptive formation tracking control for swarm systems with application to UAV swarm systems. *Neurocomputing* **2021**, *453*, 272–285. [CrossRef]
23. Zhang, S.; Zhou, Y.; Li, Z.; Pan, W. Grey wolf optimizer for unmanned combat aerial vehicle path planning. *Adv. Eng. Softw.* **2016**, *99*, 121–136. [CrossRef]

24. Azam, M.A.; Mittelmann, H.D.; Ragi, S. UAV Formation Shape Control via Decentralized Markov Decision Processes. *Algorithms* **2021**, *14*, 91. [CrossRef]
25. Shi, L.; Zhao, H.; Zhang, X. Research on Obstacle Avoidance Control Strategy of Networked Systems Based on Leader-Follower Formation Tracking. In Proceedings of the 2018 Chinese Intelligent Systems Conference, Wenzhou, China, 13–14 October 2018; Lecture Notes in Electrical Engineering. Springer: Singapore, 2019; p. 529.
26. Antoine, A.K.; De Johan, R. Cadherin mechano transduction in leader-follower cell specification during collective migration. *Exp. Cell Res.* **2019**, *376*, 86–91.
27. Hori, A.; Fukushima, M. Gauss–Seidel Method for Multi-leader–follower Games. *J. Optim. Theory Appl.* **2019**, *180*, 651–670. [CrossRef]
28. Yu, J.; Yan, C.; Huang, M. Research of consistency problem for quadrotor UAV system with leader-follower. In Proceedings of the Chinese Automation Congress (CAC 2019), Hangzhou, China, 22–24 November 2019; pp. 616–621.
29. Chen, J.M.; Wu, F.L.; Geng, C.H.; Xu, S. Consensus-based formation control approach for quadrotor UAVs. *Aero Weapon.* **2017**, *6*, 25–31.
30. Wang, P.; Yao, P.Y. Method of distributed UAVs formation with time-delay. *Comput. Meas. Control* **2016**, *24*, 181–187.
31. Lay, K.; Zhou, M. Perspective Projection for Decoding of QR Codes Posted on Cylinders. In Proceedings of the IEEE International Conference on Signal and Image Processing Applications (ICSIPA), Kuching, Malaysia, 12–14 September 2017; pp. 39–42.
32. Garrido-Jurado, S.; Munoz-Salinas, R.; Madrid-Cuevas, F.; Marin-Jimenez, M. Automatic generation and detection of highly reliable fiducial markers under occlusion. *Pattern Recognit.* **2014**, *47*, 2280–2292. [CrossRef]
33. Kam, H.; Yu, Y.; Wong, K. An Improvement on ArUco Marker for Pose Tracking Using Kalman Filter. In Proceedings of the 2018 19th IEEE/ACIS International Conference on Software Engineering, Artificial Intelligence, Networking and Parallel/Distributed Computing (SNPD), Busan, Korea, 27–29 June 2018; pp. 65–69.
34. Guo, X.; Wang, Z.; Zhou, W.; Zhang, Z. Research on Design, Calibration and Real-Time Image Expansion Technology of Unmanned System Variable-Scale Panoramic Vision System. *Sensors* **2021**, *21*, 4708. [CrossRef] [PubMed]
35. Aalerud, A.; Dybedal, J.; Hovland, G. Automatic Calibration of an Industrial RGB-D Camera Network Using Retroreflective Fiducial Markers. *Sensors* **2019**, *19*, 1561. [CrossRef]
36. Oščádal, P.; Heczko, D.; Vysocký, A.; Mlotek, J.; Novák, P.; Virgala, I.; Sukop, M.; Bobovský, Z. Improved Pose Estimation of Aruco Tags Using a Novel 3D Placement Strategy. *Sensors* **2020**, *20*, 4825. [CrossRef] [PubMed]
37. Poulose, A.; Han, D.S. Hybrid Indoor Localization Using IMU Sensors and Smartphone Camera. *Sensors* **2019**, *19*, 5084. [CrossRef] [PubMed]
38. Marut, A.; Wojtowicz, K.; Falkowski, K. ArUco markers pose estimation in UAV landing aid system. In Proceedings of the 2019 IEEE 5th International Workshop on Metrology for AeroSpace (MetroAeroSpace), Turin, Italy, 19–21 June 2019; pp. 261–266.
39. Wang, J.; Olson, E. Apriltag 2: Efficient and robust fiducial detection. In Proceedings of the 2016 IEEE/RSJ International Conference on Intelligent Robots and Systems (IROS), Daejeon, Korea, 9–14 October 2016; pp. 4193–4198.
40. Yu, J.; Jiang, W.; Luo, Z.; Yang, L. Application of a Vision-Based Single Target on Robot Positioning System. *Sensors* **2021**, *21*, 1829. [CrossRef]
41. Zhang, G.; Patricio, V.; Panagiotis, T.; Dae-Min, C. Efficient Closed-Loop Detection and Pose Estimation for Vision-Only Relative Localization in Space with A Cooperative Target. In Proceedings of the AIAA Space Conference and Exposition, San Diego, CA, USA, 4–7 August 2014.
42. Gatrell, L.; Hoff, W.; Sklair, C. Robust image features: Concentric contrasting circles and their image extraction. In Proceedings of the SPIE 1612, Cooperative Intelligent Robotics in Space II, Bellingham, WA, USA, 12–14 November 1991.
43. Edwards, M.; Hayes, M.; Green, R. High-accuracy Fiducial Markers for Ground Truth. In Proceedings of the International Conference on Image and Vision Computing New Zealand (IVCNZ), Palmerston North, New Zealand, 21–22 November 2016; pp. 261–266.
44. Krajnik, T.; Nitsche, M.; Faigl, J.; Vaněk, P.; Saska, M.; Přeučil, L.; Duckett, T.; Mejail, M. A Practical Multirobot Localization System. *J. Intell. Robot. Syst.* **2014**, *76*, 539–562. [CrossRef]
45. Bergamasco, F.; Albareli, A.; Emanuele, R.; Torsello, A. RUNE-Tag: A High Accuracy Fiducial Marker with Strong Occlusion Resilience. In Proceedings of the IEEE Conference on Computer Vision and Pattern Recognition (CVPR), Colorado Springs, CO, USA, 20–25 June 2011; pp. 113–120.
46. Waliszkiewicz, M.; Wojtowicz, K.; Rochala, Z.; Balestrieri, E. The Design and Implementation of a Custom Platform for the Experimental Tuning of a Quadcopter Controller. *Sensors* **2020**, *20*, 1940. [CrossRef]

sensors

MDPI

Article

Spherical Wrist Manipulator Local Planner for Redundant Tasks in Collaborative Environments

Marcello Chiurazzi [1,2,*], Joan Ortega Alcaide [1,2], Alessandro Diodato [1,2], Arianna Menciassi [1,2] and Gastone Ciuti [1,2]

[1] The BioRobotics Institute, Scuola Superiore Sant'Anna, 56127 Pisa, Italy
[2] Department of Excellence in Robotics and AI, Scuola Superiore Sant'Anna, 56127 Pisa, Italy
* Correspondence: marcello.chiurazzi@santannapisa.it; Tel.: +39-3356979421

Abstract: Standard industrial robotic manipulators use well-established high performing technologies. However, such manipulators do not guarantee a safe Human–Robot Interaction (HRI), limiting their usage in industrial and medical applications. This paper proposes a novel local path planner for spherical wrist manipulators to control the execution of tasks where the manipulator number of joints is redundant. Such redundancy is used to optimize robot motion and dexterity. We present an intuitive parametrization of the end-effector (EE) angular motion, which decouples the rotation of the third joint of the wrist from the rest of the angular motions. Manipulator EE motion is controlled through a decentralized linear system with closed-loop architecture. The local planner integrates a novel collision avoidance strategy based on a potential repulsive vector applied to the EE. Contrary to classic potential field approaches, the collision avoidance algorithm considers the entire manipulator surface, enhancing human safety. The local path planner is simulated in three generic scenarios: (i) following a periodic reference, (ii) a random sequence of step signal references, and (iii) avoiding instantly introduced obstacles. Time and frequency domain analysis demonstrated that the developed planner, aside from better parametrizing redundant tasks, is capable of successfully executing the simulated paths (max error = 0.25°) and avoiding obstacles.

Keywords: robotics control; local path planner; task redundancy; collision avoidance strategy; human–robot interaction

Citation: Chiurazzi, M.; Alcaide, J.O.; Diodato, A.; Menciassi, A.; Ciuti, G. Spherical Wrist Manipulator Local Planner for Redundant Tasks in Collaborative Environments. *Sensors* **2023**, *23*, 677. https://doi.org/10.3390/s23020677

Academic Editors: Luige Vladareanu, Hongnian Yu, Hongbo Wang and Yongfei Feng

Received: 2 November 2022
Revised: 21 December 2022
Accepted: 31 December 2022
Published: 6 January 2023

1. Introduction

Industrial robotic manipulators use well-established technologies that guarantee high performances in terms of velocity and accuracy. Indeed, typical values of repeatability and joint velocity for industrial manipulators are approximately 0.01 mm and 300°/s, respectively [1]. Despite the clear capabilities of industrial robots, their usage is still very much limited to applications where their workspace is exclusive and humans' presence is forbidden. The standard regulatory ISO 10218-1/2:2011 [2] and ISO/TS 15066:2016 [3] provide requirements, specifications, and guidelines to ensure safety for industrial and collaborative robotic applications and work environments. Nowadays, most industrial robots work inside fences that physically limit the access of humans into the workspace. However, certain tasks such as robotic surgery require the robot to share its workspace with humans. The need for physically close interaction between humans and machines has motivated many groups, both in academia and industry, to study new strategies for safe Human–Robot Interaction (HRI) [4,5]; the followed strategies for a safe HRI can be categorized as post-contact or pre-contact measures.

Post-contact safety measures serve to mitigate the effects of a collision once it has already occurred. Post-contact measures include soft and smooth designs of any potential contact points on the robot structure and the use of integrated sensing capabilities measuring the intensity of such impacts [6,7]; post-contact measures are used to minimize the impact of a collision but also intentional contacts [8,9].

On the other hand, pre-contact strategies use perceptive systems to provide online environment information to the robotic manipulator to generate collision-free trajectories. Path planning algorithms can be classified into: (i) global path planning algorithms, and (ii) local path planning algorithms. Global path planning algorithms solve an optimization problem searching for a free-collision path from an initial configuration to the desired one [10]. Global planners are usually able to find the optimal path in a finite amount of time; however, their computational time requirements can be a limiting factor in dynamic environments. On the other hand, local planners provide a local trajectory to the robotic arm based on the final goal and the local environment information at a certain time. Local planners require much less computational time to be executed and generally cannot guarantee that the generated trajectories will reach the final goal. Local planners are therefore adequate for tasks characterized by having a highly changing objective trajectory (e.g., teleoperation) or highly dynamic environment (e.g., collaboration with humans). Most of the local path planners in literature are based on and/or are inspired by the artificial potential field foundational method introduced by Khatib et al. in [11]. The artificial potential field method assigns a repulsive potential to the obstacles and an attractive potential to the desired goal configuration. Potential field-based methods have proved to effectively avoid collisions in real-time applications [12].

Robotic manipulators executing tasks in non-structured, dynamic environments must guarantee both a safe interaction with the environment and a safe execution of the objective task, especially in critical tasks such as the ones performed by surgical robots. Many such tasks are characterized by having an axis of redundancy aligned with the last joint of the robotic manipulator. Assuming that basic machining operations, such as milling and drilling, only require 5-DoF, the anthropomorphic robot becomes adequate and the task optimizable. The optimization method can be used to exploit the redundancy that certain tasks have. Singularities, joint limits, and collisions were optimized for redundant manipulators [13]. Lukić et al. proposed the optimization of the Cartesian stiffness of a kinematic redundant robot with a null space projection. However, they only considered maintaining position without any specified orientation, which is not the case for machining operations [14]. Several research groups have studied approaches to exploit redundancy in industrial applications. Zanchettin et al. [15] implemented a redundancy resolution criterion that maximizes the manipulator maneuverability to exploit the redundant degree of freedom available on drilling tasks. In [16], Guo et al. presented a novel method based on the Jacobian matrix for computing a performance index based on the stiffness of the robot during machining applications. These studies also paved the way for the use of robotic arms in redundant tasks related to medical scenarios, such as in Focused Ultrasound Surgery [17] or for teleoperation control of a 7-DoF robot manipulator for Minimally Invasive Surgery (MIS) [18].

The manipulation needs, found in the application described in [17], have motivated the development of the novel local planner presented in this work. In this specific robotic scenario, an anthropomorphic manipulator (i.e., an anthropomorphic arm with a spherical wrist) is equipped with a transducer able to stimulate human tissue through ultrasound energy for treating tumors in moving organs. The ultrasound energy is concentrated in a focal spot located along the central axis of the transducer. Hence, the pose of this rotation axis, combined with the manipulator end-effector (EE) linear position, determines the focal spot positioning (i.e., 5-DoF task due to symmetrical tool). The remaining DoF can be used to accomplish secondary tasks such as cable management. Similarly, there are many other scenarios where the position of the joint J_t does not affect the main task, as in welding applications. Hence, it would be useful to describe the EE angular movement decoupling the rotation of the third wrist joint J_t from the rest of the angular motions.

Aim and Organization of the Work

This work aims to develop a local planner that optimizes and simplifies the safe usage of robotic manipulators equipped with a spherical wrist executing redundant tasks in workspaces shared with dynamic obstacles (e.g., humans). The proposed path planner is based on the following features: (i) the rotation of the third wrist joint J_t must be decoupled from the rest of the EE angular motion, (ii) the resulting EE manipulator dynamics should behave as a linear dynamical system, (iii) the collision avoidance strategy must consider the entire surface of the manipulator, and (iv) all the local planner parameters must have a physical meaning.

The present work has four main sections. In Section 2, we first present the theoretical formulation that leads to the local planner and then describe the methods used to validate the proposed local planner making use of an ad hoc simulator. In Section 3, we present and discuss the results of the performed simulations. Finally, we summarize the conclusions in Section 4.

2. Materials and Methods

2.1. Local Planning for Redundant Collaborative Tasks: Theoretical Formulation

In this subsection, we present a new parametrization of the pose of the end-effector in a spherical wrist manipulator that more naturally represents the fundamental degrees of freedom of redundant tasks. The parametrization decouples the rotation of the third wrist joint J_t from the rest of the EE angular motion. We then present the theoretical computation of the disturbance vector D_{EE} based on the collision avoidance strategy. Finally, we present the control law used to implement the local path planner.

2.1.1. Task Parametrization: Separation of the Redundant Axis

The kinematic model of the robotic manipulator depends on the structure of the manipulator [19]. The spherical wrist represents one of the most widely employed joint configurations and its structure is presented in Figure 1. Figure 1 also represents the manipulator base and the manipulator EE reference system following the Denavit–Hartenberg convention [19]. This robotic structure has two important properties: (i) the pose of the $\mathbf{z_{EE}}$ axis depends only on the joints before J_t and (ii) the rotation along $\mathbf{z_{EE}}$ can be independently controlled by means of the J_t. These properties do not depend on the entire robotic structure, but they are intrinsic proprieties of the spherical wrist. We propose a parametrization that separates the EE angular movement into two rotations: (i) a rotation along the axis perpendicular to both the z-axis of the initial orientation, $\mathbf{z_s}$, and the target orientation, $\mathbf{z_t}$, and (ii) a rotation of the joint J_t to the desired rotation along the z-axis.

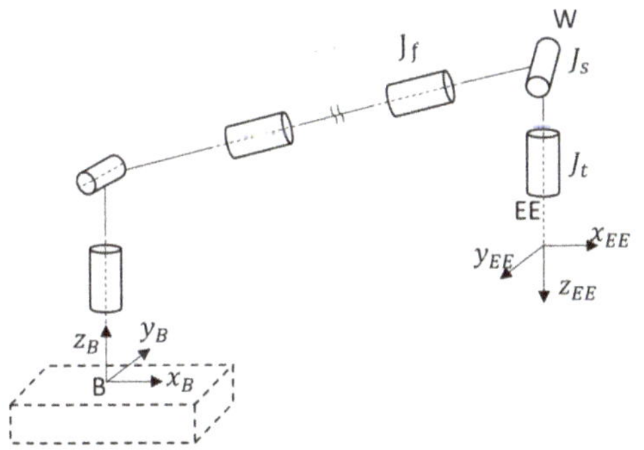

Figure 1. Kinematic model of a 6-DoF manipulator with focus on the spherical wrist, where the center of the spherical wrist (W) and the end-effector (EE) reference system are presented; a possible manipulator base reference system (B) is also represented.

In Figure 2, we present a generic motion of the z-axis together with the described parameters and rotation angles (i.e., θ and γ) along their respective axes of rotation. Figure 2b,c illustrate the parallel and perpendicular views concerning the plane defined by the $\mathbf{z_s}$ and $\mathbf{z_t}$ vectors. Figure 2b presents the θ angle rotation along the $\mathbf{x_\theta}$ axis perpendicular to the $\mathbf{z_s}$ and $\mathbf{z_t}$ plane. On the other hand, the rotation along the $\mathbf{y}_\gamma$ axis performs the out-of-plane rotation. The $\mathbf{y}_\gamma$ axis is defined to be perpendicular to the $\mathbf{x}_\theta$ axis and to the projection of $\mathbf{z}_{\mathrm{EE}}^{\theta}$ into the plane spanned by the θ angle. In the following equations, we formalize the described definitions of the rotation axes $\mathbf{x}_\theta$ and $\mathbf{y}_\gamma$.

$$\mathbf{x}_\theta = \mathbf{z_s} \times \mathbf{z_t} \tag{1}$$

$$\mathbf{y}_\gamma = \mathbf{z}_{\mathrm{EE}}^{\theta} \times \mathbf{x}_\theta \tag{2}$$

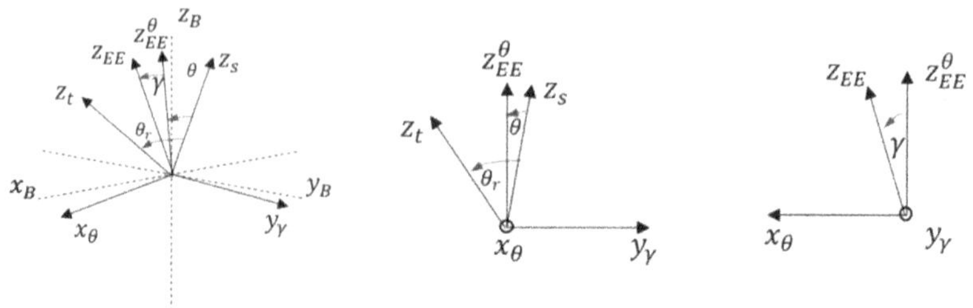

(a) (b) (c)

Figure 2. (**a**) Schematic representation of the z-axis overlapping motion for reaching the vector z_t starting from z_s. The angles θ and γ are defined relative to the rotation axis x_θ and y_γ. (**b**) Section of the plane defined by the vectors z_t and z_s spanned by the θ angle. (**c**) Section of the plane spanned by the γ angle perpendicular to the x_θ and z_{EE}^{θ} vector.

We can then compute the $\mathbf{z}_{\mathrm{EE}}$ at any instant applying the following ordered rotations to the starting z-axis ($\mathbf{z_s}$).

$$\mathbf{z}_{\mathrm{EE}} = \mathrm{R}_{\mathbf{y}_\gamma}(\gamma) R_{\mathbf{x}_\theta}(\theta)\mathbf{z_s} \tag{3}$$

The notation $\mathrm{R}_{\mathbf{a}}(b)$ refers to the rotation along the a-axis by an angle b. Based on the definitions of the rotation axis we will use the equation 3 to express the angular motion of the EE; the following expression can be used to compute the reference angle θ_r (Equation (3)) while, by definition, the reference angle γ_r is always zero.

$$\theta_r = \cos^{-1}\left(\mathbf{z_s^T z_t}\right) \tag{4}$$

More specifically, starting from a random $\mathbf{z_s}$ and using Equations (1)–(3), we can compute the $\mathbf{z}_{\mathrm{EE}}$ by multiplying $\mathbf{z_s}$ for two different rotation matrices. A first rotation is performed along $\mathbf{x}_\theta$, which is the axes and the angle needed to align $\mathbf{z_s}$ and $\mathbf{z_t}$ (target orientation). A second rotation is performed along $\mathbf{y}_\gamma$, which is the axes (perpendicular to the plane containing $\mathbf{x}_\theta$ and the projection of $\mathbf{z}_{\mathrm{EE}}$) and the angle needed to align $\mathbf{z_t}$ with $\mathbf{z}_{\mathrm{EE}}$.

Note that the definition of $\mathbf{x}_\theta$ guarantees that θ_r is always larger than or equal to zero. Given a measured EE orientation, such orientation can be expressed in the described parametrization by applying the following equation where γ_r is the reference target angle (i.e., the angle needed to reach the target orientation), whereas γ is the state variable that evolves (i.e., the real angle).

$$\gamma_r = \sin^{-1}\left(\mathbf{x}_\theta^{\mathbf{T}} \mathbf{z}_{\mathrm{EE}}\right) \tag{5}$$

$$\bar{\theta} = \cos^{-1}\left(\mathbf{z_s^T} \mathbf{z}_{\mathrm{EE}}^{\theta}\right) \tag{6}$$

Finally, we compute the last joint J_t directly applying the manipulator inverse kinematics. It is worth noting that the angle position qt of the joint J_t does not influence the z-axis overlapping motion.

Singularity Handling

The described rotation axis is not well defined when $\mathbf{z_s}$ and $\mathbf{z_t}$ are parallel. The $\mathbf{x_\theta}$ axis can be chosen as an arbitrary vector contained in the mutually perpendicular plane. If the scalar product $\mathbf{z_s} \cdot \mathbf{z_t} = -1$, an EE rotation is requested to achieve the desired orientation. This freedom of choice can be used to avoid robotic wrist singularity [19]. Hence, setting the $\mathbf{x_\theta}$ axis as the rotation axis of the joint J_f allows performing the EE rotation through only its joint angle. By doing so, the second joint J_s does not perform any movement, thus allowing it to avoid the robotic wrist singularity.

2.1.2. Disturbance Computation for Collision Avoidance

Inspired by the artificial potential field method [11], we propose to introduce a disturbance vector modifying the planned trajectory based on the distance information between obstacles O_i, i = 1, ... , N, and each manipulator link. Each obstacle contributes to such a disturbance vector introducing a virtual force $\mathbf{F_{EE_i}}$ and one virtual torque $\mathbf{T_{EE_i}}$. For each obstacle O_i, we define the distance between an obstacle and the manipulator as the minimum distance between the obstacle and each of the M manipulator links. We then compute the virtual force $\mathbf{F_{EE_i}}$ generated by the obstacles using the following piece-wise function.

$$\begin{cases} \mathbf{F_{EE_i}} = F_{MAX} - \frac{(F_{MAX} - F_W)}{d_D} \mathbf{d^m_{O_i}}; & \text{if } \left(\left\| d^m_{O_i} \right\| < d_D \right) \\ \mathbf{F_{EE_i}} = F_W - \frac{F_W}{(d_W - d_D)} \left(\mathbf{d^m_{O_i}} - d_D \right); & \text{if } \left(d_D < \left\| d^m_{O_i} \right\| < d_W \right) \\ 0; & \text{if } \left(\left\| d^m_{O_i} \right\| > d_W \right) \end{cases} \quad (7)$$

In Figure 3, we present the two linear zones: the" warning" and" danger" zones resulting from the proposed Equation (7). In these zones, each obstacle acts as linear springs with different stiffness (i.e., greater stiffness in the" danger" zone). Four parameters characterize the function: (i) the starting distance of the" warning" zone d_W, (ii) the starting distance of the "danger" zone d_D, (iii) the obstacle force F_W generated at d_W, and (iv) the maximum obstacle force F_{MAX} generated at zero distance.

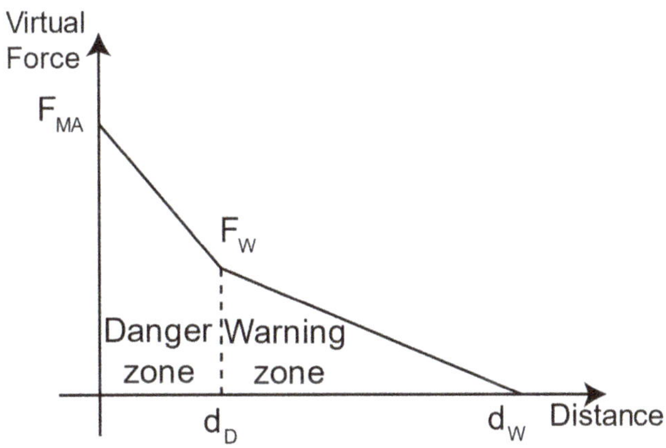

Figure 3. Virtual force generated by an obstacle at a given distance in the environment. The force is proportional to the distance, with different stiffness constants, based on the zone (i.e., "warning" and "danger" zones).

We use the virtual forces computed to generate a virtual torque. We compute the virtual torque as the direct sum of the following two torque components: (i) the torque perpendicular to the $\mathbf{z_{EE}}$ axis ($\mathbf{T^p_{EE_i}}$) and (ii) the torque along the $\mathbf{z_{EE}}$ axis ($\mathbf{T^a_{EE_i}}$). The virtual torque $\mathbf{T^a_{EE_i}}$ is non-zero only when the minimum distance $d^m_{O_i}$ is associated with the last manipulator link. The following equation presents the computation of the virtual torque

$T^a_{EE_i}$ based on the force F_{EE_i} vectors components perpendicular to the $\mathbf{z_{EE}}$ axis and the application lever arm, normalized with the maximum lever arm (i.e., $\frac{T_l}{2}$, T_l being the thickness of the last manipulator link).

$$T^{a}_{EE_i} = \frac{2}{T_l}\left(\left(\mathrm{I}_{3x3} - \mathbf{z_{EE}}\mathbf{z}^{\mathrm{T}}_{\mathbf{EE}}\right)\left(\mathbf{p}_{\mathrm{O_i}} - \mathbf{EE}\right)\right) \times \left(\mathrm{I}_{3x3} - \mathbf{z_{EE}}\mathbf{z}^{\mathrm{T}}_{\mathbf{EE}}\right)\mathrm{F}_{\mathrm{EE_i}} \tag{8}$$

We compute the virtual torque $T^p_{EE_i}$ perpendicular to the $\mathrm{z_{EE}}$ axis as the cross-product between $\mathrm{F_{EEi}}$ and the normalized lever arm along the $\mathbf{z_{EE}}$.

$$T^{p}_{EE_i} = \frac{1}{||\mathbf{z}^{\mathrm{T}}_{\mathbf{EE}}(\mathbf{EE} - \mathbf{W})||}\left(\mathbf{z_{EE}}\mathbf{z}^{\mathrm{T}}_{\mathbf{EE}}\left(\mathbf{p}_{\mathrm{O_i}} - \mathbf{EE}\right)\right) \times F_{EE_i} \tag{9}$$

Finally, we sum the force and torque contribution of each obstacle obtaining the overall virtual force and torque.

$$\mathbf{F_{EE}} = \sum_i \mathbf{F_{EE_i}} \tag{10}$$

$$\mathbf{T_{EE}} = \sum_i \mathbf{T_{EE^a_i}} + \sum_i \mathbf{T_{EE^p_i}} \tag{11}$$

Once we have the virtual torque $\mathbf{T_{EE}}$ computed in the base manipulator frame, we can express it using the transformation that we present below.

$$\mathbf{T^s_{EE}} = \begin{bmatrix} \mathbf{x}^{\mathrm{T}}_{\theta} \\ \mathbf{y}^{\mathrm{T}}_{\gamma} \\ \mathbf{z}^{\mathrm{T}}_{\mathbf{EE}} \end{bmatrix} \mathbf{T_{EE}} \tag{12}$$

If we compose the virtual force and torque expressed by the Cartesian and custom axis, respectively, we obtain the disturbance vector $\mathbf{D_{EE}}$.

$$\mathbf{D_{EE}} = \begin{bmatrix} \mathbf{F_{EE}} \\ \mathbf{T^s_{EE}} \end{bmatrix} \tag{13}$$

It is worth noting that other virtual forces/torque may be superimposed based on contact forces/torques to implement an impedance/admittance control. The measurement of the actual contact force/torque can be provided by external sensors, such as the sensitive and protective skin presented in [6,20] and/or standard load cells.

2.1.3. Control Law

The state vector $\mathbf{X}$, defined below, represents the manipulator EE pose and it is composed of the Cartesian coordinates of the EE and the angle:

$$\mathbf{X} = [x\ y\ z\ \theta\ \gamma\ q_t]^T \tag{14}$$

The decoupled nature of the state variables allows using a decentralized Multiple Input Multiple Output (MIMO) linear dynamical system to control the dynamics of $\mathbf{X}$. Each state variable is controlled through a Single Input Single Output (SISO) system with a closed-loop architecture. Figure 4 depicts the structure of the SISO control system (i.e., equal for the six state variables) and it introduces the state vector reference $\mathbf{X_r}$ and disturbance vector $\mathbf{D_{EE}}$.

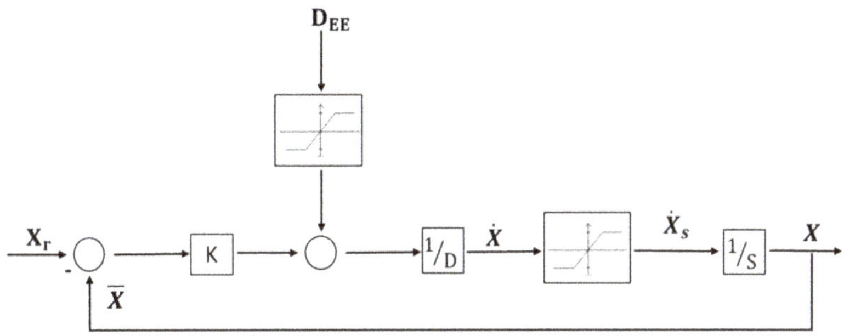

Figure 4. Schematic of the SISO linear system which controls the dynamic evolution of each state variable. The inputs are the reference state vector and the disturbance vector. The saturation for state velocity and disturbance is also reported.

Whenever the disturbance and velocities are not saturated, the system behaves linearly. Under those conditions, we can use the superimposition principle to write the transfer function from the inputs $\mathbf{X_r}$ and $\mathbf{D_{EE}}$ to the output X, as follows:

$$X = \frac{1}{\frac{D}{K}s+1}\mathbf{X_r} + \frac{\frac{1}{K}}{\frac{D}{K}s+1}\mathbf{D_{EE}} = \mathrm{F(s)}\mathbf{X_r} + \frac{1}{K}\mathrm{F(s)}\mathbf{D_{EE}} \tag{15}$$

The transfer function F(s) controls the dynamics of the state vector, parametrized through the damping D and spring K parameters (i.e., the pole of the closed-loop system is $\frac{D}{K}$). Both systems inputs equally influence the $\mathbf{X}$ dynamics with different static gains: 1 for the reference $\mathbf{X_r}$ and $\frac{1}{K}$ for the disturbance $\mathbf{D_{EE}}$. The SISO control system includes two saturations: (i) one saturates the state variable velocity and (ii) the other saturates the maximum amplitude of the disturbance. We define the following linear velocity saturation function.

$$\begin{bmatrix} \dot{\mathbf{x}}_\mathbf{s} \\ \dot{\mathbf{y}}_\mathbf{s} \\ \dot{\mathbf{z}}_\mathbf{s} \end{bmatrix} = \frac{S_l}{\left|\left|[\dot{\mathrm{x}}\ \dot{\mathrm{y}}\ \dot{\mathrm{z}}]^\mathrm{T}\right|\right|} \begin{bmatrix} \dot{\mathrm{x}} \\ \dot{\mathrm{y}} \\ \dot{\mathrm{z}} \end{bmatrix} \tag{16}$$

Similarly, we define the following saturation function for the EE angular velocity ω.

$$\omega = \begin{bmatrix} \mathbf{x}_\theta & \mathbf{y}_\gamma & \mathbf{z}_{\mathrm{EE}} \end{bmatrix} \begin{bmatrix} \dot{\theta} \\ \dot{\mathrm{y}} \\ \dot{\mathrm{z}} \end{bmatrix} \tag{17}$$

$$\begin{bmatrix} \dot{\theta}_\mathbf{s} \\ \dot{\gamma}_\mathbf{s} \\ \dot{\mathrm{q}}_{\mathrm{t_s}} \end{bmatrix} = \begin{bmatrix} \mathbf{x}_\theta & \mathbf{y}_\gamma & \mathbf{z}_{\mathrm{EE}} \end{bmatrix}^{-1} (S_a \frac{\omega}{||\omega||}) \tag{18}$$

We used just two saturation parameters to saturate the EE velocity to maintain the motion direction unchanged, following industry standards [1]. On the other hand, we may use individual saturation constants for each state variable of the disturbance signal.

2.2. Validation Methodology of the Theoretical Formulation: Simulations

In this subsection, we present the architecture, the simulation environment, and the tests that we used to validate the proposed local planner. A fundamental element of the simulator is the collision and proximity simulator (CPS). The CPS was developed and used by the authors in [21]. The local planner simulator parameters, used to validate the local planner, are presented in the following subsection, together with the representative simulated scenarios.

2.2.1. Simulator

Simulator Architecture

In Figure 5, we present the general architecture of the proposed local path planner. When a new desired EE pose is provided to the path planner, the reference block computes the state variable's reference $\mathbf{X_r}$ and the axes $\mathbf{x}_\theta$ and $\mathbf{y}_\gamma$. The reference angle θ_r is calculated using Equation (3), while the references for $\mathbf{q}_{\mathbf{t}_r}$ are computed using the manipulator inverse kinematics. The linear state variables do not need computation because they directly correspond to EE Cartesian coordinates. The inputs of the MIMO controller are the state variable reference $\mathbf{X_r}$, the $\mathbf{D_{EE}}$ disturbance vector, and the measure of the state variables $\overline{\mathbf{X}}$ provided by the block f_2. The measure of the EE Cartesian coordinate and the joint angle $\mathbf{q_t}$ are directly provided by the manipulator controller. The $\mathbf{D_{EE}}$ disturbance vector is computed based on the CPS information, as presented in the following subsection. The input of the disturbance block is the current manipulator joints angle necessary to bring the virtual manipulator in the simulator. The output of the MIMO block is the state vector $\mathbf{X}$, which is transformed into a manipulator joint trajectory $\mathbf{q_{ref}}$ by means of f_1. Block f_1 uses the manipulator inverse kinematics to compute the references of the joints before J_t is obtained from $\mathbf{X}$. The reference signal to the manipulator $\mathbf{q_{ref}}$ is obtained by adding the state variable q_t to the previously calculated joint reference.

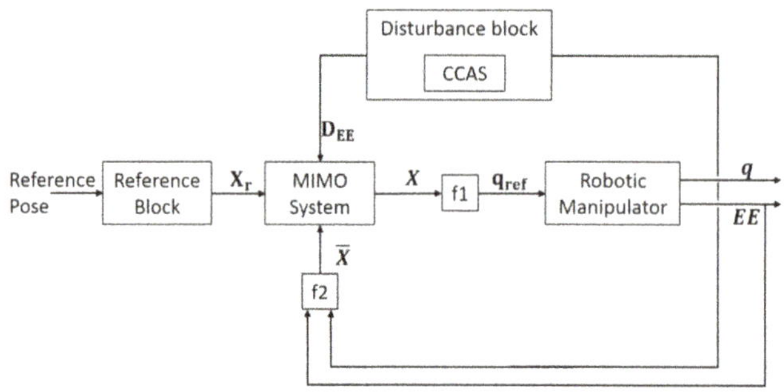

Figure 5. General architecture of the local path planner.

Collision and Proximity Simulator

The collision and proximity simulator is written in C++ language and is based on the Bullet Physics engine [22], following the performance analysis conducted in [23]. The software architecture of the simulator is based on client–server architecture; thus, different applications can interface with the CPS through a simple dedicated interface (e.g., socket applications). To reduce the computational time for collisions and proximity algorithm detection, we simplified the geometries of the manipulator links. The use of a simplified version of the manipulator links is a common practice in the development of collision simulators [24]. The working environment is displayed through an open-source viewer that can be turned off to reduce the CPS computational time. Given a set manipulator pose, the CPS outputs a list of information related to each manipulator link. In particular, the CPS output reports the minimum distance d_{O_i} (with point of application $\mathbf{p}_{\mathbf{O}_i}$ and vector $\mathbf{v}_{\mathbf{O}_i}$) between each manipulator link and each obstacle in the virtual working environment.

Simulator Parameters

In this work, we use a model of an ABB IRB120 (Zurich, Switzerland) as a representative example of an industrial manipulator with a spherical wrist. The simulator runs in Matlab (MathWorks Inc., Natick, MA, USA) and interfaces with our CPS software [20]. The model of the manipulator is equipped with a tool with maximum thickness, T_l, of 92.8 mm. The dynamics of the manipulator actuator are neglected in the performed simulation. The local planner requires two tuning steps: (i) the tuning of the MIMO system, which controls the dynamics of the manipulator, and (ii) the tuning of the collision avoidance strategy. The MIMO system is defined by the following parameters: (i) the spring parameter K, (ii) the damping parameter D, and (iii) the velocity and disturbance saturation functions. The spring parameter K is set to 1 to not amplify or attenuate the disturbance $\mathbf{D_{EE}}$. The desired linear manipulator dynamics are set to have a settling time (5%) of 3 s (i.e., a pole of the closed loop at 1 rad/s). The pole of the linear system is controlled by the ratio between K and D; therefore, the damping parameter D is set to 1. The saturation thresholds for the linear and angular velocities are set to 100 mm/s and 10°/s, respectively. The disturbance saturation for the linear state variable is set to 100 N, whereas 30 N/mm is set for the angular state variable. These settings lead to 100 mm and 30° of maximum displacement from $\mathbf{X_r}$, since the spring parameter K is 1 when obstacles appear in the workspace. The collision avoidance strategy is only defined by the parameters of Equation (7), which determine the virtual forces generated by obstacles. The parameters set in the simulations are 300 and 100 mm for the d_w and d_D, respectively, while the forces are set to 25 N (F_W) and 100 N (F_{MAX}).

2.2.2. Validation Scenarios

Three generic scenarios have been simulated using the previously described simulator. In the first scenario, the local planner is used to follow a periodic signal as would happen, for example, for a medical robot that needs to adapt its motion to the human breath. Secondly, the local planner is requested to follow a random sequence of step signals that could represent, for example, a set of motions required for welding or teleoperating a robot. Finally, a set of scenarios are simulated to validate the suitability of the local planner to avoid collision with obstacles. It is worth noting that given the linear nature of the local planner, the superimposition principle can be applied to separately investigate the manipulator's EE response to the reference signal $\mathbf{X_{ref}}$ and the disturbance $\mathbf{D_{EE}}$. The robot references generated by the local planner in all cases have been analyzed both in the time and frequency domains. The time domain analysis compares the EE trajectories with the related reference and nominal signals. The nominal signals are computed by exciting the nominal linear system (i.e., F(s)) with the related reference signals. The EE linear motion analysis is performed only by studying the state variable x. This is possible because the Cartesian coordinates are decoupled. On the other hand, angular motion requires a complete EE angular movement investigation (i.e., roll, pitch, and qt angles). The frequency analysis is performed by comparing the spectrum of the joint reference $\mathbf{q_{ref}}$ with the spectrum of nominal dynamics (which uses the RPY parametrization). This serves to investigate how the inverse kinematics affect the joint reference $\mathbf{q_{ref}}$ spectrum, also evaluating its suitability for standard manipulator actuator joints. All the simulations are performed ensuring no velocity saturation occurs.

Periodic Signal

The reference signals used for the periodic signal following the scenario are generated using the roll, pitch, and yaw (RPY) parametrization performed in local axes. The 6-DoF sinusoidal trajectories are composed of three harmonic frequencies (i.e., 0.4, 0.2, and 0.1 rad/s), both for the linear and angular coordinates. We have used the following reference trajectories for the EE Cartesian position and orientation.

$$\begin{bmatrix} EE_r^x \\ EE_r^y \\ EE_r^z \end{bmatrix} = 50 \begin{bmatrix} \sin(0.4t) \\ \sin(0.2t) \\ \sin(0.1t) \end{bmatrix} + \begin{bmatrix} 300 \\ 0 \\ 200 \end{bmatrix} \tag{19}$$

$$\begin{bmatrix} R_r \\ P_r \\ q_{t_r} \end{bmatrix} = 25 \begin{bmatrix} \sin(0.4t) \\ \sin(0.2t) \\ \sin(0.1t) \end{bmatrix} \tag{20}$$

Sequence of Step Signals

A sequence of 100 6-DoF step reference signals has been randomly generated using the roll, pitch, and yaw (RPY) parametrization in local axes. It is worth noting that the roll and pitch angles define the pose of the target axis $\mathbf{z_t}$, whereas the yaw angle is directly related to the angle position qt of the joint J_t [18]. The EE Cartesian position for the 6-DoF step reference is randomly generated in a cube with 200 mm side centered.

Figure 6 reports angular motion from an initial to the desired orientation of the manipulator's EE (depicted in blue). In red, the time evolution of the EE orientation sampled at 0.1 s is reported. The inset represents the θ dynamical response for the depicted angular motion at $[300, 0, 200]^T$ mm, whereas the EE orientations are randomly generated using RPY parametrization with a maximum amplitude of 25°.

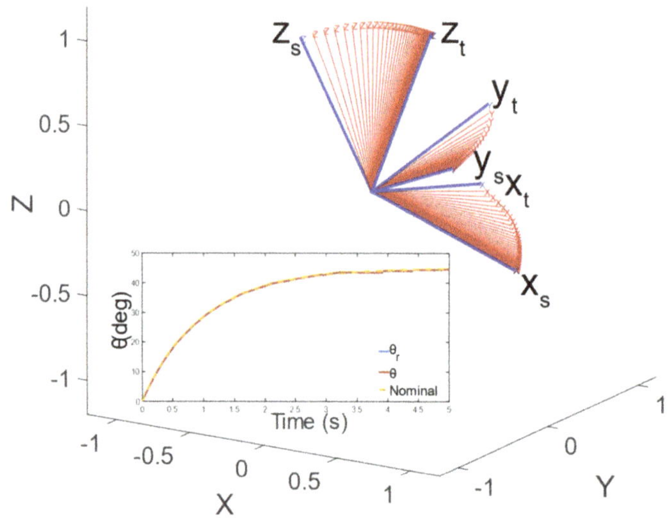

Figure 6. Angular motion from an initial to the desired orientation of the manipulator's EE (depicted in blue). In red, the time evolution of the EE orientation sampled at 0.1 s is reported. The inset represents the θ dynamical response for the depicted angular motion.

Close-Obstacle Collision Avoidance

The collision avoidance strategy is assessed by inserting obstacles (represented as spheres) in the workspace without varying the EE reference position ($[300, 0, 300]^T$ mm with zero RPY angles). Six different configurations of obstacles are chosen as the case studies. The first three simulations include a single obstacle positioned at different $\mathbf{z_b}$ coordinates (i.e., 350, 450, and 550 mm) with x_b = 300 mm and y_b = −150 mm. The other simulations include multiple obstacles (i.e., 2 and 4 spheres) to assess the superposition of the proposed collision avoidance strategy. Two simulations are performed with two obstacles: one has the obstacles on the same side of the manipulator, y_b = −150 mm) and the other has the obstacles on opposite sides, one in y_b = −150 mm and one in y_b = 150 mm). The last simulation is performed in a symmetric configuration with four obstacles placed around the manipulator at different z_b coordinates.

3. Results

3.1. Time Domain Analysis Results

In Figure 7, we report the evolution of x, the nominal dynamics, and the relative step reference signal x_r. As can be observed, the dynamics of x follow the nominal dynamical response with the tuned settling time. Indeed, the maximum error between the real and nominal dynamics is negligible (i.e., ∼6–10 mm). Figure 6 shows the angular motion trajectory (in red), sampled at 10 Hz, from a starting orientation to a target orientation (in blue). In the absence of any disturbances, the motion of the $\mathbf{z_{EE}}$ axis evolves along the plane defined by the $\mathbf{z_s}$ and $\mathbf{z_t}$ vectors, driven by the state variable θ. As can be seen in Figure 6, the θ dynamics are equal to the desired and nominal dynamics tuned with the K and D parameters. The angle position qt belongs to $\mathbf{X}$; thus, it evolves identically to the nominal response. Hence, the linear and angular EE motions are linked to a linear dynamical system with the imposed settling time for step references. Figure 8a,b report the dynamic evolution of the coordinates x and qt, their nominal dynamics, and the relative signals reference (see Equations (19) and (20)). The roll and pitch dynamics are reported in Figure 8c,d, respectively. The graphs present an almost perfect match between the nominal and real dynamics; indeed, the errors between them are 0.08 and 0.25° for roll and pitch angles, respectively.

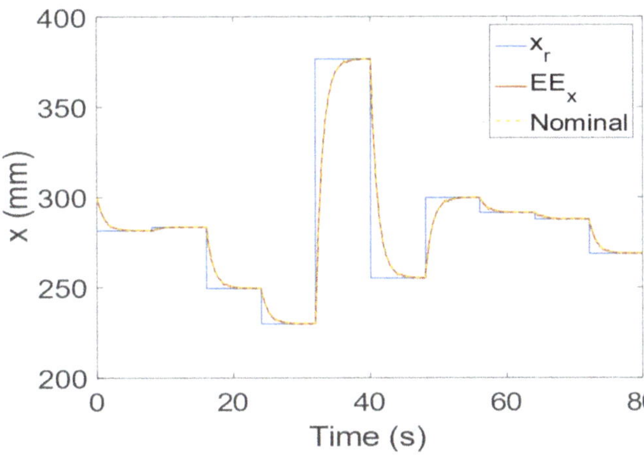

Figure 7. Dynamic evolution of the x coordinate with the relative reference and nominal signals.

3.2. Frequency Domain Analysis Results

The results of the frequency analysis for step and sinusoidal paths are reported in Figure 9a,b, respectively. The graphs report the mean and the maximum spectrum of the joint's references $\mathbf{q_{ref}}$ and the mean spectrum of the nominal dynamics (parametrized with RPY angle). Figure 9a shows that the mean and maximum $\mathbf{q_{ref}}$ spectra are very similar to the spectrum of the nominal dynamics. Therefore, the non-linearity introduced by the manipulator inverse kinematics does not significantly affect the $\mathbf{q_{ref}}$ spectrum. On the other hand, differences between the nominal spectrum and $\mathbf{q_{ref}}$ spectrum can be observed for the sinusoidal path. The manipulator inverse kinematics introduces some components multiple of the exciting input frequencies (i.e., ultra-harmonic frequencies), highlighted in Figure 9b. Nevertheless, the non-desired ultra-harmonic frequencies are attenuated after the linear system band-pass, becoming negligible with the increase in frequency. Indeed, the maximum value of the $\mathbf{q_{ref}}$ spectrum is 19.87 (100%), whereas the maximum values after 1 rad/s and 1 Hz are 0.23 (1.16 %) and 0.02 (0.10 %), respectively. Therefore, the dynamics of the joint reference $\mathbf{q_{ref}}$ are suitable for typical robotic manipulator actuator joints, since its band-pass is larger than 1 Hz [1,25].

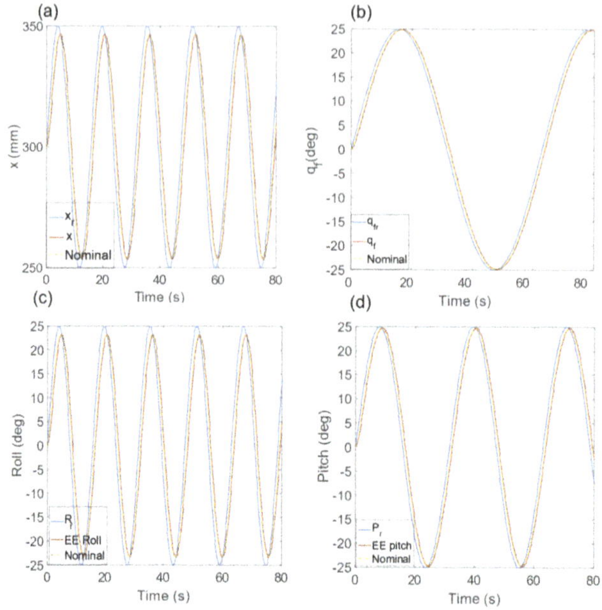

Figure 8. Dynamic evolution of x (**a**), q_t (**b**), roll (**c**), and pitch (**d**) variables compared with the nominal dynamics and the relative reference signal for the sinusoidal input.

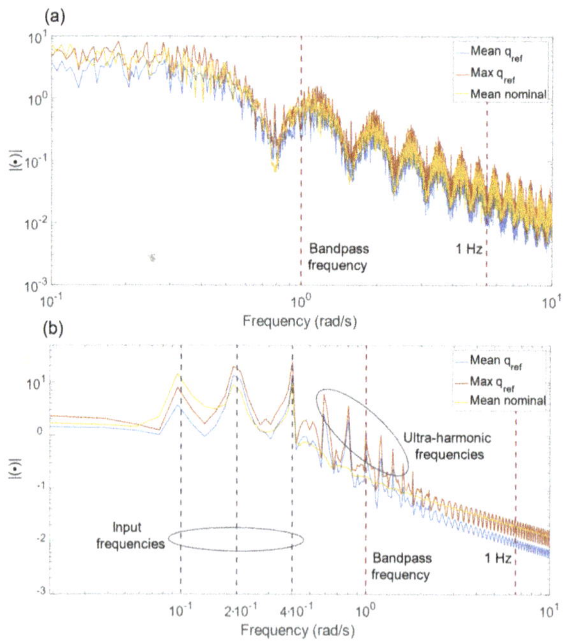

Figure 9. (**a**) Frequency analysis for the step path. The spectra of the mean and the maximum q_{ref} signal are presented, compared with the spectrum of the nominal dynamics highlighting the band-pass frequency of F(s). (**b**) Frequency analysis for the sinusoidal path. The spectra of the mean and the maximum q_{ref} signal are depicted, compared with the spectrum of the nominal dynamics highlighting some notable frequencies.

3.3. Close-Obstacle Collision Avoidance

Figure 10 report the initial poses of the validation scenarios. The x_b coordinate is fixed to 300 mm for all the simulated obstacles, as can be observed in Figure 10a. This choice allows us to describe the EE movements through just two of the state variables (y and γ) without loss of generality. Indeed, the forces produced by the obstacles are principally exerted along $\mathbf{y_b}$. These forces cause a torque along the $\mathbf{x_b}$ axis because the lever arm is mainly along $\mathbf{z_b}$. Subject to this potential field, the resultant EE motion is mainly a translation along $\mathbf{y_b}$ and a rotation along $\mathbf{x_b}$. We have decided to describe this rotation with the state variable γ, responsible for the collision avoidance strategy. The results presented in Figure 10 show how the value of γ increases and the value of y decreases when the obstacle z_B coordinate increases. As could be expected, the local planner responds to the configuration presented in Figure 10d, where the obstacle is closer to the manipulator's wrist than to the manipulator EE, by separating the wrist from the obstacle and keeping the EE close to the Cartesian reference position (i.e., $y_r = 0$).

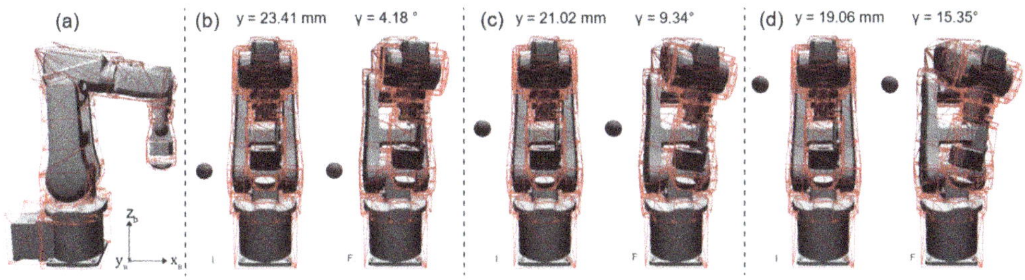

Figure 10. (**a**) Lateral view of the robotic manipulator with one obstacle. The direction of the base reference system axes is also reported. (**b**) The initial (I.) and final (F.) pose of the manipulator when the obstacle is placed at 350 mm on the z_B coordinate. (**c**) The initial and final pose of the manipulator when the obstacle is placed at 450 mm on the z_B coordinate. (**d**) The initial and final pose of the manipulator when the obstacle is placed at 550 mm on the z_B coordinate.

Figure 11 illustrates the resulting dynamics of the state variables y, γ, q_t, and the time response of the minimum distance for the three performed simulations with one obstacle. Figure 11a,b present that the fastest change of the state variables happens when the obstacle is at 550 mm due to the initial obstacle distance (i.e., 58 mm versus 85 mm, as highlighted in Figure 11d). During the initial phase, the distance constantly increases because the angular disturbance saturation is active (the torque is 50.09 N/m at 1 s on state variable γ). The resulting response allows us to conclude that the state variable's responses can be esteemed as a saturated linear dynamical response with different steady-state values. Figure 11c shows that the state variable q_t remains zero for the obstacle at 550 mm given that the obstacle is closer to the penultimate manipulator link than to the last manipulator link. Figure 12 reports the final poses of the validation scenarios. Figure 12a reports the results of the simulations with two obstacles on the same side of the manipulator. The final value of the state variables y and γ is larger than those achieved in the one-obstacle simulations, as expected given the addictive nature of the collision avoidance strategy. The results of the simulation with obstacles on different sides of the manipulator are presented in Figure 12b, resulting in a negative y due to the proximity of the lower obstacle to the EE. Finally, the results of the four obstacles simulation presented in Figure 12c show no significant manipulator motion, as can be expected from the symmetrical obstacle configuration.

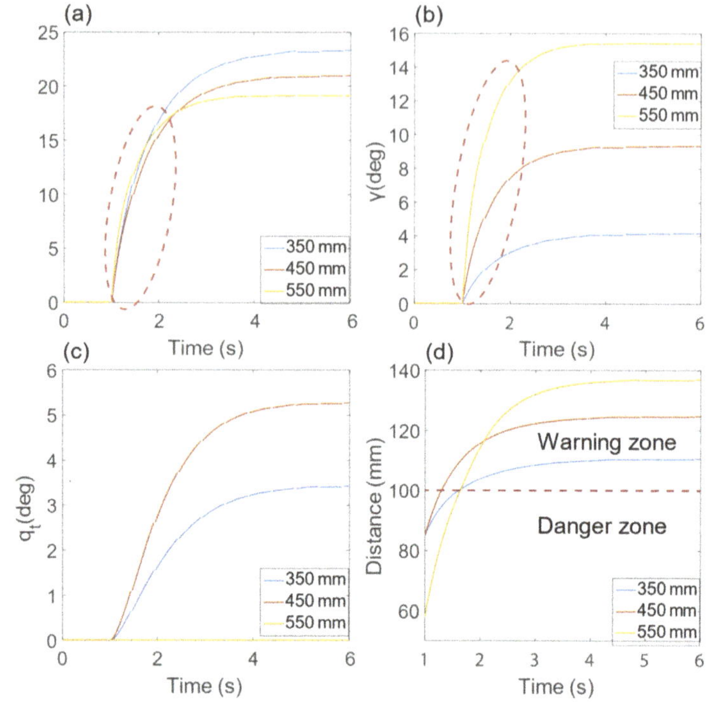

Figure 11. Dynamic evolution of the y (**a**), γ (**b**), q_t (**c**) state variables and time response (**d**) of the minimum distance for the three performed simulations with one obstacle.

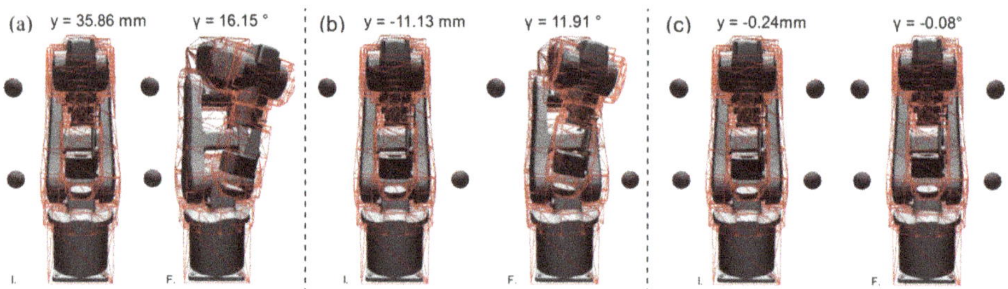

Figure 12. (**a**) Initial and final pose of the manipulator when two obstacles are placed on the same manipulator side. (**b**) The initial (I.) and final (F.) pose of the manipulator when two obstacles are placed on different manipulator sides. (**c**) The initial and final pose of the manipulator with four symmetric obstacles.

4. Conclusions

The described local planner provides a more natural way of describing 5-DoF tasks by using a parametrization of the EE orientation that decouples the rotation of the third wrist joint J_t from the rest of the EE angular motion. The developed parametrization represents the physical behavior of the manipulator in a decoupled manner, facilitating both the interpretation and the tuning of the control parameters. Indeed, θ represents the in-plane rotation along the minimal path, the γ angle represents the out-of-plane rotation, and qt is the position of the third joint of the spherical wrist. The proposed local planner, based on a decentralized MIMO linear system with closed-loop architecture, has been demonstrated to allow the imposition of the EE dynamics to behave as a first-order linear system, facilitating any desired tuning of the EE dynamic response. Approaches using robot redundancy allow us to solve and locally optimize the robot path planning in a dynamic non-structured environment where the manipulator employs potential field approaches. In this regard, the presented approach enables industrial and medical applications where robot stiffness and dexterity can greatly improve task efficiency. It is worth noting that the proposed parametrization can be easily adapted to control 7-DoF manipulators by adding the elbow angle introduced in [26,27] into the state vector **X**. Additionally, the proposed local planner integrates a custom collision avoidance strategy that has proven to successfully deform the reference trajectory to maintain the manipulator separated from surrounding obstacles. The proposed collision avoidance strategy has proven to enhance human safety with a computationally efficient and simple-to-tune disturbance vector that does not require setting control points onto the robotic manipulator.

Author Contributions: Conceptualization, M.C., A.D., J.O.A. and G.C.; methodology, M.C., J.O.A. and A.D; software, A.D.; validation, M.C. and J.O.A.; formal analysis, J.O.A. and A.D.; investigation, M.C., J.O.A. and A.D.; resources, G.C. and A.M.; data curation, M.C. and A.D.; writing—original draft preparation, M.C., J.O.A. and A.D.; writing—review and editing, M.C., A.D., A.M. and G.C.; visualization, M.C., J.O.A. and A.D.; supervision, A.M. and G.C.; project administration, A.M. and G.C.; funding acquisition, A.M. and G.C. All authors have read and agreed to the published version of the manuscript.

Funding: The work described in this paper was partially supported by the European Commission within the frameworks of the FUTURA European Project—FP7/2007-2013 (GA: 611963) and Endoo European Project—H2020-ICT-24-2015 (GA: 688592).

Institutional Review Board Statement: Not applicable.

Informed Consent Statement: Not applicable.

Data Availability Statement: Starting from random initial conditions/constraints (i.e., obstacle position, number of obstacle), as described in Sections 2.2.1 and 2.2.2, data about the relative distances between the robot manipulator and obstacles were computed by our CPS software [20]; the model presented in Section 2.1.3 was then used to compute the robot trajectories in the cartesian space.

Acknowledgments: The authors wish to thank the partners involved in both the FUTURA (www.futuraproject.eu/beneficiaries) and Endoo European projects (https://cordis.europa.eu/project/id/688592/it).

Conflicts of Interest: The authors declare no conflict of interest.

References

1. *IRB 120 ABB's 6 Axis Robot—For Flexible and Compact Production*; ABB Robotics: Zurich, Switzerland, 2021. Available online: https://new.abb.com/products/robotics/industrial-robots/irb-120 (accessed on 31 October 2022).
2. Svenska Institutet för Standarder. *Robots for Industrial Environments-Safety Requirements*; Svenska Institutet för Standarder: Stockholm, Sweden, 2006.
3. Matthias, B. *ISO/TS 15066*; Collaborative Robots Present Status. International Organization for Standardization: Geneva, Switzerland, 2016.
4. Haddadin, S.; Albu-Schäffer, A.; Hirzinger, G. Requirements for Safe Robots: Measurements, Analysis and New Insights. *Int. J. Robot. Res.* **2009**, *28*, 1507–1527. [CrossRef]
5. Hentout, A.; Aouache, M.; Maoudj, A.; Akli, I. Human–robot interaction in industrial collaborative robotics: A literature review of the decade 2008–2017. *Adv. Robot.* **2019**, *33*, 764–799. [CrossRef]
6. Mazzocchi, T.; Diodato, A.; Ciuti, G.; De Micheli, D.M.; Menciassi, A. Smart sensorized polymeric skin for safe robot collision and environmental interaction. In Proceedings of the IEEE International Conference on Intelligent Robots and Systems, Hamburg, Germany, 28 September–2 October 2015; pp. 837–843. [CrossRef]
7. Zinn, M.; Roth, B.; Khatib, O.; Salisbury, J.K. A New Actuation Approach for Human Friendly Robot Design. *Int. J. Robot. Res.* **2004**, *23*, 379–398. [CrossRef]
8. O'Neill, J.; Lu, J.; Dockter, R.; Kowalewski, T. Practical, stretchable smart skin sensors for contact-aware robots in safe and collaborative interactions. In Proceedings of the IEEE International Conference on Robotics and Automation, Washington, DC, USA, 26–30 May 2015; pp. 624–629. [CrossRef]
9. García, J.G.; Robertsson, A.; Ortega, J.G.; Johansson, R. Sensor Fusion for Compliant Robot Motion Control. *IEEE Trans. Robot.* **2008**, *24*, 430–441. [CrossRef]

10. Lavalle, S.M. PLANNING ALGORITHMS. Available online: http://planning.cs.uiuc.edu/ (accessed on 31 October 2022).
11. Khatib, O. Real-Time Obstacle Avoidance for manipultors and mobile robots. In *Autonomous Robot Vehicles*; Springer: New York, NY, USA, 1986; pp. 396–404.
12. Haddadin, S.; Urbanek, H.; Parusel, S.; Burschka, D.; Rossmann, J.; Albu-Schäffer, A.; Hirzinger, G. Real-time reactive motion generation based on variable attractor dynamics and shaped velocities. In Proceedings of the IEEE/RSJ 2010 International Conference on Intelligent Robots and Systems, IROS 2010—Conference Proceedings, Taipei, Taiwan, 18–22 October 2010; pp. 3109–3116. [CrossRef]
13. Xiao, W.; Huan, J. Redundancy and optimization of a 6R robot for five-axis milling applications: Singularity, joint limits and collision. *Prod. Eng.* **2012**, *6*, 287–296. [CrossRef]
14. Lukić, B.; Petrič, T.; Žlajpah, L.; Jovanović, K. KUKA LWR Robot Cartesian Stiffness Control Based on Kinematic Redundancy. In *Advances in Intelligent Systems and Computing*; Springer: Cham, Switzerland, 2020; Volume 980, pp. 310–318. [CrossRef]
15. Zanchettin, A.M.; Rocco, P.; Robertsson, A.; Johansson, R. Exploiting task redundancy in industrial manipulators during drilling operations. In Proceedings of the IEEE International Conference on Robotics and Automation, Shanghai, China, 9–13 May 2011; pp. 128–133. [CrossRef]
16. Guo, Y.; Dong, H.; Ke, Y. Stiffness-oriented posture optimization in robotic machining applications. *Robot. Comput. Manuf.* **2015**, *35*, 69–76. [CrossRef]
17. Cafarelli, A.; Mura, M.; Diodato, A.; Schiappacasse, A.; Santoro, M.; Ciuti, G.; Menciassi, A. A computer-assisted robotic platform for Focused Ultrasound Surgery: Assessment of high intensity focused ultrasound delivery. In Proceedings of the Annual International Conference of the IEEE Engineering in Medicine and Biology Society, EMBS, Milan, Italy, 25–29 August 2015; pp. 1311–1314. [CrossRef]
18. Su, H.; Sandoval, J.; Makhdoomi, M.; Ferrigno, G.; De Momi, E. Safety-Enhanced Human-Robot Interaction Control of Redundant Robot for Teleoperated Minimally Invasive Surgery. In Proceedings of the IEEE International Conference on Robotics and Automation, Brisbane, QLD, Australia, 21–25 May 2018; pp. 6611–6616. [CrossRef]
19. Siciliano, B.; Khatib, O. *Springer Handbook of Robotics*; Springer Science & Business Media: Berlin, Germany, 2008; Available online: https://link.springer.com/content/pdf/bfm:978-3-319-32552-1/1.pdf (accessed on 1 November 2022).
20. Chiurazzi, M.; Garozzo, G.G.; Dario, P.; Ciuti, G. Novel Capacitive-Based Sensor Technology for Augmented Proximity Detection. *IEEE Sens. J.* **2020**, *20*, 6624–6633. [CrossRef]
21. Chiurazzi, M.; Diodato, A.; Vetrò, I.; Alcaide, J.O.; Menciassi, A.; Ciuti, G. Intrinsically Distributed Probabilistic Algorithm for Human–Robot Distance Computation in Collision Avoidance Strategies. *Electronics* **2020**, *9*, 548. [CrossRef]
22. Takaya, K.; Asai, T.; Kroumov, V.; Smarandache, F. Simulation environment for mobile robots testing using ROS and Gazebo. In Proceedings of the 2016 20th International Conference on System Theory, Control and Computing, ICSTCC 2016—Joint Conference of SINTES 20, SACCS 16, SIMSIS 20—Proceedings, Sinaia, Romania, 13–15 October 2016; pp. 96–101. [CrossRef]
23. Balamurugan, B.; Maheswari, K.G.; Skariah, A.; Malathi, V.; Nalinipriya, G. Acceleration of bullet physics physical simulation library using GPU and demonstration on a set-Top box platform. In Proceedings of the ACM International Conference Proceeding Series, Udaipur, India, 4–5 March 2016. [CrossRef]
24. Xia, J.; Jiang, Z.; Liu, H.; Cai, H.; Wu, G. A Novel hybrid safety-control strategy for a manipulator. *Int. J. Adv. Robot Syst.* **2014**, *11*, 2014. [CrossRef]
25. Huber, J.E.; Fleck, N.A.; Ashby, M.F. The selection of mechanical actuators based on performance indices. *Proc. R. Soc. Lond.* **1997**, *453*, 2185–2205. [CrossRef]
26. Zanchettin, A.M.; Bascetta, L.; Rocco, P. Achieving Humanlike Motion: Resolving Redundancy for Anthropomorphic Industrial Manipulators. *IEEE Robot. Autom. Mag.* **2013**, *20*, 131–138. [CrossRef]
27. Zanchettin, A.M.; Rocco, P. Reactive motion planning and control for compliant and constraint-based task execution. In Proceedings of the IEEE International Conference on Robotics and Automation, Seattle, WA, USA, 26–30 May 2015; pp. 2748–2753. [CrossRef]

sensors

MDPI

Article

A Self-Collision Detection Algorithm of a Dual-Manipulator System Based on GJK and Deep Learning

Di Wu [1,2], Zhi Yu [1,2,*], Alimasi Adili [1,2] and Fanchen Zhao [1]

1 School of Computer Science and Technology, Dalian University of Technology, Dalian 116024, China
2 Chengdu Research Institute, Dalian University of Technology, Chengdu 611900, China
* Correspondence: yuzhi1357@mail.dlut.edu.cn

Abstract: Self-collision detection is fundamental to the safe operation of multi-manipulator systems, especially when cooperating in highly dynamic working environments. Existing methods still face the problem that detection efficiency and accuracy cannot be achieved at the same time. In this paper, we introduce artificial intelligence technology into the control system. Based on the Gilbert-Johnson-Keerthi (GJK) algorithm, we generated a dataset and trained a deep neural network (DLNet) to improve the detection efficiency. By combining DLNet and the GJK algorithm, we propose a two-level self-collision detection algorithm (DLGJK algorithm) to solve real-time self-collision detection problems in a dual-manipulator system with fast-continuous and high-precision properties. First, the proposed algorithm uses DLNet to determine whether the current working state of the system has a risk of self-collision; since most of the working states in a system workspace do not have a self-collision risk, DLNet can effectively reduce the number of unnecessary detections and improve the detection efficiency. Then, for the working states with a risk of self-collision, we modeled precise colliders and applied the GJK algorithm for fine self-collision detection, which achieved detection accuracy. The experimental results showed that compared to that with the global use of the GJK algorithm for self-collision detection, the DLGJK algorithm can reduce the time expectation of a single detection in a system workspace by 97.7%. In the path planning of the manipulators, it could effectively reduce the number of unnecessary detections, improve the detection efficiency, and reduce system overhead. The proposed algorithm also has good scalability for a multi-manipulator system that can be split into dual-manipulator systems.

Keywords: self-collision detection; dual-manipulator system; artificial intelligence; deep neural network; GJK algorithm

Citation: Wu, D.; Yu, Z.; Adili, A.; Zhao, F. A Self-Collision Detection Algorithm of a Dual-Manipulator System Based on GJK and Deep Learning. *Sensors* **2023**, *23*, 523. https://doi.org/10.3390/s23010523

Academic Editors: Luige Vladareanu, Hongnian Yu, Hongbo Wang and Yongfei Feng

Received: 3 December 2022
Revised: 29 December 2022
Accepted: 31 December 2022
Published: 3 January 2023

1. Introduction

Robots, especially manipulators, now play a significant part in medical [1,2], aerospace [3,4], industrial production [5,6], and other industries as a result of the ongoing advancements in science and technology, helping people solve problems by delivering distinct advantages. In recent years, with a deepening of the application of manipulators in various fields, the complexity of tasks has gradually increased, and many tasks require the cooperative operation of dual or multiple manipulators, such as the extraction and transportation of heavy objects [7]. In this context, research on the collaboration of multiple manipulators is of great significance, and the collision detection of manipulators is an indispensable part [8]. The working environment of a multi-manipulator system is typically more complex than that of a single manipulator, except for the collision detection between a manipulator and obstacle, and the self-collision problem caused by the overlapping workspace of manipulators should also be considered.

The purpose of collision detection is to find a collision that may occur during manipulation tasks and avoid collision in the subsequent path planning [9]. At present, the mainstream collision-detection methods of manipulators can be categorized into two types:

physical sensor-based and geometric simulation-based [10]. Sensor-based methods utilize physical sensors, which are usually implanted directly inside or outside the robot manipulators, and these methods are generally applicable to dynamic workspaces with external obstacles or human-machine interactions. External cameras are involved sometimes, as authors in [11] placed a dual-depth vision camera to detect the contact position when the manipulator collides with external obstacles. In addition, a torque sensor is also applicable for collision detection. In ref. [12], collision was detected by comparing the deviation between the calculated torque of kinematics and the measured torque of actual joints. The authors of [13] studied the feasibility of collision detection by using the change in the joint motor current value before and after collision, without using an additional physical joint sensor. In paper [14], external acceleration sensors were used to monitor the vibration of the manipulator in real-time, detect the collision of the manipulator through the abnormal vibration frequency, and determine the position and direction of the collision. Although physical sensor-based methods have clear advantages in many scenarios, these methods are costly and cannot be used in simulation studies. Collision detection in simulation scenes uses more geometric simulation-based methods.

The geometric simulation-based methods employ various shapes of the bounding box to envelope the manipulator and obstacle in the simulation environment and calculate the spatial position relationship between bounding boxes with respective algorithms to determine whether collision occurs between colliders [15,16]. The geometry-based method is applicable to situations where coordinates of each manipulator joint and obstacles in Cartesian space are known, such as manipulator path planning. For example, in [17], a manipulator collision constraint for subsequent path planning was established by using the geometric simulation method. Almost all geometric simulation-based methods can be divided into two steps: the establishment of the colliders and the detection of the collision relationship of colliders. The selection of the collider shape directly affects the accuracy of collision detection and the difficulty of the algorithm. Since the geometric simulation method requires real-time continuous modeling for fast-continuous collision detection, it has high requirements for the computing power of control system. Most current collision detection in simulation environments uses a regular-shaped bounding box to envelop the manipulator as the colliders. The authors in [18] used a sphere bounding box envelope manipulator for collision detection in path planning, while those of [19,20] used Oriented Bounding Box (OBB) in their studies. Since collision-detection algorithms are simpler for regular-shaped colliders, these regular-shaped bounding boxes can optimize the modeling and computing speed by simplifying the collider structure and improve the detection efficiency at the cost of a loss of the detection accuracy. This also leads to the problem that all existing methods using regular-shaped colliders have insufficient detection accuracy in manipulator systems with irregular surfaces.

Considering that there is a demand for high precision self-collision detection, in this paper, we used irregular shapes when modeling colliders. Therefore, we used the fine collision-detection algorithm to perform self-collision detection, and the Gilbert-Johnson-Keerthi algorithm (GJK algorithm) [21] is one of those algorithms. The GJK algorithm is an algorithm proposed and continuously improved by Gilbert, Johnson, and Keerthi to quickly detect the distance between two convex polyhedrons [22]. It can output the Euclidean distance of two convex polyhedrons after a finite number of iterations and determine whether a collision occurs from the overlap perspective [23]. Since its introduction, the GJK algorithm has been widely used in various collision detection scenes due to its universality and high accuracy. The authors of [24] proposed a contact-detection and resolution framework based on the GJK algorithm in the Discrete Element Method (DEM), which improves computational compatibility. Meanwhile, those of [25] proposed a GJK-TD method to solve the problem of precision instability that may exist in the application of the GJK algorithm in the DEM. The authors of [26] proposed a method to calculate mesh porosity (volume and area) based on the GJK algorithm for fluid flow modeling. Those of [27] applied the GJK algorithm to the field of robotics to optimize the gripping force of the robotic arm on the target object, via the accurate calculation of the distance between convex objects. The authors of [28] used the GJK algorithm for collision detection in Unmanned Aerial Vehicle (UAV) swarm trajectory planning and improved the distance operator by combining the usage scenarios. After simulation and actual robot validation, the GJK algorithm of the original authors was selected for self-collision detection in our research. However, the fine-detection algorithms represented by the GJK algorithm all face a problem. With an increase in the number of convex polyhedrons and vertices, those algorithms require more time to complete the detection, which cannot meet the requirement of a real-time control system.

Along with artificial intelligence (AI) technologies, most recent delegates, such as deep learning and deep reinforcement learning, are widely deployed in robotics. Benefiting from the excellent feature-extraction capability of deep learning, collision problems at hand have a new solution. Many studies combined neural networks with sensor-based methods. The authors in [29] proposed a deep neural network to learn the collision signal in a torque sensor dataset and extract the collision features of the torque signal, which eventually resulted in high detection performance and real-time generalization capability. The article [30] presented an algorithm based on convolutional neural network and momentum observers, to learn the characteristics of joint motor current values when a collision occurs in a manipulator, saving torque sensors while achieving good detection results for various hard and soft collisions. The authors of [31] used joint-position sensors and deep neural networks to detect collisions by learning the offset signals of the joint positions before and after the manipulator collision. The powerful decision-learning capability of deep reinforcement learning has also been applied to manipulator path planning; the authors in [32] proposed Deep Deterministic Policy Gradient (DDPG) and Twin Synchro-Control (TSC) algorithms to achieve the fast-continuous path planning of a dual-manipulator system for multiple tasks. Moreover, those of [33] presented a single robot arm path planning algorithm using a Twin Delayed Deep Deterministic Policy Gradient (TD3) with Hindsight Experience Replay (HER) for a smoother path. With the aforementioned applications, we hope that AI technology can also make progress in the self-collision detection of a dual-manipulator system.

In this paper, we propose corresponding solutions to the above problems: (a) the GJK algorithm was introduced to solve the problem of insufficient accuracy of self-collision detection. (b) By introducing AI technology, a two-level self-collision detection algorithm is proposed, which improves the efficiency of detection. To improve the accuracy of collider modeling, the regular shaped bounding box was not applied in our research. We chose appropriate convex point sets on the surface of the manipulators, and the point sets were divided into multiple convex polyhedrons as the colliders of self-collision detection. It is worth noting that this paper represents the first use of deep learning for the self-collision detection of a dual-manipulator system under geometric simulation. A deep neural network, DLNet, was trained to improve the detection efficiency of the GJK algorithm. First, we generated all working states for the dual-manipulator system in its workspace and detected self-collision with the GJK algorithm in these states. Therefore, we obtained the self-collision state dataset of the workspace. Then, we used the dataset for training DLNet, which can be applied directly to judge self-collision risk. Finally, the trained DLNet and GJK algorithm were combined into a two-level self-collision detection algorithm, the DLGJK algorithm, to solve the real-time self-collision detection problem in a dual-manipulator system with fast-continuous and high-precision properties. The DLGJK algorithm takes the joint motor configuration of each manipulator as input and has autonomous judgment capability. DLNet firstly outputs a Boolean result for self-collision risk. For the working state with a self-collision risk, the DLGJK algorithm enters the second level of detection, which comprises calling the GJK algorithm to perform self-collision detection. The experimental results show that compared to that with the global use of the GJK algorithm, the DLGJK algorithm significantly increases the detection efficiency in both single detection and working-path detection. In particular, the time expectation for single detection of the workspace was reduced by 97.7%. At the same time, it was proven in experiments that the

DLGJK algorithm can be applied to a multi-manipulator system, which can be split into dual-manipulator systems.

The rest of this paper is organized as follow: in Section 2, we introduce the multi-manipulator system used in this paper and introduce its kinematic modeling and the generation of colliders with high accuracy. In Section 3, we introduce the GJK algorithm and the process of collision detection mediated by the GJK algorithm. In Section 4, we introduce the process of the DLGJK algorithm and generate the training dataset. Then, we introduce the structure of DLNet and train it. In Section 5, we provide the experimental results, and the conclusion is given in Section 6.

2. Multi-Manipulator System and Collider Modeling

2.1. Kinematic Modeling of Multi-Manipulator System

As shown in Figure 1, the research in this paper was based on a mobile handling robot with four-manipulators attached. The four manipulators were named LS, LF, RF, and RS, which represents the left side arm, left front arm, right front arm, and right side arm, respectively. The load capacity of each manipulator could reach 50 kg. The robot uses SolidWorks for structural design and is manufactured in strict accordance with the design parameters.

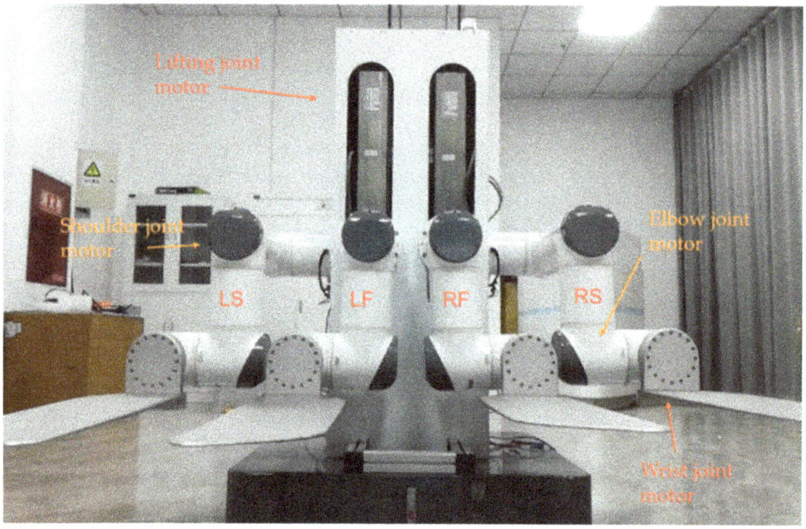

Figure 1. Front view of four-manipulator system.

There are two modes for the robot control program to control the manipulators. The first is that the manipulators move according to the specified path, and each working state in the path performs self-collision detection during path planning. The second is the real-time control mode, in which the control program controls the free movement of the manipulators in real time at the frequency of 50 times/s. In this mode, it is necessary to perform self-collision detection based on the working state in the command before each command is sent. Only the command without self-collision will be sent to the robot. With this demand, geometric simulation-based self-collision detection is more suitable for this paper.

In real-time motion planning, there is a risk of collision between two adjacent manipulators. The four-manipulator system can be divided to three dual-manipulator systems, LF-RF, RF-RS, and LF-LS. We illustrate the self-collision detection algorithm with the LF-RF dual-manipulator system.

As shown in Figure 2, each manipulator consists of four joints: the lifting joint (prismatic joint), shoulder joint, elbow joint, and wrist joint, and the wrist joint is attached to a replaceable end-effector. The configuration of the joint motor is shown in Table 1. The self-collision in the dual-manipulator system is influenced by the lift joint and shoulder joint: LF_1 represents the LF lifting joint motor value, LF_2 represents the LF shoulder joint motor value, RF_1 represents the RF lifting joint motor value, and RF_2 represents the RF shoulder joint motor value.

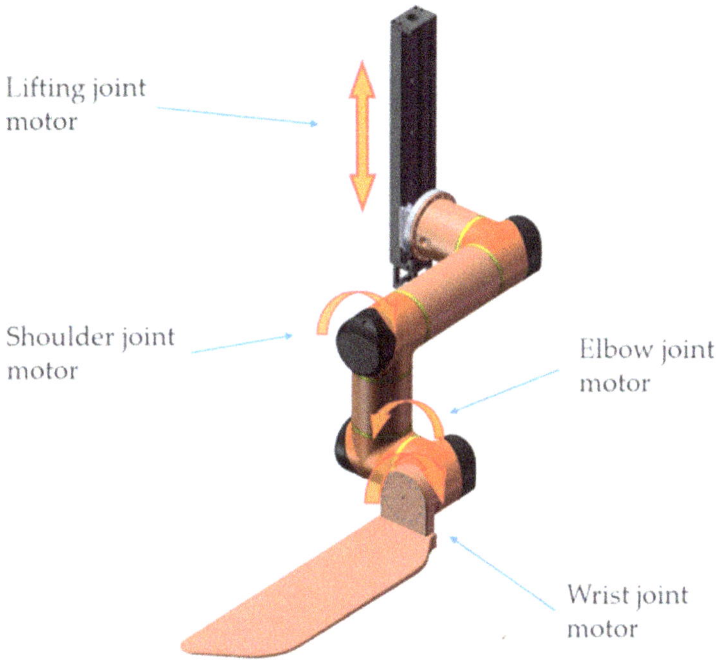

Figure 2. Single manipulator joint motor position.

Table 1. Motor configuration of single manipulator.

Motor Position	Operating Range	Motor Stepping Amount
Lifting joint motor	0~500 mm	10 mm
Shoulder joint motor	−90°~90°	0.5°
Elbow joint motor	−90°~90°	0.5°
Wrist joint motor	−90°~90°	0.5°

The D-H parameters in mechanical engineering are the four parameters associated with a particular convention, for attaching reference frames to the links of a spatial kinematic chain or robot manipulator. In this paper, as shown in Figure 3, we used the D-H method in MATLAB to model the four-manipulator system. The base coordinate system is named $\mathbf{T_0}$. The origin of $\mathbf{T_0}$ is the center of the robot chassis. We took the vertical direction pointing upwards as the positive direction of the $\mathbf{T_0}$-**Z** axis and the robot's moving forward direction as the positive direction of the $\mathbf{T_0}$-**X** axis.

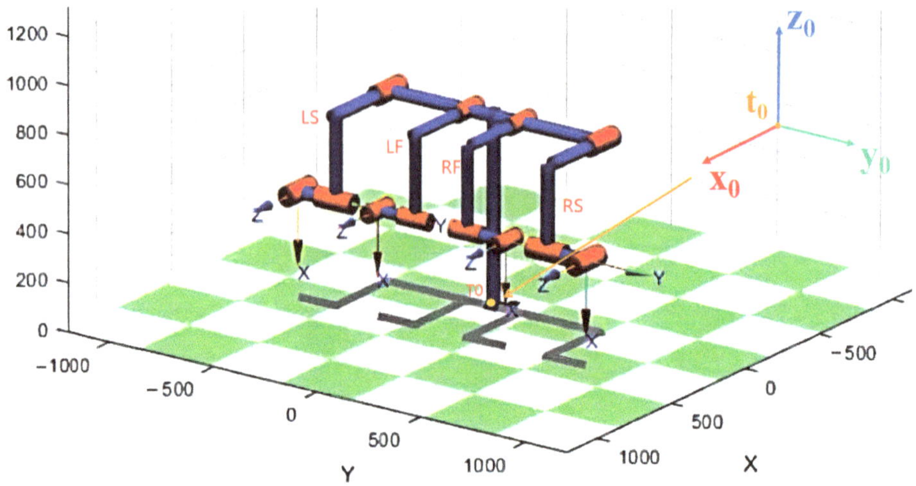

Figure 3. D-H model of four-manipulator system and base coordinate system $\mathbf{T_0}$.

It should be noted that the four-manipulator system in this paper has only one base coordinate system, $\mathbf{T_0}$, while each manipulator has its own joint coordinate system, $\mathbf{T_i}$ (i > 0). We took RF as an example, and the base coordinate system $\mathbf{T_0}$ and RF joint coordinate system **RF-$\mathbf{T_1}$**, **RF-$\mathbf{T_2}$** are shown in Figure 4. The D-H parameters of RF and LF are shown in Table 2.

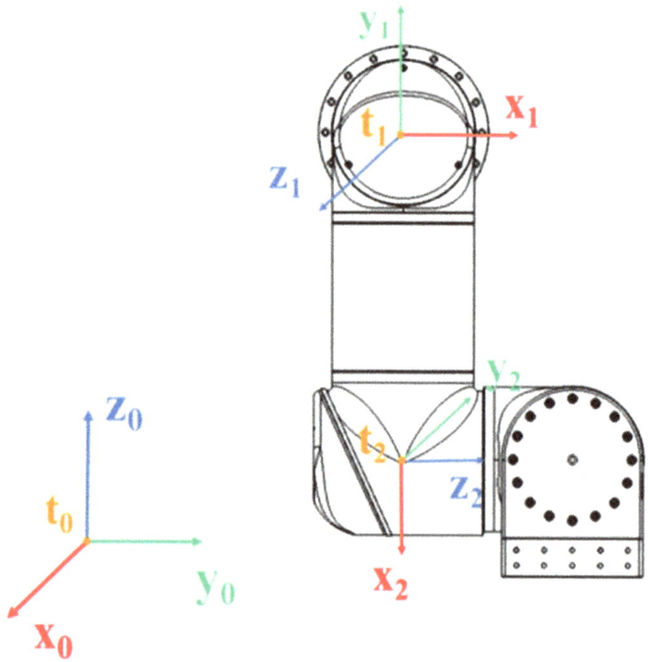

Figure 4. Front view of $\mathbf{T_0}$ and RF joint coordinate system RF-T_1, RF-T_2.

Table 2. D-H parameters of RF and LF.

Manipulator	Link	$\theta_i/(°)$	d_i/mm	a_i/mm	$\alpha_i/(°)$
RF	$l_1{}^{RF}$	90	$d_1{}^{RF}$ + 780	125	90
	$l_2{}^{RF}$	$\theta_2{}^{RF}$ − 90	351	346	−90
	$l_3{}^{RF}$	$\theta_3{}^{RF}$	182	0	90
	$l_4{}^{RF}$	$\theta_4{}^{RF}$	0	0	0
LF	$l_1{}^{LF}$	90	$d_1{}^{LF}$ + 780	−125	90
	$l_2{}^{LF}$	$\theta_2{}^{LF}$ + 90	351	346	−90
	$l_3{}^{LF}$	$\theta_3{}^{LF}$	182	0	90
	$l_4{}^{LF}$	$\theta_4{}^{LF}$	0	0	0

Based on the D-H parameters, the kinematic model of each manipulator was established, and the pose transformation matrix between two links i and $i + 1$ was obtained as follows:

$$ {}^{i-1}_{i}T = \begin{bmatrix} \cos\theta_i & -\sin\theta_i\cos\alpha_i & \sin\theta_i\sin\alpha_i & a_i\cos\theta_i \\ \sin\theta_i & \cos\theta_i\cos\alpha_i & -\cos\theta_i\sin\alpha_i & a_i\sin\theta_i \\ 0 & \sin\alpha_i & \cos\alpha_i & d_i \\ 0 & 0 & 0 & 1 \end{bmatrix} \tag{1} $$

To calculate the transformation relationship between $\mathbf{T_i}$ and $\mathbf{T_0}$, we established the pose transformation matrix of the i-th link in space as follows:

$$ {}^{0}_{i}T = {}^{0}_{1}T\,{}^{1}_{2}T\,{}^{2}_{3}T \cdots {}^{i-1}_{i}T \tag{2} $$

2.2. Collider Construction of Manipulators

Conventional geometric simulation-based methods use regular-shaped bounding boxes, such as spheres, cylinders, and cubes as colliders. The modeling of these colliders is simple, and the algorithm for distance calculation is relatively simple. For example, the distance between spheres can be converted to calculate the distance between the centers of spheres, and the distance between cylinders can be converted to calculate the distance between axes [34]. However, this modeling method of the colliders will affect the modeling accuracy at the irregular outer surface, thereby affecting the self-collision detection accuracy at these positions. If the distances between colliders are large and the loss of accuracy at these positions is acceptable, these methods can be used for collision detection.

Different from other studies, there were irregular outer surfaces at the joints of the manipulators used in this paper. These irregular surfaces were only a few millimeters away from the other manipulator in many working states. Therefore, these positions were the focus areas of this paper. Our task requirements exceeded the detection accuracy of conventional geometric simulation-based methods, resulting in undetected self-collisions that have occurred or false self-collision warnings. These conventional methods are not suitable for our manipulators, and we needed to study a method with higher detection accuracy.

To improve the detection accuracy, we selected a certain number of points on the surface of each manipulator to envelop them. The selected points of each manipulator were accurately measured, calculated using the SolidWorks (version 2021) modeling software and confirmed on the actual robot. After the high-precision collider modeling of the manipulators, the distance calculation method based on the regular-shape collider cannot be used, and thus, we introduced the GJK algorithm. Since the GJK algorithm can only detect the collision relationship between convex shapes, as shown in Figure 5, each manipulator was divided into multiple convex colliders. All colliders of manipulators were established in their own $\mathbf{T_2}$ coordinate system.

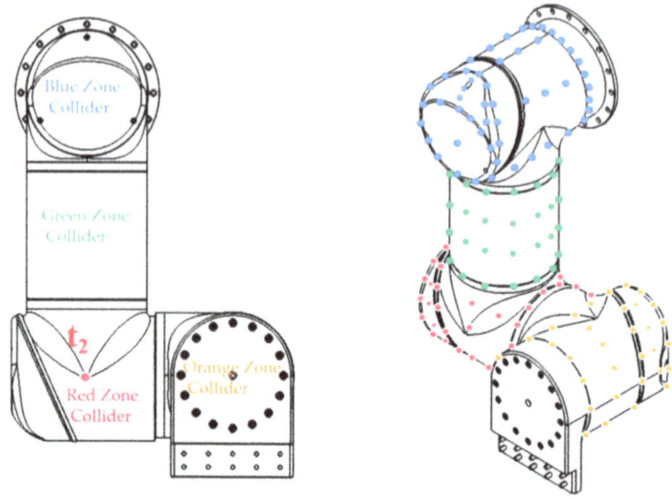

Figure 5. The point set of RF colliders.

In order to detect the spatial position relationship between the colliders of each manipulator, these colliders needed to be converted from $\mathbf{T_2}$ to $\mathbf{T_0}$. Therefore, the pose transformation matrix of each manipulator needed to be calculated. Taking RF as an example, from Equation (1) we can obtain:

$$ {}_{1}^{0}T^{\mathrm{RF}} = \begin{bmatrix} 0 & 0 & 1 & 0 \\ 1 & 0 & 0 & 125 \\ 0 & 1 & 0 & d_1^{\mathrm{RF}} + 780 \\ 0 & 0 & 0 & 1 \end{bmatrix} \tag{3} $$

$$ {}_{2}^{1}T^{\mathrm{RF}} = \begin{bmatrix} \cos(\theta_2^{\mathrm{RF}} - 90) & 0 & -\sin(\theta_2^{\mathrm{RF}} - 90) & 346\cos(\theta_2^{\mathrm{RF}} - 90) \\ \sin(\theta_2^{\mathrm{RF}} - 90) & 0 & 0 & 346\sin(\theta_2^{\mathrm{RF}} - 90) \\ 0 & -1 & \cos(\theta_2^{\mathrm{RF}} - 90) & 351 \\ 0 & 0 & 0 & 1 \end{bmatrix} \tag{4} $$

Then, from Equation (2) we can obtain the transformation matrix between the **RF-T**$_\mathbf{2}$ and $\mathbf{T_0}$ as follows:

$$ {}_{2}^{0}T^{\mathrm{RF}} = {}_{1}^{0}T^{\mathrm{RF}}\,{}_{2}^{1}T^{\mathrm{RF}} = \begin{bmatrix} 0 & -1 & \sin(\theta_2^{\mathrm{RF}}) & 351 \\ \sin(\theta_2^{\mathrm{RF}}) & 0 & \cos(\theta_2^{\mathrm{RF}}) & 346\sin(\theta_2^{\mathrm{RF}}) + 125 \\ -\cos(\theta_2^{\mathrm{RF}}) & 0 & 0 & -346\cos(\theta_2^{\mathrm{RF}}) + d_1^{\mathrm{RF}} + 780 \\ 0 & 0 & 0 & 1 \end{bmatrix} \tag{5} $$

According to the robot forward kinematics, with the manipulator joint motors angle data, we can calculate the matrix ${}_{2}^{0}T$ in real-time:

$$ pos_0 = {}_{2}^{0}T \cdot pos_2 \tag{6} $$

According to Equation (6), we can convert the coordinates of the colliders from $\mathbf{T_2}$ to the uniform base frame $\mathbf{T_0}$, where pos_0 represents the generated point set of colliders in $\mathbf{T_0}$ and pos_2 represents the generated point set of colliders in $\mathbf{T_2}$. Hence, during the movement of the system, we can obtain the point sets representing corresponding colliders in $\mathbf{T_0}$ in real-time.

3. GJK Algorithm for Dual-Manipulator Self-Collision Detection

3.1. Introduction of GJK Algorithm

3.1.1. Minkowski Difference

Before introducing the GJK algorithm, we first introduced the Minkowski difference. Assuming A and B are two convex polyhedrons in Cartesian space, a is a vector in A and b is a vector in B. The Minkowski difference between A and B is defined as:

$$A - B = \{a - b | a \in A, b \in B\} \tag{7}$$

We named the convex polyhedron formed by $A - B$ as C, $C = A - B$. The distance between A and B can be expressed as follows:

$$d(A, B) = \min\{\| \ x - y \ \| \ : x \in A, y \in B\} \tag{8}$$

assuming that $v(C)$ represents the point nearest to the origin in C and satisfies the following equation:

$$\|v(C)\| = \min\{\|x\| : x \in C\} \tag{9}$$

According to Equations (8) and (9), we obtained:

$$d(A, B) = v(C) \tag{10}$$

Which proves that calculating the minimum distance between A and B can be translated into determining whether C contains the origin.

In other words, if there is a collision between convex polyhedron A and B, the convex polyhedron C ($C = A - B$) must contain the origin. This is a very important property of the Minkowski difference in convex polyhedron collision detection.

3.1.2. Basic Principle of GJK Algorithm

Before describing the basic principle of the GJK algorithm, we needed to understand two definitions.

Definition 1: *Point P belongs to the convex polyhedron C. For a given direction vector d, if point P satisfies equation:*

$$d \cdot P = \max\{d \cdot V | V \in C\} \tag{11}$$

then point P is called the support point of C in direction d. The function to find the support point is called the support function, written as $S_{(C)}$, the finding direction is written as V_{dir}.

Definition 2: *For convex polyhedron C, a simplex is a convex tetrahedron formed by any four vertices in C. If the selected vertices are different, the simplex formed is also different. Selected vertex q is constructed by $S_{(C)}$ along different V_{dir} and satisfies the equation:*

$$q = S_{(C)}(A, V_{dir}) - S_{(C)}(B, V_{dir}) \tag{12}$$

The GJK algorithm uses the Minkowski difference property described in Section 3.1.1 to compute the minimum distance between two convex polyhedrons. For convex polyhedron A and B, the GJK algorithm iteratively searches the point with the closest distance to the origin in C ($C = A - B$). The GJK algorithm generates a simplex in every iteration process, and the simplex generated at the k-th iteration process is denoted as W_k. v_k is the point nearest to the origin in W_k and can be calculated by choosing the Johnson operator [21] or the improved operator [28,35,36] depending on the situation. If v_k is the origin, then W_k contains the origin, which means that C contains the origin, and thus, a collision occurs between A and B. If v_k is not the origin, then the algorithm updates V_{dir} according to the rule and obtains the new vertex q_{k+1}, replacing a vertex in W_k with q_{k+1} to get W_{k+1} and continue to determine whether W_{k+1} contains the origin.

The GJK algorithm terminates the loop in two cases:

(a) v_k is the origin, A and B collide, and the GJK algorithm is exited;
(b) The dot product of q_{k+1} and V_{dir} is less than zero ($\text{dot}(V_{q_{k+1}O}, V_{dir}) < 0$), at this time, the simplex containing the origin cannot be found in C, no collision occurs between A and B, and the GJK algorithm is exited.

3.2. *GJK Self-Collision Detection for Dual-Manipulator System*

As shown in Figure 6, by inputting the real-time joint motor configuration (height data and angle data) of the dual-manipulator system, the transformation matrix between $\mathbf{T_0}$ and $\mathbf{T_2}$ are obtained. After converting all colliders to a unified coordinate system, the GJK algorithm determines the real-time self-collision detection results of the colliders. The collision mark is recorded as CheckGJK, which is equal to 1 when a self-collision occurs.

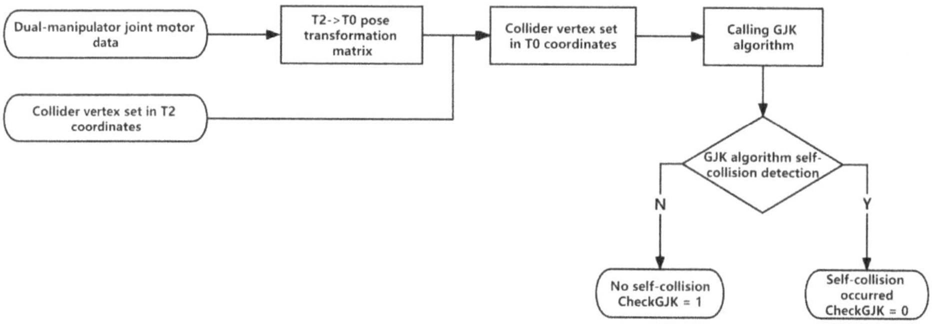

Figure 6. Flowchart of GJK algorithm self-collision detection.

4. DLGJK Algorithm

4.1. *Structure of DLGJK Algorithm*

Figure 7 shows the flowchart of the DLGJK algorithm. The DLGJK algorithm consists of DLNet and the GJK algorithm, and the input of the DLGJK algorithm is the real-time joint motors configuration of the dual-manipulator system. First, the DLGJK algorithm uses DLNet to make a judgment, and if there is no self-collision risk, the DLGJK algorithm is directly quit; if there is a risk of self-collision, the DLGJK algorithm calls the GJK algorithm to perform self-collision detection, and the GJK algorithm will detect whether self-collision occurs in the current working state.

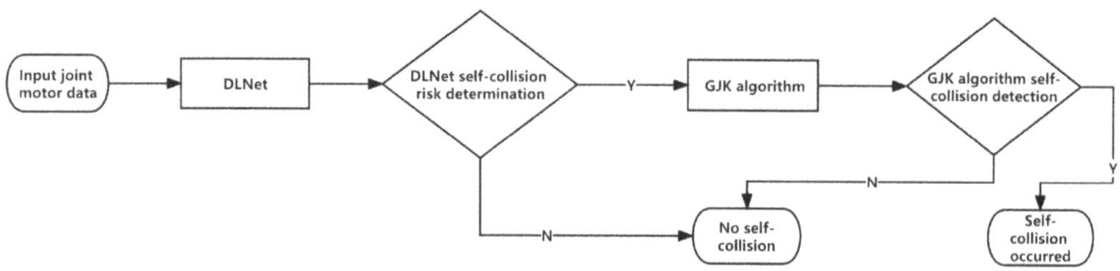

Figure 7. Flowchart of DLGJK algorithm self-collision detection.

The overall workflow of collision detection consists of two layers; the first layer is DLNet for risk checking, the second layer is GJK for risky situations, which are determined as such from first layer DLNet.

The segment judgment process of DLNet is closer to human thinking. When we judge whether there is a collision between manipulators, we present the judgment that there is no self-collision risk for manipulators with a long distance. As the distance between the manipulators gets closer and closer, we will present the judgment that there is a risk of self-collision and that self-collision detection is needed. After DLNet learns the relationship between workspace self-collision states and joint motors data, the motors data can replace the distance as the judgment basis of DLNet, so that DLNet can imitate our thinking logic for self-collision risk judgment.

Ideally, the working state of the dual-manipulator system and the self-collision detection result of the DLGJK algorithm should contain the following three cases:

As shown in Figure 8, the system has no self-collision risk and no self-collision occurs: the DLNet judges that there is no self-collision and the DLGJK algorithm returns the information that no self-collision is detected.

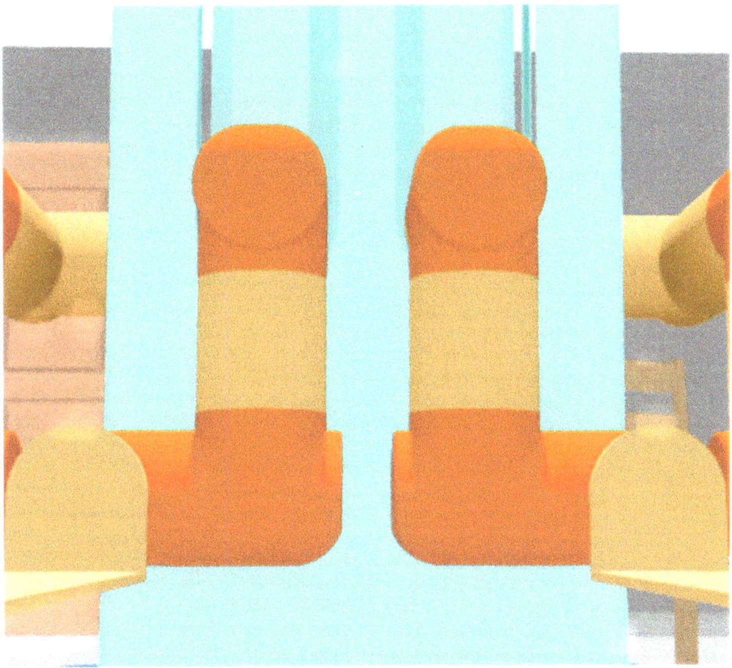

Figure 8. Dual-manipulator LF-RF without risk of self-collision.

As shown in Figure 9, the system has a self-collision risk, but no self-collision occurs: the DLNet judges that there is a self-collision risk and the GJK algorithm does not detect a self-collision, finally the DLGJK algorithm returns the information that no self-collision is detected.

As shown in Figure 10, a self-collision occurs in the system: the DLNet judges that there is a risk of self-collision, the GJK algorithm detects a self-collision, and finally the DLGJK algorithm returns the information that a self-collision occurs.

Therefore, the DLNet must be accurate in judging the no-self-collision working state. That is, if DLNet judges that there is no risk of self-collision, the dual-manipulator system must be in a no self-collision state; if the DLNet judges that there is a risk of self-collision, the system may have a self-collision. Then, the DLGJK algorithm must call the GJK algorithm for self-collision detection and returns the final result. The implementation logic will be introduced in the Section 4.3.

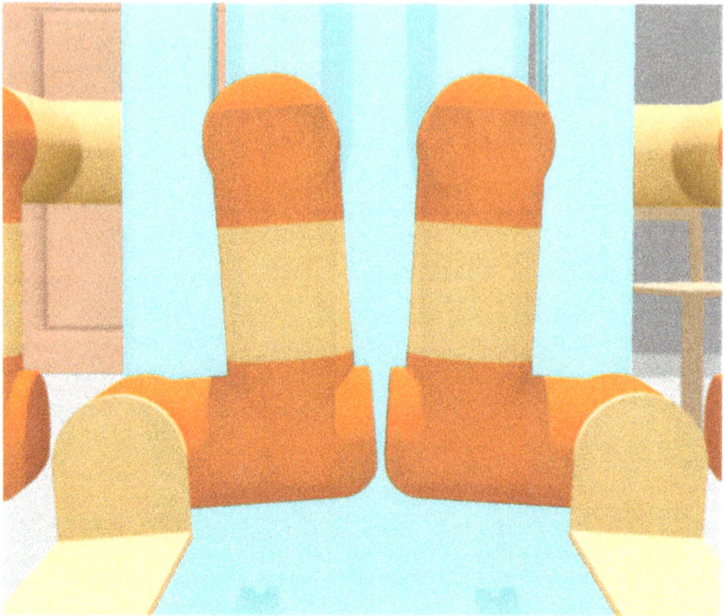

Figure 9. Dual-manipulator LF-RF with risk of self-collision.

Figure 10. Dual-manipulator LF-RF with self-collision.

4.2. Structure and Training of DLNet

4.2.1. Gathering DLNet Training Data

In order to obtain the dataset required for training the DLNet, it is necessary to generate the workspace data of the dual-manipulator system. As described in the previous section, the self-collision of the system studied in this paper is mainly affected by the motor motions of the lifting joint motors (LF_1, RF_1) and shoulder joint motors (LF_2, RF_2). According to the value ranges and step amounts of LF_1, LF_2, RF_1, and RF_2, the dual-manipulator system workspace dataset is generated exhaustively, and the GJK algorithm is called to perform self-collision detection on all data. Finally, the self-collision state dataset of the workspace in the format [LF_1, LF_2, RF_1, RF_2, CheckGJK] is obtained, written as the Space-Col dataset.

The study of the Space-Col dataset shows that for the dual-manipulator system used in this paper, when LF_2 and RF_2 are constant and the height difference between LF_1 and RF_1 is unchanged, the values of LF_1 and RF_1 have no effect on the self-collision state. That means only three variables: the height difference between LF_1 and RF_1, the LF_2, and the RF_2 can represent the relative states between two manipulators. As shown in Figure 11, the above conclusion means that, under the condition that the angle of the shoulder joint motors is unchanged, two manipulators lifting or falling the same height at the same time will not change the self-collision state.

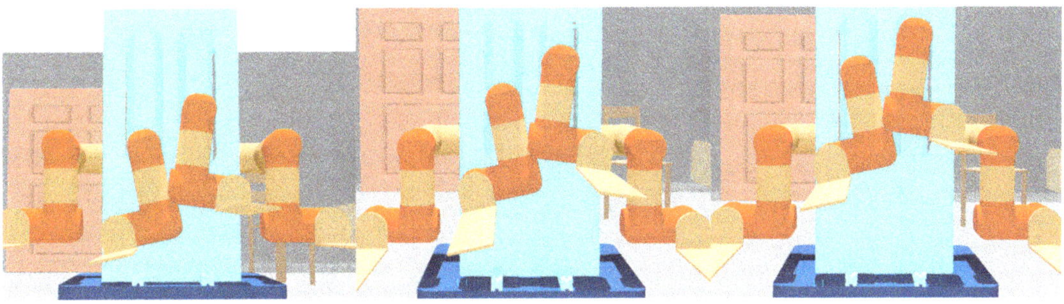

Figure 11. Dual-manipulator LF-RF lift the same height at the same time.

The height difference between LF_1 and RF_1 is denoted as the Hvalue. We used the Hvalue to replace LF_1 and RF_1 in the Space-Col dataset. After the data were de-duplicated, the training dataset in the format of [Hvalue, LF_2, RF_2, CheckGJK] was obtained and written as the DL-Train dataset.

4.2.2. Structure and Parameters of DLNet

The DL-Train dataset was used to train the DLNet. According to the characteristics of the dataset, we used a five-layer fully connected neural network to construct DLNet. The x-input of DLNet is the Hvalue, LF_2, and RF_2, and the y-input is CheckGJK. The output of the network is the probability of self-collision of the dual-manipulator system in the respective working state, denoted as OutDL.

The DLNet includes the input-layer, hidden-layer, and output-layer. The number of neurons in the input-layer is set to three (x-input) and the number of neurons in the output-layer is set to one (OutDL). The trial-and-error method was used to determine the number of hidden-layers and the number of neurons in the hidden-layers. The final number of hidden-layers was determined to be three, and the numbers of neurons were 12, 24, and 6, respectively. As shown in Figure 12, the final topology of DLNet was determined to be 3:12:24:6:1.

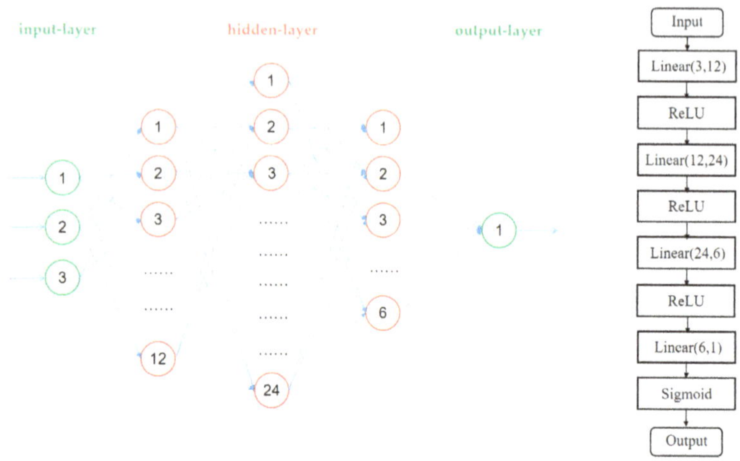

Figure 12. Topology and model structure of DLNet.

For the selection of the activation function, the ReLU function that enables faster network training was selected as the activation function of hidden-layers, while the output of the output-layer is essentially a binary problem; therefore, the Sigmoid function, which is more suitable for the binary problem, was selected as the activation function of the output-layer. Since the DL-Train dataset features are clearly distributed, after experimental verification, the Stochastic Gradient Descent (SGD) was selected as the optimization method and the BinaryCrossEntropyLoss (BCELoss) function was selected as the loss function.

It is worth noting that since the DL-Train dataset actually contains all the working states of the dual-manipulator system used in this paper, it is unnecessary to consider the overfitting problem. As long as the DLNet can learn the DL-Train dataset well, it can judge all working states of the dual-manipulator system. Model training proceeds until the loss value converges, and the loss changes in the training process are shown in Figure 13. In this paper, accuracy was not an important indicator for evaluating the DLNet training results. We will select a threshold in the following part and process the network output to achieve 100% accuracy in judging no self-collision working states.

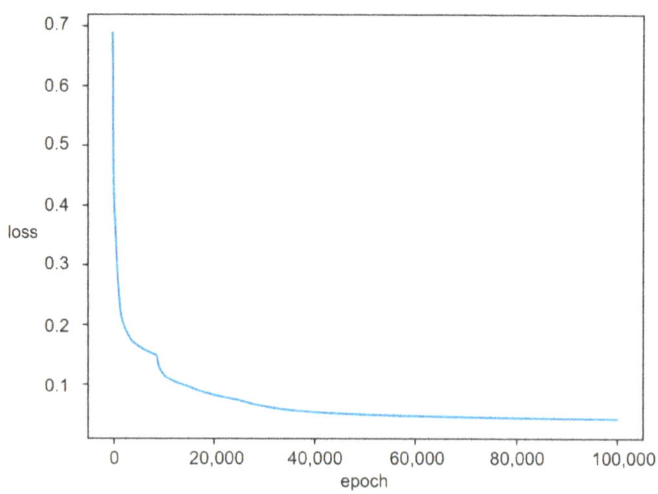

Figure 13. Change in the loss value during DLNet training.

4.3. Judgment Logic of DLNet for Self-Collision

As described in Section 4.1, the DLNet must be accurate in judging the no-self-collision working state. The output value (OutDL) of the DLNet is the predicted value of self-collision in the current working state. The value of OutDL has a range of [0, 1], where OutDL = 1 means that no self-collision occurs and OutDL = 0 means that self-collision occurs. The closer the OutDL is to 0, the higher the probability of self-collision occurring. Associating the model x-input with the OutDL, we obtained the DLNet output dataset in the format [Hvalue, LF2, RF2, OutDL], written as the DL-Out dataset.

As the self-collision judgment basis of the DLNet, we need to select a critical threshold (K) between 0 and 1. If $0 < \text{OutDL} \leq K$, the DLNet judges that there is a self-collision risk; if $K < \text{OutDL} \leq 1$, the DLNet judges that there is no self-collision risk. The selection of K with this logic should satisfy the following requirements:

$0 \leq \text{OutDL} \leq K$, the DLNet judges that there is a risk of self-collision, and at this time, the dual-manipulator system should be in a state with a risk of self-collision or a self-collision has occurred, and the final detection result of the DLGJK algorithm needs to be given by the GJK algorithm.

$K < \text{OutDL} \leq 1$, the DLNet judges that there is no risk of self-collision, and at this time, the dual-manipulator system should be in a state without self-collision risk, and the final detection result of the DLGJK algorithm is directly given by the DLNet.

Thus, the key point is: for a selected K, for all data in the DL-Out dataset that satisfy $K < \text{OutDL} \leq 1$, the detection result given by the GJK algorithm (CheckGJK) should be equal to 1. Therefore, the verification method for whether this K satisfies the requirements is as follows: determine all data in the DL-Out dataset that meet $K < \text{OutDL} \leq 1$, map these data to the DL-Train dataset, and verify whether all corresponding CheckGJK values are equal to 1. If the CheckGJK values of all data are equal to 1, this K satisfies the requirements.

For the DLNet, the range of K to satisfy the requirements should be an interval belonging to (0, 1). As shown in Figure 14, the search process for K can gradually approach 1 through dichotomy and finally find the K that satisfies the requirements.

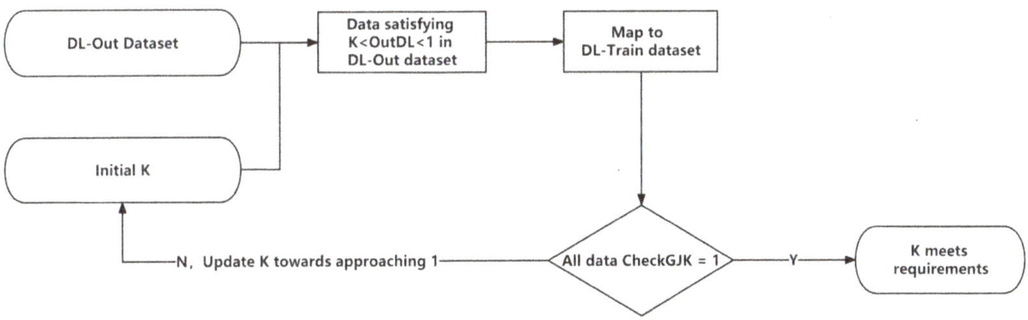

Figure 14. Flowchart for finding the K-value that satisfies the requirements.

Assuming that the minimum satisfying K is K_{min}, as shown in Figure 15, the selected K gradually approaches from K_{min} to 1, and the DLNet is more and more cautious in judging self-collision. At the same time, the self-collision judgement distance of colliders will be larger and larger, and the GJK algorithm will be called more often for self-collision detection. We can adjust the judgement distance of DLNet for self-collision by adjusting K.

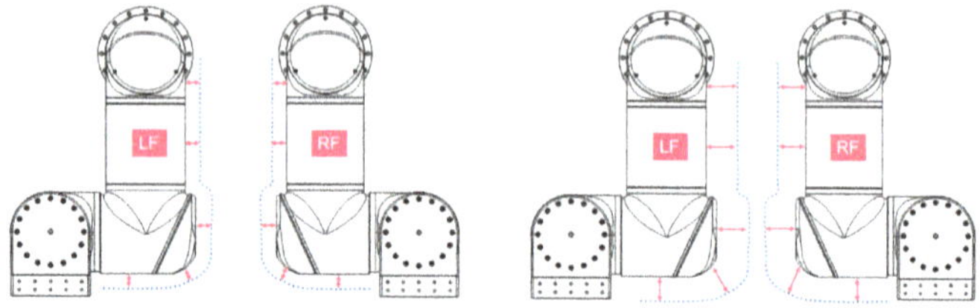

Figure 15. The detection distance increases with an increase in K.

The pseudo-code of the DLGJK algorithm for self-collision judgment of the LF-RF dual-manipulator system (Algorithm 1) is as follows:

Algorithm 1 DLGJK self-collision detection of the LF-RF dual-manipulator system

1. Input: motor data, containing motor data of 8 joints of the system.
2. Extract [LF_1, LF_2, RF_1, RF_2].
3. Hvalue $\leftarrow$ LF_1-RF_1.
4. Call the DLNet, input [Hvalue, LF_2, RF_2]

If OutDL > K:
Return no self-collision occurs in the system, exit DLGJK algorithm;
If OutDL $\leq$ K:
Continue to execute the next step.

5. Call GJK algorithm, input [LF_1, LF_2, RF_1, RF_2]

If GJK algorithm detects no self-collision:
Return no self-collision occurs in the system, exit DLGJK algorithm;
If GJK algorithm detects the occurrence of self-collision:
Return self-collision occurs in the system, exit DLGJK algorithm.

The four-manipulator system used in this paper can be regarded as three dual-manipulator systems and can perform self-collision detection simultaneously in the control system. Since the initial distance and relative position between each pair of manipulators are different, the DLNet and K (the K below refers to K_{min}) should be retrained for different dual-manipulator systems. The pseudo-code of the DLGJK algorithm for self-collision detection of the four- manipulator system (Algorithm 2) is as follows:

Algorithm 2 DLGJK self-collision detection of the four-manipulator system

1. Input: motor data, containing motor data of 16 joints of the system.
2. Extract [LF_1, LF_2, RF_1, RF_2], [RS_1, RS_2, RF_1, RF_2], [LS_1, LS_2, LF_1, LF_2].
3. Apply DLGJK algorithm simultaneously for three groups of dual-manipulator systems:
   DLGJK algorithm detection for LF-RF, input [LF_1, LF_2, RF_1, RF_2]:
      If self-collision is detected:
         Return LF-RF occurs self-collision, exit DLGJK algorithm;
      If no self-collision is detected:
         Return LF-RF no self-collision;:
   DLGJK algorithm detection for RS-RF, input [RS_1, RS_2, RF_1, RF_2]
      If self-collision is detected:
         Return RS-RF occurs self-collision, exit DLGJK algorithm;
      If no self-collision is detected:
         Return RS-RF no self-collision;:
   DLGJK algorithm detection for LS-LF, input [LS_1, LS_2, LF_1, LF_2
      If self-collision is detected:
         Return LS-LF occurs self-collision, exit DLGJK algorithm;
      If no collision is detected:
         Return LS-LF no self-collision;
4. If no self-collision occurs in the three groups of dual-manipulator systems, then no self-collision occurs in the four-manipulator system, exit DLGJK algorithm.

5. Experiment and Discussion

5.1. Experimental Platform and Simulation Environment

The research in this paper was based on a mobile handling robot with four manipulators. The simulation system environment is Windows 10 × 64, Intel i5-11600KF 3.90 GHz, DDR4 64.0 GB, NVIDIA GeForce RTX 3070 Ti, and 1T SSD. The deep-learning environment is based on the python3.9 pytorch framework, version 1.11.0. The robot control program was written on QT Creator platform, version 5.15.2, and the programming language is C++. The simulation software is Webots, version 2021b.

The simulation environment should be as close as possible to the real physical environment, so that the simulation manipulator can reflect the situation of the real manipulator in real time and ensure that the algorithms and data in the simulation environment can be used in the real environment. We directly imported the output model of SolidWorks into Webots to ensure a high degree of unity among the SolidWorks model, Webots model, and real robot. After our measurement and test, there was no visible error between the physical environment robot and the simulation environment robot. Figure 16 shows the Webots simulation model.

Figure 16. Webots model of four-manipulator handling robot.

5.2. Single Detection Time of DLGJK Algorithm

5.2.1. Single Detection Time of DLNet and GJK Algorithm

In this section, we calculated the single-detection time by dividing the detection time of the dataset by the amount of data in the dataset. We took RF-LF as an example; since the DL-Train dataset had covered the entire workspace of RF-LF, we used the DLNet to detect the DL-Train dataset ten times. For a comparison, we used the GJK algorithm to detect the Space-Col dataset ten times as well, in order to control variables; data with the same amount as the DL-Train dataset were randomly selected from the Space-Col dataset for the GJK algorithm. The results of ten detection times are shown in Table 3.

Table 3. Dataset collision detection time of DLNet and GJK (ten detection times).

Algorithm	1	2	3	4	5	6	7	8	9	10
GJK	15,020.7985 s	15,024.0230 s	15,011.7995 s	15,001.7229 s	15,003.6697 s	15,033.8485 s	15,046.9780 s	15,007.4476 s	15,021.8630 s	15,024.3327 s
DLNet	1.5952 s	1.5773 s	1.5603 s	1.6240 s	1.6471 s	1.5634 s	1.6002 s	1.6001 s	1.5970 s	1.6033 s

As shown in Table 4, the average single-detection time of DLNet (T_{DL}) is 0.12 μs, and the average single-detection time of the GJK algorithm (T_{GJK}) is 1129 μs, and the judgment speed of DLNet for self-collision is much faster than the detection speed of the GJK algorithm, which is one of the reasons why the DLGJK algorithm can improve detection efficiency.

Table 4. Single self-collision detection time comparison of DLNet and GJK.

Algorithm	Dataset Data Amount	Average Dataset Detection Time	Average Single-Detection Time
GJK	13,292,742	15,019.6483 s	1129 μs
DLNet	13,292,742	1.5969 s	0.12 μs

5.2.2. Theoretical Single-Detection Time of DLGJK Algorithm

According to the working logic of the DLGJK algorithm, the single-detection time of DLGJK algorithm should be discussed in different situations: for the working states without a self-collision risk, the single-detection time of the DLGJK algorithm is denoted as T_1, $T_1 = T_{DL} = 0.12$ μs; for the working states with a self-collision risk or self-collision occurrence, the single-detection time of the DLGJK algorithm is denoted as T_2, $T_2 = T_{DL} + T_{GJK} = 1129.12$ μs, with the results recorded in Table 5. We could observe that the DLGJK algorithm takes much less time than the GJK algorithm in a single detection for the state without a self-collision risk and does not increase the detection time for the state with a self-collision risk.

Table 5. Single self-collision detection time of DLGJK.

Working Conditions	Time-Consuming Equation	Single-Detection Time
No self-collision risk	$T_1 = T_{DL}$	0.12 μs
With self-collision risk	$T_2 = T_{DL} + T_{GJK}$	1129.12 μs

5.2.3. Actual Single-Detection Time of the DLGJK Algorithm

For the workspace of the RF-LF dual-manipulator system, the single-detection time of the DLGJK algorithm should be calculated as the time mathematical expectation of its single detection, denoted as:

$$E(T_{DLGJK}) = T_1(1 - P) + T_2P \tag{13}$$

P is the probability of the DLGJK algorithm calling GJK algorithm in a single detection. We used the DLGJK algorithm and DL-Train dataset to detect the self-collision states of the RF-LF workspace. In the DLGJK algorithm, the first-level frequency is the frequency of calling DLNet, which is called globally during algorithm execution; the second-level frequency is the frequency of calling the GJK algorithm, which is called according to the judgment result of DLNet.

Compared to the global use of the GJK algorithm, the probability of the DLGJK algorithm calling the GJK algorithm and the time expectation of a single self-collision detection are shown in Table 6.

Table 6. RF-LF workspace self-collision detection time expectation of Global GJK and DLGJK.

Algorithm	Number of Times Calling GJK	P	Single Detection-Time Expectation
Global GJK	13,292,742	100%	$E(T_{GJK}) = T_{GJK} = 1129$ µs
DLGJK	306,463	2.3%	$E(T_{DLGJK}) = T_1 \times 97.7\% + T_2 \times 2.3\% = 26.09$ µs

We can observe that for the RF-LF system, compared to that with the global use of the GJK algorithm, the single self-collision detection time when using the DLGJK algorithm is reduced by 97.7%, and the number of times calling the GJK algorithm (DLGJK second-level frequency) is effectively reduced, which reduces the system overhead.

For the four-manipulator system, we used the same method to calculate the single-detection time expectation for LF-LS and RF-RS, and the results are shown in Tables 7 and 8.

Table 7. LF-LS workspace self-collision detection time expectation of Global GJK and DLGJK.

Algorithm	Number of Times Calling GJK	Single-Detection Time	P	Single-Detection Time Expectation
Global GJK	13,292,742	$T_{GJK(LF\text{-}LS)} = 1134$ µs	100%	$E(T_{GJK}) = T_{GJK(LF\text{-}LS)} = 1134$ µs
DLGJK	471,702	$T_{1(LF\text{-}LS)} = T_{DL(LF\text{-}LS)} = 0.12$ µs $T_{2(LF\text{-}LS)} = T_{DL(LF\text{-}LS)} + T_{GJK(LF\text{-}LS)} = 1134.12$ µs	3.5%	$E(T_{DLGJK})_{(LF\text{-}LS)} = T_{1(LF\text{-}LS)} \times 96.5\% + T_{2(LF\text{-}LS)} \times 3.5\% = 39.81$ µs

Table 8. RF-RS workspace self-collision detection time expectation of Global GJK and DLGJK.

Algorithm	Number of Times Calling GJK	Single Detection Time	P	Single-Detection Time Expectation
Global GJK	13,292,742	$T_{GJK(RF\text{-}RS)} = 1131$ µs	100%	$E(T_{GJK}) = T_{GJK(RF\text{-}RS)} = 1131$ µs
DLGJK	450,981	$T_{1(RF\text{-}RS)} = T_{DL(RF\text{-}RS)} = 0.12$ µs $T_{2(RF\text{-}RS)} = T_{DL(RF\text{-}RS)} + T_{GJK(RF\text{-}RS)} = 1131.12$ µs	3.4%	$E(T_{DLGJK})_{(RF\text{-}RS)} = T_{1(RF\text{-}RS)} \times 96.6\% + T_{2(RF\text{-}RS)} \times 3.4\% = 38.57$ µs

Since the collision detection of each group of dual-manipulator systems is calculated in parallel in the robot control system, as 39.81 µs, the maximum values of $E_{(TDLGJK)}$, $E_{(TDLGJK)(RF\text{-}RS)}$, and $E_{(TDLGJK)(LF\text{-}LS)}$ are taken as the time expectation of the DLGJK algorithm single detection for the four-manipulator system. As shown in Figure 17, compared to that when using the GJK algorithm globally, using the DLGJK algorithm can significantly reduce the single-detection time expectation, improve the detection efficiency, and effectively reduce the number of times calling the GJK algorithm.

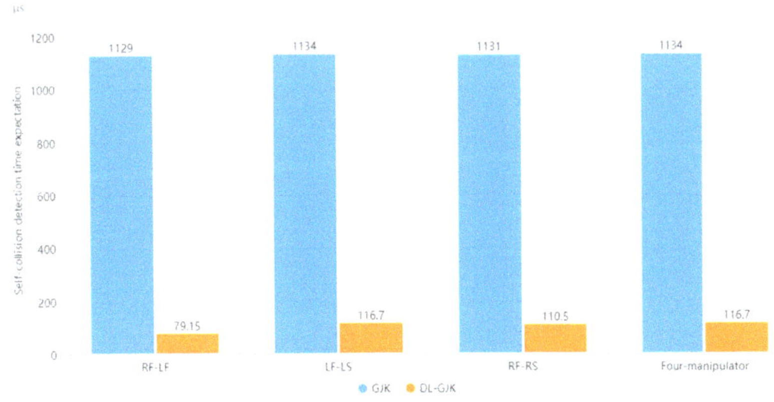

Figure 17. Single-detection time expectation of system workspace.

For the real-time control system, the single-detection time of the DLGJK algorithm meets the requirement, and the detection speed far exceeds the standard for most of the working states.

5.3. DLGJK Algorithm Self-Collision Detection for Working Path

Self-collision detection is an important process of path planning for multiple manipulators. In this part, we use the DLGJK algorithm to detect the working path of the dual-manipulator system and the four-manipulator system. The global GJK algorithm can also be used for comparison.

For the dual-manipulator system, a working path consisting of 800 motion-state sequences in the actual task of RF-LF is used. For the four-manipulator system, we also used a working path consisting of 800 motion-state sequences, which is a total of 2400 motion-state sequences for the three groups of dual-manipulator systems. The experimental results are shown in Figure 18.

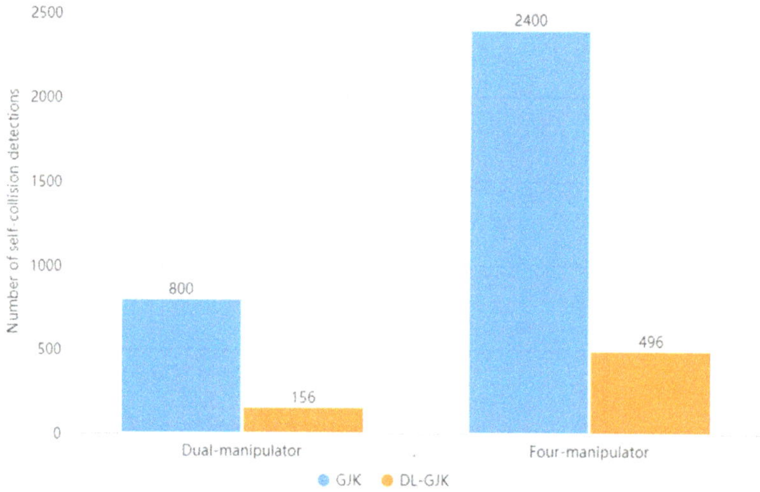

Figure 18. Number of detections for manipulator working path.

During the movement of the RF-LF, the GJK algorithm is called 800 times when the GJK algorithm is used globally, while it is called 156 times when the DLGJK algorithm is used. When using the DLGJK algorithm, the number of self-collision detections is reduced by 80.5%.

During the movement of the whole system, the GJK algorithm is called 2400 times when the GJK algorithm is used globally and 496 times when the DLGJK algorithm is used. In the case of using the DLGJK algorithm, the number of self-collision detections is reduced by 79.4%.

The experimental results show that for the system used in this paper, since most of the working states in the working path have no self-collision risk, compared to that when using the GJK algorithm globally, the DLGJK algorithm improves detection efficiency by saving the number of detections with no self-collision risk. At the same time, it can effectively reduce the time spent on self-collision detection and reduce the system overhead.

6. Conclusions

To solve the problem of real-time self-collision detection with high-precision in a multi-manipulator control system, we propose a two-level self-collision detection algorithm based on the GJK algorithm and deep learning, the DLGJK algorithm. The proposed algorithm has made great progress in the accuracy and efficiency of self-collision detection. When applying the DLGJK algorithm for self-collision detection, the DLNet is firstly used to independently judge whether there is self-collision risk in the current working state of the system. For the working state without a self-collision risk, the GJK algorithm is not called; for the working state with a self-collision risk, the DLGJK algorithm enters the second level of detection such that the GJK algorithm is called to perform self-collision detection.

For the dual-manipulator system, the experimental results show that the DLGJK algorithm takes much less single-detection time than the GJK algorithm for the working state without self-collision and does not increase the detection time for the working state with a self-collision risk. For the system workspace, compared to that with the global use of the GJK algorithm, DLGJK algorithm can reduce the single-detection time expectation by 97.7%. For the working path, the DLGJK algorithm effectively reduces the number of self-collision detections, which improves the detection efficiency and reduces the system overhead in self-collision detection.

The proposed approach also has good scalability for multiple-manipulator systems that can be divided into dual-manipulator systems, and we used a four-manipulator system to verify this.

Author Contributions: Conceptualization, D.W. and Z.Y.; methodology, Z.Y. and A.A.; software, Z.Y., F.Z. and A.A.; validation, D.W., Z.Y. and A.A.; formal analysis, Z.Y.; investigation, Z.Y.; resources, Z.Y. and A.A.; writing—original draft preparation, Z.Y.; writing—review and editing, D.W. and A.A.; visualization, Z.Y. and F.Z.; project administration, D.W. All authors have read and agreed to the published version of the manuscript.

Funding: This research was funded by the Chengdu Research Institute, Dalian University of Technology, grant number XM01006.

Institutional Review Board Statement: Not applicable.

Informed Consent Statement: Not applicable.

Data Availability Statement: Not applicable.

Conflicts of Interest: The authors declare no conflict of interest.

References

1. Tang, W.X.; Cheng, C.; Ai, H.P.; Chen, L. Dual-arm robot trajectory planning based on deep reinforcement learning under complex environment. *Micromachines* **2022**, *13*, 254. [CrossRef]
2. Shen, Y.; Guo, D.J.; Long, F.; Mateos, L.A.; Ding, H.Z.; Xiu, Z.; Hellman, R.B.; King, A.; Chen, S.X.; Zhang, C.K. Robots under COVID-19 pandemic: A comprehensive survey. *IEEE Access* **2021**, *9*, 1590–1615. [CrossRef]
3. Zhu, Y.K.; Qiao, J.Z.; Long, F.; Guo, L. Adaptive sliding mode disturbance observer-based composite control with prescribed performance of space manipulators for target capturing. *IEEE T. Ind. Electron.* **2019**, *66*, 1973–1983. [CrossRef]
4. Zhang, T.; Yue, X.K.; Ning, X.; Yuan, J.P. Stabilization and parameter identification of tumbling space debris with bounded torque in postcapture. *Acta Astronaut.* **2016**, *123*, 301–309. [CrossRef]
5. Arents, J.; Abolins, V.; Judvaitis, J.; Vismanis, O.; Oraby, A.; Ozols, K. Human–robot collaboration trends and safety aspects: A systematic review. *J. Sens. Actuator Netw.* **2021**, *10*, 48.
6. Robla-Gomez, S.; Becerra, V.M.; Llata, J.R.; Gonzalez-Sarabia, E.; Torre-Ferrero, C.; Perez-Oria, J. Working Together: A review on safe human-robot collaboration in industrial environments. *IEEE Access* **2017**, *5*, 26754–26773. [CrossRef]
7. Pan, T.Y.; Wells, A.M.; Shome, R.; Kavraki, L.E. A general task and motion planning framework for multiple manipulators. In Proceedings of the International Conference on Intelligent Robots and Systems (IROS), Electronic Network, Prague, Czech Republic, 27 September–1 October 2021; pp. 3168–3174.
8. Ostyn, F.; Vanderborght, B.; Crevecoeur, G. Comparison of collision detection techniques for high-Speed industrial robot actuators with overload clutch. In Proceedings of the International Conference on Advanced Intelligent Mechatronics (AIM), Electronic Network, Delft, The Netherlands, 12–16 July 2021; pp. 448–453.
9. Haddadin, S.; De-Luca, A.; Albu-Schaffer, A. Robot collisions: A survey on detection, isolation, and identification. *IEEE T. Robot* **2017**, *33*, 1292–1312. [CrossRef]
10. Sivcev, S.; Rossi, M.; Coleman, J.; Omerdic, E.; Dooly, G.; Toal, D. Collision detection for underwater ROV manipulator systems. *Sensors* **2018**, *18*, 1117. [CrossRef] [PubMed]
11. Hoang, X.B.; Pham, P.C.; Kuo, Y.L. Collision detection of a HEXA parallel robot based on dynamic model and a multi-dual depth camera system. *Sensors* **2022**, *22*, 5923. [CrossRef]

12. Huang, S.F.; Gao, M.; Liu, L.; Chen, J.H.; Zhang, J.W. Collision detection for cobots: A back-input compensation approach. *IEEE-Asme T. Mech.* 2022; *accepted.*
13. Park, K.M.; Park, Y.; Yoon, S.; Park, F.C. Collision detection for robot manipulators using unsupervised anomaly detection algorithms. *IEEE-Asme T. Mech.* 2021; *accepted.*
14. Min, F.Y.; Wang, G.; Liu, N. Collision detection and identification on robot manipulators based on vibration analysis. *Sensors* **2019**, *19*, 1080. [CrossRef]
15. Kong, M.X.; Bai, Y.H. An efficient collision detection algorithm for the dual-Robot coordination system. In Proceedings of the Advanced Information Technology, Electronic and Automation Control Conference (IAEAC), Chongqing, China, 12–14 October 2018; pp. 1533–1537.
16. Gottschalk, S.; Lin, M.C.; Manocha, D. OBBTree: A hierarchical structure for rapid interference detection. In Proceedings of the International Conference on Computer Graphics and Interactive Techniques, New Orleans, LA, USA, 4–9 August 1996.
17. Schulman, J.; Duan, Y.; Ho, J.; Lee, A.; Awwal, I.; Bradlow, H.; Pan, J.; Patil, S.; Goldberg, K.; Abbeel, P. Motion planning with sequential convex optimization and convex collision checking. *Int. J. Robot. Res.* **2014**, *33*, 1251–1270. [CrossRef]
18. Salehian, S.S.M.; Figueroa, N.; Billard, A. A unified framework for coordinated multi-arm motion planning. *Int. J. Robot. Res.* **2018**, *37*, 1205–1232.
19. Park, K.W.; Kim, M.; Kim, J.S.; Park, J.H. Path planning for multi-Arm Manipulators using Soft Actor-Critic algorithm with position prediction of moving obstacles via LSTM. *Appl. Sci.* **2022**, *12*, 9837. [CrossRef]
20. Prianto, E.; Kim, M.; Park, J.H.; Bae, J.H.; Kim, J.S. Path planning for multi-arm manipulators using deep reinforcement learning: Soft actor-critic with hindsight experience replay. *Sensors* **2020**, *20*, 5911. [CrossRef] [PubMed]
21. Gilbert, E.G.; Johnson, D.W.; Keerthi, S.S. A fast procedure for computing the distance between complex objects in 3-dimensional space. *IEEE J. Robot. Autom.* **1988**, *4*, 193–203. [CrossRef]
22. Gilbert, E.G.; Foo, C.P. Computing the distance between smooth objects in 3-dimensional space. In Proceedings of the International Conference On Robotics and Automation, Scottsdale, AZ, USA, 4–9 May 1989.
23. Cameron, S. Enhancing GJK: Computing minimum and penetration distances between convex polyhedron. In Proceedings of the International Conference On Robotics and Automation, Albuquerque, NM, USA, 20–25 April 1997.
24. Huang, S.; Huang, L.C.; Lai, Z.S.; Bae, J.H.; Kim, J.S. An extension of the Fourier series-based particle model to the GJK-based contact detection and resolution framework for DEM. *Comput. Part. Mech.* **2022**, *9*, 381–391. [CrossRef]
25. Descantes, Y.; Tricoire, F.; Richard, P. Classical contact detection algorithms for 3D DEM simulations: Drawbacks and solutions. *Comput. Geotech.* **2019**, *114*, 103134. [CrossRef]
26. Ferreira, T.D.; Santos, R.G.; Vianna, S.S.V. A coupled finite volume method and Gilbert-Johnson-Keerthi distance algorithm for computational fluid dynamics modelling. *Comput. Method. Appl. Mech. Eng.* **2019**, *352*, 417–436. [CrossRef]
27. Zheng, Y.; Yamane, K. Ray-shooting algorithms for robotics. *IEEE Trans. Autom. Sci. Eng.* **2013**, *10*, 862–874. [CrossRef]
28. Sabetghadam, B.; Cunha, R.; Pascoal, A. A distributed algorithm for real-time multi-drone collision-free trajectory replanning. *Sensors* **2022**, *22*, 1855. [CrossRef]
29. Heo, Y.J.; Kim, D.; Lee, W.; Kim, H.; Park, J.; Chung, W.K. Collision detection for industrial collaborative robots: A deep learning approach. *IEEE Robot. Autom. Lett.* **2019**, *4*, 740–746. [CrossRef]
30. Park, K.M.; Kim, J.; Park, J.; Park, F.C. Learning-based real-dime detection of robot collisions without joint torque sensors. *IEEE Robot. Autom. Lett.* **2021**, *6*, 103–110. [CrossRef]
31. Sharkawy, A.N.; Koustoumpardis, P.N.; Aspragathos, N. Neural network design for manipulator collision detection based only on the joint position sensors. *Robotica* **2020**, *38*, 1737–1755. [CrossRef]
32. Kim, M.; Han, D.K.; Park, J.H.; Kim, J.S. Motion planning of robot manipulators for a smoother path using a twin delayed deep deterministic policy gradient with hindsight experience replay. *Appl. Sci.* **2020**, *10*, 575. [CrossRef]
33. Liu, C.Z.; Gao, J.Y.; Park, J.H.; Bi, Y.Z.; Shi, X.Y.; Tian, D.K. A multitasking-oriented robot arm motion planning scheme based on deep reinforcement learning and wwin synchro-control. *Sensors* **2020**, *12*, 3515. [CrossRef]
34. Liu, Z.Y.; Zhang, L.H.; Qin, X.H.; Li, G. An effective self-collision detection algorithm for multi-degree-of-freedom manipulator. *Meas. Sci. Technol.* **2022**, *34*, 015901. [CrossRef]
35. Montanari, M.; Petrinic, N.; Barbieri, E. Improving the GJK algorithm for faster and more reliable distance queries between convex objects. *ACM Trans. Graph.* **2017**, *36*, 30. [CrossRef]
36. Dyllong, E.; Luther, W. The GJK distance algorithm: An interval version for incremental motions. *Numer. Algorithms* **2004**, *37*, 127–136. [CrossRef]

sensors

MDPI

Article

Method of Changing Running Direction of Cheetah-Inspired Quadruped Robot

Meng Ning [1], Jun Yang [1], Ziqiang Zhang [2,*], Jun Li [2], Zhi Wang [2], Longxing Wei [1] and Pengjin Feng [1]

1 Jiangsu Key Laboratory of Advanced Food Manufacturing Equipment & Technology, School of Mechanical Engineering, Jiangnan University, Wuxi 214122, China
2 Faculty of Materials and Manufacturing, Beijing University of Technology, Beijing 100124, China
* Correspondence: zzq06520011@163.com

Abstract: The rapid change of motion direction during running is beneficial to improving the movement flexibility of the quadruped robot, which is of great relevance to its research. How to make the robot change its motion direction during running and achieve good dynamic stability is a problem to be solved. In this paper, a method to change the running direction of the cheetah-inspired quadruped robot is proposed. Based on the analysis of the running of the cheetah, a dynamic model of the quadruped robot is established, and a two-level stability index system, including a minimum index system and a range index system, is proposed. On this basis, the objective function based on the stability index system and optimization variables, including leg landing points, trunk movement trajectory, and posture change rule, are determined. Through these constraints, the direction changes with good dynamic stability of the cheetah-inspired quadruped robot during running is realized by controlling the leg parameters. The robot will not roll over during high-speed movement. Finally, the correctness of the proposed method is proven by simulation. This paper provides a theoretical basis for the quadruped robot's rapid change of direction in running.

Keywords: quadruped robot; change of running direction; dynamic model; stability index system; simulation analysis

Citation: Ning, M.; Yang, J.; Zhang, Z.; Li, J.; Wang, Z.; Wei, L.; Feng, P. Method of Changing Running Direction of Cheetah-Inspired Quadruped Robot. *Sensors* **2022**, *22*, 9601. https://doi.org/10.3390/s22249601

Academic Editors: Luige Vladareanu, Hongnian Yu, Hongbo Wang and Yongfei Feng

Received: 6 November 2022
Accepted: 4 December 2022
Published: 7 December 2022

1. Introduction

Most quadrupeds have the ability to run fast. For example, the cheetah is the fastest-running land animal in the world, and its speed can reach 104.4 km/h [1]. Antilocapra americana can run very fast, up to 100 km/h, and has good endurance [2]. In particular, to catch a fast-moving target or escape quickly, the running direction of the creature is not constant, thus its running is no longer a plane motion but a motion in a 3D space. Therefore, for the quadruped robot, how to achieve a rapid change of motion direction in running is a problem to be solved [3].

Many researchers have studied the movement mechanism of the quadruped during running [4]. For example, Kamimura et al. [5] hypothesized that the three characteristics of the small vertical movement of their center of mass, small whole-body pitching movement, and large spine bending movement enhance the running ability of the cheetah. The hypothesis was then verified by a model with a spine joint and a torsional spring. In addition, the running of bipedal creatures, such as birds [6,7] or humans [8,9], has also been studied. On this basis, many researchers have studied the running of bio-inspired quadruped robots. To make the quadruped robot have good dynamic performance in running, the research mainly focuses on structural design [10,11], a control algorithm based on the dynamic model [12–14], an energy transfer mechanism [15], and environmental adaptability [16–18]. In terms of prototype, the most representative quadruped robot with running ability is the Cheetah robot developed by the Massachusetts Institute of Technology (MIT). Based on the research on the design principles for highly efficient legged robots and hierarchical controllers, the running speed of the Cheetah robot can reach 6 m/s and has good dynamic performance [19–22]. In addition to quadruped robots, many researchers have studied the running of biped robots [23,24] and hexapod robots [25,26], and have achieved good research results.

Creatures often do not run in only one direction, and they have the ability to move at high speed in 3D space [27,28]. The research on the motion abilities of bio-inspired robots has also expanded from plane motion to 3D space [29,30]. For examples, Di Carlo et al. [22] presented the implementation of model predictive control (MPC) to determine ground reaction forces for a torque-controlled quadruped robot, and the developed MIT Cheetah 3 can realize a full 3D gallop. Sullivan et al. [31] studied the effects of varying step width on the 3D running stability of a bipedal amputee-inspired robot. The research results showed that to obtain narrower step widths, as seen in human locomotion, a roll and yaw control would be needed. In addition to controlling the motion parameters of the robot itself, the robot can change motion direction during running by using auxiliary mechanisms. For example, Kim et al. [32] were inspired by a basilisk lizard's ability to run and steer on water surfaces for a hexapedal robot, which can steer on water by rotating its tail, and the controlled steering locomotion was stable. Kohut et al. [33] presented a running robot that used aerodynamic forces to turn. The research results showed that the robot is capable of stably turning in a 1.2 m radius at 1.6 ms, and the aerodynamic steering is superior for high-speed turns at high forward velocity. In particular, jumping is also a high-speed movement. Many researchers have studied the structure [34–36] and control algorithms [37,38] of the robot so that it can achieve fast steering when jumping.

For quadruped robots with running ability, the existing research mainly focuses on running in a plane. Research on the high-speed motion mechanism of the quadruped robot in 3D space is relatively rare. The difficulty of research on the 3D running of robots is mainly reflected in two aspects: the motion of the robot in 3D space involves many dynamic performance indices and variables to be optimized, and the coupling degree between them is high [39]; conversely, the change of direction in the high-speed motion of the robot can easily cause sudden changes in performance indices [40]. Guaranteeing the stable high-speed movement of the robot is difficult. To make the robot achieve good dynamic stability in high-speed steering, taking the steering running of the cheetah as a reference, a method of changing the running direction of a bio-inspired robot is proposed in this paper. A two-level stability index system, including minimum index system and range index system, is established based on the dynamic model of the robot, and the optimization variables, including leg landing points, trunk movement trajectory, and posture change rule, are determined. Then, the optimal leg input parameters can be obtained based on the improved bee colony algorithm. The analysis results show that the robot can turn quickly while running and has good dynamic stability by using the proposed method.

The remainder of the paper is structured as follows. Section 2 establishes the dynamic model and stability index system, and presents the optimization method of leg parameters. Section 3 shows examples to illustrate the feasibility of the method. Finally, Section 4 discusses the results. This paper provides a theoretical basis for the realization of rapid steering in the running of the quadruped robot.

2. Methods

2.1. Research Objectives

Cheetahs often need to change movement direction frequently during hunting. When the cheetah runs in a plane, the angle of leg adduction/abduction is almost zero. When the cheetah needs to change the motion direction during high-speed movement, the adduction/abduction angle is large. Figure 1a shows θ_1 and θ_2 are the angles between the leg and the vertical direction in the front view, which are 36.6° and 64.2°, respectively, in the illustrated state. With the cooperation of muscle-driving forces, the cheetah can realize steering movement during running. In particular, for the movement gait, cheetahs use a rotatory gallop with the footfall order of right fore, left fore, left hind, and right hind during curve running [41].

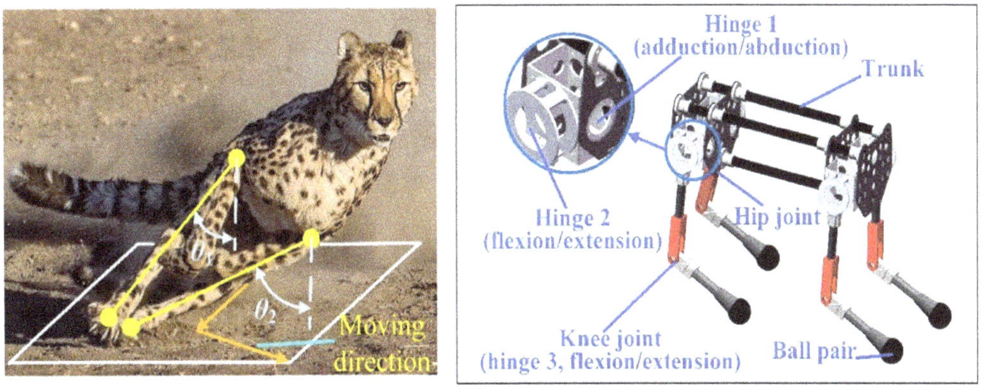

(a) (b)

Figure 1. (**a**) Moment when the cheetah changes its movement direction during running. The legs of the cheetah have larger adduction/abduction angles than the cheetah moving in one plane. (**b**) 3D model of the cheetah-inspired quadruped robot. The hip joint has 2 DOFs, and the knee joint has 1 DOF.

The 3D model of the cheetah-inspired quadruped robot is shown in Figure 1b. The hip joints of each leg have 2 degrees of freedoms (DOF) for adduction/abduction and flexion/extension movements. The axes of the two hinges intersect. The knee joint has 1 DOF for flexion/extension movement. In addition, the leg is in point contact with the ground, which can be equivalent to a 3-DOF ball pair. At this time, each leg has 6 DOFs and no constraints on the trunk. By controlling the leg postures and driving forces of the cheetah-inspired robot, the robot can simulate the cheetah to change motion direction quickly during high-speed motion.

2.2. Establishment of Dynamic Model

During running, the cheetah's two forelegs land first and its two hindlegs land later [41]. For simplicity, the two forelegs are assumed to land simultaneously. When the trunk moves to the lowest point, both forelegs leave the ground at the same time, and both hindlegs land. The trajectory of the trunk during the turning of the robot in the leg landing phase is shown in Figure 2a. When the forelegs of the robot land on the ground, its trunk moves along the trajectory O_1O_2 (O_1 is the position of the center of mass of the trunk at the moment when the forelegs land, and O_2 is the lowest point of the trunk). When the center of mass of the trunk reaches O_2, the movement direction of the trunk is changed, and the robot leaves the ground along the trajectory O_2O_3 (O_3 is the position of center of mass of the trunk at the moment when the hindlegs leave the ground). In the following text, the "trunk descending phase" and "trunk ascending phase" refer to the above two processes. Trajectories O_1O_2 and O_2O_3 are not coplanar, and the trajectory is not necessarily a straight line. The mechanism diagram of the cheetah-inspired quadruped robot is shown in Figure 2b. The coordinate origin of the fixed coordinate system O_0–$X_0Y_0Z_0$ coincides with the projection point of the lowest point O_2 of the trunk motion trajectory on the ground. The directions of the coordinate axes are shown in Figure 2b. The coordinate origin of the moving coordinate system O_t–$X_tY_tZ_t$ coincides with the geometric center of the trunk, and the friction between the legs and the ground during the movement is ignored.

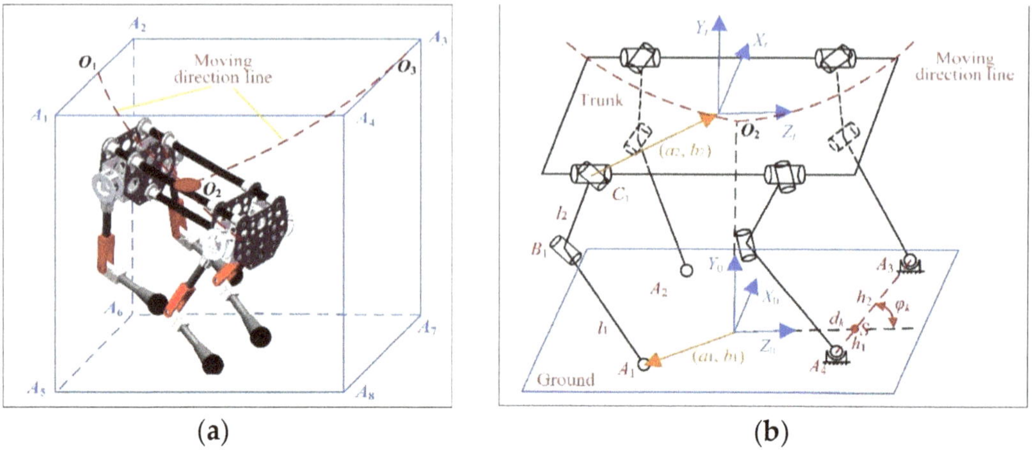

Figure 2. (**a**) Trajectory of the trunk of the cheetah-inspired quadruped robot in the process of changing the motion direction in the leg landing phase. The trajectory O_1O_2 of the center of mass of the trunk in the descending phase and the trajectory O_2O_3 in the ascending phase are not coplanar. (**b**) Mechanism diagram of the cheetah-inspired quadruped robot.

First, the motion law of the trunk must be determined. Trajectories O_1O_2 and O_2O_3 can be expressed as

$$\mathbf{S}_t(x, y, z) = \mathbf{S}_t\left(\sum_{q=0}^{n} d_{qi}t^q, \sum_{q=0}^{n} e_{qi}t^q, \sum_{q=0}^{n} f_{qi}t^q\right), \ i = 1,\ 2 \tag{1}$$

where t is the time, a_q, b_q, and c_q are the polynomial coefficients, and (x_1, y_1, z_1) and (x_2, y_2, z_2) are the coordinates of points O_1 and O_2, respectively. Equation (1) can also reflect the change of velocity and acceleration of the trunk by derivation. In particular, some boundary conditions are known. For example, at the moment when the forelegs of the robot land on the ground and the trunk reaches the lowest point O_2, the position and the velocity of the center of mass of the trunk are known. The velocity of the trunk at point O_1 is also known according to the motion parameters of the previous cycle (a running cycle is defined from the moment of robot landing to the next landing moment). Therefore, a coupling relationship between the polynomial coefficients may exist.

During the movement of the trunk along trajectories O_1O_2 and O_2O_3, the posture of the trunk can be represented by the ZYX Euler angle.

$$Q = \begin{pmatrix} c\alpha c\beta & c\alpha s\beta s\gamma - s\alpha c\gamma & c\alpha s\beta c\gamma + s\alpha s\gamma & x \\ s\alpha c\beta & s\alpha s\beta s\gamma + c\alpha c\gamma & s\alpha s\beta c\gamma - c\alpha s\gamma & y \\ -s\beta & c\beta s\gamma & c\beta c\gamma & z \\ 0 & 0 & 0 & 1 \end{pmatrix}, \tag{2}$$

where "s" and "c" refer to "sin" and "cos", respectively, and α, β, and γ are the Euler angles of the motion coordinate system O_t–$X_tY_tZ_t$ relative to the fixed coordinate system O_0–$X_0Y_0Z_0$. The change of trunk posture can be expressed as a polynomial function:

$$\boldsymbol{\Phi}_t(\alpha, \beta, \gamma) = \boldsymbol{\Phi}_t\left(\sum_{q=0}^{n} a_{qi}t^q, \sum_{q=0}^{n} b_{qi}t^q, \sum_{q=0}^{n} c_{qi}t^q\right) \ i = 1,\ 2 \tag{3}$$

Similarly, boundary conditions can be set according to actual requirements to reduce the number of polynomial coefficients to be optimized.

If the position and the posture of the trunk are determined, the leg posture can be reflected through the contact points between the legs and the ground. Taking the foreleg landing as an example, the contact points can be determined by four parameters, h_1, h_2, d_k, and φ_k, as shown in Figure 2b. h_1 and h_2 are the distances from the two landing points to the intersection S of A_3A_4 (A_3 and A_4 are the two landing points of forelegs) and the Z_0 axis, respectively. d_k is the distance from the coordinate origin of O_0–$X_0Y_0Z_0$ to S. φ_k is the angle between A_3A_4 and the positive direction of the Z_0 axis. At this time, the coordinates of the two landing points A_3 and A_4 can be expressed as

$$\boldsymbol{A}_i = \left[(-1)^i h_i \sin\varphi_k \quad 0 \quad d_k + (-1)^i h_i \cos\varphi_k\right] \; i = 3,\ 4 \tag{4}$$

The calculation method of the landing points is the same for the case of hindleg landing. The kinematic equation of the i-th leg can be expressed as

$${}^{0}T_t = {}^{0}T_{i1}\,{}^{i1}T_{i2}\,{}^{i2}T_{i3}\,{}^{i3}T_{ti}, \tag{5}$$

where

$${}^{0}T_{i1} = \begin{pmatrix} c\theta_{i1}c\theta_{i2} & c\theta_{i1}s\theta_{i2}s\theta_{i3} - s\theta_{i1}c\theta_{i3} & c\theta_{i1}s\theta_{i2}c\theta_{i3} + s\theta_{i1}s\theta_{i3} & l_{i1} + l_{i3}c\theta_{i1}c\theta_{i2} \\ s\theta_{i1}c\theta_{i2} & s\theta_{i1}s\theta_{i2}s\theta_{i3} + c\theta_{i1}c\theta_{i3} & s\theta_{i1}s\theta_{i2}c\theta_{i3} - c\theta_{i1}s\theta_{i3} & l_{i3}s\theta_{i1}c\theta_{i2} \\ -s\theta_{i2} & c\theta_{i2}s\theta_{i3} & c\theta_{i2}c\theta_{i3} & l_{i2} - l_{i3}s\theta_{i2} \\ 0 & 0 & 0 & 1 \end{pmatrix},$$

$${}^{i1}T_{i2} = \begin{pmatrix} s\theta_{i4} & -s\theta_{i4} & 0 & l_{i4}c\theta_{i4} \\ s\theta_{i4} & c\theta_{i4} & 0 & l_{i4}s\theta_{i4} \\ 0 & 0 & 1 & 0 \\ 0 & 0 & 0 & 1 \end{pmatrix},\; {}^{i2}T_{i3} = \begin{pmatrix} c\theta_{i5} & 0 & s\theta_{i5} & 0 \\ s\theta_{i5} & 0 & -c\theta_{i5} & 0 \\ 0 & 1 & 0 & 0 \\ 0 & 0 & 0 & 1 \end{pmatrix},\; {}^{i3}T_{ti} = \begin{pmatrix} c\theta_{i6} & -s\theta_{i6} & 0 & l_{i5}c\theta_{i6} \\ s\theta_{i6} & c\theta_{i6} & 0 & l_{i5}s\theta_{i6} \\ 0 & 0 & 1 & l_{i6} \\ 0 & 0 & 0 & 1 \end{pmatrix}$$

θ_{i1}, θ_{i2}, and θ_{i3} are the rotation angles of the ball pair. θ_{i4} is the rotation angle of the knee joint. θ_{i5} and θ_{i6} are the rotation angles of hinges 2 and 1, respectively, as shown in Figure 1b. (a_{i1}, b_{i1}) is the position vector of point A_i in the fixed coordinate system O_0–$X_0Y_0Z_0$, l_{i1} is the length of link A_iB_i, l_{i2} is the length of link B_iC_i, and (a_{i2}, b_{i2}) is the position vector of point C_i in the moving coordinate system O_t–$X_tY_tZ_t$. For Equation (5), when the position and the posture of the trunk and the position of the landing points are determined, the joint angle θ_{ij} (j = 1, 2, . . . , 6) can be obtained by numerical solution. At this time, the position vector of any point on the link can be expressed as

$$r_{ip} = r_{ipx}\vec{i} + r_{ipy}\vec{j} + r_{ipz}\vec{k} \tag{6}$$

On the basis of solving the kinematics, the dynamic model of the robot should be established. By calculating the first and second derivatives of Equation (5), the angular velocities and angular accelerations of the joints can be expressed as

$$\begin{cases} \dot{\theta}_{ij} = f_1(\boldsymbol{V}_t, \boldsymbol{W}_t) | \boldsymbol{V}_t = (v_{tx}, v_{ty}, v_{tz}), \boldsymbol{W}_t = \left(\dot{\alpha}, \dot{\beta}, \dot{\gamma}\right) \\ \ddot{\theta}_{ij} = f_1(\boldsymbol{V}_t, \boldsymbol{W}_t, \boldsymbol{A}_t, \boldsymbol{T}_t) | \boldsymbol{A}_t = (a_{tx}, a_{ty}, a_{tz}), \boldsymbol{T}_t = \left(\ddot{\alpha}, \ddot{\beta}, \ddot{\gamma}\right) \end{cases}, \tag{7}$$

where $\boldsymbol{V}_t$ and $\boldsymbol{W}_t$ are the velocity and the angular velocity of the trunk, respectively; $\boldsymbol{A}_t$ and $\boldsymbol{T}_t$ are the acceleration and the angular acceleration of the trunk, respectively.

By calculating the first and second derivatives of Equation (6), the velocity and the acceleration of the joint points and centers of mass of the links can be obtained as

$$\boldsymbol{V}_{ij} = \sum_{j=1}^{6}\left(a_{ij}\theta_{ij} + b_{ij}\dot{\theta}_{ij}\right) = \sum_{j=1}^{6}\left(a_{ij}F(\alpha, \beta, \gamma, x, y, z) + b_{ij}\dot{F}(\alpha, \beta, \gamma, x, y, z)\right) \tag{8}$$

$$A_{ij} = \sum_{j=1}^{6}\left(c_{ij}\theta_{ij} + d_{ij}\dot{\theta}_{ij} + e_{ij}\ddot{\theta}_{ij}\right) = \sum_{j=1}^{6}\left(c_{ij}F(\alpha,\beta,\gamma,x,y,z) + d_{ij}\dot{F}(\alpha,\beta,\gamma,x,y,z) + e_{ij}\ddot{F}(\alpha,\beta,\gamma,x,y,z)\right) \quad (9)$$

On this basis, the angular velocity and the angular acceleration of each link can be obtained by

$$\boldsymbol{V}_{i,j+1} = \boldsymbol{V}_{i,j} + \boldsymbol{\omega}_i \times \boldsymbol{L}_i \quad (10)$$

$$\dot{\boldsymbol{V}}_{i,j+1} = \dot{\boldsymbol{V}}_{i,j} + \dot{\boldsymbol{\omega}}_i \times \boldsymbol{L}_i + \boldsymbol{\omega}_i \times (\boldsymbol{\omega}_i \times \boldsymbol{L}_i) \quad (11)$$

where $\boldsymbol{V}_{i,j}$ and $\dot{\boldsymbol{V}}_{i,j}$ are the velocity and the acceleration of the j-th joint of the i-th link, respectively. $\boldsymbol{V}_{i,j+1}$ and $\dot{\boldsymbol{V}}_{i,j+1}$ are the velocity and the acceleration of the (j + 1)-th joint of the i-th link, respectively. $\boldsymbol{\omega}_i$ and $\dot{\boldsymbol{\omega}}_i$ are the angular velocity and the angular acceleration of the i-th link, respectively. $\boldsymbol{L}_i$ is the direction vector of the i-th link.

The driving torques can be obtained by establishing the Lagrange dynamic equation. The total kinetic energy of the robot can be expressed as

$$E_k = \sum_{i=1}^{2}\sum_{j=1}^{2}\left(\frac{1}{2}\,{}^0V_{ij}{}^T m_{ij}\,{}^0V_{ij} + \frac{1}{2}\,{}^0\omega_{ij}{}^T\,{}^0I_{ij}\,{}^0\omega_{ij}\right) + \left(\frac{1}{2}\,{}^0V_t{}^T m_t\,{}^0V_t + \frac{1}{2}\,{}^0\omega_t{}^T\,{}^0I_t\,{}^0\omega_t\right), \quad (12)$$

where m_{ij} and m_t are the masses of the j-th link of the i-th leg and the trunk, respectively. ${}^0V_{ij}$ and ${}^0\omega_{ij}$ are the velocity and the angular velocity of the j-th link of the i-th leg in the fixed coordinate system, respectively. ${}^0V_t$ and ${}^0\omega_t$ are the velocity and the angular velocity of the trunk in the fixed coordinate system, respectively. ${}^0I_{ij}$ and ${}^0I_t$ are the moment of inertia in the fixed coordinate system, which can be expressed as

$${}^0I_{ij(t)} = {}^0T_{ij(t)}\,{}^{ij}I_{ij(t)}\,{}^0T_{ij(t)}{}^T, \quad (13)$$

where ${}^0T_{ij(t)}$ is the transformation matrix of the j-th link of the i-th leg (or the trunk) in the fixed coordinate system. The total potential energy of the robot can be expressed as

$$E_p = \sum_{i=1}^{2}\sum_{j=1}^{2}(m_{ij}gh_{ij}) + m_t g h_t, \quad (14)$$

where h_{ij} and h_t are the distances from the center of mass of the link and the trunk to the ground, respectively, which can be obtained by kinematic analysis.

The trunk of the robot has 6 DOFs when two legs land at the same time. The drives are installed at the hip and knee joints of the legs because the ball pair formed by the contact between the legs and the ground is passive motion. At this time, the Lagrange dynamic equation can be written as

$$\tau_{ij} = \frac{d}{dt}\frac{\partial E_k}{\partial \dot{q}_{ij}} - \frac{\partial E_k}{\partial q_{ij}} + \frac{\partial E_p}{\partial q_{ij}}, \quad (15)$$

where $q_{ij} = (\theta_{i1}, \theta_{i2}, \theta_{i3}, \theta_{i4}, \theta_{i5}, \theta_{i6})$, and $\dot{q}_{ij} = \left(\dot{\theta}_{i1}, \dot{\theta}_{i2}, \dot{\theta}_{i3}, \dot{\theta}_{i4}, \dot{\theta}_{i5}, \dot{\theta}_{i6}\right)$.

Through the method detailed above, the dynamic model of the cheetah-inspired quadruped robot moving at a high speed in 3D space can be established.

2.3. Establishment of Stability Index System

On the basis of establishing the dynamic model, the stability index system must be set up so that the robot has good dynamic performance by optimizing the leg parameters. A two-level stability index system is proposed, including a minimum index system and range index system.

The indices contained in the minimum index system should be as small as possible during robot movement. It includes the total inertia moment, the angular velocity of the trunk, the zero moment point (ZMP), and the energy consumption of the robot in a motion cycle.

(1) Total inertia moment. During the high-speed movement of the robot, it should maintain good stability without overturning and rolling over. During the descending and ascending phases of the trunk, the mean and the variance of the total inertia moment and the total inertia moment of the robot at the moment of leaving the ground should be as small as possible. The total inertia moment at the k-th time can be expressed as

$$\boldsymbol{M}_{Ik} = \sum_{i=1}^{2}\sum_{j=1}^{2}\left(\boldsymbol{r}_{ijk} \times \boldsymbol{F}_{ijk} + \boldsymbol{M}_{ijk}\right) + \boldsymbol{r}_{tk} \times \boldsymbol{F}_{tk} + \boldsymbol{M}_{tk}, \quad (16)$$

where $\boldsymbol{F}_{ij}$ and $\boldsymbol{F}_t$ are the inertia forces of the j-th link of the i-th leg and the trunk, respectively. $\boldsymbol{r}_{ij}$ and $\boldsymbol{r}_t$ are the vectors of the center of mass of the j-th link of the i-th leg and the trunk in the fixed coordinate system, respectively. $\boldsymbol{M}_{ij}$ and $\boldsymbol{M}_t$ are the inertia moments. The above indices can be expressed as

$$\begin{cases} D = \left|\forall D\left(\boldsymbol{M}_{ij(t)}\right) - \forall D\left(\boldsymbol{M}_{kp}\right)\right| \\ E = \left|\forall E\left(\boldsymbol{M}_{ij(t)}\right)\right| \\ V = End\left(\boldsymbol{M}_{ij(t)}\right) \end{cases}, \quad (17)$$

where D, E, and V represent the mean, the variance, and the end value, respectively.

(2) Angular velocity of the trunk. A small total inertia moment can make the robot have a small angular acceleration, but further ensuring that the trunk has a small angular velocity at the moment of leaving the ground is still necessary to prevent the robot from turning during a long flight time. The angular velocity of the robot can be obtained according to Equations (10)–(11).

$$(\boldsymbol{\omega}_r, \boldsymbol{\alpha}_r) = g\left(\boldsymbol{\theta}_{ij}, \dot{\boldsymbol{\Phi}}, \ddot{\boldsymbol{\Phi}}\right) \quad (18)$$

(3) ZMP. ZMP can be expressed as [42]

$$\begin{cases} X_{ZMP} = \dfrac{\sum\limits_{i=1}^{4} m_{ij}\left(\ddot{y}_{ij}+g\right)x_{ij}+m_t\left(\ddot{y}_t+g\right)x_t-\sum\limits_{i=1}^{4} m_{ij}\ddot{x}_{ij}y_{ij}-m_t\ddot{x}_t y_t}{\sum\limits_{i=1}^{4} m_i\left(\ddot{y}_{ij}+g\right)+m_t\left(\ddot{y}_t+g\right)} \\ Y_{ZMP} = 0 \\ Z_{ZMP} = \dfrac{\sum\limits_{i=1}^{4} m_{ij}\left(\ddot{y}_{ij}+g\right)z_{ij}+m_t\left(\ddot{y}_t+g\right)z_t-\sum\limits_{i=1}^{4} m_{ij}\ddot{z}_{ij}y_{ij}-m_t\ddot{z}_t y_t}{\sum\limits_{i=1}^{4} m_i\left(\ddot{y}_{ij}+g\right)+m_t\left(\ddot{y}_t+g\right)} \end{cases} \quad (19)$$

where (x_{ij}, y_{ij}, z_{ij}) and (x_t, y_t, z_t) are the position coordinates of the center of mass of the j-th link of the i-th leg and the trunk in the fixed coordinate system, respectively.

(4) Energy consumption. The energy consumption of the robot in high-speed motion should be as small as possible. The total energy consumption can be expressed as

$$C = \int_0^T \sum_{i=1}^{2}\sum_{j=1}^{3}\left|P_{ij}(t)\right|dt = \int_0^T \sum_{i=1}^{2}\sum_{j=1}^{3}\left|\tau_{ij}(t)\omega_{ij}(t)\right|dt, \quad (20)$$

where P_{ij} is the instantaneous power of the j-th joint of the i-th leg, τ_{ij} is the joint torque, and ω_{ij} is the joint angular velocity.

The indices contained in the range index system are considered to meet the requirements within given ranges. This includes the driving torques of the legs and the leg swing angle.

(1) Driving torques. The mean value of the discrete points of the driving torques for different joints should be in a small range. In this way, motors with the same model can be selected, reducing the difficulty of robot prototype development and control. The variances of the joint torque should also be in a small range to ensure the smoothness of torque changes, and prevent excessive torque changes from affecting the service life of the motor. The above indices can be expressed as

$$\begin{cases} D = \left|\forall D(\tau_{ij}) - \forall D\left(\tau_{kp}\right)\right| \\ E = \left|\forall E(\tau_{ij})\right| \end{cases}, \tag{21}$$

where D and E represent the mean and the variance, respectively.

(2) Leg swing angle. The leg swing angle refers to the angle between the line between the hip joint and the landing point and the vertical direction. If the leg swing angle is too large, the robot easily loses stability due to small friction. Therefore, the leg swing angle should be smaller than the given values. The leg swing angle can be expressed as

$$\boldsymbol{\Psi} = \left(\arccos\frac{z(R_{i6}) - z(R_{i1})}{y(R_{i6}) - y(R_{i1})}\right), \tag{22}$$

where R_{ij} is the position vector of the j-th joint of the i-th leg.

Through the above analysis, a two-level stability index system including the minimum index system and the range index system is established. Among them, the constraints for total inertia moment, angular velocity of the trunk, ZMP, and leg swing angle determine the feasibility of robot motion, and the constraints for energy consumption and driving torques determine the performance advantages of robot long-term movement. The stability index system provides a basis for the subsequent optimization of the motion parameters of the robot.

2.4. Leg parameter Optimization Method

According to the analysis results of the biological mechanism in Section 2.1, the leg postures and the driving torques of the robot during high-speed movement must be determined, which can be obtained through optimization.

The optimization variables include leg posture parameters and trunk motion parameters. The former includes h_{1i}, h_{2i}, d_{ki}, and φ_{ki} (I = 1, 2), as shown in Figure 2b. The latter includes the polynomial coefficients shown in Equations (1) and (3). In particular, the polynomial coefficients are different in the descending and ascending phases of the trunk.

The optimization objective function can be expressed as

$$\begin{aligned} & Z = Min\sum_{i=1}^{n} w_i f_i(x_1, \ldots, x_n) \\ & s.t.\boldsymbol{\Gamma} \end{aligned} \tag{23}$$

where

$$\begin{aligned}
f_1 &= (D|\boldsymbol{M}_{Ik}| - min(D|\boldsymbol{M}_{Ik}|))/(max(D|\boldsymbol{M}_{Ik}|) - min(D|\boldsymbol{M}_{Ik}|)) \\
f_2 &= (E|\boldsymbol{M}_{Ik}| - min(E|\boldsymbol{M}_{Ik}|))/(max(E|\boldsymbol{M}_{Ik}|) - min(E|\boldsymbol{M}_{Ik}|)) \\
f_3 &= (End(|\boldsymbol{M}_{Ik}|) - min(|\boldsymbol{M}_{Ik}|))/(max(|\boldsymbol{M}_{Ik}|) - min(|\boldsymbol{M}_{Ik}|)) \\
f_4 &= (|D(ZMP, A_iA_{i+1})| - min|D(ZMP, A_iA_{i+1})|)/max(|D(ZMP, A_iA_{i+1})| - min|D(ZMP, A_iA_{i+1})|) \\
f_5 &= (|E(ZMP, A_iA_{i+1})| - min|E(ZMP, A_iA_{i+1})|)/max(|E(ZMP, A_iA_{i+1})| - min|E(ZMP, A_iA_{i+1})|) \\
f_6 &= (C - minC)/(maxC - minC)
\end{aligned}$$

f_1 and f_2 represent the mean and variance of the discrete points of the total inertia moment of the robot in the descending and ascending phases, respectively. f_3 represents the total inertia moment of the robot at the moment when it leaves the ground. f_4 and f_5 represent the mean and the variance of the distance from the ZMP to the line between the two landing points, respectively. f_6 represents the energy consumption. In particular, Equation

(3) is derived, and the zero angular velocity of the trunk at the end of the descending and ascending phases can be taken as the boundary condition instead of being listed as the objective function. The relationship between polynomial coefficients and time can be obtained and used as the constraints for optimization. This can ensure that the angular velocity of the trunk of the robot is zero when it leaves the ground, and that the robot has good stability. f_i (i = 1, 2, . . . , 6) should be as small as possible, which corresponds to the minimum index system. w_i is the weight coefficient, which is determined by analytic hierarchy process (AHP). The weight coefficient can be expressed as

$$w_i = \frac{w_j^0}{\sum\limits_{j=1}^{n} w_j^0}, \tag{24}$$

where w_i^0 are the values obtained by adding rows after the standardization of the judgment matrix. In particular, the consistency of the judgment matrix must be checked to ensure that the scoring of experts is logical and does not appear contradictory. Consistency index can be expressed as

$$CR = \frac{\lambda_{max} - n/n - 1}{RI}, \tag{25}$$

where $\lambda_{\max}$ is the maximum eigenvalue of the judgement matrix, and RI is an average random consistency index, which can be obtained by looking up the table.

For Equation (23), $\boldsymbol{\Gamma}$ is the constraints, which can be expressed as

$$\begin{cases} \left|\forall D(\tau_{ij}) - \forall D\left(\tau_{kp}\right)\right| \le Z_D and \left|\forall E(\tau_{ij})\right| \le Z_E \\ \boldsymbol{\Psi} \le \boldsymbol{\Psi}_o \end{cases}, \tag{26}$$

where the first formula indicates that the mean and the variance of the driving torques should meet the range requirements, and Z_D and Z_E are the given reference values. The second formula indicates that the angle between the leg and the ground should be less than the given value $\boldsymbol{\Psi}_0$. Equation (26) is consistent with the range index system.

For the above optimization variables and objective functions, an improved bee colony algorithm is applied in this paper, and the optimization is shown in Algorithm 1. First, the initial ranges of optimization variables $\boldsymbol{Q}$, the kinematic feasible region $\boldsymbol{O}$ (make sure the trunk is in the workspace), and the maximum value $\boldsymbol{Z}(i)_{max}$ and minimum value $\boldsymbol{Z}(i)_{min}$ of the objective function are given. A set of optimization variables $\boldsymbol{W}(j)$ is taken from the initial range $\boldsymbol{Q}^{range}$, and each item in the optimization objective function $\boldsymbol{Z}(j)$ and the motion parameters $\boldsymbol{O}(j)$ are calculated based on bee colony algorithm H_{rule}^{G} and range constraints $\boldsymbol{M}$. By judging the value of the objective function, $\boldsymbol{Q}^{range}$, $\boldsymbol{Z}(i)^{min}$, and $\boldsymbol{Z}(i)^{max}$ are updated and assigned to Q_{new}^{range},$Z((\mathrm{i}))_{new}^{min}$, and $Z(i)_{new}^{max}$, respectively, to obtain the approximate accurate values. While carrying out the accurate dimensionless processing of the objective function, the design efficiency is improved through the accurate constraints of the ranges. On this basis, values are taken from Q_{new}^{range}, the objective function $\boldsymbol{Z}(j)$ is calculated, and Q_{new}^{range},$Z(i)_{new}^{min}$, and $Z(i)_{new}^{max}$ are simultaneously updated to improve the constraint accuracy continuously. In particular, when the ratio of the total number of cycles to the current number of cycles is a positive natural number, the result obtained by the previous generation calculation is used as a reference to reduce the ranges by multiplying the scale coefficient k (k < 1) to improve the calculation efficiency. Finally, the minimum value of the objective function is obtained, and the optimization variables are output.

Algorithm 1 Leg parameters optimization

Nomenclature:

Q% Ranges of optimization variables
W% Optimization variables
Z% Optimization objective function
O% Kinematic feasibility constraints
M% Range constraints
H_{rule}^{G}% Bee colony algorithm

Set Q^{range}, O^{range}, $Z(i)^{min}$, $Z(i)^{max}$, and M
For j=1, ..., N_1
Select $W(j)$ from Q^{range}
Calculate $Z(j)$ and (j) by H_{rule}^{G} and$M$
If $O(j) \in O^{range}$
Update Q^{range},$Z(i)^{min}$ and $Z(i)^{max}$ *by* $Z(j)$
$Q_{new}^{range} = Q^{range}$, $Z(i)_{new}^{min}$ $Z(i)^{min}$ and $Z(i)_{new}^{max} = Z(i)^{max}$
End If
End For
For j = 1, ..., N_2
Select (j) fromQ_{new}^{range}
Calculate $Z(j)$ byH_{rule}^{G} and M
Update Q_{new}^{range}, $Z(i)_{new}^{min}$ and $Z(i)_{new}^{max}$ *by* $Z(j)$
If N_2 / N^*
Update Q_{new}^{range}
End if
Calculate Z by $Z(i)_{new}^{min}$ and $Z(i)_{new}^{max}$
If $Z \leq Z_{best}$
Copy Z into Z_{best}
End if
End For

In particular, for the above optimization process, parallel calculation is used in the process of employed bees, on-looker bees, and scout bees to find honey sources, and the extreme value of the objective function is dynamically updated after the calculation for each kind of bee is completed. At the same time, the dynamic parameters for the scout bees are added, and the working threshold of the scout bees is adjusted dynamically according to the convergence of the objective function. The above process can improve the convergence speed and enhances the ability of global optimal search.

3. Results

3.1. Examples

To prove the feasibility of the method proposed in this paper, two examples are given. The structural parameters of the robot are shown in Table 1. The variable (a_2, b_2) represents the coordinates of the hip joint in the moving coordinate system O_t–$X_tY_tZ_t$, as shown in Figure 2b. The thigh and the calf legs are cylinders, and the section radius r and length h are given in Table 1. For example 1, the known parameters are shown in Table 2. v_1 and v_2 are the velocities of the trunk at points O_1 and O_3, respectively; (x_1, y_1, z_1) and (x_2, y_2, z_2) are the coordinates of points O_1 and O_2, respectively. $\mathbf{\Phi}_0$ is the trunk posture angle at the moment of landing. $\mathbf{\Psi}_0$, Z_D, and Z_E are the given values shown in Equation (26).

Table 1. Structural parameters of the cheetah-inspired quadruped robot.

Size of Thigh/[r, h]/m	Size of Calf/[r, h]/m	Size of Trunk/m	Mass of Thigh/Kg	Mass of Calf/Kg	Mass of Trunk/Kg	(a_2, b_2)/m
0.02/0.24	0.02/0.28	0.18 × 0.2 × 0.6	0.2	0.3	1.8	(0.12, 0.26)

Table 2. Known values during optimization for example 1.

v_1/(m/s)	v_2/(m/s)	(x_1, y_1, z_1)/m	(x_2, y_2, z_2)/m	Φ_0/°	Ψ_0/°	Z_D/Z_E/(Nm)
(0, 0, 0.22)	(1.73, 0.87, 3.26)	(0.13, 0.35, −0.2)	(0, 0.3, 0)	(25, 10, 0)	60	5.0/10

To ensure the motion stability of the robot, the trunk movement trajectory and posture change rule are assumed cubic functions, and the polynomial coefficients need to be determined. In the descending phase of the trunk, the trajectory equation and the posture equation of the trunk have 12 undetermined polynomial coefficients. The position and the velocity of the trunk at O_1 and O_2 are known, the angle and angular velocity of the trunk at O_1 and O_2 are known, and the trunk does not rotate around the Z_t axis. By substituting the boundary conditions into Equations (1) and (3), all polynomial coefficients can be expressed as functions of time. In the ascending phase of the trunk, the position and the velocity of the trunk at O_2, the velocity direction of the trunk at O_3, the trunk angle and the angular velocity at O_2, and the trunk angular velocity at O_3 are known. The relationship between the undetermined coefficients and the movement time can also be obtained by substituting the boundary conditions into Equations (1) and (3). However, not all polynomial coefficients can be expressed in time. Two coefficients in Equation (1) and three coefficients in Equation (3) still need to be determined. To sum up, the optimization variables involved in the trunk motion to be determined include t_1 (movement time of trunk in the descending phase), t_2 (movement time of trunk in the ascending phase), a_{12}, a_{22}, d_{12}, d_{22}, and d_{32}. The optimization variables also include leg landing point parameters h_{1i}, h_{2i}, d_{ki}, and φ_{ki}. The initial ranges of the optimization variables are listed randomly in Table 3. The weight coefficients are w_1 = 0.0755, w_2 = 0.0464, w_3 = 0.5984, w_4 = 0.1305, w_5 = 0.0623, and w_6 = 0.0869. For the hierarchical bee colony algorithm, the number of honey sources is 100, the number of leading bees is 100, and the maximum number of iterations is 100. The optimization results obtained by the method proposed in this paper are shown in Table 3.

Table 3. Initial parameter ranges and optimization results for example 1.

	h_{11}/m	h_{21}/m	d_{k1}/m	φ_{k1}/°	h_{12}/m	h_{22}/m	d_{k2}/m	
Initial ranges	[0, 0.2]	[0, 0.3]	[−0.1, 0.1]	[0, 180]	[0, 0.6]	[0, 0.6]	[−0.1, 0.4]	
	φ_{k2}/°	t_1/s	t_2/s	a_{12}	a_{22}	d_{12}/°	d_{22}/°	d_{32}/°
	[0, 180]	[0.5, 1]	[0.1, 0.5]	[10, 61]	[0, 15]	[−15, 0]	[10, 45]	[−30, 30]
Optimization results	h_{11}/m	h_{21}/m	d_{k1}/m	φ_{k1}/°	h_{12}/m	h_{22}/m	d_{k2}/m	
	0.17	0.04	0.08	74.12	0.10	0.33	−0.02	
	φ_{k2}/°	t_1/s	t_2/s	a_{12}	a_{22}	d_{12}/°	d_{22}/°	d_{32}/°
	53.29	0.8	0.3	17	7.55	−13	32.69	20

Figure 3a,b show the motion sequence when the robot changes motion direction during running. In the descending phase of the trunk, the two forelegs of the robot are in contact with the ground, and the center of mass of the trunk moves 243.72 mm in 0.8 s. In the ascending phase of the trunk, the two hindlegs of the robot are in contact with the ground, and the center of mass of the trunk moves 492.58 mm in 0.3 s. Figure 3c shows the trajectory of the center of mass of the trunk. When the forelegs of the robot touch the ground, the motion direction vector of the trunk is (0, 0, 1). At the moment when the hindlegs of the robot leave the ground, the motion direction vector of the trunk is (1.74, 0.5, 1.84). From the top view, the included angle of the direction vector is 28.08°, and the running direction of the robot changes clearly. Figure 3d shows the change of trunk posture. The proper change of body posture is conducive to keeping the good dynamic stability of the robot. The angles of the robot around the three axes at the moment of leaving the ground are −13.01°,

32.69°, and 19.81°. The changes of angular velocities obtained by the method described in Section 2.4 are shown in Figure 3e. The angular velocity of the robot at the moment of leaving the ground is zero, and the trunk of the robot will not rotate significantly in the flight phase. Figure 3f shows the positions of the landing points of the legs. In the descending phase of the trunk, the coordinates of the landing point of the two forelegs are (200, 0, and 243.81 mm) and (−62.01, 0, and −107.17 mm). In the ascending phase of the trunk, the landing point coordinates of the two hindlegs are (−151.93, 0, and 0.04 mm) and (−32.88, 0, and 99.98 mm). The leg landing points are no longer symmetrical along the Z_0 axis, and the legs have evident adduction/abduction angles. The maximum leg swing angles of the forelegs are 41.04° and 41.09°, and the maximum leg swing angles of the hindlegs are 45.09° and 41.00°. This outcome is consistent with the analysis results of the movement mechanism of the cheetah when it turns during running, as shown in Figure 1a.

The dynamic performance of the cheetah-inspired quadruped robot during steering is shown in Figure 4. The change of the total inertia moment of the robot is shown in Figure 4a. In the descending phase of the trunk, the amplitude of the total inertia moment of the robot is small and changes gently. When the trunk reaches the lowest point O_2, the total inertia moments of the robot along the three axes are 0.99, −0.12, and −0.73 N·m. In the ascending phase of the trunk, the total inertia moment increases substantially but then decreases rapidly because the robot needs to obtain a large acceleration in a short time. When the trunk reaches point O_3, the total inertia moments of the robot along the three axes are −4.64, 0.94, and −0.31 N·m. Figure 4b shows the changes of the total inertia moment before and after optimization. "*B*" and "*A*" refer to before and after optimization, respectively. $E(M_{tI})$, $m(M_{tI})$, and $V(M_{tI})$ represent the end value, the mean, and the variance of the total inertia moment, respectively. The total inertia moment before optimization is calculated by substituting the initial parameters. Figure 4b shows that the total inertia moment decreases considerably after optimization. In the descending phase of the trunk, the maximum reductions of $E(M_{tI})$, $m(M_{tI})$, and $V(M_{tI})$ after optimization are 54.22%, 47.79%, and 78.96%, respectively. In the ascending phase of the trunk, the maximum reductions of $E(M_{tI})$, $m(M_{tI})$, and $V(M_{tI})$ after optimization are 99.6%, 97.7%, and 99.9%, respectively. The dynamic stability of the robot is remarkably improved. Figure 4c shows the distance from ZMP to the connecting line between the two landing points during the descending phase of the trunk. The average value of the distance is 9.08 mm. ZMP is near the connecting line of two points. The deviation is small compared with the size of the robot, and the robot has good dynamic stability. Figure 4d shows the mean and variance of driving torques. "J-1," "J-2," and "J-3" represent hinges 1, 2, and 3, respectively, as shown in Figure 1b. The maximum difference between the mean values of driving torques of the different joints is only 2.8 N/m, and the driving torques change smoothly with a slight difference in amplitude. Moreover, the energy consumption of the robot during movement is 27.96 J. The above analysis results reveal that the optimized indices that are contained in the minimum index system are very small, and the indices contained in the range index system are within reasonable ranges. The robot has good dynamic stability by using the parameters of the leg postures and the driving torques obtained by the method proposed in this paper.

For example 1, the robot turns left during running from the top view, thus the projection of the motion direction vector on the ground of the robot at the moment of leaving the ground is counterclockwise relative to that of the robot at the moment of landing. To prove the feasibility of the method proposed in this paper further, an example of the robot turning to the right is given. The known values remain unchanged, as shown in Table 2. The initial range of optimization variables and optimization results are shown in Tables 4 and 5.

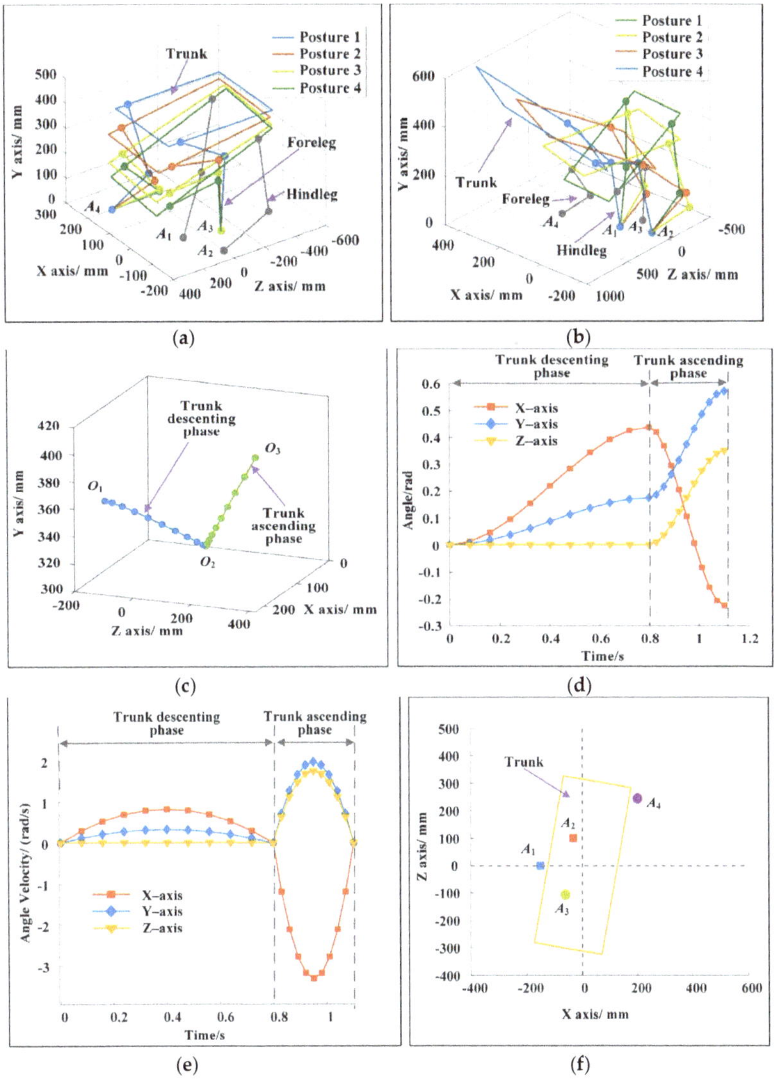

Figure 3. (**a**) Motion sequence of the robot in the descending phase of the trunk for example 1. (**b**) Motion sequence of the robot in the ascending phase of the trunk for example 1. (**c**) Movement trajectory of the trunk for example 1. In the descending and ascending phases of the trunk, the trajectories are cubic functions. (**d**) Changes of trunk posture for example 1. In the descending phase of the trunk, the angle changes of the trunk around the three axes are 25°, 10°, and 0°. In the ascending phase of the trunk, the angle changes of the trunk around the three axes are 38.01°, −22.69°, and −20.00°. (**e**) Changes of trunk angular velocity for example 1. The angular velocity of the robot at the moment of leaving the ground is zero. (**f**) Landing points of the forelegs and the hindlegs for example 1.

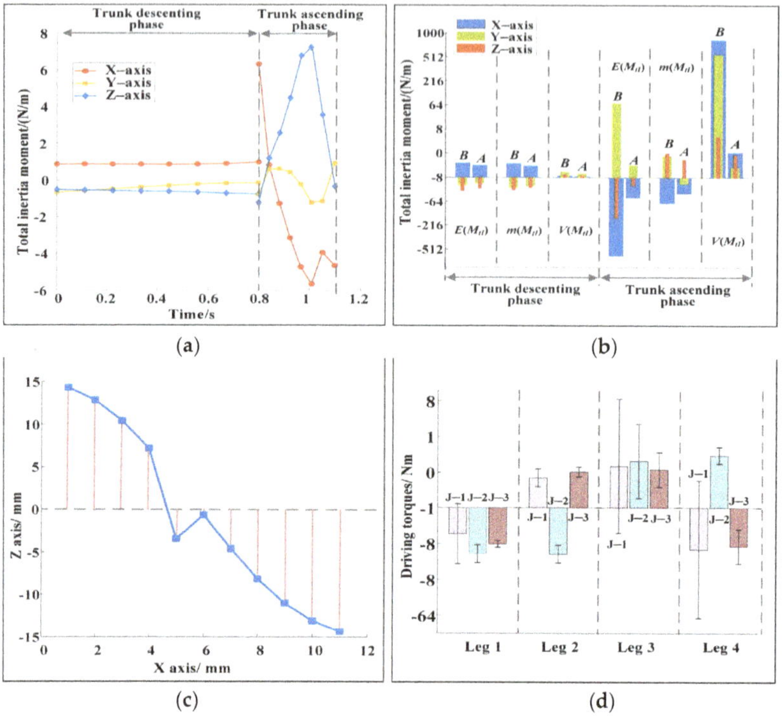

Figure 4. (**a**) Change of the total inertia moment of the robot in the descending and the ascending phases after optimization for example 1. (**b**) Changes of the total inertia moment of the robot before and after optimization for example 1. The maximum reduction of the end value, the mean, and the variance of the total inertia moment of the robot after optimization are 99.6%, 97.7%, and 99.9%, respectively, and the decreases are evident. (**c**) Change of ZMP during the descending phase of the trunk for example 1. ZMP changes near the connecting line of the landing points of two legs, showing good stability. (**d**) Mean and variance of the driving torques for example 1. The maximum difference of the mean value is 2.8 N·m, and the maximum variance is 7.16 N·m. The driving torques are within reasonable ranges.

Table 4. Known values during optimization for example 2.

v_1/(m/s)	v_2/(m/s)	(x_1, y_1, z_1)/m	(x_2, y_2, z_2)/m	Φ_0/°	Ψ_0/°	Z_D/Z_E/(Nm)
(0, 0, 0.25)	(−1.60, 0.80, 3.00)	(0.13, 0.35, −0.2)	(0, 0.3, 0)	(25, −10, 0)	60	5.0/10

Table 5. Initial parameter ranges and optimization results for example 2.

Initial ranges	h_{11}/m	h_{21}/m	d_{k1}/m	φ_{k1}/°	h_{12}/m	h_{22}/m	d_{k2}/m	
	[0, 0.3]	[0, 0.2]	[−0.1, 0.1]	[0, 180]	[0, 0.6]	[0, 0.6]	[−0.1, 0.4]	
	φ_{k2}/°	t_1/s	t_2/s	a_{12}	a_{22}	d_{12}/°	d_{22}/°	d_{32}/°
	[0, 180]	[0, 1]	[0, 0.5]	[10, 61]	[0, 15]	[−15, 0]	[−45, −10]	[−30, 30]
Optimization results	h_{11}/m	h_{21}/m	d_{k1}/m	φ_{k1}/°	h_{12}/m	h_{22}/m	d_{k2}/m	
	0.02	0.25	−0.13	0.05	0.03	0.15	0.001	
	φ_{k2}/°	t_1	t_2	a_{12}	a_{22}	d_{12}/°	d_{22}/°	d_{32}/°
	44.67	0.8	0.22	26.86	10	−15	−12	12.88

The optimization results for example 2 are shown in Figure 5. Figure 5a,b show the motion sequence of the robot for example 2. In the descending phase of the trunk, the center of mass of the trunk moves 243.72 mm in 0.8 s. In the ascending phase of the trunk, the center of mass of the trunk moves 337.3 mm in 0.22 s. Figure 5c shows the change of trunk posture. Similarly, the angular velocity of the trunk at the moment of leaving the ground is zero. Figure 5d shows the positions of the landing points of the legs. The maximum leg swing angles of the forelegs and hindlegs are (53.30°, 48.10°) and (33.75°, 27.71°), respectively. The dynamic performance of the cheetah-inspired quadruped robot during steering is shown in Figure 5e,f. Figure 5e shows the changes of the total inertia moment before and after optimization. Similarly, the total inertia moment before optimization is calculated by substituting the initial parameters. Compared with those before optimization, in the descending phase of the trunk, the maximum reductions of $E(M_{tI})$, $m(M_{tI})$, and $V(M_{tI})$ after optimization are 45.8%, 46.9%, and 68.8%, respectively. In the ascending phase of the trunk, the maximum reductions of $E(M_{tI})$, $m(M_{tI})$, and $V(M_{tI})$ after optimization are 98.89%, 90.2%, and 97.57%, respectively. Moreover, the total inertia moments of the robot around the three axes at the moment of leaving the ground are −4.7069, −0.5166, and −3.9464 N·m within small ranges. This finding shows that the robot has good dynamic stability. Figure 5f shows the mean and the variance of the driving torques. The maximum difference between the mean values of driving torques of the different joints is only 5.88 N/m, and the variance is not too large.

3.2. Simulation

Two examples are simulated with Webots to verify that the robot can turn quickly while running and has good dynamic stability, and the simulation videos are shown in Supplementary Materials. Each example contains two continuous running cycles. The structural parameters of the robot are consistent with theoretical calculation. Since the robot has a long flight time during running, the stability of the robot is directly reflected by the rotation angle of its trunk. For simulation example 1, the robot turns left continuously while running. Taking the joint angles and driving torques obtained by theoretical calculation as input for the first running cycle, the input parameters of the robot in the second running cycle can be calculated by the same method. The top view of the motion sequences of the robot in two cycles is shown in Figure 6a. O_1, O_2 and O_3 refer to the position of the center of mass of the trunk shown in Figure 2a, and O_4 refers to the highest point of the robot in the flight phase. The robot rotates 28.08° around the vertical axis in both cycles, and the motion direction changes substantially. The trunk rotation angles corresponding to Figure 6a is shown in Figure 6c. In the descending and ascending phases of the trunk of the robot in the first running cycle, the trunk rotation angles are exactly the same as those shown in Figure 3d. From one perspective, it proves the correctness of theoretical calculation; conversely, it can also show that the robot moves according to the predetermined rules in the descending and ascending phases of trunk, without movement failure, such as rollover. In the flight phase, the trunk posture of the robot almost remains unchanged. The maximum rotation angles of the trunk in two cycles around the three axes are −2.95°, 3.75°, and 3.32°. This finding shows that the robot has small angular velocity at the moment of leaving the ground, which can be seen in Figure 6e, and it also proves the correctness of the proposed two-level stability index system. For simulation example 2, the top views of the motion sequences of the robot and the trunk rotation angle are shown in Figure 6b,d, respectively. The robot rotates −28.08° around the vertical axis in both cycles. In the descending and ascending phases of the trunk of the robot in the first cycle, the trunk rotation angles are exactly the same as those shown in Figure 4c. In the flight phase, the maximum rotation angles of the trunk in two cycles around the three axes are 1.88°, 0.92°, and −3.72°. The change of the angular velocity of the trunk corresponding to simulation example 2 is shown in Figure 6f, and the angular velocity of the robot at the moment of leaving the ground in two cycles is approximately zero. The rotation angles of the trunk in the flight phases and the angular velocity of the trunk at the moment of leaving the ground are within small ranges, and the robot shows good dynamic stability.

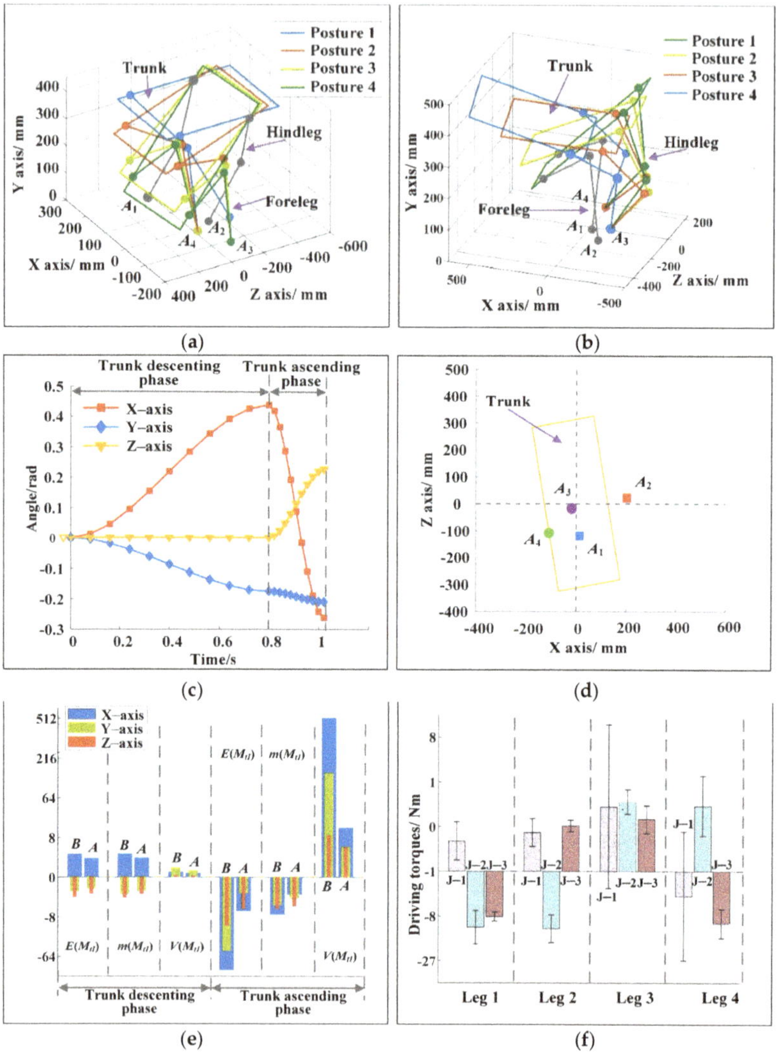

Figure 5. (**a**) Motion sequence of the robot in the descending phase of the trunk for example 2. (**b**) Motion sequence of the robot in the ascending phase of the trunk for example 2. (**c**) Changes of trunk posture for example 2. In the descending phase of the trunk, the angle changes of the trunk around the three axes are 25°, −10°, and 0°. In the ascending phase of the trunk, the angle changes of the trunk around the three axes are −40.01°, −12°, and 12.88°. (**d**) The landing points of the forelegs and hindlegs for example 2. (**e**) Changes of the total inertia moment of the robot before and after optimization for example 2. The maximum reductions of the end value, the mean, and the variance of the total inertia moment of the robot after optimization are 98.9%, 90.2%, and 97.6%, respectively, and the decreases are evident. (**f**) Mean and variance of the driving torques for example 2. The maximum difference of the mean value is 5.88 N·m, and the maximum variance is 6.12 N·m. The driving torques are within reasonable ranges.

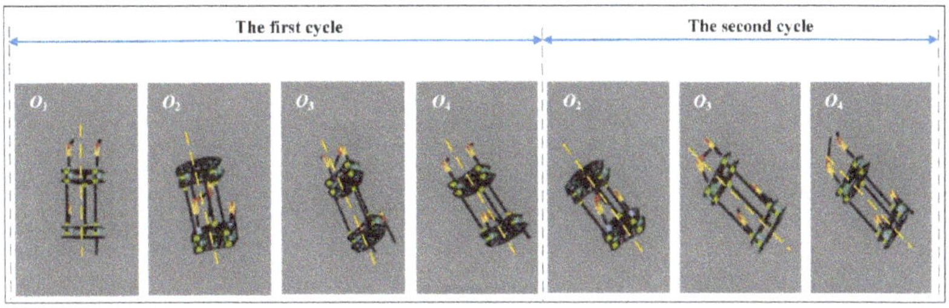

(**a**)

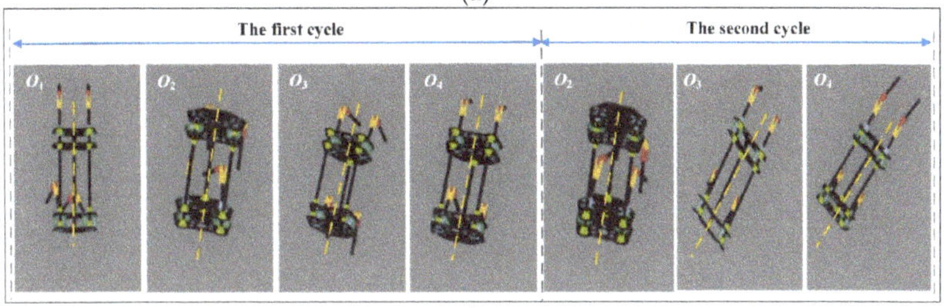

(**b**)

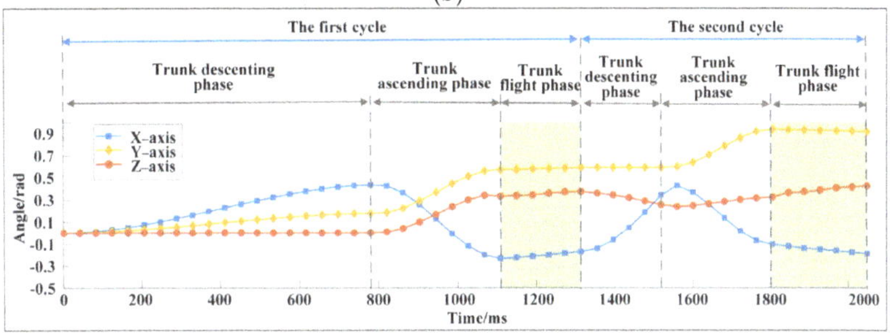

(**c**)

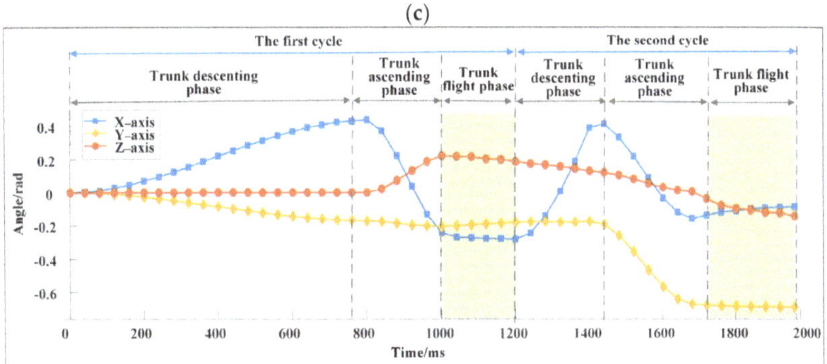

(**d**)

Figure 6. *Cont.*

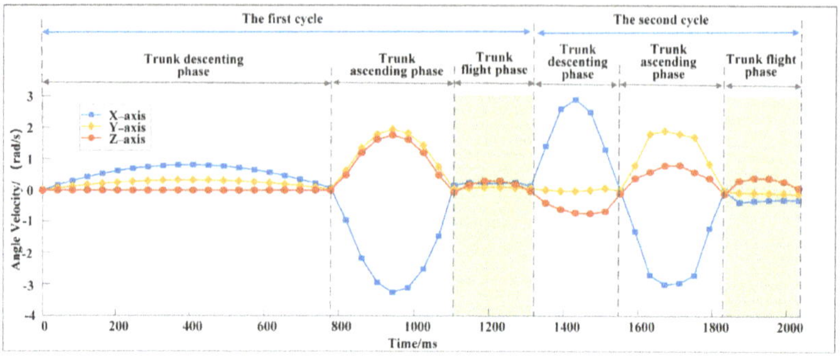

(**e**)

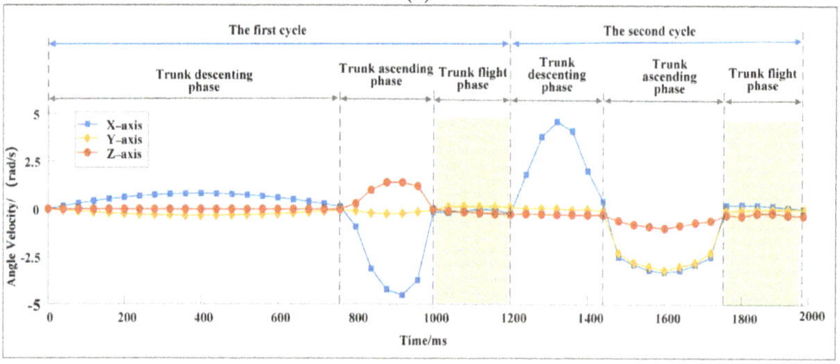

(**f**)

Figure 6. (**a**) Top view of the motion sequences of the robot for simulation example 1. The robot rotates 28.08° around the vertical axis in both cycles, and the direction of motion changes considerably. (**b**) Top view of the motion sequences of the robot for simulation example 2. The robot rotates −28.28° around the vertical axis in both cycles. (**c**) Change of trunk posture for simulation example 1. The changes of the maximum rotation angles of the trunk in the flight phase are −2.95°, 3.75°, and 3.32°. (**d**) The change of trunk posture for simulation example 2. The changes of the maximum rotation angles of the trunk in the flight phase are 1.88°, 0.92°, and −3.72°. (**e**) Change of trunk angular velocity of the trunk for simulation example 1. (**f**) Change of trunk angular velocity of the trunk for simulation example 2.

The above simulation results show that the proposed method in this paper can make the trunk posture of the robot stable and achieve good dynamic stability in high-speed steering motion by controlling the leg postures and the driving torques. The cheetah-inspired quadruped robot does not overturn or roll over due to excessive velocity and change of movement direction, so that the movement fails.

4. Discussion

In this paper, the main research objective is to propose a method to maintain the dynamic stability of the robot during steering running. Therefore, a two-level stability index system, including a minimum index system and a range index system, is proposed based on the dynamic model, and optimization objective functions are established based on the index system. The optimization variables include not only leg posture parameters, but also the trunk movement trajectory and posture parameters. Through the coordination of leg postures and driving torques obtained by the improved bee colony algorithm, the legged robot can achieve good dynamic performance [42–44]. The method proposed in this paper can make the quadruped robot achieve fast steering in running, and the following factors need to be considered.

(1) Changes in trunk posture. Figures 3 and 5 show that the posture of the trunk changes during the descending and ascending phases. If the trunk is forced to remain horizontal without a posture change, although the trunk looks more stable, keeping the total inertia moment within a small range at the moment of the robot leaving the ground is difficult. The robot turns over evidently in the flight phase, which leads to motion failure. Figure 7a shows the change of the total inertia moment of the robot when the trunk is forced horizontally. The total inertia moments of the robot at the moment of leaving the ground are −26.43, 5.41, and 7.40 N·m. They are substantially larger than those shown in Figures 4 and 5. Moreover, the change of the trunk angle should be reasonable. For example, Figure 7b shows a set of calculated results for trunk angle changes. Although the total inertia moment of the robot corresponding to Figure 7b is within a reasonable range and the robot is stable, the pitch angle of the robot at the moment of leaving the ground is 41.28°, which is not conducive to the stability of the robot in the next cycle. Figures 3d and 5c show that the pitch angle of the trunk is relatively small at the moment of leaving the ground, and this is conducive to the robot maintaining good dynamic stability.

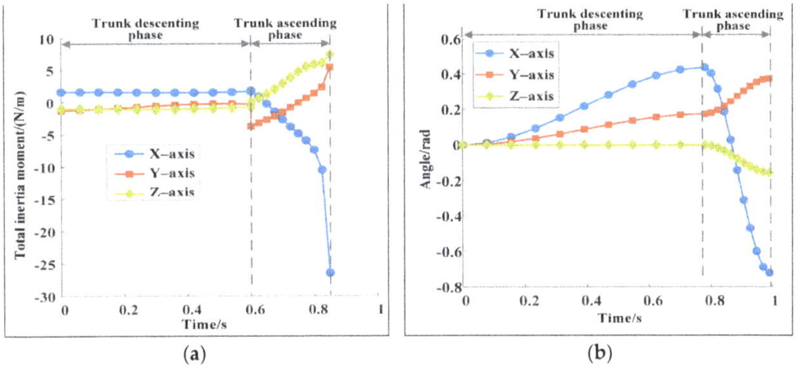

Figure 7. (**a**) Change of the total inertia moment when the trunk is forced horizontally. The maximum value of the total inertia moment is 27.97 N·m, which is much greater than the value shown in Figure 4a. (**b**) A possible trunk posture change rule. Although the corresponding total inertia moment is within a reasonable range, the maximum pitching angle of the trunk is 41.28°, which is not conducive to the stability of the robot.

(2) Coupling of multiple parameters. High-speed motion in 3D space has many dynamic stability indices, and the coupling degree between indices is high. For example, a large coupling relationship exists between the steering angle, the velocity, the total inertia moment of the robot at the moment of leaving the ground, and ZMP. When the velocity of the robot at the moment of leaving the ground increases—that is, when the forward distance of the robot in a cycle increases—or the steering angle is too large, always staying near the connecting line the landing points of the two legs is difficult for the ZMP of the robot and the total inertia moment increases, thus the robot has difficulty maintaining good stability. For example, when the velocity of the trunk increases from 3.5 m/s to 5 m/s at the moment of leaving the ground, the total inertia moment after optimization remarkably increases from 6.16 N·m to 14.21 N·m. Although it can increase the movement time of the trunk in the ascending phase to reduce the total inertia moment, the difficulty of obtaining the optimal solution increases. Therefore, the motion parameters of the robot must be reasonably determined to achieve continuous, stable motion.

(3) Determination of weight coefficients. For the optimization objective function shown in Equation (23), the weight coefficients influence the results. For the examples shown in Section 3.1, the weight coefficients are determined by AHP. f_3 and f_4 have a great influence on dynamic stability, and their weight coefficients are large; f_1, f_2, f_5, and f_6 have minimal influence on dynamic stability, and their weight coefficients are relatively small. If the

weight coefficients are changed to w_i=1/i, the optimization results show that the total inertia moments of the robot after optimization at the moment of leaving the ground are −21.31, 4.35, and −5.29 N·m. The dynamic stability clearly deteriorates. Therefore, using experts' experience to determine the importance of the indices to determine the weight coefficients is reasonable.

However, due to the complexity of the optimization objective functions and the large number of optimization variables, the current optimization efficiency cannot meet the real-time requirements. The robot needs to complete the motion planning in advance under the known terrain to achieve complex high-speed movement. In the future, on the basis of the method proposed in this paper, the data set can be established and the method to maintain the dynamic stability of the robot during steering running based on deep neural network can be further proposed. The efficiency of the algorithm will be further improved, making it possible for the robot to complete high-speed steering movement in real time.

5. Conclusions

The steering of the quadruped robot during high-speed running is of great importance for improving its movement flexibility. However, too many optimization variables, high coupling of multiple performance indices, and high velocity make the research difficult. Therefore, taking the cheetah-inspired quadruped robot as the research object, the method of changing the running direction of the robot was proposed to make the robot turn quickly in the process of high-speed movement and have good dynamic stability. (1) On the basis of establishing the dynamic model of the cheetah-inspired quadruped robot running, a two-level dynamic stability index system was proposed, including a minimum index system and a range index system, which cover almost all of the indices that affect the dynamic stability of the robot. (2) The optimization objective function based on the dynamic stability index system and optimization variables are determined. Then, the optimal values were obtained based on the improved bee colony algorithm. By controlling the leg posture parameters and the corresponding driving torques, the robot can change the motion direction during high-speed movement. (3) According to the method proposed in this paper, two examples were given: The robot turned 28.08° to the left and −28.08° to the right during forward running when viewed from the top view. The calculation results showed that the total inertia moment of the robot was in a small reasonable range, and the angular velocity of the robot at the moment of leaving the ground was approximately zero, which proved that the robot had good dynamic stability. The simulation results show that there is no obvious change in the posture of the trunk of the robot during the flight phase, and the robot can land stably, which also proved the correctness of the method. The method proposed in this paper can provide a theoretical basis for the realization of high-speed movement of the robot in 3D space and had good applicability.

Supplementary Materials: The following supporting information can be downloaded at: https://www.mdpi.com/article/10.3390/s22249601/s1, Video S1: Simulation results of rapid steering in the running of the quadruped robot.

Author Contributions: Methodology, M.N. and Z.Z.; software, J.Y. and Z.W.; validation, J.L. and L.W.; writing, original draft preparation, Z.Z. and P.F.; writing—review and editing, Z.Z. and J.Y.; project administration, M.N.; funding acquisition, Z.Z. All authors have read and agreed to the published version of the manuscript.

Funding: This research was funded by the National Natural Science Foundation of China (Grant Number 51805010).

Data Availability Statement: The original data contributions presented in the paper are included in the article. Further inquiries can be directed to the corresponding authors.

Conflicts of Interest: The authors declare no conflict of interest.

References

1. Hudson, P.E.; Corr, S.A.; Payne-Davis, R.C.; Clancy, S.N.; Lane, E.; Wilson, A.M. Functional anatomy of the cheetah (*Acinonyx jubatus*) hindlimb. *J. Anat.* **2010**, *218*, 363–374. [CrossRef] [PubMed]
2. Lindstedt, S.L.; Hokanson, J.F.; Wells, D.J.; Swain, S.D.; Hoppeler, H.; Navarro, V. Running energetics in the pronghorn antelope. *Nature* **1991**, *353*, 748–750. [CrossRef] [PubMed]
3. Park, H.W.; Park, S.; Kim, S. Variable-speed quadrupedal bounding using impulse planning: Untethered high-speed 3D Running of MIT Cheetah 2. In Proceedings of the 2015 IEEE International Conference on Robotics and Automation (ICRA), Seattle, WA, USA, 26–30 May 2015; 2015; pp. 5163–5170.
4. Kropff, E.; Carmichael, J.E.; Moser, E.I.; Moser, M.B. Frequency of theta rhythm is controlled by acceleration, but not speed, in running rats. *Neuron* **2021**, *109*, 1029–1039. [CrossRef] [PubMed]
5. Kamimura, T.; Sato, K.; Aoi, S.; Higurashi, Y.; Wada, N.; Tsuchiya, K.; Sano, A.; Matsuno, F. Three characteristics of cheetah galloping improve running performance through spinal movement: A modeling study. *Front. Bioeng. Biotechnol.* **2022**, *10*, 825638. [CrossRef]
6. Mikolajczyk, T.; Mikolajewska, E.; Al-Shuka, H.F.N.; Malinowski, T.; Klodowski, A.; Pimenov, D.Y.; Paczkowski, T.; Hu, F.W.; Giasin, K.; Mikolajewski, D.; et al. Recent advances in bipedal walking robots: Review of gait, drive, sensors and control systems. *Sensors* **2022**, *22*, 4440. [CrossRef]
7. Rubenson, J.; Sawicki, G.S. Running birds reveal secrets for legged robot design. *Sci. Robot.* **2022**, *64*, abo2147. [CrossRef]
8. Kamimura, T.; Sato, K.; Murayama, D.; Kawase, N.; Sano, A. Dynamical effect of elastically supported wobbling mass on biped running. In Proceedings of the IEEE/RSJ International Conference on Intelligent Robots and Systems (IROS), Electr Network, Prague, Czech Republic, 27 September–1 October 2021; pp. 4071–4078.
9. Huang, B.; Chen, W.B.; Liang, J.J.Y.; Cheng, L.F.; Xiong, C.H. Characterization and categorization of various human lower limb movements based on kinematic synergies. *Front. Bioeng. Biotechnol.* **2022**, *9*, 793746. [CrossRef]
10. Bidgoly, H.J.; Vafaei, A.; Sadeghi, A.; Ahmadabadi, M.N. Learning approach to study effect of flexible spine on running behavior of a quadruped robot. In Proceedings of the 13th International Conference on Climbing and Walking Robots and the Support Technologies for Mobile Machines, Nagoya Inst Technol, Nagoya, Japan, 31 August–3 September 2010; pp. 1195–1201.
11. Phan, L.T.; Lee, Y.H.; Lee, Y.H.; Lee, H.; Kang, H.; Choi, H.R. Study on effects of spinal joint for running quadruped robots. *Intell. Serv. Robot.* **2019**, *13*, 29–46. [CrossRef]
12. Lee, J.; Hyun, D.J.; Ahn, J.; Kim, S.; Hogan, N. On the dynamics of a quadruped robot model with impedance control: Self-stabilizing high speed trot-running and period-doubling bifurcations. In Proceedings of the 2014IEEE/RSJ International Conference on Intelligent Robots and Systems (IROS), Chicago, IL, USA, 14–18 September 2014; pp. 4907–4913.
13. Gonzalez-Luchena, I.; Gonzalez-Rodriguez, A.G.; Gonzalez-Rodriguez, A.; Adame-Sanchez, C.; Castillo-Garcia, F.J. A new algorithm to maintain lateral stabilization during the running gait of a quadruped robot. *Robot. Auton. Syst.* **2016**, *83*, 57–72. [CrossRef]
14. Krasny, D.P.; Orin, D.E. Generating high-speed dynamic running gaits in a quadruped robot using an evolutionary search. *IEEE Trans. Syst. Man Cybern. Part B (Cybern.)* **2004**, *34*, 1685–1696. [CrossRef]
15. Cherouvim, N.; Papadopoulos, E. Novel energy transfer mechanism in a running quadruped robot with one actuator per Leg. *Adv. Robot.* **2010**, *24*, 963–978. [CrossRef]
16. Zhang, Z.G.; Kimura, H. Rush: A simple and autonomous quadruped running robot. *Proc. Inst. Mech. Eng. Part I J. Syst. Control Eng.* **2009**, *223*, 323–336. [CrossRef]
17. Zhang, Z.G.; Masuda, T.; Kimura, H.; Takase, K. Towards realization of adaptive running of a quadruped robot using delayed feedback control. In Proceedings of the IEEE International Conference on Robotics and Automation, Rome, Italy, 10–14 April 2007; pp. 4325–4330.
18. Zhang, Z.G.; Fukuoka, Y.; Kimura, H. Adaptive running of a quadruped robot on irregular terrain based on biological concepts. In Proceedings of the 20th IEEE International Conference on Robotics and Automation (ICRA), Taipei, Taiwan, 14–19 September 2003; pp. 2043–2048.
19. Seok, S.; Wang, A.; Chuah, M.Y.; Otten, D.; Lang, J.; Kim, S. Design principles for highly efficient quadrupeds and implementation on the MIT Cheetah robot. In Proceedings of the IEEE International Conference on Robotics and Automation (ICRA), Karlsruhe, Germany, 6–10 May 2013; pp. 3307–3312.
20. Hyun, D.J.; Seok, S.; Lee, J.; Kim, S. High speed trot-running: Implementation of a hierarchical controller using proprioceptive impedance control on the MIT Cheetah. *Int. J. Robot. Res.* **2014**, *33*, 1417–1445. [CrossRef]
21. Park, H.-W.; Wensing, P.M.; Kim, S. High-speed bounding with the MIT Cheetah 2: Control design and experiments. *Int. J. Robot. Res.* **2017**, *36*, 167–192. [CrossRef]
22. Di Carlo, J.; Wensing, P.M.; Katz, B.; Bledt, G.; Kim, S. Dynamic locomotion in the MIT Cheetah 3 through convex model-predictive control. In Proceedings of the 25th IEEE/RSJ International Conference on Intelligent Robots and Systems (IROS), Madrid, Spain, 1–5 October 2018; pp. 7440–7447.
23. Melo, L.C.; Melo, D.C.; Maximo, M.R.O.A. Learning humanoid robot running motions with symmetry incentive through proximal policy optimization. *J. Intell. Robot. Syst.* **2021**, *102*, 54. [CrossRef]

24. Boroujeni, M.G.; Daneshmand, E.; Righetti, L.; Khadiv, M. A unified framework for walking and running of bipedal robots. In Proceedings of the 20th International Conference on Advanced Robotics (ICAR), Electr Network, Ljubljana, Slovenia, 6–10 December 2021.
25. Yang, W.S.; Lu, W.C.; Lin, P.C. Legged robot running using a physics-data hybrid motion template. *IEEE Trans. Robot.* **2021**, *37*, 1680–1695. [CrossRef]
26. Leng, X.K.; Piao, S.H.; Chang, L.; He, Z.C.; Zhu, Z. Dynamic running hexapod robot based on high-performance computing. *J. Supercomput.* **2020**, *76*, 844–857. [CrossRef]
27. Krasny, D.P.; Orin, D.E. Evolution of a 3D gallop in a quadrupedal model with biological characteristics. *J. Intell. Robot. Syst.* **2010**, *60*, 59–82. [CrossRef]
28. Ballen-Moreno, F.; Bautista, M.; Provot, T.; Bourgain, M.; Cifuentes, C.A.; Munera, M. Development of a 3D relative motion method for human-robot interaction assessment. *Sensors* **2022**, *22*, 2411. [CrossRef]
29. Wu, A.; Geyer, H. The 3-D spring–mass model reveals a time-based deadbeat control for highly robust running and steering in uncertain environments. *IEEE Trans. Robot.* **2013**, *29*, 1114–1124. [CrossRef]
30. Kang, N.; Cho, J.U.; Park, J.H. Rapid change of running direction for biped robots. In Proceedings of the 14th IEEE-RAS International Conference on Humanoid Robots (Humanoids), Madrid, Spain, 18–20 November 2014; pp. 475–480.
31. Sullivan, T.; Seipel, J. 3D dynamics of bipedal running: Effects of step width on an amputee-inspired robot. In Proceedings of the IEEE/RSJ International Conference on Intelligent Robots and Systems (IROS), Chicago, IL, USA, 14–18 September 2014; pp. 939–944.
32. Kim, H.; Jeong, K.; Sitti, M.; Seo, T. Steering control of a water-running robot using an active tail. In Proceedings of the IEEE/RSJ International Conference on Intelligent Robots and Systems (IROS), Daejeon, Republic of Korea, 9–14 October 2016; pp. 4945–4950.
33. Kohut, N.J.; Zarrouk, D.; Peterson, K.C.; Fearing, R.S. Aerodynamic steering of a 10 cm high-speed running robot. In Proceedings of the IEEE/RSJ International Conference on Intelligent Robots and Systems (IROS), Tokyo, Japan, 3–8 November 2013; pp. 5593–5599.
34. Chen, R.; Yuan, Z.; Guo, J.L.; Bai, L.; Zhu, X.Y.; Liu, F.Q.; Huayan, P.; Liming, X.; Yan, P.; Jun, L.; et al. Legless soft robots capable of rapid, continuous, and steered jumping. *Nat. Commun.* **2021**, *12*, 7028. [CrossRef] [PubMed]
35. Jung, G.P.; Cho, K.J. Froghopper-inspired direction-changing concept for miniature jumping robots. *Bioinspir. Biomim.* **2016**, *11*, 056015. [CrossRef] [PubMed]
36. Kalouche, S. GOAT: A legged robot with 3D agility and virtual compliance. In Proceedings of the IEEE/RSJ International Conference on Intelligent Robots and Systems (IROS), Vancouver, BC, Canada, 24–28 September 2017; pp. 4110–4117.
37. Shi, H.R.; Yong, X.; Liu, J.L.; Jiang, X.Y.; Jie, Y. Marsbot: A monopod robot capable of achieving three-dimensional dynamic and stable jumping. *Proc. Inst. Mech. Eng. Part I-J. Syst. Control Eng.* **2021**, *236*, 552–565.
38. Yim, J.K.; Singh, B.R.P.; Wang, E.K.; Featherstone, R.; Fearing, R.S. Precision robotic leaping and landing using stance-phase balance. *IEEE Robot. Autom. Mag.* **2020**, *5*, 3422–3429. [CrossRef]
39. Chiu, J.-R.; Huang, Y.C.; Chen, H.C.; Tseng, K.Y.; Lin, P.C. Development of a running hexapod robot with differentiated front and hind leg morphology and functionality. In Proceedings of the IEEE/RSJ International Conference on Intelligent Robots and Systems (IROS), Electr Network, Las Vegas, NV, USA, 24 October 2020–24 January 2021; pp. 3710–3717.
40. Yamakawa, Y.; Matsui, Y.; Ishikawa, M. Development of a real-time human-robot collaborative system based on 1 kHz visual feedback control and its application to a peg-in-hole task. *Sensors* **2021**, *21*, 663. [CrossRef] [PubMed]
41. Ichikawa, H.; Matsuo, T.; Haiya, M.; Higurashi, Y.; Wada, N. Gait characteristics of cheetahs (*acinonyx jubatus*) and greyhounds (*canis lupus familiaris*) running on curves. *Mammal Study* **2018**, *43*, 199–206. [CrossRef]
42. Zhang, Z.; Wang, L.; Liao, J.; Zhao, J.; Zhou, Z.; Liu, X. Dynamic stability of bio-inspired biped robots for lateral jumping in rugged terrain. *Appl. Math. Model.* **2021**, *97*, 113–137. [CrossRef]
43. Zhang, L.; Li, D.; Yang, F.; Liu, C. Development and attitude control of a hexapod bionic-robot. In Proceedings of the IEEE International Conference on Robotics and Biomimetics (IEEE ROBIO), Qingdao, China, 3–7 December 2016; pp. 77–82.
44. Liu, Y.B.; Wang, C.B.; Zhang, H.; Zhao, J. Research on the posture control method of hexapod robot for rugged terrain. *Appl. Sci.* **2020**, *10*, 19. [CrossRef]

sensors

Article

Prediction of Metal Additively Manufactured Surface Roughness Using Deep Neural Network

Min Seop So [1], Gi Jeong Seo [2], Duck Bong Kim [2] and Jong-Ho Shin [1,*]

1 Department of Industrial Engineering, Chosun University, Gwangju 61452, Korea
2 Department of Manufacturing and Engineering Technology, Tennessee Tech University, Cookeville, TN 38505, USA
* Correspondence: jhshin@chosun.ac.kr; Tel.: +82-(0)10-4086-8005

Abstract: In recent years, manufacturing industries (e.g., medical, aerospace, and automobile) have been changing their manufacturing process to small-quantity batch production to flexibly cope with fluctuations in demand. Therefore, many companies are trying to produce products by introducing 3D printing technology into the manufacturing process. The 3D printing process is based on additive manufacturing (AM), which can fabricate complex shapes and reduce material waste and production time. Although AM has many advantages, its product quality is poor compared to conventional manufacturing systems. This study proposes a methodology to improve the quality of AM products based on data analysis. The targeted quality of AM is the surface roughness of the stacked wall. Surface roughness is one of the important quality indicators and can cause short product life and poor structure performance. To control the surface roughness, the resultant surface roughness needs to be predicted in advance depending on the process parameters. Various analysis methods such as data pre-processing and deep neural networks (DNN) combined with sensor data are used to predict surface roughness in the proposed methodology. The proposed methodology is applied to field data from operated wire + arc additive manufacturing (WAAM), and the analysis result shows its effectiveness, with a mean absolute percentage error (MAPE) of 1.93%.

Keywords: wire + arc additive manufacturing; surface roughness; deep neural network; arc welding

Citation: So, M.S.; Seo, G.J.; Kim, D.B.; Shin, J.-H. Prediction of Metal Additively Manufactured Surface Roughness Using Deep Neural Network. *Sensors* **2022**, *22*, 7955. https://doi.org/10.3390/s22207955

Academic Editors: Luige Vladareanu, Hongnian Yu, Hongbo Wang and Yongfei Feng

Received: 13 September 2022
Accepted: 11 October 2022
Published: 19 October 2022

1. Introduction

Additive manufacturing (AM) is a production method in which raw materials such as thermoplastics, ceramic powders, paper, plastic films, or metals are stacked layer by layer. Due to the characteristics of this process, AM has several advantages: (1) manufacturing products with complicated shapes; (2) producing small-quantity batches quickly; and (3) saving materials compared to subtractive manufacturing methods [1–3]. AM can be processed via various forms, such as extrusion, jetting, light polymerization, sintering, directed energy deposition (DED), lamination, and powder bed fusion (PBF) [4]. Among them, metal AM (i.e., DED, PBF) is attracting more attention since many machinery components should be produced with metal.

When focusing on metal AM, PBF uses high-energy power sources such as lasers or electron beams to melt or sinter material powder. The cost of the equipment and materials for PBF is high, and production speed is relatively low. In analogy to PBF, DED uses a focused energy source. However, in DED, the material is simultaneously melted as it is deposited by a nozzle, which helps to reduce material waste. One of the representative forms of DED is wire + arc additive manufacturing (WAAM), which uses metal wire as the feedstock and an arc as an energy source. Since the material in WAAM is deposited through a metal wire, the amount of metal used can be minimized. In addition, arc welding requires cheaper equipment than PBF or other DED methods. Despite its many advantages, WAAM is one of the lesser-known metal AM technologies. However, it has huge potential for large-scale metal AM applications across various industries.

Although WAAM has many benefits, most companies still hesitate to adopt it into their processes due to certain drawbacks. Additive processes based on arc welding can raise many problems, such as spatter, porosity, undercutting, deformation, cracks, and slag. In addition, the surface quality of layers stacked by WAAM is poor. The high heat energy of arc welding induces high residual stress and distortion, which deteriorates part accuracy and surface roughness. Therefore, additional post-processing, such as machining, is necessary, which leads to increased manufacturing costs.

To improve the quality of WAAM products and to reduce additional processing costs, it is important to control the surface roughness. Unlike the conventional definition of surface roughness used in the cutting process, surface roughness in WAAM is defined as the side of the wall built by stacked layers (see Figure 1). Since WAAM products are produced as stacked layers through welding, they can have harsh surface conditions compared to products produced by cutting, also known as the stair-stepping effect [5].

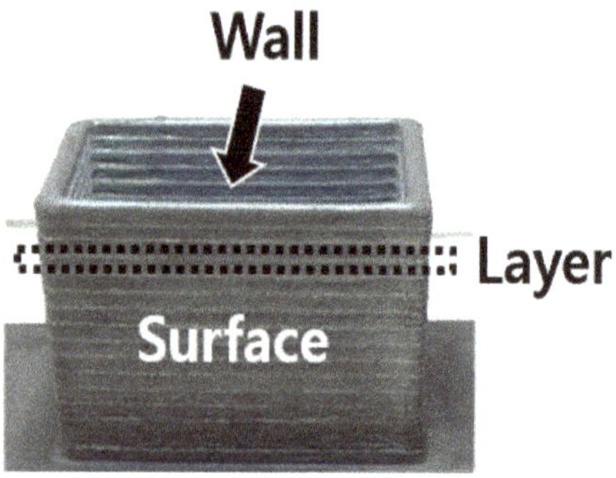

Figure 1. Surface roughness of WAAM product.

To reduce the additional finishing processes required for the surface roughness of stacked layers, additional layers must be deposited as flat as possible. The shape of the additionally stacked layers is decided by process parameters such as voltage, current, and feed rate [2,5–7]. In a case where a proper set of process parameters has been defined, the stair-stepping effect of the wall in WAAM can be reduced. In finding the near-optimal process parameters, it is necessary to predict the resultant surface roughness depending on the process parameters. This study proposes a methodology to predict surface roughness when an additional layer is stacked under a specific set of process parameters. The proposed method consists of data pre-processing to utilize raw data as input/output variables for the predictive model and implements machine learning algorithms such as DNN to predict surface roughness. Different statistical methods such as correlation analysis are also applied to verify the effectiveness of the prediction model. The usefulness and feasibility of the proposed methodology are proved by the experimental data collected from the gas metal arc welding (GMAW)-WAAM system. The remainder of the paper is organized as follows: Section 2 reviews the related work to analyze the influence of process parameters on surface roughness and on predictions of surface roughness. Sections 3 and 4 presents the data analysis-based predictive modelling approach to predict surface roughness, and Section 5 provides conclusions and directions for future work.

2. State of the Art

This section discusses the previous works related to surface roughness measurement and the process parameters affecting surface roughness during AM processes as well as some prediction models for surface roughness.

2.1. Definition of Surface Roughness

In general, surface roughness is defined as regular or irregular unevenness on a surface. Product surface embodies a complex microshape made of a series of peaks and troughs of varying heights, depths, and spacings. In the case of large components, the effect of surface roughness can be negligible since it only affects small areas within micron ranges. However, surface roughness is more critical as more components are being miniaturized [8]. Therefore, many research works have tried to define surface roughness precisely and to control it during manufacturing.

Surface roughness can be measured by various methods depending on different definitions [9–13]. The mostly used measurement method for surface roughness is the average distance between the surface and mean surface profiles (see Figure 2). As shown in Figure 2, the shaded area should be summed and divided by the length L to calculate the surface roughness.

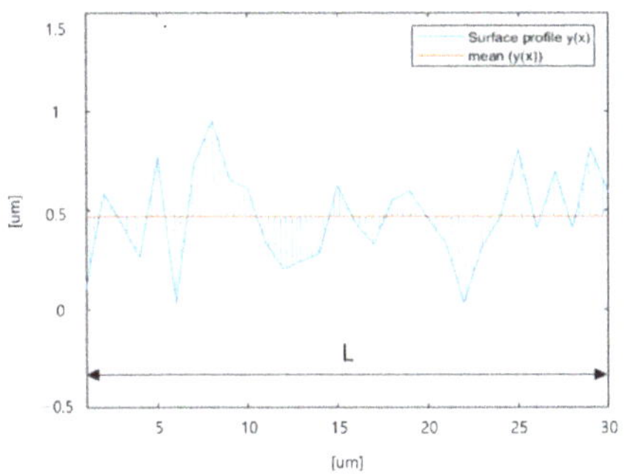

Figure 2. Calculation of surface roughness using surface profile.

Lee [9] suggested surface waviness by calculating the effective area (EA) ratio from the cross-section of an orthogonally cut wall. The EA ratio is calculated by dividing the whole area of the cross-section of a wall by the area of the largest inscribed rectangle. Since surface waviness is calculated from one cross-section of the wall, it is challenging for it to represent the general surface roughness of the whole side of the wall. To overcome this limitation, some research works have tried to obtain as much data from the wall surface as possible. Some researchers [10,11] measured surface roughness by calculating the distances between the surface profile points and the above mean plane defined by the surface profile. Since more wall points are considered when calculated using 3D scanner data to measure surface roughness, the surface roughness is more accurate. Since the surfaces of the walls in WAAM products are highly uneven, considering more points when measuring surface roughness is desirable. Therefore, this study uses cloud points from the surface measured by a 3D scanner.

2.2. Process Parameters Related to Surface Roughness

Chan et al. [14] conducted a study regarding the effect of surface roughness on product life. According to this study, surface roughness causes a reduction in product life expectancy. Sahin [15] explained the effects of surface roughness on product performance, such as tensile strength and fatigue strength. Dawood et al. [11] analyzed the influence of surface roughness on microstructures and mechanical properties. According to these works, surface roughness is one of the most important factors of product quality, and it should be controlled carefully. Considering WAAM, the surface roughness becomes more prevalent at a macroscale, so the fineness of the walls created by WAAM is not as important. The important aspect of surface roughness in WAAM is that the uneven surface caused by the stair-stepping effect requires more post-processing. However, more post-processing cannot guarantee sufficient wall thickness.

Some research works are dedicated to finding the relation between the control variables of processing and surface roughness. Xiong et al. [5] studied the influence of process parameters on surface roughness in the case of gas metal arc welding (GMAW). In this study, process parameters such as the inter-layer temperature, wire feed speed, and travel speed are shown to be closely related to surface roughness. Galantucci et al. [16] analyzed the effect of the process parameters on surface roughness in fused filament fabrication (FDM)-based AM via the design of the experiments. This study proved that the surface roughness deteriorates with increasing slice height and raster width. In other work, the five shape measurements of beads (layer thickness, build angle, raster angle, raster width, and air gap) seem to be essential variables to change surface roughness [17]. Strano et al. [18] studied the effect of layer thickness on surface roughness for steel 316 alloy parts made by selective laser melting (SLM). Zhou et al. [1] chose four important parameters (layer thickness, printing saturation, heater power ratio, and drying time) when developing a prediction model for surface roughness since those are highly effective. Yamaguchi et al. [19] studied the effect of heat input and argon gas on surface roughness. This study showed that increasing the heat input deteriorates the surface roughness and that argon gas helps surface roughness more than other shield gases. Bhushan and Sharma [6] investigated the impact of welding factors such as rotational speed and welding speed regarding the surface roughness of friction stir-welded AA6061-T651. Their results showed that the rotational speed of 1400 rpm and the welding speed of 20 mm/min resulted in the finest surface roughness. Chinchanikar et al. [7] carried out an investigation regarding the effects of different combinations of process parameters (rotational speed and feed rate) on surface roughness when welding aluminum 6063 alloy. Dinovitzer et al. [2] analyzed the influence of travel speed and current on surface roughness. According to this analysis, increasing travel speed and decreasing current worsen the surface roughness. From the previous works, it is proven that various process parameters effect surface roughness, and this study focuses on two of them (i.e., feed rate and travel speed) as control variables.

2.3. *Prediction of Surface Roughness*

Swarna and Arumaikkannu [20] proposed a non-contact method for estimating the surface roughness in SLM-customized implants using an artificial neural network (ANN). The ANN developed in the study was used to predict surface roughness after training using scan data from a femur bone. The prediction accuracy reached 97.2%. Ahn et al. [21] developed a prediction model to estimate the surface roughness of a whole area and the distribution of the surface roughness in a sampled area using interpolation. Strano et al. [18] predicted the surface roughness by considering the stair-stepping effect for SLM specimens, thus helping to minimize the need for post-processing. Boschetto et al. [22] developed an ANN model to determine the surface roughness of FDM parts. The model is used to optimize the effect of process parameters in the product development stage. Wu et al. [23] proposed a data fusion approach to predict surface roughness in FDM processes. This study combines three kinds of sensor data (vibration, temperature of the extruder and table, melt-pool temperature) with various artificial intelligence (AI) models. Vahabli and Rahmait [17] also used an ANN model to predict surface roughness. Chen and Zhao [24] adopted a backward propagation neural network (BP-NN) to predict surface roughness. Xia et al. [25] developed a prediction model to predict the surface roughness in WAAM processes. This study calculated the surface roughness using a laser scanner and combines three kinds of parameters (welding speed, wire feed speed, and overlap ratio) with a genetic algorithm–adaptive neuro fuzzy inference system (GA-ANFIS). The prediction model shows its performance with a MAPE of 14.15%. Yaseer and Chen [26] investigated the layer roughness in WAAM processes. This study explored a layer-roughness prediction method based on multilayer perceptron (MLP) and random forest combined with weaving path. Their results show that random forest achieved better performance in terms of MAPE, the value of which is about 5.64%.

As described in the previous literature, many studies have tried to predict surface roughness depending on process parameters and using various methods in the finishing process. Recently, some researchers have tried to predict surface roughness in situ; however, to our knowledge, using previously stacked layers as input data has not been considered. Studies predicting the surface roughness of stacked layers in situ during WAAM are still lacking. Therefore, this study focuses on developing a prediction model for surface roughness in situ during WAAM by considering process parameters and previously stacked layers using an AI model.

3. Prediction Model of Surface Roughness

The stair-stepping effect can be minimized by properly setting process parameters such as current, voltage, and feed rate. However, there are numerous possible combinations that only use three parameters. In finding the near-optimal ones, it is necessary to be able to predict the surface quality depending on a set of process parameters. Then, each set should be assessed and compared to search for the best process setting. This section will show how the surface roughness can be predicted depending on various process parameter settings. Finding the best set of process parameters among many candidates will be carried out in future work.

3.1. Measurement of Surface Roughness

The first step in predicting surface roughness is to define it precisely. As previously described, the surfaces of walls made via WAAM are harsher than those of a conventionally manufactured (i.e., cutting, drilling, punching, etc.) product. However, the basic concept of measuring the surface roughness is same. The important difference from the conventional definition of surface roughness is that the surface roughness of the wall in the WAAM product is generated layer by layer at the macrolevel. Since the surface roughness is redefined whenever a new layer is stacked in the WAMM process, the surface roughness in this study is defined between two consecutive stacked layers, as shown in Figure 3.

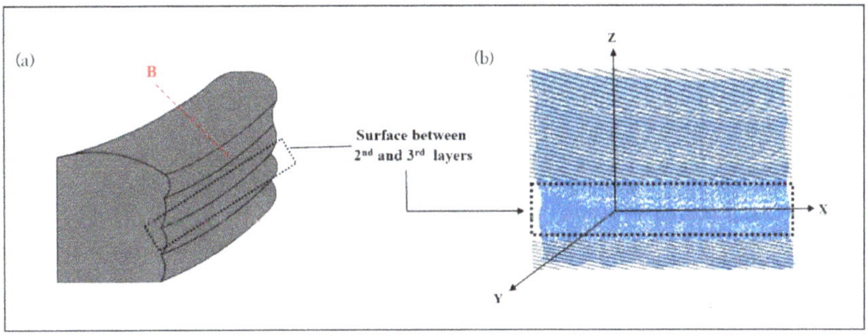

Figure 3. (**a**) Surface of WAAM product between second and third layers. (**b**) Reconstruction of WAAM product between second and third layers by CMM.

The method used for measuring surface roughness is depicted in Figure 4. The main concept of defining surface roughness is to measure the variation in the surface profile between consecutively stacked layers. The starting and ending point between two layers is set to the widest area of each layer when the WAAM wall is cut orthogonally. The actual profile is obtained using a coordinate measuring machine (CMM, model: Hexagon Romer Arm 7525SIE) as points clouds (see Figure 4b).

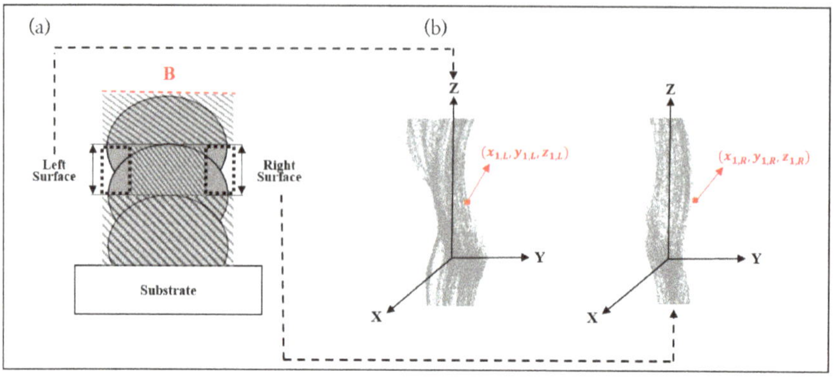

Figure 4. (**a**) Schematic diagram of cross-section of WAAM product. (**b**) Reconstruction of surface profile of both sides of a WAAM product between second and third layers by CMM.

Generally, the surface roughness is measured using one cross-section cut from the wall (See Figure 3 red in B and Figure 4 red in B). So that it is limited to representing the whole surface area of the wall (See Figure 4). In this study, the surface profile measured by CMM is expressed as three-dimensional coordinates ($(x_{k,L}, y_{k,L}, z_{k,L})$ for the left-wall side and $(x_{k,R}, y_{k,R}, z_{k,R})$ for the right-wall side) of the point clouds extended from one cross-section and can include the characteristics of the whole surface area of the wall (see Figures 3a and 4b). The numerical equation to calculate the surface roughness between two layers, which considers the wall's whole surface area, is formulated as Equation (1).

$$\text{Surface rouhgness} = (\frac{\frac{\sum_{k=1}^{n}\left(y_{k,L}-\overline{y_L}\right)^2}{n} + \frac{\sum_{k=1}^{m}\left(y_{k,R}-\overline{y_R}\right)^2}{m}}{2} \quad (1)$$

where $y_{k,L}$ is the observed y coordinate value of the kth point cloud on the left surface profile of the wall. The index of k ranges from 1 to n since there are n points on the left side of the wall. Additionally, $\overline{y_L}$ is the mean of the y-values for the point clouds on the left surface. On the other hand, $y_{k,R}$ is the observed y-values of the right-side surface profile of the wall. The point clouds on the right side of the wall consist of m points. The deviation in the left side of the wall is calculated by subtracting the observed $y_{k,L}$ value of each point from the mean ($\overline{y_L}$) and then squaring and adding all of them and then dividing by the total number of observed point clouds from the surface profile on the left. The deviation in the right side of the wall also follows the same method. The surface roughness is measured as the mean of the deviation in both sides since the manufactured wall is composed of a left and right side.

3.2. Experimental Set-Up

The experimental setup in this study is based on gas tungsten arc welding–cold metal transfer (GMAW)-CMT, as shown in Figure 5. This system consists of a robot manipulator (Fanuc ArcMate 120iC) and a welding power source (Fronius TPS 400i) equipped with a welding torch (Fronius WF 25i Robacta Drive). The process parameters were controlled using the robot and power-source controllers. A coordinate measuring machine (CMM) was also installed to obtain 3D point clouds of the wall surface between two stacked layers.

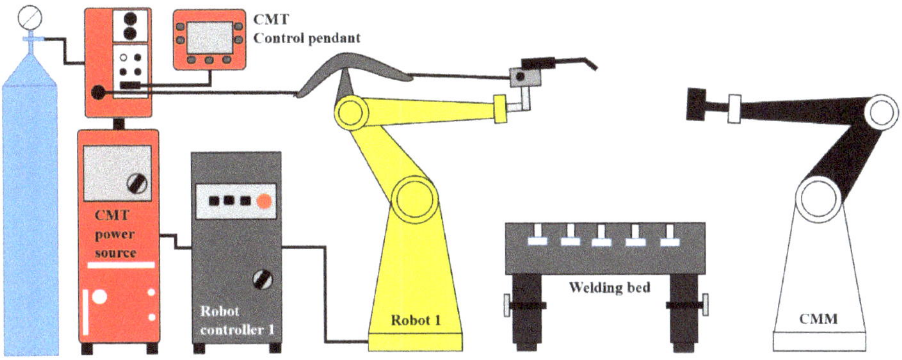

Figure 5. Environment of the experimental set-up.

A wall made by (GMAW)-CMT was built on a stainless steel 316 L substrate with the dimensions 6 × 2 × 0.25 inches. A bead deposition experiment was conducted on the substrate using stainless steel 316 L as a wire material, and the deposition direction was unaltered. Both middle sides of the substrate were clamped to the stage to prevent distortion, and wire was fed at an angle of 30° from the top surface towards inside.

Since the welding is processed by a robot arm, there can be positioning accuracy problems. The wall roughness should be controlled at the macrolevel in this work. Therefore, processing errors caused by robot arm movement are not considered in this paper.

3.3. Data Collection and Pre-Processing

3.3.1. Process Parameters

The process parameters of (GMAW)-CMT deposition are shown in Table 1. The dynamic (or controlling) process parameters are newly set whenever the next layer is deposited. The static parameters are fixed until the process is finished. The travel speed can vary from 1 to 12,000 cm/min, with one-unit increments. The feed rate can be set from 100 to 1000 cm/min and changes in increments of 10 units. The deposited layer is cooled to 100 °C before the next layer is stacked to reduce the influence of heat.

Table 1. WAAM process parameters.

Parameters		Unit	Values
Dynamic process parameters	Travel speed	cm/min	1~12,000
	Feed rate	cm/min	100~1000
Static process parameters	Previous layer temperature	°C	100
	Arc length (bead to arc distance)	mm	5
	Wire diameter	mm	1.2
	Wire feeding angle	Degree	30
	Shielding gas	%	100
	Flow rate	L/min	20

3.3.2. Bead Shape

As mentioned in Section 2.2, process parameters (travel speed and feed rate) highly influence the surface roughness. In addition, the bead shape (angle, width, height, and bead location (layer)) of the previous layer (see Figure 6) also plays an important role in shaping newly stacked layers, deciding the surface roughness. Therefore, this study considers the bead shape and dynamic process parameters in Table 1 as the input data to develop an AI model for predicting the surface roughness. According to previous studies, the hardness of the bottom layer deposited using a WAAM process is not constant due to mechanical properties. Therefore, the substrate and bottom layer are not used at actual worksites [27–29]. Thus, only the data for the beads deposited above the first layer of the wall are used in model development (Figure 6).

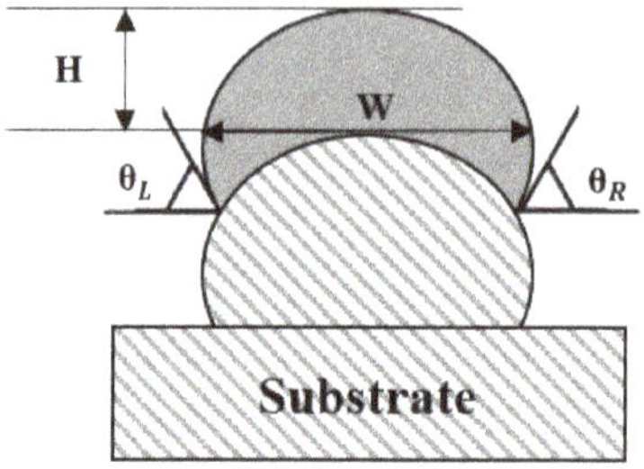

Figure 6. Schematic diagram of bead shape.

In Figure 6, W represents the width, which is the widest distance between each layer. Each layer's height (H) is the distance from the top of the previous layer to the top of the next layer. The angles for both sides (θ_{Left}, θ_{Right}) of each layer are measured based on the narrowest area between two stacked layers.

3.3.3. Data Collection

To collect experimental data regarding dynamic process parameters and bead shape, 27 thin walls with five layers were fabricated using the (GMAW)-CMT system. The three combinations of dynamic process parameters shown in Table 2 are set to deposit the layers.

Table 2. WAAM dynamic process parameters.

Combination No.	Feed Rate	Travel Speed
1	480	30
2	560	31
3	650	33

The process for collecting and pre-processing data such as the dynamic process parameters and bead shape is shown in Figure 7.

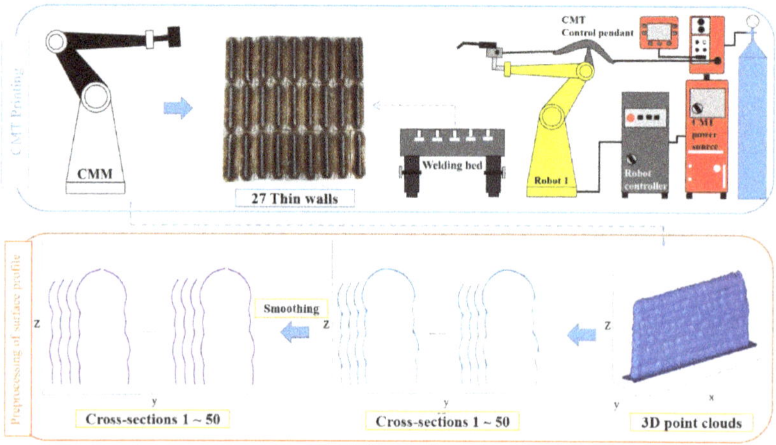

Figure 7. Pre-process and process for data collection.

Generally, the bead shape is measured by one cross-section of the wall so that it has a limited capability in representing the whole-wall characteristics. To improve this limitation, point clouds of the surface profile are cut into 50 cross-sections at regular intervals for each wall. The surface profile of each cross-section composed of point clouds is converted to one line using the smoothing method (see lower image of Figure 7). Then, using each cross-section, the bead shape is measured as described in Section 3.3.2. The mean of the bead shape of all cross-sections represents the bead shape of the whole area of each wall. Next, the input and output data used to train the model are defined by the measured bead shape, dynamic process parameters, and surface roughness.

3.4. Model Development

3.4.1. Definition of Input Data and Output Data and Normalization

To develop an AI model, defining the input and output data is a prerequisite. The collected data (explained in Section 3.3), such as the dynamic process parameters and bead shape of the previously stacked layer, are adopted as the features of the input layer of the AI model, and one resulting property (surface roughness between the consecutively stacked layers of a wall) is adopted as the output-layer variable (refer Table 3). Collected structural data, samples of dynamic process parameters, bead shape, and surface roughness obtained from the experiments are described in Table 3.

Table 3. Input and output structure.

Index	# of Thin Wall	Input Data								Output Data
		Layer	θ_L (°)	θ_R (°)	Width (mm)	Height (mm)	Travel Speed (cm/min)	Feed Rate (cm/min)		Surface Roughness
1	1	2nd	102.11	101.94	6.95	2.06	30	480		1.0363
2	1	3rd	100.98	99.87	6.91	3.73	31	560		1.1303
⋮	⋮	⋮	⋮	⋮	⋮	⋮	⋮	⋮		⋮
80	27	3rd	99.37	100.2	7.36	2.76	31	560		1.0393
81	27	4th	100.05	99.29	7.46	2.76	31	560		1.0474

The first two columns in Table 3: 'Index' and 'Number of thin walls', represent an index of the two consecutive layers processed in each wall. In each wall, there are four consecutive layers. The third column indicates the data measured from the processed layer in the previous deposition, and the bead shape is expressed from the fourth column to the seventh. The eighth and ninth columns show the dynamic process parameters for the layer currently being processed. The last column is for the output value of the surface roughness between the previous layer and the layer currently being processed under the given process parameter are in (the eighth and ninth columns).

Normalization is performed for each variable since the measured values have different value ranges. The aim is to reduce the influence of the deviations caused by the differences in the measurement range of each variable. In addition, normalization can reduce the learning time of machine learning models and prevent decreases in accuracy caused by heavy computations [30]. In this study, the robust scaler normalization is used, where it is represented in Table 4.

Table 4. Data normalization.

Index	# of Thin Wall	Layer	θ_L (°)	θ_R (°)	Width (mm)	Height (mm)	Travel Speed (cm/min)	Feed Rate (cm/min)	Surface Roughness
		Input Data							Output Data
1	1	−0.5	−0.69	−3.19	0.64	0.65	−1	−8	1.0363
2	1	0	−0.76	3.4	0.23	0.05	0	0	1.1303
⋮	⋮	⋮	⋮	⋮	⋮	⋮	⋮	⋮	⋮
80	27	0	−0.14	−0.4	−0.35	0.14	0	0	1.0393
81	27	0.5	0	−0.4	−0.1	−0.12	0	0	1.0474

3.4.2. DNN Model Development

There are various kinds of machine learning models. ANN is a single-layer perceptron structure, which has limitations in solving nonlinear problems. To cover this limitation, a deep learning model with multiple hidden layers using backpropagation is proposed. Recently, DNN has been widely used in various areas and has shown good performance. Hence, the authors adopted a DNN-based model. DNN is one of the core models of deep learning and has a structure comprising multiple hidden layers. It has the advantages of understanding the complex structure of large datasets and learning various non-linear relationships. The proposed structure is shown in Figure 8. The structure of DNN can vary according to the hyper parameters (number of hidden layers, optimizer, learning rate). Therefore, finding the best structure for DNN requires trial and error.

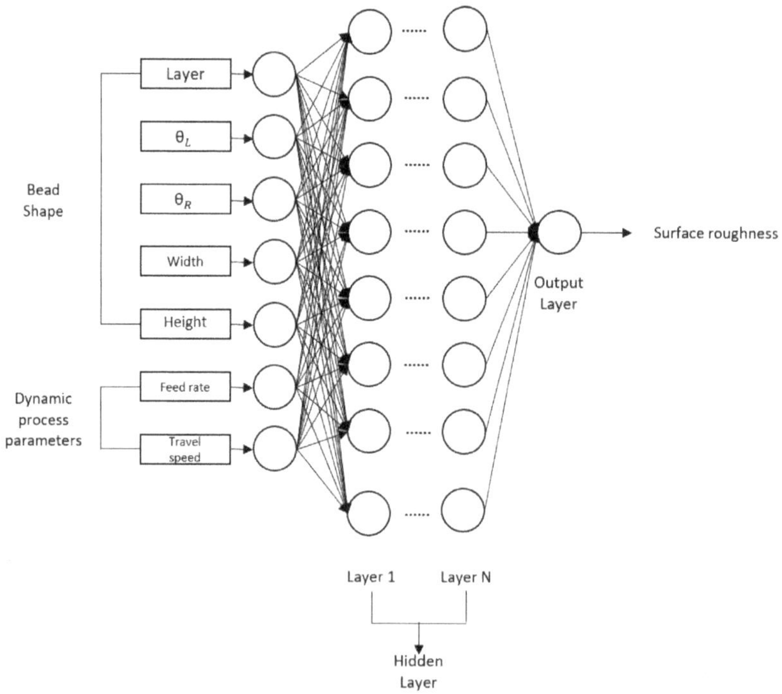

Figure 8. Schematic diagram of the deep neural network for the prediction of surface roughness.

4. Model Evaluation

To evaluate the prediction performance of the used DNN model, mean absolute percentage error (MAPE) and root mean squared error (RMSE) are adopted as performance measures (refer to Equations (2) and (3)). Since MAPE represents the averaged difference in the percentage between real and predicted values, a lower value means better performance. The range of MAPE ranges from 0 to 100. RMSE is used to represent the precision of the model, and a lower value means the better precision. The range of RMSE become from 0 to ∞. The formulae for MAPE and RMSE are as expressed in Equations (2) and (3).

$$\text{MAPE} = \frac{100}{n}\sum_{t=1}^{n}\left|\frac{A_t - F_t}{A_t}\right| \tag{2}$$

$$\text{RMSE} = \sqrt{\sum_{t=1}^{n}\frac{(A_t - F_t)^2}{n}} \tag{3}$$

In Equations (2) and (3), A_t represents the actual surface roughness calculated by CMM data, and F_t is the surface roughness predicted by the used model. The whole data set is split into 80% training data and 20% testing data. The training data set is only used to learn the model, and the testing data set is used to see how well the model performs under the new process parameter settings. Table 5 shows the results of the performance measures depending on the tested prediction models. Some conventional predictive models, such as regression and support vector regression (SVR), are also tested to compare them with DNN.

Table 5. Results of performance comparison.

Model	Model Parameters							Result	
Regression	Degree							Mape (%)	Rmse
1	Linear							67.33	0.97
2	Polynomial(quadratic)							7.75	0.13
3	Polynomial(cubic)							18.08	0.3
SVR	C			Degree	Epsilon	Kernel		Mape (%)	Rmse
1	1			3	0.1	rbf		8.31	0.109
2	1.3			2	0.1	Poly		8.43	0.111
3	1.5			4	0.1	sigmoid		12.2	0.183
DNN	Activation Function	Layer	Drop Out	Weight Initialization	Optimizer	Learning Rate	Epoch	Mape (%)	Rmse
1	Relu	(7, 64, 32, 28, 1)	0.2	He initialization	RMSprop	1×10^{-2}	10,000	10.45	0.145
2	Relu	(7, 64, 32, 16, 1)	None	He initialization	Adam	1×10^{-4}	15,000	1.93	0.03
3	Relu	(7, 32, 16, 1)	0.3	He initialization	SGD	1×10^{-3}	30,000	11.39	0.16

From Table 5, the prediction accuracy of the polynomial (quadratic) regression model gives the best results, with an MAPE of 7.75 % and an RMSE of 0.126. As a result, linear regression is not enough to explain the data set, and polynomial (cubic) regression is over-fit on the training data set. SVR does not achieve large variance of accuracy depending on the hyper parameters of the model. However, the error rate of SVR has an MAPE of 8.31%, but that it still is not enough to explain the data set. On the other hand, the prediction accuracy of the DNN model with the following hyper parameters: Activation function = Relu; Layer = (input layer (7), hidden layer (64, 32, 16), and output layer (1); value in () means number of nodes of each layer); Drop out = None; Weight initialization = He initialization; Optimizer = Adam; Learning_rate = 1×10^{-4}; and Epoch = 15,000, gives the best result, with MAPE = 1.93% and RMSE = 0.03. Figure 9a shows the residual error between the actual surface roughness and the predicted surface roughness as a graph. To validate the prediction accuracy of the second DNN model with the highest one, the correlation between the real value and the value predicted by the DNN model is plotted. Correlation analysis is commonly used to infer the relationship between two variables. The value of the Pearson correlation shows a positive correlation when the value of each variable increases or decreases together. When the value of one variable increases and the value of the other variable decreases, it shows a negative correlation. When the value of one variable change and the value of one variable remains the same, it means there is no correlation between the two variables. The correlation coefficient, 'r', always satisfies $-1 \leq r \leq 1$. In the case of no correlation, the value of r is close to 0. When r is more than 0.6 or less than −0.6, the correlation between the variables is strong. In the DNN model used in this study, the correlation coefficient between the actual and predicted value is r = 0.97, which means that they have a strong correlation. Figure 9b shows the relationship between the actual surface roughness and the predicted surface roughness as a graph.

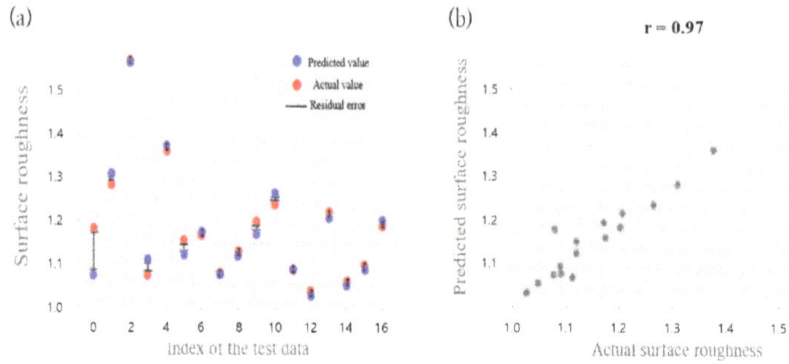

Figure 9. (**a**) Residual error plot of real values and predicted values. (**b**) Scatter plot of real values and predicted values.

5. Conclusions and Discussion

Concerning the comparison with related work, the proposed method is able to predict surface roughness in situ. If the surface roughness can be reduced in situ by predicting the surface roughness depending on the process parameters, there will be less post-processing, and material waste will be reduced. To achieve this, some studies have proposed AI models based on process parameters. Some of the researchers who have tried to predict surface roughness in situ have used process parameters (welding speed, wire feed speed, and overlap ratio). However, there have been few investigations of the bead geometry of previously stacked layers, which has a huge potential to reduce surface roughness. Additionally, researchers have previously defined surface roughness using the top surface of a bead. However, the surface roughness of the side of a bead also requires post-processing in multi-layer processes.

Therefore, this paper proposed a prediction model for surface roughness between consecutively stacked layers in a thin wall produced via WAAM that depended on process parameters and the bead shape of the previously processed layer using DNN. The targeted WAAM process was a (GMAW)-CMT system that could monitor and collect dynamic process parameters. Two kinds of dynamic parameters (travel speed and feed rate) are focused on the (GMAW)-CMT process. The bead shape was measured by the CMM that was installed and maintained a 3D position as point clouds in a thin wall. These data are used as input data in the used DNN model, which can predict surface roughness under given process parameters. Commonly, when measuring surface roughness, one cross-sectional of bead is used. This has limitations in representing the whole area of a wall. To cover this limitation, we propose an extension of the cross section to the whole area of the wall using point clouds with a smoothing method. In addition, robust scaler was adopted to reduce the influence of the deviations caused by the difference in the measurement range of each variable during the analysis.

Some conventional predictive models such as regression and SVR were also adopted, and the prediction performances were compared with the used DNN model. According to the experimental results, the DNN model showed the best performance among them. The best DNN model has predication accuracy of about 98%, with a high correlation between the real and predicted values. Using the developed model, surface roughness can be estimated when a new layer is stacked under a diverse combination of bead shapes and dynamic process parameters. In the process results achieved under a specific operation parameter, the best operation parameter can be searched. Then, a search algorithm or reinforced learning should be adopted. This will be carried out in other authors' future research.

Author Contributions: Writing—review and editing, writing—original draft, data analysis, and data gathering, M.S.S.; data gathering and conceptualization, G.J.S.; project administration, conceptualization, review and editing, and supervision, D.B.K.; writing—review and editing, conceptualization, supervision, and funding acquisition, J.-H.S. All authors have read and agreed to the published version of the manuscript.

Funding: This research was supported by the Ministry of Science, ICT (MSIT), Korea, under the High-Potential Individuals Global Training Program (No. 2020-0-01539) supervised by the Institute for Information & Communications Technology Planning & Evaluation (IITP). This material is based upon work supported by the National Science Foundation under Grant No. 2015693.

Institutional Review Board Statement: Not applicable.

Informed Consent Statement: Not applicable.

Data Availability Statement: Not applicable.

Conflicts of Interest: The authors declare no conflict of interest.

Abbreviations

AI	artificial intelligence
AM	additive manufacturing
ANN	artificial neural network
BP-NN	backward propagation neural network
CMM	coordinate-measuring machine
DED	directed energy deposition
DNN	deep neural networks
EA	effective area
FDM	fused filament fabrication
GA-ANFIS	genetic algorithm–adaptive neuro fuzzy inference system
GMAW-CMT	gas metal arc welding–cold metal transfer
MAPE	mean absolute percentage error
MLP	multi-layer perceptron
PBF	powder bed fusion
RMSE	root mean squared error
SLM	selective laser melting
SVR	support vector regression
WAAM	wire + arc additive manufacturing

References

1. Zhou, Y.; Chen, H.; Tang, Y.; Gopinath, S.; Xu, X.; Zhao, Y.F. Simulation and optimization framework for additive manufacturing processes. In Proceedings of the 2014 International Conference on Innovative Design and Manufacturing (ICIDM), Montreal, QC, Canada, 13–15 August 2014; IEEE: Piscataway, NJ, USA, 2014; pp. 34–40.
2. Dinovitzer, M.; Chen, X.; Laliberte, J.; Huang, X.; Frei, H. Effect of wire and arc additive manufacturing (WAAM) process parameters on bead geometry and microstructure. *Addit. Manuf.* **2019**, *26*, 138–146. [CrossRef]
3. Le, V.T.; Mai, D.S.; Tran, V.C.; Doan, T.K. *Additive Manufacturing of Thin-Wall Steel Parts by Gas Metal Arc Welding Robot: The Surface Roughness, Microstructures and Mechanical Properties, Further Advances in Internet of Things in Biomedical and Cyber Physical Systems*; Springer: Berlin/Heidelberg, Germany, 2021; pp. 43–54.
4. Frazier, W.E. Metal additive manufacturing: A review. *J. Mater. Eng. Perform.* **2014**, *23*, 1917–1928. [CrossRef]
5. Xiong, J.; Li, Y.; Li, R.; Yin, Z. Influences of process parameters on surface roughness of multi-layer single-pass thin-walled parts in GMAW-based additive manufacturing. *J. Mater. Process. Technol.* **2018**, *252*, 128–136. [CrossRef]
6. Bhushan, R.K.; Sharma, D. Investigation of mechanical properties and surface roughness of friction stir welded AA6061-T651. *Int. J. Mech. Mater. Eng.* **2020**, *15*, 7. [CrossRef]
7. Chinchanikar, S.; Gharde, S.; Gadge, M. Investigation of tool forces, weld bead micro-hardness and surface roughness during friction stir welding of Aluminium 6063 alloy. *Adv. Mater. Process. Technol.* **2020**, 1–9. [CrossRef]

8. Suh, C.H.; Jung, Y.-C.; Kim, Y.S. Effects of thickness and surface roughness on mechanical properties of aluminum sheets. *J. Mech. Sci. Technol.* **2010**, *24*, 2091–2098. [CrossRef]
9. Lee, S.H. Optimization of cold metal transfer-based wire arc additive manufacturing processes using gaussian process regression. *Metals* **2020**, *10*, 461. [CrossRef]
10. Xiong, J.; Li, Y.-J.; Yin, Z.-Q.; Chen, H. Determination of surface roughness in wire and arc additive manufacturing based on laser vision sensing. *Chin. J. Mech. Eng.* **2018**, *31*, 74.
11. Dawood, H.I.; Mohammed, K.S.; Rahmat, A.; Uday, M. The influence of the surface roughness on the microstructures and mechanical properties of 6061 aluminium alloy using friction stir welding. *Surf. Coat. Technol.* **2015**, *270*, 272–283. [CrossRef]
12. Léger, D.; Perrin, J. Real-time measurement of surface roughness by correlation of speckle patterns. *JOSA* **1976**, *66*, 1210–1217. [CrossRef]
13. Bhushan, B. Surface Roughness Analysis and Measurement Techniques. In *Modern Tribology Handbook, Two Volume Set*; CRC Press: Boca Raton, FL, USA, 2000; pp. 79–150.
14. Chan, K.S.; Koike, M.; Mason, R.L.; Okabe, T. Fatigue life of titanium alloys fabricated by additive layer manufacturing techniques for dental implants. *Metall. Mater. Trans. A* **2013**, *44*, 1010–1022. [CrossRef]
15. Sahin, M. Effect of surface roughness on weldability in aluminium sheets joined by cold pressure welding. *Ind. Lubr. Tribol.* **2008**, *60*, 249–254. [CrossRef]
16. Galantucci, L.M.; Lavecchia, F.; Percoco, G. Experimental study aiming to enhance the surface finish of fused deposition modeled parts. *CIRP Ann.* **2009**, *58*, 189–192. [CrossRef]
17. Vahabli, E.; Rahmati, S. Improvement of FDM parts' surface quality using optimized neural networks–medical case studies. *Rapid Prototyp. J.* **2017**, *23*, 825–842. [CrossRef]
18. Strano, G.; Hao, L.; Everson, R.M.; Evans, K.E. Surface roughness analysis, modelling and prediction in selective laser melting. *J. Mater. Process. Technol.* **2013**, *213*, 589–597. [CrossRef]
19. Yamaguchi, M.; Komata, R.; Furumoto, T.; Abe, S.; Hosokawa, A. Influence of Metal Transfer Behavior Under Ar And CO_2 Shielding Gases On Geometry And Surface Roughness of Single And Multilayer Structures in GMAW-Based Wire Arc Additive Manufacturing of Mild Steel. *Int. J. Adv. Manuf. Technol.* **2021**, *119*, 911–926. [CrossRef]
20. Swarna Lakshmi, K.; Arumaikkannu, G. Evaluation of Surface Roughness in Additive Manufactured customised implant using Artificial Neural Network based on 2D Fourier transform–A Machine Vision approach. *Biomed. Res.* **2015**, *26*, 34–40.
21. Ahn, D.; Kim, H.; Lee, S. Surface roughness prediction using measured data and interpolation in layered manufacturing. *J. Mater. Process. Technol.* **2009**, *209*, 664–671. [CrossRef]
22. Boschetto, A.; Giordano, V.; Veniali, F. 3D roughness profile model in fused deposition modelling. *Rapid Prototyp. J.* **2013**, *19*, 240–252. [CrossRef]
23. Wu, D.; Wei, Y.; Terpenny, J. Predictive modelling of surface roughness in fused deposition modelling using data fusion. *Int. J. Prod. Res.* **2019**, *57*, 3992–4006. [CrossRef]
24. Chen, H.; Zhao, Y.F. Learning algorithm based modeling and process parameters recommendation system for binder jetting additive manufacturing process. In Proceedings of the International Design Engineering Technical Conferences and Computers and Information in Engineering Conference, American Society of Mechanical Engineers, Boston, MA, USA, 2–5 August 2015; p. V01AT02A029.
25. Xia, C.; Pan, Z.; Polden, J.; Li, H.; Xu, Y.; Chen, S. Modelling and prediction of surface roughness in wire arc additive manufacturing using machine learning. *J. Intell. Manuf.* **2022**, *33*, 1467–1482. [CrossRef]
26. Yaseer, A.; Chen, H. Machine learning based layer roughness modeling in robotic additive manufacturing. *J. Manuf. Process.* **2021**, *70*, 543–552. [CrossRef]
27. Wang, L.; Xue, J.; Wang, Q. Correlation between arc mode, microstructure, and mechanical properties during wire arc additive manufacturing of 316L stainless steel. *Mater. Sci. Eng.* **2019**, *751*, 183–190. [CrossRef]
28. Wu, W.; Xue, J.; Zhang, Z.; Yao, P. Comparative study of 316L depositions by two welding current processes. *Mater. Manuf. Process.* **2019**, *34*, 1502–1508. [CrossRef]
29. Haselhuhn, A.S.; Wijnen, B.; Anzalone, G.C.; Sanders, P.G.; Pearce, J.M. In situ formation of substrate release mechanisms for gas metal arc weld metal 3-D printing. *J. Mater. Process. Technol.* **2015**, *226*, 50–59. [CrossRef]
30. Liu, Z. A method of SVM with normalization in intrusion detection. *Procedia Environ. Sci.* **2011**, *11*, 256–262. [CrossRef]

sensors

MDPI

Article

sEMG-Based Gain-Tuned Compliance Control for the Lower Limb Rehabilitation Robot during Passive Training

Junjie Tian [1], Hongbo Wang [1,2], Siyuan Zheng [1], Yuansheng Ning [1], Xingchao Zhang [1], Jianye Niu [1,*] and Luige Vladareanu [3,*]

1 Parallel Robot and Mechatronic System Laboratory of Hebei Province, Yanshan University, Qinhuangdao 066004, China
2 Academy for Engineering & Technology, Fudan University, Shanghai 200433, China
3 Institute of Solid Mechanics of the Romanian Academy, 010141 Bucharest, Romania
* Correspondence: jyniu@ysu.edu.cn (J.N.); luigiv@arexim.ro (L.V.)

Abstract: The lower limb rehabilitation robot is a typical man-machine coupling system. Aiming at the problems of insufficient physiological information and unsatisfactory safety performance in the compliance control strategy for the lower limb rehabilitation robot during passive training, this study developed a surface electromyography-based gain-tuned compliance control (EGCC) strategy for the lower limb rehabilitation robot. First, the mapping function relationship between the normalized surface electromyography (sEMG) signal and the gain parameter was established and an overall EGCC strategy proposed. Next, the EGCC strategy without sEMG information was simulated and analyzed. The effects of the impedance control parameters on the position correction amount were studied, and the change rules of the robot end trajectory, man-machine contact force, and position correction amount analyzed in different training modes. Then, the sEMG signal acquisition and feature analysis of target muscle groups under different training modes were carried out. Finally, based on the lower limb rehabilitation robot control system, the influence of normalized sEMG threshold on the robot end trajectory and gain parameters under different training modes was experimentally studied. The simulation and experimental results show that the adoption of the EGCC strategy can significantly enhance the compliance of the robot end-effector by detecting the sEMG signal and improve the safety of the robot in different training modes, indicating the EGCC strategy has good application prospects in the rehabilitation robot field.

Keywords: sEMG; lower limb rehabilitation robot; compliance control; training mode; MOTOmed; continuous passive motion; straight leg raise; feature analysis

Citation: Tian, J.; Wang, H.; Zheng, S.; Ning, Y.; Zhang, X.; Niu, J.; Vladareanu, L. sEMG-Based Gain-Tuned Compliance Control for the Lower Limb Rehabilitation Robot during Passive Training. *Sensors* **2022**, *22*, 7890. https://doi.org/10.3390/s22207890

Academic Editor: M. Osman Tokhi

Received: 14 September 2022
Accepted: 14 October 2022
Published: 17 October 2022

1. Introduction

Lower limb motor dysfunction is a common sequela of stroke patients. The elderly is a high-risk group for stroke, and as the population ages, the incidence of stroke increases dramatically [1,2]. The plasticity of the human brain and central nervous system is the basis of rehabilitation medicine. Through the training exercise of specific tasks and the use of the motor relearning program of the nervous system, the motor function of the patient's lower limbs can be effectively restored [3–5]. Rehabilitation robotics, as an emerging technology developed in the rehabilitation field, has advantages in clinical and biomechanical measurements compared with conventional therapy [6]. In addition, the rehabilitation robot is relatively easy to manage and control, which can help patients perform predetermined training actions accurately and repeatedly and improve the effectiveness of rehabilitation treatment [7]. In recent years, the design and control strategies of rehabilitation robots have become research hotspots in the fields of rehabilitation engineering and robotics.

With the development of robotics and rehabilitation theory, various lower limb rehabilitation robots have been designed. Lower limb rehabilitation robots are mainly divided into exoskeleton type and end-effector type [8]. In the exoskeleton robot system, there is a one-to-one correspondence between the robot and human joints. The exoskeleton robot system can be worn on the human body and usually has a compact structure [9]. The lower limb exoskeleton robot MotionMaker adopts the integrated design of the seat and lower limb motion mechanism, which can carry out passive, semi-active, and active training modes [10]. Li et al. designed a lower limb exoskeleton rehabilitation robot which can assist the patient in carrying out gait training [11]. Feng et al. designed a lower limb rehabilitation robot for passive training of stroke patients, and the moving seat can be adjusted or separated from the robot to meet the rehabilitation demands of patients at different stages [12]. Akdoğan et al. produced a therapeutic exercise robot Physiotherabot, which can perform active and passive movements and learn specific exercise movements [13]. In the end-effector robot system, pedals or platforms are used to generate limb motion from the distal end of the lower limb without requiring alignment between the robot and human joints. Wang et al. designed a rigid-flexible end-effector lower limb rehabilitation robot, which consists of a rigid mobile device and a flexible drive system, which can realize the adduction/abduction and internal/external rotation movement of the lower limb [14]. Bouri et al. developed a parallel robot Lambda that can be used to guide the movement of the lower limb and carry out rehabilitation training of the hip, knee, and ankle joints [15]. Saglia et al. developed a 3-UPS/U parallel mechanism, which can perform rehabilitation training of the human ankle joint [16].

According to the active participation degree of patients, rehabilitation training can be divided into three categories: passive training, semi-active training, and active training [17]. In the passive training process, the rehabilitation robot guides the affected limb to move along a predetermined trajectory for rehabilitation training [18]. For the passive training modes of lower limb rehabilitation robots, the typical ones include MOTOmed training mode, continuous passive motion (CPM) training mode, and straight leg raise (SLR) training mode [19–22]. In the MOTOmed training mode, the end trajectory of the robot is a circular trajectory; In the CPM training mode, the end trajectory of the robot is a linear trajectory; In the SLR training mode, the end trajectory of the robot is an arc trajectory. In order to improve the safety and comfort of patients during passive rehabilitation training, numerous studies have been conducted on the compliance control strategy of the lower limb rehabilitation robot. Wang et al. [23] proposed a fuzzy sliding mode variable admittance controller based on safety evaluation and supervision for the cable-driven lower limb rehabilitation robot, which can switch between active training mode and passive training mode and adjust the parameters of the admittance controller. Li et al. [24] designed a multi-modal control scheme for exoskeleton rehabilitation robots, including robot-assisted mode, robot-dominant mode, and safety-stop mode, and verified the effectiveness of the scheme in upper-limb and lower-limb exoskeleton robot systems. Zhou et al. [25] proposed a trajectory deformation algorithm, which can realize the desired trajectory planning of participants based on the interaction force in the process of human-robot interaction and improve robot compliance and motion smoothness. Chen et al. proposed a reference trajectory adaptive compliance control algorithm, which combines impedance control and motion trajectory planning [26]. Huo et al. developed a lower limb exoskeleton impedance modulation strategy, which can provide proper power and balance assistance during sit-to-stand movements [27]. Compared with the position control strategy, the compliance control strategy is beneficial in avoiding excessive force between the human and the robot and has a wider application in the field of rehabilitation robots [28].

The sEMG-based control strategies of the lower limb rehabilitation robot mainly include the sEMG-based continuous control strategy and the sEMG-triggered control strategy [29]. Many studies have been carried out on the sEMG-based continuous control strategy, in which the lower limb motion intention recognition is performed using the sEMG signal and torque assistance proportional to the sEMG signals is provided to generate the desired motions. Khoshdel et al. proposed an sEMG-based robust impedance control strategy for the lower limb rehabilitation robots and the sEMG signals were used to estimate the exerted force [30]. Yao et al. developed an adaptive admittance control scheme consisting of an admittance filter, an inner position controller, and an sEMG-driven musculoskeletal model [31]. Xie et al. proposed an adaptive trajectory planning method based on sEMG signals and interactive forces for lower limb rehabilitation robots and planned three periodic trajectories using sEMG signals [32]. Different from the sEMG-based continuous control, the robot assistance is triggered when the sEMG signals reach a certain threshold in the sEMG-triggered control strategy. Meng et al. proposed an active interactive controller based on motion recognition and adaptive impedance control. Using the root mean square (RMS) feature of the sEMG signal integrated with the support vector machine (SVM) classifier, it can predict the motion intention of the lower limbs and trigger robot assistance [33]. Lin et al. designed an sEMG-triggered controller for the artificial muscle-driven lower limb rehabilitation robot, and the methods of discrete wavelet transformation and the support vector machine are used to predict the lower limb movement intention [34]. Compared with force and position signals, the sEMG signals can reflect the activity level of specific muscle groups, which can monitor and control the movement of limbs in more detail [35].

However, the above-mentioned compliance control strategies for lower limb rehabilitation robots using sEMG signals are mainly aimed at active training scenarios. Existing passive training control strategies mainly rely on force and position information and lack the intelligent sEMG-based compliance adjustment function, resulting in an unsatisfactory safety performance of lower limb rehabilitation robots [36]. Moreover, in the passive training process of lower limbs, the essential purpose of adopting different training modes is to perform specific training effects on different muscle groups. The fusion of the force, position and sEMG signals in the compliance control strategy, monitoring the muscle activation degree in real time, and controlling the motion of the robot, encompass a significant problem to be solved in the control strategy development of the lower limb rehabilitation robot [36].

Aiming at the problems above, based on the hybrid end-effector lower limb rehabilitation robot (HE-LRR) developed in our research group [37], this paper proposes an sEMG-based gain-tuned compliance control (EGCC) strategy. In the passive training process, the lower limbs follow the robot end effector to move in three-dimensional space. The human body keeps the lower limbs relaxed and does not actively contract muscles. The sEMG signal collected under this condition is intended to monitor the muscle condition and protect the patient by enhancing robot compliance. The rationality of the control strategy is verified through simulation and experimental research under three training modes: MOTOmed, CPM, and SLR. The rest of this paper is organized as follows. Section 2 contains the introduction of the configuration design of the HE-LRR. The EGCC strategy is proposed in Section 3. The simulation research of the EGCC strategy without sEMG information is performed in Section 4. In Section 5, the sEMG acquisition and feature analysis are carried out, and the EGCC strategy comprehensive experiment is conducted. Section 6 presents the conclusions and prospects for the EGCC strategy.

2. Robot Configuration

There are mainly three types of lower limb movement for the human body, namely moving in the sagittal plane, stepping in the coronal plane, and turning around the longitudinal axis of the human body [38]. HE-LRR is designed in accordance with ergonomic considerations, which includes a base frame, a hybrid (2UPS+U)&(R+RPR) mechanism, and a pedal unit. Here U, P, R, and S represent a universal pair, a prismatic pair, a revolute pair, and a spherical pair, respectively. Figure 1 shows the virtual prototype of the HE-LRR and the pedal unit. The HE-LRR allows people to sit or lie on the opposite side of the machine while their feet are connected to the robot end effector, and they receive rehabilitation training.

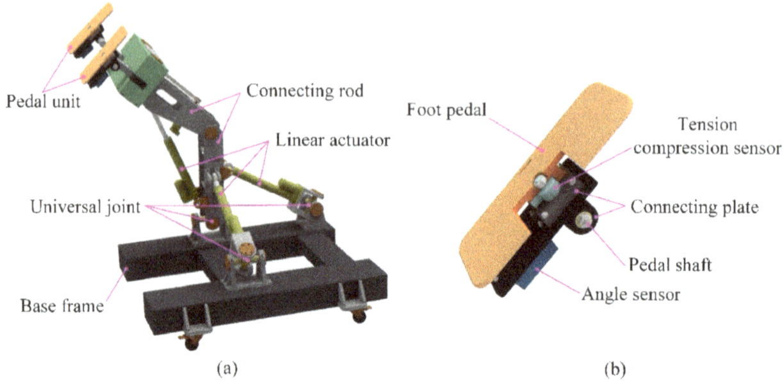

Figure 1. (**a**) The virtual prototype of the HE-LRR; (**b**) structure of pedal unit.

According to the simplified rotation characteristics of the hip joint where two rotation axes are orthogonal, the parallel part of the lower limb rehabilitation robot is designed as a (2-UPS+U) mechanism, including two UPS branches and one U branch chain. Using linear actuators, the parallel part is driven to rotate around the cross axis, thereby assisting the lower limbs in achieving rehabilitation training in the sagittal and coronal planes. In order to realize the rotary motion of the knee joint, the RPR branch chain is introduced into the parallel part, and the linear actuator is used as the driving unit. Rehabilitation training requirements for patients with multiple degrees of freedom can be met by the coordinated movements of (2-UPS+U)&(R+RPR) mechanisms. The (R+RPR) mechanism is superior to rotary motor driving, and it can reduce the mass and inertia of the kinematic joint of the robot and increase its bearing capacity.

The pedal unit is composed of a foot pedal, a pedal shaft, connecting plates, a tension compression sensor, and an angle sensor. The foot pedal is utilized to guide the distal end of the lower limb to move while the pedal shaft is used to connect the pedal unit with the hybrid mechanism. The tension compression sensor is embedded in the pedal unit to record the man-machine contact force, and the angle force is installed on the connecting plate to acquire the angle information of the pedal unit.

3. EGCC Strategy

There are two typical impedance control strategies applied in rehabilitation robots: the force-based impedance control strategy and the position-based impedance control strategy. Although the force-based impedance control strategy can realize force tracking, the controller relies on the dynamic characteristics between the robot and the environment, making it difficult to implement control in practice. Compared with the force-based impedance control, the position-based impedance control has more stable performance [39,40]. In this section, the passive training of the lower limb rehabilitation robot adopts a position-based impedance control strategy. The impedance control model is as follows:

$$M_d \Delta \ddot{X} + B_d \Delta \dot{X} + K_d \Delta X = F \tag{1}$$

where, M_d, B_d, K_d are the target inertia matrix, damping matrix, and stiffness matrix of the impedance model; F is the man-machine contact force acting on the robot end effector; ΔX is the position correction amount of the robot end effector.

Using Laplace transformation, the position correction amount in the Laplace domain can be derived as follows:

$$\Delta X(s) = \frac{F(s)}{M_d s^2 + B_d s + K_d} \tag{2}$$

where, s is the complex number frequency parameter.

The block diagram of the position-based impedance control is shown in Figure 2. The man-machine contact force F passes through the impedance control model to generate the position correction amount ΔX, which is superimposed on the reference position X_r to generate the desired position X_d, which is sent to the position controller after the inverse kinematics solution, so that the actual position tracks the desired position.

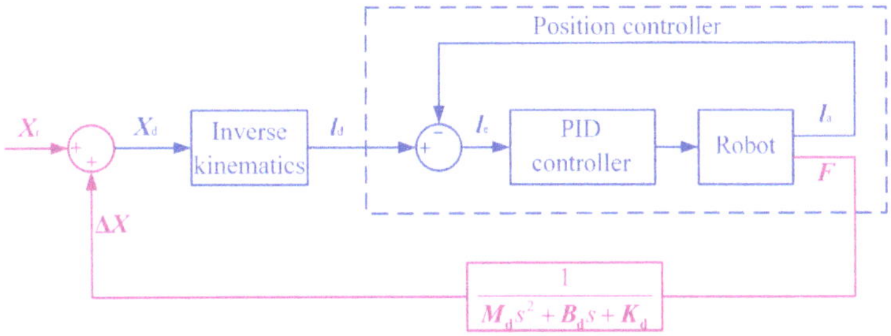

Figure 2. Position-based impedance control strategy diagram.

The above position-based impedance control strategy is suitable for not only controlling the robot to move along a preset trajectory, but also maintaining a certain flexibility during the movement. The method is to convert the end contact force into the position correction amount through the impedance control model. In order to improve the compliance and safety of the control strategy, the sEMG information needs to be integrated into the above position-based impedance control strategy. The modified EGCC strategy diagram is shown in Figure 3.

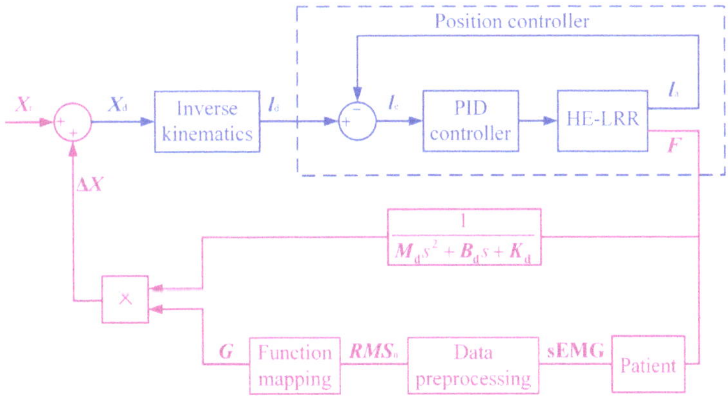

Figure 3. EGCC strategy diagram for the HE-LRR.

From the original sEMG signal of the patient's target muscle group to the gain parameter, it needs to go through two processes: data preprocessing and function mapping. In the process of data preprocessing, the high-frequency and low-frequency signals are filtered out of the sEMG signal through the band-pass filter, and then the time-domain features with the intuitive physical significance are obtained through feature extraction. The root mean square (RMS) can reflect the average power of the sEMG signal, so the RMS feature value is used to evaluate the characteristics of the sEMG signal, and the calculation formula is as follows:

$$RMS_j = \sqrt{\frac{1}{W}\sum_{i=1}^{W} x_i^2} \tag{3}$$

where j represents the j-th segment in the original sEMG data sequence, x_i is the i-th original data in the segment data, and W is the sliding window width.

In order to improve the generalization ability of the model, the sEMG signals after feature extraction need to be normalized. The normalization calculation formula is as follows:

$$RMS_{\mathrm{n}} = \frac{RMS - RMS_{\mathrm{min}}}{RMS_{\mathrm{max}} - RMS_{\mathrm{min}}} \tag{4}$$

where RMS represents the sEMG signal after feature extraction; RMS_{min} and RMS_{max} are the minimum and maximum values of RMS, respectively; RMS_{n} is the normalized sEMG signal. RMS_{min} and RMS_{max} are constants in different training modes and can be obtained through sEMG signal acquisition and feature analysis (see Section 5.2). Here the gain parameter G is set to be 1, that is, the sEMG signal is not included in the control strategy during the sEMG acquisition experiment.

After the normalization processing, the normalized sEMG signals RMS_{n} of different muscle groups can be obtained according to Equation (4) respectively. In the "Function mapping" block, the maximum value of the muscle groups' normalized sEMG signals is compared with the threshold value of the normalized sEMG signal RMS_{t}, and the gain parameter G can be calculated according to the following equation:

$$G = \begin{cases} 1 & RMS_{\mathrm{n}} \leq RMS_{\mathrm{t}} \\ a(RMS_{\mathrm{n}} - RMS_{\mathrm{t}})^2 + 1 & RMS_{\mathrm{n}} > RMS_{\mathrm{t}} \end{cases} \tag{5}$$

When the normalized sEMG signal does not exceed the threshold value, the gain parameter is equal to 1. Otherwise, there is a quadratic functional relationship between the gain parameter and the normalized sEMG signal. Thus, in the passive training process of the lower limb rehabilitation robot, the position correction amount is jointly affected by the inertia parameter, damping parameter, stiffness parameter, and gain parameter. When the normalized sEMG threshold is constant, the maximum value of the gain parameter G is determined by the parameter a. If the parameter a is too large, the position correction amount will be too large, it will become more difficult for the robot end effector to move near the set trajectory, and the patient will not be able to receive standardized rehabilitation training. If the parameter a is too small, the position correction amount is too small, and the robot end effector will have no apparent sEMG-based compliance enhancement effect in the EGCC strategy. Therefore, the parameter a should be kept within a moderate range.

4. Simulation and Results

4.1. Impedance Control Parameter Influence Analysis

In the passive training process, it is important to select appropriate inertia parameters, damping parameters, and stiffness parameters when applying the impedance control model. Therefore, it is necessary to analyze the influence of impedance control parameters on the control performance. The transfer function of the impedance control model is:

$$G(s) = \frac{\Delta X(s)}{F(s)} = \frac{1}{M_{\mathrm{d}}s^2 + B_{\mathrm{d}}s + K_{\mathrm{d}}} \tag{6}$$

For the convenience of analysis, considering the impedance control model in a single direction, Equation (6) can be simplified to Equation (7):

$$G(s) = \frac{1}{ms^2 + bs + k} \tag{7}$$

where, m, b, and k are the inertia parameter, damping parameter, and stiffness parameter, respectively. Equation (7) is transformed into the standard form:

$$G(s) = \frac{1}{k} \frac{\omega_n^2}{s^2 + 2\xi\omega_n s + \omega_n^2} \tag{8}$$

where, ω_n is the undamped natural frequency; ξ is the damping ratio.

The response curves of position correction amount under different inertia parameters are shown in Figure 4. The simulation parameters are set to {F = 1 N, b = 0.10 N·s/mm, k = 0.25 N/mm}. When m = 0.001 N·s^2/mm, $\xi > 1$, the system is in the overdamped state; when m = 0.01 N·s^2/mm, $\xi = 1$, the system is in the critically damped state; when m = 0.02, 0.03 N·s^2/mm, $\xi < 1$, the system is in the underdamped state. The response curves of the position correction amount under different damping parameters are shown in Figure 5. The simulation parameters are set to {F = 1 N, m = 0.01 N·s^2/mm, k = 0.25 N/mm}. When b = 0.20 N·s/mm, $\xi > 1$, the system is in the overdamped state; when b = 0.10 N·s/mm, $\xi = 1$, the system is in the critically damped state; when b = 0.03, 0.05 N·s/mm, $\xi < 1$, the system is in the underdamped state. When the system is in the overdamped or critically damped state, the response curve has no overshoot and oscillation, and the rise time and settling time of the critically damped system are shorter than those of the overdamped system. When the system is in the underdamped state, as the damping ratio decreases, the overshoot increases and the settling time becomes longer.

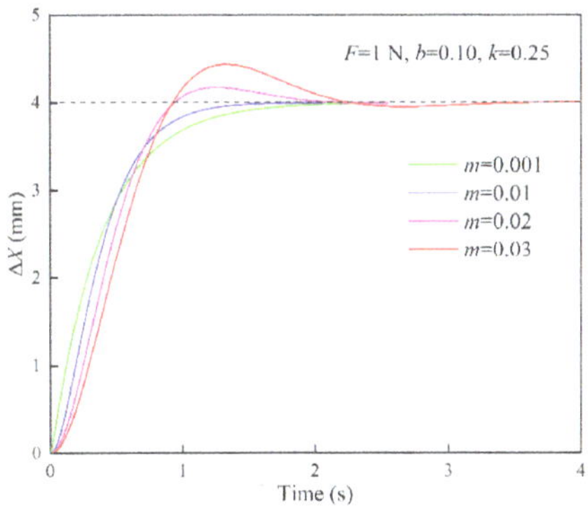

Figure 4. Response curves of position correction amount under different inertia parameters (m: N·s^2/mm; b: N·s/mm; k: N/mm).

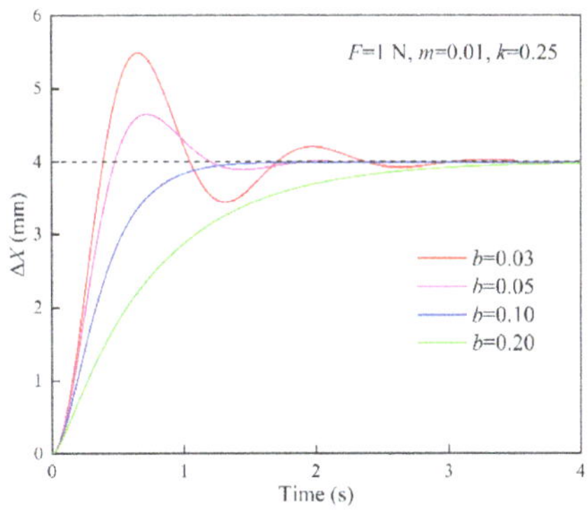

Figure 5. Response curves of position correction amount under different damping parameters (m: N·s^2/mm; b: N·s/mm; k: N/mm).

The response curves of the position correction amount under different stiffness parameters are shown in Figure 6. The simulation parameters are set to {F = 1 N, m = 0.005 N·s^2/mm, b = 0.06 N·s/mm}. When k = 0.12 N/mm, $\xi > 1$, the system is in the overdamped state; when k = 0.18 N/mm, $\xi = 1$, the system is in the critically damped state; when k = 0.24, 0.30 N/mm, $\xi < 1$, the system is in the underdamped state. With the change of the stiffness parameter, it is found that the steady-state value of the response curve changes significantly. As the stiffness parameter increases, the steady-state value decreases, that is, the position correction amount becomes smaller, thus the robot's compliance worsens.

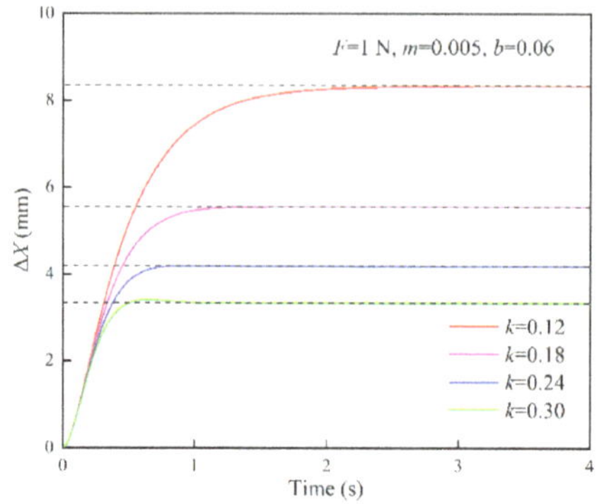

Figure 6. Response curves of position correction amount under different stiffness parameters (m: N·s^2/mm; b: N·s/mm; k: N/mm).

Through the above analysis, applying the impedance control model to the passive training of the rehabilitation robot is to improve the compliance of the rehabilitation robot and achieve the purpose of protecting the patient. The response curve needs to show no overshoot and no oscillation. In addition, the settling time should be shortened as much as possible. Therefore, the impedance model parameters should be set to the critically damped state. Since the steady-state value of the position correction amount is only affected by the stiffness parameter, the stiffness parameter can be reduced to increase the robot's compliance.

4.2. Impedance Control Strategy Simulation

When simulating the passive training impedance control strategy, it is necessary to add the impedance control model on the basis of the previous position control simulation. In the simulation environment, the man-machine contact force is set to be:

$$\begin{cases} F_y = \sin t + \sin 2t + \sin 4t \\ F_z = \cos t + \cos 2t + \cos 4t \end{cases} \tag{9}$$

where, F_y and F_z are the components of the man-machine contact force in the Y-direction and Z-direction, respectively.

In the MOTOmed training mode, the reference trajectory of the robot end effector is a circular trajectory. The reference trajectory parameters are set to {the center coordinates (x_0, y_0, z_0) = (0, −670, 470) and the radius r = 90.00 mm}. The impedance model parameters are selected from a set of parameters in the critically damped state: {m = 0.01 N·s^2/mm, b = 0.10 N·s/mm, k = 0.25 N/mm}. The comparison between the reference trajectory and the simulated trajectory of MOTOmed training is shown in Figure 7a. It can be seen that under the action of the man-machine contact forces F_y and F_z, the simulated trajectory has a certain degree of offset compared with the reference trajectory, the coordinate where the maximum position offset occurs is (0, −689.77, 567.59) and the maximum offset is 9.73 mm (Y-direction: −0.32 mm, Z-direction: 9.72 mm). In the CPM training mode, the reference trajectory of the robot end effector is a beeline trajectory, and the coordinates of the starting point and the end point are set to be (0, −575, 300) and (0, −775, 300), respectively. The impedance control parameters and the contact force function are the same as those of the circular trajectory. The comparison between the CPM training reference trajectory and the simulated trajectory is shown in Figure 7b. Compared with the reference trajectory, the coordinate of the maximum position offset on the simulated trajectory is (0, −602.70, 309.72) and the maximum offset is 9.73 mm (Y-direction: −0.33 mm, Z-direction: 9.72 mm). In the

SLR training mode, the reference trajectory of the robot is an arc trajectory, the coordinate of the starting point of the reference trajectory is $(x_0, y_0, z_0) = (0, -822.5, 613.5)$, and the coordinate of the end point is $(x_0, y_0, z_0) = (0, -639.8, 326.3)$, the radius $r = 892.00$ mm. The comparison between the SLR training reference trajectory and the simulated trajectory is shown in Figure 7c. Compared with the reference trajectory, the coordinate of the maximum position offset of the simulated trajectory is (0, −774.39, 567.70), and the maximum offset is 9.73 mm (*Y*-direction: −0.32 mm, *Z*-direction: 9.72 mm). From the above analysis, it is found that in the three training modes, the maximum offset values of the simulated trajectories are the same, which is related to the same settings of man-machine contact force and impedance control parameters in the simulation.

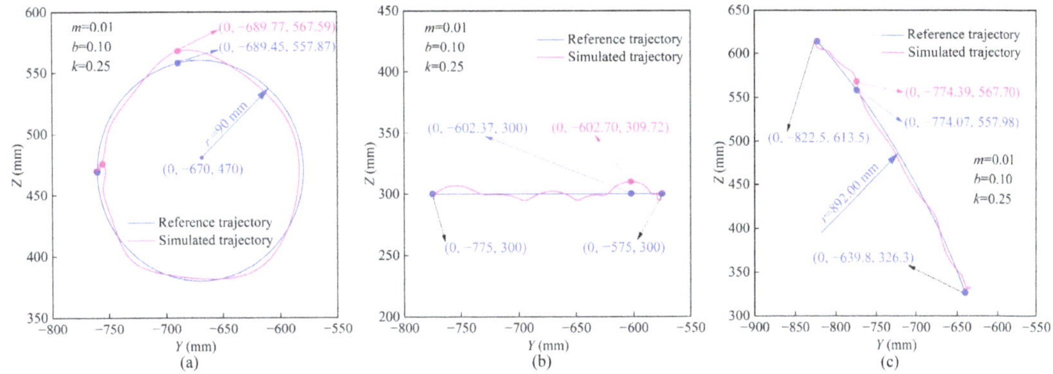

Figure 7. Reference trajectories and simulated trajectories under different training modes: (**a**) MOTOmed training; (**b**) CPM training; (**c**) SLR training; (m: N·s^2/mm; b: N·s/mm; k: N/mm).

The contact force and position correction amount in *Y*-direction are shown in Figure 8a. It can be seen that within the simulation time of 0–10 s, the *Y*-direction contact force fluctuates within a certain range, and at the time of 6.80 s, the contact force reaches the maximum value of 2.23 N. The fluctuation trend of the position correction amount in the *Y*-direction is consistent with that of the contact force, but there is a certain delay between the position correction amount and the contact force. At the moment of 7.20 s, the position correction amount reaches the maximum value of 6.74 mm. The contact force and position correction amount in the *Z*-direction are shown in Figure 8b. Within the simulation time of 0–10 s, the position correction amount lags behind the contact force. At the time of 6.28 s, the contact force in the *Z*-direction reaches the maximum value of 3.00 N. At the moment of 6.63 s, the *Z*-direction position correction amount achieves the maximum value of 9.72 mm. By comprehensive analysis of the above results, the time at which the maximum position offset occurs is 6.63 s in the three training modes. The maximum offsets in the three training modes are the same, indicating that the position offset is determined by the man-machine contact force and not affected by the training mode. Through the above simulations of MOTOmed training, CPM training, and SLR training, it can be shown that under the action of man-machine contact force, the rehabilitation robot shows a certain compliance by generating the position correction amount to adapt to changes of the man-machine contact force.

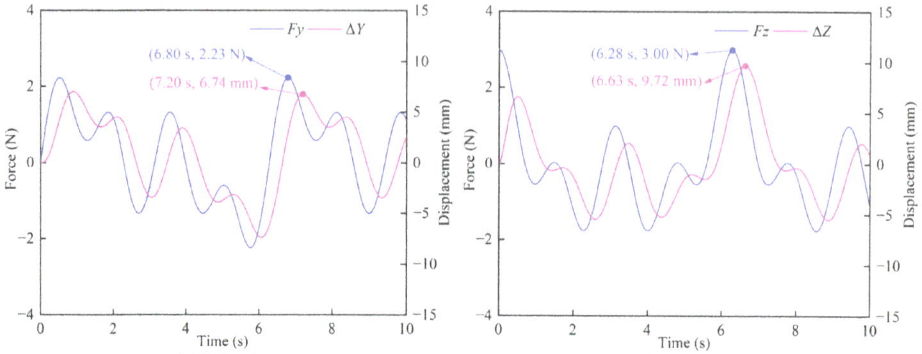

(a) *Y*-direction (b) *Z*-direction

Figure 8. The comparison of the contact force and the position correction amount in different directions (**a**) *Y*-direction; (**b**) *Z*-direction.

5. Experimental Verification

5.1. Robot Prototype and Control System

The control system of the lower limb rehabilitation robot consists of the controlling unit, the driving unit, the actuating unit, the sensing unit, the sEMG acquisition unit, and the power unit, as shown in Figure 9.

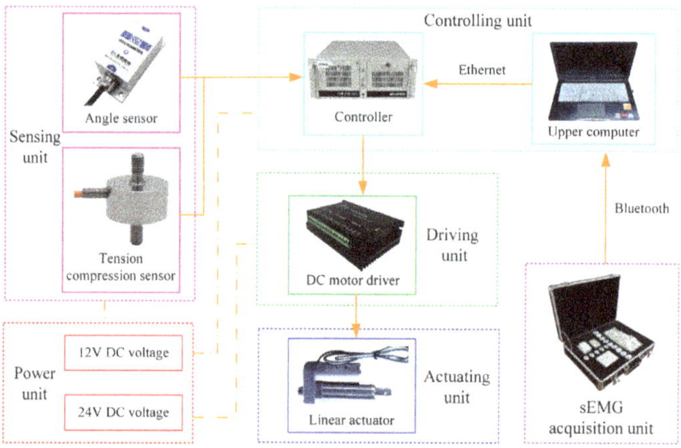

Figure 9. Frame diagram of lower limb rehabilitation robot control system.

The biosignal acquisition tool (PLUX wireless biosignals S.A., Biosignals Researcher, Lisbon, Portugal) collects sEMG signals in real-time through electromyography electrodes pasted on the target muscle groups of the lower limbs and transmits the signals to the upper computer (DELL Technologies Co., Ltd., Vostro 5370, Round Rock, TX, USA) through Bluetooth. Filter processing and feature value calculation are carried out within the set time period, and the feature value is transmitted to the controller through the Ethernet. The industrial controller (Advantech Technology Co., Ltd., IPC610, Suzhou, China) is used as the controller. In addition to receiving instructions from the upper computer in real-time, it can also receive signals from the tension compression sensor (HY chuangan Technologies Co., Ltd., HYLY-019, Bengbu, China) and the angle sensor (BEWIS Sensing Technologies Co., Ltd., BWK220, Wuxi, China). At the same time, the controller sends instructions to the DC motor driver (Magicon Intelligent Technologies Co., Ltd., MC-FBLD-6600, Shenzhen, China), and drives the linear actuators (Suzhou Yuancheng mingchuang Electromechanical

Equipment Co., Ltd, LEC606, Suzhou, China) to perform telescopic movement. The linear actuator has a built-in incremental encoder, which can record the motion position of the DC motor to facilitate the position-based closed-loop control of the linear actuator. Angle sensors, tension compression sensors, and DC motor drivers require 12 V or 24 V DC voltage, which is provided by the power unit.

The prototype of HE-LRR was manufactured and integrated with the control system, which is shown in Figure 10. Universal casters with brakes are installed at the bottom of the base frame to facilitate the movement of the robot and improve the stability during rehabilitation training. The patient's feet are placed on the foot pedal to carry out the rehabilitation training. During the implementation of this study, five healthy participants (age: 24–31 years old; height: 1670–1870 mm; thigh length: 405–455 mm; calf length: 385–420 mm) were recruited to take part in the experiment following the procedures for healthy participants as approved by the China Rehabilitation Research Center (CRRC-IEC-RF-SC-005-01), and the basic information of the participants is listed in Table 1. There were no known muscular or neurological disorders among the healthy participants. All participants completed the experimental protocol safely and reported no physical discomfort.

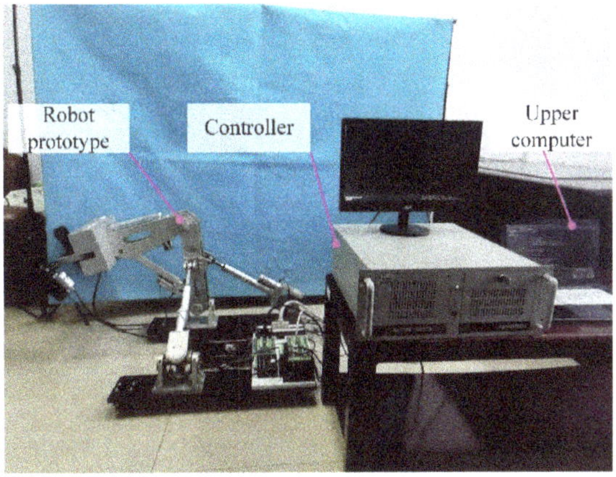

Figure 10. Prototype of the HE-LRR and the control system.

Table 1. Basic information of the participants in the experiments.

Number	Age (year)	Height (mm)	Thigh Length (mm)	Calf Length (mm)
1	31	1790	430	405
2	28	1720	430	400
3	24	1870	455	420
4	30	1670	405	385
5	28	1690	415	400

The experimental procedure is shown in Figure 11. In the subsection of Signal Acquisition and Feature Analysis, the experimental processes include signal acquisition preparation, signal acquisition, signal preprocessing. and signal characteristic analysis. In the subsection of EGCC Strategy Comprehensive Experiment, the research is carried out in the order of the determination of model parameters, experimental verification, comparative analysis of experimental results. and experimental conclusion.

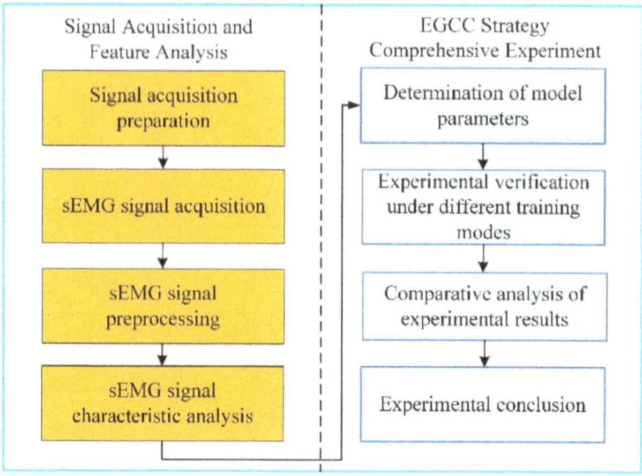

Figure 11. Flowchart of the experimental procedure.

5.2. Signal Acquisition and Feature Analysis

Before the sEMG signal acquisition experiment, the biceps femoris (BF), rectus femoris (RF), tibialis anterior (TA), and peroneus longus (PL) were selected as the target muscle groups of the lower limbs, and the surface electrodes were pasted on the corresponding skin positions of the muscle groups. The positions of the four target muscle groups of the lower limbs and the sensor sticking positions are shown in Figure 12. In the sEMG signal acquisition process, the subjects were given instructions to keep their lower limbs relaxed and not to contract their muscles actively. Their feet followed the robot end effector to move in space. Each subject participated in 12 groups of experiments for each training mode (MOTOmed, CPM or SLR). Impedance parameter settings in the 12 groups of experiments are shown in Table 2. In each group of experiments, the subjects performed 10 cycles of training.

The sampling frequency of the sEMG acquisition unit is 1000 Hz, and the sampling period is 1 ms. The collected original sEMG signals are in the range of 0–10 μV. After passing through the band-pass filter with a passband of 10–500 Hz, the feature value is extracted from the filtered sEMG signal and the RMS feature value is used for the time-domain quantitative analysis of the sEMG signal. Figure 13 shows the sEMG signals before and after RMS feature extraction. It can be seen that the signal characteristic of violent fluctuations is eliminated after RMS feature extraction. At the same time, the sEMG signal after the RMS feature extraction can well reflect the change trend of the original signal (before RMS feature extraction) and shows good regularity and stability. The maximum RMS values of the sEMG signal of the subjects in different training modes are extracted and statistical analysis is carried out to obtain the average value and standard deviation.

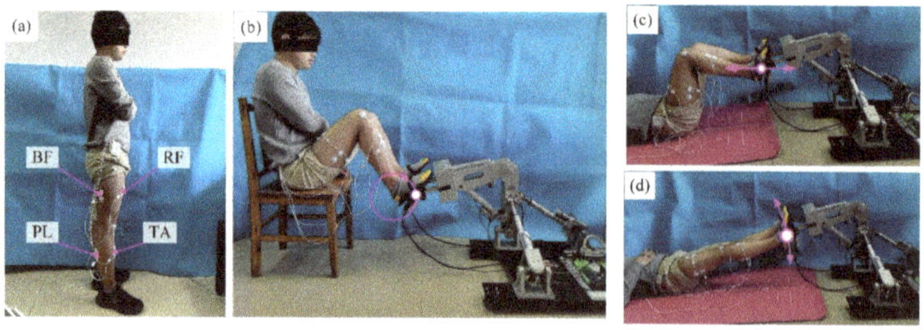

Figure 12. (**a**) Target muscle groups and sensor sticking positions; (**b**) MOTOmed training mode; (**c**) CPM training mode; (**d**) SLR training mode.

Table 2. Impedance parameter setting in the 12 groups of experiments.

Group Number	Inertia Parameter (N·s^2/mm)	Damping Parameter (N·s/mm)	Stiffness Parameter (N/mm)
1	0.001	0.10	0.25
2	0.01	0.10	0.25
3	0.02	0.10	0.25
4	0.03	0.10	0.25
5	0.01	0.03	0.25
6	0.01	0.05	0.25
7	0.01	0.10	0.25
8	0.01	0.20	0.25
9	0.005	0.06	0.12
10	0.005	0.06	0.18
11	0.005	0.06	0.24
12	0.005	0.06	0.30

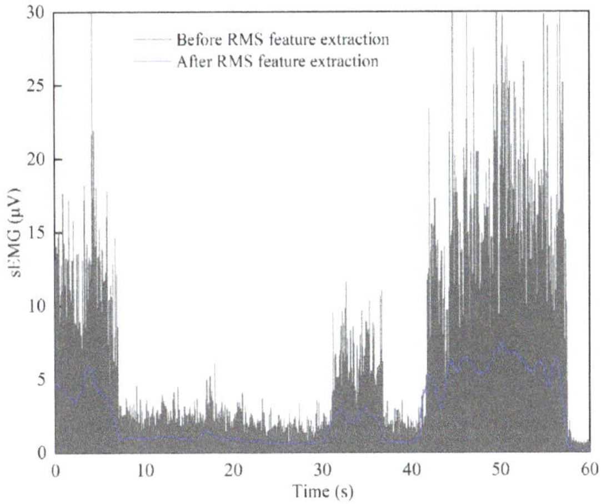

Figure 13. sEMG signals before and after RMS feature extraction.

Figure 14 displays the maximum RMS values of the sEMG signal in different training modes. In the MOTOmed training mode, under the condition of different impedance control parameters, the maximum RMS values of the four muscle groups are shown in Figure 14a. It can be seen that when the damping parameter and stiffness parameter are fixed values (b = 0.10 N·s/mm, k = 0.25 N/mm), the RMS values of the four muscles are at a higher level under the underdamped state (m = 0.02, 0.03 N·s^2/mm) and the RMS values of the four muscles are at a lower level when under the overdamped or critically damped state (m = 0.001, 0.01 N·s^2/mm). Similarly, when the inertia parameter and stiffness parameter are fixed values (m = 0.01 N·s^2/mm, k = 0.25 N/mm), the four muscles obtain relatively high RMS values of the sEMG signals in the underdamped state. When the inertia parameter and damping parameter are fixed values (m = 0.005 N·s^2/mm, b = 0.06 N·s/mm), the maximum RMS values of the muscle groups except for the PL muscle increase with the increase of the stiffness parameter. This is because when the stiffness parameter increases, the offset degree of the robot in response to the action of the man-machine contact force decreases, and the compliance of the HE-LRR robot is reduced, resulting in the situation where the muscle activation level cannot be released and maintained at a high level.

In the CPM training mode, under different impedance control parameters, the maximum RMS values of the four muscle groups are shown in Figure 14b. It can be seen that different muscles can obtain higher RMS values in the underdamped state, which is similar to the MOTOmed training mode. The difference is that the maximum RMS value is 8.26 ± 0.25 μV (TA muscle) in the CPM training mode, while the maximum RMS value is

9.24 ± 0.23 μV (BF muscle) in the MOTOmed training mode. In the SLR training mode, under different impedance control parameters, the maximum RMS values of the four muscles are shown in Figure 14c. It can be seen that, when m = 0.005 N·s²/mm, b = 0.06 N·s/mm, k = 0.30 N/mm, the maximum RMS value of the sEMG signal is 8.30 ± 0.24 μV (BF muscle), and when m = 0.005 N·s²/mm, b = 0.06 N·s/mm, k = 0.24 N/mm, the maximum RMS value is 7.89 ± 0.28 μV (RF muscle).

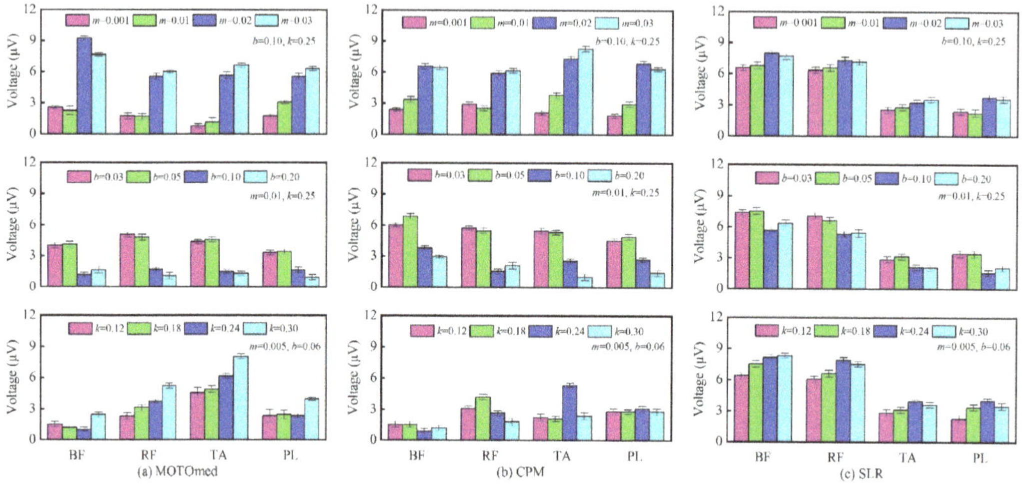

Figure 14. Maximum RMS value of sEMG signal in different training modes (**a**) MOTOmed mode; (**b**) CPM mode; (**c**) SLR mode (m: N·s²/mm; b: N·s/mm; k: N/mm).

Comprehensive analysis, when the participants participate in the three training modes in a relaxed state, the RMS range of sEMG for target muscle groups is 0–9.24 μV in MOTOmed training, the RMS range of sEMG is 0–8.26 μV in CPM training, and the RMS range of sEMG is 0–8.30 μV in the SLR training (since the minimum values of RMS of different subjects were close to zero, here the lower bound value of the RMS range is determined to be zero). In the MOTOmed training mode, $RMS_{\min}$ and $RMS_{\max}$ are determined as 0 μV and 9.24 μV; in the CPM training mode, $RMS_{\min}$ and $RMS_{\max}$ are determined as 0 μV and 8.26 μV; in the SLR training mode, $RMS_{\min}$ and $RMS_{\max}$ are determined as 0 μV and 8.30 μV. The feature analysis results show that there exists a difference in the RMS range under different training modes, which proves that adopting different training modes can carry out targeted rehabilitation training for different muscle groups, so as to achieve a better effect of lower limb rehabilitation training. In particular, after RMS feature extraction, the regularity and stability of the sEMG signals are further improved, which can meet the needs of the EGCC strategy. Moreover, taking the maximum RMS values in this subsection as the reference values for normalization processing can improve the generalization ability of the EGCC strategy.

5.3. EGCC Strategy Comprehensive Experiment

In order to verify the control effect of EGCC strategy, validation experiments were carried out under different training modes. The participants kept their lower limbs in a relaxed state during the training process. After normalization processing, the normalized sEMG threshold was set at 0.50, 0.75, and 1.00, respectively. The inertia parameter m, damping parameter b, and stiffness parameter k in the EGCC strategy were set at 0.01 N·s²/mm, 0.10 N·s/mm, and 0.25 N/mm, respectively. For the convenience of comparison, the coefficient a was set to be 5 in the following EGCC strategy comprehensive experiment.

The experimental results of the actual end trajectory and gain parameter of the lower limb rehabilitation robot under different training modes are shown in Figure 15. It can be seen that in the MOTOmed training mode, the actual trajectories in the three groups of experiments deviate to a certain extent compared with the reference trajectory (Figure 15a). When the normalized sEMG threshold is 0.50, 0.75, and 1.00, the maximum values of the position correction amount are 17.22 mm, 12.03 mm, and 8.33 mm, respectively. As can be seen from Figure 15b, when the normalized sEMG thresholds are 0.50 and 0.75, the gain parameter fluctuates locally. When the normalized sEMG threshold is 0.50, the maximum value of the gain parameter is 2.09. When the normalized sEMG threshold is 0.75, the maximum value of the gain parameter is 1.24, which shows that the decrease of the normalized sEMG threshold is beneficial in improving the compliance of HE-LRR.

In the CPM training mode, when the normalized sEMG thresholds are 0.50, 0.75, and 1.00, the maximum values of the position correction amount are 21.75 mm, 13.71 mm, and 7.69 mm, respectively, while the maximum values of the gain parameter are 2.09, 1.24, and 1.00, respectively. In the SLR training mode, when the normalized sEMG thresholds are 0.50, 0.75, and 1.00, the maximum values of the position correction amount are 16.98 mm, 11.74 mm, and 5.92 mm, and the maximum values of the gain parameter are 2.08, 1.27, and 1.00, respectively. Comparing the results in the three training modes, although the maximum values of the position correction amount are different, the gain parameters are relatively close to each other. This is because when the normalized sEMG thresholds are 0.50, 0.75, and 1.00, the gain parameters have a maximum value of 2.25, 1.3125, and 1.00, respectively, which enables the position correction amount of the lower limb rehabilitation robot to be maintained within a certain range to prevent secondary damage caused by excessive offset.

In addition, it can be seen from Figure 15b,d,f that the gain parameter is larger than 1.00 in a relatively short time. Since there is a clear functional relationship between the gain parameter and normalized sEMG threshold, it shows that the normalized sEMG can recover below the threshold in a short time. This is due to the fact that as the gain parameter increases, the position offset occurring in the direction of the man-machine contact force increases and the compliance of the lower limb rehabilitation robot is enhanced, which is conducive to the recovery of muscle activation. When the normalized sEMG threshold is set as 1.00, the EGCC strategy can be used to identify abnormal sEMG signals and increase the compliance of the lower limb rehabilitation robot to protect the participant. In conclusion, the EGCC strategy can play a significant role in regulating the compliance of the lower limb rehabilitation robot and increasing the safety of the participant.

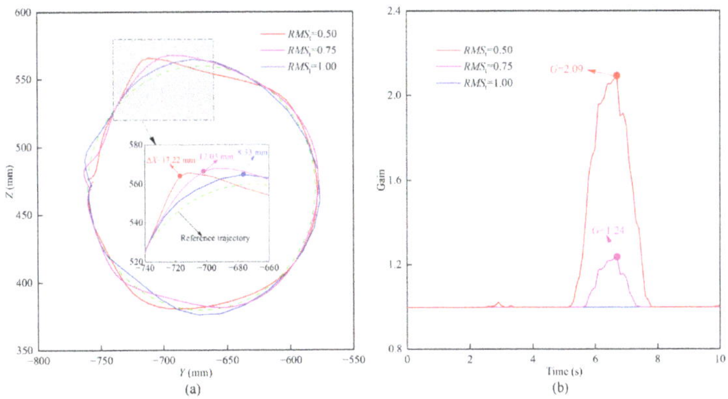

Figure 15. *Cont.*

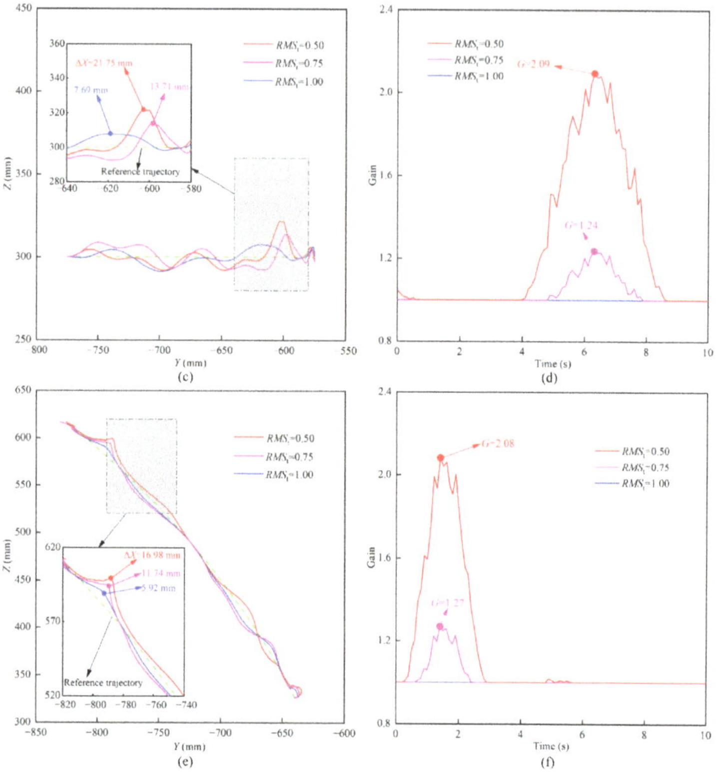

Figure 15. EGCC experimental results of HE-LRR. (**a**) Actual trajectories in the MOTOmed training mode; (**b**) gain parameters in the MOTOmed training mode; (**c**) actual trajectories in the CPM training mode; (**d**) gain parameters in the CPM training mode; (**e**) actual trajectories in the SLR training mode; (**f**) gain parameters in the SLR training mode.

6. Conclusions and Future Work

Aiming at the problems of insufficient physiological information and unsatisfactory safety performance in the existing compliance control strategies for the lower limb rehabilitation robot during passive training, this paper developed an sEMG-based gain-tuned compliance control strategy and carried out simulation and experimental research based on this control strategy. The main conclusions are as follows:

(1) The EGCC strategy without sEMG information was simulated and analyzed. The influence of impedance control parameters on the position correction amount of the robot end effector was studied through simulation, and the change rules of the robot end trajectory, man-machine contact force and position correction amount analyzed, providing a basis for establishing a gain-tuned control strategy fusing the sEMG information.

(2) The experimental acquisition and feature analysis of sEMG signals were carried out to determine the influence of impedance control parameters on the RMS values of sEMG under different training modes and the normal range of RMS values. The preprocessed sEMG has good regularity and stability, which can provide a reference for the normalization processing of sEMG signals in the EGCC strategy.

(3) Based on the lower limb rehabilitation robot control system, the control effect of EGCC strategy was studied in different training modes. The influences of the normalized EMG threshold on the robot's end trajectory and the gain parameter were analyzed. The results prove that EGCC strategy can play a significant role in improving the

compliance and safety of the lower limb rehabilitation robot, which validates the rationality of the EGCC strategy.

Although the control strategy in this paper was verified in the end-effector robot system, the basic methodology can also be applied in the exoskeleton lower limb robot system. There are still some shortcomings in the current research work, for example, the simulation and experimental research of the EGCC strategy were mainly carried out in three training modes: MOTOmed, CPM, and SLR, and the normalized sEMG threshold was required to be set manually. Future research work will be committed to solving the problems of the EGCC strategy validation in various training modes as well as the autonomous learning and optimization of the EGCC strategy model.

Author Contributions: Methodology, J.T. and J.N.; software, S.Z. and Y.N.; validation, X.Z.; writing—original draft preparation, J.T. and S.Z.; writing—review and editing, J.T. and J.N.; project administration, J.N. and L.V.; funding acquisition, J.N. and H.W. All authors have read and agreed to the published version of the manuscript.

Funding: This research was partially funded by the National Key Research and Development Program under Grant 2019YFB1312500, National Natural Science Foundation of China under Grant U1913216, Science and Technology (S&T) Program of Hebei under Grant 216Z1803G and E2020103001, and is also partially funded by Shanghai Clinical Research Center for Aging and Medicine (19MC1910500).

Institutional Review Board Statement: The study was conducted in accordance with the Declaration of Helsinki and approved by the Ethics Committee of China Rehabilitation Research Center (protocol code: 2020-006-1 and date of approval: March 2020).

Informed Consent Statement: Informed consent was obtained from all subjects involved in the study.

Data Availability Statement: The original data contributions presented in the study are included in the article; further inquiries can be directed to the corresponding authors.

Acknowledgments: The authors would like to take this opportunity to express thanks to Doctor Ying Liu from Qinhuangdao Haigang hospital for his assistance in the design and implementation of experimental schemes.

Conflicts of Interest: The authors declare no conflict of interest.

Abbreviations

EGCC	Electromyography-based gain-tuned compliance control
sEMG	Surface electromyography
CPM	Continuous passive motion
SLR	Straight leg raise
SVM	Support vector machine
HE-LRR	Hybrid end-effector lower limb rehabilitation robot
BF	Biceps femoris
RF	Rectus femoris
TA	Tibialis anterior
PL	Peroneus longus
RMS	Root mean square

References

1. Rea, M.; Rana, M.; Lugato, N.; Terekhin, P.; Gizzi, L.; Brötz, D.; Fallgatter, A.; Birbaumer, N.; Sitaram, R.; Caria, A. Lower limb movement preparation in chronic stroke: A pilot study toward an fNIRS-BCI for gait rehabilitation. *Neurorehabil. Neural Repair* **2014**, *28*, 564–575. [CrossRef] [PubMed]
2. Yang, J.; Zhao, Z.; Du, C.; Wang, W.; Peng, Q.; Qiu, J.; Wang, G. The realization of robotic neurorehabilitation in clinical: Use of computational intelligence and future prospects analysis. *Expert Rev. Med. Devices* **2020**, *17*, 1311–1322. [CrossRef]
3. Turner, D.L.; Ramos-Murguialday, A.; Birbaumer, N.; Hoffmann, U.; Luft, A. Neurophysiology of robot-mediated training and therapy: A perspective for future use in clinical populations. *Front. Neurol.* **2013**, *4*, 184. [CrossRef] [PubMed]
4. Ottoboni, L.; Merlini, A.; Martino, G. Neural stem cell plasticity: Advantages in therapy for the injured central nervous system. *Front. Cell. Dev. Biol.* **2017**, *5*, 52. [CrossRef] [PubMed]
5. Huo, C.C.; Zheng, Y.; Lu, W.W.; Zhang, T.Y.; Wang, D.F.; Xu, D.S.; Li, Z.Y. Prospects for intelligent rehabilitation techniques to treat motor dysfunction. *Neural Regen. Res.* **2021**, *16*, 264–269.

6. Chang, W.H.; Kim, Y.H. Robot-assisted therapy in stroke rehabilitation. *J. Stroke* **2013**, *15*, 174–181. [CrossRef]
7. Eiammanussakul, T.; Sangveraphunsiri, V. A lower limb rehabilitation robot in sitting position with a review of training activities. *J. Healthc. Eng.* **2018**, *2018*, 1927807. [CrossRef] [PubMed]
8. Molteni, F.; Gasperini, G.; Cannaviello, G.; Guanziroli, E. Exoskeleton and end-effector robots for upper and lower limbs rehabilitation: Narrative review. *PM&R* **2018**, *10*, S174–S188.
9. Glowinski, S.; Krzyzynski, T.; Bryndal, A.; Maciejewski, I. A kinematic model of a humanoid lower limb exoskeleton with hydraulic actuators. *Sensors* **2020**, *20*, 6116. [CrossRef]
10. Bouri, M.; Abdi, E.; Bleuler, H.; Reynard, F.; Deriaz, O. Lower limbs robotic rehabilitation case study with clinical trials. In *New Trends in Medical and Service Robots*; Springer: Berlin/Heidelberg, Germany, 2014; pp. 31–44.
11. Li, W.; Liu, K.; Li, C.; Sun, Z.; Liu, S.; Gu, J. Development and evaluation of a wearable lower limb rehabilitation robot. *J. Bionic Eng.* **2022**, *19*, 688–699. [CrossRef]
12. Feng, Y.; Wang, H.; Du, Y.; Chen, F.; Yan, H.; Yu, H. Trajectory planning of a novel lower limb rehabilitation robot for stroke patient passive training. *Adv. Mech. Eng.* **2017**, *9*, 1687814017737666. [CrossRef]
13. Akdoğan, E.; Adli, M.A. The design and control of a therapeutic exercise robot for lower limb rehabilitation: Physiotherabot. *Mechatronics* **2011**, *21*, 509–522. [CrossRef]
14. Wang, K.Y.; Yin, P.C.; Yang, H.P.; Tang, X.Q. The man-machine motion planning of rigid-flexible hybrid lower limb rehabilitation robot. *Adv. Mech. Eng.* **2018**, *10*, 1687814018775865. [CrossRef]
15. Bouri, M.; Le Gall, B.; Clavel, R. A new concept of parallel robot for rehabilitation and fitness: The Lambda. In Proceedings of the IEEE International Conference on Robotics and Biomimetics (ROBIO), Guangxi, China, 19–23 December 2009; pp. 2503–2508.
16. Saglia, J.A.; Tsagarakis, N.G.; Dai, J.S.; Caldwell, D.G. Control strategies for patient-assisted training using the ankle rehabilitation robot (ARBOT). *IEEE ASME Trans. Mechatron.* **2012**, *18*, 1799–1808. [CrossRef]
17. Li, F.; Zhang, H.; Dong, W.; Li, J.; Li, W.; Sun, L. Surface Electromyography and Force Study for Progressive Rehabilitation Training during Different Modes. In Proceedings of the International Conference on Advanced Robotics and Mechatronics (ICARM), Shenzhen, China, 18–21 December 2020; pp. 157–162.
18. Xu, G.; Song, A.; Pan, L.; Gao, X.; Liang, Z.; Li, J.; Xu, B. Clinical experimental research on adaptive robot-aided therapy control methods for upper-limb rehabilitation. *Robotica* **2014**, *32*, 1081–1100. [CrossRef]
19. Shen, C.; Liu, F.; Yao, L.; Li, Z.; Qiu, L.; Fang, S. Effects of MOTOmed movement therapy on the mobility and activities of daily living of stroke patients with hemiplegia: A systematic review and meta-analysis. *Clin. Rehabil.* **2018**, *32*, 1569–1580. [CrossRef] [PubMed]
20. Bartík, P.; Vostrý, M.; Hudáková, Z.; Šagát, P.; Lesňáková, A.; Dukát, A. The Effect of Early Applied Robot-Assisted Physiotherapy on Functional Independence Measure Score in Post-Myocardial Infarction Patients. *Healthcare* **2022**, *10*, 937. [CrossRef] [PubMed]
21. Golgouneh, A.; Bamshad, A.; Tarvirdizadeh, B.; Tajdari, F. Design of a new, light and portable mechanism for knee CPM machine with a user-friendly interface. In Proceedings of the Artificial Intelligence and Robotics (IRANOPEN), Qazvin, Iran, 9 April 2016; pp. 103–108.
22. Lee, C.; Oh, S. Robust assistive force control of leg rehabilitation robot. In Proceedings of the IEEE International Conference on Advanced Intelligent Mechatronics (AIM), Munich, Germany, 3–7 July 2017; pp. 634–638.
23. Wang, Y.L.; Wang, K.Y.; Li, X.; Mo, Z.J.; Wang, K.C. Control strategy and experimental research of a cable-driven lower limb rehabilitation robot. *IEEE Access* **2021**, *9*, 79182–79195. [CrossRef]
24. Li, X.; Pan, Y.; Chen, G.; Yu, H. Multi-modal control scheme for rehabilitation robotic exoskeletons. *Int. J. Robot. Res.* **2017**, *36*, 759–777. [CrossRef]
25. Zhou, J.; Li, Z.; Li, X.; Wang, X.; Song, R. Human–Robot Cooperation Control Based on Trajectory Deformation Algorithm for a Lower Limb Rehabilitation Robot. *IEEE ASME Trans. Mechatron.* **2021**, *26*, 3128–3138. [CrossRef]
26. Chen, J.; Huang, Y.; Guo, X.; Zhou, S.; Jia, L. Parameter identification and adaptive compliant control of rehabilitation exoskeleton based on multiple sensors. *Measurement* **2020**, *159*, 107765. [CrossRef]
27. Huo, W.; Moon, H.; Alouane, M.A.; Bonnet, V.; Huang, J.; Amirat, Y.; Vaidyanathan, R.; Mohammed, S. Impedance Modulation Control of a Lower-Limb Exoskeleton to Assist Sit-to-Stand Movements. *IEEE Trans. Robot.* **2021**, *38*, 1230–1249. [CrossRef]
28. Zhang, X.; Yue, Z.; Wang, J. Robotics in lower-limb rehabilitation after stroke. *Behav. Neurol.* **2017**, *2017*, 3731802. [CrossRef] [PubMed]
29. Meng, W.; Liu, Q.; Zhou, Z.; Ai, Q.; Sheng, B.; Xie, S.S. Recent development of mechanisms and control strategies for robot-assisted lower limb rehabilitation. *Mechatronics* **2015**, *31*, 132–145. [CrossRef]
30. Khoshdel, V.; Akbarzadeh, A.; Naghavi, N.; Sharifnezhad, A.; Souzanchi-Kashani, M. sEMG-based impedance control for lower-limb rehabilitation robot. *Intell. Serv. Robot.* **2018**, *11*, 97–108. [CrossRef]
31. Yao, S.; Zhuang, Y.; Li, Z.; Song, R. Adaptive admittance control for an ankle exoskeleton using an EMG-driven musculoskeletal model. *Front. Neurorobotics* **2018**, *12*, 16. [CrossRef] [PubMed]
32. Xie, P.; Qiu, S.; Li, X.; Du, Y.; Wu, X.; Guo, Z. Adaptive trajectory planning of lower limb rehabilitation robot based on emg and human-robot interaction. In Proceedings of the International Conference on Information and Automation (ICIA), Zhejiang, China, 31 July–4 August 2016; pp. 1273–1277.
33. Meng, W.; Zhu, Y.; Zhou, Z.; Chen, K.; Ai, Q. Active interaction control of a rehabilitation robot based on motion recognition and adaptive impedance control. In Proceedings of the International Conference on Fuzzy Systems (FUZZ-IEEE), Beijing, China, 6–11 July 2014; pp. 1436–1441.

34. Lin, C.J.; Chuang, H.C.; Hsu, C.W.; Chen, C.S. Pneumatic artificial muscle actuated robot for lower limb rehabilitation triggered by electromyography signals using discrete wavelet transformation and support vector machines. *Sens. Mater.* **2017**, *29*, 1625–1636.
35. Campagnini, S.; Liuzzi, P.; Mannini, A.; Riener, R.; Carrozza, M.C. Effects of control strategies on gait in robot-assisted post-stroke lower limb rehabilitation: A systematic review. *J. NeuroEng. Rehabil.* **2022**, *19*, 52. [CrossRef]
36. Shi, D.; Zhang, W.; Zhang, W.; Ding, X. A review on lower limb rehabilitation exoskeleton robots. *Chin. J. Mech. Eng.* **2019**, *32*, 1–11. [CrossRef]
37. Wang, L.; Tian, J.; Du, J.; Zheng, S.; Niu, J.; Zhang, Z.; Wu, J. A Hybrid Mechanism-Based Robot for End-Traction Lower Limb Rehabilitation: Design, Analysis and Experimental Evaluation. *Machines* **2022**, *10*, 99. [CrossRef]
38. Types of Body Movements. Available online: https://pressbooks.bccampus.ca/humanbiomechanics/chapter/9-5-types-of-body-movements (accessed on 11 October 2022).
39. Liang, X.; Wang, W.; Hou, Z.G.; Ren, S.; Wang, J.; Shi, W.; Peng, L.; Su, T. Position based impedance control strategy for a lower limb rehabilitation robot. In Proceedings of the 2019 41st Annual International Conference of the IEEE Engineering in Medicine and Biology Society (EMBC), Berlin, Germany, 23–27 July 2019; IEEE: Piscataway, NJ, USA, 2019; pp. 437–441.
40. Pan, L.; Song, A.; Xu, G.; Li, H.; Zeng, H.; Xu, B. Safety supervisory strategy for an upper-limb rehabilitation robot based on impedance control. *Int. J. Adv. Robot. Syst.* **2013**, *10*, 127. [CrossRef]

sensors

MDPI

Article

Human–Robot Cooperative Strength Training Based on Robust Admittance Control Strategy

Musong Lin [1], Hongbo Wang [1,2,3], Congliang Yang [1], Wenjie Liu [1], Jianye Niu [1,4,*] and Luige Vladareanu [5,*]

1 Hebei Provincial Key Laboratory of Parallel Robot and Mechatronic System, Yanshan University, Qinhuangdao 066004, China
2 Academy for Engineering & Technology, Fudan University, Shanghai 200433, China
3 Shanghai Clinical Research Center for Aging and Medicine, Shanghai 200040, China
4 Key Laboratory of Advanced Forging & Stamping Technology and Science of Ministry of Education, Yanshan University, Qinhuangdao 066004, China
5 Robotics and Mechatronics Department, Institute of Solid Mechanics of Romanian Academy, 010141 Bucharest, Romania
* Correspondence: jyniu@ysu.edu.cn (J.N.); luige.vladareanu@vipro.edu.ro (L.V.)

Abstract: A stroke is a common disease that can easily lead to lower limb motor dysfunction in the elderly. Stroke survivors can effectively train muscle strength through leg flexion and extension training. However, available lower limb rehabilitation robots ignore the knee soft tissue protection of the elderly in training. This paper proposes a human–robot cooperative lower limb active strength training based on a robust admittance control strategy. The stiffness change law of the admittance model is designed based on the biomechanics of knee joints, and it can guide the user to make force correctly and reduce the stress on the joint soft tissue. The controller will adjust the model stiffness in real-time according to the knee joint angle and then indirectly control the exertion force of users. This control strategy not only can avoid excessive compressive force on the joint soft tissue but also can enhance the stimulation of quadriceps femoris muscles. Moreover, a dual input robust control is proposed to improve the tracking performance under the disturbance caused by model uncertainty, interaction force and external noise. Experiments about the controller performance and the training feasibility were conducted with eight stroke survivors. Results show that the designed controller can effectively influence the interaction force; it can reduce the possibility of joint soft tissue injury. The robot also has a good tracking performance under disturbances. This control strategy also can enhance the stimulation of quadriceps femoris muscles, which is proved by measuring the muscle electrical signal and interaction force. Human–robot cooperative strength training is a feasible method for training lower limb muscles with the knee soft tissue protection mechanism.

Keywords: rehabilitation robot; human–robot interaction; admittance control; robust control; active strength training

Citation: Lin, M.; Wang, H.; Yang, C.; Liu, W.; Niu, J.; Vladareanu, L. Human–Robot Cooperative Strength Training Based on Robust Admittance Control Strategy. *Sensors* **2022**, *22*, 7746. https://doi.org/10.3390/s22207746

Academic Editor: Carlo Alberto Avizzano

Received: 25 August 2022
Accepted: 8 October 2022
Published: 12 October 2022

1. Introduction

The independent walking ability of the elderly is the basic premise to ensure the quality of life [1]. However, limb weakness increases with age and the impact of cardiovascular disease often leads to physical disability in the elderly [2]. According to statistics, there are more than millions new incident stroke cases worldly in every year, and there is a high probability of losing walk ability among the survivors [3,4]. Facing such a large number of disabled people, more rehabilitation physicians and rehabilitation training equipment are needed to help them regain lower limb strength, stand up again and return to society [5,6]. As a new type of intelligent medical robot, rehabilitation robot can effectively improve limb disabilities caused by aging or sequela and their therapeutic effect has been proved by many clinical experiments [7–9].

Muscle weakness is well established as the primary impairment that affects walking after stroke, and strength training can effectively promote the recovery of muscle strength [10,11]. The effectiveness of strength training has also been proven by some resistance training [12,13]. The quadriceps femoris is the biggest human skeletal muscle at the front of the thigh, and it plays a vital role in extending the knee, flexing the hip and maintaining an upright position. Leg flexion and extension is a strength training exercise that can effectively enhance the quadriceps, so the research of related equipment has also attracted much attention. The American Harley Company proposed a rehabilitation device X-10, which uses variable pressure technology to reduce the pain in the patient's treatment and improve the patient's joint mobility [14]; Another similar device is a sitting rehabilitation device developed by King Wangut University of Technology, which is suitable for home training but only has one free rotation and a small range of motion [15]. They all belong to the same type of rehabilitation equipment using a moving platform. They send the terminal force and joint torque into the control feedback loop to ensure the safety of training respectively, but the training effect on the hip joint is not obvious. The University of Tsukuba and a partner company developed an exoskeleton robot called HAL, which can directly provide active or passive lower limb flexion and extension training to bedridden patients. The range of motion and the walking ability of the patients is improved after training, but the strength of the quadriceps femoris does not change significantly [16,17]. Italy and Poland developed a new 3-DOF bionic exoskeleton, which can be used for rehabilitation after joint surgery, ligament, and cartilage injuries [18].

In robot-assist active training fields, the robot needs to be able to extract the patient's motion intention according to the interaction information and assist the patient to complete the training action. The effectiveness of impedance control and force-position hybrid control have been verified on the rehabilitation machine LOKOMAT, and these methods have improved the interactivity of human–machine cooperative training [19]. Wu et al. developed an admittance control strategy induces the active participation of patients [20]; an optimization method based on admittance control was proposed to compensate the weight and friction of the exoskeleton [21]. A lower rehabilitation robot called LOPES II allows different active training intensities through admittance control [22]. Impedance controllers are also applied in robot-assist active training for joint or lower limb rehabilitation [23,24]. Some researchers use sEMG (surface electromyography) or EEG (electroencephalography) signals for guiding rehabilitation robots to complete active training [25–27]. Courtney et al developed an algorithm for adjusting functional electrical stimulation to help patients taking active training [28].

Including the research mentioned above and other we can find, none have mentioned the protection of the knee soft tissue. However, the physiological functions of the elderly gradually degenerate, and soft tissues such as the meniscus, cartilage and ligaments are relatively fragile [29,30]. For the main user groups of rehabilitation therapy, it is necessary to avoid damage to their joint soft tissues during rehabilitation strength training. The National Strength and Conditioning Association has studied knee joint biomechanics during the human squat and pointed out the conclusion. That is, the tibiofemoral compressive force will peak at 130 degrees of knee flexion, and the menisci and articular cartilage bear significant amounts of stress [31]. Soft tissue such as ligaments are at great risk of injury at this moment [32]. Patellofemoral compressive force, tibiofemoral compressive force and tibiofemoral shear force will gradually decrease with knee extension, while quadriceps muscle activity will peak at approximately 80 to 90 degrees of knee flexion and remain relatively stable thereafter [33,34]. In the human–machine cooperative leg flexion and extension training, it is necessary to timely control the interaction force depending on the knee joint angle in order to reduce the possibility of joint soft tissue injury.

In this paper, a human–machine cooperative leg flexion and extension training based on a robust admittance control strategy is proposed, which fully considers the protection of knee soft tissue based on biomechanics. The performance device is the sitting and lying lower limb rehabilitation robot (LLR-II) developed by our team. In this training, LLR-II responds according to the interaction force and assists the patient performs a full lower limb flexion and extension similar to a leg press. Compared with single knee flexion and extension training, this training can maintain and improve the mobility of each joint of the lower limbs, and can effectively exercise the muscles of the hips, knees and ankles. Firstly, according to the biomechanics of the knee joint, the change law of the stiffness of the main admittance model is designed, and the flexibility of the training is increased by the subsidiary admittance control. The controller will adjust the model stiffness according to the joint angle during the training, and it could avoid excessive compressive force on the soft tissue and increase the stimulation of the quadriceps. Then, the joint tracking performance is improved by two-input robust motion control by compensating the motion control disturbances caused by model uncertainty, interactive forces, and external noise. Finally, the testing experiment of this human–machine cooperative leg flexion and extension training is conducted.

2. LLR-II Rehabilitation Robot

The LLR-II is an intelligent robotic system that can intervene early and provide a variety of rehabilitation training and more details can be found in our published papers [35,36]. LLR-II can be divided into four modules which include two symmetrical training modules, a seat module and an electric control module, as shown in Figure 1. The LLR-II is assembled by connecting the underframe of each module and each module can be moved independently for installation and transportation. The right training module is equipped with a touch display and an emergency stop button and the width between the two training modules can be adjusted according to the user's body shape. The height of the seat module is adjustable and it can help medical staff transfer patients. In addition, in order to adapt to different people, the length of the upper and lower mechanical legs can be adjusted through the internal electric linear actuator.

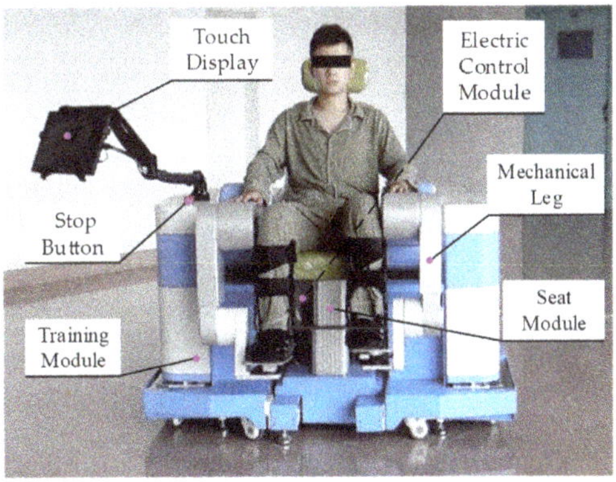

Figure 1. Structure of LLR-II.

2.1. *Structural Design of LLR-II*

The mechanical leg of LLR-II is a three joint series mechanical mechanism, and the three joints correspond to the hip, knee and ankle joints of the human body, respectively. Its joint drive train is composed of flange structures, as shown in Figure 2. The high torque motors of the hip and knee joints adjust the fixed positions through timing belts, which are located at the bottom of the training module and the rear end of the mechanical leg respectively. Hip and knee joint transmission structures are similar, and both of them are consist of a synchronous pulley, a reducer and a torque sensor (Figure 2a). The ankle joint equips with a frameless motor, and the integration of the ankle joint is effectively improved by directly connecting the motor and the reducer (Figure 2b).

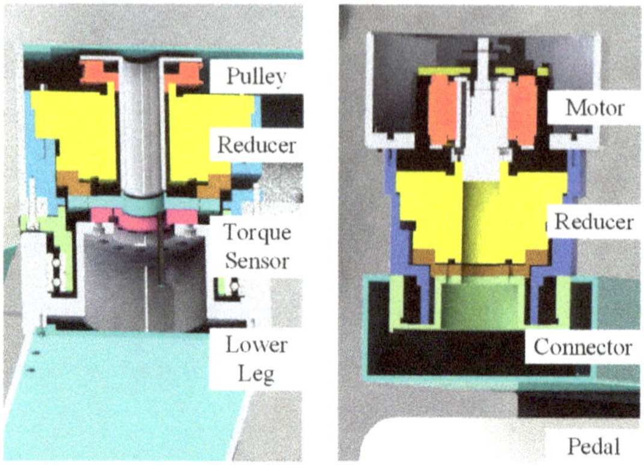

(a) (b)

Figure 2. Section view of joint drivetrain: (**a**) knee joint and (**b**) ankle joint.

The electric control system of LLR-II can be divided into four parts as follows: central control section, drive control section, sensor feedback section and human–robot interaction section (Figure 3). The central control section mainly includes the host computer and related data acquisition equipment, which is responsible for the advanced operations and coordinates other parts. The drive control section is mainly composed of the joint motor, the electric linear actuator and the related communication control equipment. The sensor feedback section mainly includes the torque sensor, the angle sensor of the joint, the six-dimensional force sensor and the potentiometer. The interaction operation is mainly realized through a touch display screen. In addition, the LLR-II also has multimedia functions such as virtual reality and voice control.

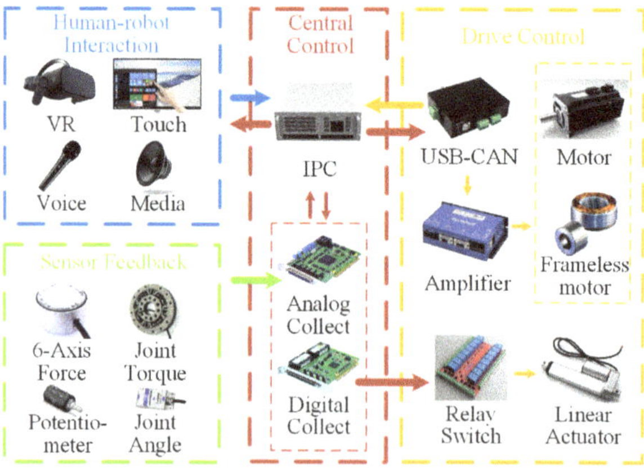

Figure 3. Electric control system. The arrow represents the direction of information transmission.

2.2. *Mechanical Leg Model Analysis*

The mechanical leg of LLR-II is a series manipulator working in the sagittal plane, and its physical model can be simplified as a 3R structure, as shown in Figure 4.

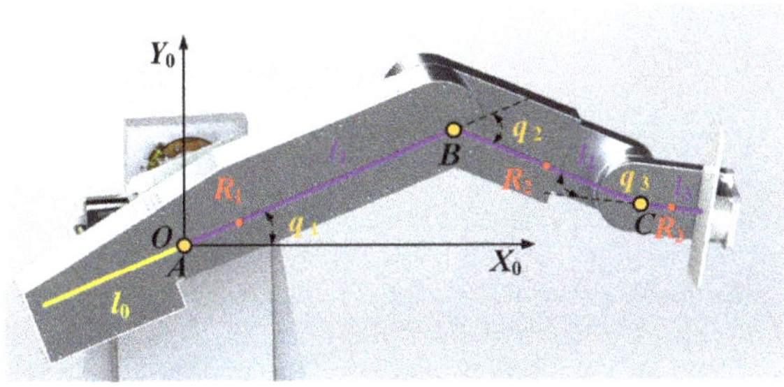

Figure 4. Mechanism model of the mechanical leg.

Establish a global coordinate system $\{O\text{-}X_0Y_0Z_0\}$ at the hip joint rotation center point A. B and C represent the rotation centers of the knee and ankle joints respectively. q_1, q_2 and q_3 are the joint variables of the three rotating joints, l_1, l_2 and l_3 respectively represent the distance between the rotating joints, l_0 represents the distance between the counterweight mess center and the hip rotating joint; R_1, R_2 and R_3 represent the distance between the link mass center and the rotation center, respectively. The kinematic model of LLR-II is the same as the standard 3R mechanism, and its kinematics forward and inverse solutions can be calculated by the D-H method and geometric method. The results are shown in Equations (1) and (2) below:

$$T = \begin{bmatrix} n_x & o_x & a_x & p_x \\ n_y & o_y & a_y & p_y \\ n_z & o_z & a_z & p_z \\ 0 & 0 & 0 & 1 \end{bmatrix} = \begin{bmatrix} \cos q_{123} & -\sin q_{123} & 0 & l_3\cos q_{123} + l_2\cos q_{12} + l_1\cos q_1 \\ \sin q_{123} & \cos q_{123} & 0 & l_3\sin q_{123} + l_2\sin q_{12} + l_1\sin q_1 \\ 0 & 0 & 1 & 0 \\ 0 & 0 & 0 & 1 \end{bmatrix}, \tag{1}$$

$$\begin{array}{c} q_1 = \text{Atan2}(K,\ \pm\sqrt{1-K^2}) - \text{Atan}\,2(A,\ B) \\ q_2 = \text{Atan2}(B - l_1\sin q_1,\ A - l_1\cos q_1) - q_1 \\ q_3 = \text{Atan2}(n_y,\ n_x) - q_1 - q_2 \end{array}, \tag{2}$$

where

$$\begin{array}{c} A = p_x - l_3 n_x \\ B = p_y - l_3 n_y \\ K = \frac{A^2+B^2+l_1^2-l_2^2}{2l_1\sqrt{A^2+B^2}} \\ q_{1\ldots i} = q_1 + \ldots + q_i \end{array}.$$

The dynamic equation of the mechanism can be obtained through the Lagrangian equation, and the controlled system model of the robot can be obtained as follows:

$$\boldsymbol{M}(\boldsymbol{q})\ddot{\boldsymbol{q}} + \boldsymbol{C}(\boldsymbol{q},\dot{\boldsymbol{q}})\dot{\boldsymbol{q}} + \boldsymbol{g}(\boldsymbol{q}) + \boldsymbol{J}^T(\boldsymbol{q})\boldsymbol{F} = \boldsymbol{u}, \tag{3}$$

where $\boldsymbol{M}(\boldsymbol{q})$ is a diagonal matrix consisting of the inertia matrix and drive train inertia. $\boldsymbol{C}(\boldsymbol{q},\dot{\boldsymbol{q}})$ represents the matrix of Coriolis and centrifugal forces and $\boldsymbol{g}(\boldsymbol{q})$ represents the gravitational vector. $\ddot{\boldsymbol{q}}$, $\dot{\boldsymbol{q}}$ and $\boldsymbol{q}$ are the joint acceleration, velocity and position vectors. $\boldsymbol{J}(\boldsymbol{q})$ is the Jacobian matrix of the mechanism and $\boldsymbol{F}$ represents the human–robot interaction force. $\boldsymbol{u}$ is the control input vector.

Unlike the standard 3R structure, this mechanism has a counterweight used for lightening the motor load, as the yellow line shown in Figure 4. The leg length adjustment function is adjusting the position of the rotation center point A and it means that the relative position of the link mass center point R_1 in the global coordinate system will change under the influence of the counterweight and the leg length change. The Lagrangian quantity change caused by the mass center position change will exacerbate the system uncertainty in the dynamic control. Therefore, it is necessary to calculate the mass center position of the link l_1, as shown in Equation (4) below:

$$R_1 = \frac{m(l_1 - l_0) - 2m_0 l_0}{2m + 2m_0}, \tag{4}$$

where m_0 is the mass of the counterweight and m is the mass of the first link (without counterweight). In Lagrangian dynamics, the change of the mass center position will directly change the translational kinetic energy and gravitational potential energy of the first link, and the moment of inertia in the angular kinetic energy term also needs to be recalculated according to Equation (4) after length adjustment.

3. Robust Admittance Control Strategy

The control strategy of the rehabilitation robot is different from the general industrial robot; it needs to fully consider human–robot interactions to ensure the safety of patients. Rehabilitation robots should be able to respond to different levels of interaction and maximize the movement potential of patients. Biomechanical research has shown that pushing force should be avoided when the knee is flexed at a wide angle, and there is also an efficient training range for the quadriceps. In addition, due to the large interactive force of the active training, it has high requirements for the robustness of the control algorithm. Therefore, a robust admittance control strategy for lower limb strength training is proposed, which combines robust control and admittance control. The strategy block diagram is shown in Figure 5. This strategy indirectly controls the user's force through variable stiffness admittance control, and it can avoid excessive compressive force on the joint soft tissue and increase muscle group stimulation. Dual input robust control adds an error compensation term that can be used for compensating force interference, and it improves the tracking performance of the machine joints.

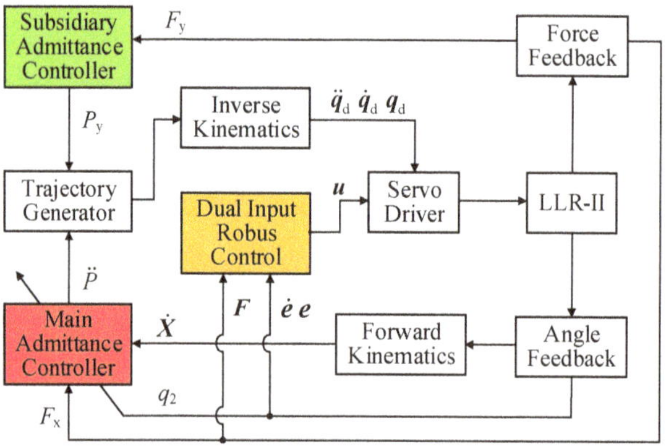

Figure 5. Admittance robust control block diagram.

3.1. Variable Stiffness Admittance Control

Admittance control is a control strategy that describes the relationship between force and motion through a spring damping model, and both admittance control and impedance control use the same model. The input and output of admittance control are force and position, respectively. The end force of the series robot can be easily obtained by force sensors, so this method is often used in human–robot interactions. The admittance control strategy proposed in this paper includes two control laws, and its function is shown in Figure 6. The effect of the main control law is changing the model stiffness according to the knee joint angle; it can protect the knee joint and increase the stimulation of the quadriceps muscle (the stiffness change is plotted on a trajectory with color mapping in Figure 6, the bright part indicates high stiffness). The subsidiary control law allows a small deviation of the training trajectory, which increases the flexibility of the training action. When the user's vertical force will lead to a large deviation of the trajectory, the subsidiary control law will ensure the trajectory by resisting the user's force (as arrows shown in Figure 6).

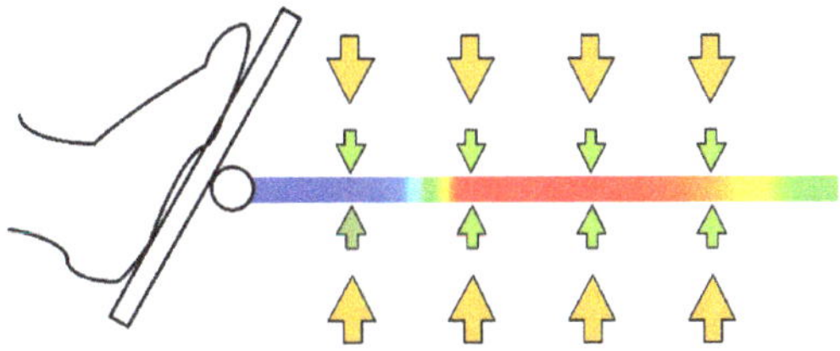

Figure 6. Working schematic diagram of admittance controller.

The input of the subsidiary admittance control is the interaction force $F_y(s)$ in the vertical direction, and the output is the end position $P_y(s)$ in the vertical direction. Its transfer function is shown in Equation (5):

$$G(s) = \frac{P_y(s)}{F_y(s)} = \frac{1}{M_{dy}s^2 + B_{dy}s + K_{dy}}, \tag{5}$$

where M_{dy}, B_{dy} and K_{dy} represent inertia, damping and stiffness. The system will compare the expected position with the set offset threshold. If output exceeds the set allowable offset, the excess part will be limited. Two outputs of the subsidiary control and main control will be sent to the trajectory generator, and the generator will obtain the actual end position based on vector calculation before inverse kinematics. With smaller model parameters, the compliant and constrained training trajectory can be achieved.

The model of main admittance control is a second-order model with varying stiffness along the motion trajectory and the output $\ddot{P}$ is the desired end acceleration. When receiving an interaction force exceeding the threshold, the end of the machine will accelerate. When the interaction force is deficient, the end of the machine will decelerate to stop according to the admittance parameters. Its control law is designed as follows:

$$M_{dx}\ddot{P} + B_{dx}\|\dot{\boldsymbol{X}}\|_2 + \boldsymbol{K}_{var}(q_2)D = F_x, \tag{6}$$

where F_x is the extracted effective interaction force; D is a constant with the same dimension as the end position; $\dot{\boldsymbol{X}}$ represents the end velocity vector of the robot. M_{dx} and B_{dx} are the inertia and damping of the model and the model stiffness $\boldsymbol{K}_{var}$ is a piecewise function of the knee joint angle, designed as follows:

$$\boldsymbol{K}_{var} = \begin{cases} k_1 + \frac{(k_2-k_1)[L(q_2)-L_0]^2}{[L_1-L_0]^2} & -120^\circ \le q_2 < -100^\circ \\ \frac{k_2+k_3}{2} - \frac{k_3-k_2}{2}\cos(\pi\frac{L(q_2)-L_1}{L_2-L_1}) & -100^\circ \le q_2 < -90^\circ \\ k_3 - k_4 \exp\left[k_5\frac{L(q_2)-L}{L-L_2}\right] & -90^\circ \le q_2 \le 0^\circ \end{cases}.$$

$L(q_2)$ is a function of the knee joint angle and leg length; it represents the end position of the robot. L_0, L_1 and L_2 represent the end position scalars of the robot when the knee joint is at $-120°$, $-100°$ and $-90°$; L represents the total length of the training trajectory. The constant coefficients k_i (i = 1, 2 ...) are all parameters of this function and the amplitude of stiffness can be adjusted by changing these parameters.

In this training process, the motion range of the knee joint is $-120°$ to $0°$, which covers 80% normal motion range of the human body. The purpose of this design is to stretch the muscles of the knee joint and maintain joint mobility. In addition, the controller will adjust the model stiffness in real-time according to the knee joint, and this can protect the knee soft tissue and increase the stimulation effect on the quadriceps. At the beginning of the training (120° of knee flexion), the model stiffness is set at a low level. This is because, in this angle range, it will put greater stress on the knee soft tissue when the leg extends with resistance forces. Training in this situation for a long time might cause damage to the knee joint. When the knee joint is flexed to 100°, the model stiffness begins to rise rapidly. When the knee joint is flexed to 90°, the stiffness reaches the highest level, which marks the training entering the strong stimulation phase. At this stage, the force of the lower limbs mainly depends on the contraction of the quadriceps femoris, and the training effect can be improved by correctly exerting force in this stage. In the final stage, the stiffness decreases slowly with a negative exponential trend. Considering the lower limb is not easy to exert force when it is close to full extension, this design can extend the stimulation movement and ensure that the user can complete the leg extension.

3.2. Dual Input Robust Control

Robot dynamics control needs to solve the tracking error problem caused by external disturbance or model inaccuracy. For most of the series robots, the model inaccuracy mainly comes from the uncertainty of the dynamic parameters (the deviation between the theoretical reference model and the actual model). This uncertainty is generally changeless and can be reduced by optimizing parameters through classical algorithms. The model structure of the LLR-II is rather special as the first link mass center position becomes a variable under the influence of the counterweight structure and the length adjustment. Therefore, the parameters of the dynamic model will change greatly after the mechanical leg length adjustment because the mass center change will lead to the change of Lagrangian variables. That is to say, the parameter uncertainty of the LLR-II model is also a variable. Although the reference model will be updated according to Equation (4), there is still a deviation from the actual model. Adding to the influence of the large fluctuation interaction force, common classical algorithms cannot adapt to such variable parameter systems.

This paper proposes a dual input robust control considering the s interactive force effect, and it is used for reducing the influence of model uncertainty, noise interference and the impact of interactive forces on machine tracking performance. The design control law is as follows:

$$u = \hat{M}(q)a + \hat{C}(q,\dot{q})v + \hat{g}(q) + \hat{J}^T(q)\hat{F} - Kr, \tag{7}$$

where $\hat{M}$, $\hat{C}$, $\hat{g}$ and $\hat{J}$ are estimated values defined by the corresponding symbols (theoretical reference value); K and Λ are two constant positive gain matrices; v, a and r are defined as follows:

$$\begin{cases} v = \dot{q}_{\mathrm{d}} - \Lambda e \\ a = \dot{v} = \ddot{q}_{\mathrm{d}} - \Lambda \dot{e} \\ r = \dot{q} - v = \dot{e} + \Lambda e \end{cases}.$$

Another simplified form of the control input can be obtained by linearizing the parameters of Equation (4):

$$u = Y(q,\dot{q},a,v)\hat{\theta} + Z(q)\hat{\pi} - Kr, \tag{8}$$

where the functions Y and Z are the regressors of the first three terms and the fourth terms on the left side of Equation (4). $\hat{\theta}$ and $\hat{\pi}$ are the parameter vectors of the corresponding estimated model (two control inputs). Substituting Equation (8) into Equation (4) and linearizing the parameters, the designed closed-loop system equation can be obtained:

$$M(q)\dot{r} + C(q,\dot{q})r + Kr = Y(\hat{\theta} - \theta) + Z(\hat{\pi} - \pi). \tag{9}$$

As mentioned above, considering the uncertainty of model parameters, the following design is made:

$$\hat{\theta} = \theta_0 + \delta\theta;\ \hat{\pi} = \pi_0 + \delta\pi, \tag{10}$$

where θ_0 and π_0 are the constant vectors of the corresponding parameter vectors (the theoretical calculation values); $\delta\theta$ and $\delta\pi$ are two design control terms used for compensating the disturbance caused by uncertainty. For the above uncertainty (the difference between the actual value and the calculated value), it can be expressed as:

$$\|\widetilde{\theta}\| = \|\theta - \theta_0\| \leq \rho; \ \|\widetilde{\pi}\| = \|\pi - \pi_0\| \leq \sigma, \tag{11}$$

where $\widetilde{\theta}$ represents the parameter uncertainty of the dynamic model and $\widetilde{\pi}$ represents the uncertainty of the link length and the interaction force. Selecting the upper bound constants σ and ρ. The designs of $\delta\boldsymbol{\theta}$ and $\delta\boldsymbol{\pi}$ are as follows:

$$\delta\theta = \begin{cases} -\rho\frac{Y^T r}{\|Y^T r\|} & \|Y^T r\| > \varepsilon \\ -\rho\frac{Y^T r}{\varepsilon} & \|Y^T r\| \leq \varepsilon \end{cases}, \tag{12}$$

$$\delta\pi = \begin{cases} -\sigma\frac{Z^T r}{\|Z^T r\|} & \|Z^T r\| > \eta \\ -\sigma\frac{Z^T r}{\eta} & \|Z^T r\| \leq \eta \end{cases}, \tag{13}$$

where ε and η are two positive constants used to ensure the continuity of the design term.

In order to analyze the stability of the designed closed-loop system by the Lyapunov second method, the following Lyapunov function is selected:

$$V = \frac{1}{2}r^T M(q)r + e^T \Lambda K e. \tag{14}$$

Taking the derivative of Equation (14) along the system (9):

$$\dot{V} = -\dot{e}^T K\dot{e} - e^T\Lambda^T K\Lambda e + r^T Y(\widetilde{\theta} + \delta\theta) + r^T Z(\widetilde{\pi} + \delta\pi). \tag{15}$$

According to the Lyapunov second method, if a Lyapunov function derivative along the system direction is strictly negative definite, it can be determined that the system is asymptotically stable. No matter what state the system starts from, the error will eventually converge to zero. However, in order to ensure Equation (15) is negative definite, additional constraints need to be found. First, rewrite Equation (15) into the following form:

$$\dot{V} = -A^T Q A + r^T Y(\widetilde{\theta} + \delta\theta) + r^T Z(\widetilde{\pi} + \delta\pi), \tag{16}$$

where $A^T = [e^T, \dot{e}^T]$, $Q = \mathrm{diag}[\Lambda^T K\Lambda,\ K]$. Although the first term of Equation (16) can be determined to be semi-negative definite, there are four possible combinations of the last two terms. Since the structures of these two items are similar, the last item is used as an example for analysis. First, when $\|Z^T r\| > \eta$, according to the Cauchy-Schwartz inequality we can obtain:

$$(Z^T r)^T(\widetilde{\pi} + \delta\pi) = (Z^T r)^T(\widetilde{\pi} - \sigma\frac{Z^T r}{\|Z^T r\|}) \leq \|Z^T r\|(\|\widetilde{\pi}\| - \sigma) < 0. \tag{17}$$

When $\|Z^T r\| \leq \eta$, we can be obtained:

$$(Z^T r)^T(\widetilde{\pi} + \delta\pi) \leq (Z^T r)^T(\sigma\frac{Z^T r}{\|Z^T r\|} - \sigma\frac{Z^T r}{\eta}) = -\frac{\sigma}{\eta}\|Z^T r\|^2 + \sigma\|Z^T r\|. \tag{18}$$

When the designed item is in the state of Equation (17), the judgment condition is satisfied. When the design item is in the state of Equation (18), Equation (18) can be regarded as a quadratic function about $\|Z^T r\|$. Its maximum value $\sigma\eta/2$ at $\|Z^T r\| = \eta/2$ can be obtained, and then the conditions for guaranteeing the Equation (15) is negative definite can be obtained.

According to the designed terms $\delta\boldsymbol{\theta}$ and $\delta\boldsymbol{\pi}$, two maximum values $\sigma\eta/2$ and $\rho\varepsilon/2$ can be obtained respectively. It is not difficult to find that if $A^T Q A$ is always greater than the sum of these two maximum values, Equation (16) is less than zero forever in all cases (four combinations). In other words, when Equation (19) is satisfied:

$$A^T Q A > (\sigma\eta + \rho\varepsilon)/2. \tag{19}$$

Using the matrix eigenvalue relation $A^T Q A \geq \lambda_{\min}\|A\|^2$ (where $\lambda_{\min}$ is the minimum eigenvalue of the matrix Q), the constraints that guarantee Equation (15) is negative definite could be obtained:

$$\|A\| > [(\sigma\eta + \rho\varepsilon)/2\lambda_{\min}]^{1/2}. \tag{20}$$

When Equation (20) is satisfied, $\dot{V}$ can be guaranteed to be less than zero. Therefore, according to Lyapunov second method, the tracking error of system (9) under the designed control law is uniformly ultimately bounded. That is to say, selecting appropriate coefficients in Equations (12) and (13) can ensure that the error continuously approaches a sufficiently small upper error bound, and a good tracking performance could be obtained.

4. Experiment

In order to verify the function, feasibility and effectiveness of the proposed lower limb flexion and extension strength training, eight stroke survivors were selected to participate in the test experiment using LLR-II. Every subject confirmed the protocol of the experiment, and research was carried out following the principles of the Declaration of Helsinki. All experiments were conducted under the premise of ensuring the subject's safety, and sufficient time was given to familiarize the subjects with LLR-II before the formal experiment. The training trajectory is a straight line passing through the hip joint and parallel to the ground, and its starting point and length are determined according to the user's leg length and knee joint rotation range. The knee joint angle range of all training trajectories in experiments was consistent. Due to the height difference of subjects, the horizontal position coordinates of the training trajectory are also different. For normalized analysis, the horizontal position in this part is represented by percentage of total track length.

To test the controller performance on guiding users to generate the force, the training interaction force was recorded through the six-dimensional force sensor. In the experiment, each subject was required to maintain higher training speed in three groups of training. Figure 7 shows the changes in knee joint angle q_2, model stiffness $\boldsymbol{K}_{\text{var}}$ and effective interaction force F_{x} during training. In the experiment, the adjustment constant coefficients k_{i} (i = 1, 2 . . .) of $\boldsymbol{K}_{\text{var}}$ are set to 0.3, 0.8, 2.5, 1.5, 6. The average of the end interaction force was calculated, and error bars were plotted based on its standard deviation, as the red line and the orange area shown in the figure. With the stiffness change based on the knee joint angle, the interaction force also displayed a similar trend. Although the strength levels of different subjects were inconsistent, the data results show that the controller has achieved the function of guiding the user to make forces.

To analyze the tracking performance of the dual input robust controller, joint angle data in training were recorded as shown in Figure 8. Observing average error curves, it can be found that the absolute values of each joint steady-state error are close to about 0.5°. The result shows that the controller has good tracking ability, and it is in line with the final boundedness proved before. Moreover, it can be found that the two joint errors (orange and purple lines) and error bars (yellow and green areas) appear to be fluctuations in the half of the trajectory. The maximum standard deviation of the hip joint is 0.29°, while the knee joint is 0.16°. This is due to the rapid force increase when the subject tries to adapt to the model stiffness change. The interaction force influence is different to two joints, but the controller can make adjustments to adapt to different sudden interference. It shows that the designed robust controller has strong robustness.

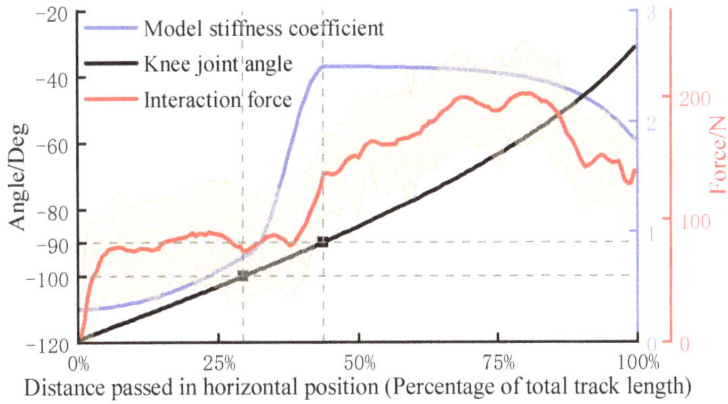

Figure 7. Performance testing of admittance control.

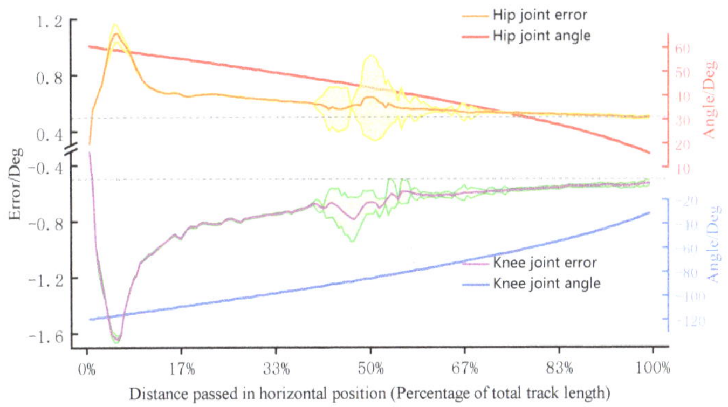

Figure 8. Joint tracking performance.

The EMG signal is a physiological indicator that can directly reflect neuromuscular activity [37–39]. This experiment verifies the effectiveness of this strength training by collecting the quadriceps EMG signal during training. The quadriceps femoris is divided into rectus femoris, vastus medialis, vastus lateralis and vastus intermedius. Since the vastus intermedius is located in the deep part of the muscle group, only the EMG signals of the other three muscles were collected in this experiment. EMG device information and electrode patch positions are shown in Figure 9. The positions of the electrode patches are selected under the doctor's guidance.

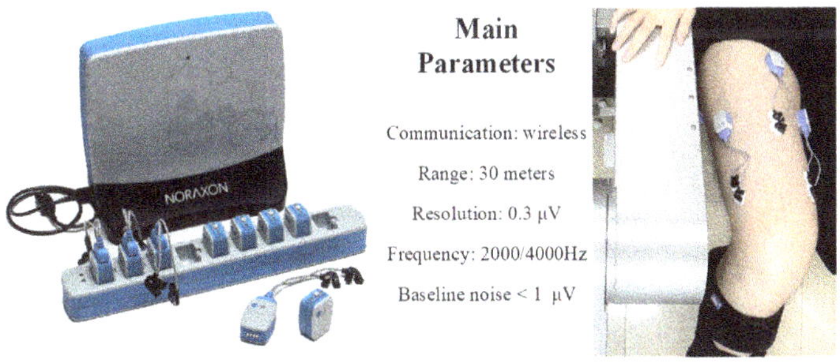

Figure 9. Parameters of EMG device and electrode patch positions.

Figure 10 shows the changes in the EMG signals and terminal interaction force of each muscle during a 10-min training. In order to extract the features of EMG signals, the original data was processed by high and low-pass filtering, absolute value taking and smoothing, respectively. The interaction force collected by the force sensor was also plotted in the figure. It can be found that all the data in the training action area are significantly higher.

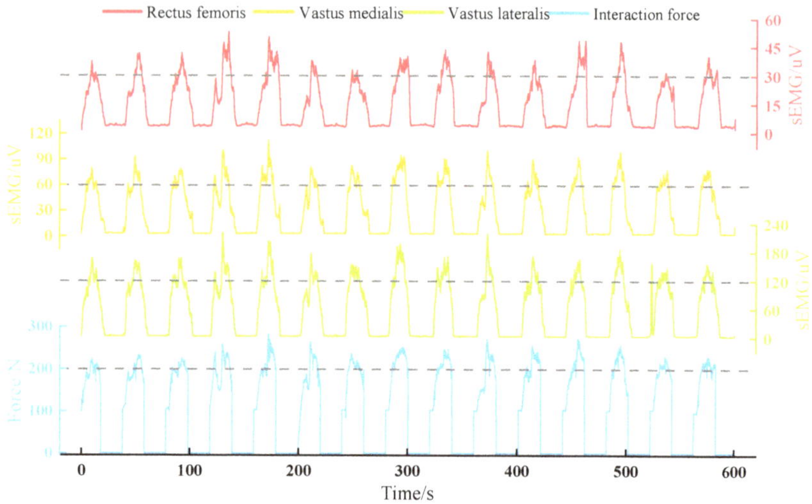

Figure 10. Changes of EMG and interaction force during the training (Dashed line for value reference).

5. Discussion

The model stiffness of the admittance controller can be adjusted in real-time according to the knee joint angle during training, thereby avoiding excessive compressive force on the knee joint soft tissue and enhancing the muscle stimulation. Through the result of the controller performance experiment, it can be found that the model stiffness $\boldsymbol{K}_{\mathrm{var}}$ changes strictly depending on the knee joint angle according to the designed function during training, as the blue line shown in Figure 7. Under the effect of stiffness adjustment, the subject only needs about 90 N to maintain the target training speed when the knee joint flexes more than 90°. This shows that this controller successfully guides users to avoid making forces in the posture that soft tissue is the main bearing object. Meanwhile, the quadriceps femoris enter the most active area when the knee extends to about 90°, and all subjects reported that the training speed at this stage was significantly slowed down. This is due to the change in stiffness, which led to the reduction of the model output acceleration. In order to maintain the training speed, the average interaction force of subjects can reach around 200 N. The results above show that designing a variable stiffness admittance model can indirectly control the terminal interaction force, and it can reduce the possibility of joint soft tissue injury and enhance exertion force in the effective training range. Moreover, the designed robust admittance control can ensure joint tracking performance even under the strong influence of interaction force, and it makes the robot meet the task requirements of this active strength training. In experiments, the peak value of the terminal interaction force was basically above 200 N. The EMG peak value of the vastus lateralis muscle was around 150 uV; the peak value of the vastus medialis muscle was around 75 uV; the peak value of the rectus femoris muscle is around 45 uV. The signal performance of these muscles is consistent with the results of related lower body training studies [33], and obvious signal increase means that the quadriceps femoris is in an active state. These prove that the target muscle group has received effective stimulations under this active strength training method.

There are some limitations in this study and they need to be further studied. Firstly, we design a robust admittance controller strategy to guide users to generate the force correctly during training, and it can be regarded as a method of avoiding soft tissue bearing too much stress under the biomechanics theory support. However, we are unable to provide accurate data on the reduction of soft tissue stress or the actual contribution of this method so far. We planned to conduct a controlled experiment, but it may put control group subjects at risk of injury. We believe that we still need to find a non-invasive method for measuring joint stress to provide strong proof for our work. On the other hand, we selected eight stroke survivors for testing under the recommendation of doctors, and we obtained the result that this training provides effective stimulation to the target muscle group through the sEMG information. Obviously, the sample data are not enough to conclude stronger results, and we ignored to study of the intervention of this training to different types of stroke survivors. Although we believe that the training efficiency can be increased (compared to other same type training) by guiding users to generate forces intensively in an efficient range, there is still a lack of clinical trial data that can quantify the rehabilitation effect of this strength training. We have to recognize that the work shown in the paper is still preliminary research, and more testing experiments need to be carried out later.

We think the rehabilitation robot research should not only consider the training effect but ignore the potential hidden dangers, especially for the elderly group of stroke survivors. In the robot-assist rehabilitation field, few researchers have focused on knee joint protection. This research presents a solution as an attempt to this research gap, but its clinical effect needs a long-term follow-up observation. However, this research still proposes a new point to robot-assisted training: potential negative factors should be considered in order to provide better rehabilitation medical devices for the elderly.

6. Conclusions

In order to avoid an excessive compressive force on the joint soft tissues and increase the stimulation to the target muscle during the leg flexion and extension training, this paper proposes a human–robot cooperative lower limb active strength training based on a robust admittance control strategy. The robust admittance control strategy mainly includes variable stiffness admittance control and dual input robust control. The variation law of admittance model stiffness is designed according to the knee joint biomechanics. The main controller can adjust the stiffness of the model in real-time according to the angle of the knee joint and indirectly control the exertion force of users; the subsidiary admittance control can increase the training flexibility and compliance. Dual input robust control can improve joint tracking performance under the influence of the disturbance caused by the model uncertainty, interactive forces, and external noise. The experiment results show that the designed controller can effectively reduce the possibility of joint soft tissue injury and enhance the stimulation of the quadriceps, and this active training method is effective for exercising the quadriceps. In order to evaluate the efficacy of this strategy, it will be applied to more clinical experiments in future works.

Author Contributions: Conceptualization, H.W., J.N. and L.V.; methodology, M.L.; software, C.Y.; formal analysis, W.L.; writing—original draft preparation, M.L.; writing—review and editing, H.W. and J.N. All authors have read and agreed to the published version of the manuscript.

Funding: This work was funded by the National Key Research and Development Program of China (2019YFB1312500), the National Natural Science Foundation of China (U1913216), and the Science and Technology (S&T) Program of Hebei under Grant, China (E2020103001, 216Z1803G).

Institutional Review Board Statement: The study was conducted according to the guidelines of the Declaration of Helsinki, and approved by Ethics Committee of China Rehabilitation Research Center (protocol code 2020-006-1; date of approval 25 February 2020).

Informed Consent Statement: Informed consent was obtained from all subjects involved in the study.

Data Availability Statement: Not applicable.

Acknowledgments: This research is partially supported by Shanghai Clinical Research Center for Aging and Medicine (19MC1910500).

Conflicts of Interest: The authors declare no conflict of interest.

References

1. Feng, Y.; Wang, H.; Du, Y.; Chen, F.; Yan, H.; Yu, H. Trajectory planning of a novel lower limb rehabilitation robot for stroke patient passive training. *Adv. Mech. Eng.* **2017**, *9*, 1687814017737666. [CrossRef]
2. Feng, Y.; Wang, H.; Lu, T.; Vladareanuv, V.; Li, Q.; Zhao, C. Teaching training method of a lower limb rehabilitation robot. *Int. J. Adv. Rob. Syst.* **2017**, *13*, 57. [CrossRef]
3. Johnson, C.O.; Nguyen, M.; Roth, G.A.; Nichols, E.; Alam, T.; Abate, D.; Abd-Allah, F.; Abdelalim, A.; Abraha, H.N.; Abu-Rmeileh, N.M.; et al. Global, regional, and national burden of stroke, 1990–2016: A systematic analysis for the global burden of disease study 2016. *Lancet Neurol.* **2019**, *18*, 439–458. [CrossRef]
4. Ochi, M.; Wada, F.; Saeki, S.; Hachisuka, K. Gait training in subacute non-ambulatory stroke patients using a full weight-bearing gait-assistance robot: A prospective, randomized, open, blinded-endpoint trial. *J. Neurol. Sci.* **2015**, *353*, 130–136. [CrossRef]
5. Maciejasz, P.; Eschweiler, J.; Gerlach-Hahn, K.; Jansen-Troy, A.; Leonhardt, S. A survey on robotic devices for upper limb rehabilitation. *J. Neuroeng. Rehabil.* **2014**, *11*, 3. [CrossRef] [PubMed]
6. Wang, H.; Feng, Y.; Yu, H.; Wang, Z.; Vladareanuv, V.; Du, Y. Mechanical design and trajectory planning of a lower limb rehabilitation robot with a variable workspace. *Int. J. Adv. Rob. Syst.* **2018**, *15*, 1729881418776855. [CrossRef]
7. Colombo, R.; Pisano, F.; Micera, S.; Mazzone, A.; Delconte, C.; Carrozza, M.; Dario, P.; Minuco, G. Robotic techniques for upper limb evaluation and rehabilitation of stroke patients. *IEEE Trans. Neural Syst. Rehabil. Eng.* **2005**, *13*, 311–324. [CrossRef]
8. Mazzoleni, S.; Puzzolante, L.; Zollo, L.; Dario, P.; Posteraro, F. Mechanisms of motor recovery in chronic and subacute stroke patients following a robot-aided training. *IEEE Trans. Haptics* **2014**, *7*, 175–180. [CrossRef]
9. Aprile, I.; Iacovelli, C.; Goffredo, M.; Cruciani, A.; Galli, M.; Simbolotti, C.; Pecchioli, C.; Padua, L.; Galafate, D.; Pournajaf, S.; et al. Efficacy of end-effector robot-assisted gait training in subacute stroke patients: Clinical and gait outcomes from a pilot bi-centre study. *NeuroRehabilitation* **2019**, *45*, 201–212. [CrossRef]
10. Tole, G.; Raymond, M.J.; Williams, G.; Clark, R.A.; Holland, A.E. Strength training to improve walking after stroke: How physiotherapist, patient and workplace factors influence exercise prescription. *Physiother. Theory Pract.* **2022**, *38*, 1198–1206. [CrossRef]
11. Liu, Y.; Li, X.L.; Zhu, A.; Zheng, Z.; Zhu, H. Design and evaluation of a surface electromyography-controlled lightweight upper arm exoskeleton rehabilitation robot. *Int. J. Adv. Rob. Syst.* **2021**, *18*, 17298814211003461. [CrossRef]
12. Khadanga, S.; Savage, P.D.; Ades, P.A. Resistance Training for Older Adults in Cardiac Rehabilitation. *Clin. Geriatr. Med.* **2019**, *35*, 459–468. [CrossRef]
13. Kristensen, J.; Burgess, S. A comparison of two 3-week resistance training programmes commonly used in short-term military rehabilitation. *J. R. Army Med. Corps* **2013**, *159*, 35–39. [CrossRef]
14. Halley, D.; Paul Ewing, B.M. The X-10: A revolution in knee rehabilitation. *Reconstr. Rev.* **2013**, *3*, 11–16.
15. Wannaphan, P.; Chanthasopeephan, P. Position controlled knee rehabilitation orthotic device for patients after total knee replacement arthroplasty. *Iop Conf.* **2016**, *157*, 12–30. [CrossRef]
16. Yoshioka, T.; Sugaya, H.; Kubota, S.; Onishi, M.; Kanamori, A.; Sankai, Y.; Yamazaki, M. Knee-extension training with a single-joint hybrid assistive limb during the early postoperative period after total knee arthroplasty in a patient with osteoarthritis. *Case Rep. Orthop.* **2016**, *9*, 9610745. [CrossRef]
17. Fukaya, T.; Mutsuzaki, H.; Yoshikawa, K.; Sano, A.; Mizukami, M.; Yamazaki, M. The training effect of early intervention with a hybrid assistive limb after total knee arthroplasty. *Case Rep. Orthop.* **2017**, *7*, 6912706. [CrossRef]
18. Olinski, M.; Gronowicz, A.; Handke, A.; Ceccarelli, M. Design and characterization of a novel knee articulation mechanism. *Int. J. Appl. Mech. Eng.* **2016**, *21*, 611–622. [CrossRef]
19. Riener, R.; Lunenburger, L.; Jezernik, S.; Anderschitz, M.; Colombo, G.; Dietz, V. Patient-cooperative strategies for robot-aided treadmill training: First experimental results. *IEEE Trans. Neural Syst. Rehabil. Eng.* **2005**, *13*, 380–394. [CrossRef] [PubMed]
20. Wu, Q.; Wang, X.; Chen, B.; Wu, H. Development of a minimal-intervention-based admittance control strategy for upper extremity rehabilitation exoskeleton. *IEEE Trans. Syst. Man Cybern.-Syst.* **2018**, *48*, 1005–1016. [CrossRef]
21. Aguirre-Ollinger, G.; Colgate, J.E.; Peshkin, M.A.; Goswami, A. Design of an active one-degree-of-freedom lower-limb exoskeleton with inertia compensation. *Int. J. Rob. Res.* **2011**, *30*, 486–499. [CrossRef]
22. Meuleman, J.; van Asseldonk, E.; van Oort, G.; Rietman, H.; van der Kooij, H. LOPES II-design and evaluation of an admittance controlled gait training robot with shadow-leg approach. *IEEE Trans. Neural Syst. Rehabil. Eng.* **2016**, *24*, 352–363. [CrossRef]
23. dos Santos, W.M.; Siqueira, A.A.G. Optimal impedance via model predictive control for robot-aided rehabilitation. *Control Eng. Pract.* **2019**, *93*, 104177. [CrossRef]
24. Rosado, W.M.A.; Ortega, A.B.; Valdes, L.G.V.; Ascencio, J.R.; Beltrán, C. Active rehabilitation exercises with a parallel structure ankle rehabilitation prototype. *IEEE Lat. Am. Trans.* **2017**, *15*, 786–794. [CrossRef]
25. Zhang, F.; Hou, Z.G.; Cheng, L.; Wang, W.; Chen, Y.; Hu, J.; Peng, L.; Wang, H. iLeg—A lower limb rehabilitation robot: A proof of concept. *IEEE Trans. Hum.-Mach. Syst.* **2016**, *46*, 761–768. [CrossRef]

26. Huang, Y.; Song, R.; Argha, A.; Savkin, A.V.; Celler, B.G.; Su, S.W. Continuous description of human 3D motion intent through switching mechanism. *IEEE Trans. Neural Syst. Rehabil. Eng.* **2020**, *28*, 277–286. [CrossRef] [PubMed]
27. Li, M.; Liang, Z.; He, B.; Zhao, C.-G.; Yao, W.; Xu, G.; Xie, J.; Cui, L. Attention-controlled assistive wrist rehabilitation using a low-cost EEG sensor. *IEEE Sens. J.* **2019**, *19*, 6497–6507. [CrossRef]
28. Rouse, C.A.; Downey, R.J.; Gregory, C.M.; Cousin, C.A.; Duenas, V.H.; Dixon, W.E. FES Cycling in Stroke: Novel Closed-Loop Algorithm Accommodates Differences in Functional Impairments. *IEEE Trans. Biomed. Eng.* **2020**, *67*, 738–749. [CrossRef] [PubMed]
29. Reininga, I.H.F.; Stevens, M.; Wagenmakers, R.; Bulstra, S.K.; Akker-Scheek, I.V.D. Minimally invasive total hip and knee arthroplasty-implications for the elderly patient. *Clin. Geriatr. Med.* **2012**, *28*, 447–458. [CrossRef]
30. Leslie, M. Knee osteoarthritis management therapies. *Pain Manag. Nurs. Off. J. Am. Soc. Pain Manag. Nurses* **2000**, *1*, 51–57. [CrossRef] [PubMed]
31. Nisell, R.; Ekholm, J. Joint load during the parallel squat in powerlifting and force analysis of in vivo bilateral quadriceps tendon rupture. *Scand. J. Sports Sci.* **1986**, *8*, 63–70.
32. Li, G.; Zayontz, S.; Most, E.; DeFrate, L.E.; Suggs, J.F.; Rubash, H.E. In situ forces of the anterior and posterior cruciate ligaments in high knee flexion: An in vitro investigation. *J. Orthop. Res.* **2004**, *22*, 293–297. [CrossRef]
33. Escamilla, R.F. Knee biomechanics of the dynamic squat exercise. *Med. Sci. Sports Exerc.* **2001**, *33*, 127–141. [CrossRef] [PubMed]
34. Escamilla, R.F.; Fleisig, G.S.; Zheng, N.; Barrentine, S.W.; Wilk, K.E.; Andrews, J.R. Biomechanics of the knee during closed kinetic chain and open kinetic chain exercises. *Med. Sci. Sports Exerc.* **1998**, *30*, 556–569. [CrossRef] [PubMed]
35. Yan, H.; Wang, H.; Vladareanu, L.; Lin, M.; Vladareanu, V.; Li, Y. Detection of participation and training task difficulty applied to the multi-sensor systems of rehabilitation robots. *Sensors* **2019**, *19*, 4681. [CrossRef]
36. Feng, Y.; Wang, H.; Vladareanu, L.; Chen, Z.; Jin, D. New Motion Intention Acquisition Method of Lower Limb Rehabilitation Robot Based on Static Torque Sensors. *Sensors* **2019**, *19*, 3439. [CrossRef]
37. Marin, C.; Marti, M.J.; Tolosa, E.; Alvarez, R.; Montserrat, L.; Santamaria, J. Muscle activity changes in spasmodic torticollis after botulinum toxin treatment. *Eur. J. Neurol.* **1995**, *1*, 243–247. [CrossRef]
38. Falla, D.; Jull, G.; O'Leary, S.; Dall'Alba, P. Further evaluation of an EMG technique for assessment of the deep cervical flexor muscles. *J. Electromyogr. Kinesiol.* **2006**, *16*, 621–628. [CrossRef]
39. Okubo, Y.; Kaneoka, K.; Imai, A.; Shiina, I.; Tatsumura, M.; Izumi, S.; Miyakawa, S. Comparison of the activities of the deep trunk muscles measured using intramuscular and surface electromyography. *J. Mech. Med. Biol.* **2010**, *10*, 611–620. [CrossRef]

sensors

MDPI

Article

Navigation Path Based Universal Mobile Manipulator Integrated Controller (NUMMIC)

Taehyeon Kim [1], Myunghyun Kim [2], Sungwoo Yang [2] and Donghan Kim [2,*]

[1] Department of Electronic Engineering, Kyung Hee University, Yongin 17104, Korea
[2] AgeTech-Service Convergence Major, Department of Electronic Engineering, Kyung Hee University, Yongin 17104, Korea
* Correspondence: donghani@khu.ac.kr

Abstract: As the demand for service robots increases, a mobile manipulator robot which can perform various tasks in a dynamic environment attracts great attention. There are some controllers that control mobile platform and manipulator arm simultaneously for efficient performance, but most of them are difficult to apply universally since they are based on only one mobile manipulator model. This lack of versatility can be a big problem because most mobile manipulator robots are made by connecting a mobile platform and manipulator from different companies. To overcome this problem, this paper proposes a simultaneous controller which can be applied not only to one model but also to various types of mobile manipulator robots. The proposed controller has three main characteristics, which are as follows: (1) establishing a pose that motion planning can be carried out in any position, avoiding obstacles and stopping in a stable manner at the target coordinates, (2) preventing the robot from collision with surrounding obstacles while driving, (3) defining a safety area where the manipulator does not hit the obstacles while driving and executing the manipulation accordingly. Our controller is fully compatible with Robot Operating System (ROS) and has been used successfully with three different types of mobile manipulator robots. In addition, we conduct motion planning experiments on five targets, each in two simulation worlds, and two motion planning scenarios using real robots in real-world environments. The result shows a significant improvement in time compared to existing control methods in various types of mobile manipulator and demonstrates that the controller works successfully in the real environment. The proposed controller is available on GitHub.

Keywords: mobile manipulator; motion planning; simultaneous control; path analysis; ROS

Citation: Kim, T.; Kim, M.; Yang, S.; Kim, D. Navigation Path Based Universal Mobile Manipulator Integrated Controller (NUMMIC). *Sensors* **2022**, *22*, 7369. https://doi.org/10.3390/s22197369

Academic Editors: Luige Vladareanu, Hongnian Yu, Hongbo Wang and Yongfei Feng

Received: 13 September 2022
Accepted: 24 September 2022
Published: 28 September 2022

1. Introduction

With the development of artificial intelligence and control technology, the era has come when the service robot directly interacts with humans. The service robot is expected to have an important role in our daily life [1]. However, a current service robot is mostly only used in the same way as a mobile robot, or manipulator robot. A converged platform, in which the manipulator is loaded onto the mobile robot, is called a mobile manipulator, and since it can accomplish unstructured tasks in dynamic environments, it maximizes the use of the robots and is of especially great value in the service area [2]. This is the reason for the current research on mobile manipulators.

There are two types of mobile manipulator controllers, one for sequential control and the other for simultaneous control. Today, most of the mobile manipulator controllers in a real environment such as the field of industry use sequential control. This control method, which is shown in the Figure 1a, controls the manipulator and moves its end-effector to the goal pose after it moves the mobile robot to the manipulable location in a single goal pose. This is due not only to legal reasons, including safety concerns, but also to maintain precision and dexterity [3,4]. On the other hand, the simultaneous control method, which is shown in the Figure 1b, calculates the desired pose of a mobile robot to a single goal pose, as well as calculating how to manipulate the end-effector to reach the goal pose while the robot moves to the corresponding desired pose. After that, it executes the algorithm controlling both the mobile robot and the manipulator at the same time. Simultaneous control of the mobile manipulator has a great advantage for efficiency, and work is continuously being carried out in this area [5–7].

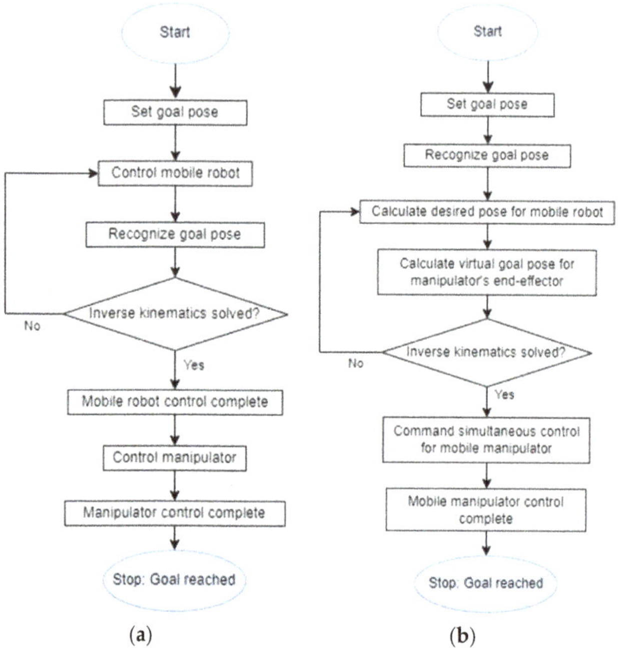

Figure 1. (**a**) Flowchart of the algorithm controlling mobile manipulator sequentially. (**b**) Flowchart of the algorithm controlling the mobile manipulator simultaneously.

Meanwhile, because of its complexity, the typical simultaneous controller is designed to control one fixed structured mobile manipulator [8]. However, most of the mobile manipulator robots currently used do not come from one company in the form of a finished product, but are used by combining the mobile platform and the manipulator arm of different companies. This increases the possibility of each user using different mobile manipulator platforms and this situation makes it hard to apply existing simultaneous controllers built on a single model. This paper proposes the Navigation path-based Universal Mobile Manipulator Integrated Controller (NUMMIC), which is a type of kinematic controller. NUMMIC is able to control the mobile platform and manipulator simultaneously by simply changing a few parameters to overcome the existing kinematic controller's limitations. Since most of the existing kinematic controllers need as detailed as possible characteristics of models for precise operation, it is challenging to use it with various types of mobile manipulators. However, in NUMMIC, the parameters required by the algorithm are minimized for stable simultaneous control. Accordingly, it can be applied to various types of mobile manipulators. Here, the only hardware it requires is a mobile manipulator which has a single arm on a mobile platform with Light Detection and Ranging (LiDAR) and Inertial Measurement Unit (IMU) sensor, and the software required is the Unified Robot Description Format (URDF) [9], available on ROS [10] for each part. Any mobile manipulator that satisfies these conditions can be used by the proposed controller with a few parameter revisions. This is possible because the controller performance is based on the platform's navigation control and does not need other sensors except for LiDAR and

IMU sensors during motion planning. Also, it tunes the lower-level kinematic controller rather than directly controlling the hardware at the lower end.

NUMMIC, which is suggested in this paper, is composed of three substructures: a Manipulation Enabled Pose (MEP) setting based on a LiDAR sensor, an optimized end-effector default pose, and a Manipulation Safety Section (MSS) setting based on path curvature. These substructures elaborately control the move_base package [11] and the MoveIt package [12], which are publicly provided by the ROS as mentioned, and make simultaneous control of the mobile manipulator of the target object possible in different environments and positions. Since the entire controller is operated by coordinating the lower kinematic controller packages, the controller is easily compatible with various mobile manipulators which have different specifications.

The specific structure of NUMMIC can be found in Figure 2. For a detailed explanation of the substructures, the desired pose, which is called Manipulation Enabled Pose (MEP), is needed. This pose which allows the mobile manipulator to be controlled simultaneously using global path is found by MEP setting based on LiDAR sensor. The second substructure, the optimized end-effector default pose, derives the location in which there is least deviation of time, regardless of the position of the target object and its designation as a manipulator's default pose. This idea is based on the fact that, in the operating environment, the manipulator's manipulation is restricted to limited directions. The last substructure, the Manipulation Safety Section (MSS) setting based on path curvature, supports the safe simultaneous control of the mobile manipulator. According to its control algorithm, manipulation is operated at the same time as the mobile platform moves. If the manipulation is being executed or has already completed its execution and the platform moves with the stretched manipulator, the possibility of colliding with obstacles near the path will become much higher. To prevent this, an algorithm from this substructure locates the area which is in no danger of colliding with nearby objects and only performs the manipulation when the mobile platform passes through the area. This area is called the Manipulation Safety Section (MSS).

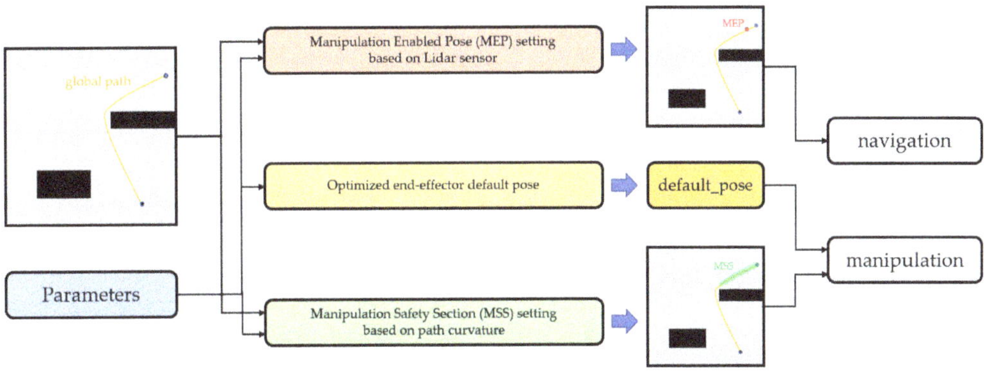

Figure 2. Diagram of NUMMIC's substructures.

In summary, this work suggests the controller, NUMMIC, for simultaneous control of the mobile manipulator. NUMMIC is able to perform in a stable manner the motion planning towards the target object in any environment when its target coordinates are given. This process takes less time compared to the sequential control algorithm, due to the simultaneous control of the mobile platform and the manipulator. Since this NUMMIC controller coordinates the move_base and MoveIt packages, which can be used publicly at ROS, it can be applied to various manipulator robots with different specifications if some parameters in the controller are modified.

To validate our proposal, we present an experiment for motion planning towards given target coordinates using the mobile manipulator robot in a simulation environment.

To show the motion planning in different environments we use two different maps with various obstacles for the simulation and designate various points in the map as target coordinates. Also, to show that NUMMIC can be used in mobile manipulators with different specifications, we run the simulation with three different types of mobile manipulator: one in which UR3 [13] of universal robot is attached to Husky UGV [14] from Clearpath corporation, another one which has a UR5 [15] manipulator with the same mobile platform, and a third that has Kinova corporation's Gen3 lite [16] manipulator on Jackal UGV [17]. Finally, we conduct an experiment using NUMMIC with a mobile manipulator, in which Husky UGV is attached to a UR3 manipulator in a real environment.

In Section 2 we explain existing approaches to mobile manipulator control. In Section 3 we describe the structure of NUMMIC in detail, including (1) its three substructures (2) the architecture based on ROS using these substructures. We present the experiments in both simulation and within a real environment, discussing the results obtained in Sections 4 and 5. Lastly, the conclusions of the evaluation and future works are presented in Section 6.

2. Related Work

Because of the mobile manipulator's capability, various related studies are conducted on the premise that it is used at different fields. The many fields of application include industry [18,19], which is mentioned above, but also construction [20], agriculture [21–23], disaster [24], and healthcare [25,26].

For a robot to execute complex works in these different fields and environments, it needs a highly qualified manipulation ability. In particular, the efficient control of the mobile manipulator in unstructured dynamic environments is important, but this issue is not completely solved. In Reference [27], it minimizes execution time for the pick-up task by deriving the optimal trajectory of joint space, applying a random profile approach (RPA). There are some works whose methods of control focus on the manipulator's end-effector. [28]. One of those works carries out sampling of the waypoint with the end-effector's target position and orientation trajectory and implements an optimized planner using the Genetic Algorithm for continuous movement of the mobile manipulator. The work in [29] efficiently generates a path without collision in complex environments by suggesting the Optimized Hierarchical Mobile Manipulator Planner (OHMP), which is composed of two steps: two-dimensional mobile motion planning and three-dimensional manipulator motion planning. Recently, due to the development of deep learning, research into mobile manipulator control using reinforcement learning is also being conducted. In [30], the authors suggest a system in which the mobile manipulator robot learns action-related places through experience-based learning with the environment. In Reference [31], they offer a mobile manipulator system with a more efficient framework by decoupling the state-of-the-art deep reinforcement learning control and visual perception.

The controller suggested in this research works as a controlling move_base, which is a package for navigation and MoveIt, the manipulator control package, on the upper level. There are some studies to find improved action by the selection in which it uses an existing controller in normal situations and replaces the motion with a new controller or adjusts the existing one in particular situations. In Reference [32], the controller normally uses move-base to drive the mobile robot and then when the robot faces the narrow space, it regenerates appropriate waypoints for passing the space. Also, in the work of Reference [33], the author suggests an algorithm which executes a more efficient exploration using Gmapping [34] and the move-base package. Moreover, in the same context, other studies are conducted which extend the function of move_base with a higher-level controller [35–37] or uses the MoveIt package [38–40] for operation in specific higher-level environments. Although it is not related to replacing or tuning the controller itself, as with reference [41], there are also some studies on user-friendly interfaces, replacing RViz [42], the 3D visualization tool which gives order to the existing move_base, and MoveIt packages, to a VR-based interface. In the case of the controllers suggested in the studies mentioned, they are activated by replacing or tuning the existing ROS packages in certain environments but have the limitation that they have to be controlled with RViz or terminals. However, in this paper, the authors make a Virtual Reality-based control interface in which the user has access intuitively at higher level. This seems consistent with the approach direction that suggests a higher-level controller which gives order to a lower one without directly handling the lower kinematic controller of the move-base and MoveIt packages.

3. Controller Description

The objective of the controller is to control the mobile manipulator simultaneously in various environments. For its successful operation, when the mobile manipulator receives the position of the target object, it should firstly be able to calculate the pose where it can execute the manipulation towards the target and move to the corresponding pose. The flow chart of NUMMIC for this operation can be found in Figure 3.

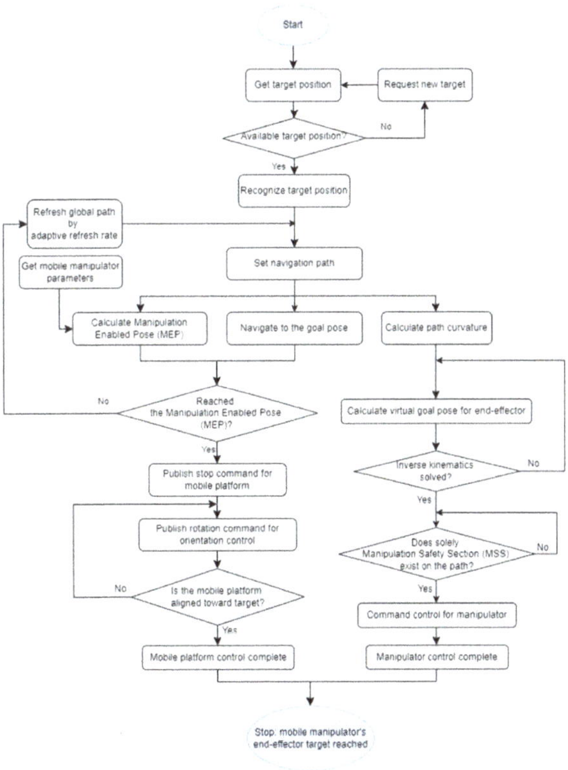

Figure 3. Execution flowchart of NUMMIC.

Following the order of the flow chart, after receiving the available position of the target, NUMMIC sets the navigation path through the global path planner [43] in the move-base package with scan data from the LiDAR sensor attached at the mobile platform. If MEP, a position where the manipulation for the target on navigation path is successfully executed, is specified, the mobile platform of the mobile manipulator can be located on the MEP controlled using move-base. This process is based on some parameters of the mobile manipulator and the information about the position of the target.

At the same time, two additional processes are required for the efficient and stable control of the mobile manipulator, which are the designation of the manipulator's default pose and the setting for MSS using path's curvature analysis. The designation of the suggested default pose is based on the idea that the generated trajectory at manipulation is likely to be a straight line since the mobile manipulator is aligned to face the target object when it stops at MEP. The default pose proposed in this paper is a point where, no matter what value the z-coordinate of the target object has, deviation of the distance from default pose's coordinate to the target, i.e., the trajectory of end-effector during manipulation, is minimized and the manipulator does not hit the surrounding obstacles. Since the state of the manipulator not performing any action while the mobile manipulator drives is defined as the default pose, there is no part related to the calculation of default pose in NUMMIC flow chart of Figure 3. As seen in Figure 2, although the part suggesting an optimized default pose exists in parallel with other substructures, it is decided in advance by the parameters of mobile manipulator and used in NUMMIC rather than being performed in the main operation of NUMMIC. This default pose is calculated with the manipulator's workspace and some parameters including mobile robot's footprint, and by using it to control the manipulator it can reduce the average planning time for target objects in various locations.

The setting for MSS using path's curvature analysis, like MEP generating algorithm, uses a navigation path to find the area with a high risk of collision between the manipulator and surroundings while the mobile robot drives. This operation can also be seen in the flow chart of Figure 3 through the *Calculate path curvature* block on the rightmost side following the *Set navigation path*. The global path generated by the global path planner from move-base is split into steps according to the granularity value, and it analyzes the curvature at each path's interval using the difference of radian values at these steps. It distinguishes the area where there is a possibility of the mobile manipulator colliding with nearby obstacles or not depending on the analyzed curvature, the width of mobile manipulator, and the manipulation distance. Finally, it performs the manipulation only if there is MSS, the area which has no risk for the manipulator to collide with the surroundings on its path between the mobile manipulator and the target object according to the path analysis.

3.1. Manipulation Enabled Pose (MEP) Setting Based on LiDAR Sensor

In this part, the executed operations are as follows: (1) setting the MEP for the manipulation towards the given target and control the mobile platform for the movement to the pose, (2) stopping the MEP using the algorithm which controls the velocity proportional to distance and (3) rotation control based on P-controller to perfectly align the target and the mobile manipulator. These three operations are executed sequentially.

To set the MEP, the controller calculates the Manipulable Area. Manipulable Area is an area in which the mobile manipulator can manipulate the target. The controller then generates a global path to the target using move-base and makes the mobile manipulator drive along the path. Here, the calculation of the Manipulable Area is as follows. A pose is assumed in which the mobile manipulator stopping at MEP performs the manipulation towards the target. Figure 4 shows the pose in the simulation. Here, the first joint from the manipulator's base link becomes the central axis of the recommended workspace. Using the characteristics of NUMMIC algorithm, only values of x and z coordinates in 3-dimensional space during the manipulation are needed since the coordinates of the base link of the mobile manipulator and the target are aligned after the control of the mobile platform. Assuming the radius of the manipulator's recommended workspace to be d_m, z-coordinates of target be t_z, and z-coordinates of manipulator's first joint from the ground be m_z, the angle between the line from the target, which is perpendicular to the ground, and the line extended from target to manipulator's first joint is as follows:

$$\theta = \cos^{-1}\left(\frac{|t_z - m_z|}{d_m}\right) \quad (1)$$

The definition of the distance on the x-axis from the base link of the mobile platform to the first joint of the manipulator as d_{bm}, r_m, a radius of Manipulable Area is as follows:

$$r_m = d_m \sin\theta + d_{bm} \quad (2)$$

Thus r_m, the radius of Manipulable Area is a distance between the perpendicular foot of a point where the target meets the recommended workspace to the ground, and the perpendicular foot of a base link to the ground.

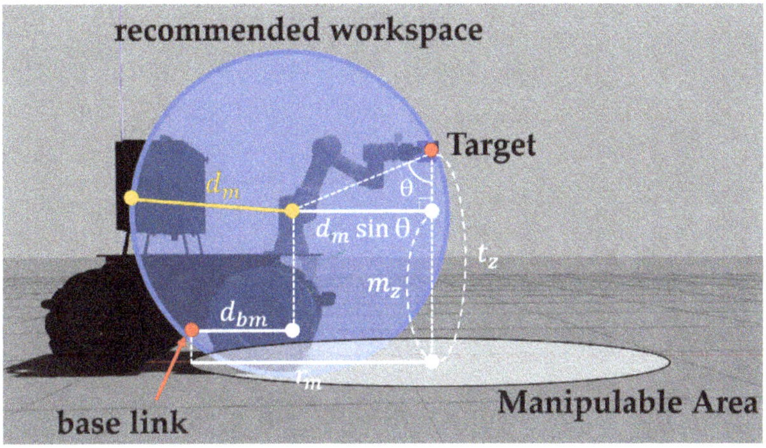

Figure 4. Schematic representation for the correlation between mobile manipulator's recommended workspace, target, and r_m.

Second, the controller stops the mobile manipulator when it is determined that the mobile manipulator has entered the Manipulable Area while driving along the path. If a signal is sent instantaneously, a significant error occurrs since the controller controls the mobile robot with move-base. To prevent this, the suggested controller in this paper defines the area equivalent to twice the radius of the Manipulable Area as sigmoid distance proportional speed control area and adjusts the velocity of the mobile platform in this area. The velocity decelerates along the shape of the sigmoid function in proportion to the distance from the target point. When v_x is the translational velocity of mobile platform, v_{max} is the maximum velocity of mobile platform, v_{stop} is the velocity when mobile platform is stopped, and d is the distance between the mobile platform and the MEP, then the formula of the sigmoid function is as follows.

$$v_x = \frac{v_{max} - v_{stop}}{e^{-d} + 1} + v_{stop} \tag{3}$$

To converge to the velocity v_{stop} when it reaches the target point, the function is shifted to the positive direction as follows:

$$v_x = \frac{v_{max} - v_{stop}}{e^{-d+6} + 1} + v_{stop} \tag{4}$$

Finally, assuming the radius of predefined sigmoid distance proportional speed control area to be r_{sa}, the coefficient to decelerate after entering the area is revised.

$$v_x = \frac{v_{max} - v_{stop}}{e^{-\frac{12}{r_{sa}}d+6} + 1} + v_{stop} \tag{5}$$

In order to verify how the mobile platform of the mobile manipulator is controlled through the above Formula (5), a graph is drawn assuming the specific situation. Because the maximum speed of Husky UGV which is used in the experiment of the paper is 1 m/s, v_{max} is set at 1 m/s and the targeting velocity at stop is set at 0 m/s. Then, assuming that r_{sa} about particular target A is 1.2 m, a graph of the corresponding sigmoid function is drawn as Figure 5. From this graph, it can be expected that as the mobile manipulator goes beyond the sigmoid distance proportional speed control area and approaches the target, its speed will decrease and stops in a stable manner at MEP.

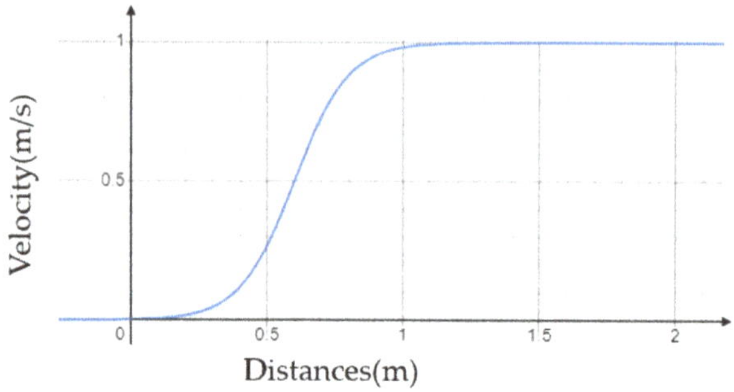

Figure 5. A distance-velocity graph for applying sigmoid distance proportional speed control at a point 1.2 m away from the target with a mobile platform which has a maximum speed of 1 m/s.

After the mobile platform is stopped by the sigmoid distance proportional speed control algorithm, it rotates the platform to face toward the coordinates of target object. This rotational control is composed of simple P-control which multiplies the gain value to the difference of mobile platform's yaw value and target one, and this gain can be modified according to the needs of the user at NUMMIC's configuration, even though it is specified to 0.25 as default.

The final pose of the mobile manipulator becomes the MEP through a series of control processes for detailed alignment of the mobile platform including the designation of MEP by target coordinates and specification of the mobile manipulator, stop at the position, and rotational control. The graphical explanation about MEP can be found in Figure 6. Figure 6a shows where the MEP is located on the path, based on the creation of a navigation path which has the position of target object from the mobile manipulator as goal on RViz. Figure 6b shows the Manipulable Area, a circular area with radius r_m that has the target object as a center when the mobile manipulator is located closer to the target object, and the sigmoid distance proportional speed control area with radius $2r_m$ which also has target object as a center. In this case, the intersection of the navigation path from the mobile manipulator to target object and the Manipulable Area becomes the position of the MEP.

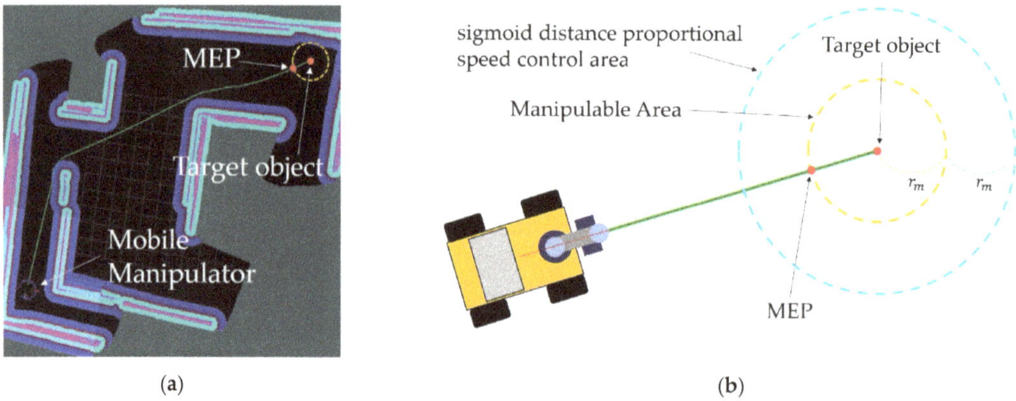

Figure 6. Schematic description of the Manipulation Enabled Pose (MEP). (**a**) shows where the MEP is located on the navigation path. (**b**) shows the Manipulable Area and the sigmoid distance proportional speed control area according to r_m.

3.2. Optimized End-Effector Default Pose

The default pose of the end-effector suggested in this paper is a pose in which there is no collision when the mobile manipulator drives, and it does not lose much time in the planning of the manipulation, whatever value the target's z-coordinate has. The z-coordinate of the suggested pose is assumed to be k, and distance at x-axis from the base link of manipulator to the front footprint value on move-base of the mobile platform to be d_{fm}, which can be described as Figure 7. Figure 7a represents d_m, the radius of mobile manipulator's recommended workspace, d_{fm}, the distance on the x-axis from the manipulator's base link to the front footprint of the mobile platform, and d_{bm}, the distance on x-axis from the mobile manipulator's base link to the manipulator arm's base link. Figure 7b represents an arbitrary position of the target (blue point) and the expected position of default pose (green point on the green line) through a circle with the first joint from the manipulator's base link as the origin and d_m as the radius. A red point is the target which has a minimum z value among the target, and a purple point is the target which has a maximum z value. This range can be modified by controller's parameter values. X, expected planning trajectory distance value from default pose to the target object, can be derived as follows:

$$X = \sqrt{\left(x - d_{fm}\right)^2 + \left(\sqrt{d_m^2 - x^2} - k\right)^2} \tag{6}$$

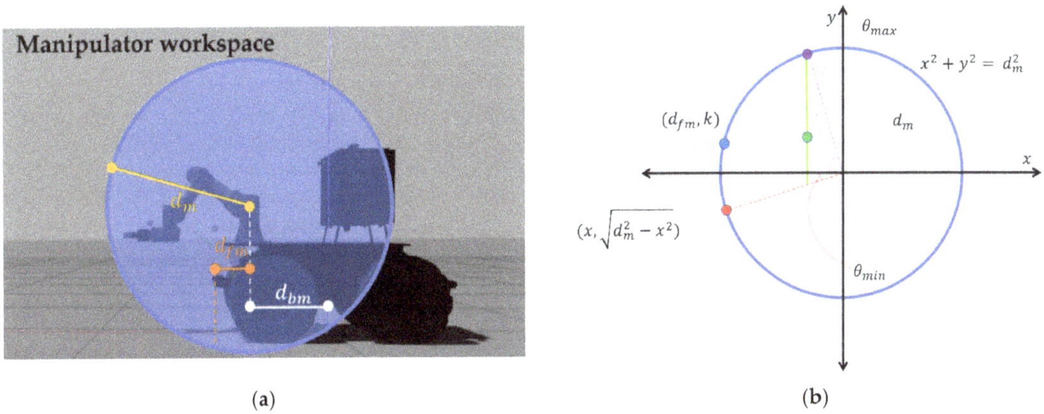

Figure 7. Schematic description of the position for the default pose. (**a**) represents d_m, d_{fm}, d_{bm} on the simulation mobile manipulator model. (**b**) represents the expected position of default pose (green point) in a simplified drawing.

To find a default pose required by the controller, the formula should be expressed as the mean value and variance of continuous probability variable as follows:

$$E_{distance}(X) = \int_{-d_m}^{-d_{fm}} x\sqrt{\left(x - d_{fm}\right)^2 + \left(\sqrt{d_m^2 - x^2} - k\right)^2}\, dx = m \tag{7}$$

$$V_{distance}(X) = \int_{-d_m}^{-d_{fm}} (x - m)^2\sqrt{\left(x - d_{fm}\right)^2 + \left(\sqrt{d_m^2 - x^2} - k\right)^2}\, dx \tag{8}$$

When the $V_{distance}(X)$ is minimum, k becomes the z-coordinate of manipulator's default pose. Although the above expression is suitable for understanding the concept of suggested default pose, it is difficult to calculate the desired k value due to its complexity. Thus, for ease of calculation, we exchanged the values of x and y-axis, and the values in the range of integrals are replaced by discrete ones which take into consideration the manipulator's operating range and limits in control. The revised formula is given below.

Here, z_{max} is the value in which the maximum height for the mobile manipulator to perform manipulation is subtracted by the z-coordinate value of manipulator's first joint from the base link, and z_{min} is the value in which the minimum height for manipulation is subtracted by the z-coordinate value of manipulator's first joint.

$$X_2 = \sqrt{(x-k)^2 + \left(\sqrt{d_m^2 - x^2} - d_{fm}\right)^2} \tag{9}$$

$$E_{distance}(X_2) = \int_{z_{min}}^{z_{max}} x\sqrt{(x-k)^2 + \left(\sqrt{d_m^2 - x^2} - d_{fm}\right)^2}\,dx = m_2 \tag{10}$$

$$V_{distance}(X_2) = \int_{z_{min}}^{z_{max}} (x-m_2)^2\sqrt{(x-k)^2 + \left(\sqrt{d_m^2 - x^2} - d_{fm}\right)^2}\,dx \tag{11}$$

As in Expressions (6)–(8), when the $V_{distance}(X_2)$ is minimum, k becomes the z-coordinate of manipulator's default pose $(z_{min} \leq k \leq z_{max})$. Finally, the k value which is derived from the above calculation is designated as the z-coordinate of the default pose and d_{fm}, the distance to the front footprint of the mobile platform based on the manipulator's base link is designated as the x-coordinate of the default pose. After defining the y-coordinate as the nearest point to 0 where the manipulator can move satisfying these two values, and inputting the orientation value so that the end-effector looks at the front of the mobile manipulator in the corresponding position, the default pose is set.

3.3. Manipulation Safety Section (MSS) Setting Based on Path Curvature

For successful simultaneous control of the mobile manipulator in various environments which include obstacles, it is necessary to prevent the manipulator from colliding with its surroundings. For this reason, in this paper, we analyze the global path where the mobile manipulator drives and make the manipulator decide whether there is a large curve that it might bump into when it is stretched forward along the path from the current position to the target. Assuming the radius of Manipulable Area about specific target of mobile manipulator to be r_m, the width of the mobile platform to be w_m, and the mobile manipulator to be a material particle that moves along the global path, the curvature radius ρ about the differential length of the path is required.

Generally, this curvature radius ρ, which is decided by the arc between two adjacent points of the trace, is expressed as follows:

$$\rho = \frac{ds}{d\theta} \tag{12}$$

Meanwhile, the global path from move-base is in the form of an array composed of numerous x and y coordinates. Differential length, which is called path step in this paper, can be decided using the difference between the sequential values of these x and y coordinates. Each of these path steps has a certain distance value and they are preset in advance which can be checked at the configuration of move-base package. This differential length is called path granularity, which refers to ds of above Formula (12). $d\theta$ can also be derived from the angular difference of each continuous path step. The equation for calculating the curvature radius by applying the above is as follows:

$$\rho = \frac{path\ granularity}{difference\ of\ path\ step\ angular} \tag{13}$$

Using curvature radius ρ and width of mobile platform w_m, the area where the manipulator does not collide with nearby obstacles while the mobile platform passes specific path step with its stretched arm can be calculated. This area corresponds to the space between the arc of a circle whose radius is equal to the curvature radius ρ plus half of w_m, and the arc of a circle whose radius is same as the value, ρ is subtracted by half of w_m. This is described as the green space at Figure 8. If the curvature of the path is large enough for the end-effector to be outside the green space when the manipulation is executed at that moment, the path step, which includes the base link (a green dot inside the mobile platform in Figure 8) of the mobile manipulator, is treated as not belonging to MSS. Algorithm 1 is a pseudo-code based on Python for deciding the MSS by global path.

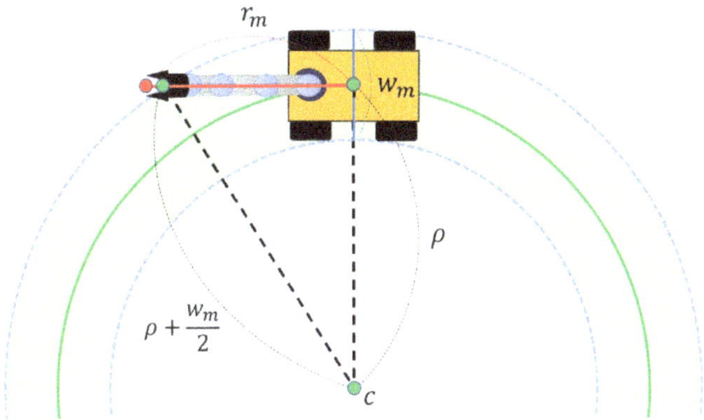

Figure 8. Schematic description for the calculation of Manipulation Safety Section (MSS).

After distinguishing the MSS and the section which is not on the global path from the mobile manipulator's start point towards the target, if only the MSS exists on the remaining path from the path step, which is closest to the location where the mobile manipulator is driving, to the target, manipulator's planning will be executed. Through the process, mobile manipulator can be controlled by simultaneous control without collision in complex environments including obstacles.

3.4. ROS-Based Architecture

NUMMIC is implemented through the Python scripts based on ROS, and it controls a whole mobile manipulator with move_base, which controls the mobile platform, and MoveIt, which controls the manipulator, solving inverse kinematics. The structure of NUMMIC packages on ROS is shown as Figure 9.

Controller.launch executes the nodes at the same time which are required for operating NUMMIC package through python scripts inside the script folder. *default_pose_cal.launch* executes the python script which calculates the position of proposed default pose using the value inside *controller_param.yaml* for the user to control the default pose that is proposed in this paper before operating NUMMIC. *controller_param.yaml* file obtains the specification of the mobile manipulator and additional setting parameters related to the operation of the controller and sends them to each node through *rospy.get_param* function. A brief description about input and additional parameters at *controller_param.yaml* file can be found in Table 1. *goal_nav.py*, *goal_nav_stop_combine.py*, and *orientation_check.py* are the Python scripts for the MEP setting, stop at MEP, and detailed rotational control after stopping. *curvature_check.py* sends the decision about MSS and its result to *manipulation.py*. *manipulation.py* executes the manipulation to locate at the proposed default pose, which is calculated in advance by the manipulator based on MSS, or at virtual goal pose, which is to reach the target coordinates for the end-effector or manipulator when the mobile platform is stopped at MEP. *default_pose_calculator.py* calculates the position of default pose which will be used with this controller according to the parameter values set by the user. Figure 10 represents how the communication using the topics works in the process in which NUMMIC controls the mobile manipulator through the external move-base package and MoveIt package on ROS. The proposed controller is released as an open-source repository on GitHub [44].

Algorithm 1: Determining the Manipulation Safety Section (MSS) from curvature of global path

Data: Path data: path_msg [[path_msg[0]$_x$, path_msg[0]$_y$], [path_msg[1]$_x$, path_msg[1]$_y$], ... [path_msg[N − 1]$_x$, path_msg[N − 1]$_y$]]; Path granularity: pg; Width of mobile robot: w_m; Radius of Manipulable Area: r_m

Result: Manipulation Safety Section (MSS) on the global path

```
path = []
path_angular = []
path_angular_modified = []
MSS = []
path_step = N - 1
path_offset = round(r_m/pg)
# Get path data
for i = 0 to path_step do:
    path.append([path_msg[i]_x, path_msg[i]_y])
end for
# Calculate path step angular
for i = 0 to path_step−1 do:
    yaw_x = path[i + 1][0]−path[i][0]
    yaw_y = path[i + 1][1]−path[i][1]
    angular = atan2(yaw_y, yaw_x)
    if angular < 0:                                   # Match the signs of the angular
        angular = 2π + angular
    end if
    path_angular.append(angular)
end for
# Get difference of path step's angular
for i = 0 to path_step−2 do:
    angular_modified = path_angular[i + 1]−path_angular[i]
    if angular_modified < −π:
        angular_modified = 2π + angular_modified
    elif angular_modified > π:
        angular_modified = 2π−angular_modified
    end if
    if i ≥ ((path_step−2)−path_offset):               # Exclude the path step belonging to Manipulable Area
        angular_modified = 0
    end if
    path_angular_modified.append(|angular_modified|)
end for
# Get MSS
for i = 0 to path_step−2 do:
    if path_angular_modified[i] == 0:
        radius_of_curvature = 0
    else:
        radius_of_curvature = (pg/path_angular_modified[i])
    end if
    if radius_of_curvature == 0:                      # Position with True values on this array is MSS
        MSS.append(True)
    elif sqrt(radius_of_curvature + (w_m/2))^2 −(radius_of_curvature)^2) > r_m:
        MSS.append(True)
    else:
        MSS.append(False)
    end if
end for
```

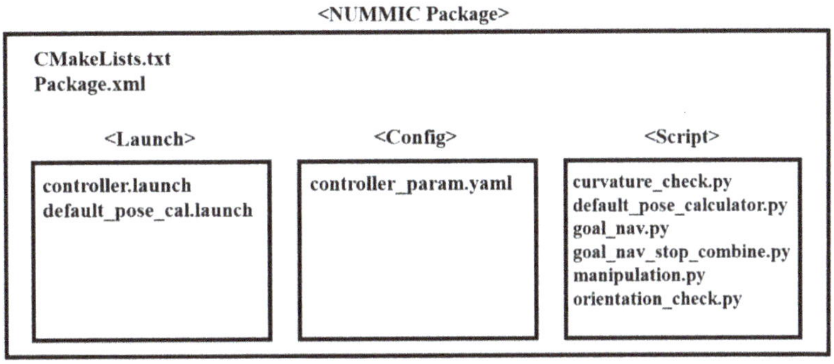

Figure 9. Structure of NUMMIC Package based on ROS.

Table 1. Parameters that can be set in *controller_param.yaml* of NUMMIC Package, and brief description about them.

Parameter	Description
/first_joint_height	z-axis distance from ground to manipulator's first joint (m).
/between_base_link	x-axis distance from mobile robot's base_link to manipulator's base_link (m).
/recommended_reach	Manipulator's recommended workspace (m).
/mobile_robot_width	Width of the mobile robot (m).
/base_link_offset	Height of the mobile robot's base_link (m).
/orientation_kP_value	kP value in orientation control.
/refresh_cycle	Global path refresh cycle (s).
/granularity	The step size to take between points on a given navigation trajectory (m).
/m_bl_to_ft	x-axis distance from manipulator's base link to front footprint (m).
/z_max	Maximum z value in manipulation (m).
/z_min	Minimum z value in manipulation (m).

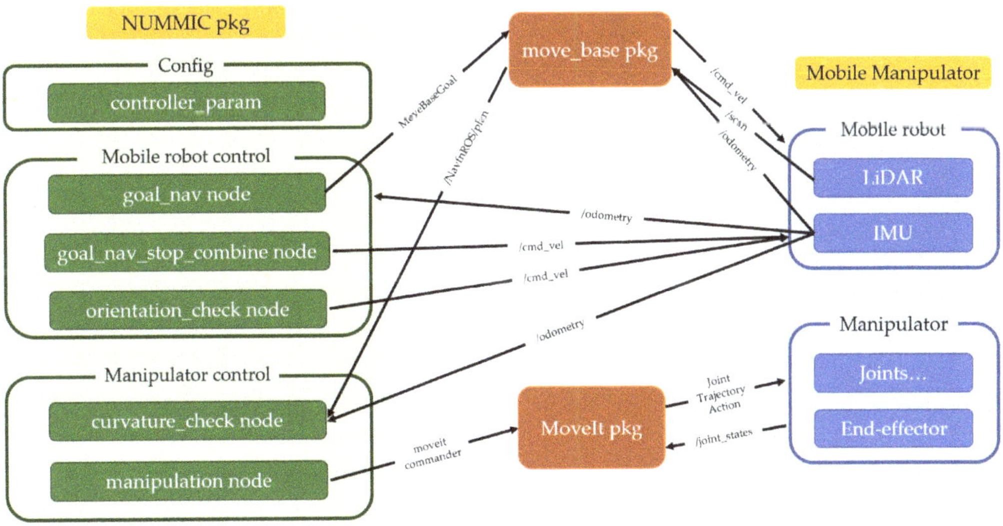

Figure 10. Topic exchanges between nodes in NUMMIC package based on ROS.

4. Experimental Setup

Prior to the experiment evaluating the suggested controller, we would like to explain the simulation world for the experiment, give a detailed specification of mobile manipulator, and the parameter values of NUMMIC and navigation package.

4.1. Simulation Worlds and Robotics Platforms

The simulation is performed for three different mobile manipulator platforms in two different worlds. Each simulation world, corresponding map files, and target coordinates are described at Figure 11. Among them, the simulation experiment in the first world involves the mobile manipulator, which always moves from the origin when motion planning for each target. Throughout this experiment, we can evaluate the mobile manipulator with the suggested controller on whether it can perform the motion planning from a fixed point to different places, avoiding the obstacles. The experiment in the second world involves the mobile manipulator that moves from MEP of previous target when it executes the motion planning for each target. Throughout the experiment, it is possible to verify that mobile manipulators existing in various locations can once again carry out motion planning towards different locations while avoiding obstacles. Also, since Test world #2 has a room-like structure in the middle, the mobile manipulator should pass through a narrow gap and exit the structure for motion planning toward Target 3 after Target 2. The experiment in such an environment is required to determine whether a collision exists during driving, which is important in a word of mobile manipulator using simultaneous control, and also it will be possible to verify the usefulness of the decision for MSS at the controller.

World	Test world #1	Test world #2
Appearance		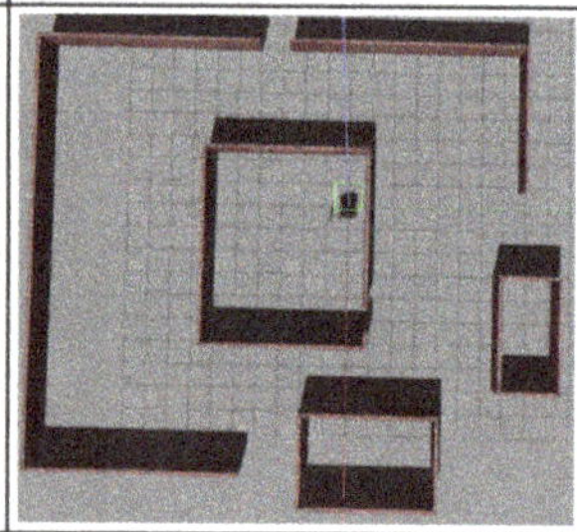
Map	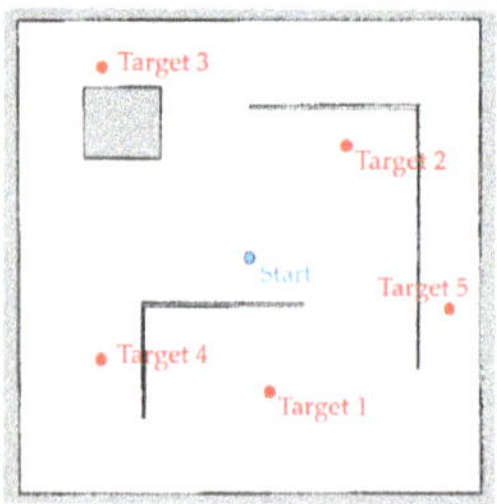	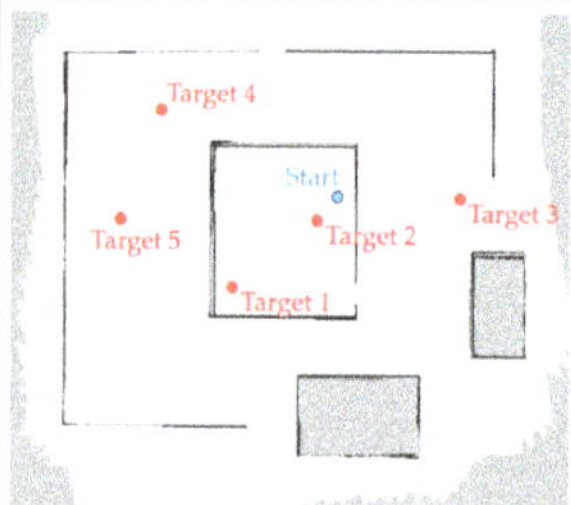
Target #	[x, y, z] coordinates (m)	
1	[6, 1, 0.4]	[4, −5, 0.35]
2	[−4, 5, 0.533]	[1, −1, 0.6]
3	[−8.5, −7, 0.6]	[0, 6, 0.533]
4	[4.5, −7, 0.7]	[−5, −9, 0.533]
5	[2, 9, 0.5]	[1, −11, 0.8]

Figure 11. Appearance of Test worlds for each simulation tests, their map files, and $[x, y, z]$ coordinates of target points.

As mentioned previously, the mobile manipulators used for the experiments are three different types: Husky UGV with UR3 (Husky_UR3), Husky UGV with UR5 (Husky_UR5), and Jackal UGV with Kinova Gen3 lite (Jackal_Kinova). The hardware specifications of each mobile manipulator can be found in Figure 12. In addition, there are some remarks for each mobile manipulator used in the experiment. First, Husky_UR3 and Husky_UR5 share the same mobile platform but since Husky_UR3 has a bracket structure between the mobile platform and the manipulator, and Husky_UR5 does not. The height of the first joint from the manipulator's base link is higher at Husky_UR3. Second, for the UR series provided by Universal Robots, there is a recommended reach separate from the maximum reach, but the Gen3 lite model from Kinova does not have the recommended reach described in the manual. Thus, when we used NUMMIC in the case of the UR series, the recommended reach value described in the manual was used for the parameters, but in the case of Gen3 lite, we reduced the appropriate value in the maximum reach and used it as recommended reach.

Model	Husky_UR3	Husky_UR5	Jackal_Kinova
Appearance			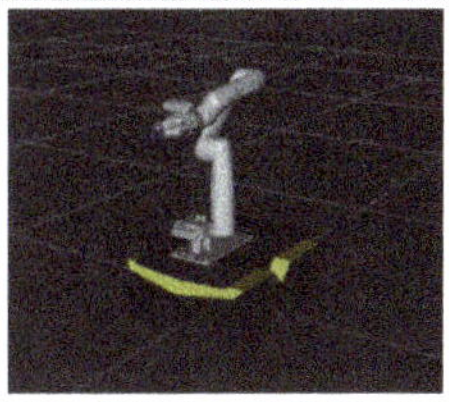
Mobile platform	**Husky UGV** External dimensions: 990 × 670 × 390 mm Internal dimensions: 296 × 411 × 155 mm Weight: 50 kg Payload: 75 kg Max speed: 1.0 m/s LiDAR: SICK-TIM571	**Husky UGV** External dimensions: 990 × 670 × 390 mm Internal dimensions: 296 × 411 × 155 mm Weight: 50 kg Payload: 75 kg Max speed: 1.0 m/s LiDAR: SICK-TIM571	**Jackal UGV** External dimensions: 508 × 430 × 250 mm Internal dimensions: 250 × 100 × 85 mm Weight: 17 kg Payload: 20 kg Max speed: 2.0 m/s LiDAR: SICK-TIM571
Manipulator	**UR3** Weight: 11 kg Payload: 3 kg Reach: 500 mm Degrees of freedom: 6 rotating joints Recommended reach: 450 mm	**UR5** Weight: 18.4 kg Payload: 5 kg Reach: 850 mm Degrees of freedom: 6 rotating joints Recommended reach: 750 mm	**Gen3 lite** Weight: 5.4 kg Payload: 0.5 kg Reach: 760 mm Degrees of freedom: 6 rotating joints

Figure 12. Hardware specifications of three mobile manipulators.

4.2. NUMMIC Parameters

In order to perform simultaneous control successfully for the mobile manipulator, it is necessary to put a proper parameter value according to the specifications of the mobile manipulator to be used. Although each parameter value is described sufficiently in the previous Section 3.4, this section will further explain why these values are added by the specifications. Parameters for each mobile manipulator used for experiments are represented at Table 2.

In the case of */first_joint_height*, Husky_UR3 and Husky_UR5, using similar manipulator and the same mobile platform, should have almost same value, but as described above, Husky_UR3 has a larger value due to the difference in bracket structure. The Jackal_Kinova model has the lowest platform height but its value is higher because of the structural characteristics of the manipulator. For the */between_base_link* parameter, Husky_UR3 and Husky_UR5 have the same value because the bracket structure mentioned earlier only affects the height, and Jacal_Kinoval's is close to 0 since the manipulator is attached to the center of the mobile platform. The values of */recommended_reach*, */mobile_robot_width*, and */base_link_offset* are input based on the hardware specification manual, and since only for Jackal_Kinova model */recommended_reach* value is not listed on the manual, the parameter which is obtained by subtracting the arbitrary value from the maximum value is used. High */orientation_KP_value* will reduce the time to control rotation but reduce the accuracy of motion planning, and vice versa. In this experiment, the same value is applied to all mobile manipulator models for variable control. Also, the */refresh_cycle* value is the same for each model due to variable control, even though reducing the value can affect better driving with more system loading. */granularity* and */m_bl_to_ft* are written based on the parameter values in the move_base package of mobile platforms used for each mobile manipulator. Therefore, for models using the same Husky UGV, the same parameter value is applied on the NUMMIC. In the case of */z_max* and */z_min*, the user can enter any value as long as the mobile manipulator specification allows it, but here, the value corresponding to the limit value of the specification is added. */z_max* is the z value that the manipulator can extend beyond the footprint of the mobile platform as much as possible, and */z_min* is the height value of LiDAR sensor attached to the mobile platform. The reason why */z_min* is set in this way is that if */z_min* is smaller than the height of LiDAR, the LiDAR sensor may be covered by manipulator and interfere with driving.

Table 2. Parameter values of NUMMIC package for each mobile manipulator used in experiments.

Parameters	Husky_UR3	Husky_UR5	Jackal_Kinova
/first_joint_height	0.533	0.474	0.52
/between_base_link	0.331	0.331	0.01
/recommended_reach	0.45	0.75	0.71
/mobile_robot_width	0.67	0.67	0.43
/base_link_offset	0.13	0.13	0.065
/orientation_KP_value	0.25	0.25	0.25
/refresh_cycle	3	3	3
/granularity	0.025	0.025	0.02
/m_bl_to_ft	0.169	0.169	0.25
/z_max	0.95	1.204	1.184
/z_min	0.312	0.312	0.25

4.3. Other Parameters

Since NUMMIC is operated at upper level of the move_base stack and MoveIt package, fine-tuning of these packages is significant for successful operation. In particular, the adjustment of parameters related to navigation plays a major role for the mobile manipulator to move successfully and efficiently to the MEP. In fact, this process should be delicately determined according to different specifications of each mobile manipulator and the configuration of the map, but in this paper, only the minimum parameter values are modified based on the default value in GitHub code supporting for each mobile platform from their companies. Because a duration of time, the time spent on Manipulation for evaluating algorithms in this paper is measured from the moment when the mobile manipulator enters the sigmoid distance proportional speed control area until the manipulation is completed. Fine-tuning of the parameter values might improve the total driving time or position error of end-effector but considering that the results of each algorithm are compared in this paper, the overall conclusion will be maintained.

Thus, we use Navfn [45] for the global path planner, and DWA planner [46] for the local path planner [47] based on navigation parameters in the repository for Husky UGV [48] and the repository for Jackal UGV [49]. *Inflation_radius* and *min_vel_x* values are modified slightly. For successful manipulation without collision at any points near the wall, the *inflation_radius* value is fixed at 0.1. Also, at Test world #2, to check whether designation of MSS is successfully carried out, the mobile manipulator should pass through the narrow gap between walls. Thus, we modify *min_vel_x* value to −0.1 and make the mobile platform temporarily move backward to pass the gap easily. The pose estimate of the mobile manipulator robot is performed by AMCL [50] that the most commonly used Monte-Carlo Localization (MCL) algorithm implemented on ROS. With the MoveIt package, the basic setting is performed based on the URDF of each manipulator arm using the supported MoveIt Setup Assistant [51]. Here, KDL Kinematics Plugin [52] was chosen for the kinematics solver.

5. Experimental Results

This section covers the analysis of the results of experiment for verifying our proposed controller's performance. In Section 5.1 we analyze the results for a total of 45 times of the manipulation test with three different mobile manipulators from Target 1 to 5 in the Test world #1 simulation environment. In Section 5.2 we repeat the previous motion planning test in Test world #2 and analyze the results. Lastly, in Section 5.3, we conduct two different motion planning scenarios four times each with an actual Husky_UR3 mobile manipulator robot in real environments and analyze the results for this experiment.

5.1. Experiment #1: Simulated Robots in Test World #1

Table 3 shows the comparison of the average duration of time value with respect to the result of motion planning for each target using Conventional algorithms and the NUMMIC suggested in this paper. The first algorithm for comparison is the sequential controller (SC) which controls the mobile manipulator in a sequential manner. This controller executes the manipulation after its mobile platform has completely finished moving. Because it is possible to compare performance with NUMMIC when it can do motion planning for various points in the map, only the idea of MEP of NUMMIC algorithm is applied in the process of driving the mobile platform. The second algorithm, simply combined only with move_base and MoveIt (OMM), controls only the mobile platform and manipulator arm simultaneously and does not contain the velocity control which is used with NUMMIC for stability in the motion planning process and MSS decision. Duration is a measure of the time between when the mobile manipulator enters the sigmoid distance proportional speed control area and when the manipulation is completed. The reason why duration is defined in this way is that when the overall motion planning time is calculated, the duration of time varies significantly, depending on the distance from the origin to target, thus it is difficult to compare each time for different control methods. Table 4 represents the average values of the Euclidean distance error of x-axis, y-axis, and x-y plane for target coordinates and the mobile manipulator's end-effector at the end of motion planning separately for each pre-mentioned algorithm. The reason why the error value about z-axis is not in the table is that the error on z-axis is always maintained at 0 compared to the errors on x-axis and y-axis which changed significantly by each algorithm.

Table 3. The result comparing the average values of duration using different algorithms for each mobile manipulator in Test world #1.

Average Duration of Time (S)	SC	OMM	NUMMIC
Husky_UR3	26.2	10.97	16.22
Husky_UR5	25.01	9.2	14.99
Jackal_Kinova	23.12	8.59	12.68

Table 4. The average values of error of end-effector after motion planning using different algorithms for each mobile manipulator in Test world #1.

Average Error (cm)	SC			OMM			NUMMIC		
	x	y	ED *	x	y	ED	x	y	ED
Husky_UR3	0.7	0.54	0.95	3.32	3.34	5.28	0.68	0.46	0.83
Husky_UR5	0.9	0.42	1.03	6.42	4.06	8.18	0.62	0.72	0.99
Jackal_Kinova	1.14	1.04	1.68	6.2	4.66	8.05	1.58	1.18	2.17

* Euclidean distance.

The result shows that the duration was reduced by about 41% for every mobile manipulator robot when we use NUMMIC for motion planning compared to the motion planning with the existing Sequential Controller. The simultaneous control of only move_base and MoveIt can reduce the time more drastically than the method proposed in this paper, but accuracy of motion planning becomes significantly lower. In fact, the control method using only move_base and MoveIt is about +400 to +700% which is a huge surge compared to Sequential Controller. On the other hand, NUMMIC has fewer errors than that of the controller with only move_base and MoveIt, which has −12% of decreasing error or +29% increasing error with Sequential Controller.

The reason for this result seems to be closely related to which process the errors in this experiment mainly come from. Since every error is shown on the x-axis and the y-axis, not on the z-axis, it is estimated that the errors in the end-effector position are caused mostly by the navigation process. There are various factors for the cause of errors in the navigation process including the error from the localization between the map file and driving environment, the error by the slip of wheel, and the error that occurs when starting and stopping. These navigation errors affect the motion planning of the mobile manipulator to make errors, and in the case of OMM, which has a particularly large error, it seems that a larger error has accumulated during the stopping at the MEP. Here, it suddenly stopped without velocity control in the sigmoid distance proportional speed control area, which is one of the NUMMIC's internal algorithm. Therefore, it takes less duration than NUMMIC, but a large slip occurs during a sudden stop and causes a large error in the end-effector position. On the other hand, in the case of NUMMIC, when entering a preset area, it stops in a stable manner at the MEP by sigmoid distance proportional speed control. This process makes a little time loss but it is still faster than Sequential Controller and, in terms of accuracy, it is not significantly different from Sequential Controller.

5.2. *Experiment #2: Simulated Robots in Test World #2*

The overall procedure is similar with previous Section 5.1. Table 5 compares the average value of duration for each target by algorithm, and Table 6 represents the average value of the Euclidean distance of the x-axis, y-axis, and x-y plane for the target coordinates and the mobile manipulator's end-effector after motion planning is completed by each algorithm. However, there is a noticeable point which differs between Tables 3 and 4 in Section 5.1. In the case of the control method with OMM applied to Husky_UR5, when the motion planning toward Target 3 from the position of Target 2 is executed, the manipulator always hits the wall and fails to execute. Thus, the tables below show the average value except for that result.

Table 5. The result comparing the average values of duration by different algorithms for each mobile manipulator in Test world #2.

Average Duration of Time (S)	SC	OMM	NUMMIC
Husky_UR3	23.92	9.98	15.25
Husky_UR5	24.73	11.37	15.5
Jackal_Kinova	22.72	8.19	13.49

Table 6. The average values of error of end-effector after motion planning by different algorithms for each mobile manipulator in Test world #2.

Average Error (cm)	SC			OMM			NUMMIC		
	x	y	ED *	x	y	ED	x	y	ED
Husky_UR3	0.36	0.66	0.79	5.3	5.68	8.12	0.32	0.62	0.72
Husky_UR5	0.38	0.58	0.77	1.88	2.58	3.62	0.62	0.84	1.15
Jackal_Kinova	1.7	1.52	2.48	4.22	4.86	6.77	1.52	1.08	2.14

* Euclidean distance.

Through the table, the experiment conducted in the Test world #2 shows similar results to 5.1 for all mobile manipulator robots. For NUMMIC, the duration is reduced by about 38% compared to the existing Sequential Controller. And for the method with only move_base and MoveIt, the duration greatly decreases compared to NUMMIC but there is a problem that the error on the end-effector position becomes too large.

Additionally, there are several results that can be established with this experiment. One of them is the collision between the manipulator and the wall during the motion planning from Target 2 to Target 3 with Husky_UR5 and the controller with only move_base and MoveIt, which are mentioned previously. This controller simply controls the mobile platform and the manipulator arm simultaneously without any additional tuning, and it might cause serious problem in the motion planning process. In the case of the manipulator of Husky_UR3 and Jackal_Kinova, there isn't any collision because of their short reach, but Husky_UR5's manipulator, which has relatively long reach, can hit the obstacles. This situation can be seen in Figure 13a. In the second scene of the figure, the mobile manipulator reaches out its arm and tries to pass through a narrow gap in the third scene, resulting in a collision, which causes a completely distorted costmap, as in fourth and fifth scene. With NUMMIC, as shown in Figure 13b, this collision does not occur because it goes through the process of determining the MSS through the global path. In fact, it does not implement the manipulation because there is an area with the risk of collision on the remaining global path until the second scene of Figure 13b. However, from the third scene, which depicts the mobile robot passing a narrow gap, it starts the manipulation and successfully completes the motion planning for the target point in the fifth scene.

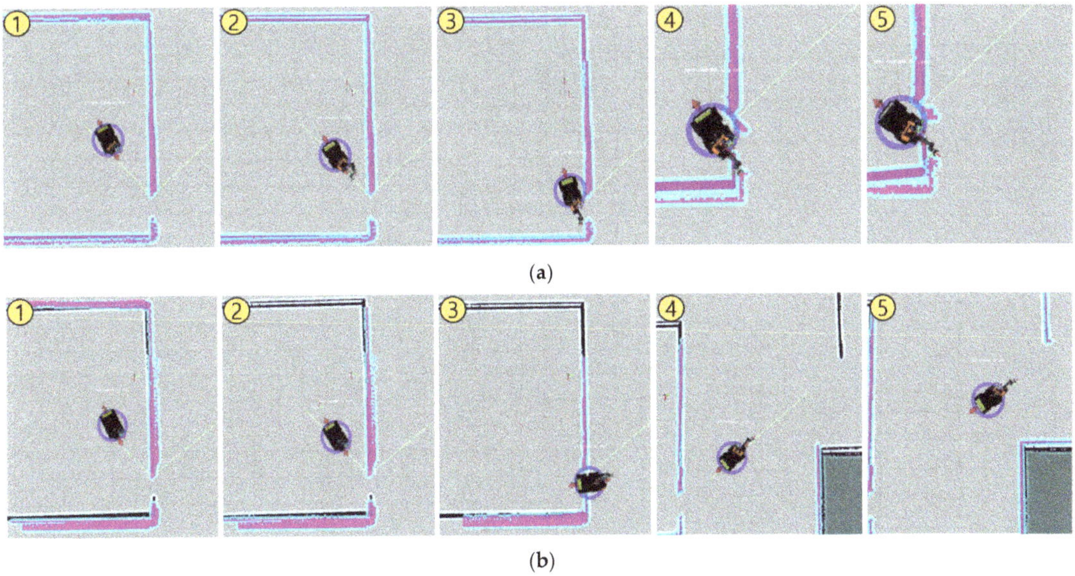

Figure 13. Both snapshots (**a**,**b**) show the process of motion planning from Target 2 to Target 3 in Test world #2 using Husky_UR5. (**a**) uses only move_base and MoveIt, and (**b**) uses the proposed NUMMIC controller.

In addition, although the tendency for the result values of each controller is maintained, the case with Jackal UGV always shows less duration and greater error compared with Husky UGV. This result seems to be because Jackal UGV itself has a higher maximum speed than Husky UGV, and the linear and angular accelerations in [48,49] GitHub repository which are referred to in this paper are set according to this property.

5.3. Experiment #3: Real Robot in a Real Environment

Lastly, we conducted Experiment #3 with a real Husky_UR3 robot to check whether NUMMIC works in real-world environment without any problems. The hardware specification of Husky_UR3 and the NUMMIC's parameter values are identical to the ones from the previous simulation. The map file of an actual environment is shown in Figure 14. This experiment is composed of two scenarios. In the first scenario, T01_Target [3, 0, 0.533] is designated as target coordinates based on the T01_Start point and the motion planning with NUMMIC is executed. Four motion planning experiments are repeated for the same point, and after each planning is completed, a laser point is applied to the end-effector to lower the foot of the perpendicular to measure which point is manipulated. In the second scenario, T02_Target [2.795, −7, 0.587] is set as target coordinates based on the T02_Start point and the motion planning with NUMMIC is done. In this scenario, the mobile manipulator must turn a corner before motion planning the target because of the structure of the hallway. In the same manner, four motion plannings are repeated for the same target, and the error between the position of end-effector and target coordinates is measured by the foot of the perpendicular in which a laser point is applied to the end-effector.

Figure 14. Map file of a real environment for the experiment. Each blue point, named T01_Start and T02_Start, represents the starting point of the mobile manipulator in the first and second scenarios. Each red point, named T01_Start and T02_Start, represents the target point of the mobile manipulator in the first and second scenarios.

Figure 15 shows the motion planning from T01_Start to T01_Target point sequentially. Since there is no collision risk zone on the path to the target, manipulation is performed at the same time as driving (Second scene of Figure 15). After that, when it enters within a specific distance from the target point, the motion planning is successfully performed by the distance proportional speed control using sigmoid function and stopping at the MEP. Figure 16 depicts motion planning from T02_Start to T02_Target point. In this scenario, there is a high-curvature point on the path, which is an area at risk of collision, thus before passing the section, the manipulator maintains the default pose (second scene of Figure 16) and the moment it passes the section, it starts manipulation (third scene of Figure 16).

In this way, the NUMMIC operates as designed, but in terms of accuracy, the result is clearly worse than that of the simulation. Table 7 compares the average values of the error between the target coordinates and the mobile manipulator's end-effector position after finishing each motion planning experiments: T01 and T02. In an actual experiment, since there is an uneven floor or an error on the manipulation that does not appear in the simulation, the error in the z-axis occurred even if it is not large compared to that in the x-y

plane. Therefore, errors are also stated based on all x, y, z axes and Euclidean distance in three dimensions.

Figure 15. Snapshots of the experiment in the first scenario at real environment.

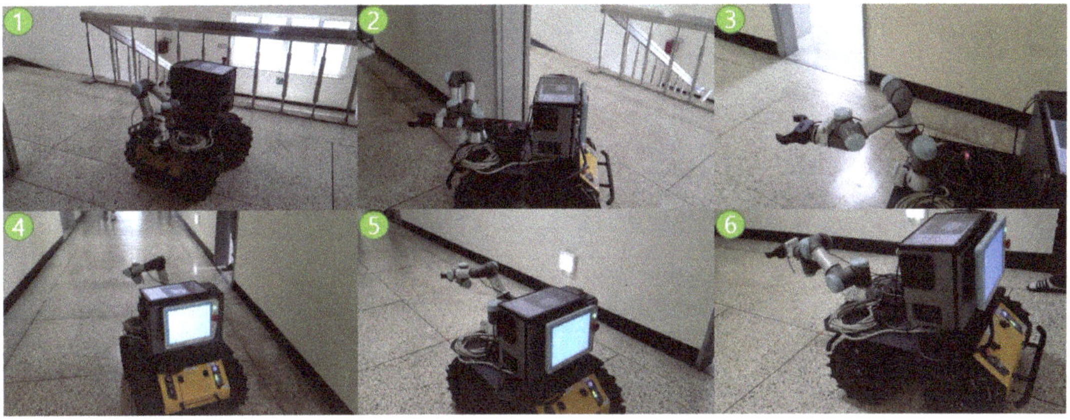

Figure 16. Snapshots of the experiment in the second scenario at real environment.

Table 7. The error values of end-effector position after motion planning in a real environment. T01 is the result of the first scenario, and T02 is the result of the second scenario.

Average Error (cm)	x	y	z	Euclidean Distance
T01	2.3	2.1	0.075	3.62
T02	3.08	8.05	0.15	9.2

However, similar to the previous simulation, this result is estimated to have accumulated larger errors in the navigation process rather than derived from NUMMIC itself. In fact, prior experiments show that a significant number of errors are caused by problems from the navigation process. Since more varied non-systematic errors are easier to intervene in in real environments, the increase in errors in real environments compared to the simulation is a phenomenon that occurs in most navigation-related experiments. In the experiment of T02, which has particularly larger errors than in the simulation, most of the causes seem to have been due to the localization process between the map and the real environment, and this can be estimated in relation to the direction in which the error is large. T01 shows a relatively uniform error in the x-axis and y-axis, but the error of the y-axis in T02 is much larger than that of the x-axis. This is because in the T02 scenario the robot drives on a straight hallway and this environment lacks a point to grasp the feature, which creates a large error in the direction due to the characteristics of the localization algorithm. Thus, we can conclude that although NUMMIC operates in the same way as the simulation, due to the characteristic of the real environment, a larger error is accumulated in the navigation stage, which focuses on localization, and the manipulation stage. We expect that the errors in the entire motion planning process can also be overcome by installing additional sensors or algorithms to reduce errors from the localization stage.

6. Conclusions

In this paper, we proposed the NUMMIC for the mobile manipulator robot, which is able to execute in a stable manner motion planning in various environments with simultaneous control and has more time benefits than the traditional sequential control method. Here, the various environments mean that the mobile manipulator can work under various surroundings including obstacles, while also meaning that the controller can be used in different types of mobile manipulator model. What makes it possible are the structural characteristics of NUMMIC, which is composed of the designation of the MEP that selects a stable position for manipulation at different environments, the designation of the default pose position of the manipulator to help manipulation efficiently, and the safety check for the manipulator during the motion planning toward target. These three aspects control the mobile platform and the manipulator arm by tuning the move_base and MoveIt packages. Thus, any mobile manipulator platform can use this controller only if it is a mobile manipulator, the mobile platform is attached to a single manipulator arm with LiDAR and IMU sensor, and it has a URDF about the robot. This controller was tested in simulations by two different maps and three mobile manipulator platforms which have different specifications and confirmed that it operated in any environment in a stable manner. Also, in the test with real robots, the overall operation was similar to the simulation results, even though there were some errors caused by the localization process.

In the future, we will focus on reducing errors in motion planning which are inferred from the localization process and the grasping algorithm. For those, we suppose that the process for obtaining data about the grasped object using an additional camera on the wrist near the manipulator's end effector is needed. Using NUMMIC, it will be able to reduce the error in motion planning with the method continuously checking whether it can grasp the target object at current MEP or not when the camera captures the target object while the robot moves to MEP for grasping. Also, if the grasping algorithm is added to the final process of NUMMIC using the data, this simultaneous controller for mobile manipulator can be used instantly for work such as pick and place in various environments.

Author Contributions: Conceptualization, T.K.; methodology, T.K. and M.K.; software, T.K.; validation, T.K. and D.K.; formal analysis, T.K.; investigation, T.K. and S.Y.; resources, T.K., M.K. and S.Y.; writing—original draft preparation, T.K.; writing—review and editing, T.K., M.K., S.Y. and D.K.; visualization, T.K.; supervision, D.K. All authors have read and agreed to the published version of the manuscript.

Funding: This research was funded by the Ministry of Trade, Industry and Energy (MOTIE), South Korea, under the Industrial Technology Innovation Program under Grant 20004315, 20009008 and the Korea Institute for Advancement of Technology, Grant P0017033 and the BK21 plus program through the National Research Foundation (NRF) funded by the Ministry of Education of Korea (No.5120200313836) and partly supported by the Institute of Information & Communications Technology Planning & Evaluation (IITP) grant funded by the Korean government (MSIT) (No.RS-2022-00150000, Artificial Intelligence Convergence Innovation Human Resources Development (Kyung Hee University)).

Institutional Review Board Statement: Not applicable.

Informed Consent Statement: Not applicable.

Data Availability Statement: Not applicable.

Acknowledgments: We would like to thank the anonymous reviewers and academic editor for their comments and suggestions. T.K. would like to thank his brother, Gyeongmin, for his support and help.

Conflicts of Interest: The authors declare no conflict of interest.

References

1. Belanche, D.; Casaló, L.V.; Flavián, C.; Schepers, J. Service robot implementation: A theoretical framework and research agenda. *Serv. Ind. J.* **2020**, *40*, 203–205. [CrossRef]
2. Jae-Bong, Y.; Seung-Joon, Y. Mobile Manipulation for the HSR Intelligent Home Service Robot. In Proceedings of the 16th International Conference on Ubiquitous Robots (UR), Jeju, Korea, 24–27 June 2019.
3. Chen, F.; Selvaggio, M.; Caldwell, G.D. Dexterous Grasping by Manipulability Selection for Mobile Manipulator with Visual Guidance. *IEEE Trans. Ind. Inform.* **2019**, *15*, 1202–1210. [CrossRef]
4. Zhou, K.; Ebenhofer, G.; Eitzinger, C.; Zimmermann, U.; Walter, C.; Saenz, J.; Castaño, P.L.; Hernández, A.F.M.; Oriol, N.J. Mobile Manipulator Is Coming to Aerospace Manufacturing Industry. In Proceedings of the IEEE International Symposium on Robotic and Sensors Environments (ROSE), Timisoara, Romania, 16–18 October 2014.
5. Andaluz, V.H.; Sásig, E.R.; Chicaiza, W.D.; Velasco, P.M. Linear Algebra Applied to Kinematic Control of Mobile Manipulators. *IT Converg. Secur.* **2017**, *449*, 297–306.
6. Mashali, M.; Wu, L.; Alqasemi, R.; Dubey, R. Controlling a Non-Holonomic Mobile Manipulator in a Constrained Floor Space. In Proceedings of the 2018 IEEE International Conference on Robotics and Automation (ICRA), Brisbane, Australia, 21–25 May 2018.
7. Zhou, S.; Yazhini, C.P.; Peter, C.Y.C. Simultaneous Base and End-Effector Motion Control of a Nonholonomic Mobile Manipulator. In Proceedings of the 6th International Conference on Automation, Robotics and Applications, Queenstown, New Zealand, 17–19 February 2015.
8. Sandakalum, T.; Ang, M.H., Jr. Motion Planning for Mobile Manipulators—A Systematic Review. *Machines* **2022**, *10*, 97. [CrossRef]
9. Sucan, I.; Kay, J. Urdf. Available online: https://wiki.ros.org/urdf (accessed on 25 May 2022).
10. Garage, W.; Stanford Artificial Intelligence Laboratory; Open Robotics. Robotic Operating System. Available online: www.ros.org (accessed on 6 December 2021).
11. Marder-Eppstein, E. Move_Base. Available online: https://wiki.ros.org/move_base (accessed on 6 December 2021).
12. Loan, A.S.; Chitta, S. MoveIt. Available online: https://moveit.ros.org (accessed on 6 December 2021).
13. Universal Robot Ur3. Available online: https://www.universal-robots.com/products/ur3-robot/ (accessed on 2 May 2022).
14. Husky Unmanned Ground Vehicle. Available online: https://clearpathrobotics.com/husky-unmanned-ground-vehicle-robot/ (accessed on 2 May 2022).
15. Universal Robot Ur5. Available online: https://www.universal-robots.com/products/ur5-robot/ (accessed on 2 May 2022).
16. Discover Our Gen3 Lite Robot. Available online: www.kinovarobotics.com/product/gen3-lite-robots (accessed on 23 June 2022).
17. Jackal Unmanned Ground Vehicle. Available online: https://clearpathrobotics.com/jackal-small-unmanned-ground-vehicle/ (accessed on 23 June 2022).
18. Ventator, E.; Lee, G.S.; Newman, W. Hardware and software architecture of ABBY: An industrial mobile manipulator. In Proceedings of the 2013 IEEE International Conference on Automation Science and Engineering (CASE), Madison, WI, USA, 17–20 August 2013.
19. Meng, J.; Wang, S.; Li, G.; Jiang, L.; Zhang, X.; Lui, C.; Xie, Y. Iterative-learning error compensation for autonomous parking of mobile manipulator in harsh industrial environment. *Robot. Comput.-Integr. Manuf.* **2021**, *68*, 102077. [CrossRef]
20. Štibinger, P.; Broughton, G.; Majer, F.; Rozsypálek, Z.; Wang, A.; Jindal, K.; Zhou, A.; Thakur, D. Mobile Manipulator for Autonomous Localization, Grasping and Precise Placement of Construction Material in a Semi-Structured Environment. *IEEE Robot. Autom. Lett.* **2021**, *6*, 2595–2602. [CrossRef]
21. Vatavuk, I.; Vasiljević, G.; Kovačić, Z. Task Space Model Predictive Control for Vineyard Spraying with a Mobile Manipulator. *Agriculture* **2022**, *12*, 381. [CrossRef]
22. Colucci, G.; Botta, A.; Tagliavini, L.; Cavallone, P.; Baglieri, L.; Quaglia, G. Kinematic Modeling and Motion Planning of the Mobile Manipulator Agri.Q for Precision Agriculture. *Machines* **2022**, *10*, 321. [CrossRef]
23. Vineet, S.; Deshmukh, D.; Pratihar, D.K.; Deb, A.K.; Ray, H.; Bhattacharyya, H. Dynamic Analysis of Tracked Mobile Manipulator Used in Agriculture. In Proceedings of the 2021 IEEE 18th India Council International Conference, Guwahati, India, 19–21 December 2021.
24. Naazare, M.; Rosas, F.G.; Schulz, D. Online Next-Best-View Planner for 3D-Exploration and Inspection With a Mobile Manipulator Robot. *IEEE Robot. Autom. Lett.* **2022**, *7*, 3779–3786. [CrossRef]
25. Colucci, G.; Tagliavini, L.; Carbonari, L.; Cavallone, P.; Botta, A.; Quaglia, G. Paquitop.arm, a Mobile Manipulator for Assessing Emerging Challenges in the COVID-19 Pandemic Scenario. *Robotics* **2021**, *10*, 102. [CrossRef]
26. Li, Z.; Moran, P.; Dong, Q.; Shaw, R.J.; Hauser, K. Development of a tele-nursing mobile manipulator for remote care-giving in quarantine areas. In Proceedings of the 2017 IEEE International Conference on Robotics and Automation (ICRA), Singapore, 29 May–3 June 2017; pp. 3581–3586.
27. Akli, I.; Bouzouia, B.; Achour, N. Motion analysis of a mobile manipulator executing pick-up tasks. *Comput. Electr. Eng.* **2015**, *43*, 257–269. [CrossRef]
28. Vazquez-Santiago, K.; Goh, C.F.; Shimada, K. Motion Planning for Kinematically Redundant Mobile Manipulators with Genetic Algorithm, Pose Interpolation, and Inverse Kinematics. In Proceedings of the 2021 IEEE 17th International Conference on Automation Science and Engineering (CASE), Lyon, France, 23–27 August 2021; pp. 1167–1174.
29. Li, Q.; Mu, Y.; You, Y.; Zhang, Z.; Feng, C. A Hierarchical Motion Planning for Mobile Manipulator. *IEEJ Trans. Electr. Electron. Eng.* **2020**, *15*, 1390–1399. [CrossRef]

30. Stulp, F.; Fedrizzi, A.; Mösenlechner, L.; Beetz, M. Learning and Reasoning with Action-Related Places for Robust Mobile Manipulation. *J. Artif. Intell. Res.* **2012**, *43*, 1–42. [CrossRef]
31. Wang, C.; Zhang, Q.; Tian, Q.; Li, S.; Wang, X.; Lane, D.; Petillot, Y.; Wang, S. Learning Mobile Manipulation through Deep Reinforcement Learning. *Sensors* **2020**, *20*, 939. [CrossRef] [PubMed]
32. Moreno, F.-A.; Monroy, J.; Ruiz-Sarmiento, J.-R.; Galindo, C.; Gonzalez-Jimenez, J. Automatic Waypoint Generation to Improve Robot Navigation Through Narrow Spaces. *Sensors* **2020**, *20*, 240. [CrossRef] [PubMed]
33. da Silva Lubanco, D.L.; Pichler-Scheder, M.; Schlechter, T. A Novel Frontier-Based Exploration Algorithm for Mobile Robots. In Proceedings of the 2020 6th International Conference on Mechatronics and Robotics Engineering (ICMRE), Barcelona, Spain, 12–15 February 2020.
34. Gerkey, B. Gmapping. Available online: https://wiki.ros.org/gmapping (accessed on 2 May 2022).
35. Conner, D.C.; Willis, J. Flexible Navigation: Finite state machine-based integrated navigation and control for ROS enabled robots. In Proceedings of the SoutheastCon 2017, Concord, NC, USA, 30 March–2 April 2017; pp. 1–8.
36. Choi, Y.J.; Ramatryana, I.N.A.; Shin, S.Y. Cellular Communication-Based Autonomous UAV Navigation with Obstacle Avoidance for Unknown Indoor Environments. *Int. J. Intell. Eng. Syst.* **2012**, *14*, 344–352. [CrossRef]
37. Fernandez Carmona, M.; Parekh, T.; Hanheide, M. Making the Case for Human-Aware Navigation in Warehouses. In *Towards Autonomous Robotic Systems*; Lecture Notes in Computer Science; Althoefer, K., Konstantinova, J., Zhang, K., Eds.; Springer International Publishing: Cham, Switzerland, 2019; pp. 449–453.
38. Chen, L.; Wei, Z.; Zhao, F.; Tao, T. Development of a virtual teaching pendant system for serial robots based on ROS-I. In Proceedings of the 2017 IEEE International Conference on Cybernetics and Intelligent Systems (CIS) and IEEE Conference on Robotics, Automation and Mechatronics (RAM), Ningbo, China, 19–21 November 2017; pp. 720–724.
39. Wang, Z.; Gong, L.; Chen, Q.; Li, Y.; Liu, C.; Huang, Y. Rapid Developing the Simulation and Control Systems for a Multifunctional Autonomous Agricultural Robot with ROS. In *Intelligent Robotics and Applications*; Lecture Notes in Computer Science; Silva, M., Luís Lima, J., Reis, L., Sanfeliu, A., Tardioli, D., Eds.; Springer International Publishing: Cham, Switzerland, 2016; pp. 26–39.
40. Sepúlveda, D.; Fernández, R.; Navas, E.; González-de-Santos, P.; Armada, M. ROS Framework for Perception and Dual-Arm Manipulation in Unstructured Environments. In *Robot 2019: Fourth Iberian Robotics Conference*; Advances in Intelligent Systems and Computing; Silva, M., Luís Lima, J., Reis, L., Sanfeliu, A., Tardioli, D., Eds.; Springer International Publishing: Cham, Switzerland, 2019; pp. 137–147.
41. Roldán, J.J.; Peña-Tapia, E.; Garcia-Aunon, P.; Del Cerro, J.; Barrientos, A. Bringing Adaptive and Immersive Interfaces to Real-World Multi-Robot Scenarios: Application to Surveillance and Intervention in Infrastructures. *IEEE Access* **2019**, *7*, 86319–86335. [CrossRef]
42. Hershberger, D.; Gossow, D.; Faust, J. RViz. Available online: https://wiki.ros.org/rviz (accessed on 6 December 2021).
43. Lu, D. Global_Planner. Available online: https://wiki.ros.org/global_planner (accessed on 10 May 2021).
44. Qualia, T. Nummic. Available online: https://github.com/QualiaT/nummic (accessed on 15 July 2022).
45. Konolige, K.; Marder-Eppstein, E. Navfn. Available online: http://wiki.ros.org/navfn (accessed on 20 June 2022).
46. Marder-Eppstein, E. Dwa_Local_Planner. Available online: http://wiki.ros.org/dwa_local_planner (accessed on 20 June 2022).
47. Marder-Eppstein, E.; Perko, E. Base_Local_Planner. Available online: http://wiki.ros.org/base_local_platnner (accessed on 20 June 2022).
48. Husky. Available online: https://github.com/husky/husky (accessed on 20 June 2022).
49. Jackal. Available online: https://github.com/jackal/jackal (accessed on 20 June 2022).
50. Gerkey, B. Amcl. Available online: https://wiki.ros.org/amcl (accessed on 20 June 2022).
51. Ioan, A. Sucan and Sachin Chitta, MoveIt Setup Assistant. Available online: http://docs.ros.org/en/melodic/api/moveit_tutorials/html/doc/setup_assistant/setup_assistant_tutorial.html#moveit-setup-assistant (accessed on 20 June 2022).
52. Smits, R.; Aertbelien, E.; Orocos Developers. Kdl. Available online: http://wiki.ros.org/kdl (accessed on 20 June 2022).

sensors

MDPI

Article

Research on Monocular-Vision-Based Finger-Joint-Angle-Measurement System

Yongfei Feng, Mingwei Zhong and Fangyan Dong *

Faculty of Mechanical Engineering & Mechanics, Ningbo University, Ningbo 315211, China
* Correspondence: dongfangyan@nbu.edu.cn

Abstract: The quantitative measurement of finger-joint range of motion plays an important role in assessing the level of hand disability and intervening in the treatment of patients. An industrial monocular-vision-based knuckle-joint-activity-measurement system is proposed with short measurement time and the simultaneous measurement of multiple joints. In terms of hardware, the system can adjust the light-irradiation angle and the light-irradiation intensity of the marker by actively adjusting the height of the light source to enhance the difference between the marker and the background and reduce the difficulty of segmenting the target marker and the background. In terms of algorithms, a combination of multiple-vision algorithms is used to compare the image-threshold segmentation and Hough outer- and inner linear detection as the knuckle-activity-range detection method of the system. To verify the accuracy of the visual-detection method, nine healthy volunteers were recruited for experimental validation, and the experimental results showed that the average angular deviation in the flexion/extension of the knuckle was 0.43° at the minimum and 0.59° at the maximum, and the average angular deviation in the adduction/abduction of the knuckle was 0.30° at the minimum and 0.81° at the maximum, which were all less than 1°. In the multi-angle velocimetry experiment, the time taken by the system was much less than that taken by the conventional method.

Keywords: monocular vision; human joint angle measurement; visual detection method; hand disability

Citation: Feng, Y.; Zhong, M.; Dong, F. Research on Monocular-Vision-Based Finger-Joint-Angle-Measurement System. *Sensors* **2022**, *22*, 7276. https://doi.org/10.3390/s22197276

Academic Editor: Salvatore Pirozzi

Received: 21 August 2022
Accepted: 21 September 2022
Published: 26 September 2022

Publisher's Note: MDPI stays neutral with regard to jurisdictional claims in published maps and institutional affiliations.

1. Introduction

The quantitative measurement of hand-joint range of motion (ROM) is important for clinicians to assess a patient's level of hand disability and the effectiveness of intervention therapy. In the clinical setting, knuckle goniometers are often used to measure ROM due to their ease of use, portability, and affordability. However, these devices are time-consuming for single-joint angle measurements and do not allow simultaneous multi-joint angle measurements. Many experts and scholars have conducted in-depth research in the field of knuckle-angle measurement, including wearable-sensor-based knuckle-angle-measurement methods and vision-based knuckle-angle-measurement methods. Okuyama et al. developed a finger-joint-angle-measurement system based on flexible polymer sensors [1]. The system measures the flexion/extension movement of fingers by installing flexible polymer sensors on the surfaces of fingers, which can realize the detection of joint-angle changes during daily grasping movements. A three-dimensional (3-D) finger-motion-measurement system based on a soft sensor was proposed by Park et al. [2]. Changcheng et al. designed an integrated mechanical-sensor detection system, consisting of an angle-measurement device and a measurement circuit in order to achieve finger-joint measurement [3]. The effectiveness of the system was verified by joint-angle measurement, motion-law evaluation and object-grasping experiments, and the experimental results showed that the root mean square (RMS) of the DIP, PIP, and MCP angle-measurement errors were 0.36, 0.59, and 0.32 degrees, respectively [3]. It has been found that these wearable-sensor-based finger-joint-angle measurement methods have high accuracy in measuring finger joint angles, but the difficulty in wearing them has not been effectively solved in clinical applications for patients with hand motor dysfunction [4–10].

Vision-based knuckle-angle-measurement systems could realize the dynamic measurement of multi-joint angles without involving direct physical contact between the doctor and the patient's hand. Vision-based measurement systems work by first capturing an image of the entire hand and then using computer-vision techniques to estimate the hand posture [11–15]. Commercial devices (such as Leap Motion) are currently used for hand-angle measurement [16,17] and, recently, they have been used in virtual-reality headsets (such as Facebook's OculusQuest and Microsoft's HoloLens2) equipped with hand tracking for human–computer interaction. The two main problems faced by current vision-based hand-posture estimation systems are the low accuracy of the knuckle-angle measurement and the high level of restriction on the camera view [18]. Lee J.W. et al. proposed a method of measuring finger-joint angles and finger forces in the process of maximum cylindrical grip using a multi-camera photogrammetric method with markers and a pressure-sensitive film, respectively [19]. The experimental results showed that this method can be used to judge the extension/flexion direction of the knuckle.

An industrial monocular-vision-based knuckle-angle-measurement system based on the existing computer-vision detection system is proposed in this paper [20]. This knuckle-angle-measurement system consists of a hardware system, a vision system, and a control system. The hand visual markers in the hardware system can simplify the difficulty of knuckle identification, and the use of high-resolution cameras can greatly improve the accuracy of the knuckle-angle detection. The active multi-angle light-detection system consisting of the control system, hardware system, and specified light source can adjust the light-irradiation angle and light-source-irradiation intensity to the marker by adjusting the height of the light source, thus enhancing the difference between the marker and the background, making the marker easy to the segment from the background and simplifying the marker-segmentation process.

2. Biological Structure of Human Fingers and Their Movement Characteristics

2.1. Structural Composition of the Human Hand

The human hand consists of the index finger (IF), middle finger (MF), ring finger (RF), little finger (LF), and thumb (TUM). The IF, MF, RF, and LF consist of one degree of freedom (DOF) distal phalangeal (DIP), one DOF proximal phalangeal (PIP), and two-DOF metacarpophalangeal (MCP) and two-DOF carpometacarpal (CMC) joints, respectively. The thumb consists of a one-DOF distal phalangeal joint (IP), a two-DOF metacarpophalangeal joint (MCP), and a two-DOF carpometacarpal joint (TM) [21], as shown in Figure 1.

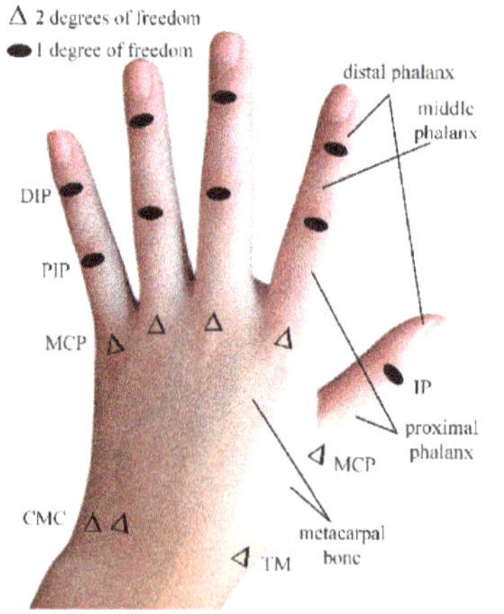

Figure 1. Structural components of the human hand.

2.2. Finger-Movement Characteristics

The movement of hand joints is mainly manifested by the abduction/adduction and flexion/extension movements of the four fingers and the thumb. The movement of human fingers has the following characteristics: (1) the DIP and PIP joints of the four fingers other than the thumb are bound to each other and meet; (2) when the MCP joint of the four fingers other than the thumb is flexed, the adjacent MCP joint is also flexed. According to the Evaluation of Rehabilitation Therapy, the ROM of the human finger joint and traditional measurement methods can be determined, as shown in Figure 2.

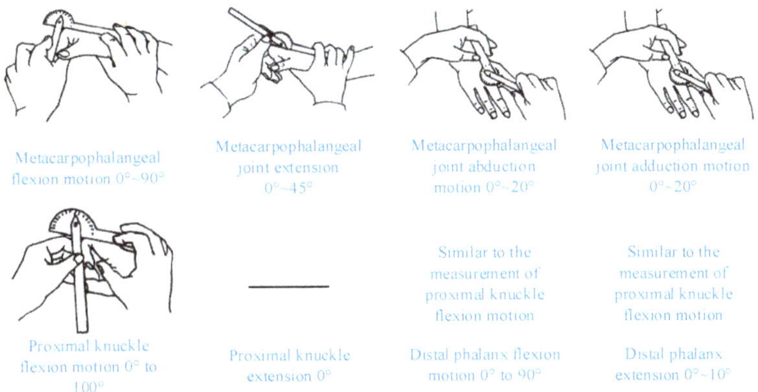

Figure 2. Human finger-joint range of motion and measurement methods.

3. Experimental-Platform Construction

Machine-vision technology has been developed, including hardware and software, but in the computer-vision measurement system, the design and layout of the lighting system is still a pivotal link, which can often significantly affect the performance of the vision-measurement system. A good illumination system can greatly enhance the difference between the measurement target and the measurement background, improve the system imaging, and make the target easier to identify and segment, thus simplifying the time and hardware cost required for program calculation. The different arrangements of light-source systems in the field of defect detection are often divided into passive multi-angle illumination-detection methods and active multi-angle illumination-detection methods. Considering the different characteristics of the two lighting methods, the active multi-angle lighting-detection method was selected as the light source arrangement method in the experimental platform.

3.1. Design of Experimental Platform

The core of the active multi-angle light-source detection method is the machine-vision-detection part; therefore, the quality of the acquired images and the speed of the image processing have a greater impact on the visual-detection effect. The quality of the camera hardware determines the quality of the image acquisition, and a high-performance, high-resolution camera can produce image data containing clear features under the irradiation of a highly stable light source, while a clear image is the basis for ensuring the stable operation of the image-processing algorithm and the detection effect of the system, which shows that the selection and design of the detection hardware are also particularly important. Based on the finger-joint-angle-measurement-system scheme, the actual system built in this study is shown in Figure 3. In Figure 3, Figure 3a represents the angle detection in the finger flexion/extension state, and Figure 3b represents the angle detection in the finger abduction/adduction state. Through this platform, high-quality multi-angle light-source-irradiated multivariate images can be acquired; subsequently, through the PC image-processing algorithm, these can be processed to segment the finger-joint identifiers in the image for the subsequent calculation of the finger-joint angle and length.

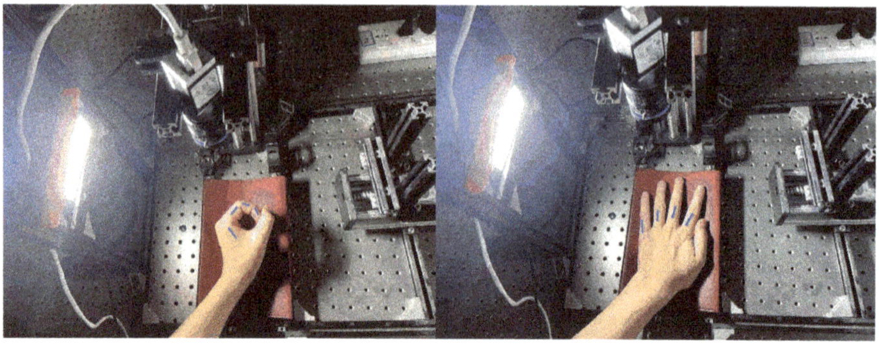

(**a**) (**b**)

Figure 3. Finger-joint-angle-detection platform.

3.2. Light-Source Selection and Solution of the Single-Reflection Matrix

Industrial cameras are at the core of the vision-inspection system, and their main role is to convert the optical signal into an electrical signal and transmit it to the processing unit. As the most important part of the industrial camera, the light-sensitive element is of two main types: CCD (charge-coupled element) and CMOS (complementary metal oxide semiconductor). Furthermore, CCD technology is more widely used. Industrial cameras have many important parameters, such as resolution, shutter time, external trigger, frame rate, etc. Therefore, the vision-inspection system should take into account the needs of the inspection task to select the most appropriate camera. Depending on the interface type of the camera, it can be divided into USB, GigE, and camera link. Considering the advantages of the data-transmission speed, ease of use, and data-transmission distance, the GigE interface camera in Basler ace was selected.

In the inspection system, the choice of industrial lens directly affects the quality of the captured image. The industrial-lens parameters, such as interface type and CCD size, should be matched with the industrial camera. In addition, the aperture of the lens controls the light intake of the industrial camera, which exerts a direct impact on the brightness of the image; the focal length directly affects the size of the field of view, representing the vertical distance from the imaging plane to the center of the lens. Considering these lens characteristics, the lens selected in this study was TEC-V7X.

The light source is another important component of the visual inspection system, which is to determine the key to clear and stable imaging. The choice of the light source should highlight the object to be detected. According to the classification of light-emitting devices in the light source, the light source can be divided into fluorescent lamps, LED lamps, halogen lamps, etc., of which LED lamps are the most common. The light source selected for this paper was the ring light source of model R50-26-13, developed by Huakang Technology Company.

The transformation of the camera coordinate system, x-y-z, into the two-dimensional image coordinate system, u-v, is shown in Equation (1).

$$\begin{bmatrix} u \\ v \\ 1 \end{bmatrix} = s \begin{bmatrix} f_x & \gamma & u_0 \\ 0 & f_y & v_0 \\ 0 & 0 & 1 \end{bmatrix} \begin{bmatrix} r_1 & r_2 & t \end{bmatrix} \begin{bmatrix} x_W \\ y_W \\ 1 \end{bmatrix} \quad (1)$$

where $\begin{bmatrix} f_x & \gamma & u_0 \\ 0 & f_y & v_0 \\ 0 & 0 & 1 \end{bmatrix}$ is the internal reference matrix of the camera and $\begin{bmatrix} r_1 & r_2 & t \end{bmatrix}$ is the external reference matrix of the camera. This leads to the formula for calculating the single-response matrix of the camera and the conversion formula for converting the pixel coordinates of the image to world coordinates as:

$$\begin{cases} \boldsymbol{H} = s\begin{bmatrix} f_x & \gamma & u_0 \\ 0 & f_y & v_0 \\ 0 & 0 & 1 \end{bmatrix}\begin{bmatrix} r_1 & r_2 & t \end{bmatrix} = s\boldsymbol{M}\begin{bmatrix} r_1 & r_2 & t \end{bmatrix} \\ s\boldsymbol{X} = \boldsymbol{H}^{-1}\boldsymbol{x} \end{cases} \tag{2}$$

where $\boldsymbol{H}$ is the single-response matrix, $\boldsymbol{x}$ is the pixel coordinate in the image, and $\boldsymbol{X}$ is the world coordinate.

The above coordinate-system-conversion Equation (2) is used to obtain the single response matrix $\boldsymbol{H}$ from the pixel-coordinate system to one of the plane-coordinate systems (W) in space. Using $\boldsymbol{H}$, two points in the pixel-coordinate system can be converted into W. The distance s1 between two points in W is calculated, after which a ruler is used to directly measure the actual distance s2 between the corresponding two points in W. The error result of comparing s1 and s2 is 0.073 mm. However, when the relative distance between W and the camera changes, the error between s1 and s2 becomes dramatically larger. Therefore, during the finger-joint-angle measurement, the position of the detection plane relative to the camera should always be constant, and $\boldsymbol{H}$ should be updated in time when the distance of the camera relative to the detection plane changes.

4. Vision-Based Finger-Joint-Angle-and-Length-Detection Method

The finger-joint angle-and-length-detection method proposed in this paper is a joint-angle-detection method for visual-identifier-segmentation reprocessing. The method mainly consists of finger-joint-identifier pasting and image acquisition, visual identifier segmentation, the edge detection of visual identifiers, and joint-angle calculation based on the different joint identifiers of the finger. In the visual-identifier-segmentation method, the HSV color-space-conversion method and image-threshold segmentation method were adopted in this study to segment the finger-joint identifiers in the image. In the finger-joint-angle-calculation method, the inner and outer edge Hough straight-line-detection method and the least-squares method of fitting a straight line are used. Therefore, a finger-joint-angle image produces 2 × 2 joint angles and lengths, and the method that is ultimately closest to the real joint angle was selected as the finger-angle detection method for this paper by comparing the four joint angles with the real joint angle.

4.1. Vision-Based Finger-Joint-Angle-and-Length-Detection Method

When detecting the angle of each finger joint, firstly, the position of each finger bone in the image is identified and, secondly, the position and joint angle of each finger joint by the intersection point and the angle between each finger bone are identified. A finger-joint identifier for which it was easy to perform image segmentation was used for the identification of finger phalanges in the image. The finger-joint identifiers of different scales are shown in Figure 4a, and the most suitable finger-joint identifier was selected by comparing the accuracy of the angle detection of the identifiers at different scales. Figure 4b shows the method of attaching the finger-joint identifiers.

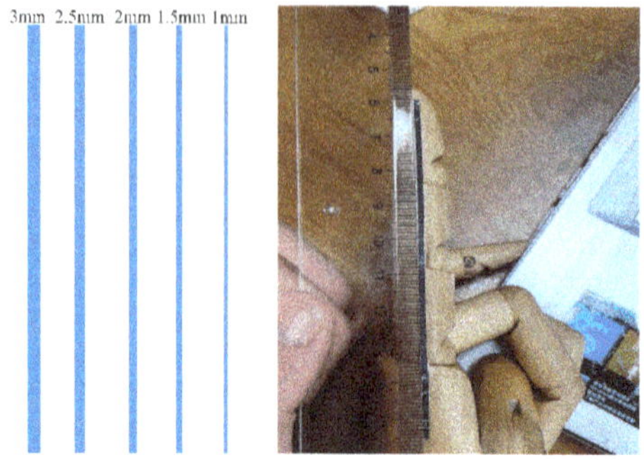

(a) (b)

Figure 4. Finger-joint markers and their method of attachment.

Since the light-source intensity and light-irradiation angle have a significant impact on the segmentation and extraction of finger-joint markers, the height of the light source can be adjusted to alter the light-irradiation angle and the light-source-irradiation intensity of the markers, enhancing the difference between the markers and the background, making it easy to segment the markers from the background and simplifying the marker-segmentation process. The image-acquisition method based on the active multi-angle light-source detection method is shown in Figure 5: (a) represents high angle lighting; (b) represents medium angle lighting; (c) represents low angle lighting.

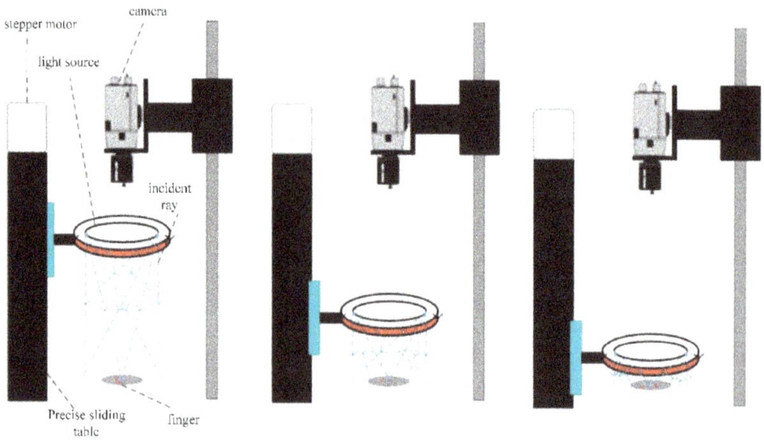

(a) (b) (c)

Figure 5. Image-acquisition method based on the active multi-angle light-source-detection method.

4.2. *Visual Marker Segmentation Methods*

To obtain a better finger-joint-angle-detection algorithm, this paper uses the HSV color-space-conversion method and the image-threshold-segmentation method to extract the target finger-joint identifier in the image and different edge-detection algorithms to obtain the identifier edge coordinates and then calculates each finger-joint pinch angle by two different finger-joint-angle-detection algorithms.

(1) HSV color-space-marker-segmentation extraction with Canny edge detection

In HSV color space, H denotes color, S denotes shade when S = 0 only grayscale image, and V denotes light and dark, indicating the brightness of the color [22,23]. The conical model of HSV color space can be formed by erecting and flattening the central axis of the RGB-color-space 3D coordinates. The RGB–HSV color-space-conversion equations are shown in Equations (3)–(5).

$$V = \max(R, G, B) \tag{3}$$

$$S = \begin{cases} \frac{V - \min(R,G,B)}{V} & V \neq 0 \\ 0 & \text{other} \end{cases} \tag{4}$$

$$H = \begin{cases} 60(G - B)/(V - \min(R, G, B)) & V = R \\ 120 + 60(B - R)/(V - \min(R, G, B)) & V = G \\ 240 + 60(R - G)/(V - \min(R, G, B)) & V = B \end{cases} \tag{5}$$

In Equations (3)–(5), R, G, and B denote the three components of the three-dimensional coordinate axes in the RGB color space. The setting ranges of the three components of HSV are H: 100~130, S: 150~255, V: 130~255. The results of the specified color-region extraction are shown in Figure 6b. Canny edge detection is currently a commonly used edge-detection algorithm. It was proposed by John Canny in 1986 [23]. It is a multi-stage algorithm consisting of image-noise reduction, the computation of the image gradient, non-maximal value suppression, and threshold screening. Its formula for image-gradient calculation for edge detection is shown in Equation (6).

$$\begin{cases} G = \sqrt{G_x^2 + G_y^2} \\ \theta = \operatorname{atan2}(G_y, G_x) \end{cases} \tag{6}$$

The θ in Equation (6) represents the gradient angle range of $-\pi$~π, which can be approximated as four angles, 0°, 45°, 90°, and 135°, representing the horizontal, vertical, and two diagonal directions, respectively. The Canny operator edge-extraction results are shown in Figure 7c.

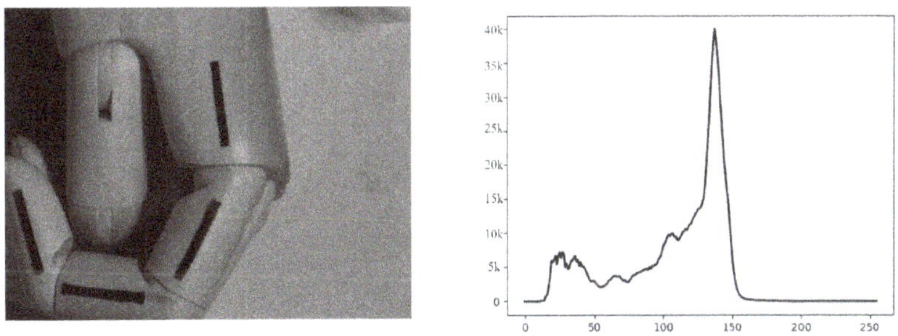

(**a**) Grayscale plot of the original image (**b**) Histogram of the grayscale plot

Figure 6. Grayscale conversion of the original image with the histogram.

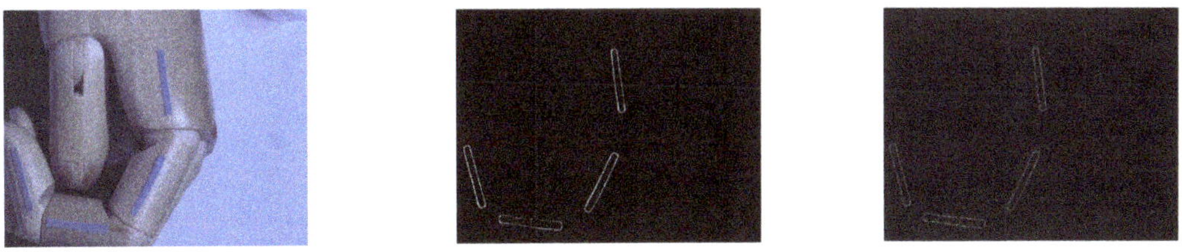

(**a**) Original image (**b**) HSV marker segmentation image (**c**) Marker edge-detection image

Figure 7. HSV marker segmentation and edge detection.

(2) Image thresholding method with edge-contour extraction

The use of image segmentation to separate the target region from the background region can prevent the need to conduct a blind search on the image and greatly improve the processing efficiency of the image [24,25]. Threshold segmentation based on the grayscale histogram is simple to compute and is suitable for grayscale images where the target and background are distributed in different grayscale ranges, as shown in Figure 7 for the histogram of the original image.

The image-segmentation formula based on different thresholds is shown in Equation (7), where T is the gray threshold; $f(x_i,y_i)$ is the gray level of the detected image point, and A and $\overline{A}$ are the set gray level of the current position image. In this study, the gray level of the target image was set as 0, and the gray level of the other images was set as 255. The above operation was performed simultaneously by scanning the image by a line from two directions using a raster scan, which can prevent missing image information for various reasons, as shown in Figure 8a for the image after threshold segmentation. Next, the image contours were detected by the fine-contours function in OpenCV and, finally, the contours of the target identifier were filtered out automatically based on the similarity of the contour-enclosing area. The results of the target-identifier contour detection are shown in Figure 8b.

$$g(x_i, y_i) = \begin{cases} \overline{A} & \text{if } f(x_i, y_i) > T \\ A & \text{if } f(x_i, y_i) \leqslant T \end{cases} \quad (7)$$

(**a**) Threshold-segmentation result (**b**) Marker-contour-detection result

Figure 8. Image-thresholding segmentation and contour-detection results.

4.3. Joint-Angle-Calculation Method Based on Different Joint Identifiers of the Finger

(1) Hough straight-line detection method for inner and outer edges

The Hough transform was improved by Richard Duda in 1972. The method transforms a point in the data space into a curve in the ρ-θ parameter space so that points with the same reference-quantity characteristics intersect in the reference space after transformation. Subsequently, the detection of the characteristic straight line is completed by judging the accumulation degree at the intersection point. The expression formula of a straight line in the data space is shown in Equation (8), where k denotes the slope and b denotes the intercept.

$$y = kx + b \quad (8)$$

The standard straight-line Hough transform uses the following parametric straight-line formula, as shown in Equation (9), where ρ is the perpendicular distance from the origin to the line and θ is the angle between ρ and the x-axis.

$$x \cos\theta + y \sin\theta = \rho \quad (9)$$

When different points on a straight line in the data space are transformed into a family of sinusoidal curves intersecting at p points in the parameter space, the detection of a straight line in the data space can be achieved by detecting the local maximum p points in the parameter space. The results of the detection of the inner and outer Hough straight lines for the target identifier are shown in Figure 9. Figure 9a represents the detection results of the Hough line on the outside of the HSV segmentation; Figure 9b represents the detection results of the Hough line inside the HSV segmentation; Figure 9c represents the detection results of the Hough line outside the threshold segmentation; and Figure 9d represents the detection results of the Hough line inside the threshold segmentation. The inner- and outer-edge Hough straight-line-detection method detects four straight lines on the inner edge and four straight lines on the outer edge of each identifier, after which the angle of each knuckle on the inner side of the identifier and the angle of each knuckle on the outer side are calculated using the finger-joint-angle-calculation method, and finally, the angle of each knuckle is found as $\theta_i = \frac{\theta_{iw}+\theta_{in}}{2}$ (i = 1, 2, 3).

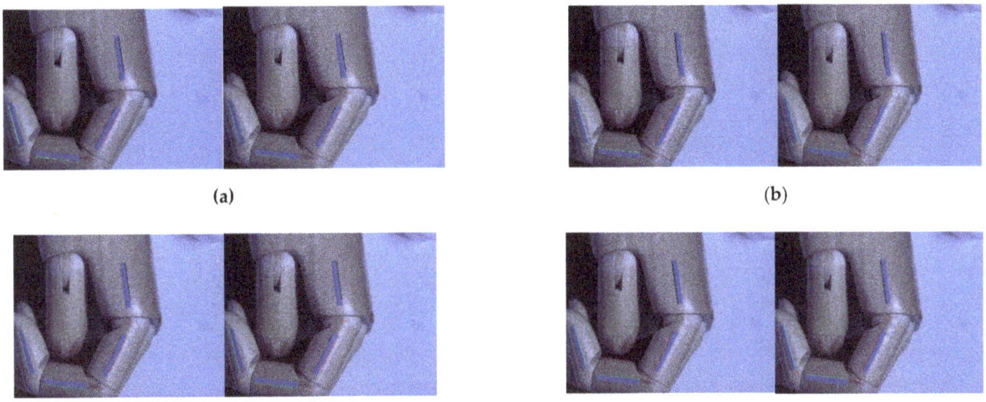

(a) (b) (c) (d)

Figure 9. Inner and outer Hough straight-line detection results.

(2) Least-squares fitting of the target identifier profile

The least-squares method was discovered by Legendre in the 19th century and takes the form shown in Equation (10). In Equation (10), y_i is the observed value, i.e., multiple samples, and y is the theoretical value, i.e., the assumed fit function. S_{ϵ^2} is the objective function, i.e., the loss function, and the objective of the least-squares method is to model the fit function when the objective function is minimized.

$$S_{\epsilon^2} = \sum(y - y_i)^2 \quad (10)$$

To fit the four joint identifiers in the image as four straight lines, this paper assumes that the number of contour coordinates of each joint identifier is n. Assume that the equation of the straight line is $y = ax + b$, where a is the slope of the line and b is the intercept of the line. The least-squares method is used to solve for a and b, whose formulas are shown in Equation (11). The results of the least-squares method for fitting the straight line to the pixel points of the target identifier are shown in Figure 10. Figure 10a represents the line-fitting result of the HSV-segmentation least-squares method. Figure 10b represents the line-fitting result of the threshold-segmentation least-squares method.

$$\begin{cases} b = \dfrac{\left(\sum\limits_{i=1}^{N} x_i^2\right)\left(\sum\limits_{i=1}^{N} y_i\right) - \left(\sum\limits_{i=1}^{N} x_i\right)\left(\sum\limits_{i=1}^{N} x_i y_i\right)}{N\left(\sum\limits_{i=1}^{N} x_i^2\right) - \left(\sum\limits_{i=1}^{N} x_i\right)^2} \\ a = \dfrac{N\left(\sum\limits_{i=1}^{N} x_i y_i\right) - \left(\sum\limits_{i=1}^{N} x_i\right)\left(\sum\limits_{i=1}^{N} y_i\right)}{N\left(\sum\limits_{i=1}^{N} x_i^2\right) - \left(\sum\limits_{i=1}^{N} x_i\right)^2} \end{cases} \tag{11}$$

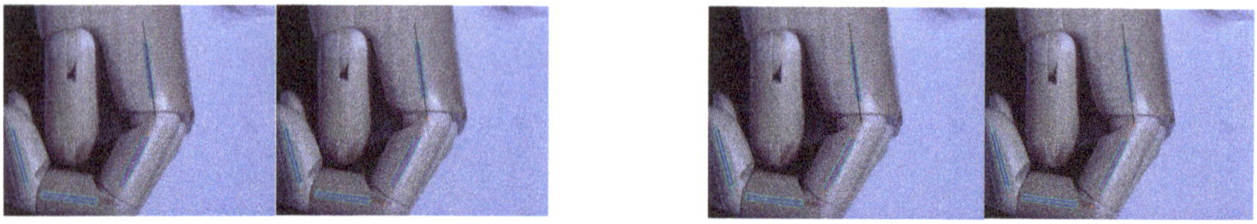

(**a**) (**b**)

Figure 10. Least-squares linear-fit results.

(3) Finger-joint-angle-calculation method

The relevant lines of finger-joint markers can be obtained by the above linear-detection methods. According to these lines, the head and tail coordinates of the four relevant lines of the four joint markers can be obtained, after which the angle between the joints of the fingers can be calculated by the formula of the angle between the two-dimensional vectors, as shown in Equation (12).

$$\theta_i = \arccos\left(\frac{\vec{a}_i \cdot \vec{b}_j}{\|a_i\| \cdot \|a_j\|}\right) \tag{12}$$

In Equation (12), $\vec{a}_i$ and $\vec{b}_j$ are the vectors of two adjacent phalangeal identifiers and θ_i is the knuckle-joint angle. The finger-joint-angle measurements using different methods are shown in Table 1. The experiments showed better results with high-angle illumination. The results obtained for the detection of the human-hand model in the case of high-angle illumination are shown in the Table 1. HSV–HOISLM represents the HSV + Hough outer- and inner-straight-line method; HSV–LSFLKADM represents HSV + the method of least-squares-fitting linear-knuckle-angle detection; TS–HOMLDM represents the threshold segmentation + Hough outer medial linear-detection method; TS–LSFLM represents the threshold-segmentation + least-squares-fitting-line method; and TKAM represents traditional knuckle-angle measurement, as shown in Figure 2.

As can be seen from Table 1, the accuracy and reliability of the visual-based finger-joint-angle measurement method were demonstrated by comparing the measurement results of multiple visual-finger-joint-angle-measurement methods with those of the conventional finger-joint-angle measurement method, in which the angular deviation between the visual-based finger-joint-angle-measurement results and the conventional finger-joint-angle-measurement results were in the range of 0° to 2°. The maximum deviation in the comparison with the conventional knuckle-angle-measurement method was 2°, the knuckle where the maximum deviation was located was the DIP joint, and the visual-angle-measurement method that caused the maximum deviation was the HSV–LSFLKADM. The visual-angle-measurement method with the smallest mean value of the deviation of the finger-joint angle in comparison with the traditional finger-joint-angle measurement method was the TS–HOMLDM; therefore, this method was selected as the finger-joint-detection method for this paper.

Table 1. Finger-joint angles measured by different methods.

	HSV + Hough Outer- and Inner-Straight-Line Method	HSV + Least-Squares-Fitting Linear-Knuckle-Angle-Detection Method	Threshold Segmentation + Hough Outer Medial Linear-Detection Method	Threshold-Segmentation + Least-Squares-Fitting-Line Method	Traditional Knuckle-Angle Measurement
MCP	145.02°	144.76°	144.95°	144.59°	145°
PIP	111.03°	109.38°	110.48°	111.26°	110°
DIP	111.83°	114.07°	112.09°	112.34°	112°
Length of proximal phalanx	26.94 mm	28.24 mm	27.37 mm	27.32 mm	27 mm
Length of middle phalanx	25.53 mm	25.53 mm	25.64 mm	25.26 mm	26 mm
Mean Angle deviation	0.407°	0.967°	0.207°	0.670°	

5. Experimental Verification

In this study, nine healthy male volunteers aged between 20 and 25 were recruited for the experiment, and three different finger-joint angles were detected using the TS–HOMLDM for visual identifiers with widths of 1.5 mm, 2 mm, and 2.5 mm, respectively, to verify the monocular vision-based finger-joint-angle measurement system (MVBFJAMS) proposed in this paper to measure the accuracy of the test in comparison with the traditional inspection method and to determine the most appropriate visual identifier width. To ensure the reliability of the experiment, we invited professional physicians to measure different volunteer knuckle angles using the traditional method first, after which our group members measured different volunteer knuckle angles using MVBFJAMS. To verify the accuracy of the MVBFJAMS for finger-joint-angle measurement during finger extension/contraction, a control experiment was conducted using the conventional measurement method and the visual measurement method. This paper also verifies the speed of the knuckle detection by the visual inspection method by comparing the time used to detect and record 30 joint-angle data by the traditional method and the visual-inspection method. Table 2 shows the knuckle-joint-retention angles for different volunteers with different markers to verify the accuracy of the visual-detection method. The finger-bone-length data are not given because the actual joint position of the finger was uncertain.

Table 2. Knuckle-retention angles under different markers in different volunteers.

	MCP (°)	PIP (°)	DIP (°)
Knuckle-hold angle under each marker	145	110	115
	160	130	110
	150	165	130

The detection method in Figure 3a was adopted for the volunteers, and the detection results for the knuckle accuracy of the different volunteers at different scales of visual markers were obtained, as shown in Table 3.

Table 3. Results of different volunteers' visual-detection angles.

Volunteer	Mark on the Scale	MCP (°)	PIP (°)	DIP (°)	Length of Proximal Phalanx (mm)	Length of Middle Phalanx (mm)
volunteer 1	1.5 mm	144.72	109.31	115.42	45.52	30.23
		160.10	130.12	109.21	44.07	31.45
		149.48	165.72	130.31	45.31	30.21
	2 mm	145.21	109.10	114.42	46.21	31.03
		161.71	132.22	109.71	44.71	30.15
		151.31	167.28	130.02	45.49	29.24
	2.5 mm	144.72	108.91	115.92	46.71	29.02
		160.40	128.93	109.27.	43.93	30.51
		147.32	164.89	133.22	46.44	29.91.
volunteer 2	1.5 mm	145.31	110.21	114.71	47.22	33.47
		159.27	130.31	111.31	47.31	32.17
		150.32	164.44	139.74	46.28	31.95
	2 mm	143.31	110.72	116.71	46.93	33.36
		160.44	129.10	110.23	47.32	32.78
		150.77	165.69	131.21	48.91	34.19
	2.5 mm	146.21	110.79	114.49	48.31	35.66
		162.99	131.44	111.22	47.76	34.54
		150.55	167.21	131.59	47.77	31.22
volunteer 3	1.5 mm	144.81	110.47	115.69	43.17	27.49
		160.77	130.21	110.48	44.21	26.36
		150.06	165.56	131.81	42.89	28.91
	2 mm	144.31	111.81	114.01	44.33	29.36
		161.17	130.79	112.58	46.96	27.22
		150.97	163.84	130.91	45.89	26.54
	2.5 mm	146.79	110.11	115.98	43.22	27.77
		160.89	129.33	111.39	45.10	29.99
		150.34	166.79	130.44	45.78	26.53
volunteer 4	1.5 mm	145.32	110.17	114.87	45.17	30.24
		160.17	130.22	109.97	44.54	29.77
		150.27	164.90	131.07	45.98	29.31
	2 mm	146.32	110.54	115.94	43.33	27.45
		159.12	130.84	110.95	44.54	26.79
		149.71	165.55	128.77	42.59	26.34
	2.5 mm	146.71	110.21	116.19	43.24	28.79
		160.77	131.44	108.22	45.77	27.32
		151.45	165.99	130.97	43.35	28.23
volunteer 5	1.5 mm	145.21	109.55	115.94	40.22	23.33
		160.56	129.53	109.84	41.57	24.35
		150.41	165.77	129.92	43.98	23.47
	2 mm	145.99	109.21	116.31	42.22	25.22
		160.77	131.74	109.55	41.31	24.51
		150.22	166.33	130.44	39.45	23.91
	2.5 mm	145.97	109.22	115.33	40.58	25.33
		161.44	130.55	110.89	41.32	24.56
		148.97	165.33	131.75	43.77	22.22

Table 3. *Cont.*

Volunteer	Mark on the Scale	MCP (°)	PIP (°)	DIP (°)	Length of Proximal Phalanx (mm)	Length of Middle Phalanx (mm)
volunteer 6	1.5 mm	145.31	109.12	114.33	40.12	30.21
		160.33	130.22	109.22	44.45	29.22
		150.22	165.72	130.33	43.43	27.34
	2 mm	145.33	110.47	115.33	39.65	28.79
		161.43	130.99	109.44	41.76	30.33
		150.67	165.33	131.65	42.22	30.67
	2.5 mm	146.12	110.22	115.48	45.97	30.15
		158.91	130.21	110.77	42.71	31.33
		149.23	163.47	131.22	42.45	29.78
volunteer 7	1.5 mm	145.33	110.32	116.12	36.45	27.13
		159.31	130.07	110.77	36.84	26.56
		150.21	165.22	129.22	37.32	26.32
	2 mm	146.71	110.42	113.41	34.78	25.72
		160.12	130.65	110.89	37.77	28.23
		151.14	164.31	130.22	37.96	27.45
	2.5 mm	145.42	110.31	114.21	39.03	29.81
		161.31	128.64	109.01	39.76	25.33
		152.12	166.21	129.13	38.78	25.91
volunteer 8	1.5 mm	145.32	110.77	114.57	43.15	27.49
		160.74	129.22	110.10	41.33	28.27
		151.12	165.33	129.38	44.54	27.39
	2 mm	145.72	110.31	116.66	42.56	29.72
		159.21	131.72	110.07	42.33	27.59
		150.56	166.77	130.33	41.12	28.23
	2.5 mm	145.32	110.07	115.21	44.45	30.02
		157.42	131.72	110.99	41.75	29.67
		150.22	166.23	129.25	45.39	28.37
volunteer 9	1.5 mm	145.31	110.23	115.76	35.46	23.57
		160.22	130.74	110.55	34.90	24.88
		159.31	165.21	130.90	37.04	24.42
	2 mm	146.13	111.31	114.31	36.24	25.56
		158.91	129.10	110.12	39.35	23.78
		149.01	165.12	131.14	37.67	24.33
	2.5 mm	143.21	109.22	115.33	38.91	24.89
		160.33	131.55	107.32	37.33	26.33
		151.33	165.77	129.22	37.57	23.91

From Tables 2 and 3, the deviations from the mean knuckle angle at different scale markers, shown in Figure 11, can be calculated.

As shown in Figure 11, the minimum-knuckle-angle mean deviation was 0.27° and the maximum-knuckle-angle mean deviation was 1.38° for the nine volunteers using visual identifiers at different scales. The knuckle-angle deviations for the nine volunteers using visual identifiers at a scale of 1.5 mm were 0.43°, 0.47°, 0.58°, 0.27°, 0.45°, 0.5°, 0.5°, 0.59°, and 0.51°, which were much smaller than the mean deviation of the knuckle angle when using other scales of visual identifiers. Therefore, the scale of a 1.5-millimeter visual marker was chosen as the test condition for the subsequent experiments. To verify the accuracy of the finger-abduction angle, three different finger-abduction-joint angles were measured using visual measures on nine volunteers, and the accuracy of the angles was verified using conventional methods. The results of the measurement of the three different abduction-joint angles are shown in Table 4.

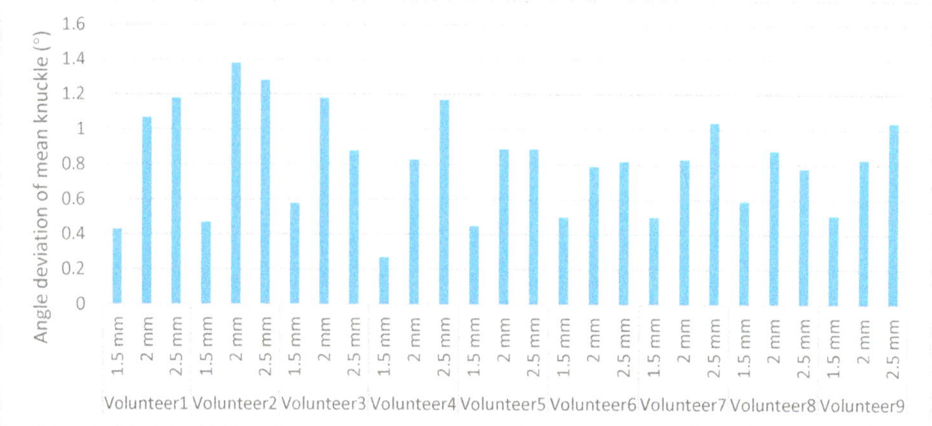

Figure 11. Deviation from the mean value of knuckle angle at different scales.

Table 4. Measurement results of abduction/adduction knuckle angle.

Volunteer	Knuckle-Angle Measurement	Measuring Angle (°)			Mean Knuckle-Angle Deviation (°)
volunteer 1	Vmm	25.73	39.21	40.39	0.63
	Tmm	25	40	40	
volunteer 2	Vmm	24.32	39.03	40.41	0.68
	Tmm	25	40	40	
volunteer 3	Vmm	23.91	40.71	40.51	0.77
	Tmm	25	40	40	
volunteer 4	Vmm	24.41	39.93	40.33	0.33
	Tmm	25	40	40	
volunteer 5	Vmm	25.22	39.35	40.61	0.49
	Tmm	25	40	40	
volunteer 6	Vmm	24.12	38.77	41.12	0.61
	Tmm	25	40	40	
volunteer 7	Vmm	24.52	39.79	40.22	0.30
	Tmm	25	40	40	
volunteer 8	Vmm	24.91	38.54	40.89	0.81
	Tmm	25	40	40	
volunteer 9	Vmm	24.33	40.95	40.87	0.83
	Tmm	25	40	40	

In Table 4, Vmm represents the visual measurement method and Tmm represent the traditional measurement method. As shown in Table 4, the maximum and minimum knuckle-angle deviations of the nine volunteers were 0.81° and 0.30°, respectively. The mean values of the knuckles were 0.63°, 0.68°, 0.77°, 0.49°, 0.33°, 0.61°, 0.30°, 0.81°, and 0.83°, respectively. Table 5 shows the average time taken to measure and record the angle data of 30 joints for the 9 volunteers using the traditional method and the visual-detection method (including the time to paste the visual marker).

Table 5. Time taken to measure and record data for 30 joint angles under different methods.

Method of Knuckle-Angle Detection	Time Taken to Measure and Record Knuckle Angles for 30 Times (s)
TMM	51.75
VMM	421.21

From Table 5, it can be seen that the time taken by the vision-based knuckle-angle-detection method is much less than that of the conventional knuckle-angle-detection method. This result was produced because the vision-based knuckle-angle-detection method not only enables the simultaneous measurement of multiple knuckles compared to the conventional knuckle-angle-detection method, but also increases the speed of the knuckle measurement and the speed at which the knuckle-angle data are recorded.

6. Conclusions

To solve the problems that the joint-angle measuring instrument takes more time to measure the angle of single joints in clinical medicine, and cannot measure the angles of multiple joints at the same time, a vision-based finger-joint-angle-measuring system was designed on the basis of the original visual-inspection system. The system consists of a hardware system, a control system, and a vision system. The active multi-angle-light-source-detection system composed of a control system and a hardware system can simplify the recognition process of visual markers by adjusting the height of the light source. The vision system is composed of an industrial camera and the knuckle-angle-detection method proposed in this paper. The knuckle-angle-detection method proposed in this paper is composed of finger-joint-marker pasting, image acquisition, visual-marker segmentation, visual-marker edge detection, and joint-angle calculation based on different finger-joint markers. In this study, each component of the method was analyzed and verified by experiments. These experiments proved that in the case of high angle illumination, the TS–HOMLDM should be adopted, and the visual marker with the scale of 1.5 mm was selected, since it had the highest measurement accuracy. The shortcomings of the current proposed MVBFJAMS are also very obvious. Firstly, the system requires a Basler ace camera, a TEC-V7X industrial lens, an R50-26-13 light source, and a computer, which makes it much more expensive than traditional knuckle-measurement methods and sensor-based methods; furthermore, the system can only achieve two-dimensional inspection at present.

The system is still in the experimental stage and has high requirements for the detection environment for light sources. Considering the complexity of the clinical environment, in order to improve the anti-interference capability of the system, we intend to add an opaque housing to the exterior of the device in the future in order to maintain the stability of the testing environment. In the next phase, we intend to add another depth camera to this system and fuse the texture information from the normal camera with the depth-camera depth information to build a model of the detector's hand. Using this approach, three-dimensional detection can then be achieved to detect the angle of each finger joint of the hand. In the meantime, we will further validate the accuracy of the system through clinical trials, as well as the accuracy of the assessment of the level of handicap and the effectiveness of the intervention treatment.

Author Contributions: Conceptualization, Y.F. and M.Z.; methodology, Y.F.; software, Y.F.; validation, Y.F. and F.D.; the main content of this manuscript was created and written by Y.F. and reviewed by all authors. All authors have read and agreed to the published version of the manuscript.

Funding: This research was funded by the Natural Science Foundation of Zhejiang Province, grant number LQ21E050008; Educational Commission of Zhejiang Province, grant number Y201941335; Science and Technique Plans of Ningbo City, grant number 202002N3133; The Major Scientific and Technological Projects in Ningbo City, grant number 2020Z082; Research Fund Project of Ningbo University, grant number XYL19029; and the K. C. Wong Magna Fund of Ningbo University.

Institutional Review Board Statement: The study was conducted according to the guidelines of theDeclaration of Helsinki, and approved by the Ethics Committee of Faculty of Mechanical Engineering & Mechanics, Ningbo University (protocol code [2022]LLSP(0315) and 2022.03.15).

Informed Consent Statement: Informed consent was obtained from all subjects involved in the study.

Data Availability Statement: Not applicable.

Conflicts of Interest: The authors declare no conflict of interest.

References

1. Okuyama, T.; Kobayashi, K.; Otsuki, M.; Tanaka, M. Measurement of finger joint angle using a flexible polymer sensor. *Int. J. Appl. Electromagn. Mech.* **2016**, *52*, 951–957. [CrossRef]
2. Park, W.; Ro, K.; Kim, S.; Bae, J. A soft sensor-based three-dimensional (3-D) finger motion measurement system. *Sensors* **2017**, *17*, 420. [CrossRef] [PubMed]
3. Kawaguchi, J.; Yoshimoto, S.; Kuroda, Y.; Oshiro, O. Estimation of finger joint angles based on electromechanical sensing of wrist shape. *IEEE Trans. Neural Syst. Rehabil. Eng.* **2016**, *25*, 1409–1418. [CrossRef] [PubMed]
4. Kitano, K.; Ito, A.; Tsujiuchi, N.; Wakida, S. Estimation of joint center and measurement of finger motion by inertial sensors. In Proceedings of the 2016 38th Annual International Conference of the IEEE Engineering in Medicine and Biology Society (EMBC), Orlando, FL, USA, 16–20 August 2016; pp. 5668–5671.
5. Zheng, Y.; Peng, Y.; Wang, G.; Liu, X.; Dong, X.; Wang, J. Development and evaluation of a sensor glove for hand function assessment and preliminary attempts at assessing hand coordination. *Measurement* **2016**, *93*, 1–12. [CrossRef]
6. Veber, M.; Bajd, T.; Munih, M. Assessing joint angles in human hand via optical tracking device and calibrating instrumented glove. *Meccanica* **2007**, *42*, 451–463. [CrossRef]
7. Lu, S.; Chen, D.; Liu, C.; Jiang, Y.; Wang, M. A 3-D finger motion measurement system via soft strain sensors for hand rehabilitation. *Sens. Actuators A Phys.* **2019**, *285*, 700–711. [CrossRef]
8. Park, Y.; Lee, J.; Bae, J. Development of a wearable sensing glove for measuring the motion of fingers using linear potentiometers and flexible wires. *IEEE Trans. Ind. Inform.* **2014**, *11*, 198–206. [CrossRef]
9. Park, Y.; Bae, J. A three-dimensional finger motion measurement system of a thumb and an index finger without a calibration process. *Sensors* **2020**, *20*, 756. [CrossRef] [PubMed]
10. Jang, M.; Kim, J.S.; Kang, K.; Kim, J.; Yang, S. Towards Finger Motion Capture System Using FBG Sensors. In Proceedings of the 2018 40th Annual International Conference of the IEEE Engineering in Medicine and Biology Society (EMBC), Honolulu, HI, USA, 18–21 July 2018; pp. 3734–3737.
11. Metcalf, C.D.; Robinson, R.; Malpass, A.J.; Bogle, T.P.; Dell, T.A.; Harris, C.; Demain, S.H. Markerless motion capture and measurement of hand kinematics: Validation and application to home-based upper limb rehabilitation. *IEEE Trans. Biomed. Eng.* **2013**, *60*, 2184–2192. [CrossRef] [PubMed]
12. Pham, T.; Pathirana, P.N.; Trinh, H.; Fay, P. A non-contact measurement system for the range of motion of the hand. *Sensors* **2015**, *15*, 18315–18333. [CrossRef] [PubMed]
13. Simon, T.; Joo, H.; Matthews, I.; Sheikh, Y. Hand keypoint detection in single images using multiview bootstrapping. In Proceedings of the IEEE Conference on Computer Vision and Pattern Recognition, Honolulu, HI, USA, 21–26 July 2017; pp. 4645–4653.
14. Mathis, A.; Mamidanna, P.; Cury, K.M.; Abe, T.; Murthy, V.N.; Mathis, M.W.; Bethge, M. Deeplabcut: Markerless pose estimation of user-defined body parts with deep learning. *Nat. Neurosci.* **2018**, *21*, 1281–1289. [CrossRef] [PubMed]
15. Oikonomidis, P.I.; Argyros, A. Using a single rgb frame for real time 3d hand pose estimation in the wild. In Proceedings of the IEEE Winter Conference on Applications of Computer Vision (WACV), Lake Tahoe, NV, USA, 12–15 March 2018; pp. 436–445.
16. Tung, J.Y.; Lulic; Gonzalez, D.A.; Tran, J.; Dickerson, C.R.; Roy, A.E.A. Evaluation of a portable markerless finger position capture device: Accuracy of the leap motion controller in healthy adults. *Physiol. Meas.* **2015**, *36*, 1025–1035. [CrossRef] [PubMed]
17. Nizamis, K.; Rijken, N.H.M.; Mendes, A.; Janssen, M.M.H.P.; Bergsma, A.; Koopman, B.F.J.M. A novel setup and protocol to measure the range of motion of the wrist and the hand. *Sensors* **2018**, *18*, 3230. [CrossRef] [PubMed]
18. Lim, G.M.; Jatesiktat, P.; Kuah, C.W.K.; Ang, W.T. Camera-based hand tracking using a mirror-based multi-view setup. In Proceedings of the 2020 42nd Annual International Conference of the IEEE Engineering in Medicine & Biology Society (EMBC), Montreal, QC, Canada, 20–24 July 2020; pp. 5789–5793.
19. Lee, J.W.; Rim, K. Measurement of finger joint angles and maximum finger forces during cylinder grip activity. *J. Biomed. Eng.* **1991**, *13*, 152–162. [CrossRef]
20. Zhu, J.J.; Ji, W.; Hua, Q. An automatic vision inspection system for detecting surface cracks of welding joint. *J. Comput. Methods Sci. Eng.* **2019**, *19*, 635–646. [CrossRef]
21. Zhang, H. *Mechanical and Control System Design of Finger Training Rehabilitation Apparatus*; Yanshan University: Qinhuangdao, China, 2016.
22. Zotin, A. Fastalgorithm of image enhancement based on nulti-scale retinex. *Procedia Comput. Sci.* **2018**, *131*, 6–14. [CrossRef]
23. Kruseaw, A.W.; Alenin, A.S.; Vaughni, I.J.; Tyo, J.S. Perceptually uniform color space for visualizing trivariate linear polarization imaging data. *Opt. Lett.* **2018**, *43*, 2426–2429. [CrossRef] [PubMed]
24. Abbas, A.K.; Bassam, R. Phonocardiography signal processing. *Morgan Claypool* **2009**, *4*, 218.
25. Papadaniil, C.D.; Hadjileontiadis, L.J. Efficient heart sound segmentation and extraction using ensemble empirical mode decomposition and kurtosis features. *IEEE J. Biomed. Health Inform.* **2014**, *18*, 1138–1152. [CrossRef]

sensors

Article

Smart Vehicle Path Planning Based on Modified PRM Algorithm

Qiongqiong Li, Yiqi Xu, Shengqiang Bu and Jiafu Yang *

College of Mechanical and Electronic Engineering, Nanjing Forestry University, Nanjing 210037, China
* Correspondence: jfyang@njfu.edu.cn; Tel.: +86-13951004006

Abstract: Path planning is a very important step for mobile smart vehicles in complex environments. Sampling based planners such as the Probabilistic Roadmap Method (PRM) have been widely used for smart vehicle applications. However, there exist some shortcomings, such as low efficiency, low reuse rate of the roadmap, and a lack of guidance in the selection of sampling points. To solve the above problems, we designed a pseudo-random sampling strategy with the main spatial axis as the reference axis. We optimized the generation of sampling points, removed redundant sampling points, set the distance threshold between road points, adopted a two-way incremental method for collision detections, and optimized the number of collision detection calls to improve the construction efficiency of the roadmap. The key road points of the planned path were extracted as discrete control points of the Bessel curve, and the paths were smoothed to make the generated paths more consistent with the driving conditions of vehicles. The correctness of the modified PRM was verified and analyzed using MATLAB and ROS to build a test platform. Compared with the basic PRM algorithm, the modified PRM algorithm has advantages related to speed in constructing the roadmap, path planning, and path length.

Keywords: smart vehicle; probabilistic roadmap algorithm; pseudo-random sampling; collision detection; path smoothing

Citation: Li, Q.; Xu, Y.; Bu, S.; Yang, J. Smart Vehicle Path Planning Based on Modified PRM Algorithm. *Sensors* **2022**, *22*, 6581. https://doi.org/10.3390/s22176581

Academic Editors: Luige Vladareanu, Hongnian Yu, Hongbo Wang and Yongfei Feng

Received: 11 July 2022
Accepted: 29 August 2022
Published: 31 August 2022

1. Introduction

In recent years, smart vehicles have received more attention with the development of emerging technologies such as cloud computing, big data, and the full-scale launch of 5G construction [1,2]. Smart vehicles have significant effects in relieving driving pressure, avoiding traffic jams, and reducing environmental pollution [3] Path planning and motion control are significant and complex navigation tasks in smart vehicles. Path planning technology is the basis of smart vehicles to make motion decisions and navigate positioning [4,5]. To achieve successful path planning and motion control to be able to reach a target safely, smart vehicles must be provided with the ability to perceive and detect obstacles to be avoided [6]. Many sensors are installed on the body of smart vehicles, which ensure that they can perceive and interpret information gathered from the environment to determine position, direction to the target, position of obstacles, and navigation in both structured or unstructured environments [7].A smart vehicle is expected to perform these tasks with the safest and shortest path, reaching the target in the shortest time, and ultimately performing the specified task without the intervention of humans. Path planning in smart vehicles refers to determining how the smart vehicle reaches its target point safely to ensure obstacle avoidance. Smart vehicle path planning is described as a multi-objective optimization problem as it requires the generation of appropriate trajectories as well as obstacle avoidance in the environment [8].

The methods of smart vehicle path planning can be classified in different ways. Ayawli et al. [7] categorized them into nature-inspired computation methods, traditional methods, and hybrid methods. Methods and strategies that imitate natural phenomena are described as nature-inspired computation methods. Meanwhile those that have nothing to do with imitating nature phenomena are described as the conventional method. Approaches that combine two or more strategies are described as hybrid methods. Nature-inspired computing consists of a metaheuristic algorithm that simulates, based on nature phenomena given by natural science [9]. A number of researchers have attempted to solve the problem of mobile robotics path planning by using nature-inspired algorithms including genetic algorithms (GA) [10,11], artificial neural networks (ANN) [12,13], simulated annealing (SA) [14], ant colony optimization (ACO) [15], particle swarm optimization (PSO) [16], and artificial bee colonies (ABC) [17].In order to take advantage of the strengths of some methods while reducing the effects of their disadvantages, some researchers combine two or more methods to provide an efficient hybrid path planning method for controlling smart vehicles. These approaches include APF combined with GA [18], APF combined with PSO [19], and fuzzy logic combined with Kalman filtering [20,21]. Conventional path planning methods have been used for many years. These methods mainly rely on distance information from the object to the smart vehicles, repulsive force and attractive force clustering, or graphical map calculations to determine the path planning of smart vehicles. Even though conventional methods of path planning are computationally expensive, they are easy to implement. Conventional methods mainly consist of the rapidly-exploring random tree (RRT) algorithm [22], probabilistic roadmap algorithm (PRM) [23], artificial potential field (APF) [24,25], sliding mode control (SMC) [11,26], A * algorithm [27], D * algorithm [28,29], and simultaneous localization and mapping (SLAM) [30].

PRM is one of the most popular sampling based planners. PRM is a space planner that uses multiple-query planning. The key idea in PRM is to distribute the nodes across the space and then connect these nodes using simple local planning and straight lines to form a graph roadmap. By connecting the available space, the PRM succeeds in exploring a faster path by reducing the search to a graph [31]. However, PRM has shortcomings, including lack of orientation in the selection of sampling points, low reuse rate of the roadmap, and low search efficiency. Moreover, due to the random sampling of nodes in PRM, there exists a narrow passage problem that generates an unconnected graph. To enhance the efficiency of sampling-based algorithms, Kantaros et al. [32] introduced bias into the sampling process. Vasile et al. [33] maintained sparsity of generated samples. Sparseness was also explored by Dobson and Berkis for PRM using different techniques [34]. Amato et al. [35] proposed parallelizing strategies; the PRM method has massive inherent parallelism, which can be easily and best exploited. Berkis et al. [36] used the probabilistic roadmap method (PRM) with bidirectional rapidly exploring random trees (BI-RRT) as the local planner to solve multiple queries for motion planning problems with single query planners. Kurniawait et al. [37] designed an improved PRM algorithm, which was based on obstacle boundary sampling and evaluated the optimal feasible region to optimize the dispersion of random sampling of the PRM algorithm. Esposito et al. [38] proposed a processing algorithm for optimizing probabilistic roadmaps. Dealing with the format of convex cells in free space with a number of nodes that requires a lot of computation, this algorithm could simplify the computation required for this step by sparse decomposition. Gao Junli et al. [39] proposed to combine the deep reinforcement learning twin-delayed deep deterministic policy gradient algorithm with the traditional PRM algorithm as a new path planner, and the experimental results showed that this incremental training mode could significantly improve search efficiency. Moreover, this new path planner effectively improved the generalization of the model. Chen Gang et al. [40] proposed an improved PRM method. Based on a virtual force field, a new sampling strategy of PRM was proposed to generate a configuration that is more appropriate for practical application in free space.

RAVANKAR et al. [41] proposed a method for global planning using a hierarchical hybrid PRM and the APF method, using a decomposition method of node distribution that used map segmentation to generate regions of high and low potential, and proposed a method to reduce the dispersion of sample sets during roadmap building. Xu Zhenfan et al. [42] changed the sampling strategy so that nodes were incrementally added and evenly distributed in the exploration region to produce the best viewpoints and PRM enabled the planner to quickly search for alternative paths and avoid dynamic obstacles for safe exploration.

Aiming to improve the shortcomings of the PRM algorithm, the main innovation of this paper is that we propose a pseudo-random sampling strategy with the main spatial axis as the reference axis, set the distance threshold between road points, and adopt a two-way incremental method for collision detections. We aim to find the shortest path between the start point and target point and shorten the time of the planning path. The key road points of the path are extracted as discrete control points of the Bessel curve. We use Bezier curve to make the path smoother, whereas the path is more like the actual driving condition of the smart vehicle.

2. Modified PRM Algorithm

2.1. PRM Algorithm

The PRM algorithm includes sampling and query phases.

Sampling phase: the PRM algorithm randomly samples in the planning space and judges the reasonableness of the sampling points by the local planner. By repeating the sampling times n to generate a collection of valid waypoints V traversing the V, the algorithm connects all the feasible paths between the waypoints to expand to the whole planning space and forms the waypoint graph. $V = \{v_1, .v_2, \ldots, v_n\}$ denotes the set of waypoints; $E = \{v_i, v_j | v_i, v_j \in V\}$ denotes the set of edges between waypoints.

Query phase: the start point q_{init} and target point q_{goal} are put into the wayfinding graph $G(V, E)$, and the algorithm enters the path search phase. We use the graph search algorithm in the wayfinding graph $G(V, E)$ to find a collision-free path connecting the start point q_{init} and target point q_{goal}.

2.2. Pseudo-Random Sampling

In the PRM algorithm, the number of sampling points generated by the random sampling strategy increases with an increase in planning space. It is difficult to achieve a global uniform distribution and easy to create redundancy in sampling points. There is a considerable probability that the shortest path occurs in the area where the starting point and target point connects. This region is regarded as a focused sampling region, referred to as the spatial principal axis region.

To construct the spatial principal axis information, we set the coordinates of the starting point to be $S(x_s, y_s)$ and the coordinates of the target point to be $G(x_g, y_g)$. Length L and declination of the spatial principal axis θ was denoted by:

$$L = \|G - S\|_2 \tag{1}$$

$$\theta = \frac{\pi}{2} - \arctan\frac{|y_g - y_s|}{|x_g - x_s|} \tag{2}$$

We designed the spatial principal axes with the length L, and number of sampling points n, then obtained the longitudinal sampling spacing N_d, as:

$$N_d = \frac{L}{n} \tag{3}$$

Referring to the random sampling method, the sampling points were symmetrically distributed in the sector area near the main axis of space, and sampling points $P_{i,j}(x, y)$ were calculated as follows:

$$x = x_s + r_d \times \cos(\theta + \phi_j) \tag{4}$$

$$y = y_s + r_d \times \sin(\theta + \phi_j) \tag{5}$$

$$r_d = i \times N_d, i = [1, 2, \ldots, n] \tag{6}$$

where (x_s, y_s) indicates the starting point of the intelligent vehicle; r_d indicates the sampling radius; sampling radius is centered on the starting point; $\phi_j \in [-\phi_m, \phi_m]$ indicates the angle of deflection of the sampling point and; ϕ_m indicates the maximum deflection angle. It is used to control the angle of the sector sampling area, that is, the range of lateral sampling.

According to Figure 1a,b, the sampling points are symmetrically distributed on both sides of the main spatial axis, and sampling range is controlled by the maximum deflection angle ϕ_m. With the increase of ϕ_m, the sampling points spread in all directions along the main spatial axis. To make the sampling point distribution more uniform, the lateral sampling range is adjusted along the main axis of space, and sampling range is adjusted in increments using $\Delta\phi = \phi_{\mathrm{m}}/n$. The distribution of sampling points after adjustment is shown in Figure 1c,d.

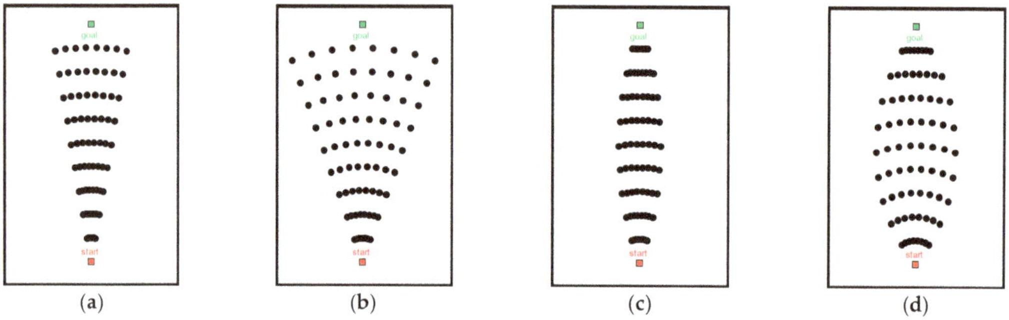

Figure 1. Sampling method based on spatial principal axis: (**a**) $\phi_m = 10$, (**b**) $\phi_m = 20$, (**c**) $\phi_m = 10$, and (**d**) $\phi_m = 20$.

Integrating the characteristics of uniform sampling, we counted the number of sampling points p in free space and the effective sampling rate of the horizontal sampling layer is defined as R:

$$R = \frac{p}{N} \tag{7}$$

where N indicates the total number of samples in the current sampling layer and the size of the effective sampling rate R reflects the connectivity of the current sampling layer. The larger R is, the better the connectivity of the sampling layer. If R is too small, this means that most of the sampling points in the sampling layer have fallen into the obstacle space. If the sampling layer edge subsequently has the same sampling interval, the chance of sampling points falling into the obstacle space will increase.

In order to improve the ability of the sampling points in avoiding obstacles, we introduced random increments Δr to adjust the sampling interval of sampling points. Based on Figure 1d, we adjust the size of the random increment Δr to get Figure 2. As the value of the random increment Δr increases, the sampling points tend to approach random distribution. With a decreasing value of Δr, the sampling points tend to approach uniform distribution.

Referring to Figure 3, hollow dots indicate the sampling points before adjusting the sampling spacing, solid dots indicate the adjusted sampling points, red markers represent the sampling points falling into the obstacle space, and black markers represent the sampling points in the free space. The effective sampling rate of the front sampling layer is low ($R = 0.3$), the radius fluctuation rate ($R = 0.8$) of the subsequent sampling layer is adjusted, and the sampling points avoid the obstacles by using the pseudo-random sampling strategy, which improves the quality of sampling point generation.

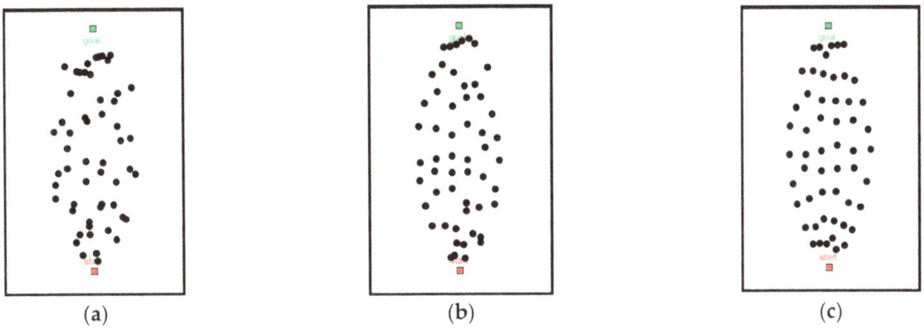

Figure 2. Pseudo-random-based sampling method: (a) $\Delta r = r$, (b) $\Delta r = 0.5r$, and (c) $\Delta r = 0.25r$.

The sampling radius after adding random increments Δr is shown in Equation (8):

$$r'_d = r_d + \Delta r \tag{8}$$

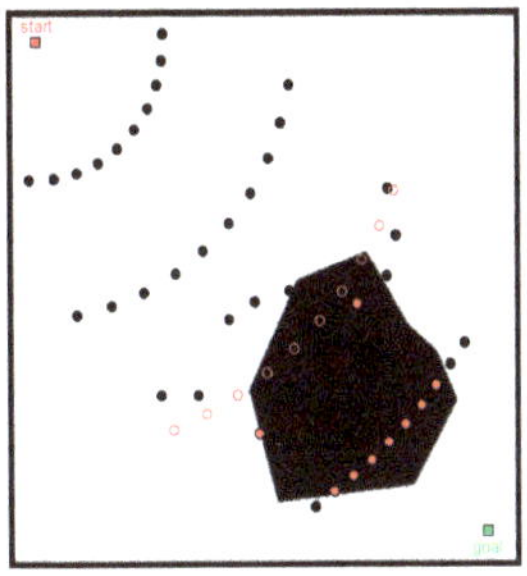

Figure 3. Schematic of sampling point adjustment.

2.3. Bidirectional Incremental Collision Detection

Collision detection is used to determine whether the connected line segments between the sample points intersect with the obstacle space, and the sample points are connected to each other by collision detection to form a roadmap $G(V, E)$. The traditional PRM algorithm usually takes an incremental detection strategy. According to a fixed step size, the planner selects discrete points and detects whether the point falls into the obstacle space. To improve the efficiency of collision detection execution, we combined this incremental detection method with the dichotomous method, proposing a two-way incremental detection strategy.

First, the two-way incremental detection method judges the reasonableness of the first and last connected sample points (Figure 4a). Then, we end the detection if the sample points belong to the obstacle space. If the sample points belong to the self-use space, we select the test point in both directions gradually along the first and last connected sample points and judge the reasonableness of the test point. If the selected test point belongs to the obstacle space, the detection is stopped to discard the path, as shown in Figure 4b. The sample points are connected to each other by collision detection, and finally form a roadmap $G(V, E)$.

2.4. Neighbouring Layer Connection Strategy

In the roadmap $G(V, E)$, the threshold distance between road points is an important factor affecting the efficiency of roadmap construction. The path formed by connecting road points in the same sampling layer is not conducive to shorten the global path length. Taking the distribution characteristics of the longitudinal sampling layer into account, we set the connection threshold of the longitudinal sampling spacing L_{TH} to screen the paths that met the threshold conditions and make the connection between road points from the full connection to adjacent sampling layer connection, improving roadmap construction efficiency.

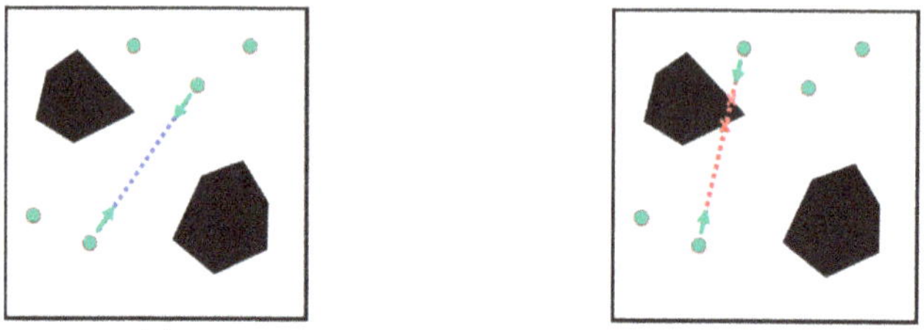

(a) (b)

Figure 4. Schematic diagram of two-way incremental detection strategy: (**a**) reasonable path and (**b**) illegal path.

The sampling points generated based on the pseudo-random sampling strategy ($N = 20$) were selected to obtain the roadmap constructed under the drive of two connection strategies, as shown in Figure 5. Figure 5a shows the wayfinding graph generated by the full connectivity strategy, with the red solid line representing the filtered paths. Figure 5b indicates the wayfinding graph generated by the neighbouring layer connectivity strategy. In terms of time consumption, the composition time using these different connection strategies was 0.906 s and 0.437 s, respectively, and the latter optimized composition efficiency by 48.2%.

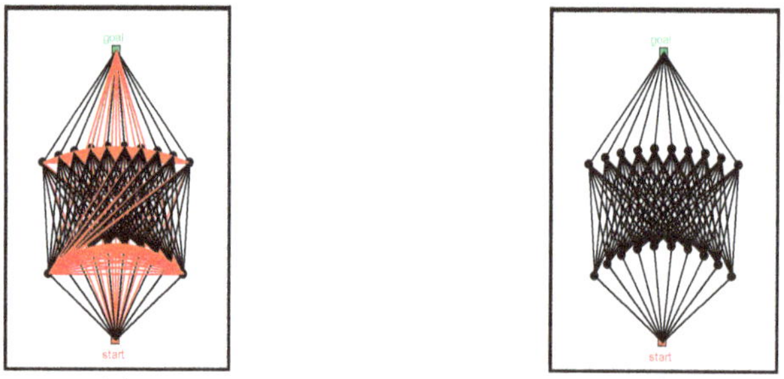

(a) (b)

Figure 5. Comparison of road signs: (**a**) full connection and (**b**) neighbouring layer connection.

3. Path Smoothing

In this paper, Bessel curves were chosen to smooth the paths planned by the modified PRM algorithm.

The n order Bessel curve expressions were defined as:

$$B(t) = \sum_{i=0}^{n} P_i b_{i,n}(t),\ (t \in [0,1]) \tag{9}$$

where P_i represents the $n+1$ control point of the Bessel curve and $b_{i,n}(t)$ represents the Bernstein basis function. The value of this function is shown in Equation (10):

$$b_{i,n}(t) = C_n^i t^i (1-t)^{n-i} = \frac{n\,!}{(n-i)\,!i\,!} t^i (1-t)^{n-i},\ i = 0,1,2,\ldots,n \tag{10}$$

In this paper, a 4th order Searle curve was chosen, and the formula is as follows:

$$B(t) = (1-t)^4 P_0 + 4P_1(1-t)^3 t + 6P_2(1-t)^2 t^2 + 4P_3(1-t)t^3 + P_4 t^4,\ t \in [0,1] \quad (11)$$

The curvature of the Bessel curve at any point $\kappa(t)$ is:

$$\kappa(t) = \frac{|B'(t) \times B''(t)|}{|B'(t)|^2} \quad (12)$$

Assuming that the planning path $path = \{P_n\}$ consists of a series of discrete points $(n \geq 5)$, the discrete points are used as the control points P_i of the Bessel curve, and the curvature of the Bessel curve $\kappa(P)$ can be obtained according to Equation (12):

$$\kappa(P) = \frac{P'_x P''_y - P'_y P''_x}{(P'^2_x + P'^2_y)^{3/2}} \quad (13)$$

The curvature of the Bessel curve at the starting point is $\kappa(0)$:

$$\kappa(0) = \frac{3|(P_1 - P_0) \times (P_2 - P_1)|}{4(P_1 - P_0)^3} \quad (14)$$

In this specific implementation, the key waypoints of the path searched by the modified PRM algorithm were extracted, discrete control points of the Bessel curve P_i were obtained by discretizing the line between key waypoints, and the discrete points were interpolated and fitted by Equation (9) to realize the smoothing of the path.

4. Simulation Test and Analysis

To verify the composition and path planning efficiency of the modified PRM algorithm, MATLAB (MATLAB2018b, MathWorks. Inc., Natick, MA, USA) was used to build a simulation experiment platform and a ROS (ROS1.0, Willow Garage. Inc., Menlo Park, CA, USA) experimental platform was used to verify the correctness of the modified PRM algorithm. Our computer configurations included: a Windows 10 operating system, 512 GB hard disk, and 8 GB RAM.

4.1. Comparison of Algorithm Composition Efficiency

The planning space of the known map is shown in Figures 6 and 7. The two algorithms kept the same total number $N = m \times n$ of sampling points in the sampling phase, where m and n represent the number of horizontal and vertical sampling points of the algorithm, respectively. We focused on the planning path length and roadmap construction time and repeated the test several times (recorded 10 times). The results are shown in Table 1 in mean values.

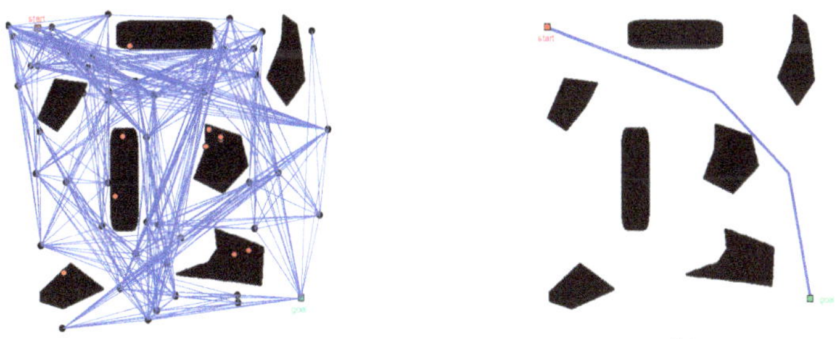

(a) (b)

Figure 6. Planning results of the basic PRM algorithm ($N = 60$): (**a**) roadmap and (**b**) planned path.

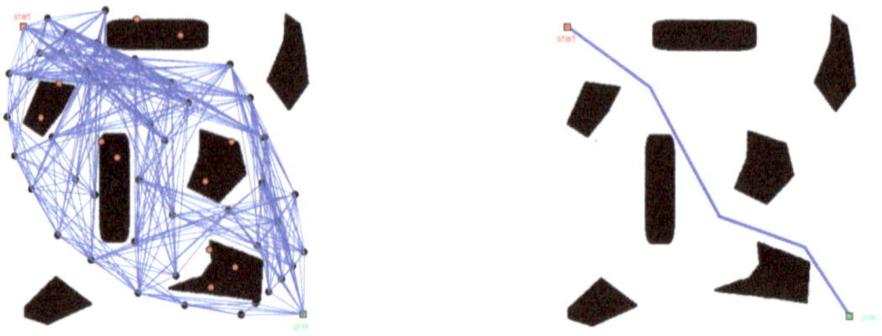

(a) (b)

Figure 7. Planning results of the modified PRM algorithm ($N = 60$): (**a**) roadmap and (**b**) planned path.

Table 1. The results of algorithm comparison.

Algorithm Name	Number of Sampling Points N	Path Length/m	Composition Time/s
PRM algorithm	30	582.1	0.958
	60	602.6	3.269
	90	615.4	10.393
Modified PRM algorithm	30	593.3	0.404
	60	590.6	2.056
	90	578.7	5.196

Taking sampling points $N = 60$ as an example, we analyzed the results of the roadmap construction (Figures 6a and 7a). The sampling points were widely distributed in the PRM algorithm and there were many redundant sampling points. On the other hand, for the roadmap constructed by the modified PRM algorithm (Figure 7a), the location selection of the sampling points had a certain orientation, mainly distributed along the main axis of space, and there were fewer redundant sampling points.

In Figures 6 and 7 and Table 1, it is shown that when the number of sampling points N is 30, the length of the planned path increases by 1.9% and composition time is reduced by 57.8%. When the number of sampling points N is 60, the length of the planned path is reduced by 1.9% and composition time is reduced by 37.1%. When the number of sampling points increase to 90, the length of the planned path is reduced by 5.9% and composition time is reduced 50%. It shows that the changes in path length according to different number N are not consistent. Compared with the PRM algorithm, there is no great advantage in path length for the modified PRM algorithm. However, the modified PRM algorithm showed great advantages in decreasing the construction time of the roadmap; the efficiency of constructing maps was significantly improved.

In Figure 8, keeping all other conditions equal, when the number of fold points of the path increased, path smoothness gradually improved as the number of sampling points increased. The overall trend of the path remains unchanged, indicating that the quality of the path solution solved by the modified PRM algorithm is stable.

To obtain Figure 9, we used the Bessel curve to deal with Figure 8b, the solid blue line indicating the modified PRM algorithm planning path and the black hollow circle logo representing the key road points, used as the Bessel curve control points. The path obtained after the smoothing process (shown by the red line) was more consistent with intelligent vehicle driving road conditions.

4.2. Comparison of Path Planning Efficiency

To verify the path planning efficiency of the modified PRM algorithm, the basic PRM algorithm was used as the comparison algorithm for the case test, where Case A is a square maze and Case B is a narrow channel. The success rate was measured by a ratio of the number of successful path searches to total search number. The results of the case test are shown in Figures 10 and 11 and Table 2.

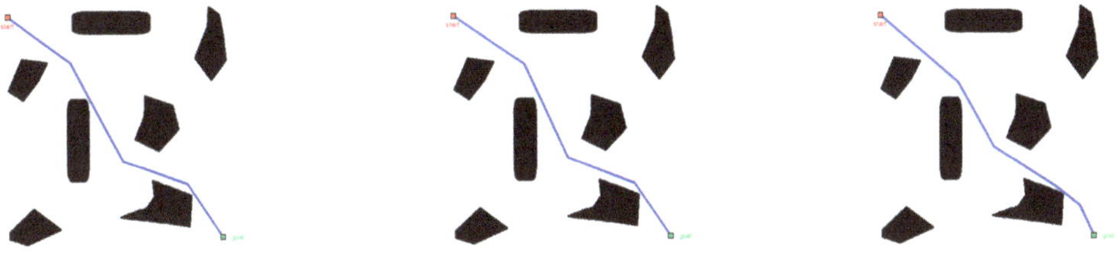

(a) (b) (c)

Figure 8. Comparison of planning results of modified PRM algorithm: (**a**) $N = 30$, (**b**) $N = 60$, and (**c**) $N = 90$.

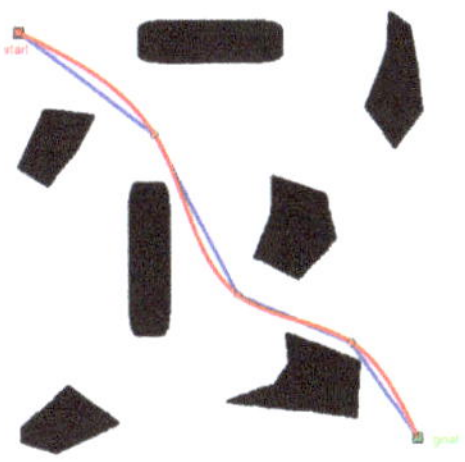

Figure 9. Path smoothing diagram.

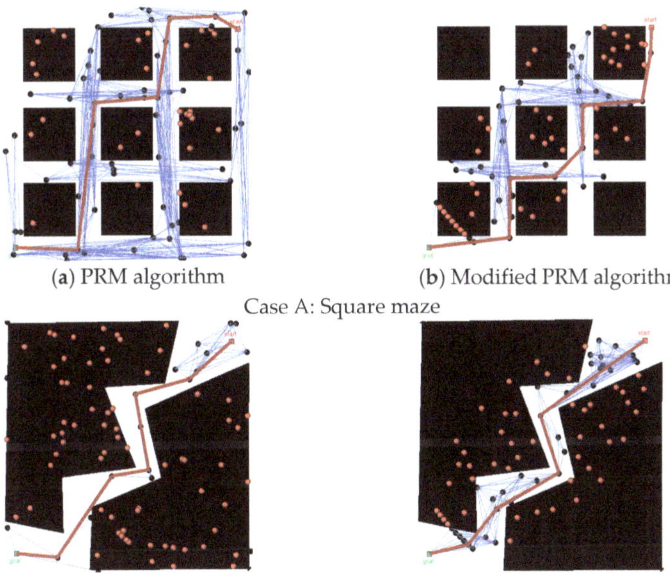

(a) PRM algorithm (b) Modified PRM algorithm

Case A: Square maze

(a) PRM algorithm (b) Modified PRM algorithm

Case B: Narrow channel

Figure 10. Comparison of algorithm planning results.

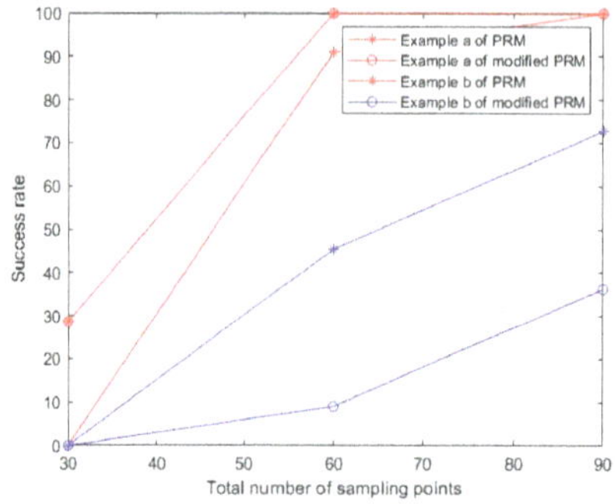

Figure 11. Algorithm success rate comparison.

Table 2. Comparison results of algorithm efficiency.

Algorithm Case	Sampling Points N	Basic PRM Algorithm			Modified PRM Algorithm		
		Path Length/m	Running Time/s	Success Rate/%	Path Length/m	Running Time/s	Success Rate/%
A	30	883.14	0.23	28.57	\	\	0
	60	869.63	0.89	100	839	0.62	90.91
	90	861.86	2.18	100	819.91	1.12	100
B	30	\	\	0	\	\	0
	60	812.1	0.28	9.09	735.51	0.29	45.45
	90	734.53	0.43	36.36	729.45	0.73	72.73

Referring to Figure 10, in the experiment of Case A, the number of sampling points falling into the obstacle space was comparable in both algorithms, but the sampling points in the self-use space were widely distributed in the PRM algorithm, which caused redundancy. In the modified PRM algorithm, the sampling points were concentrated on both sides of the main axis of the space, which improved the utilization of sampling points. In the experiment of Case B, most of the sampling points in the PRM algorithm fell into the obstacle space, and there were very few sampling points in the self-use space, which affected the quality of the path solution. In the modified PRM algorithm, the sampling points were distributed along the main axis of the space, and the larger number of sampling points in the self-use space provided the possibility of seeking a better path solution.

In Table 2 and Figure 11, for Case A, the modified PRM algorithm could not successfully plan the path when the number of sampling points was low ($N = 30$). When the number of sampling points increased to 60 ($N = 60$), the differences between the two algorithms in path length, running time, and success rate were not obvious. When the number of sampling points increased to 90 ($N = 90$), the modified PRM algorithm was better than the basic PRM algorithm in path length and running time. For Case B, when the number of sampling points was low ($N = 30$), both algorithms could not successfully plan the path, and as the number of sampling points increased, the modified PRM algorithm had a higher success rate in path planning and the quality of the path solution was more reliable.

4.3. ROS Simulation Test

In order to further verify the implementability of the modified PRM algorithm, simulation tests were designed, based on the ROS experimental platform. The composition of the ROS trolley is shown in Figure 12.

Figure 12. ROS car composition.

We mainly addressed the path planning problem of smart vehicles in a two-dimensional environment, using the function package provided by the ROS experimental platform to implement the LIDAR map building function. The test site is shown in Figure 13, and the SLAM map building effect is shown in Figure 14. Based on this environmental map, we defined the localization result of ROS itself as the starting point and specified the target point. The modified PRM algorithm was executed and the path planning results are shown in Figure 15.

Figure 13. Field map.

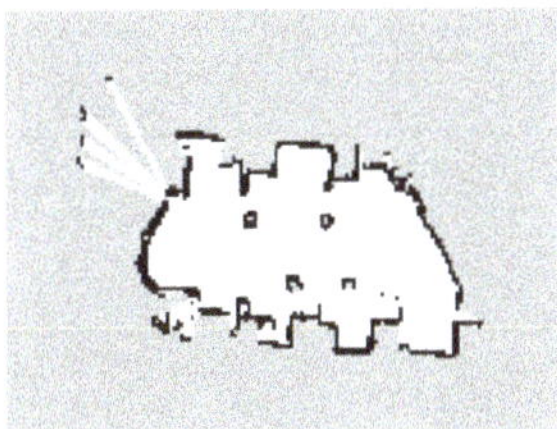

Figure 14. SLAM map.

(**a**) (**b**)

Figure 15. Path planning: (**a**) wayfinding map and (**b**) planning path.

From the simulation results, a road map was established in the SLAM map by the modified PRM algorithm. Meanwhile, the modified PRM algorithm planned a path successfully connecting the starting and target point, verifying the feasibility of the modified PRM algorithm.

5. Conclusions

In order to improve the overall quality of the PRM algorithm in path planning, a pseudo-random sampling method based on uniform sampling was designed to optimize the quality of sampling point generation. Random increments were introduced to adjust the fluctuation range of sampling points to effectively avoid the obstacle space. Due to the disadvantage of a low rate of roadmap construction, a two-way incremental collision detection strategy was used to set the connection threshold between road points to reduce the number of collision detection calls. Finally, the correctness of the modified PRM algorithm was verified and analyzed using MATLAB and ROS test platforms. The test results showed that the modified PRM algorithm has obvious advantages in enhancing the stability of the roadmap, shortening the length of the planned path, and improving the search rate of the algorithm. However, the majority of current algorithms, including the modified PRM algorithm, are model-driven, and face many limitations. These algorithms need to be further researched. Data-driven and cloud-network fusion technologies could be added to these algorithms to achieve better path planning and obstacle avoidance in smart vehicles.

Author Contributions: Conceptualization, S.B. and J.Y.; methodology, Q.L.; software, Q.L. and S.B.; validation, Q.L. and. S.B.; formal analysis, Q.L.; investigation, Y.X.; resources, Q.L.; data curation, Q.L.; writing—original draft preparation, Q.L. and. S.B.; writing—review and editing, Q.L.; visualization, Q.L.; supervision, J.Y.; project administration, J.Y.; funding acquisition, Q.L. All authors have read and agreed to the published version of the manuscript.

Funding: This research was funded by Graduate Research Innovation Program Project of Jiangsu Province, China, grant number "KYCX22_1059".

Institutional Review Board Statement: Not applicable.

Informed Consent Statement: Not applicable.

Data Availability Statement: The study did not report any data.

Conflicts of Interest: The authors declare no conflict of interest.

References

1. Shi, Y.J.; Han, Q.M.; Shen, W.M.; Wang, X. A Multi-Layer Collaboration Framework for Industrial Parks with 5G Vehicle-to-Everything Networksy. *Engineering* **2021**, *7*, 818–831. [CrossRef]
2. Zheng, Z.G.; Bashir, A.K. Graph-Enabled Intelligent Vehicular Network Data Processing. *IEEE Trans. Intell. Transp. Syst.* **2022**, *23*, 4726–4735. [CrossRef]
3. Sun, N.; Shi, H.Z.; Han, G.J.; Wang, B.; Shu, L. Dynamic Path Planning Algorithms With Load Balancing Based on Data Prediction for Smart Transportation Systems. *IEEE Access* **2020**, *8*, 15907–15922. [CrossRef]
4. Zhu, M.; Liu, X.Y.; Wang, X.D. An Online Ride-Sharing Path-Planning Strategy for Public Vehicle Systems. *IEEE Trans. Intell. Transp. Syst.* **2019**, *20*, 616–627. [CrossRef]
5. Zhu, Y.L.; Chu, K.M.; Chen, X.; Wang, X.; Su, H. Research and application of a multi-degree-of-freedom soft actuator. *Sens. Actuators A Phys.* **2022**, *338*, 113492. [CrossRef]
6. Tian, Y.; Yao, Q.Q.; Hang, P.; Wang, S. Adaptive Coordinated Path Tracking Control Strategy for Autonomous Vehicles with Direct Yaw Moment Control. *Chin. J. Mech. Eng.* **2022**, *35*, 1. [CrossRef]
7. Ayawli, B.K.; Chellali, R.; Appiah, A.Y.; Kyeremeh, F. An Overview of Nature-Inspired, Conventional, and Hybrid Methods of Autonomous Vehicle Path Planning. *J. Adv. Transp.* **2018**, *2018*, 8269698. [CrossRef]
8. Nazarahari, M.; Khanmirza, E.; Doostie, S. Multi-objective multi-robot path planning in continuous environment using an enhanced genetic algorithm. *Expert Syst. Appl.* **2019**, *115*, 106–120. [CrossRef]
9. Siddique, N.; Adeli, H. Nature Inspired Computing: An Overview and Some Future Directions. *Cogn. Comput.* **2015**, *7*, 706–714. [CrossRef] [PubMed]
10. Holland, J.H. Building blocks, cohort genetic algorithms, and hyperplane-defined functions. *Evol. Comput.* **2000**, *8*, 373–391. [CrossRef]
11. Tang, M.; Liu, Y.; Ding, F.; Wang, Z. Solution to Solid Wood Board Cutting Stock Problem. *Appl. Sci.* **2021**, *11*, 7790. [CrossRef]
12. Hoffman, M.R.; Mielens, J.D.; Omari, T.I.; Rommel, N.; Jiang, J.J.; McCulloch, T.M. Artificial neural network classification of pharyngeal high-resolution manometry with impedance data. *Laryngoscope* **2013**, *123*, 713–720. [CrossRef] [PubMed]
13. Yang, J.; Wang, Y.D.; Chen, Y.; Yu, J. Detection of Weeds Growing in Alfalfa Using Convolutional Neural Networks. *Agronomy* **2022**, *12*, 1459. [CrossRef]

14. Kirkpatrick, S.; Gelatt, C.D., Jr.; Vecchi, M.P. Optimization by Simulated Annealing. *Science* **1983**, *220*, 671–680. [CrossRef]
15. Dorigo, M.; Di Caro, G.; Gambardella, L.M. Ant algorithms for discrete optimization. *Artif. Life* **1999**, *5*, 137–172. [CrossRef]
16. Hu, X.H.; Shi, Y.H.; Eberhart, R. Recent Advances in Particle Swarm. In Proceedings of the 2004 Congress on Evolutionary Computation, Portland, OR, USA, 19–23 June 2004; IEEE: Piscataway, NJ, USA, 2004; pp. 90–97.
17. Karaboga, D.; Basturk, B. A powerful and efficient algorithm for numerical function optimization: Artificial bee colony (ABC) algorithm. *J. Glob. Optim.* **2007**, *39*, 459–471. [CrossRef]
18. Xu, X.Y.; Xie, J.; Xie, K.M. Path Planning and Obstacle-Avoidance for Soccer Robot Based on Artificial Potential Field and Genetic Algorithm. In Proceedings of the 2006 6th World Congress on Intelligent Control and Automation, Dalian, China, 21–23 June 2006; IEEE: Piscataway, NJ, USA, 2006; pp. 3494–3498.
19. Girija, S.; Joshi, A. Fast Hybrid PSO-APF Algorithm for Path Planning in Obstacle Rich Environment. *IFAC Pap.* **2019**, *52*, 25–30. [CrossRef]
20. Dai, L.; Wu, C.; Qi, J.T.; Han, J. Fuzzy Adaptive Kalman Filter Algorithm for RUAV's Integrated Navigation System. In Proceedings of the 2012 24th Chinese Control and Decision Conference (CCDC), Taiyuan, China, 23–25 May 2012; IEEE: Piscataway, NJ, USA, 2012; pp. 2865–2869.
21. Bahari, M.H.; Karsaz, A.; Pariz, N. High maneuvering target tracking using a novel hybrid kalman filter-fuzzy logic architecture. *Int. J. Innov. Comput. Inf. Control* **2011**, *7*, 501–510.
22. Simon, P. Principles of Robot Motion: Theory, Algorithms and Implementations. *Knowl. Eng. Rev.* **2007**, *22*, 209–211.
23. Lydia, E.K.; Petr, S.; Jean-Claude, L.; Overmars, M.H. Probabilistic roadmaps for path planning in high-dimensional configuration spaces. *IEEE Trans. Robot. Autom.* **1996**, *12*, 566–580.
24. Oussama, K. Real-Time Obstacle Avoidance for Manipulators and Mobile Robots. *Int. J. Robot. Res.* **1986**, *5*, 396–404.
25. Hwang, Y.K.; Ahuja, N. A potential field approach to path planning. *IEEE Trans. Robot. Autom.* **1992**, *8*, 23–32. [CrossRef]
26. Camacho, O.; Smith, C.A. Sliding mode control: An approach to regulate nonlinear chemical processes. *ISA Trans* **2000**, *39*, 205–218. [CrossRef]
27. Andrew, R.L.; Keith, P. Automated conformational analysis: Directed conformational search using the A* algorithm. *J. Comput. Chem.* **1990**, *11*, 1193–1205.
28. Carsten, J.; Ferguson, D.; Stentz, A. 3D Field D*: Improved Path Planning and Replanning in Three Dimensions. In Proceedings of the 2006 IEEE/RSJ International Conference on Intelligent Robots and Systems, Beijing, China, 9–15 October 2006; IEEE: Piscataway, NJ, USA, 2006; p. 3381.
29. Zhou, J.H.; Lin, H.Y. A self-localization and path planning technique for mobile robot navigation. In Proceedings of the 2011 9th World Congress on Intelligent Control and Automation, Taipei, Taiwan, 21–25 June 2011.
30. Cadena, C.; Carlone, L.; Carrillo, H.; Latif, Y.; Scaramuzza, D.; Neira, J.; Reid, I.; Leonard, J.J. Past, Present, and Future of Simultaneous Localization and Mapping: Toward the Robust-Perception Age. *IEEE Trans. Robot.* **2016**, *32*, 1309–1332. [CrossRef]
31. Cheng, Q.; Zhang, W.; Liu, H.; Zhang, Y.; Hao, L. Research on the Path Planning Algorithm of a Manipulator Based on GMM/GMR-MPRM. *Appl. Sci.* **2021**, *11*, 7599. [CrossRef]
32. Kantaros, Y.; Zavlanos, M.M. STyLuS*: A Temporal Logic Optimal Control Synthesis Algorithm for Large-Scale Multi-Robot Systems. *Int. J. Robot. Res.* **2020**, *39*, 812–836. [CrossRef]
33. Vasile, C.I.; Belta, C. Sampling-based temporal logic path planning. In Proceedings of the 2013 IEEE/RSJ International Conference on Intelligent Robots and Systems, Tokyo, Japan, 3–7 November 2013.
34. Dobson, A.; Bekris, K.E. Improving Sparse Roadmap Spanners. In Proceedings of the 2013 IEEE International Conference on Robotics and Automation, Karlsruhe, Germany, 6–10 May 2013; IEEE: Piscataway, NJ, USA, 2013; pp. 4106–4111.
35. Amato, N.M.; Dale, L.K. Probabilistic roadmap methods are embarrassingly parallel. In Proceedings of the 1999 IEEE International Conference on Robotics and Automation (Cat. No. 99CH36288C), Detroit, MI, USA, 10–15 May 1999.
36. Bekris, K.E.; Chen, B.Y.; Ladd, A.M.; Plaku, E.; Kavraki, L.E. Multiple query probabilistic roadmap planning using single query planning primitives. In Proceedings of the 2003 IEEE/RSJ International Conference on Intelligent Robots and Systems (IROS 2003) (Cat. No. 03CH37453), Las Vegas, NV, USA, 27–31 October 2003.
37. Kurniawati, H.; Hsu, D. *Workspace-Based Connectivity Oracle: An Adaptive Sampling Strategy for PRM Planning*; Springer: Berlin/Heidelberg, Germany, 2008; pp. 35–51.
38. Esposito, J.M.; Wright, J.N. Matrix completion as a post-processing technique for probabilistic roadmaps. *Int. J. Robot. Res.* **2019**, *38*, 388–400. [CrossRef]
39. Gao, J.; Ye, W.; Guo, J.; Li, Z. Deep Reinforcement Learning for Indoor Mobile Robot Path Planning. *Sensors* **2020**, *20*, 5493. [CrossRef]
40. Chen, G.; Luo, N.; Liu, D.; Zhao, Z.; Liang, C. Path planning for manipulators based on an improved probabilistic roadmap method. *Robot. Comput.-Integr. Manuf.* **2021**, *72*, 102196. [CrossRef]
41. Ravankar, A.A.; Ravankar, A.; Emaru, T.; Kobayashi, Y. HPPRM: Hybrid Potential Based Probabilistic Roadmap Algorithm for Improved Dynamic Path Planning of Mobile Robots. *IEEE Access* **2020**, *8*, 221743–221766. [CrossRef]
42. Xu, Z.F.; Deng, D.; Shimada, K. Autonomous UAV Exploration of Dynamic Environments Via Incremental Sampling and Probabilistic Roadmap. *IEEE Robot. Autom. Lett.* **2021**, *6*, 2729–2736. [CrossRef]

sensors
MDPI

Article

Model Predictive Control of a Novel Wheeled–Legged Planetary Rover for Trajectory Tracking

Jun He *, Yanlong Sun, Limin Yang and Feng Gao

State Key Laboratory of Mechanical System and Vibration, School of Mechanical Engineering, Shanghai Jiao Tong University, Shanghai 200240, China; sunyanlong@sjtu.edu.cn (Y.S.); ylm20159@sjtu.edu.cn (L.Y.); fengg@sjtu.edu.cn (F.G.)
* Correspondence: jhe@sjtu.edu.cn

Abstract: Amid increasing demands for planetary exploration, wide-range autonomous exploration is still a great challenge for existing planetary rovers, which calls for new planetary rovers with novel locomotive mechanisms and corresponding control strategies. This paper proposes a novel wheeled–legged mechanism for the design of planetary rovers. The leg suspension utilizes a rigid–flexible coupling mechanism with a hybrid serial–parallel topology. First, the kinematic model is derived. Then, a control strategy for the wheeled–legged rover that includes a trajectory tracking module based on the model predictive control, the steering strategy, and the wheel speed allocation algorithm is proposed. After that, three groups of cosimulations with different trajectories and speeds, and experiments are carried out. Results of both the simulations and experiments validate the proposed control method.

Keywords: mobile robot; advanced intelligent control; wheeled–legged; trajectory tracking; model predictive control

Citation: He, J.; Sun, Y.; Yang, L.; Gao, F. Model Predictive Control of a Novel Wheeled–Legged Planetary Rover for Trajectory Tracking. *Sensors* **2022**, 22, 4164. https://doi.org/10.3390/s22114164

Academic Editors: Luige Vladareanu, Hongnian Yu, Hongbo Wang and Yongfei Feng

Received: 19 April 2022
Accepted: 28 May 2022
Published: 30 May 2022

1. Introduction

The planetary rovers that were deployed for the exploration of the moon and Mars, such as Curiosity and Perseverance, are purely wheeled robotic systems [1,2]. They adopt the passive rocker–bogie suspension configuration. There are two identical linkage mechanisms on each side of the rover, which consist of a rocker and a bogie. A differential mechanism is adopted to connect the two linkage mechanisms. One wheel is fixed at one end of the rocker, while the bogie has two wheels that are mounted on the other end of the rocker. Recently, China's Zhurong Mars rover adopted an active rocker–bogie suspension. There was a novel angle-adjusting mechanism between the two rockers to generate a wheel-step motion that could help the rover avoid wheel slip sinkage [3]. Although many remarkable achievements have been made in the field of planetary exploration, the capability of wide-range autonomous exploration is still a great challenge for planetary rovers.

The hybrid leg–wheel mechanism can be used in the design of planetary rovers. Legged–wheeled robots have the merits of being both wheeled and legged robots. They can robustly deal with uncertainties or disturbances caused by the unstructured discontinuous terrain encountered during planetary exploration. Moreover, they have a relatively high locomotion efficiency. There are three categories of leg–wheel robotic systems that differ according to leg morphology [4]. The first one is the serial leg configuration. For example, the Jet Propulsion Laboratory (JPL) developed an articulated–wheeled lunar robot called ATHLETE [5]. Each leg was a 6R (rotational joint) serial mechanism with six degrees of freedom (DOFs). It could roll over flat smooth terrain on rotating wheels and could also use the wheels as feet to walk over irregular and steep terrain. Grand et al. [6] addressed a wheeled–legged robot called Hylos, which had 16 actively actuated DOFs, with each leg combining a two-DOF leg and the steering and rotation DOFs in the wheel. Smith et al. [7] presented the PAW, a four-legged vehicle with a T-shaped body and compliant legs. Each leg had two DOFs, including a passive prismatic joint. The second one was a leg with a parallel topology. Xu et al. [8] proposed a parallel legged–wheeled robotic system called BIT-NAZA, which had four parallel platforms with six DOFs and a 6-UPU (universal–prismatic–universal joints) configuration. There were four active wheels that were mounted on the feet of the parallel legs. Compared to their serial counterparts, parallel legged–wheeled systems usually have more payload and stiffness [9]. In addition, the actuators of the parallel leg system can be installed on the body, and the inertia of the moving part of the leg can be reduced. The electric devices comprising the actuator, such as the encoder and the torque sensor, can be easily protected [10]. Finally, there is the third category of hybrid wheeled–legged robots, namely transformable wheeled–legged vehicles, such as the Whegs series [11,12], Quattroped [13], Wheel Transformer [14], TurboQuad [15], and STEP [16]. For these robots, the wheel and leg morphology can be switched via the active joints. Transformable leg–wheel robots often adopt simple mechanical structures to simplify the control strategy. Thus, the stability and maneuverability of hybrid robots are inevitably sacrificed [17].

In spite of the excellent kinematic characteristics of the leg mechanisms discussed above, they cannot be directly applied to extraterrestrial exploration rovers because of the existence of special requirements such as maneuverability and security. For example, planetary rovers such as Curiosity [18] have additional wheels and legs to maintain a high level of security to overcome the tough terrains of the outer planet. Exploration rovers must have a fault tolerance feature to ensure the safety of the vehicle. These rovers can continue to move and carry out exploration missions even if one or multiple actuators are not working. For instance, the wheeled–legged rover ShearpTT [19] adopted self-locking gears in the actuator design for the suspension. There are two benefits to this: The first one is that the rover would not fall down when the actuator in the knee joint is invalid. The other is that the rover can support its own weight through the self-locking mechanism without the need for additional electrical energy due to the motor brake.

Legged suspension can change the center of gravity, the body posture, the distribution of contact forces, and even raise wheels to negotiate obstacles. Hence, controlling wheeled–legged robots is more complex than traditional exploration rovers with rocker–bogie suspension, especially in terms of trajectory tracking. Lamon et al. [20] proposed a control method for three-dimensional trajectory tracking. Furthermore, feedback control based on stereo vision efficiently improved the accuracy of trajectory tracking [21,22]. For rovers with independent front and rear steering and four wheels that are driven independently, path tracking becomes more complicated. Krid et al. [23] developed a dynamics-based tracking controller on a horizontal plane using a linear quadratic regulator (LQR). LQR controllers are able to track the line trajectory with quite a good accuracy. However, there is an obvious decrease in the accuracy with regard to steering. In contrast, model predictive control (MPC) can handle complex trajectories [24]. The control algorithm based on MPC can be derived in a recursive form, which is computationally more efficient than the other methods. The computing efficiency is a key evaluation index for planetary rovers because there are very limited computing resources in space. Though the MPC method has been applied to wheeled robots [25,26], there are some differences for wheeled-legged robots. First, wheeled-legged robots possess terrain-adaptive capabilities [27]. The leg length can be adjusted by changing the knee joint angle even if the wheel is always under the hip joint. The attitude angles of the robot can be controlled through changing the leg lengths. Thus, the terrain-adaptive capability needs to be involved in the trajectory tracking when the robot runs across irregular terrains. Second, having wheels that drive independently can lead to an uneven speed distribution, resulting in the occurrence of wheel slip [28]. For wheeled–legged rovers, the pose of the body, the wheel–soil contact force, and the height of the gravitational center can all be adjusted by coordinating the motion of the hip and knee joints when the wheeled–legged robot moves over rough terrain [29]. Both the motion of the hip and knee joints affect the motion characteristics of the wheel, resulting in slippage.

Therefore, it is necessary to provide a suitable speed for each wheel that is based on the motion characteristics of the whole robot on rough terrain.

In this paper, a novel wheeled–legged mechanism called TAWL is proposed for the design of planetary rovers. The leg suspension utilizes a rigid–flexible coupling mechanism with a hybrid serial–parallel topology. A kinematic model is derived first. Then, a control strategy for a wheeled–legged rover is proposed that includes a trajectory-tracking module based on MPC, the steering module, and the wheel speed allocation module. After that, a cosimulation model is established in both NX/Motion and Simulink software to verify the control strategy. Finally, experiments are also carried out to validate the proposed control method.

The remainder of the paper is organized as follows: Section 2 reports the hardware design and the kinematics of the rover; Section 3 details the control strategy; Section 4 presents the simulations, experiments, and the discussion of the results; and finally, Section 5 offers the conclusions.

2. Hardware and Kinematics of the Rover

2.1. Mechanical Structure

There are two aspects that need to be considered for leg design: First, the leg inertia must be as low as possible. Each leg has four DOFs, as illustrated in Figure 1, namely the hip abduction/adduction (HAA) joint, the hip flexion/extension (HFE) joint, the hip endo/exorotation (HEE), and the knee flexion/extension (KFE) joint. The HEE joint can also be used to steer the wheels. To reduce the rotational inertia of the robot's legs, the actuators of the HFE and KFE joints are coaxially located at the hip. The KFE joint is actuated by a pantograph mechanism. In addition, to increase the driving torques of the HFE and KFE joints, a gear reducer stage was adopted at each of their output shafts. Second, compliant mechanisms are necessary for legged robotic systems to handle uncertainties or disturbances such as ground contact collisions. A telescopic structure with a passive damped spring was used for the leg design. In addition, there are two spring ball plungers that trigger the spring–damper mechanism. When the impact force from the ground exceeds the threshold value of the spring ball plunger, the spring–damper mechanism works to dissipate the impact energy. After that, the lower leg returns to its original length with the restoring force of the spring.

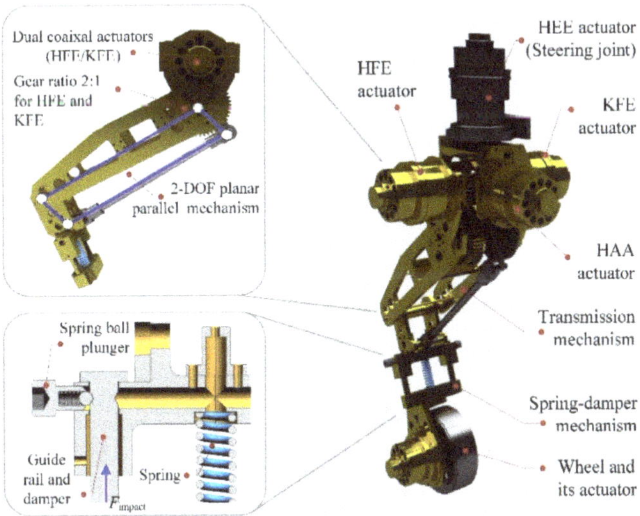

Figure 1. The leg–wheel structure.

The TAWL robot has four identical legs with wheels. The four legs are mounted to the torso in an axially symmetric distribution, as depicted in Figure 2. Its four hip joints are located on a circle with a diameter of 1.2 m. From a biological view, to obtain highly dynamic characteristics in the longitudinal direction, the ratio of the length to the width of the torso should be more than 1. However, the wheeled mode is the primary motion mode for the TAWL robot. An axially symmetrical arrangement was adopted for the robot design so that the robot would have all-directional locomotion capability in both the wheeled and legged modes (walking or trotting). Furthermore, this arrangement also increases the number of legged locomotion modes. There are at least three leg configurations for legged locomotion, i.e., the M-configuration, O-configuration, and X-configuration.

Figure 2. The TAWL robot.

2.2. Perception and Control System

There are two types of sensors: proprioceptive and exteroceptive sensors. Proprioceptive sensors contain the joint encoder, the joint torque sensor, and the inertial measurement unit (IMU), as seen in Figure 3. All of the joint angles are precisely measured by absolute encoders. Since the angle measures of each motor are absolute, the robot does not have to be homed at startup. The IMU sensor is mounted on the body and is responsible for the poses of the robot's torso. Exteroceptive sensors include visual and nonvisual sensors, which are employed to measure environmental information such as the geometrical parameters of the terrain and ground contact forces. Here, a stereo vision system was attached to the front part of the main body. Furthermore, an independent computer was implemented to deal with the vision algorithms. To improve the reliability, we did not assemble force sensors for ground contact force measurements to the end of each leg. We established a distribution measurement model and then evaluated the ground contact forces using the measurement data from the joint torque sensors.

An onboard main controller was used to run the entire control program. The main controller communicates with 20 servo drives and 16 joint torque sensors in real time via the EtherCAT industrial network protocol (Bechoff, Verl, Germany). The measurement data from the IMU sensor are transferred into the main controller according to the RS-485 serial data standard. The main controller communicates with the visual controller by means of the ADS (automation device specifications) protocol. The TAWL robot's control software was developed using the TwinCAT software platform (Bechoff, Verl, Germany), a real-time PC-based control system. In addition, there are two on-board lithium batteries that the robot can use to run for about 1.5 h.

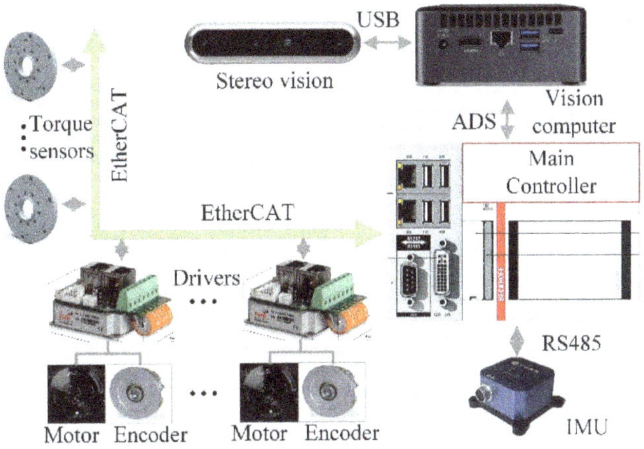

Figure 3. The perception and control system.

2.3. Kinematics of the Rover

The body frame $\{O_B—X_BY_BZ_B\}$ of the whole robot is located at the center of the plane and is composed of the centers of four hip joints. We established the D-H coordinate systems in Figure 4 for each leg. Because each leg has the same kinematic structure, the D-H parameters of the four legs are also the same. $\{O_0—x_0y_0z_0\}$ is the base frame of each leg (i.e., the leg frame), which is located at the center of the hip joint. $\{O_4—x_4y_4z_4\}$ is the wheel frame of each leg. The D-H parameters are shown in Table 1. Therefore, the transformation matrix from frame $i-1$ to i for the ith limb can be written as

$$ {}^{i-1}_{i}T = \begin{bmatrix} c\theta_i & -s\theta_i c\alpha_i & s\theta_i s\alpha_i & a_i c\theta_i \\ s\theta_i & c\theta_i c\alpha_i & -c\theta_i s\alpha_i & a_i s\theta_i \\ 0 & s\alpha_i & c\alpha_i & d_i \\ 0 & 0 & 0 & 1 \end{bmatrix} \tag{1} $$

where s and c denote the sine and cosine functions.

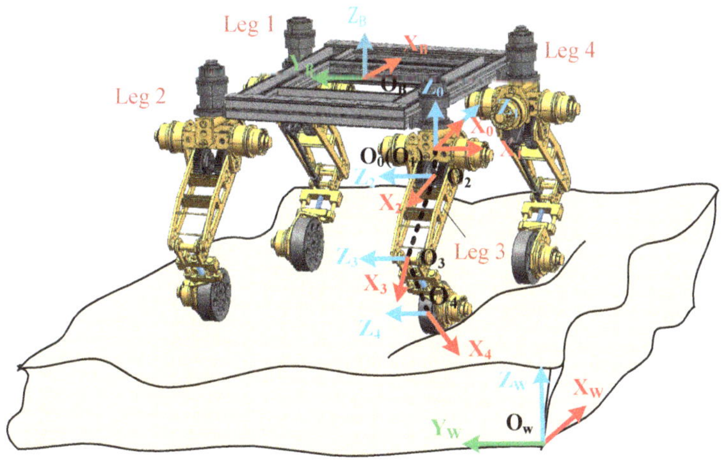

Figure 4. The coordinate systems of the rover.

Table 1. The D-H parameters.

	θ_i	d_i	α_i	a_i
1	θ_1	0	$\pi/2$	0
2	θ_2	0	$-\pi/2$	$L_1 = 87.5$
3	θ_3	0	0	$L_2 = 350$
4	θ_4	0	0	$L_3 = 310$

For the ith leg, the transformation matrix from the wheel frame to the leg frame is written as

$$\begin{aligned} {}^{0}_{4}T^{i} = {}^{0}_{1}T^{i}\,{}^{1}_{2}T^{i}\,{}^{2}_{3}T^{i}\,{}^{3}_{4}T^{i} &= \begin{pmatrix} \boldsymbol{R} & \boldsymbol{P} \\ \boldsymbol{0} & 1 \end{pmatrix} \\ &= \begin{pmatrix} -s_{34} & -c_{34} & 0 & -L_3 s_{34} - L_2 s_3 \\ c_{34}c_2 & -s_{34}c_2 & -s_2 & c_2(L_1 + L_3 c_{34} + L_2 c_3) \\ c_{34}s_2 & -s_{34}s_2 & c_2 & s_2(L_1 + L_3 c_{34} + L_2 c_3) \\ 0 & 0 & 0 & 1 \end{pmatrix}, \end{aligned} \tag{2}$$

where $s_{34} = \sin(\theta_3+\theta_4)$, $c_{34} = \cos(\theta_3+\theta_4)$, $s_2 = \sin\theta_2$, $c_2 = \cos\theta_2$, $s_3 = \sin\theta_3$, and $c_3 = \cos\theta_3$. Here, $\theta_1 = \pi/2$ and $\boldsymbol{P} = (P_x,\ P_y\ P_z)^T$. are the positions of the wheel center with respect to the leg frame.

When $\boldsymbol{P}$ is given, the rotational angle of each joint, θ_2, θ_3, and θ_4, can be obtained as

$$\theta_2 = \mathrm{atan}(P_z/P_y), \tag{3}$$

$$\theta_3 = -\mathrm{atan}\left(\frac{C}{A^2+B^2+C^2}\right) - atan\left(\frac{B}{A}\right), \tag{4}$$

$$\theta_4 = -\mathrm{atan}\left(\frac{G}{\sqrt{E^2+F^2-G^2}}\right) - atan\left(\frac{F}{E}\right) - \theta_3 \tag{5}$$

where

$$A = 2P_x L_2$$

$$B = -2\left(\sqrt{P_y{}^2 + P_z{}^2} - L_1\right)L_2$$

$$C = \left(\sqrt{P_y{}^2 + P_z{}^2} - L_1\right)^2 + L_2{}^2 + P_x{}^2 - L_3{}^2$$

$$E = 2P_x L_3$$

$$F = -2L_3\left(\sqrt{P_y{}^2 + P_z{}^2} - L_1\right)$$

$$G = \left(\sqrt{P_y{}^2 + P_z{}^2} - L_1\right)^2 + P_x{}^2 + L_3{}^2 - L_2{}^2$$

3. Control Strategy

In this section, a control architecture for the wheeled–legged rover is proposed, as depicted in Figure 5. The control strategy consists of a planning layer, a controller layer, and a physical layer. First, the planner layer generates the reference trajectory. A planned path is generally composed of discrete points that come from the operator or the planner, which is based on a vision system. Using these points, a Bezier curve was adopted to produce a reference trajectory that included the time information. Thus, the derivation of the reference trajectory yielded the reference velocity. Second, the controller layer includes an MPC module, a steering module, and a wheel speed allocation module. The MPC module calculates the optimal control inputs through the last control inputs and the current state variables. The state variables can be estimated by a data fusion algorithm such as a Kalman filter and a particle filter, which is based on the proprioceptive and exteroceptive sensors in the robotic system. Considering that the main purpose was to verify the trajectory tracking algorithm, the state variables, including the position and velocity of the robot, were measured by the vision motion capture system directly in the present experimental study. In addition, to eliminate the accumulated errors, a PID control method was added in the loop. Then, the steering module provided the speed and the steering angle of each wheel. After that, the wheel speed allocation algorithm was presented to avoid a wheel slip. Next, the leg joint angles were obtained through the inverse kinematics of the rover. Third, the physical layer received the steering angles, the wheel speeds, and the leg joint angles and sent these orders to servo drives.

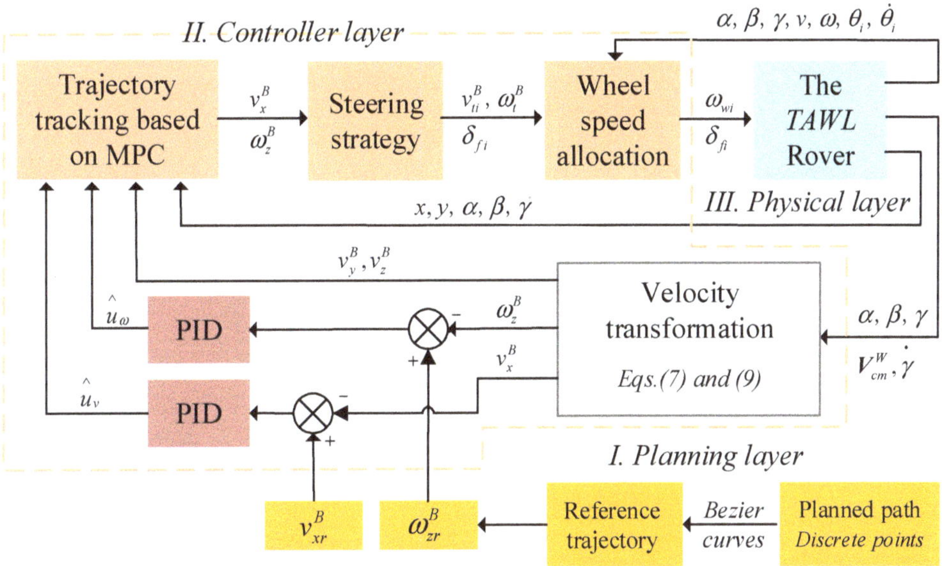

Figure 5. The rover's control strategy.

3.1. Locomotive Equations

The rotation matrix from the body frame {B} to the world frame {W} is written as

$$
{}^{W}_{B}R(\alpha,\beta,\gamma) = \begin{pmatrix} c\gamma c\beta & c\gamma s\beta s\alpha - s\gamma c\alpha & c\gamma s\beta c\alpha + s\gamma s\alpha \\ s\gamma c\beta & s\gamma s\beta s\alpha + c\gamma c\alpha & s\gamma s\beta c\alpha - c\gamma s\alpha \\ -s\beta & c\beta s\alpha & c\beta c\alpha \end{pmatrix}, \tag{6}
$$

where α, β, and γ are the fixed rotational angles with respect to the x, y, and z axes of the world frame, respectively.

Furthermore, the velocity of the centroid of the robot can be denoted by

$$
\boldsymbol{V}^{W}_{cm} = \begin{pmatrix} \dot{x} \\ \dot{y} \\ \dot{z} \end{pmatrix} = \begin{pmatrix} c\gamma c\beta & c\gamma s\beta s\alpha - s\gamma c\alpha & c\gamma s\beta c\alpha + s\gamma s\alpha \\ s\gamma c\beta & s\gamma s\beta s\alpha + c\gamma c\alpha & s\gamma s\beta c\alpha - c\gamma s\alpha \\ -s\beta & c\beta s\alpha & c\beta c\alpha \end{pmatrix} \boldsymbol{V}^{B}_{cm}, \tag{7}
$$

where $\boldsymbol{V}^{W}_{cm}$ and $\boldsymbol{V}^{B}_{cm}$ are the velocities of the body centroid for frames {W} and {B}, and $\boldsymbol{V}^{B}_{cm} = \left(v^{B}_{x}, v^{B}_{y}, v^{B}_{z}\right)^{T}$.

The yaw angle of the robot with respect to the body frame, γ^{B}, can be written as

$$
\tan\gamma = \tan\gamma^{B} c\alpha / c\beta \tag{8}
$$

where γ is the yaw angle in frame {W}.

Thus, we have

$$\dot{\gamma} = \omega_z^B c\alpha / c\beta. \tag{9}$$

Aordingly, the kinematic equation for the trajectory tracking is obtained as

$$\dot{\boldsymbol{X}} = \begin{pmatrix} \dot{x} \\ \dot{y} \\ \dot{\gamma} \end{pmatrix} = \begin{pmatrix} c\gamma c\beta & 0 \\ s\gamma c\beta & 0 \\ 0 & \frac{c\alpha}{c\beta} \end{pmatrix} \begin{pmatrix} v_x^B \\ \omega_z^B \end{pmatrix} + \begin{pmatrix} c\gamma s\beta s\alpha - s\gamma c\alpha & c\gamma s\beta c\alpha + s\gamma s\alpha \\ s\gamma s\beta s\alpha + c\gamma c\alpha & s\gamma s\beta c\alpha - c\gamma s\alpha \\ 0 & 0 \end{pmatrix} \begin{pmatrix} v_y^B \\ v_z^B \end{pmatrix} \tag{10}$$

where $\boldsymbol{X} = (x, y, \gamma)^T$, $\boldsymbol{u} = (v_x^B, \omega_z^B)^T$, and $\dot{X} = (\dot{x}, \dot{y}, \dot{\gamma})^T = f(X, u, t)$. At a reference point on the trajectory, we have $\boldsymbol{X}_r = (x_r, y_r, \gamma_r)^T$, $\dot{\boldsymbol{X}}_r = f(X_r, u_r, t) = (\dot{x}_r, \dot{y}_r, \dot{\gamma}_r)^T$, and $\boldsymbol{u}_r = (v_{xr}^B, \omega_{zr}^B)^T$.

Therefore, expanding Equation (10) in the Taylor series around the reference point $(\boldsymbol{X}_r, \boldsymbol{u}_r)$ and discarding the high order terms yields

$$\dot{X} = f(X_r, u_r, t) + \frac{\partial f(X, u, t)}{\partial X}|_{(X_r,\, u_r)}(X - X_r) + \frac{\partial f(X, u, t)}{\partial u}|_{(X_r,\, u_r)}(u - u_r) \tag{11}$$

where

$$\frac{\partial f(X,u,t)}{\partial X}|_{(X_r,\, u_r)} = \begin{pmatrix} \frac{\partial f_1(X,u,t)}{\partial x} & \frac{\partial f_1(X,u,t)}{\partial y} & \frac{\partial f_1(X,u,t)}{\partial \gamma} \\ \frac{\partial f_2(X,u,t)}{\partial x} & \frac{\partial f_2(X,u,t)}{\partial y} & \frac{\partial f_2(X,u,t)}{\partial \gamma} \\ \frac{\partial f_3(X,u,t)}{\partial x} & \frac{\partial f_3(X,u,t)}{\partial y} & \frac{\partial f_3(X,u,t)}{\partial \gamma} \end{pmatrix}$$

$$= \begin{pmatrix} 0 & 0 & -s\gamma_r c\beta v_{xr}^B + (-s\gamma_r s\alpha s\beta - c\gamma_r c\alpha)v_y^B + (-s\gamma_r s\beta c\alpha + c\gamma_r s\alpha)v_z^B \\ 0 & 0 & c\gamma_r c\beta v_{xr}^B + (c\gamma_r s\alpha s\beta - s\gamma_r c\alpha)v_y^B + (c\gamma_r s\beta c\alpha + s\gamma_r s\alpha)v_z^B \\ 0 & 0 & 0 \end{pmatrix},$$

$$\frac{\partial f(X,u,t)}{\partial u}|_{(X_r,\, u_r)} = \begin{pmatrix} \frac{\partial f_1(X,u,t)}{\partial v_x^B} & \frac{\partial f_1(X,u,t)}{\partial \omega_z^B} \\ \frac{\partial f_2(X,u,t)}{\partial v_x^B} & \frac{\partial f_2(X,u,t)}{\partial \omega_z^B} \\ \frac{\partial f_3(X,u,t)}{\partial v_x^B} & \frac{\partial f_3(X,u,t)}{\partial \omega_z^B} \end{pmatrix} = \begin{pmatrix} c\beta c\gamma_r & 0 \\ c\beta s\gamma_r & 0 \\ 0 & c\alpha / c\beta \end{pmatrix}.$$

Accordingly, the state space equation can be denoted by

$$\dot{\hat{X}} = A(t)\hat{X} + B(t)\hat{u} \tag{12}$$

where $\hat{X} = (x - x_r, y - y_r, \gamma - \gamma_r)^T$, $\dot{\hat{X}} = (\dot{x} - \dot{x}_r, \dot{y} - \dot{y}_r, \dot{\gamma} - \dot{\gamma}_r)^T$, $\hat{u} = (\hat{u}_v, \hat{u}_\omega) = (v - v_{xr}^B, \omega - \omega_{zr}^B)^T$, $A(t) = \frac{\partial f(X,u,t)}{\partial X}|_{(X_r,\, u_r)}$, and $B(t) = \frac{\partial f(X,u,t)}{\partial u}|_{(X_r,\, u_r)}$. $\hat{X}$ is the error with respect to the reference trajectory, and $\hat{u}$ is its associated perturbation control input.

Using forward differences, the approximation of $\dot{X}$ can be obtained as the following discrete-time form:

$$\hat{X}(k+1) = G_k\hat{X}(k) + H_k\hat{u}(k) \tag{13}$$

where $G_k = TA_k + \boldsymbol{I}$, and $H_k = TB_k$. T and k are the sampling period and the sampling time. $\boldsymbol{I}$ is the identity matrix.

3.2. Trajectory Tracking Model Based on MPC

3.2.1. Objective Function

A controller was designed for the wheeled–legged robot to track the desired trajectory precisely and stably. By changing the current and future inputs of the control system, the optimization problem is the minimization of a predicted performance cost, which is a quadratic function of the states and control inputs as follows:

$$J(t) = \sum_{i=1}^{N_p} \hat{X}^T(t+i|t)Q\hat{X}(t+i|t) + \sum_{j=1}^{N_c-1} \Delta\hat{u}^T(t+i|t)R\Delta\hat{u}(t+i|t) + \rho\varepsilon^2, \tag{14}$$

where N_p and N_c are the prediction and control horizons, respectively. Here, Q and R are the weighting matrices; ρ is the weight coefficient, and ε is the relaxation factor.

Let

$$\xi(k|t) = \begin{pmatrix} \hat{X}(k|t) \\ \hat{u}(k-1|t) \end{pmatrix}, \tag{15}$$

we obtain

$$\xi(k+1|t) = \hat{A}_k \xi(k|t) + \hat{B}_k \Delta \hat{u}(k|t), \tag{16}$$

$$\eta(k|t) = \hat{C}_k \xi(k|t), \tag{17}$$

where $\hat{A}_k = \begin{pmatrix} G_k & H_k \\ \mathbf{0} & I \end{pmatrix}$, and $\hat{B}_k = \begin{pmatrix} H_k \\ I \end{pmatrix}$.

Furthermore, Equations (16) and (17) can be rewritten as the following matrix form:

$$\boldsymbol{Y}(t) = \boldsymbol{\Omega}\xi(t) + \boldsymbol{\Phi}\Delta\boldsymbol{U} \tag{18}$$

where

$$\boldsymbol{Y}(t) = \begin{pmatrix} \eta(k+1|t) \\ \eta(k+2|t) \\ \cdots \\ \eta(k+N_c|t) \\ \cdots \\ \eta(k+N_p|t) \end{pmatrix}, \boldsymbol{\Omega} = \begin{pmatrix} \hat{C}_k \hat{A}_k \\ \hat{C}_k \hat{A}_k^2 \\ \cdots \\ \hat{C}_k \hat{A}_k^{N_c} \\ \cdots \\ \hat{C}_k \hat{A}_k^{N_p} \end{pmatrix}, \Delta\boldsymbol{U} = \begin{pmatrix} \Delta u(t|t) \\ \Delta u(t+1|t) \\ \cdots \\ \Delta u(t+N_c|t) \end{pmatrix}, \text{ and}$$

$$\boldsymbol{\Phi} = \begin{pmatrix} \hat{C}_k \hat{B}_k & 0 & 0 & 0 \\ \hat{C}_k \hat{A}_k \hat{B}_k & \hat{C}_k \hat{B}_k & 0 & 0 \\ \cdots & \cdots & \ddots & \cdots \\ \hat{C}_k \hat{A}_k^{N_c-1} \hat{B}_k & \hat{C}_k \hat{A}_k^{N_c-2} \hat{B}_k & \cdots & \hat{C}_k \hat{B}_k \\ \hat{C}_k \hat{A}_k^{N_c} \hat{B}_k & \hat{C}_k \hat{A}_k^{N_c-1} \hat{B}_k & \cdots & \hat{C}_k \hat{A}_k \hat{B}_k \\ \vdots & \vdots & \ddots & \vdots \\ \hat{C}_k \hat{A}_k^{N_p-1} \hat{B}_k & \hat{C}_k \hat{A}_k^{N_p-2} \hat{B}_k & \cdots & \hat{C}_k \hat{A}_k^{N_p-N_c-1} \hat{B}_k \end{pmatrix}$$

Equations (14) and (18) yield

$$\begin{aligned} \boldsymbol{J}(\boldsymbol{t}) &= \Delta\boldsymbol{U}^T(\boldsymbol{t})\boldsymbol{R}\Delta\boldsymbol{U}(\boldsymbol{t}) + \boldsymbol{Y}^T(\boldsymbol{t})\boldsymbol{Q}\boldsymbol{Y}(\boldsymbol{t}) + \rho\varepsilon^2 \\ &= \Delta\boldsymbol{U}^T(\boldsymbol{t})\boldsymbol{R}\Delta\boldsymbol{U}(\boldsymbol{t}) + (\boldsymbol{\Phi}\Delta\boldsymbol{U}(\boldsymbol{t}))^T\boldsymbol{Q}(\boldsymbol{\Phi}\Delta\boldsymbol{U}(\boldsymbol{t})) \\ &+ \mathbf{2}(\boldsymbol{\Omega}\boldsymbol{\xi}(\boldsymbol{t}))^T\boldsymbol{Q}(\boldsymbol{\Phi}\Delta\boldsymbol{U}(\boldsymbol{t})) + (\boldsymbol{\Omega}\boldsymbol{\xi}(\boldsymbol{t}))^T\boldsymbol{Q}(\boldsymbol{\Omega}\boldsymbol{\xi}(\boldsymbol{t})) + \rho\varepsilon^{\mathbf{2}}. \end{aligned} \tag{19}$$

Here, $\boldsymbol{\Omega}\xi(t)$ is not affected by the inputs and can thus be discarded. Therefore, the objective function is rewritten as a standard quadratic form:

$$\boldsymbol{J}(t) = (\Delta\boldsymbol{U}^T(t) \quad \varepsilon)\boldsymbol{H}(t)(\Delta\boldsymbol{U}^T(t) \quad \varepsilon)^T + \boldsymbol{F}(t)(\Delta\boldsymbol{U}^T(t) \quad \varepsilon)^T, \tag{20}$$

where

$$\boldsymbol{H}(\boldsymbol{t}) = \begin{pmatrix} \boldsymbol{\Phi}^T\boldsymbol{Q}\boldsymbol{\Phi} + \boldsymbol{R} & \mathbf{0} \\ \mathbf{0} & \rho \end{pmatrix}, \boldsymbol{F}(\boldsymbol{t}) = \begin{pmatrix} \mathbf{2}(\boldsymbol{\Omega}\boldsymbol{\xi}(\boldsymbol{t}))^T\boldsymbol{Q}\boldsymbol{\Phi} & \mathbf{0} \end{pmatrix}.$$

3.2.2. Constraints

There are some constraints when the wheeled–legged robot carries out trajectory tracking tasks. The amplitude of the control input $\boldsymbol{u}$ and control input increment $\Delta\boldsymbol{u}$ satisfy

$$\boldsymbol{u}_{min}(\boldsymbol{t}+\boldsymbol{k}|\boldsymbol{t}) \leq \boldsymbol{u}(\boldsymbol{t}+\boldsymbol{k}|\boldsymbol{t}) \leq \boldsymbol{u}_{max}(\boldsymbol{t}+\boldsymbol{k}|\boldsymbol{t}),\ k = 0, 1 \cdots N_c - 1, \tag{21}$$

$$\Delta\boldsymbol{u}_{min}(t+k|t) \leq \Delta\boldsymbol{u}(t+k|t) \leq \Delta\boldsymbol{u}_{max}(t+k|t),\ k = 0, 1 \cdots N_c - 1, \tag{22}$$

where $\boldsymbol{u_{min}}$ and Δu_{min} are the predefined lower bounds, and $\boldsymbol{u_{max}}$ and Δu_{max} are the predefined upper bounds. Furthermore, the variable to be solved in the objective function are the control increment in the control horizon. Therefore, the constraints need be converted into the product form of the control increment and the transformation matrix.

The following relationship exists:

$$\boldsymbol{u}(t+k|t) = \boldsymbol{u}(t+k-1|t) + \Delta \boldsymbol{u}(t+k|t). \tag{23}$$

Furthermore, Equation (23) can be reformulated as a matrix form:

$$\boldsymbol{U}(t) = \boldsymbol{E}\Delta \boldsymbol{U}(t) + \boldsymbol{U}(t-1) \tag{24}$$

where

$$\boldsymbol{U}(t) = \begin{pmatrix} u(t|t) \\ u(t+1|t) \\ \vdots \\ u(t+N_c-1|t) \end{pmatrix}, \boldsymbol{E} = \begin{pmatrix} I & 0 & 0 & 0 \\ I & I & 0 & 0 \\ \vdots & \vdots & \ddots & \vdots \\ I & I & I & I \end{pmatrix},$$

$$\Delta \boldsymbol{U}(t) = \begin{pmatrix} \Delta u(t|t) \\ \Delta u(t+1|t) \\ \vdots \\ \Delta u(t+N_c-1|t) \end{pmatrix}, \boldsymbol{U}(t-1) = \begin{pmatrix} u(t-1) \\ u(t-1) \\ \vdots \\ u(t-1) \end{pmatrix}.$$

Moreover, from Equations (19) and (23), we obtain

$$\boldsymbol{U}_{min}(t) \leq \boldsymbol{E}\Delta \boldsymbol{U}(t) + \boldsymbol{U}(t-1) \leq \boldsymbol{U}_{max}(t), \tag{25}$$

where

$$\boldsymbol{U}_{min}(t) = \begin{pmatrix} u_{min}(t|t) \\ u_{min}(t+1|t) \\ \vdots \\ u_{min}(t+N_c-1|t) \end{pmatrix}, \ \boldsymbol{U}_{max}(t) = \begin{pmatrix} u_{max}(t|t) \\ u_{max}(t+1|t) \\ \vdots \\ u_{max}(t+N_c-1|t) \end{pmatrix}.$$

For the control increment, we have

$$\Delta \boldsymbol{U}_{min}(t) \leq \Delta \boldsymbol{U}(t) \leq \Delta \boldsymbol{U}_{max}(t), \tag{26}$$

where

$$\Delta \boldsymbol{U}_{min}(t) = \begin{pmatrix} \Delta u_{min}(t|t) \\ \Delta u_{min}(t+1|t) \\ \vdots \\ \Delta u_{min}(t+N_c-1|t) \end{pmatrix}, \ \Delta \boldsymbol{U}_{max}(t) = \begin{pmatrix} \Delta u_{max}(t|t) \\ \Delta u_{max}(t+1|t) \\ \vdots \\ \Delta u_{max}(t+N_c-1|t) \end{pmatrix}.$$

Accordingly, Equations (20), (25) and (26) yield the following quadratic programming problem

$$\begin{gathered} J(t) = (\Delta \boldsymbol{U^T}(t) \quad \varepsilon)\boldsymbol{H}(t)(\Delta \boldsymbol{U^T}(t) \quad \varepsilon)^T + \boldsymbol{F}(t)(\Delta \boldsymbol{U^T}(t) \quad \varepsilon)^T, \\ s.t.\ \boldsymbol{U_{min}}(t) \leq \boldsymbol{E}\Delta \boldsymbol{U}(t) + \boldsymbol{U}(t-1) \leq \boldsymbol{U_{max}}(t), \\ \Delta \boldsymbol{U_{min}}(t) \leq \Delta \boldsymbol{U}(t) \leq \Delta \boldsymbol{U_{max}}(t). \end{gathered} \tag{27}$$

Sving Equation (27) in each control cycle leads to a series of control increments in the control time domain:

$$\Delta U^*(t) = \left(\Delta u^*(t|t) \quad \Delta u^*(t+1|t) \quad \cdots \quad \Delta u^*(t+N_c-1)\right), \tag{28}$$

Furthermore, the first element in the sequence was adopted for the actual control increment

$$u^*(t|t) = u(t-1|t) + \Delta u^*(t|t). \quad (29)$$

Finally, by repeating the above process in each control cycle, the desired trajectory is tracked.

3.3. Steering Strategy

Using the aforementioned MPC method, we can obtain the optimal control inputs, $u^*(t|t) = \left(v_x^B,\ \omega_z^B\right)$. Furthermore, the speed and the steering angle of each wheel need to be derived. In the present study, the steering strategy in which all of the wheels make the uniform circular motion was adopted, as seen in Figure 6.

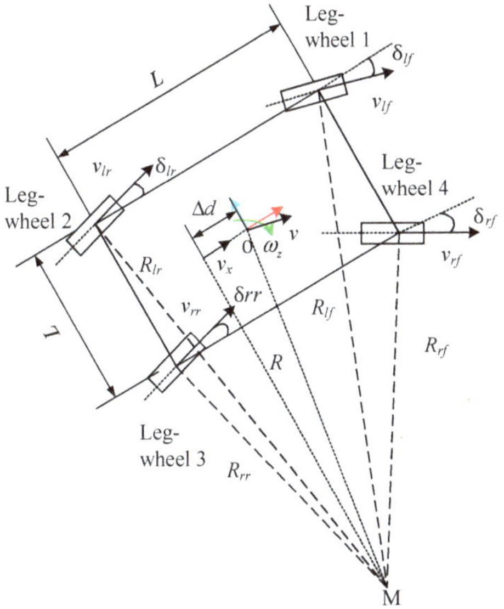

Figure 6. The steering strategy.

The point M is the steering center and the steering radius of the robot R is

$$R = \frac{v_x^B}{\omega_z^B}, \quad (30)$$

where $\omega_z^B \neq 0$. Furthermore, the steering radii of the four wheels are written as

$$\begin{cases} R_{rf} = \sqrt{\left(\frac{L}{2} - \Delta d\right)^2 + \left(R - \frac{L}{2}\right)^2} \\ R_{lf} = \sqrt{\left(\frac{L}{2} - \Delta d\right)^2 + \left(R + \frac{L}{2}\right)^2} \\ R_{rr} = \sqrt{\left(\frac{L}{2} + \Delta d\right)^2 + \left(R - \frac{L}{2}\right)^2} \\ R_{lr} = \sqrt{\left(\frac{L}{2} + \Delta d\right)^2 + \left(R + \frac{L}{2}\right)^2} \end{cases}. \quad (31)$$

According to Ackermann's principle, the wheel speeds and the steering angles are obtained as follows:

$$\begin{cases} \omega_{rf} = \frac{\omega_z^B R_{rf}}{R_w} \\ \omega_{lf} = \frac{\omega_z^B R_{lf}}{R_w} \\ \omega_{rr} = \frac{\omega_z^B R_{rr}}{R_w} \\ \omega_{lr} = \frac{\omega_z^B R_{lr}}{R_w} \end{cases} \quad (32)$$

$$\begin{cases} \delta_{rf} = sign(k)\tan^{-1}\frac{\frac{L}{2}-\Delta d}{R-L/2} \\ \delta_{lf} = sign(k)\tan^{-1}\frac{\frac{L}{2}-\Delta d}{R+L/2} \\ \delta_{rr} = -sign(k)\tan^{-1}\frac{\frac{L}{2}+\Delta d}{R-L/2} \\ \delta_{lr} = -sign(k)\tan^{-1}\frac{\frac{L}{2}+\Delta d}{R+L/2} \end{cases} \tag{33}$$

where ω_{rf}, ω_{lf}, ω_{rr}, and ω_{lr} are the wheel speeds, and δ_{rf}, δ_{lf}, δ_{rr}, and δ_{lr} are the steering angles. Here, $sign(k)$ is a signum function, and $sign(k) = -1$ when the wheel rotates clockwise; $sign(k) = 1$ when the wheel rotates anticlockwise. When $\omega_z^B = 0$ in Equation (30), the four steering angles are all zero, i.e., $\delta_{rf} = \delta_{lf} = \delta_{rr} = \delta_{lr} = 0$.

3.4. Wheel Speed Allocation (WSA)

The WSA module calculates the suitable speed for each wheel according to the motion characteristics of the whole robot on rough terrain.

First, according to the kinematic equations, the linear velocity of the wheel center and the angular velocity of the lower leg (i.e., Frame 4) in Figure 4 are written as

$$\begin{pmatrix} \boldsymbol{v}_{iw} \\ \boldsymbol{\omega}_{iw} \end{pmatrix} = \begin{pmatrix} {}^4_BR_i & {}^4_BR_i\boldsymbol{S}_{iw} \\ 0 & {}^4_BR_i \end{pmatrix}\begin{pmatrix} \boldsymbol{v}_{i0}^B \\ \boldsymbol{\omega}_{i0}^B \end{pmatrix} + {}^4_0R_iJ_i\begin{pmatrix} \dot{\theta}_{i1} \\ \dot{\theta}_{i2} \\ \dot{\theta}_{i3} \\ \dot{\theta}_{i4} \end{pmatrix}, \tag{34}$$

where $\boldsymbol{S}_{iw}$ is the position vector of the wheel center with respect to the body frame; ${}^4_BR_i$ is the rotation transformation matrix from the body frame to frame 4; ${}^4_0R_i$ is the rotation transformation matrix from the leg frame to frame 4; J_i is the Jacobian matrix with respect to the leg frame; i = 1–4 denotes the leg number; and $\boldsymbol{v}_{i0}^B$ and $\boldsymbol{\omega}_{i0}^B$ are the linear and angular velocities of the leg frame with respect to the body frame, which are given by

$$\begin{pmatrix} \boldsymbol{v}_{i0}^B \\ \boldsymbol{\omega}_{i0}^B \end{pmatrix} = \begin{pmatrix} \boldsymbol{\omega}^B \times (\boldsymbol{O}_{0i} - \boldsymbol{M}) \\ \boldsymbol{\omega}^B \end{pmatrix}, \tag{35}$$

where $\boldsymbol{\omega}^B$ is the angular velocity of the body.

Second, the ideal (no-slip) linear velocity of the wheel center comes from the driving motor and the rotation of the lower leg, which can be denoted by

$$||v_{iw}|| = (\omega_{iwz} + \omega_{id})R_w, \tag{36}$$

where ω_{iwz} is the projection of $\boldsymbol{\omega}_{iw}$ on the direction of the wheel axis.

Accordingly, the rotational speeds of the wheel motors are obtained by

$$\omega_{id} = \frac{||\boldsymbol{v}_{iw}||}{R_w} - \omega_{iwz}. \tag{37}$$

4. Results and Discussion

4.1. Simulations

The numerical program of the control strategy was first developed using MATLAB software. Then, the joint simulation model was established by SIMULINK and UG Motion software. UG motion software provides the joint angles as well as the pitch and roll angles for each control block. In the meantime, the control blocks calculate the joint angles and wheel speeds and provide them to the virtual prototype. There are some system and control parameters that can be grouped into three categories, namely the input parameters, the output parameters, and the control parameters, as seen in Table 2. The input parameters include the points on the reference path, the desired yaw angle of the robot body, and the desired linear and angular velocities of the robot body. The output parameters are the linear and angular velocities of the robot body from the MPC and the steering angles and the wheel speeds. In addition, there are control parameters, including the prediction and control horizons, the weight coefficient and the relaxation factor, and the PID parameters to control the linear and angular velocities of the robot body.

Table 2. The system and control parameters.

Categories	Terminology	Definition
Input parameters	x^w_{cr}, y^w_{cr}	Points on reference path
	γ^w_r	Desired yaw angle of body
	v^B_{xr}, ω^B_{zr}	Desired linear and angular velocities of body
Control parameters	N_p, N_c	Prediction and control horizons
	ρ, ε	Weight coefficient and the relaxation factor
	k_{p1}, k_{i1}, k_{d1}	PID parameters for control of the linear velocity of body
	k_{p2}, k_{i2}, k_{d2}	PID parameters for control of the angular velocity of body
Output parameters	$u^*(t\|t) = (v^B_x, \omega^B_z)$	The linear and angular velocities of the body
	$\delta_{rf}, \delta_{lf}, , \delta_{lr}$	Steering angles
	ω_{id}.	Rotational speeds of the wheel motors

First, the WSA module was verified. For the simulation, the terrain included two trapezoid and two arc obstacles. The posture as well as the linear and angular velocities of the body, the joint angles and the angular velocities of the joints, and the driving speeds of the wheels were all measured using the virtual model in UG Motion software. Note that the terrain with the obstacles led to the changes of rover attitude angles (α, β). Here, the terrain-adaptive algorithm in [27] was adopted to control the rover attitude. With this algorithm, the robot attitude was almost kept unchanged in irregular terrains. Then, the practical linear velocity of the wheel centers and the practical angular velocity of the wheels were calculated according to Equations (36) and (37). Therefore, the slip percent could be obtained from

$$\mu = \frac{((\omega_{id} + \omega_{iwz})R_w - v_i)}{(\omega_{id} + \omega_{iwz})R_w} \times 100\%, \tag{38}$$

where R_w is the radius of the wheel; ω_{id} is the practical angular velocity of the wheel, which can be measured by the wheels' encoders; and v_i is the practical linear velocity of the wheel center. Figure 7 shows the comparison of the slippage percentages with and without the WSA module. Without the WSA module, the slippage reached up to 0.25, while with the WSA, the maximum of the slippage was less than 0.13. It was found that wheel slip was obviously decreased by the WSA component.

Second, the trajectory tracking based on MPC was verified. An arc trajectory with a radius of 30 m in the plane was selected for the validation simulation. In the simulations, there were three speeds, i.e., 0.1 m/s, 0.2 m/s, and 0.4 m/s. The control parameters for the simulations of the linear trajectory were: N_p = 6; N_c = 3; ρ = 10; $\varepsilon = 0$ for the lower limit and $\varepsilon = 10$ for the upper limit. The PID parameters for the linear velocity were set as: $k_{p1} = 2$, $k_{i1} = 1$, $k_{d1} = 0$. Since there was only a linear velocity in the body frame, the PID module for the control of angular velocities did not work. Figures 8–10 show the trajectory tracking results for three speeds. It was found that the robot could track the corresponding target values within a short period of time under the three different speeds. There was a large increase in trajectory errors at the beginning of the tracking process. The reason for this is that the initial direction of the target speed was the same as the x axis in the global coordinate system. There was an obvious delay before the actual speed reached the target value, and the speed error was relatively larger at the beginning. Furthermore, it was found that there were obvious overshoots in the velocity responses from the MPC method in the beginning. These overshoots facilitated trajectory tracking, and thus, the forward velocity of the robot could approximate the desired value quickly. In the meantime, the overshoot increased as the desired speed increases. The overshoot at 0.4 m/s was the largest one among the three forward speeds. It should also be noted that the final velocity response errors increased as the target speed increased. However, as a whole, the trajectory errors for the three speeds were all relatively small, validating the MPC module and the whole control strategy.

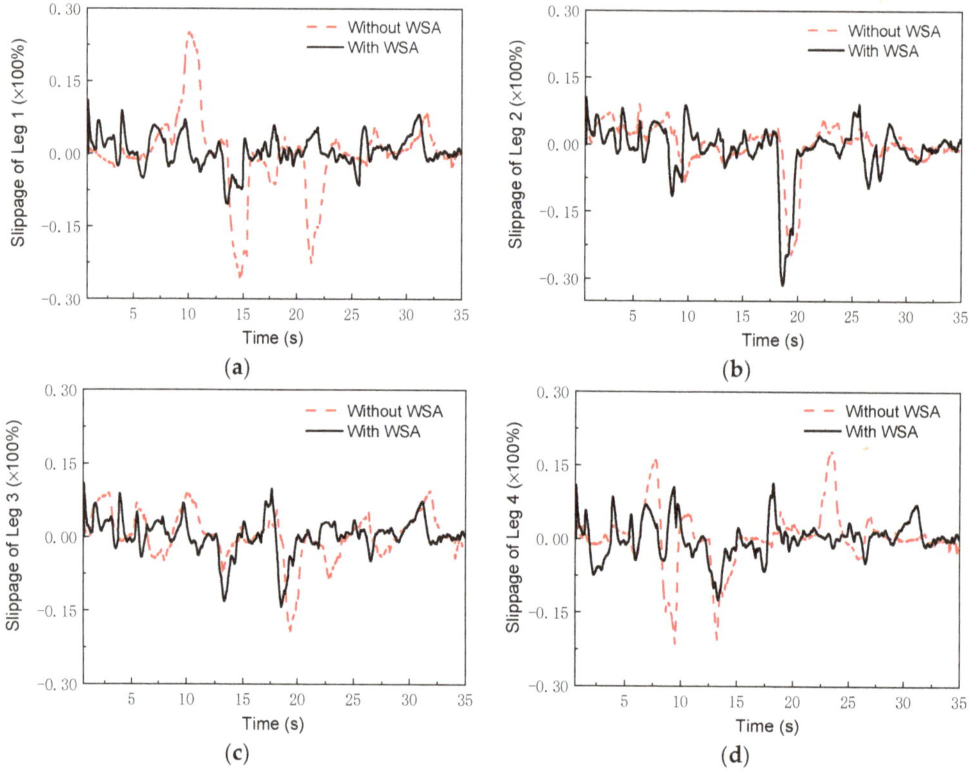

Figure 7. Slippage in simulations: (**a**) leg 1; (**b**) leg 2; (**c**) leg 3; (**d**) leg 4.

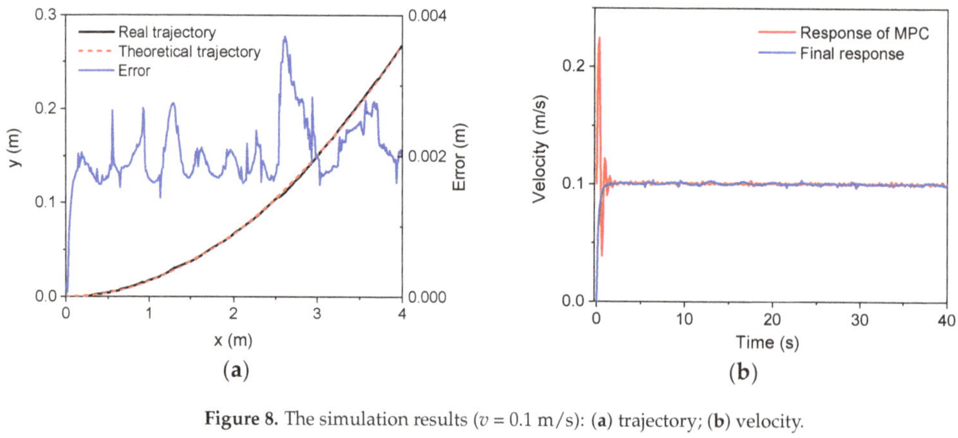

Figure 8. The simulation results (v = 0.1 m/s): (**a**) trajectory; (**b**) velocity.

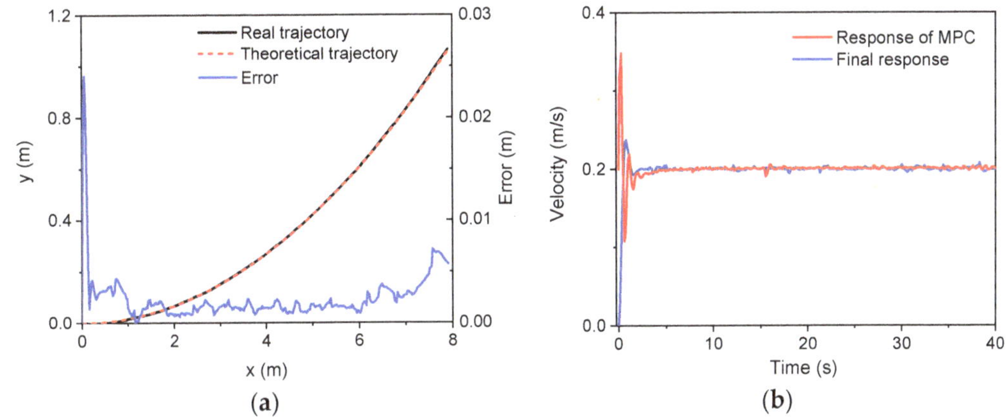

Figure 9. The simulation results (v = 0.2 m/s): (**a**) trajectory; (**b**) velocity.

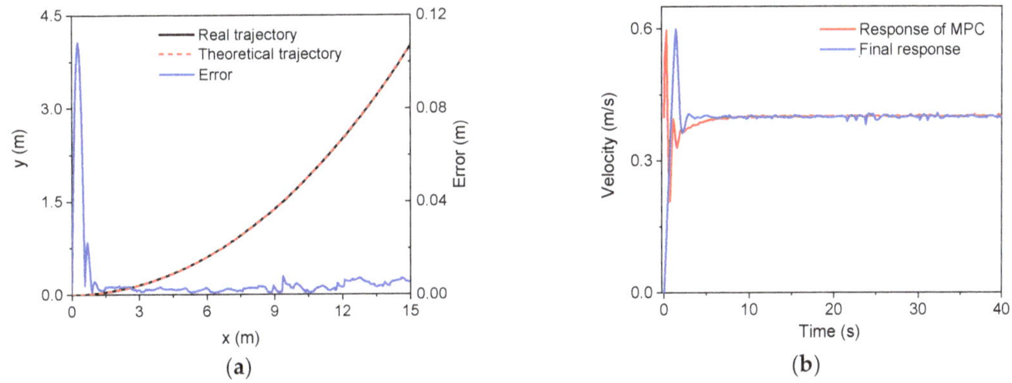

Figure 10. The simulation results (v = 0.4 m/s): (**a**) trajectory; (**b**) velocity.

To further validate the control strategy, a more complicated trajectory, i.e., an S-type trajectory was selected for the tracking simulations. The S-type trajectory consisted of two semicircles with a radius of R = 20 m, which can be described as follows:

$$x_{cr}^{w} = \begin{cases} R\sin(\omega_z t),\ 0 \le t < T_s \\ R\sin[-\omega_z(t - T_s)], T_s \le t \le 2T_s \end{cases}, \tag{39}$$

$$y_{cr}^{w} = \begin{cases} R - R\cos(\omega_z t),\ 0 \le t < T_s \\ 2R - R\cos(\omega_z T_s) - R\cos[-\omega_z(t - T_s)], T_s \le t \le 2T_s \end{cases}, \tag{40}$$

$$\gamma_{cr}^{w} = \begin{cases} \omega_z t,\ 0 \le t < T_s \\ \omega_z T_s - \omega_z(t - T_s), T_s \le t \le 2T_s \end{cases}, \tag{41}$$

where $v_x = 0.4\ \text{m/s}; \omega_z = v_x/R; T_s = \pi/\omega_z$. During the simulation, the control parameters were set as: N_p = 6; N_c = 3; $\rho = 10$; $\varepsilon = 0$ for the lower limit and $\varepsilon = 10$ for the upper limit. The PID parameters for the linear velocity were set as: $k_{p1} = 0.7$, $k_{i1} = 0$, $k_{d1} = 5$. Figure 11 gives the comparisons of the theoretical and real trajectories and velocities. It was found that the robot could track well the reference trajectory and the reference velocity when running along the S-type trajectory. Furthermore, the errors in the x and y coordinates were very small, the relative error of which were less than 2% and 1.75%, respectively, as seen in Figure 12.

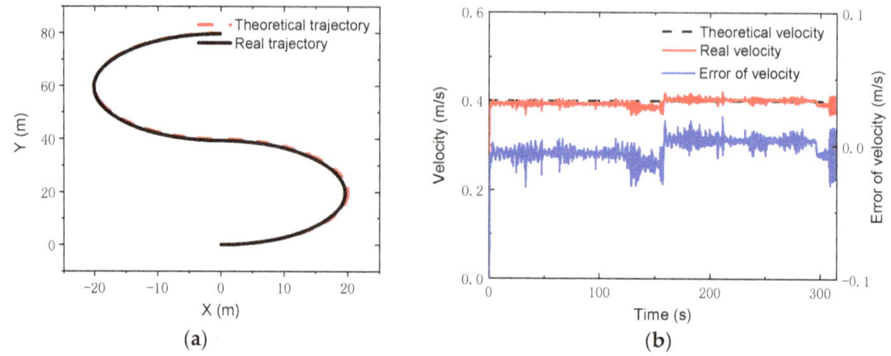

Figure 11. S-type trajectory and velocity: (**a**) trajectories; (**b**) velocities and errors.

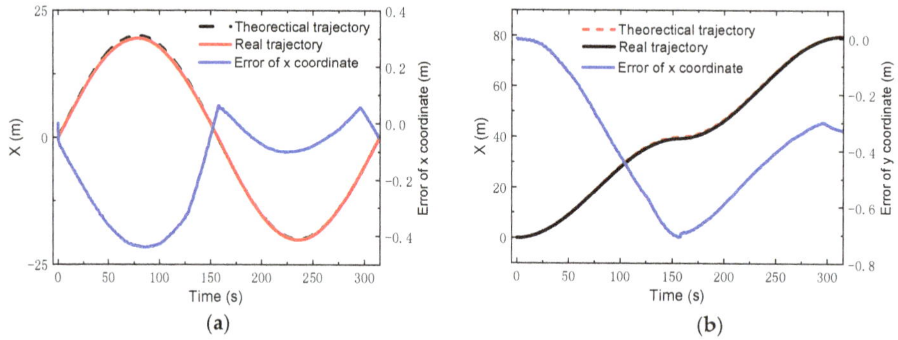

Figure 12. Coordinates and errors for S-type trajectory: (**a**) x coordinate; (**b**) y coordinate.

In addition, tracking simulations for high speeds were also carried out. Two speeds, i.e., $v_x = 2$ m/s and 4 m/s, were chosen, which were ten times as large as the speeds in the previous simulations. A circle trajectory with a radius of R = 35 m was selected for the simulations, which can be described by

$$\begin{cases} x_{cr}^{w} = R\sin(\omega_z t) \\ y_{cr}^{w} = R - R\cos(\omega_z t) \\ \gamma_r^{w} = \omega_z t \end{cases}, \tag{42}$$

where $\omega_z = v_x/R$. The control parameters for the simulations of the linear trajectory were set as: N_p = 6; N_c = 3; $\rho = 10$; for the lower limit and $\varepsilon = 10$ for the upper limit. The PID parameters for the linear velocity were set as: $k_{p1} = 2$, $k_{i1} = 1$, $k_{d1} = 0$. Figure 13 gives the changes of the real velocities. It was found that the robot could still track the reference velocity after a relatively short time. Moreover, with the control, the robot could track the reference trajectories of both the x coordinate and the y coordinate, depicted in Figures 14 and 15. Compared to the lower speed, the position errors increased. However, the relative errors of the position points were small. The maxima of the relative position errors at 2 m/s and 4 m/s were less than 3% and 8.5%, respectively.

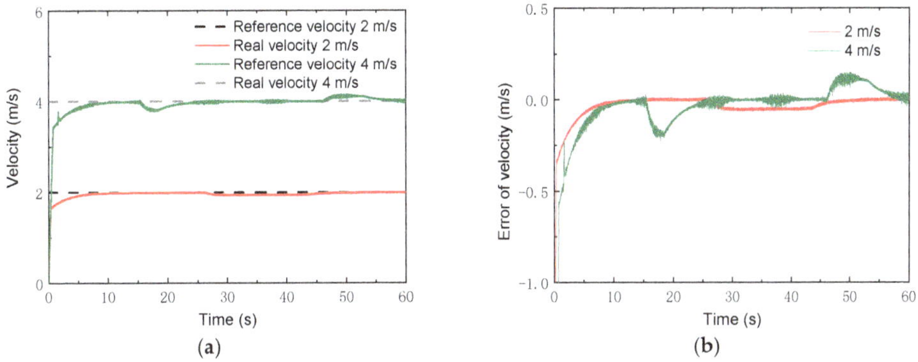

Figure 13. Velocity results with higher speeds: (**a**) velocity; (**b**) error of velocity.

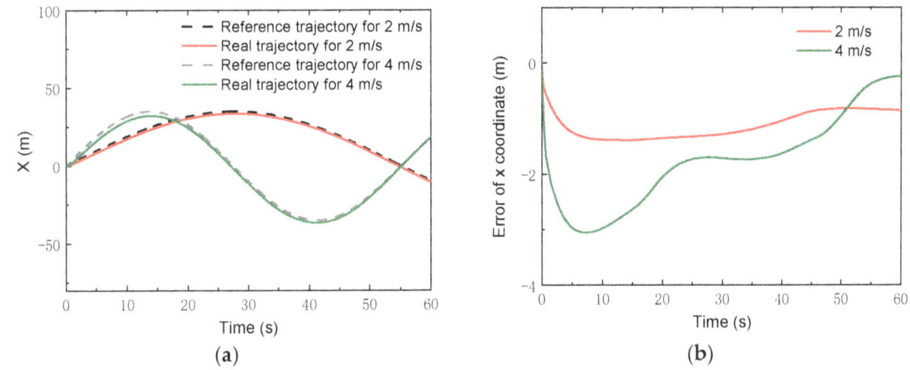

Figure 14. x Coordinates with higher speeds: (**a**) x coordinate; (**b**) error of x coordinate.

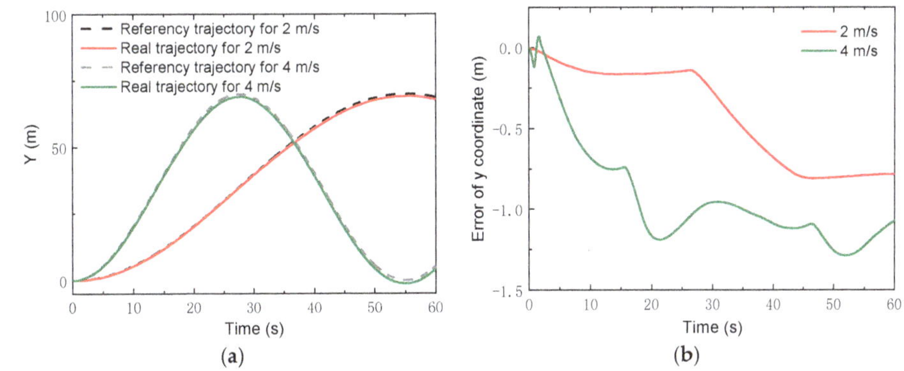

Figure 15. y Coordinates with higher speeds: (**a**) y coordinate; (**b**) error of y coordinate.

4.2. Experiments

To further verify the control strategy, an experimental setup based on the NOKOV vision motion capture system was established that consisted of six cameras, as shown in Figure 16. An L-type tool was used for the benchmark calibration of the vision system. After there were enough cameras placed around the robot, the c vision capture system was calibrated. The L-type tool was mounted on the body, as seen in Figure 17. There are four markers on the L-type tool. The cameras recognize the markers, and thus, the vision frame (i.e., the global coordinate system) can be established. According to the geometrical relationship between the mounting location of the L-type tool and the robot's body frame, the initial transformation matrix between the vision frame and the body frame could be obtained. Serval markers were bonded to the body of the rover, and thus, the body coordinate system could be established in the world coordinate system. Therefore, the real motion trajectory of the rover could be measured in real time and sent to the rover control system. To clarify the effectiveness of the WSA module, a terrain with a flat surface and two trapezoids was employed in the experiments. Since the terrain included obstacles, the terrain-adaptive algorithm [27] was adopted, similar to the simulations. During the experiments, the control parameters for the MPC module were set as: $N_p = 6$; $N_c = 3$; $\rho = 10$; $\varepsilon = 0$ for the lower limit and $\varepsilon = 10$ for the upper limit. The PID parameters for the control of linear velocities were set as: $k_{p1} = 8$, $k_{i1} = 0$, $k_{d1} = 0.2$. Figure 18 shows the slippage in the experiments. Note that the slippages of Leg 1 and 4 (Leg 2 and 3) are almost the same because they suffer the same terrain condition. It was found that the average slippage of all of the legs demonstrated an obvious decrease after WSA control, up to 20%. Figure 19 shows the experimental results of trajectory tracking. As it can be seen, the rover could strictly track the reference trajectory. The deflection with respect to the reference trajectory was less than 2% F.S., which is a relatively small error. Accordingly, the control strategy was validated by the experiments.

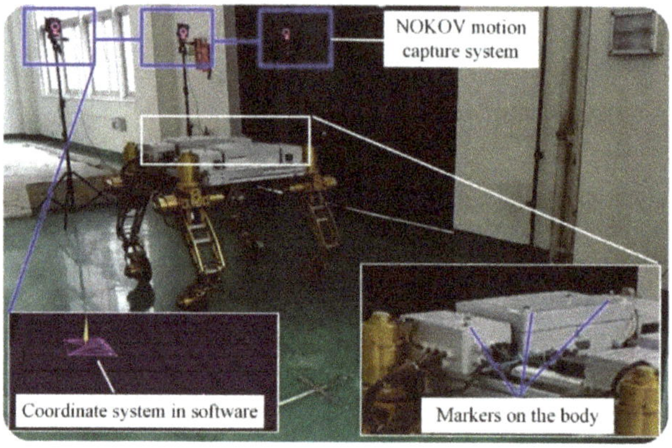

Figure 16. The experimental setup.

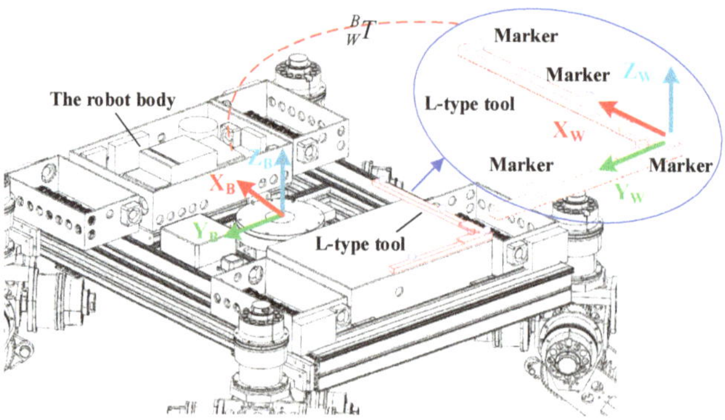

Figure 17. The calibration of the vision frame.

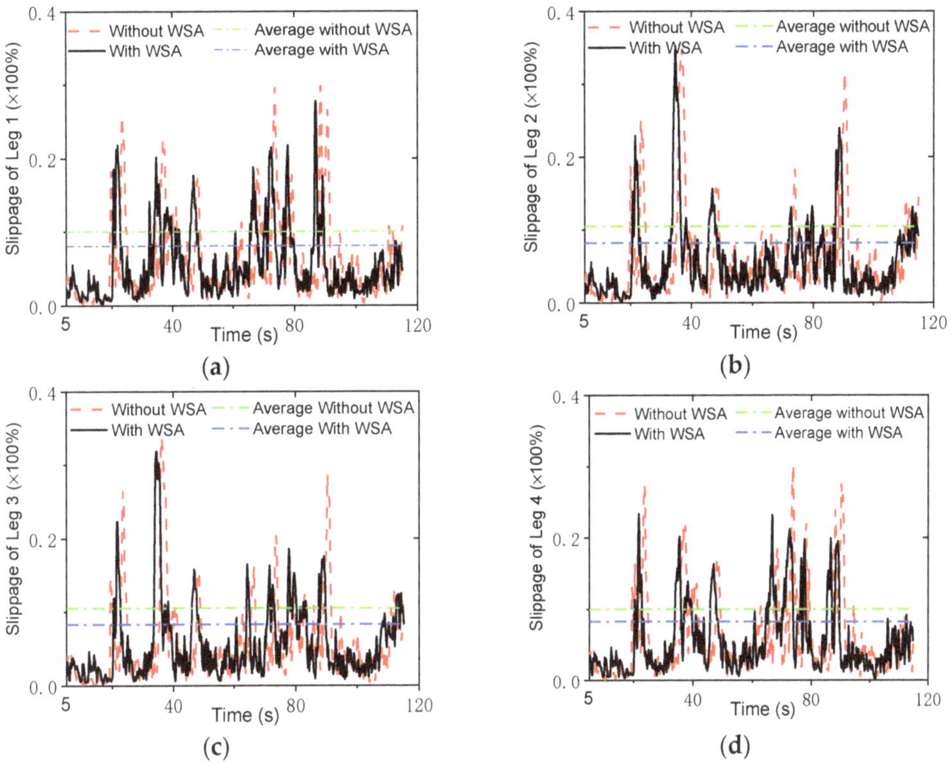

Figure 18. Slippage in the experiments: (**a**) Leg 1; (**b**) Leg 2; (**c**) Leg 3; (**d**) Leg 4.

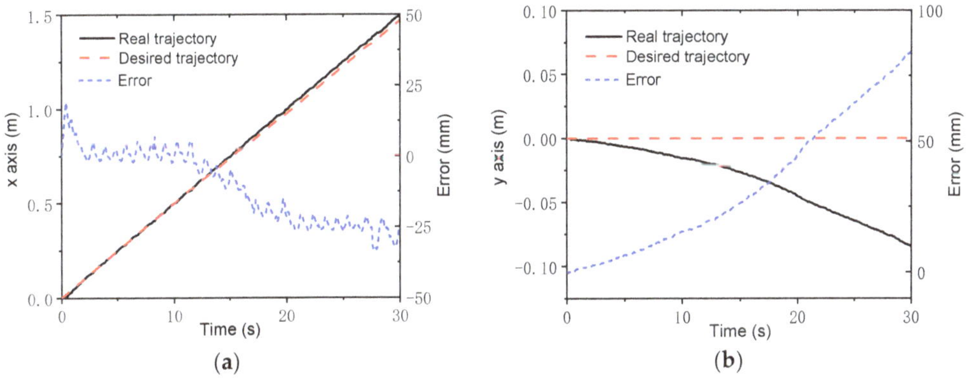

Figure 19. Experimental trajectory tracking results: (**a**) x axis; (**b**) y axis.

5. Conclusions

In this paper, a novel wheeled–legged planetary rover with four legs was proposed, and each leg had four DOFs with an actuated wheel. The articulated legs utilized a serial–parallel hybrid configuration, and it had the merits of both serial and parallel mechanisms. Moreover, the legs had a rigid–flexible coupling structure that could conform to unstructured terrain using both active and passive compliance. The kinematics equations of the rover were derived. Then, a control scheme including trajectory tracking, the steering strategy, and the WSA module was proposed. A trajectory tracking model based on MPC that could handle the line and arc trajectory with quite a good accuracy was established. In addition, the WSA was introduced into the control strategy to decrease the slippage. After that, to validate the control method, three groups of cosimulations, i.e., tracking an arc trajectory, tracking a S-type trajectory, and trajectory tracking with high speeds were carried out. Finally, trajectory tracking experiments were conducted through a vision motion capture system. It was found that the average slippage of all of the legs decreased obviously after WSA control, with a slippage up to 20% in our experiments. Moreover, the rover could strictly track the reference trajectory. With respect to the reference trajectory, the deflection was found to be less than 2% F.S., which is a relatively small error. Accordingly, the proposed control strategy was thoroughly verified by the simulations and experiments.

Author Contributions: Conceptualization, J.H. and Y.S.; methodology, J.H. and Y.S.; software, Y.S. and L.Y.; investigation, Y.S. and L.Y.; writing—original draft, J.H.; writing—review and editing, J.H.; supervision, F.G.; funding acquisition, J.H. All authors have read and agreed to the published version of the manuscript.

Funding: This research was funded by National Natural Science Foundation of China, grant no. 52175022, the State Key Laboratory of Mechanical System and Vibration, grant no. MSVZD202106, and Shanghai R&D public service platform project, grant no. 19DZ2291400.

Institutional Review Board Statement: Not applicable.

Informed Consent Statement: Not applicable.

Data Availability Statement: Data will be made available upon reasonable request by the corresponding author.

Conflicts of Interest: The authors declare no conflict of interest.

References

1. Rankin, A.; Maimone, M.; Biesiadecki, J.; Patel, N.; Levine, D.; Toupet, O. Driving curiosity: Mars rover mobility trends during the first seven years. In Proceedings of the IEEE Aerospace Conference, Big Sky, MT, USA, 7–14 March 2020.
2. Dodge, R.; Parsons, D.; Abid, M.; Chrystal, K.; Kartolov, B. Dynamics associated with the Corer on M2020 Perseverance Rover. In Proceedings of the IEEE Aerospace Conference, Big Sky, MT, USA, 6–13 March 2021.
3. Zheng, J.; Gao, H.; Yuan, B.; Liu, Z.; Yu, H.; Ding, L.; Deng, Z. Design and terramechanics analysis of a Mars rover utilizing active suspension. *Mech. Mach. Theory* **2018**, *128*, 125–149. [CrossRef]
4. Michaud, F.; Letourneau, D.; Arsenault, M.; Bergeron, Y.; Cadrin, R.; Gagnon, F.; Legault, M.A.; Millette, M.; Paré, J.F.; Tremblay, M.C.; et al. Multi-modal locomotion robotic platform using leg-track-wheel articulations. *Auton. Robots* **2005**, *18*, 137–156. [CrossRef]
5. Hauser, K.; Bretl, T.; Latombe, J.C.; Harada, K.; Wilcox, B. Motion Planning for Legged Robots on Varied Terrain. *Int. J. Robot. Res.* **2008**, *27*, 1325–1349. [CrossRef]
6. Grand, C.; Benamar, F.; Plumet, F.; Bidaud, P. Stability and traction optimization of a reconfigurable wheel-legged robot. *Int. J. Robot. Res.* **2004**, *23*, 1041–1058. [CrossRef]
7. Smith, J.A.; Poulakakis, I.; Trentini, M.; Sharf, I. Bounding with active wheels and liftoff angle velocity adjustment. *Int. J. Robot. Res.* **2010**, *29*, 414–427. [CrossRef]
8. Xu, K.; Wang, S.; Yue, B.; Wang, J.; Peng, H.; Liu, D.; Chen, Z.; Shi, M. Adaptive impedance control with variable target stiffness for wheel-legged robot on complex unknown terrain. *Mechatronics* **2020**, *69*, 102388. [CrossRef]
9. He, J.; Gao, F. Type Synthesis for bionic quadruped walking robots. *J. Biol. Eng.* **2015**, *12*, 527–538. [CrossRef]
10. He, J.; Gao, F. Mechanism, actuation, perception, and control of highly dynamic multi-legged robots: A Review. *Chin. J. Mech. Eng.* **2020**, *33*, 79. [CrossRef]
11. Lewinger, W.A.; Harley, C.M.; Ritzmann, R.E.; Branicky, M.S.; Quinn, R.D. Insect-like antennal sensing for climbing and tunneling behavior in a biologically-inspired mobile robot. In Proceedings of the IEEE International Conference on Robotics and Automation, Barcelona, Spain, 18–22 April 2005.
12. Daltorio, K.A.; Wei, T.E.; Gorb, S.N.; Ritzmann, R.E.; Quinn, R.D. Passive foot design and contact area analysis for climbing mini-whegs. In Proceedings of the IEEE International Conference on Robotics and Automation, Rome, Italy, 10–14 April 2007.
13. Chen, S.C.; Huang, K.J.; Chen, W.H.; Shen, S.Y.; Li, C.H.; Lin, P.C. Quattroped: A leg–wheel transformable robot. *IEEE/ASME Trans. Mechantron.* **2014**, *19*, 730–742. [CrossRef]
14. Kim, Y.S.; Jung, G.P.; Kim, H.; Cho, K.J.; Chu, C.N. Wheel transformer: A wheel-leg hybrid robot with passive transformable wheels. *IEEE Trans. Robot.* **2014**, *30*, 1487–1498. [CrossRef]

15. Chen, W.H.; Lin, H.S.; Lin, Y.M.; Lin, P.C. TurboQuad: A novel leg–wheel transformable robot with smooth and fast behavioral transitions. *IEEE Trans. Robot.* **2017**, *33*, 1025–1040. [CrossRef]
16. Kim, Y.; Lee, Y.; Lee, S.; Kim, J.; Kim, H.S.; Seo, T. STEP: A new mobile platform with 2-DOF transformable wheels for service robots. *IEEE/ASME Trans. Mechantron.* **2020**, *25*, 1859–1868. [CrossRef]
17. Sun, T.; Xiang, X.; Su, W.; Wu, H.; Song, Y. A transformable wheel-legged mobile robot: Design, analysis and experiment. *Robot. Auton. Syst.* **2017**, *98*, 30–41. [CrossRef]
18. Grotzinger, J.P.; Crisp, J.; Vasavada, A.R.; Anderson, R.C.; Baker, C.J.; Barry, R.; Blake, D.F.; Conrad, P.; Edgett, K.S.; Ferdowski, B.; et al. Mars science laboratory mission and science investigation. *Space Sci. Rev.* **2012**, *170*, 5–56. [CrossRef]
19. Cordes, F.; Kirchner, F.; Babu, A. Design and field testing of a rover with an actively articulated suspension system in a Mars analog terrain. *J. Field Robot.* **2018**, *35*, 1149–1181. [CrossRef]
20. Lamon, P. 3D-position tracking and control for all-terrain robots. *Adv. Robot.* **2008**, *43*, 33–51.
21. Chwa, D. Robust distance-based tracking control of wheeled mobile robots using vision sensors in the presence of kinematic disturbances. *IEEE Trans. Ind. Electron.* **2016**, *63*, 6172–6183. [CrossRef]
22. Liang, Z.; Chen, J.; Wang, Y. Equivalent acceleration imitation for single wheel of manned lunar rover by varying torque on earth. *IEEE/ASME Trans. Mechatron.* **2019**, *25*, 282–293. [CrossRef]
23. Krid, M.; Amar, F.B. A dynamic based path tracking controller for a fast rover with independent steering and drive. In Proceedings of the CLAWAR 2011, Paris, France, 6–8 September 2011.
24. Yang, H.; Zhao, H.; Xia, Y.; Zhang, J. Nonlinear MPC with time-varying terminal cost for tracking unreachable periodic references. *Automatica* **2021**, *123*, 109337. [CrossRef]
25. Liu, X.; Wang, W.; Li, X.; Liu, F.; He, Z.; Yao, Y.; Ruan, H.; Zhang, T. MPC-based high-speed trajectory tracking for 4WIS robot. *ISA Trans.* **2022**, *123*, 413–424. [CrossRef]
26. Ding, T.; Zhang, Y.; Ma, G.; Cao, Z.; Zhao, X.; Tao, B. Trajectory tracking of redundantly actuated mobile robot by MPC velocity control under steering strategy constraint. *Mechatronics* **2022**, *84*, 102779. [CrossRef]
27. Sun, Y.L.; He, J.; Xing, Y. Multi-target coordinated control of wheel-legged Mars rover. *Acta Aeronutica Astronaut. Sin.* **2021**, *42*, 524246.
28. Li, W.; Ding, L.; Gao, H.; Tavakoli, M. Haptic tele-driving of wheeled mobile robots under nonideal wheel rolling, kinematic control and communication time delay. *IEEE Trans. Syst. Man Cybern. Syst.* **2020**, *50*, 336–347. [CrossRef]
29. Chen, C.; Shu, M.; Wang, Y.; Ding, L.; Gao, H.; Liu, H.; Zhou, S. Simultaneous control of trajectory tracking and coordinated allocation of rocker-bogie planetary rovers. *Mech. Syst. Signal Proc.* **2021**, *151*, 107312. [CrossRef]

sensors MDPI

Article

The Hybrid Position/Force Walking Robot Control Using Extenics Theory and Neutrosophic Logic Decision

Ionel-Alexandru Gal, Alexandra-Cătălina Ciocîrlan and Luige Vlădăreanu *

Institute of Solid Mechanics of the Romanian Academy, 15 C. Mille, 010141 Bucharest, Romania; alexandru.gal@imsar.ro (I.-A.G.); alexandra.ciocirlan@imsar.ro (A.-C.C.)
* Correspondence: luige.vladareanu@vipro.edu.ro; Tel.: +40-21-315-7478

Abstract: This paper presents a hybrid force/position control. We developed it for a hexapod walking robot that combines multiple bipedal robots to increase its load. The control method integrated Extenics theory with neutrosophic logic to obtain a two-stage decision-making algorithm. The first stage was an offline qualitative decision-applying Extenics theory, and the second was a real-time decision process using neutrosophic logic and DSmT theory. The two-stage algorithm separated the control phases into a kinematic control method that used a PID regulator and a dynamic control method developed with the help of sliding mode control (SMC). By integrating both control methods separated by a dynamic switching algorithm, we obtained a hybrid force/position control that took advantage of both kinematic and dynamic control properties to drive a mobile walking robot. The experimental and predicted results were in good agreement. They indicated that the proposed hybrid control is efficient in using the two-stage decision algorithm to drive the hexapod robot motors using kinematic and dynamic control methods. The experiment presents the robot's foot positioning error while walking. The results show how the switching method alters the system precision during the pendulum phase compared to the weight support phase, which can better compensate for the robot's dynamic parameters. The proposed switching algorithm directly influences the overall control precision, while we aimed to obtain a fast switch with a lower impact on the control parameters. The results show the error on all axes and break it down into walking stages to better understand the control behavior and precision.

Keywords: hybrid position/force control; sliding mode control; decision method; neutrosophic logic; extension set

Citation: Gal, I.-A.; Ciocîrlan, A.-C.; Vlădăreanu, L. The Hybrid Position/Force Walking Robot Control Using Extenics Theory and Neutrosophic Logic Decision. *Sensors* **2022**, *22*, 3663. https://doi.org/10.3390/s22103663

Academic Editor: Gregor Klancar

Received: 18 March 2022
Accepted: 9 May 2022
Published: 11 May 2022

1. Introduction

Worldwide, practical robot applications are diversifying more and more in the new world of robotics, automation, and artificial intelligence [1]. Researchers and engineers are working on developing solutions and solving problems for all kinds of robots. This research will enhance human motion and workspace investigation through different sensors and automate tasks for unattended robots [2]. Into this category falls every type of robot control method that can improve robot control and behavior, with or without autonomous capabilities [3]. For a robot to be capable of accomplishing a designated task, it must reject most of the uncertainties and disturbances within the work environment. The robot must also handle information from several sensors and fuse the data to reach a close decision to the truth value.

Most mobile robots combine kinematic and dynamic control methods to solve such a problem, each designated for certain joints in the robot structure. However, for a highly versatile robot structure, a hybrid position/force method is used. Although the technique is not new, having begun with Raibert and Craig [4], it has the attention of robotic control research, and it continues to bring adaptability to the robots using it. In recent years, different approaches have been researched. Zhang et al. [5] created a hybrid control method that could adjust the joint dynamic parameters online. The process allowed rough modeling of the robot parameters and left the fine-tuning to the control algorithm. A similar approach used a neural network to autocalibrate the control parameters [6]. Still, not all hybrid methods can use mechanical parameters because they increase the system's complexity. For a robot with a simple structure for which the kinematic or dynamic equations are easier to define, a classic approach to hybrid control can be easier to implement. Some examples include the hybrid method with impedance control [7] or even the backstepping method with a Hamilton controller [8]. Applications of the hybrid control method can be found in all types of robots, from a robot used for mechanical tests [9] to an upper limb rehabilitation robot [10]. Because of its versatility, the hybrid position/force control was chosen as the primary control method for the walking robot.

As we know, hybrid control combines a kinematic control method for joints that do not require compensation of weight and inertia and a dynamic control method that can handle these parameters and reject environmental disturbances. The kinematic approach is used for positioning control of the robot and the dynamic approach for the force and torque control. Consequently, a classic proportional-integrative-derivative (PID) regulator was chosen for the position control and a sliding mode control (SMC) method [11] for the force and torque control. The main reason for using a SMC method was its robustness in the presence of external disturbances and uncertainties. Many scientists have used the control method to improve industrial robot trajectory [12], mobile robot trajectory in dynamic environments [13], n-link serial manipulator control [14], balance control of a two-wheel robot [15], and even airplane fuselage inspection [16]. SMC is not a perfect control method, and it has drawbacks, one of which is the chattering effect that it can introduce. New research is published every year [17] on eliminating the chattering impact in a general manner or for a specific robot structure or purpose.

Using multiple regulators or control methods on the same robot structure can separate the robot joints statically into two categories, starting with the design of the control law. However, this is not desirable if one needs to build a versatile robot. Hence, a real-time decision method must determine the degree of freedom (joints) controlled by each method. A combination of techniques and control methods was thus selected. The first one, Extenics [18] or extension logic [19], entails defining the control parameters and robot properties or abilities and is used by scientists to configure problem-solving algorithms [18] and even design toys for children with special needs [20].

For the proposed robot structure, Extenics helped ease the process of organizing the parameters of each control method and provided the offline means of solving potential conflicts, uncertainties, or mismatching of sensor data and regulators.

Neural networks [21,22] were considered for the decision method, but the process of training the network was too extensive for the proposed robot. Another possibility was using swarm optimization [23] to predict what the robot needs in terms of control methods. This also overcomplicated the control system, and it should be handled in future work. For the presented robot, neutrosophic logic [24] and the Dezert–Smarandache Theory (DSmT) [25] were chosen. DSmT combined with Extenics is used to manage decision making [20] and provides excellent results by combining the mapping process of Extension logic with the sensor fusion of DSmT in uncertain and contradictory conditions. As an extension of fuzzy logic, neutrosophic logic and DSmT have been used by researchers to develop applications [26] for aviation parking [27], multi-UAV surveillance [28], obstacle avoidance in unknown environments [29], and environmental detection and estimation [30].

A different approach in designing the decision algorithm of a hybrid system is using time triggers or an event-driven mechanism [31] with an event generation mechanism [32] to ensure control of the system at the precise times of important defined events. This approach is safe for robots in a known environment, but it can fail or make inconsistent decisions for robots moving inside unknown and unstructured environments.

To develop a mobile walking robot, one can reference many highly advanced robots, some designed by renowned institutes [33], that use dynamic control methods to provide stability and error rejection for the control architecture. While efficient mathematical solutions [34] are desired for a control law to give it low computational requirements, these can be difficult to obtain when the robot model is complex. Moreover, the dynamic control of any robot must overcome external disturbances [35] and reject any influence from other sources, including within the sensor information.

Here, we propose and describe a mobile walking robot hybrid position/force control that can be used within a group of linked robots. The research aim to obtain a control algorithm and method using both kinematic and dynamic control methods and an intelligent switching method between them. As a result, several experiments were conducted to improve the performance of the developed hybrid control, taking advantage of the extension set and neutrosophic logic. The extension set and neutrosophic logic were used to enhance the decision making required by the hybrid control, the first as an offline set of characteristics to extend the system's definition, and the second as an online switching mechanism that works with uncertain and contradictory information. The resulting hybrid control using a two-stage decision algorithm was a robot control method that took advantage of the best properties of the kinematic and dynamic control laws while the robot was fulfilling its tasks in uncertain environments. The data fusion provided by the neutrosophic theory in contradictory or uncertain conditions improved the decision switching mechanism, while the overall reference tracking of the robot did not decrease. The computational requirements of the proposed hybrid control were reduced because of the kinematic control method when the robot did not require dynamic compensation.

The paper is divided into six main sections. Section 2 provides a visual description of the robot used in the experiments. Section 3 presents the offline decision using the extension set, while Section 4 presents the decision method based on neutrosophic logic that takes advantage of DSmT [25]. The hybrid control is presented in Section 5 with an in-depth analysis of the kinematic (Section 5.1) and SMC dynamic (Section 5.2) control methods. Sections 6 and 7 contain the conducted experiments and simulations with the obtained results. In the end, Section 8 presents this paper's conclusions.

2. System Description

Figure 1 presents the robot structure. The robot was a hexapod [36], and its design was selected to avoid stability problems. Future research will consider the stability of a single bipedal mobile walking robot. As can be seen, the robot platform was divided into three modules, resulting in a modular robot that could be further extended or reconfigured. Figure 1b presents the kinematic structure of the hexapod robot leg. Each leg had three degrees of freedom, ensuring the 3D positioning of the foot.

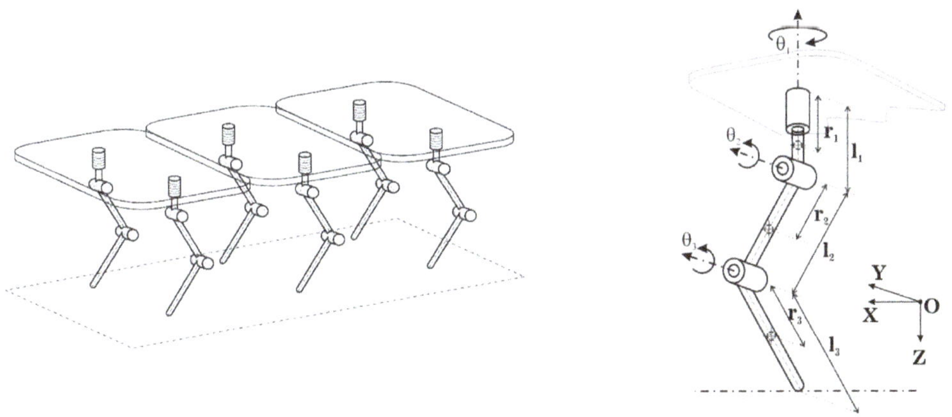

(a) (b)

Figure 1. The robot structure: (**a**) the hexapod walking robot; (**b**) kinematic structure of the robot leg.

In the robot structure, aluminum was considered for rectangular bars with height, width, and length dimensions $h_i \times w_i \times l_i$ and weight m_i. h_i and w_i with the dimensions of h_i = 3 cm and w_i = 3 cm. Table 1 presents the robot dimensions used in the testing and simulations presented throughout the paper.

Table 1. Robot values.

Dimension	Value
r_1	0.05 [m]
l_1	0.1 [m]
m_1	0.25 [kg]
r_2	0.25 [m]
l_2	0.5 [m]
m_2	1.25 [kg]
r_3	0.35 [m]
l_3	0.7 [m]
m_3	1.76 [kg]

l_i and r_i represent, respectively, leg segment dimensions and the distance from the joint axis to the center of mass for each leg segment, and m_i is the segment's mass.

3. Extenics Theory and Extension Set Applied to Robots

Extenics is a scientific field that uses modeling and formal methods to extend elements or physical objects. The models and methods are then used to solve contradictory problems that cannot be solved in their defined form and conditions [37,38].

Because contradictory problems are omnipresent in any field, Extenics aims to define a set of methods that allows solving contradictory issues using virtual simulation with the help of computers.

The central parts of extension theory are the base element theory, extension set theory, and extension logic [39].

The fundamental element used to describe objects in extension theory is defined as:

$$M = (O_m, c_m, v_m) \tag{1}$$

where M is the object element for which O_m is the object, c_m is the characteristic, and v_m is the measure. If one characteristic exists, the other matter element can be of only one dimension. If the object has more characteristics, however, the multidimension matter element is be defined as:

$$M = \begin{bmatrix} O_m, & c_{m1}, & v_{m1} \\ & c_{m2}, & v_{m2} \\ & \vdots & \vdots \\ & c_{mn}, & v_{mn} \end{bmatrix} = (O_m, C_m, V_m). \tag{2}$$

If a hybrid control is used, then a multidimension matter element is used, described by many characteristics specific to the chosen control methods.

For a hybrid position/force control, the following matter element can be defined:

$$R_0 = \begin{bmatrix} \text{Robot Control} & \text{Control Type} & \text{Hybrid Control} \\ & \text{Overall Computation Speed} & \text{Good} \\ & \text{Refference Tracking Speed} & \text{Very Good} \\ & \text{Refference Tracking Error} & \text{Very Good} \\ & \text{Inertia Compensation} & \text{Good} \\ & \text{Disturbance Rejection} & \text{Good} \end{bmatrix}. \tag{3}$$

By using Extenics principle 2.2 [40], which Ren et al. [18] used to design low carbon products, the object from Equation (3) can be extended and decomposed into two matter elements for which O_1 and O_2 are defined as kinematic control and dynamic control, respectively. The two objects have the same characteristics as the primary object (called "hybrid control") but with different values:

$$R_1 = \begin{bmatrix} \text{Robot Control,} & \text{Control Type} & \left\{ \begin{matrix} \text{Kinematic Control} \\ \text{PID Control} \end{matrix} \right\} \\ & \text{Overall Computation Speed,} & \text{Very Good} \\ & \text{Refference Tracking Speed,} & \text{Very Good} \\ & \text{Refference Tracking Error,} & \text{Good} \\ & \text{Inertia Compensation,} & \text{Very Poor} \\ & \text{Perturbance Rejection} & \text{Poor} \end{bmatrix}, \quad (4)$$

$$R_2 = \begin{bmatrix} \text{Robot Control,} & \text{Control Type} & \left\{ \begin{matrix} \text{Dynamic Control} \\ \text{PID Sliding Control} \end{matrix} \right\} \\ & \text{Overall Computation Speed,} & \text{Average} \\ & \text{Refference Tracking Speed,} & \text{Good} \\ & \text{Refference Tracking Error,} & \text{Very Good} \\ & \text{Inertia Compensation,} & \text{Very Good} \\ & \text{Perturbance Rejection} & \text{Very Good} \end{bmatrix}. \quad (5)$$

As can be seen, the two matter elements from Equations (4) and (5) describe the control types, the kinematic and the dynamic, briefly. The matter elements are customized for control types, but numerous other features can be added for which the matter characteristics are different according to the desired control type.

The contradiction between the two control types is found using the matter element characterization. The kinematic type has a better computational speed for a real-time controller. Still, when a robot is subject to inertial forces, it has worse positioning error and tracking speed. On the other hand, the dynamic control method takes into consideration the inertial forces that act on a robot and has a better tracking error. However, although the tracking error is better, the tracking speed is worse. The overall computational speed is greatly diminished, owing to the many calculations inside the control loop.

As a simple reference trajectory, an ideal trajectory of the foot (Figure 2) was used. When a robot foot has the role of support (the unbroken line in Figure 2), precise control is needed that considers the weight and inertia of the robot, so the robot's position does not oscillate on the vertical axis during the support phase. Additionally, the joints of a robot leg must complete or partially support the overall robot weight, including the other legs in the advancing stage. The dotted line in Figure 2 represents the leg balance trajectory when a robot takes a step for which the positioning is not required to be precise but must be fast and smooth. During the second motion phase, the leg joints support only their leg weight.

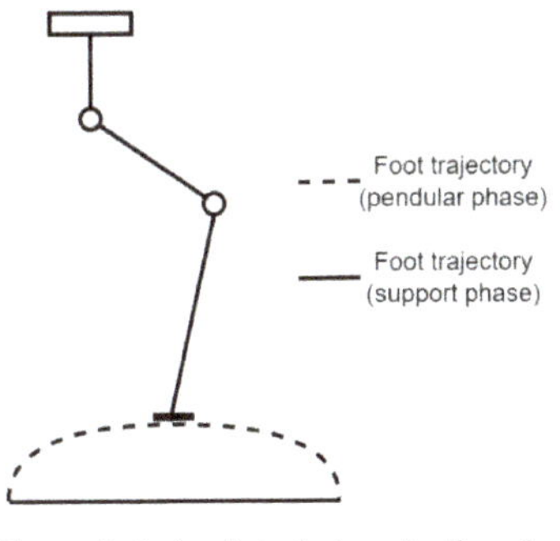

Figure 2. A simple trajectory for the robot foot.

Knowing the gross characterization of the two types of trajectories that a robot foot takes, the problem of choosing the control type is solved by checking the properties of the two matter elements defined by Equations (4) and (5).

Thereby, to control the robot during the uniform pull and weight support phase, the matter element R_2 was chosen. Its properties provided better precision in tracking the position reference and considered the robot's inertia to compensate for the robot's weight and inertial motion forces.

When the robot foot must follow a curve in space during the advancing phase, the robot's weight was not supported by it, so we used matter element R_1. The R_1 properties better corresponded to the robot motion criteria. The kinematic controller was used when the robot needed to make a forward or reverse motion that was not in direct contact with the support plane. High positioning precision was not required for the advancing movement, only a faster speed to position the foot as quickly as possible on the next support point.

One of the properties of the two matter elements is "overall computation speed," which indicates how many mathematical operations are needed to compute the actual reference for each separate joint. Therefore, a kinematic controller is much more efficient in computational requirements, performing fewer mathematical operations than a dynamic one. Results have indicated that a kinematic controller supplies not only a better tracking speed but also minimal resource consumption.

When defining and separating the control type that is best for the job, a real-time switching method was required. Thus, with the help of neutrosophic logic, the robot leg phase was determined, based not on reference values but on sensor information. According to the data calculated by Extenics theory on which type of control law to use, a hybrid control could be obtained to resolve the transition problem between kinematic and dynamic control laws. As an offline result, it could be reiterated for future datasets to enhance control properties or add a second layer of details and properties.

4. Neutrosophic Logic in Robot Control

As defined in [41], neutrosophic logic is the foundation of neutrosophic mathematics. Neutrosophic logic works with neutrosophic sets that generalize fuzzy sets and describe neutrosophic elements. The elements are based on <A>, <anti A>, and <neutral A>, where <A> is an attribute, <anti A> is the opposite of the attribute, and <neutral A> is the neutral area between <A> and <anti A>.

In neutrosophic logic, every affirmation *Af* is *T*% true, *I*% undetermined (uncertain), or *F*% false. Therefore, we can say *Af* (*T*, *I*, *F*), where *T*, *I*, and *F* are standard or non-standard subsets of the interval $]^{-}0, 1^{+}[$ [41].

If *U* is the work universe and *M* is a set included in *U*, then one element *x* from *U* is written as *x* (*T*, *I*, *F*) according to set *M* and belongs to the same set in the following way: element *x* is *t*% true in set *M*; element *x* is *i*% undetermined in set *M* (either true or false); and element *x* is *f*% false in set *M*. The value of *t* varies in *T*, *i* varies in *I*, and *f* varies in *F* [42,43].

As described in the current paper, the robot control diagram presented used both kinematic and dynamic elements. At a specific time, the robot used only one of the control methods to maximize and optimize computing and motion speed or the positioning error. A precision element was needed to switch between the two control types. Using Extenics and extension theory, the contradictory elements were defined to separate the two control types between which the decision algorithm switched using neutrosophic theory.

The classic neutrosophic theory [25] chooses between the two control methods. The general equation is presented in Relation (6) and defines the generalized basic belief assignment:

$$m(C) = \sum_{\substack{A, B \in D^{\Theta} \\ A \cap B = C}} m_1(A) \cdot m_2(B), \forall C \in D^{\Theta} \tag{6}$$

where D^{Θ} is a hyperpower set from the frame $\Theta = \{\theta_1, \theta_2, \ldots, \theta_n\}$ of n exhaustive elements and $A, B \in 2^{\Theta}$. The basic belief assignment is $(\cdot) : 2^{\Theta} \to [0,1]$, where $2^{\Theta} = \{\varnothing, \theta_1, \theta_2, \theta_3, \theta_1 \cup \theta_2, \theta_1 \cup \theta_3, \theta_2 \cup \theta_3, \theta_1 \cup \theta_2 \cup \theta_3\}$ when $\Theta = \{\theta_1, \theta_2, \theta_3\}$.

In the case of the presented robot, two belief assignments were assigned to the two observers. The two observers were the force and proximity sensors that must determine which type of control was required at one time.

The experimental data for the two observers are presented in Table 2. These values divided the sensors' measurement interval in a decision percentage, where the force sensor was more likely to decide on a dynamic control (75%) than the proximity sensor (65%). The rate was reversed for the kinematic control and was the same for the uncertain interval.

Table 2. Observer experimental data.

θ	**Force Sensor** $m_1(\theta)$	**Proximity Sensor** $m_2(\theta)$
θ_D *	0.75	0.65
θ_C **	0.2	0.3
$\theta_D \cup \theta_C$ ***	0.05	0.05

* θ_D = dynamic control; ** θ_C = kinematic control; *** $\theta_D \cup \theta_C$ is the indeterminate area.

The values meant that the decision could be computed with a certain approximation by using Equation (6) if the robot was in contact with the support surface, according to the data received from the sensors, and a decision was made whether it would switch from one control type to another. The kinematic control type was used in the foot balancing phase and the dynamic control type in the support phase. The decision was made between the two contradictory objects, defined with the help of Extenics and extension theory.

Table 3 presents the cases in which the meutrosophic values $m_1(\theta_D)$, $m_1(\theta_C)$, $m_2(\theta_D)$, $m_2(\theta_C)$, $m_1(\theta_D \cup \theta_C)$, or $m_2(\theta_D \cup \theta_C)$ can be found in any combination for A and B to correspond to Equation (6), meaning that $A \cap B = C$. The results were obtained using Equation (6) and represent the neutrosophic probabilistic values of truth (certainty of a valid value), falsity (assurance of a false value), uncertainty (the unknown state between two possible outcomes), and contradiction (two observers provide contradictory information with high certainty for both).

Table 3. The experimental data after using Equation (6).

$C = A \cap B$	m (C)	
φ	0	-
θ_D	0.5575	Truth value for θ_D and falsity value for θ_C
θ_C	0.085	Truth value for θ_C and falsity value for θ_D
$\theta_D \cup \theta_C$	0.0025	Uncertainty between θ_C and θ_D
$\theta_D \cap \theta_C$	0.355	The contradiction between θ_C and θ_D

The values from Table 3 were computed in Equation (7).

$$
\begin{aligned}
m(\phi) &= 0 \\
m(\theta_D) &= m_1(\theta_D) \times m_2(\theta_D \cup \theta_C) + m_1(\theta_D \cup \theta_C) \times m_2(\theta_D) + m_1(\theta_D) \times m_2(\theta_D) = 0.5575 \\
m(\theta_C) &= m_1(\theta_C) \times m_2(\theta_D \cup \theta_C) + m_1(\theta_D \cup \theta_C) \times m_2(\theta_C) + m_1(\theta_C) \times m_2(\theta_C) = 0.085 \\
m(\theta_D \cup \theta_C) &= m_1(\theta_D \cup \theta_C) \times m_2(\theta_D \cup \theta_C) = 0.0025 \\
m(\theta_D \cap \theta_C) &= m_1(\theta_D) \times m_2(\theta_C) + m_1(\theta_C) \times m_2(\theta_D) = 0.355
\end{aligned}
\tag{7}
$$

where $m(\theta_D)$ and $m(\theta_C)$ are the probabilistic values of certainty to choose a certain control law; $m(\theta_D \cup \theta_C)$ is the probabilistic uncertainty value of the two sensors; and $m(\theta_D \cap \theta_C)$ is the probabilistic contradiction values between the two sensors. As a test, when all five values are added, their sum must be equal to 1 (100%): $m(\varphi) + m(\theta_D) + m(\theta_C) + m(\theta_D \cup \theta_C) + m(\theta_D \cap \theta_C) = 1$.

Using the computed values, each observer's decision (force and proximity sensor) had a certain probability that each of the two control systems required to control the robot.

Table 4 presents all cases presented in Figure 3a,b for the force sensor and proximity sensor where X and α were defined according to the sensor type.

Table 4. Control probability.

$C = A \cap B$	A (Force Sensor)	B (Proximity Sensor)	m (C)	Control Type
φ	φ	φ	0	Robot stopped
θ_D	θ_D	$\theta_D \cup \theta_C$	0.5575	Dynamic Control
	$\theta_D \cup \theta_C$	θ_D		
	θ_D	θ_D		
θ_C	θ_C	$\theta_D \cup \theta_C$	0.085	Cinematic Control
	$\theta_D \cup \theta_C$	θ_C		
	θ_C	θ_C		
$\theta_D \cup \theta_C$	$\theta_D \cup \theta_C$	$\theta_D \cup \theta_C$	0.0025	Uncertainty
$\theta_D \cap \theta_C$	θ_D	θ_C	0.355	Contradiction
	θ_C	θ_D		

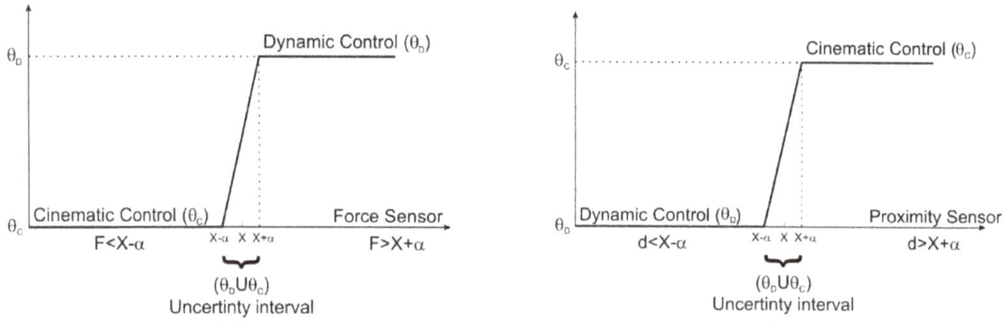

Figure 3. Control-deciding graphs: (**a**) force sensor graph; (**b**) proximity sensor graph.

For the last two cases in Table 4, the $C = \theta_D \cup \theta_C$ or $C = \theta_D \cap \theta_C$ uncertainty in decision making was due to the sensor values, leading to a contradiction. If, in the case of uncertainty, the control type running at that time could be kept, in the case of contradiction between sensor data, a decision must be made on which control should be used. Because the contradiction could appear only under specific conditions, a decision was made to use the same type of control as the robot in the case of uncertainty.

One exceptional or typical case is the robot stepping on very uneven ground. The force sensor indicates that the foot is on the floor, but the proximity sensor does not provide the same conclusion since it reads a value greater than the reference threshold. Therefore, the decision should be to switch to a dynamic controller. On the other hand, if a kinematic control is used and the foot is subject to external factors, the force sensor records high peak values in short periods, leading to the chattering effect. The algorithm switched from kinematic to dynamic control for any case of uncertainty. To prevent additional chattering effects, the algorithm switched the control method when the force sensor retained its contradictory value for a minimum Δt time interval. The time threshold provided a precision control law in uneven terrain and contradictory cases between input sensors and observers.

A supplementary condition was required in addition to the selected requirements for the control type. The condition was bound to the way the robot moves. Because the dynamic control was slower to compensate for high errors and its stationary points were unnecessary, we chose the control law based on robot kinematics to save computing time.

One could argue that the switching control law is unnecessary and uses simple triggers that act as switching mechanisms. However, a simple control switch cannot decide between options when the information received is inaccurate, which is one of the main reasons the neutrosophic switching mechanism was chosen and used.

5. The Walking Robot Leg Control Architecture

To control a walking robot, one has to design a control law for each leg, and the control has many walking phases that depend directly on the reference signal of the foot. Therefore, the design of a general control law is needed to control foot position and the motor's torque according to the computed reference and to use the sensor signal (force and proximity) for environmental interaction and detection.

Figure 4 presents the general control diagram for one leg of the walking robot. The graph contains a reference generation block to generate the foot trajectory using detailed data chosen to test the control law.

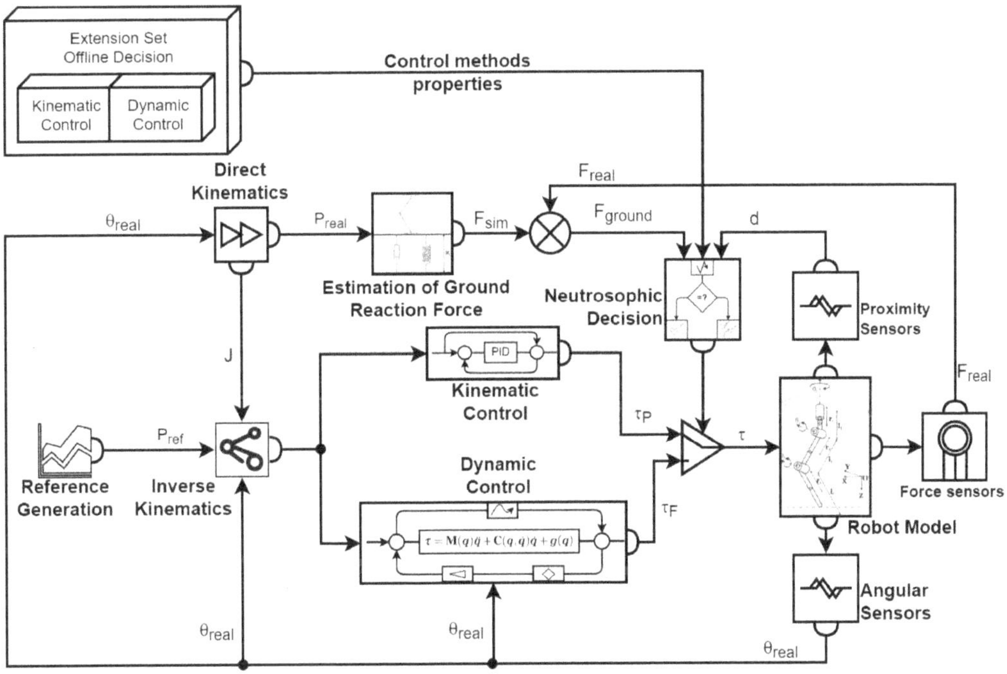

Figure 4. The general control diagram.

The reference generation was made in the operational space, and the data were converted to the joint space from the operational space by using inverse kinematics. An inverse kinematics algorithm based on the Jacobian transpose was used and is presented in

Equation (8). Compared to other algorithms, it provides a reference speed for the leg joint motors and not the angular position reference.

$$\begin{array}{ll} 1. & \Delta e = e_{goal} - e_{real} \\ 2. & JJTde = J \times J^T \times \Delta e \\ 3. & \alpha = \frac{\Delta e^T \times JJTde}{JJTde^T \times JJTde} \\ 4. & \Delta\theta = \left(\alpha \times J^T \times \Delta e\right)^T \end{array} . \tag{8}$$

The speed reference value cannot be used to control the robot joints by the dynamic controller because the dynamic controller needs the angular reference for all the degrees of freedom it controls, and this is the reason why the angular values for each joint were computed using the foot position as the origin. The equations are:

$$\begin{aligned} q_1 &= \arctan\left(\frac{Mx}{My}\right) \\ q_2 &= 2 \times \arctan\left(\frac{\sin q_2}{\sin^2 q_2 + \cos^2 q_2} + \cos q_2\right) \\ q_3 &= \arctan\left(-\frac{\sin q_3}{\cos q_3}\right) \end{aligned} \tag{9}$$

where the sine and cosine values are given by

$$\begin{aligned} \cos q_2 &= \frac{(Mz - l_1) \times (l_2 + l_3 \cos q_3) + Mx \times l_3 \sin q_3}{(Mz - l_1)^2 + Mx^2 + My^2}, \\ \sin q_2 &= \sqrt{1 - \cos^2 q_2}, \\ \cos q_3 &= \frac{(Mz - l_1)^2 + Mx^2 + My^2 - l_2^2 - l_3^2}{2 l_2 l_3}, \\ \sin q_3 &= \sqrt{1 - \cos^2 q_3}. \end{aligned} \tag{10}$$

For Equation (9) to be valid and to condition the leg posture, additional conditions were added:

$$\begin{array}{ll} 1: & if\ \text{My} = 0\ then\ \ \text{q1} = 0 \\ 2: & q_1 \in \left(-\frac{\pi}{2}, \frac{\pi}{2}\right) \\ 3: & q_3 \leq 0 \end{array} . \tag{11}$$

The two sensors' data (proximity and force) were used as input signals for the neutrosophic block to decide. Because generated information was used, the two sensors were simulated. Therefore, the proximity sensor had a function based on the calculated distance from the foot to the support surface considered a plane, but to which a sinusoidal signal was added to generate the measurement error of the sensor. Regarding the force sensor, the foot–ground interaction was simulated using the system from Figure 5. The simulation was achieved with the help of a damper and a spring.

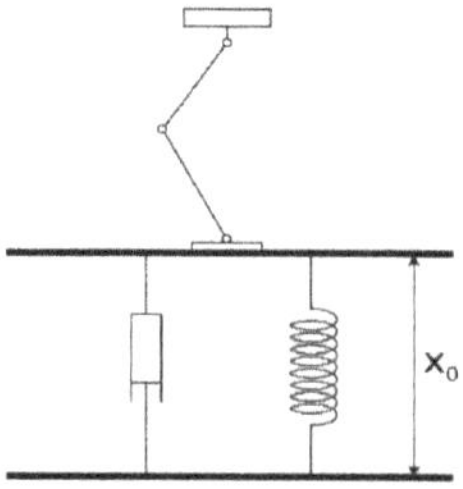

Figure 5. Interaction between the robot and ground surface.

The equation used for contract modeling and determining the reaction force of ground interaction was the classical one:

$$F_{tot} = -(k \cdot x + c \cdot \dot{x}) \quad (12)$$

where k and c are the constants of the spring and damper, respectively.

Having the two parameters, reaction force and proximity distance, as inputs for the decision method, the two control methods are defined in the following sections.

5.1. The Kinematic Control Method

This method used the data provided by the computing algorithm of inverse kinematics (Figure 6) and fed the output to the PI (proportional-integration) regulator that drove the robot joint motors.

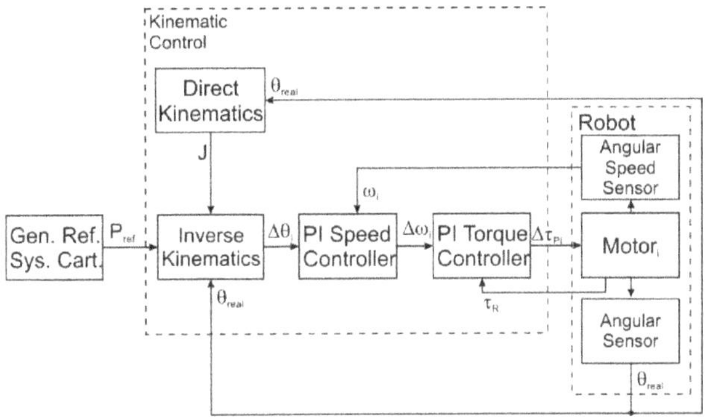

Figure 6. The kinematic control diagram.

As previously described in the Extenics method, the control method has fewer calculations. Still, the positioning error is not the best because of the inverse kinematics method. It does not consider the inertial force that the robot experiences during the actual motion.

The main component of the controller is the Jacobian matrix:

$$J = \begin{bmatrix} -s_1(l_2s_2 + l_3s_{23}) & c_1(l_2c_2 + l_3c_{23}) & l_3c_1c_{23} \\ c_1(l_2s_2 + l_3s_{23}) & s_1(l_2c_2 + l_3c_{23}) & l_3s_1c_{23} \\ 0 & -l_2s_2 - l_3s_{23} & -l_3s_{23} \end{bmatrix} \quad (13)$$

where $s_i = \sin(\theta_i)$, $c_i = \cos(\theta_i)$, $s_{ij} = \sin(\theta_i + \theta_j)$, and $c_{ij} = \cos(\theta_i + \theta_j)$.

The matrix was computed from the direct kinematics equations and was used to find the foot position in the operational space:

$$M(x, y, z) = \begin{bmatrix} c_1(l_2s_2 + l_3s_{23}) \\ s_1(l_2s_2 + l_3s_{23}) \\ l_1 + l_2c_2 + l_3c_{23} \end{bmatrix}. \quad (14)$$

The entire kinematic control loop was based on the Jacobian matrix. First, the matrix containing the actual angular joint position was calculated. After it followed its transpose matrix and the operational space reference position, the positioning error $\Delta\theta$ was obtained.

The positioning error was sent to two PI (proportional-integrative) feedback control loops for controlling the angular speed and motor torque. Thereby, the torque control for each joint was obtained, and the switch from one controller to another (from the kinematic control to the dynamic one, and vice versa) was more accessible since they both used torque to control the robot joints.

The transpose Jacobian method is not new and is based on using the transpose matrix of the Jacobian instead of the inverse matrix. Therefore, $\Delta\theta$ was computed using Equation (15):

$$\Delta\dot{q} = \alpha J^T e \tag{15}$$

for specific values of constant α.

The transpose-Jacobian-matrix-based algorithm presented in Equation (8) eliminated stability problems. The algorithm was also chosen because it had a higher computation speed than the control values of other algorithms, even if the computed values were not as precise as the inverse-Jacobian-matrix-based method [44].

Because the method of solving the inverse kinematics problem uses the Jacobian matrix, the final results are always formed by angular speeds that the robot joints must follow. Therefore, the control is suitable for PI and PID regulators and for controlling angular velocities. The downside is that the method cannot be used to compute a dynamic control reference since it needs a precise joint angular value. In contrast, if the values given by the Jacobian-based inverse kinematic problem are integrated, the result is not as accurate as is required.

5.2. The Dynamic Control Method

The dynamic control method used the same reference data as the kinematic one. Nevertheless, it computed the torque reference of the motors considering kinematic parameters, the inertial ones provided by the inertia matrix, and the Coriolis and gravity force effects supplied by the Coriolis and gravity matrices.

Figure 7 presents the dynamic control diagram. The most critical control blocks are shown, including those that compute the inertial parameters and values used by the slide control block. The three control blocks that formed the dynamic controller from Figure 7 were the PID error controller, the fuzzy controller, and the slide control. The first block passed the positioning error through a PID controller so that the control method could consider the error variations. Using the PID error controller data, the fuzzy amplification was obtained through the membership functions presented in Figure 8a,b. The command torque for each motor joint could be calculated after computing the fuzzy gain, using the inertial data and the reference values [45].

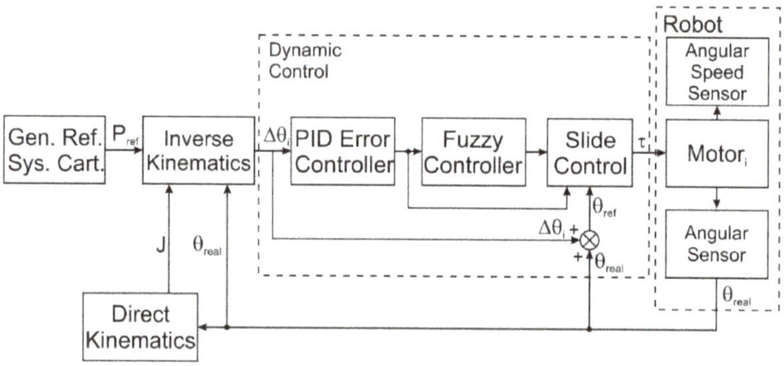

Figure 7. The dynamic control scheme.

All the control values were computed from the presented robot structure, characteristics, structural weights, and measurements.

For Figure 8a,b the abbreviations are N = Negative, P = Positive, ZE = zero, S = Small, M = Medium, B = Big, and V = Very. For the membership functions, Table 5 presents the values for the membership parameters so the gain value K_{fuzzy} could be chosen. The membership functions that provided the gain were selected according to the values of the two parameters s and $\dot{s}$, where s represents the error through the PID error controller and $\dot{s}$

is its derivate. A constant gain was not desired for each case, leading to a standard-step fuzzy controller, but a function-based one was selected.

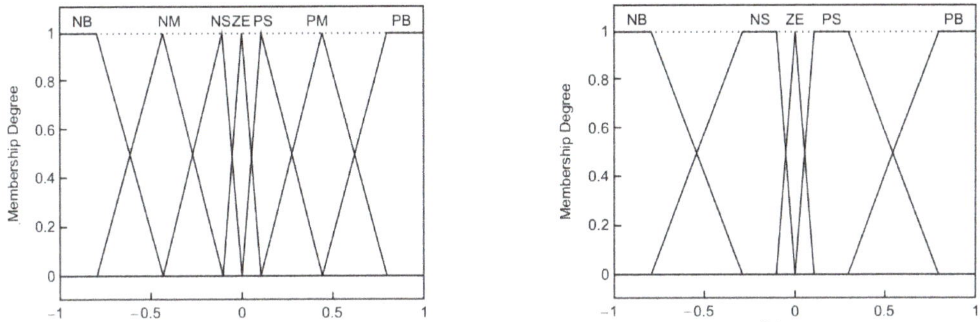

(a) (b)

Figure 8. Membership functions: (**a**) member function for input s; (**b**) member function for input $\dot{s}$.

Table 5. The output fuzzy gain computation.

	s	NB	NM	NS	Z	PS	PM	PB
$\dot{s}$		$S < -2$	$-2 < = S < -1$	$-1 < = S < 0$	$S = 0$	$0 < S < = 1$	$1 < S < = 2$	$2 < S$
NB	$\dot{s} < -10$	S	VS	S	M	B	VB	VB
N	$-10 \leq \dot{s} < 0$	M	S	VS	S	M	B	VB
Z	$\dot{s} = 0$	B	M	S	VS	S	M	B
PS	$0 < \dot{s} \leq 10$	VB	B	M	S	VS	S	M
PB	$10 < \dot{s}$	VB	VB	B	M	S	VS	S

Using Table 5 data, the parabola in Figure 9 was considered for computing the K_{fuzzy} gain, according to the two inputs s and $\dot{s}$. The parabola equation was computed from Equation (16):

$$y(x) = 2x^2 + 50, \quad (16)$$

and we modified it to introduce the fuzzy parameters:

$$K_{fuzzy}(\dot{s}) = 2(\dot{s} - 10 \cdot s)^2 + 50. \quad (17)$$

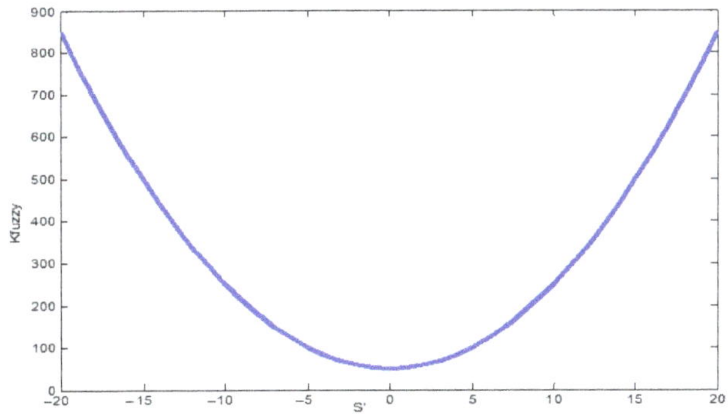

Figure 9. Parameter K_{fuzzy} for s = 0 and $\dot{s}$ between −20 and 20.

Equation (15) now provides the K_{fuzzy} parameter in the dynamic control.

The sliding control was made with the help of the slide control block (Figure 7). The control type was inspired by Shafiei [12] and modified to match the robot kinematic structure used, a design with three degrees of freedom instead of the two used by Shafiei [12]. Following that, the dynamic equations that allowed the dynamic controller's development are presented.

The basic dynamic control equation was:

$$H(q)\ddot{q} + C(q,\dot{q})\dot{q} + G(q) + \tau_d = \tau. \tag{18}$$

From Equation (18), the signal for motor torque control was calculated. All the parameters from Equation (18) are required to be known. The unknown values are the torque τ, the matrices H (inertial parameters), C (Coriolis and centrifugal forces), and G (gravity effect), which are given by the following equations, in which the angles θ from the joint space are equal to the ones in the operational space:

$$H = M = \begin{bmatrix} M_{11} & M_{12} & M_{13} \\ M_{21} & M_{22} & M_{23} \\ M_{31} & M_{32} & M_{33} \end{bmatrix} \tag{19}$$

where M is the inertial parameters matrix.

The inertial matrix parameters can be computed using the following:

$$\begin{gathered}
T(\theta,\dot{\theta}) = \tfrac{1}{2}\dot{q}^T \cdot M \cdot \dot{q} = \tfrac{1}{2}\textstyle\sum_{i,j} M_{ij}(q)\dot{q}_i\dot{q}_j \geq 0, \\
T(\theta,\dot{\theta}) = \tfrac{1}{2}m_1(\dot{\bar{x}}_1^2 + \dot{\bar{y}}_1^2 + \dot{\bar{z}}_1^2) + \tfrac{1}{2}m_2(\dot{\bar{x}}_2^2 + \dot{\bar{y}}_2^2 + \dot{\bar{z}}_2^2) + \tfrac{1}{2}m_3(\dot{\bar{x}}_3^2 + \dot{\bar{y}}_3^2 + \dot{\bar{z}}_3^2) + \tfrac{1}{2}I_{z_1}\dot{\theta}_1^2 + \tfrac{1}{2}I_{z_2}\left(\dot{\theta}_1 + \dot{\theta}_2\right)^2 + \\
\tfrac{1}{2}I_{z_3}\left(\dot{\theta}_1 + \dot{\theta}_2 + \dot{\theta}_3\right)^2 \\
\bar{x}_1 = 0,\ \dot{\bar{x}}_1 = 0, \\
\bar{y}_1 = 0, \dot{\bar{y}}_1 = 0, \\
\bar{z}_1 = r_1,\ \dot{\bar{z}}_1 = 0, \\
\bar{x}_2 = r_2\mathrm{sin}q_2{\cdot}\mathrm{cos}q_1,\quad \dot{\bar{x}}_2 = -r_2\mathrm{sin}q_1 - \mathrm{sin}q_2{\cdot}\dot{q}_1 + r_2\mathrm{cos}q_1{\cdot}\mathrm{cos}q_2{\cdot}\dot{q}_2, \\
\bar{y}_2 = r_2\mathrm{sin}q_2{\cdot}\mathrm{sin}q_1,\quad \dot{\bar{y}}_2 = r_2\mathrm{cos}q_1{\cdot}\mathrm{sin}q_2{\cdot}\dot{q}_1 + r_2\mathrm{sin}q_1{\cdot}\mathrm{cos}q_2{\cdot}\dot{q}_2, \\
\bar{z}_2 = l_1 + r_2\mathrm{cos}q_2,\quad \dot{\bar{z}}_2 = -r_2\mathrm{sin}q_2{\cdot}\dot{q}_2, \\
\bar{x}_3 = \mathrm{cos}q_1(l_2\mathrm{sin}q_2 + r_3\mathrm{sin}(q_2+q_3)), \\
\bar{y}_3 = \mathrm{sin}q_1(l_2\mathrm{sin}q_2 + r_3\mathrm{sin}(q_2+q_3)), \\
\bar{z}_3 = l_1 + l_2\mathrm{cos}q_2 + r_3\mathrm{cos}(q_2+q_3), \\
\dot{\bar{x}}_3 = -\mathrm{sin}q_1(l_2\mathrm{sin}q_2 + r_3\mathrm{sin}(q_2+q_3))\dot{q}_1 + \mathrm{cos}q_1(l_2\mathrm{cos}q_2 + r_3\mathrm{cos}(q_2+q_3))\dot{q}_2 + r_3\mathrm{cos}q_1\mathrm{cos}(q_2+q_3)\dot{q}_3, \\
\dot{\bar{y}}_3 = \mathrm{cos}q_1(l_2\mathrm{sin}q_2 + r_3\mathrm{sin}(q_2+q_3))\dot{q}_1 + \mathrm{sin}q_1(l_2\mathrm{cos}q_2 + r_3\mathrm{cos}(q_2+q_3))\dot{q}_2 + r_3\mathrm{sin}q_1\mathrm{cos}(q_2+q_3)\dot{q}_3 \\
\dot{\bar{z}}_3 = -(l_2\mathrm{sin}q_2 + r_3\mathrm{sin}(q_2+q_3))\dot{q}_2 - r_3\mathrm{sin}(q_2+q_3)\dot{q}_3, \\
I_{xi} = \tfrac{m_i}{12}\left(w_i^2 + h_i^2\right),\ I_{yi} = \tfrac{m_i}{12}\left(l_i^2 + h_i^2\right),\ I_{zi} = \tfrac{m_i}{12}\left(l_i^2 + w_i^2\right)
\end{gathered} \tag{20}$$

where $\bar{x}_i, \bar{y}_i, \bar{z}_i, \dot{\bar{x}}_i, \dot{\bar{y}}_i, \dot{\bar{z}}_i$ are the coordinates of the center of mass for each element of a leg, and, respectively, their first derivate; and I_{xi}, I_{yi}, and I_{zi} represent the inertia tensors of each leg element.

By using inertia matrix requirement parameters, the inertia matrix elements were computed by the following equations:

$$
\begin{gathered}
M_{11} = r_2^2 m_2 + r_3^2 m_3 + l_2^2 m_3 + \tfrac{1}{12} l_1^2 m_1 + \tfrac{1}{12} w^2 m_1 + \tfrac{1}{12} l_2^2 m_2 + \tfrac{1}{12} w^2 m_2 + \tfrac{1}{12} l_3^2 m_3 + \tfrac{1}{12} w^2 m_3 + \\
2 l_2 r_3 m_3 \sin(q_2 + q_3) - \cos^2(q_2)(l_2^2 m_3 + r_2^2 m_2) - r_3^2 m_3 \cos^2(q_2 + q_3), \\
M_{12} = \tfrac{1}{6} l_2^2 m_2 + \tfrac{1}{6} w^2 m_2, \\
M_{21} = \tfrac{1}{6} w^2 m_3 + \tfrac{1}{6} l_3^2 m_3, \\
M_{22} = r_2^2 m_2 + l_2^2 m_3 + r_3^2 m_3 + \tfrac{1}{12} w^2 m_2 + \tfrac{1}{12} l_2^2 m_2 + \tfrac{1}{12} l_3^2 m_3 + \tfrac{1}{12} w^2 m_3 + 2 l_2 r_3 m_3 [\sin q_2 \sin(q_2 + q_3) + \cos q_2 \cos(q_2 + q_3)], \\
M_{23} = 2 l_2 r_3 m_3 [\sin q_2 \cdot \sin(q_2 + q_3) + \cos q_2 \cdot \cos(q_2 + q_3)], \\
M_{31} = \tfrac{1}{6} l_3^2 m_3, \\
M_{32} = \tfrac{1}{6} w^2 m_3 + \tfrac{1}{6} l_3^2 m_3 + 2 r_3^2 m_3, \\
M_{33} = r_3^2 m_3 + \tfrac{1}{12} l_3^2 m_3 + \tfrac{1}{12} w^2 m_3.
\end{gathered} \tag{21}
$$

The Coriolis matrix was computed using the following equation:

$$
C_{ij}(q, \dot{q}) = \sum_{k=1}^{3} \Gamma_{ijk} \dot{q}_k = \frac{1}{2} \sum_{k=1}^{3} \left(\frac{\partial M_{ij}}{\partial q_k} + \frac{\partial M_{ik}}{\partial q_j} - \frac{\partial M_{kj}}{\partial q_i} \right) \dot{q}_k \tag{22}
$$

for which the Γ_{ijk} parameters are:

$$
\begin{gathered}
\Gamma_{111} = \Gamma_{122} = \Gamma_{123} = \Gamma_{132} = \Gamma_{133} = \Gamma_{212} = \Gamma_{213} = \Gamma_{221} = \Gamma_{222} = \Gamma_{231} = \Gamma_{312} = \Gamma_{313} = \Gamma_{321} = \Gamma_{323} = \Gamma_{331} = \\
\Gamma_{333} = 0, \\
\Gamma_{112} = \begin{pmatrix} 2 l_2 m_3 r_3 (\sin q_2 \cos(q_2 + q_3) + \cos q_2 \sin(q_2 + q_3)) + 2 l_2^2 m_3 \cos q_2 \sin q_2 + \\ + 2 m_2 r_2^2 \cos q_2 \sin q_2 + 2 m_3 r_3^2 \cos(q_2 + q_3) \sin(q_2 + q_3) \end{pmatrix} \dot{q}_2, \\
\Gamma_{113} = (2 l_2 m_3 \sin q_2 \cos(q_2 + q_3) + 2 m_3 r_3^2 \cos(q_2 + q_3) \sin(q_2 + q_3)) \dot{q}_3 \\
\Gamma_{121} = \begin{pmatrix} 2 l_2 m_3 r_3 (\sin q_2 \cos(q_2 + q_3) + \cos q_2 \sin(q_2 + q_3)) + 2 l_2^2 m_3 \cos q_2 \sin q_2 + \\ + 2 m_2 r_2^2 \cos q_2 \sin q_2 + 2 m_3 r_3^2 \cos(q_2 + q_3) \sin(q_2 + q_3) \end{pmatrix} \dot{q}_1, \\
\Gamma_{131} = (2 l_2 m_3 \sin q_2 \cos(q_2 + q_3) + 2 m_3 r_3^2 \cos(q_2 + q_3) \sin(q_2 + q_3)) \dot{q}_1 \\
\Gamma_{211} = -\begin{pmatrix} 2 l_2 m_3 r_3 (\sin q_2 \cos(q_2 + q_3) + \cos q_2 \sin(q_2 + q_3)) + 2 l_2^2 m_3 \cos q_2 \sin q_2 + \\ + 2 m_2 r_2^2 \cos q_2 \sin q_2 + 2 m_3 r_3^2 \cos(q_2 + q_3) \sin(q_2 + q_3) \end{pmatrix} \dot{q}_1, \\
\Gamma_{223} = 2 l_2 m_3 r_3 (\sin q_2 \cos(q_2 + q_3) - \cos q_2 \sin(q_2 + q_3)) \dot{q}_3, \\
\Gamma_{232} = 2 l_2 m_3 r_3 (\sin q_2 \cos(q_2 + q_3) - \cos q_2 \sin(q_2 + q_3)) \dot{q}_2, \\
\Gamma_{233} = 4 l_2 m_3 r_3 (\sin q_2 \cos(q_2 + q_3) - \cos q_2 \sin(q_2 + q_3)) \dot{q}_3, \\
\Gamma_{311} = -(2 l_2 m_3 \sin q_2 \cos(q_2 + q_3) + 2 m_3 r_3^2 \cos(q_2 + q_3) \sin(q_2 + q_3)) \dot{q}_1, \\
\Gamma_{322} = -2 l_2 m_3 r_3 (\sin q_2 \cos(q_2 + q_3) - \cos q_2 \sin(q_2 + q_3)) \dot{q}_2, \\
\Gamma_{332} = -2 l_2 m_3 r_3 (\sin q_2 \cos(q_2 + q_3) - \cos q_2 \sin(q_2 + q_3)) \dot{q}_2.
\end{gathered} \tag{23}
$$

The last part of the dynamic equation is given by Equation (24), which computed the gravity effect matrix on the robot leg:

$$
G(q) = N(q, \dot{q}) = \frac{\partial U}{\partial q} = \begin{bmatrix} \frac{\partial U}{\partial q_1} \\ \frac{\partial U}{\partial q_2} \\ \frac{\partial U}{\partial q_3} \end{bmatrix} \tag{24}
$$

where

$$
\begin{gathered}
U(q) = m_1 x_1 g + m_1 y_1 g + m_1 z_1 g + m_2 g(x_2 + y_2 + z_2) + m_3 g(x_3 + y_3 + z_3) \\
= m_1 r_1 g + m_2 g(l_1 + r_2 \cos q_2 + r_2 \sin q_2 (\sin q_1 + \cos q_1)) + \\
+ m_3 g(l_1 + l_2 \cos q_2 + r_3 \cos(q_2 + q_3) + (\sin q_1 + \cos q_1)(l_2 \sin q_2 + r_3 \sin(q_2 + q_3)))
\end{gathered} \tag{25}
$$

and its derivative components are:

$$\frac{\partial U}{\partial q_1} = m_2 r_2 g \sin q_2(-\sin q_1 + \cos q_1) + m_3 g(-\sin q_1 + \cos q_1)(l_2 \sin q_2 + r_3 \sin(q_2 + q_3))$$
$$\frac{\partial U}{\partial q_2} = m_2 g(-r_2 \sin q_2 + r_2 \cos q_2(\cos q_1 + \sin q_1))$$
$$+ m_3 g[-l_2 \sin q_2 - r_3 \sin(q_2 + q_3) + (\sin q_1 + \cos q_1)(l_2 \cos q_2 + r_3 \cos(q_2 + q_3))]$$
$$\frac{\partial U}{\partial q_3} = m_3 g[-r_3 \sin(q_2 + q_3) + r_3 \cos(q_2 + q_3)(\sin q_1 + \cos q_1)]. \quad (26)$$

Using the dynamic control equations, the PID sliding control can be developed, which computes the torque τ used in the joint motor torque control so that the position vector q can track the desired trajectory q_d. The tracking error vector is defined as:

$$e = q_d - q. \quad (27)$$

Sliding motion control requires a sliding surface, given by Equation (28), and contains both the derivative term and the integral one:

$$s = \dot{e} + \lambda_1 e + \lambda_2 \int_0^t e dt \quad (28)$$

where λ_i is a positive diagonal matrix; it turns out that, for $s = 0$, a stable sliding surface is obtained (as shown by Shafiei in [12]). The dynamic robot equations can be written by using the sliding surface equation:

$$H\dot{s} = -Cs + f + \tau_d - \tau \quad (29)$$

where

$$f = H(\ddot{q}_d + \lambda_1 \dot{e} + \lambda_2 e) + C\left(\dot{q}_d + \lambda_1 e + \lambda_2 \int_0^t e dt\right) + G. \quad (30)$$

The control module input becomes:

$$\tau = \hat{f} + K_v s + K \mathrm{sgn}(s) \quad (31)$$

where

$$\hat{f} = \hat{H}(\ddot{q}_d + \lambda_1 \dot{e} + \lambda_2 e) + \hat{C}\left(\dot{q}_d + \lambda_1 e + \lambda_2 \int_0^t e dt\right) + \hat{G}. \quad (32)$$

Equation (32) represents a force estimation f, and $K_v s = K_v \dot{e} + K_v \lambda_1 e + K_v \lambda_2 \int_0^t e dt$ is the outer PID loop; K_v and K are positive diagonal matrices built so that the stability conditions are fulfilled and guaranteed. The *sgn*(*s*) function is the sign function. The function can also be written as:

$$\left|\tilde{f}\right| = \left|\tilde{H}(\ddot{q}_d + \lambda_1 \dot{e} + \lambda_2 e) + \tilde{C}\left(\dot{q}_d + \lambda_1 e + \lambda_2 \int_0^t e\, dt\right) + \tilde{G}\right| \le F \quad (33)$$

where $\tilde{f} = f - \hat{f}$, $\tilde{H} = H - \hat{H}$, and $\tilde{G} = G - \hat{G}$. The vector F is:

$$F = \left|\tilde{H}(\ddot{q}_d + \lambda_1 \dot{e} + \lambda_2 e)\right| + \left|\tilde{C}\left(\dot{q}_d + \lambda_1 e + \lambda_2 \int_0^t e\, dt\right)\right| + \left|\tilde{G}\right|. \quad (34)$$

To control the system states $(e, \dot{e})$ and to reach the sliding surface $s = 0$ in a limited time by staying on the surface, the control law should be formulated so that Condition (35) is fulfilled:

$$\frac{1}{2}\frac{d}{dt}\left[s^T H s\right] < \eta\left(s^T s\right)^{\frac{1}{2}},\ \eta > 0. \quad (35)$$

Using the sign function in the control law, high oscillations in the control torque are found as the undesired phenomenon called chattering. To overcome this drawback, a saturation function was used (36) for the discontinuous part of the control law:

$$sat\left(\frac{s}{\varphi}\right) = \left\{ \begin{array}{cc} 1 & s \geq \varphi \\ \frac{s}{\varphi} & -\varphi < s < \varphi \\ -1 & s \leq -\varphi \end{array} \right\}. \tag{36}$$

As a result, a layer ϕ around the sliding surface was obtained so that, when the robot foot trajectory was inside the layer, it remained there. The values of λ_1, λ_2, K, and K_v were adjusted to better position the mobile walking robot foot.

6. Hybrid Control Simulation

The simulation was built with the help of MATLAB Simulink software to test the proposed methods and control laws. Figure 10 presents the diagram of the main components of the hybrid controller. The reference generation block for the OXYZ axis in the Cartesian space is shown in Figure 11, and the constant generation block defining the walking robot is presented in Figure 12. All the values were sent to a reference system on the robot structure, illustrated in Figure 1b. The foot's vertical position was at a distance of 1.1 m from the origin set on the robot platform, not the foot.

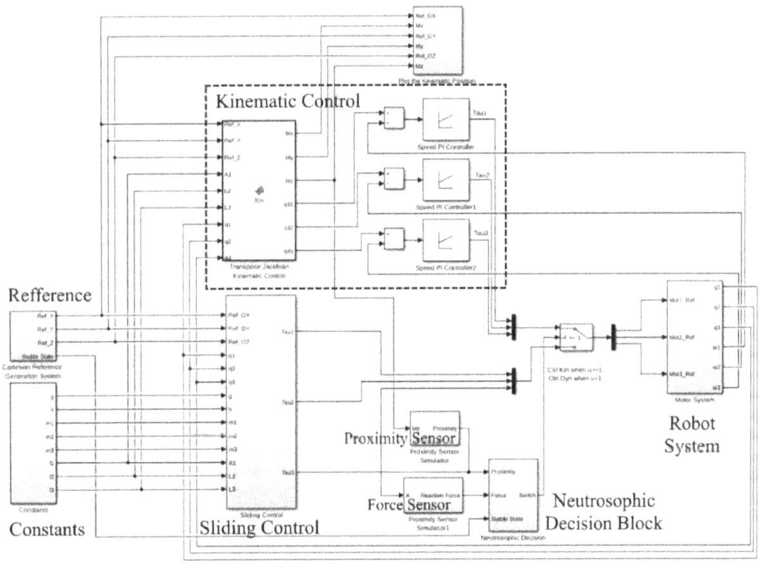

Figure 10. MATLAB Simulink diagram for the hybrid control.

The three lines in Figure 11 represent the reference system as follows: the top signal (green line) is the reference for the robot foot on the OZ axis, the trapezoidal signal (blue line) is the reference for the robot foot on the OX axis, and for the OY axis, a zero-value signal was used (purple line). These three datasets represent the Cartesian position of the robot foot for a complete cycle of a leg's walking step. The reference on the OY axis is the heading direction of the robot and has a trapezoidal shape because the foot is moving relative to the robot platform.

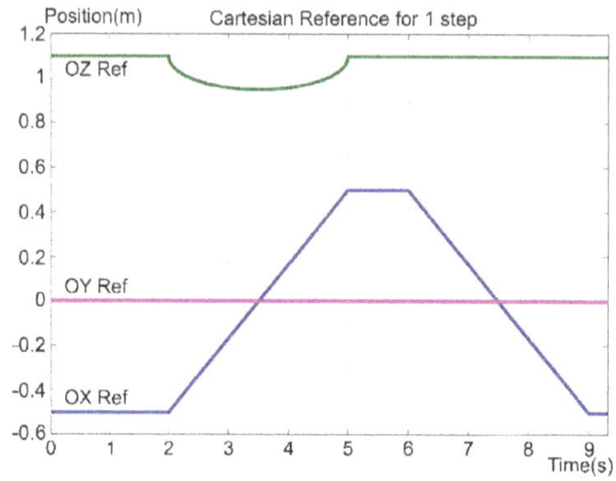

Figure 11. Foot reference signals.

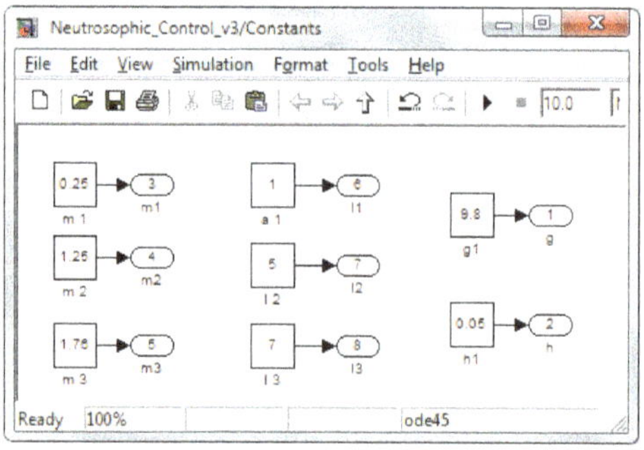

Figure 12. Constant values.

Figure 13 shows the diagram corresponding to the sliding control method made in MATLAB Simulink in which all the described elements are found. With their help, the command signal for the three joint motors was calculated.

Algorithm 1 controlled the kinematic control block. It computed the angular speeds using the Jacobian matrix and the formula from Equation (8), which provided the angular reference speed.

Figures 14 and 15 present the simulation diagrams for the two sensors used in determining which control law should be used at a particular moment in time according to the switching algorithm based on neutrosophic logic.

Using what was presented in Section 4 regarding the neutrosophic decision, the neutrosophic control switching block was implemented. It is illustrated in Figure 16 with its inputs and outputs. The two inputs already described are shown, bringing proximity and force information into the switching mechanism. In addition to these two, there was a third input called stable-state, and it provided the block with additional information. When the robot was homing or reached specific points, it was controlled only by the kinematic control law. The solution was chosen to save computing power and provide a higher speed for arriving at the initial position (homing phase).

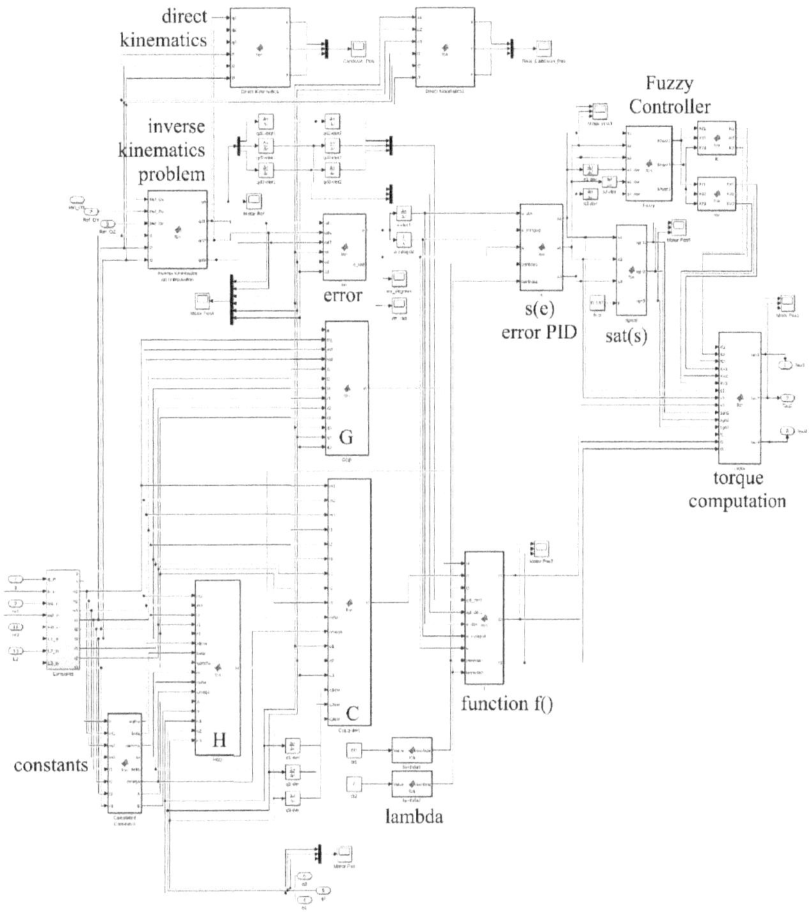

Figure 13. The sliding control diagram made in MATLAB Simulink.

Algorithm 1 The kinematic control block

```
function [Mx, My, Mz, qd]= fcn(Ref_X, Ref_Y, Ref_Z, A1, L2, L3, q1, q2, q3)
fi1 = q1; fi2 = q2; fi3 = q3;
J11 = −sind(fi1) × (L2 × sind(fi2)+L3 × sind(fi2 + fi3));
J12 = L2 × cosd(fi1) × cosd(fi2)+L3 × cosd(fi1) × cosd(fi2 + fi3);
J13 = L3 × cosd(fi1) × cosd(fi2 + fi3);
J21 = cosd(fi1) × (L2 × sind(fi2)+L3 × sind(fi2 + fi3));
J22 = L2 × sind(fi1) × cosd(fi2)+L3 × sind(fi1) × cosd(fi2 + fi3);
J23 = L3 × sind(fi1) × cosd(fi2 + fi3);
J31 = 0;
J32 = −L2 × sind(fi2) −L3 × sind(fi2 + fi3);
J33 = −L3 × sind(fi2 + fi3);
Jb =[J11 J12 J13; J21 J22 J23; J31 J32 J33];
Mx = cosd(fi1) × (L2 × sind(fi2)+L3 × sind(fi2 + fi3));
My = sind(fi1) × (L2 × sind(fi2)+L3 × sind(fi2 + fi3));
Mz = L2 × cosd(fi2)+L3 × cosd(fi2 + fi3)+A1;
M_err =[Ref_X − Mx; Ref_Y − My; Ref_Z − Mz];
JJTde = Jb × Jb'xM_err;
qd = alpha × Jb' × M_err;
```

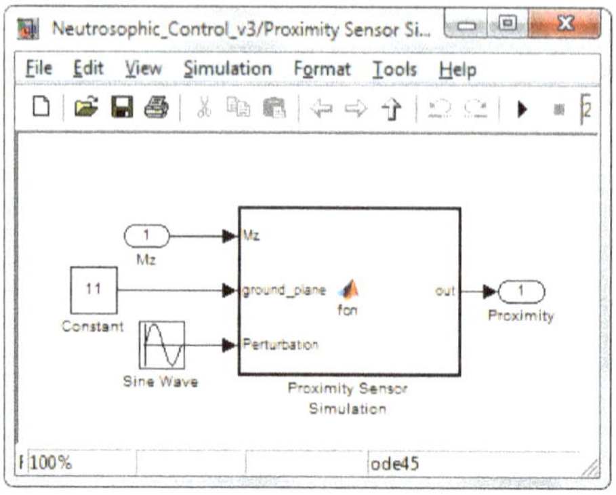

Figure 14. Proximity sensor simulation.

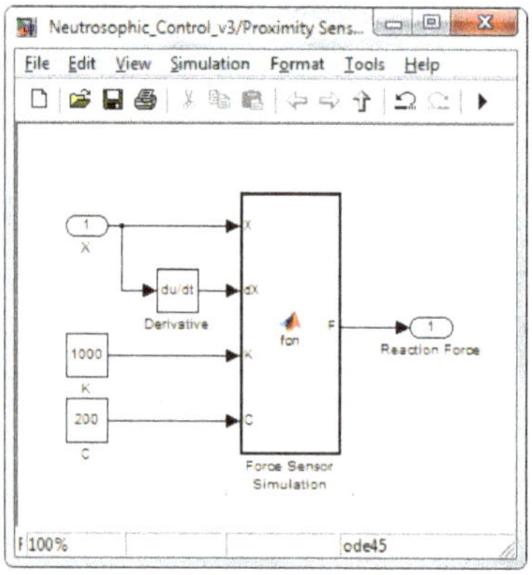

Figure 15. Force sensor simulation.

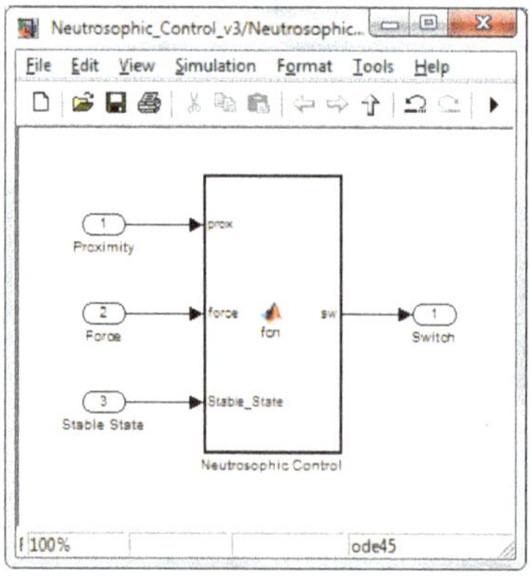

Figure 16. Neutrosophic switching diagram.

The actual neutrosophic switching block followed the detailed conditions already described.

7. Experimental Results

Following the simulation results, we observed several things. One of them was that, to successfully simulate the control law, which was bounded by the interaction between the support surface and the robot, different conditions were needed by the decision and control methods. This case was observed during the support phase, for which the robot leg must hold the entire robot weight and carry out the forward robot motion. The force and proximity sensors must have values that assumed the support surface contact in actual case conditions. In contrast, in simulation conditions, if the positioning control error placed the robot foot slightly above the support surface, then the sensors could affect the control laws and the entire system. Consequently, the switching mechanism was built with the condition that switched the control law when there was permanent contact with the support surface. An example is the homing motion of the foot, for which the robot was controlled only through the kinematic control method.

Figure 17 presents the reference and position tracking for the robot foot in the operational space in Cartesian coordinates on the OX axis. The positioning error on the OX axis is shown in Figure 18. The movement represents the forward direction of motion for the robot and its legs. Thus, three steps are presented, for which the trapezoidal shape of the signal represents the forward and retreat motion relative to the robot platform. The movement was computed according to the reference system relative to the robot platform. Because the reference was considered in the robot's operational space, the first coordinate system was selected at the point where the first joint of the robot was placed.

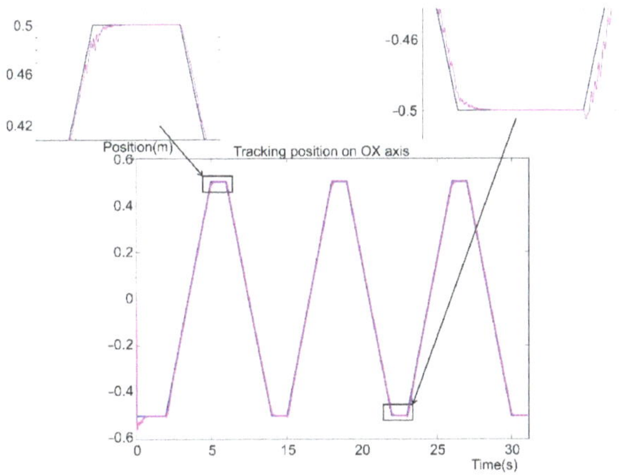

Figure 17. Foot reference and position tracking on the OX axis.

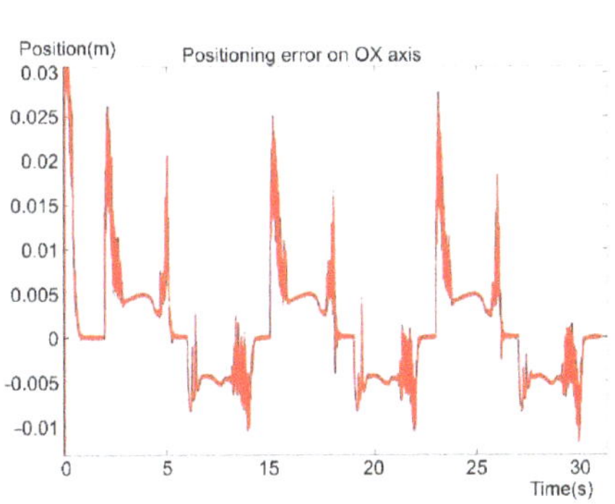

Figure 18. Foot positioning error on the OX axis.

On average, the error on the OX axis was below 1 cm, but there were some spikes in the error signal. The high amplitude errors were due to the sudden change in the reference speed, which was used in controlling the angular velocity through the torque of the joint's motor. The high amplitude errors were found at the points where the reference changed its path slope and control type. The error had a more continuous shape when the kinematic control was in place, and in the case of the dynamic control, the error tended to oscillate.

Figure 19 presents the robot foot's reference, positioning, and error signals on the OY axis. The reference value was zero, and the positioning error was less than 1 mm. On the other two axes, spikes were found in the error signal at the moment when the control law changed.

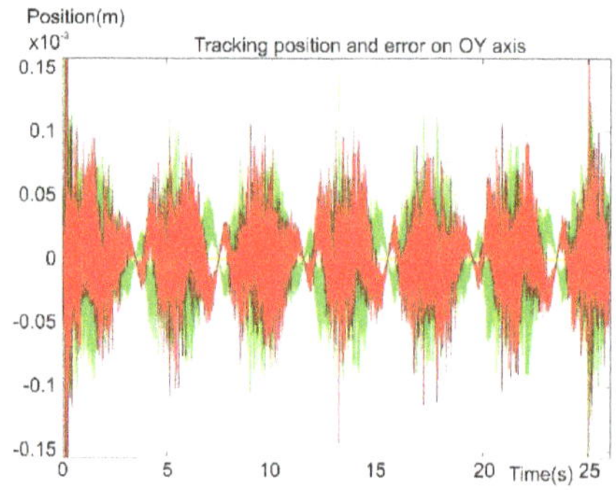

Figure 19. Foot tracking position on the OY axis.

Figure 20 presents the diagram for the reference and positioning signals of the robot foot on the OZ axis, which corresponds to the perpendicular axis on the support surface, meaning the vertical motion. The diagram presents the foot position during the leg's swing phase. The leg was positioned on the vertical axis so it would not hit an obstacle or the support surface. Also, the vertical trajectory of the foot was in the support phase, for which the reference was zero. The foot followed a continuous and uniform reference value during the swing phase. In the support and moving-forward phase, a positioning error was observed. The error may have been due to the platform weight compensating at the moment the robot foot crossed the point of intersection with the platform center of the vertical gravity axis. The positioning error became zero on the OZ axis.

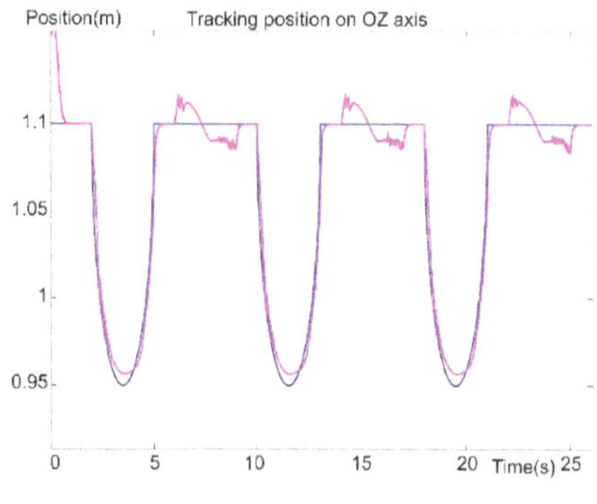

Figure 20. Foot reference and position tracking on the OZ axis.

Figures 17–21 present, in the same time frame, the motion of the robot leg stepping three times to move the robot forward. The diagrams show all motion stages for the robot foot to complete a step. They present reference and tracking signals. The homing occurred in the first second of the simulation, and a high error was observed. In the time interval of [2–5 s], the leg moved on the vertical axis and forward, controlled by the kinematic control law to reach a new position for the foot. In the next second of the virtual experiment at [5–6 s], the control method reached the vertical reference position to allow the robot leg to support the robot's weight. Between 6 and 9 s, the leg moved backward in relation to the robot platform and was controlled by the dynamic SMC method. A different error pattern is observed in Figures 18 and 21, considering that the robot leg supported the weight at this stage. After this stage was completed, the next step continued in the same manner, excluding the homing sequence.

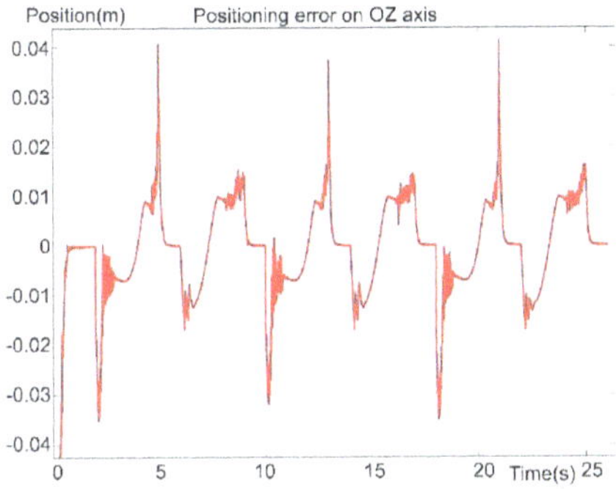

Figure 21. Foot positioning error on the OZ axis.

In Figure 21, a maximum error of 4 cm was found at the amplitude peaks and an average value of 1 cm. The high amplitude values appeared as described above when the control laws were switched, which is the subject of future work to stabilize the system at the switch. The error peaks were also due to the sudden shape-change of the reference signal. By changing from a curve signal to a straight line, the derivative part of the controller received an extremely high value, which in turn affected the control signal. The influence should be attenuated or removed entirely in future work.

8. Conclusions

To summarize and conclude the results, Figure 22 presents the robot foot trace in a 3D space with the reference pattern. All three steps overlap in the same diagram. The coordinates are given in the Cartesian space. The first stage that was easily found was the homing curve, seen in the lower section of the image. The maximum error was found at the start or end of a step, where the reference system must be improved to avoid sharp changes of direction. For the simulation, a fixed Cartesian coordinates system was considered, with the origin placed in the first joint where the robot top platform joined with to the robot leg. The shape of the horizontal motion was not uniform. The trajectory had minor errors in the range of millimeters and hundreds of micrometers when the control method was not changed, and we considered the shape of the foot trajectory as close to the reference.

Overall, as presented, the dynamic controller was better at following a continuous reference than a simple positioning kinematic controller. Although the positioning was more precise when a dynamic-based controller was used, sudden changes were added in the reference value when changing from a linear trajectory to a half ellipse. Since these were the points where the decision algorithm should also switch the used control method, these points of interest became essential areas of disturbance in the system. We will dedicate our attention to mitigating the reference and switching effects in the reference-tracking algorithm in future work.

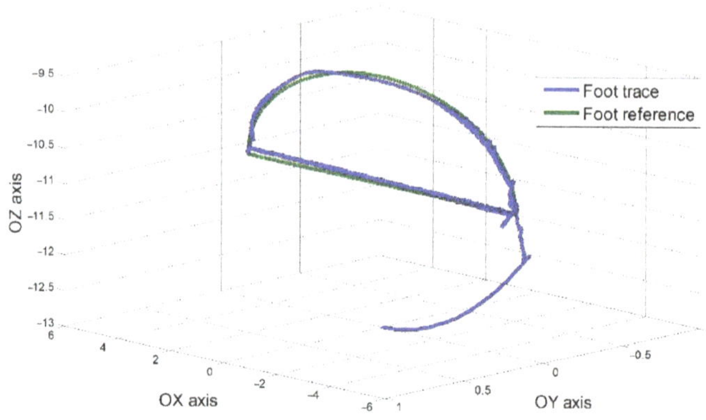

Figure 22. Foot trace in Cartesian coordinates.

The dynamic controller tended to be slower than the kinematic controller in compensating for the disturbance, but it did not override the PI kinematic controller. Moreover, the PI kinematic controller oscillated around the reference value when the robot leg was subjected to exterior forces. The gravitational acceleration acted upon the entire leg when high gains were used inside the control loops to lower the reference tracking time. It resulted in a high tracking error on the vertical axis during the kinematic control. The reference tracking time was considered the time difference between the change to the kinematic control method and until the foot reached the target point, with an error small enough to consider that the position was reached. The target position was chosen near the support surface but far enough for the leg to lower its speed before hitting the surface.

A PI kinematic-based controller was used during the swing motion of the robot leg because high precision was not required to move the robot foot. Instead, a constant foot speed was needed to reach the point of contact with the support surface in a short time. In addition, along with the positioning precision, the controller did not need to compensate for the gravity and inertial forces during the leg and robot motion and could have severe and undesired consequences in the support phase. Therefore, we concluded that a dynamic-based controller was required to compensate for all the inertial forces and to better track the reference.

Finally, the proposed hybrid control efficiently used the two control methods for the mobile walking robot leg. The biggest problem was found during the transition between the two control techniques.

The main conclusion of the paper was on the decision algorithm side. By having a two-stage decision, the information that could be analyzed offline between simulations defined the outline of the critical decision in each case or phase of the robot. The final algorithm distinguished between robot motion phases and rejected contradictory conditions at the online stage.

The consequence of the presented hybrid force/position control with a two-stage decision algorithm was that it can successfully be used and further developed for other types of robots or tasks.

Our future work will focus on studies for removing the high peaks of positioning error. At the same time, new, improved simulations are required to visualize the leg motion cycle.

Author Contributions: Conceptualization, I.-A.G. and L.V.; simulation, I.-A.G.; validation, I.-A.G., L.V. and A.-C.C.; investigation, I.-A.G. and L.V.; resources, I.-A.G. and A.-C.C.; writing—original draft preparation, I.-A.G.; writing—review and editing, I.-A.G., L.V. and A.-C.C.; supervision, L.V. All authors have read and agreed to the published version of the manuscript.

Funding: This research received no external funding.

Institutional Review Board Statement: Not applicable.

Informed Consent Statement: Not applicable.

Data Availability Statement: Not applicable.

Acknowledgments: This work was supported by the Institute of Solid Mechanics of the Romanian Academy and by an interacademic project of IMSAR–Yanshan University: "Joint Laboratory of Intelligent Rehabilitation Robot" (KY201501009), a collaborative research agreement between Yanshan University, China, and the Romanian Academy by IMSAR, RO.

Conflicts of Interest: The funders had no role in the design of the study; in the collection, analyses, or interpretation of data; in the writing of the manuscript; or in the decision to publish the results.

Glossary

θ_i	robot leg join rotation
θ_{ref}	robot joint angular position reference
θ_{real}	robot joint angular position measured by angular sensors
$\Delta\theta_i$	leg joint positioning error
ω_i	joint angular speed
$\Delta\omega_I$	joint angular speed error
r_i	distance from the previous joint axis to the *i*th leg segment center of mass
l_i	length of the *i*th leg segment
m_i	mass of the *i*th leg segment
P_{ref}	position reference of the robot foot
P_{real}	real position of the robot foot
J	Jacobian matrix
J_{ij}	Jacobian matrix element with coordinates *i* (row) and *j* (column)
F_{sim}	simulated ground reaction force
F_{real}	real force given by force sensors placed on robot foot
F_{ground}	ground reaction force
d	distance from robot foot to the ground given by proximity sensors
s_i	$sin(\theta_i)$
c_i	$cos(\theta_i)$
s_{ij}	$sin(\theta_i + \theta_j)$
c_{ij}	$cos(\theta_i + \theta_j)$
τ_P	joint torque computed by position control
τ_F	joint torque computed by force control
τ	joint torque selected by the decision algorithm
q_i	leg joint used by the dynamic control method
s	sliding surface error in terms of SMC
SMC	sliding motion control
O_m	extension theory object
c_m	extension theory characteristic
v_m	extension theory measure
m (C)	the neutrosophic generalized basic belief assignment
D^θ	a hyperpower set
θ_C	neutrosophic kinematic state
θ_D	neutrosophic dynamic state
$\theta_D \cup \theta_C$	neutrosophic uncertain state
$\theta_D \cap \theta_C$	neutrosophic contradiction state

References

1. Gao, Z.; Wanyama, T.; Singh, I.; Gadhrri, A.; Schmidt, R. From Industry 4.0 to Robotics 4.0-a Conceptual Framework for Collaborative and Intelligent Robotic Systems. *Procedia Manuf.* **2020**, *46*, 591–599. [CrossRef]
2. Bragança, S.; Costa, E.; Castellucci, I.; Arezes, P.M. A Brief Overview of the Use of Collaborative Robots in Industry 4.0: Human Role and Safety. In *Occupational and Environmental Safety and Health*; Springer: Cham, Switzerland, 2019; Volume 202, pp. 641–650. [CrossRef]
3. Yao, X.-Y.; Ding, H.-F.; Ge, M.-F. Task-space tracking control of multi-robot systems with disturbances and uncertainties rejection capability. *Nonlinear Dyn.* **2018**, *92*, 1649–1664. [CrossRef]
4. Craig, J.J.; Raibert, M.H. A Systematic Method of Hybrid Position/Force Control of a Manipulator. In Proceedings of the COMPSAC 79, Computer Software and the IEEE Computer Society's Third International Applications Conference, Chicago, IL, USA, 6–8 November 1979; IEEE: Piscataway, NJ, USA, 1979; pp. 446–451.
5. Wu, J.; Zhang, B.; Wang, L.; Yu, G. An iterative learning method for realizing accurate dynamic feedforward control of an industrial hybrid robot. *Sci. China Technol. Sci.* **2021**, *64*, 1177–1188. [CrossRef]
6. Liu, H.; Yan, Z.; Xiao, J. Pose error prediction and real-time compensation of a 5-DOF hybrid robot. *Mech. Mach. Theory* **2022**, *170*, 104737. [CrossRef]
7. Huynh, B.-P.; Wu, C.-W.; Kuo, Y.-L. Force/Position Hybrid Control for a Hexa Robot Using Gradient Descent Iterative Learning Control Algorithm. *IEEE Access* **2019**, *7*, 72329–72342. [CrossRef]
8. Sun, W.; Wu, Y.; Wang, L. Trajectory tracking of constrained robotic systems via a hybrid control strategy. *Neurocomputing* **2018**, *330*, 188–195. [CrossRef]
9. Le Flohic, J.; Paccot, F.; Bouton, N.; Chanal, H. Application of Hybrid Force/Position Control on Parallel Machine for Mechanical Test. *Mechatronics* **2018**, *49*, 168–176. [CrossRef]
10. Islam, M.R.; Assad-Uz-Zaman, M.; Al Zubayer Swapnil, A.; Ahmed, T.; Rahman, M.H. An Ergonomic Shoulder for Ro-bot-Aided Rehabilitation with Hybrid Control. *Microsyst. Technol.* **2021**, *27*, 159–172. [CrossRef]
11. Shafiei, S.E. *Sliding Mode Control of Robot Manipulators via Intelligent Approaches*; INTECH Open Access Publisher: London, UK, 2010; ISBN 953-307-099-4.
12. Yang, X.; Liu, H.; Xiao, J.; Zhu, W.; Liu, Q.; Gong, G.; Huang, T. Continuous Friction Feedforward Sliding Mode Controller for a TriMule Hybrid Robot. *IEEE/ASME Trans. Mechatron.* **2018**, *23*, 1673–1683. [CrossRef]
13. Xie, Y.; Zhang, X.; Meng, W.; Zheng, S.; Jiang, L.; Meng, J.; Wang, S. Coupled fractional-order sliding mode control and obstacle avoidance of a four-wheeled steerable mobile robot. *ISA Trans.* **2020**, *108*, 282–294. [CrossRef]
14. Zaare, S.; Soltanpour, M.R. Adaptive fuzzy global coupled nonsingular fast terminal sliding mode control of n-rigid-link elastic-joint robot manipulators in presence of uncertainties. *Mech. Syst. Signal. Process.* **2021**, *163*, 108165. [CrossRef]
15. Jmel, I.; Dimassi, H.; Hadj-Said, S.; M'Sahli, F. Adaptive Observer-Based Sliding Mode Control for a Two-Wheeled Self-Balancing Robot under Terrain Inclination and Disturbances. *Math. Probl. Eng.* **2021**, *2021*, 8853441. [CrossRef]
16. Feng, X.; Wang, C. Robust Adaptive Terminal Sliding Mode Control of an Omnidirectional Mobile Robot for Aircraft Skin Inspection. *Int. J. Control. Autom. Syst.* **2020**, *19*, 1078–1088. [CrossRef]
17. Cheng, X.; Liu, H.; Lu, W. Chattering-Suppressed Sliding Mode Control for Flexible-Joint Robot Manipulators. In Proceedings of the Actuators, Orlando, FL, USA, 20–24 June 2021; Multidisciplinary Digital Publishing Institute: Basel, Switzerland, 2021; Volume 10, p. 288.
18. Ren, S.; Gui, F.; Zhao, Y.; Zhan, M.; Wang, W.; Zhou, J. An Extenics-Based Scheduled Configuration Methodology for Low-Carbon Product Design in Consideration of Contradictory Problem Solving. *Sustainability* **2021**, *13*, 5859. [CrossRef]
19. Cai, W.; Yang, C.Y.; He, B. *Preliminary Extension Logic*; Automation Institute on Chinese Academy: Beijing, China, 2003.
20. Wu, S. Research on Toy Design for Special Children Based on Sensory Integration Training, D-S Theory, and Extenics: Taking Physical Toys for ADHD Children as an Example. *Sci. Program.* **2022**, *2022*, 1395265. [CrossRef]
21. Melinte, D.O.; Travediu, A.-M.; Dumitriu, D.N. Deep Convolutional Neural Networks Object Detector for Real-Time Waste Identification. *Appl. Sci.* **2020**, *10*, 7301. [CrossRef]
22. Melinte, D.O.; Vladareanu, L. Facial Expressions Recognition for Human–Robot Interaction Using Deep Convolutional Neural Networks with Rectified Adam Optimizer. *Sensors* **2020**, *20*, 2393. [CrossRef]
23. Yan, H.; Wang, H.; Vladareanu, L.; Lin, M.; Vladareanu, V.; Li, Y. Detection of Participation and Training Task Difficulty Applied to the Multi-Sensor Systems of Rehabilitation Robots. *Sensors* **2019**, *19*, 4681. [CrossRef]
24. Smarandache, F. A unifying field in logics: Neutrosophic logic. In *Neutrosophy, Neutrosophic Probability, Set, and Logic*; American Research Press: Rehoboth, MA, USA, 2002.
25. Smarandache, F.; Dezert, J. *An Introduction to DSmT*; Smarandache, F., Dezert, J., Eds.; American Research Press: Rehoboth, MA, USA, 2009.
26. Smarandache, F.; Vlădăreanu, L. Applications of Neutrosophic Logic to Robotics: An Introduction. In Proceedings of the 2011 IEEE International Conference on Granular Computing, Kaohsiung, Taiwan, 8–10 November 2011; IEEE: Piscataway, NJ, USA, 2011; pp. 607–612.
27. Saqlain, M.; Saeed, M. Fuzzy Logic Controller for Aviation Parking with 5G Communication Technology. In *Intelligent and Fuzzy Techniques in Aviation 4.0*; Springer: Berlin/Heidelberg, Germany, 2022; pp. 41–62.

28. Li, H.; Xie, X.; Du, P.; Xi, J. Cooperative Object Recognition Method of Multi-UAVs Based on Decision Fusion. In Proceedings of the 2021 33rd Chinese Control and Decision Conference (CCDC), Kunming, China, 22–24 May 2021; IEEE: Piscataway, NJ, USA, 2021; pp. 5424–5429.
29. Chai, H.; Lv, S.; Fang, M. Obstacle Avoidance by DSmT for Mobile Robot in Unknown Environment. In Proceedings of the 2019 4th International Conference on Automation, Control and Robotics Engineering, Shenzhen, China, 19–21 July 2019; pp. 1–6.
30. Yuan, S.; Guo, P.; Han, X.; Luan, F.; Zhang, F.; Liu, T.; Mao, H. DSmT-Based Ultrasonic Detection Model for Estimating Indoor Environment Contour. *IEEE Trans. Instrum. Meas.* **2019**, *69*, 4002–4014. [CrossRef]
31. Liu, J.; Wei, L.; Cao, J.; Fei, S. Hybrid-Driven H∞ Filter Design for T–S Fuzzy Systems with Quantization. *Nonlinear Anal. Hy-brid Syst.* **2019**, *31*, 135–152. [CrossRef]
32. Aslam, M.S.; Qaisar, I.; Saleem, M.A. Quantized Event-triggered feedback control under fuzzy system with time-varying delay and Actuator fault. *Nonlinear Anal. Hybrid. Syst.* **2019**, *35*, 100823. [CrossRef]
33. Bledt, G.; Powell, M.J.; Katz, B.; Di Carlo, J.; Wensing, P.M.; Kim, S. MIT Cheetah 3: Design and Control of a Robust, Dynamic Quadruped Robot. In Proceedings of the 2018 IEEE/RSJ International Conference on Intelligent Robots and Systems (IROS), Madrid, Spain, 1–5 October 2018; pp. 2245–2252.
34. Zhang, J.; Jin, L.; Yang, C. Distributed Cooperative Kinematic Control of Multiple Robotic Manipulators with an Improved Communication Efficiency. *IEEE/ASME Trans. Mechatron.* **2021**, *27*, 149–158. [CrossRef]
35. Zhang, B.; Wu, J.; Wang, L.; Yu, Z. Accurate dynamic modeling and control parameters design of an industrial hybrid spray-painting robot. *Robot. Comput. Manuf.* **2019**, *63*, 101923. [CrossRef]
36. Ion, I.; Vladareanu, L.; Simionescu, I.; Vasile, A. The Gait Analysis for Modular Walking Robot MERO Walks on the Slope. *Nature* **2008**, *6*, 8.
37. Vladareanu, V.; Schiopu, P.; Deng, M.; Yu, H. Intelligent extended control of the walking robot motion. In Proceedings of the 2014 International Conference on Advanced Mechatronic Systems, Kumamoto, Japan, 10–12 August 2014; pp. 489–495. [CrossRef]
38. Vladareanu, L.; Vladareanu, V.; Yu, H.; Mitroi, D.; Ciocîrlan, A.-C. Intelligent Control Interfaces Using Extenics Multidimen-sional Theory Applied on VIPRO Platforms for Developing the IT INDUSTRY 4.0 Concept. *IFAC-Pap.* **2019**, *52*, 922–927.
39. Wen, C.; Chun-Yan, Y.; Bin, H. New Development of the Basic Theory of Extenics. *Eng. Sci.* **2003**, *5*, 80–87.
40. Cai, W.; Yang, C.; Smarandache, F.; Vladareanu, L.; Li, Q.; Zou, G.; Zhao, Y.; Li, X. *Extenics and Innovation Methods*; CRC Press Leiden: Boca Raton, FL, USA, 2013; ISBN 1-306-50052-4.
41. Smarandache, F. Foundations of Neutrosophic Logic and Set and Their Applications to Information Fusion, Tutorial. In Proceedings of the 17th International Conference on Information Fusion, Salamanca, Spain, 7 July 2014.
42. Peng, J.-J.; Wang, J.-Q.; Wang, J.; Zhang, H.-Y.; Chen, X.-H. Simplified neutrosophic sets and their applications in multi-criteria group decision-making problems. *Int. J. Syst. Sci.* **2014**, *47*, 2342–2358. [CrossRef]
43. Broumi, S.; Bakali, A.; Bahnasse, A. Neutrosophic Sets: An Overview. 2018, pp. 403–434. Available online: https://books.google.co.kr/books?hl=zh-TW&lr=&id=pftuDwAAQBAJ&oi=fnd&pg=PA408&dq=Neutrosophic+Sets:+An+Overview&ots=Ietca2c5tz&sig=mMXdkKa8sePH9cQ8GRleW5XcM-E&redir_esc=y#v=onepage&q=Neutrosophic%20Sets%3A%20An%20Overview&f=false (accessed on 17 March 2022).
44. Buss, S.R. Introduction to Inverse Kinematics with Jacobian Transpose, Pseudoinverse and Damped Least Squares Methods. *IEEE J. Robot. Autom.* **2004**, *17*, 16.
45. Gal, A.; Vladareanu, L.; Munteanu, M.S.; Melinte, O. PID Sliding Motion Control by Using Fuzzy Adjustment. In Proceedings of the SISOM 2012 and Session of the Commission of Acoustics, Bucharest, Romania, 30–31 May 2012.

sensors

MDPI

Article

Control Design for Uncertain Higher-Order Networked Nonlinear Systems via an Arbitrary Order Finite-Time Sliding Mode Control Law

Maryam Munir [1], Qudrat Khan [2], Safeer Ullah [3], Tayyaba Maryam Syeda [3] and Abdullah A. Algethami [4,*]

1 Department of Electrical Engineering, HITEC University, Taxila 47080, Pakistan; maryam_munir96@yahoo.com
2 Centre for Advanced Studies in Telecommunications (CAST), COMSATS University, Islamabad 45550, Pakistan; qudratullahqau@gmail.com
3 Department of Electrical and Computer Engineering, COMSATS University, Islamabad 45550, Pakistan; safeer_iiui@yahoo.com (S.U.); s.tayyaba38@gmail.com (T.M.S.)
4 Department of Mechanical Engineering, College of Engineering, Taif University, Taif 11099, Saudi Arabia
* Correspondence: a_algethami@tu.edu.sa; Tel.: +966-50-635-4615

Abstract: The authors proposed an arbitrary order finite-time sliding mode control (SMC) design for a networked of uncertain higher-order nonlinear systems. A network of $n + 1$ nodes, connected via a directed graph (with fixed topology), is considered. The nodes are considered to be uncertain in nature. A consensus error-based canonical form of the error dynamics is developed and a new arbitrary order distributed control protocol design strategy is proposed, which not only ensures the sliding mode enforcement in finite time but also confirms the finite time error dynamics stability. Rigorous stability analysis, in closed-loop, is presented, and a simulation example is given, which demonstrates the results developed in this work.

Keywords: arbitrary order sliding mode; networked system; finite-time systems; nonlinear system

Citation: Munir, M.; Khan, Q.; Ullah, S.; Syeda, T.M.; Algethami, A.A. Control Design for Uncertain Higher-Order Networked Nonlinear Systems via an Arbitrary Order Finite-Time Sliding Mode Control Law. *Sensors* **2022**, *22*, 2748. https://doi.org/10.3390/s22072748

Academic Editors: Luige Vladareanu, Hongnian Yu, Hongbo Wang and Yongfei Feng

Received: 6 January 2022
Accepted: 29 March 2022
Published: 2 April 2022

Publisher's Note: MDPI stays neutral with regard to jurisdictional claims in published maps and institutional affiliations.

1. Introduction

In consensus, locally communicating agents reach an agreement which is mostly met via distributed control strategies [1]. These agreements (consensus) finds very impressive applications in formation control [2–4], sensor networks [5], smart grid applications [6], and rendezvous control of non-holonomic agents [7,8]. In the context of consensus, cooperative control has been one of the main areas of research, which is subdivided into two main classes called the leaderless control (for instance; [9]), and the leader–follower control [10,11]. In the leader–follower systems, a distributed control strategy is generally designed for the followers to follow the leader, which shares information through a properly defined network topology. Thus far, the leader–follower problems and their solutions via various methodologies, for electro-mechanical (or second-order) systems, is extensively addressed in the existing literature (see, for example; [12–19]). Das and Lewis [14,15] developed distributed laws of adaptive nature for the cooperative tracking of single and double integrator systems in uncertain scenarios. Nonetheless, the requirement of knowing the Laplacian matrix's non-zero eigenvalue limits its applicability. Cooperative control of higher-order uncertain networked systems was an expansion of [14,15] in Brunovsky form.

The authors, in [11], presented a second-order sliding mode control (SOSMC) technique for the consensus of a network of higher-order nonlinear systems. Their presented results were excellent. However, a distributed law was developed to compensate the bounded uncertainties caused by inputs and states, which raises theoretical concerns. Furthermore, asymptotic convergence does not ensure consensus accuracy. In [20], second-order linear networked systems were designed to compensate matched and mismatched uncertain disturbances. The researchers, in [13], studied a second-order linear network system under an unknown disturbance. Furthermore, second-order SMC based distributed laws were proposed for uncertain second-order linear networked systems in [21] that resulted in finite time error stabilisation. Their presented results were satisfactory; nevertheless, they were confined to linear systems with matching uncertainty. Furthermore, this algorithm demonstrated sensitivity to perturbations during the reaching phase.

An integral SMC law with an extended observer and neural networks was developed to estimate and compensate the uncertain disturbance of matched type, respectively. A distributed control approach based on integral sliding modes (ISM) and subject to fixed topology and the directed graph was devised for uncertain nonlinear networked systems under matched uncertainties [22]. This technique alleviates the reaching phase, resulting in increased robustness. It was, nonetheless, confined to electromechanical systems. In terms of applications, Ref. [23] proposed adaptive formation control algorithms for a class of non-holonomic mobile robots. These approaches mainly focused on the stability of a network of linear and nonlinear second-order agents even in bounded uncertainties. However, their performance can be affected due to the existence of all system dynamics in the sliding manifold.

To maintain the convergence of finite-time consensus mismatches at zero, a distributed control system based on a terminal sliding mode control (TSMC) technique was devised. However, the existence of the singularity in the surface may reduce its significance [24,25]. In [12], an uncertain network of first-order Multi Input Multi-Output (MIMO) systems was focused where neural networks (NNs) were utilized for the uncertain dynamic estimation. In order to alleviate the approximation error, a robustness signal was also used. Nevertheless, it was ultimately bounded. The control researcher, in [26], investigated uncertain MIMO second-order networked systems with a fixed topology and undirected graph and developed a distributed TSMC, based on Chebyshev Neural Networks (CNNs), to compensate the external disturbances and uncertain dynamics. An approach based on NNs was designed to estimate the uncertain input channels and drift terms and compensate the uncertainties. Nevertheless, this strategy was influential in the asymptotic stability of tracking error dynamics to the limited neighborhood of the origin. Ref. [27] investigated networked MIMO higher-order systems for synchronization applications. While applying NNs, these MIMO agents were controlled through the unknown non-singular control gains. The limits of the error dynamics may not have been easily decreased by modifying the controller gains. The control gains must be properly selected to guarantee the asymptotic convergence. Ref. [28]'s methodology was enhanced in [29] by including a neuro-adaptive sliding mode strategy. However, this led to several limitations, such as the fact that the boundedness of the approximated NNs' weights cannot always be ensured using the proposed tuning laws. Additionally, ensuring the boundedness of the control input is quite challenging.

At this stage, it was realized to develop a terminal sliding mode like a strategy that must confirm finite time error dynamics convergence and show robustness to cross-coupling of the agents and matched disturbances from the very beginning. Therefore, this paper studies the cooperative tracking control of higher-order nonlinear systems subject to uncertainties like parametric variations and matched bounded disturbances. The distributed control laws are developed on novel sliding surfaces of the error dynamics. The designed sliding manifold, which involves some discontinuous terms of the errors, seems analogous to the proportional-integral type, which helps in the elimination of the critical reaching phase. Consequently, robustness is guaranteed from the very start. Having established sliding modes, the error dynamics seem analogous to terminal attractor like in [30] which exhibits finite convergence. Thus, all the error dynamics converge in finite time, which results in high precision. In addition, our proposed work solves the theoretical shortcoming of [11] and the uncertain terms are now depending on the states information of the agents. The rest of the paper is organised as follows: Section 2 is about the problem formulation and mathematical preliminaries. In Sections 3 and 4, the detailed controller design procedure and the stability analysis are discussed, respectively. The illustrative example is mentioned in Section 5. Finally, Section 6 concludes the article.

2. Problem Formulation

Definitions

In this study, a network of $n+1$ nodes is considered which share information via a directed graph (with fixed topology). These networked nodes include one leader and n followers. The followers are assumed under the action of uncertainties. The following state space equations represent the dynamical model of an ith follower:

$$\begin{aligned}\dot{x}_{ij} &= x_{ij+1} \\ \dot{x}_{in} &= f_i(x_i) + g_i(x_i)u_i + \Delta_i(x_i,t)\end{aligned} \tag{1}$$

where $i = 1,2,\ldots,n$, $j = 1,2,\ldots,n-1$, $x_i = [x_{i1}, x_{i2}, \ldots, x_{in}]^T \in \Re^n$ is the measurable state vector, $\Delta_i(x_i,t)$ is the uncertainty, u_i represents the control input which is to be applied to the system, and f_i and g_i are the system distribution and drift functions, respectively. For the sake of the detailed description, the following assumptions are made:

Assumption 1. *It is assumed that $g_i(x_i)$ $\forall$ $x_i \in \Re^n$ is non singular, which will guarantee the controllability of each network agent.*

Assumption 2. *The uncertainty $\Delta_i(x_i,t)$ is assumed to be norm bounded i.e.,*

$$||\Delta_i(x_i,t)|| \leq C_i \tag{2}$$

where $i = 1,2,\ldots,n$, $||.||$, and C_i represents Euclidean norm and a positive constant, respectively.

The leader is governed by the following state space model:

$$\begin{aligned}\dot{x}_{0r} &= x_{0r+1}, \\ \dot{x}_{0n} &= f_0(t,x_0)\end{aligned} \tag{3}$$

where $r = 1,2\ldots,n-1$, $x_0 = [x_{01}, x_{02}, \ldots, x_{0n}]^T \in \Re^n$ is state vector of the leader and $f_0(t,x_0)$ is the continuous bounded function, which derive the leader. Suppose that the origin is an equilibrium for $f_0(t,x_0)$ i.e., $f_0(t,0) = 0$ and the nonlinear function $f_0(t,x_0)$ (leader driving force) is considered to be bounded and smooth. The vector set $\mathcal{V} = \{\mathcal{V}_0, \mathcal{V}_1, \ldots, \mathcal{V}_n\}$ represents the relationship between the leader and the follower nodes while $\mathcal{G} = \{\mathcal{V}, \mathcal{E}\}$ is the related directed graph in which node i can transfer data with node j, but node j cannot send back the information to node i. On the other hand, in an undirected graph, both way communication takes place. The mathematical expression for the adjacency matrix is given as follows:

$$A_i = \begin{bmatrix} 0 & 0 & \ldots & 0 \\ a_{10} & a_{11} & \ldots & a_{1n} \\ a_{20} & a_{21} & \ldots & a_{2n} \\ \vdots & \ldots & \ddots & \vdots \\ a_{n0} & a_{n1} & \ldots & a_{nn} \end{bmatrix}$$

Subgraph $\bar{\mathcal{G}} = \{\bar{\mathcal{V}}, \bar{\mathcal{E}}\}$ can be obtained by dropping the first row and first column of the above adjacency matrix; thus, one has

$$\bar{A}_i = \begin{bmatrix} a_{11} & a_{12} & \dots & a_{1n} \\ a_{21} & a_{22} & \dots & a_{2n} \\ \dots & \dots & \ddots & \vdots \\ a_{n1} & a_{n2} & \dots & a_{nn} \end{bmatrix}$$

The Laplacian matrix for the followers topology is defined to be $\bar{L} = \bar{D} - \bar{A} \in \Re^{n\times n}$, where $D = diag[\bar{d}_1, \bar{d}_2, \dots, \bar{d}_n]$ with $\bar{d}_i = \sum_{j=1}^{n} a_{ij}$. In addition, note that $a_{ij} = 0$ if $(\mathcal{V}_j, \mathcal{V}_i) \notin \mathcal{E}$ and $a_{ij} = 0$ otherwise. The matrix $\bar{B} = diag[b_1, b_2, \dots, b_n]$ shows the connection between the followers and the leader with $b_i = 0$ if the follower is not connected to the leader and $b_i = 1$ in case of the connection to the leader. A is time-invariant throughout the paper. Since we are considering a directed graph, matrix A is not necessarily to be symmetric. In contrast, in the case of the undirected graph, the symmetry is necessary for A. $\bar{L} + \bar{B}$ must be non-singular for the distributed control of all the networked agents. Similarly, $\bar{D}$ remains non-singular.

The main objective of the current work is that the follower states must have consensus with the leader states (in other words, the followers must follow the leader). In order to complete the task, the consensus error between the leader and the ith follower must be forced to zero. Therefore, the consensus error is defined as follows:

$$e_{ik} = \sum_{j=1, j\neq i}^{n} a_{ij}(x_{ik} - x_{jk}) + b_i(x_{ik} - x_{0k}) \tag{4}$$

where $k = 1, 2, .., n$. Based on the consensus error Equation (4), the consensus error dynamics can be expressed as follows:

$$\begin{aligned} \dot{e}_{i1} &= e_{i2} \\ \dot{e}_{i2} &= e_{i3} \\ &\vdots \\ \dot{e}_{in} &= \left(\sum_{j=1, j\neq i}^{n} a_{ij} + b_i\right)\left(f_i(x) + g_i(x)u_i\right) - \sum_{j=1, j\neq i}^{n} a_{ij}\left(f_j(x) + g_j(x)u_j\right) \\ &\quad - b_i f_0(x,t) + h_i(x,t) \end{aligned} \tag{5}$$

with

$$h_i(x,t) = \left(\sum_{j=1, j\neq i}^{n} a_{ij} + b_i\right)\Delta_i(x,t) - \sum_{j=1, j\neq i}^{n} a_{ij}\Delta_j(x,t)$$

representing the uncertainty terms in lumped form. In this equation, it is clearly shown that the uncertainties depends only on the system states.

Remark 1. *The compact form of (5) can also be written in the following form:*

$$\begin{aligned} \dot{\Sigma}_1 &= \Sigma_2 \\ \dot{\Sigma}_2 &= \Sigma_3 \\ &\vdots \\ \dot{\Sigma}_n &= (\bar{L} + \bar{B})\left(f(x) + g(x)u + \Delta(x,t) - \bar{\mathbf{1}} f_0(t,x)\right) \end{aligned} \tag{6}$$

where

$$\Sigma_1 = [e_{11}, e_{21}, e_{31}, \dots, e_{n1}],$$

$$\Sigma_2 = [e_{12}, e_{22}, e_{32}, \dots, e_{n2}],$$

$$\vdots$$

$$\Sigma_n = [e_{1n}, e_{2n}, e_{3n}, \ldots, e_{nn}],$$

and $f(x) = [f_1(x_1), f_2(x_2), \ldots, f_n(x_n)]^T$, $g(x) = diag[g_1(x_1), g_2(x_2), \ldots, g_n(x_n)]$, $\bar{1} = [11 \ldots 1]^T$, $u = [u_1, u_2, \ldots, u_n]^T$ *and* $\Delta(t, x) = [\Delta_1(t, x_1), \Delta_2(t, x_2), \ldots, \Delta_n(t, x_n)]^T$.

Now, the problem at hand becomes an error regulation problem which will, in other words, provide a consensus among the leader and n followers. The task can be accomplished by a robust nonlinear sliding mode strategy which will nullify the effects of uncertain terms and will ensure finite time error dynamics convergence. In the following section, a novel finite-time sliding mode strategy is presented.

3. Control Problem Design

The main task here is to drive the error dynamics (5) states to the equilibrium in the presence of disturbances. To achieve this goal, a novel sliding surface based sliding mode control protocol is presented. The proposed sliding surface helps in the finite time convergence of the consensus error dynamics (5) to equilibrium and also establishes finite time sliding mode. The newly proposed sliding surface, for follower i, can be defined as follows:

$$s_i = (e_{in} + \sum_{j=1}^{n-1} a_{ij}e_{ij}) + \int_0^t \sum_{j=1}^{n} \Big(b_{ij}|e_{ij}|^{\alpha_{ij}} sign(e_{ij}) + c_{ij}|e_{ij}|^{\beta_{ij}} sign(e_{ij})\Big) d\tau \quad (7)$$

In expanded form, this surface can be defined as follows:

$$\begin{aligned} s_i &= e_{in} + a_{i1}e_{i1} + a_{i2}e_{i2} + \ldots + a_{i(n-1)}e_{i(n-1)} \\ &+ \int_0^t (b_{i1}|e_{i1}|^{\alpha_{i1}} sign(e_{i1}) + \ldots + b_{in}|e_{in}|^{\alpha_{in}} sign(e_{in}) \\ &+ c_{i1}|e_{i1}|^{\beta_{i1}} sign(e_{i1}) + \ldots + c_{in}|e_{in}|^{\beta_{in}} sign(e_{in})\Big) d\tau \end{aligned} \quad (8)$$

Remark 2. *In the above Equation (8), the terms α_i and β_i are chosen as follows [31]:*

$$\alpha_{i-1} = \frac{\alpha_i \alpha_{i+1}}{2\alpha_{i+1} - \alpha_i}, \beta_i = \frac{\beta_i \beta_{i+1}}{2\beta_{i+1} - \beta_i}$$

where $\alpha_{n+1} = 1$, $\alpha_n = \alpha$ *and* $\beta_{n+1} = 1$, $\beta_n = \beta$, α, $\beta \in \Re$. *In addition,* $\alpha_i \in (0, 1)$ *and* $\beta_i \in (1, 1+ \in)$ *where* $\in > 0$.

By taking the derivative of the above equation, one may obtain the following expression:

$$\begin{aligned} \dot{s_i} &= \dot{e}_{in} + a_{i1}\dot{e}_{i1} + a_{i2}\dot{e}_{i2} + \ldots + a_{i(n-1)}\dot{e}_{i(n-1)} \\ &+ (b_{i1}|e_{i1}|^{\alpha_{i1}} sign(e_{i1}) + \ldots + b_{in}|e_{in}|^{\alpha_{in}} sign(e_{in}) \\ &+ c_{i1}|e_{i1}|^{\beta_{i1}} sign(e_{i1}) + \ldots + c_{in}|e_{in}|^{\beta_{in}} sign(e_{in})\Big) \end{aligned} \quad (9)$$

Substituting the values from (5) in (9), it becomes as follows:

$$\begin{aligned}\dot{s}_i = &(\sum_{j=1,j\neq i}^{n} a_{ij} + b_i)(f_i(x) + g_i(x)u_i)\\ &- \sum_{j=1,j\neq i}^{n} a_{ij}(f_j(x) + g_j(x)u_j) - b_i f_0(x,t) + h_i(x,t)\\ &+ a_{i1}e_{i2} + a_{i2}e_{i3} + \ldots + a_{i(n-1)}e_{in}\\ &+ b_{i1}|e_{i1}|^{\alpha_{i1}} sign(e_{i1}) + \ldots + b_{in}|e_{in}|^{\alpha_{in}} sign(e_{in})\\ &+ c_{i1}|e_{i1}|^{\beta_{i1}} sign(e_{i1}) + \ldots + c_{in}|e_{in}|^{\beta_{in}} sign(e_{in})\end{aligned} \tag{10}$$

Now, our objective is to calculate the equivalent control law [29], to ensure the Filippove sense solutions [32] in sliding modes. Posing $\dot{s}_i = 0$ and calculating for u_i, while, assuming $h_i(x,t) = 0$, one may obtain

$$\begin{aligned}u_{i(eq)} = &\Big((\sum_{j=1,j\neq i}^{n} a_{ij} + b_i)g_i\Big)^{-1} \times \Big(-(\sum_{j=1,j\neq i}^{n} a_{ij} + b_i)f_i\\ &+ \sum_{j=1,j\neq i}^{n} a_{ij}(f_j + g_j u_j) + b_i f_0(x,t)\\ &- a_{i1}e_{i2} - a_{i2}e_{i3} - \ldots - a_{i(n-1)}e_{in}\\ &- b_{i1}|e_{i1}|^{\alpha_{i1}} sign(e_{i1}) - \ldots - b_{in}|e_{in}|^{\alpha_{in}} sign(e_{in})\\ &- c_{i1}|e_{i1}|^{\beta_{i1}} sign(e_{i1}) - \ldots - c_{in}|e_{in}|^{\beta_{in}} sign(e_{in})\Big)\end{aligned} \tag{11}$$

This control component governs the system trajectories exactly on the sliding surface $s_i = 0$ [1]. To ensure the robustness against uncertainties of a matched kind, the overall control law is considered as an algebraic sum of the aforementioned equivalent control component and a discontinuous control component i.e.,

$$u_i = u_{i(eq)} + u_{i(dis)} \tag{12}$$

where

$$u_{i(dis)} = -K_i sign(s_i) \tag{13}$$

with K_i being the switching gain. Thus, the final distributed control protocol can be obtained by putting (11) and (13) in (12). The control law defined in (12) ensures the convergence of system states to zero in finite time. The following stability analysis presents the detailed presentation of sliding mode enforcement and the finite-time convergence of the system states.

4. Stability Analysis

Now, at this stage, it is necessary to present the stability of the proposed control protocol in a close loop under the effect of the uncertainty. Therefore, the following theorem is stated.

Theorem 1. *The finite sliding mode can be enforced along the nonlinear sliding surface (8) by the control protocol (12). If the switching gain is chosen as follows*

$$K_i \geq |h_i(x,t)| + \eta,$$

the trajectories of (5) also converge in finite time to the equilibrium.

Proof. A Lyapunov function of the following form is considered to prove the theorem:

$$v_i(s_i) = \frac{1}{2}s_i^2 \tag{14}$$

The time derivative of (14) along (10) becomes

$$\dot{v}_i(s_i) = s_i\dot{s}_i$$

$$\begin{aligned}\dot{v}_i(s_i) =& s_i\Bigg(\Big(\sum_{j=1,j\neq i}^{n} a_{ij} + b_i\Big)(f_i(x) + g_i(x)u_i) - \sum_{j=1,j\neq i}^{n} a_{ij}(f_i(x) + g_i(x)u_i) \\ &- b_i f_0(x,t) + h_i(x,t) + a_{i1}e_{i2} + a_{i2}e_{i3} + \ldots + a_{i(n-1)}e_{in} \\ &+ b_{i1}|e_{i1}|^{\alpha_{i1}} sign(e_{i1}) + \ldots + b_{in}|e_{in}|^{\alpha_{in}} sign(e_{in}) \\ &+ c_{i1}|e_{i1}|^{\beta_{i1}} sign(e_{i1}) + \ldots + c_{in}|e_{in}|^{\beta_{in}} sign(e_{in})\Bigg)\end{aligned} \tag{15}$$

Incorporating (12) in (15) (with components in (11) and (13)), it reduces to

$$\dot{v}_i(s_i) = s_i(h_i(x,t) - K_i sign(s_i))$$

$$\dot{v}_i(s_i) = s_i h_i(x,t) - s_i K_i sign(s_i) \tag{16}$$

Using the identity $s_i sign(s_i) = |s_i|$, (16) becomes

$$\dot{v}_i(s_i) = s_i h_i(x,t) - K_i|s_i|$$

$$\begin{aligned}\dot{v}_i(s_i) &\leq |s_i||h_i(x,t)| - K_i|s_i| \\ \dot{v}_i(s_i) &\leq -|s_i|(K_i - |h_i(x,t)|)\end{aligned} \tag{17}$$

The sliding mode along (8) can be ensured, if one chooses

$$K_i - |h_i(x,t)| \geq \eta_i > 0 \tag{18}$$

$$K_i \geq |h_i(x,t)| + \eta_i$$

where η_i refers to small positive constants. Thus, using (18), (17) becomes

$$\dot{v}_i = -\eta_i|s_i|$$

$$\dot{v}_i \leq -\sqrt{2}\eta_i {v_i}^{1/2} \tag{19}$$

The time t_s taken for the trajectory of the proposed system to reach the sliding surface can be found by integrating (19) as

$$t_s \leq \frac{1}{2\bar{\eta}_i} \ln\Big(\bar{\eta}_i v^{\frac{1}{2}} s_i(0)\Big) : \quad \text{where } \bar{\eta}_i = \sqrt{2}\eta_i$$

This equation certifies the finite time convergence of sliding mode along (8) [33]. The establishment of sliding mode along (8) means that the system trajectories now evolve on the manifold $s_i = 0$. Thus, one may have

$$\begin{aligned}& e_{in} + a_{i1}e_{i1} + a_{i2}e_{i2} + \ldots + a_{i(n-1)}e_{i(n-1)} \\ &+ \int_0^t (b_{i1}|e_{i1}|^{\alpha_{i1}} sign(e_{i1}) + \ldots + b_{in}|e_{in}|^{\alpha_{in}} sign(e_{in}) \\ &+ c_{i1}|e_{i1}|^{\beta_{i1}} sign(e_{i1}) + \ldots + c_{in}|e_{in}|^{\beta_{in}} sign(e_{in})\Big)d\tau = 0\end{aligned} \tag{20}$$

Equation (20) can also be written as

$$\begin{aligned}&\dot{e}_{in} + b_{in}|e_{in}|^{\alpha_{in}} sign(e_{in}) + c_{in}|e_{in}|^{\beta_{in}} sign(e_{in})\\&+ (a_{i(n-1)}\dot{e}_{i(n-1)} + b_{i(n-1)}|e_{i(n-1)}|^{\alpha_{i(n-1)}} sign(e_{i(n-1)})\\&+ c_{i(n-1)}|e_{i(n-1)}|^{\beta_{i(n-1)}} sign(e_{i(n-1)}) + \ldots + a_{i1}\dot{e}_{i1}\\&+ b_{i1}|e_{i1}|^{\alpha_{i1}} sign(e_{i1}) + c_{i1}|e_{i1}|^{\beta_{i1}} sign(e_{i1}) = 0\end{aligned} \tag{21}$$

Equation (21) holds only if

$$\begin{aligned}&\dot{e}_{in} + b_{in}|e_{in}|^{\alpha_{in}} sign(e_{in}) + c_{in}|e_{in}|^{\beta_{in}} sign(e_{in}) = 0\\&\dot{e}_{i(n-1)} + \frac{b_{i(n-1)}}{a_{i(n-1)}}|e_{i(n-1)}|^{\alpha_{i(n-1)}} sign(e_{i(n-1)})\\&+ \frac{c_{i(n-1)}}{a_{i(n-1)}}|e_{i(n)}|^{\beta_{i(n-1)}} sign(e_{i(n-1)}) = 0\\&\vdots\\&\dot{e}_{i1} + \frac{b_{i1}}{a_{i1}}|e_{i1}|^{\alpha_{i1}} sign(e_{i1}) + \frac{c_{i1}}{a_{i1}}|e_{i1}|^{\beta_{i1}} sign(e_{i1}) = 0\end{aligned} \tag{22}$$

These equations in (22) are finite time stable terminal attractors [30], which confirm that $e_{ij} \to 0$ in finite time and stays at zero for all subsequent times. This proves the theorem. □

5. Illustrative Example

This design strategy presented above is validated in this section via the simulation study of a numerical example. The example is conducted according to the topology shown in Figure 1, which consists of one leader and four followers. The leader and the followers, considered here, are governed by third-order uncertain systems. In addition, the agents are operated under uncertainties of the matched kind. The descriptions of the considered systems are presented in the following study.

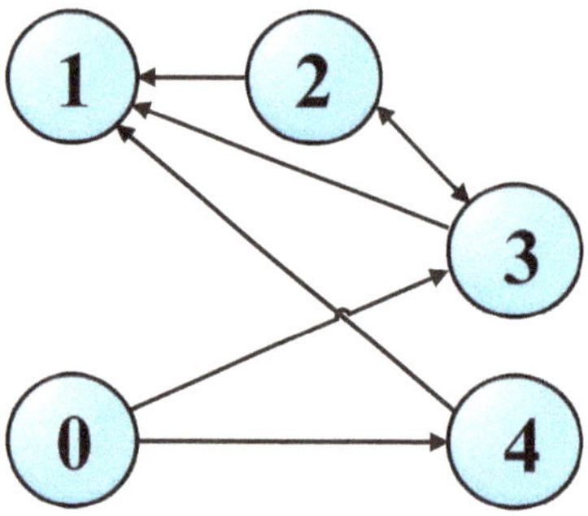

Figure 1. Topology of the system network of one leader and four followers.

5.1. Systems Description

The dynamics of the leader are

$$\begin{aligned}\dot{x}_{01} &= x_{02}\\\dot{x}_{02} &= x_{03}\\\dot{x}_{03} &= -x_{02} - 2x_{03} + 1 + 3\sin(2t) + 2\cos(2t)\end{aligned} \tag{23}$$

The governing equations of the followers are written as follows:

$$\begin{aligned}\dot{x}_{13} &= x_{12}\sin(x_{11}) + \cos^2(x_{13}) + (0.1 + x_{12}^2)u_1 + \xi_1 \\ \dot{x}_{23} &= -x_{21}x_{22} + 0.01x_{21} - 0.01x_{21}^2 + (1 + \sin^2(x_{21}))u_2 + \xi_2 \\ \dot{x}_{33} &= x_{32} + \sin(x_{33}) + (1 + \cos^2(x_{32}))u_3 + \xi_3 \\ \dot{x}_{43} &= -3(x_{41} + x_{42} - 1)^2(x_{41} + x_{42} + x_{43} - 1) - x_{42} \\ &\quad - x_{43} + 0.5\sin(2t) + \cos(2t) + (1 + 0.5x_{42}^2)u_4 + \xi_4\end{aligned} \tag{24}$$

where the term ξ_i represents the matched uncertainties in the follower dynamics. That is, ξ_1 is matched uncertainty in follower 1 and so on.

Since the graph is directed, so the Laplacian and adjacency matrices are written as follows:

$$A = \begin{bmatrix} 0 & 0 & 0 & 0 & 0 \\ 0 & 0 & 1 & 1 & 1 \\ 0 & 0 & 0 & 1 & 0 \\ 1 & 0 & 1 & 0 & 0 \\ 1 & 0 & 0 & 0 & 0 \end{bmatrix} \quad \bar{L} = \begin{bmatrix} 3 & -1 & -1 & -1 \\ 0 & 1 & -1 & 0 \\ 0 & -1 & 1 & 0 \\ 0 & 0 & 0 & 0 \end{bmatrix}$$

and

$$\bar{B} = diag[0, 0, 1, 1]$$

The main task here is that the followers should follow the leader trajectory. For achieving this task, one needs to design a controller by following the steps mentioned in the previous section.

5.2. Controller Design

Since four followers and one leader are considered, the consensus errors, which will be steered to zero, are therefore defined as follows:

$$e_{ij} = \sum_{j=1}^{4} a_{ij}(x_{i1} - x_{j1}) + b_i(x_{i1} - x_{01}); \quad i = 1, 2, 3, 4$$

The related sliding manifolds are defined as follows:

$$\begin{aligned} s_i &= e_{i4} + a_{i3}e_{i3} + a_{i2}e_{i2} + a_{i1}e_{i1} + \\ &\int_0^t b_{i1}|e_{i1}|^{\alpha_{i1}} sign(e_{i1}) + \ldots + b_{i4}|e_{i4}|^{\alpha_{i4}} sign(e_{i4}) \\ &+ c_{i1}|e_{i1}|^{\beta_{i1}} sign(e_{i1}) + \ldots + c_{i4}|e_{i4}|^{\beta_{i4}} sign(e_{i1}) d\tau \end{aligned} \tag{25}$$

where $i = 1, 2, 3, 4$.

The expression for controllers are given below

$$\begin{aligned} u_1 = &\Big(\big(\sum_{j=1, j\neq i}^{4} a_{1j} + b_1 \big) g_i \Big)^{-1} \times \Big(-\big(\sum_{j=1, j\neq i}^{4} a_{1j} + b_1 \big) f_1 + \sum_{j=1, j\neq i}^{4} a_{1j}(f_1 + g_1 u_1) \\ &+ b_1 f_0(x, t) - a_{11}e_{12} - a_{12}e_{13} - \ldots - a_{13}e_{14} \\ &- b_{11}|e_{11}|^{\alpha_{11}} sign(e_{11}) - \ldots - b_{14}|e_{14}|^{\alpha_{14}} sign(e_{14}) \\ &- c_{11}|e_{11}|^{\beta_{11}} sign(e_{11}) - \ldots - c_{14}|e_{14}|^{\beta_{14}} sign(e_{1n}) \Big) \\ &- u_{1(dis)} \end{aligned} \tag{26}$$

$$
\begin{aligned}
u_2 =&\Big(\big(\sum_{j=1,j\neq i}^{4} a_{2j} + b_2\big) g_2\Big)^{-1} \times \Big(-\big(\sum_{j=1,j\neq i}^{4} a_{2j} + b_2\big) f_2 + \sum_{j=1,j\neq i}^{4} a_{2j}(f_2 + g_2 u_2) \\
&+ b_2 f_0(x,t) - a_{21}e_{22} - a_{22}e_{23} - \ldots - a_{23}e_{24} - \\
&b_{21}|e_{21}|^{\alpha_{21}} sign(e_{21}) - \ldots - b_{24}|e_{24}|^{\alpha_{24}} sign(e_{24}) - \\
&c_{21}|e_{21}|^{\beta_{21}} sign(e_{21}) - \ldots - c_{24}|e_{24}|^{\beta_{24}} sign(e_{24})\Big) \\
&- u_{2(dis)}
\end{aligned} \tag{27}
$$

$$
\begin{aligned}
u_3 =&\Big(\big(\sum_{j=1,j\neq i}^{4} a_{3j} + b_3\big) g_3\Big)^{-1} \times \Big(-\big(\sum_{j=1,j\neq i}^{4} a_{3j} + b_3\big) f_3 + \sum_{j=1,j\neq i}^{4} a_{3j}(f_3 + g_3 u_3) \\
&+ b_3 f_0(x,t) - a_{31}e_{32} - a_{32}e_{33} - \ldots - a_{33}e_{34} - \\
&b_{31}|e_{31}|^{\alpha_{31}} sign(e_{31}) - \ldots - b_{34}|e_{34}|^{\alpha_{34}} sign(e_{34}) - \\
&c_{31}|e_{31}|^{\beta_{31}} sign(e_{31}) - \ldots - c_{34}|e_{34}|^{\beta_{34}} sign(e_{34})\Big) \\
&- u_{3(dis)}
\end{aligned} \tag{28}
$$

$$
\begin{aligned}
u_4 =&\left(\big(\sum_{j=1,j\neq i}^{4} a_{4j} + b_4\big) g_4\right)^{-1} \times \left(-\big(\sum_{j=1,j\neq i}^{4} a_{4j} + b_4\big) f_4 + \sum_{j=1,j\neq i}^{4} a_{4j}(f_4 + g_4 u_4)\right. \\
&+ b_4 f_0(x,t) - a_{41}e_{42} - a_{42}e_{43} - \ldots - a_{43}e_{44} - \\
&b_{41}|e_{41}|^{\alpha_{41}} sign(e_{41}) - \ldots - b_{44}|e_{44}|^{\alpha_{44}} sign(e_{44}) - \\
&c_{41}|e_{41}|^{\beta_{41}} sign(e_{41}) - \ldots - c_{44}|e_{44}|^{\beta_{44}} sign(e_{44})\Big) \\
&- u_{4(dis)}
\end{aligned} \tag{29}
$$

These distributed control algorithms are used in the closed-loop, and the consensus with the leader trajectories is met, which will be discussed below.

5.3. The Simulation Results' Discussion

The network of the four followers agents and one leader, which we are sharing information through the network topology shown in Figure 1 are simulated under the action of the distributed control protocols designed above. The leader and followers were initialized from different initial conditions, and the controller's gains were chosen according to the values reported in Table 1. The simulations are performed in the MATLAB environment while using an S-function. The numerical solver is used with a fixed step Euler Method with a step size of 0.01 s.

All the followers were operated under the influence of time-varying sinusoidal disturbances to show the robustness of the proposed distributed control protocols. The consensus in positions, velocities, and accelerations among the followers and leader is displayed in Figures 2–4, respectively. The corresponding position errors convergence, velocities error convergence, and accelerations' errors convergence are shown in Figures 5–7, respectively. It is obvious that the consensus armong the states of leader and followers is quite fascinating even in the presence of disturbances.

Table 1. Parameters of the controllers used in the simulation.

α_{11}	α_{12}	α_{13}	α_{14}	α_{21}	α_{22}	α_{23}	α_{24}
0.5	0.2	0.02	0.22	0.12	0.32	0.12	0.02
α_{31}	α_{32}	α_{33}	α_{34}	α_{41}	α_{42}	α_{43}	α_{44}
0.3	0.32	0.42	0.22	0.12	0.12	0.21	0.22
β_{11}	β_{12}	β_{13}	β_{14}	β_{21}	β_{22}	β_{23}	β_{24}
0.01	0.22	0.22	0.32	0.22	0.32	0.12	0.42
β_{31}	β_{32}	β_{33}	β_{34}	β_{41}	β_{42}	β_{43}	β_{44}
0.5	0.02	0.42	0.22	0.2	0.52	0.42	0.52
b_{11}	b_{12}	b_{13}	b_{14}	b_{21}	b_{22}	b_{23}	b_{24}
15	21.2	15.2	15.2	25.2	8.2	15.2	6.2
b_{31}	b_{32}	b_{33}	b_{34}	b_{41}	b_{42}	b_{43}	b_{44}
10	20.2	25.2	81.2	14.2	4.2	25.2	23.2
c_{11}	c_{12}	c_{13}	c_{14}	c_{21}	c_{22}	c_{23}	c_{24}
5.4	25.2	15.2	35.2	45.2	18.2	15.2	25.2
c_{31}	c_{32}	c_{33}	c_{34}	c_{41}	c_{42}	c_{43}	c_{44}
5.6	2.2	15.2	5.2	25.2	8.2	22.2	6.2

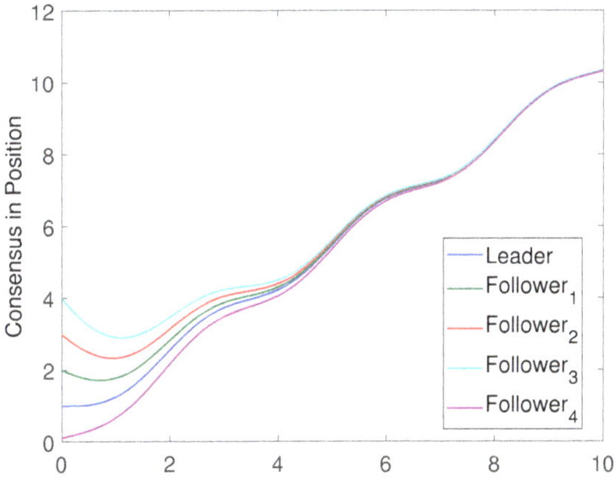

Figure 2. Position consensus of the four followers with leader position trajectory.

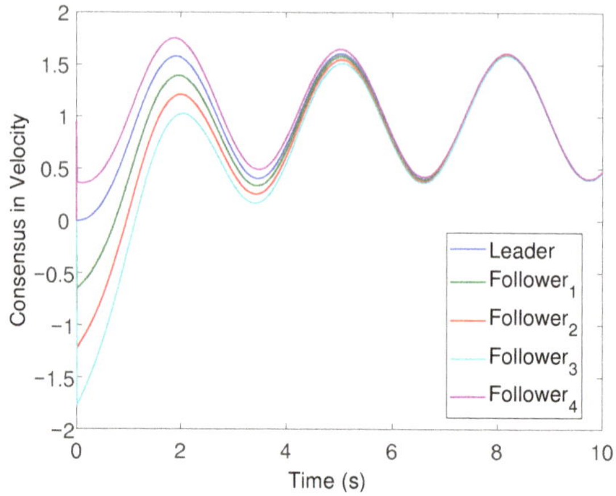

Figure 3. Velocity consensus of the four followers with leader velocity trajectory.

Figure 8 shows the control effort history of each control input. Under the proposed control algorithm, one may obtain almost noise-free control, which reduces chattering (because the noises also cause chattering). The relevant sliding manifolds, which ensure that sliding mode from the very start (as shown in Figure 9) converges to zero in finite time, which ensures the robustness of the designed controller. Having looked at the simulation results, it is evident that the newly designed control protocols offer excellent benefits in terms of robust consensus established from the beginning, which is an appealing attribute of the proposed design. Hence, it is important to conclude that this protocol design is suitable for the consensus of higher-order systems operating under uncertain conditions.

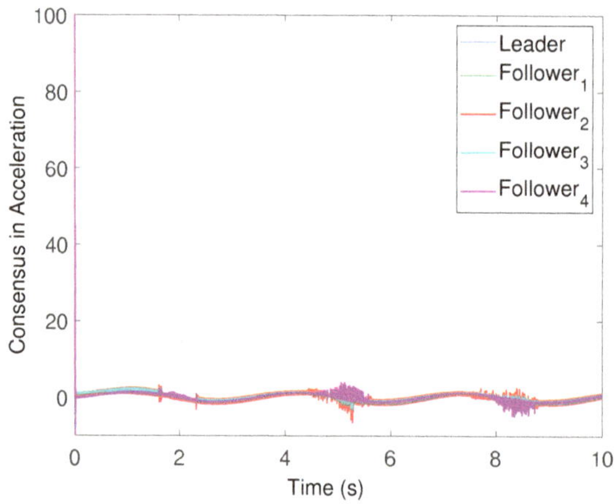

Figure 4. Acceleration consensus of the four followers with leader acceleration trajectory.

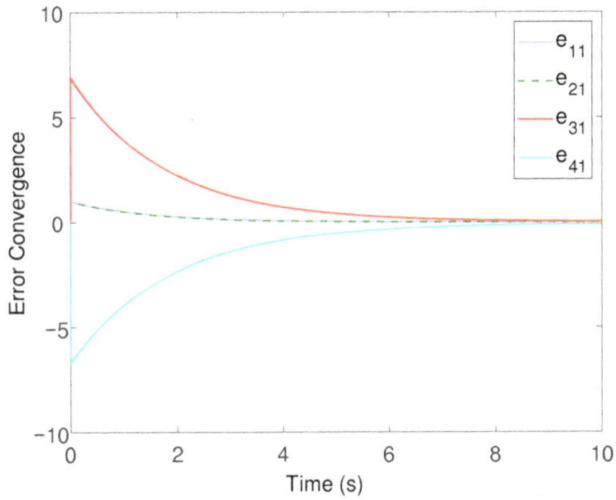

Figure 5. Position errors' convergence.

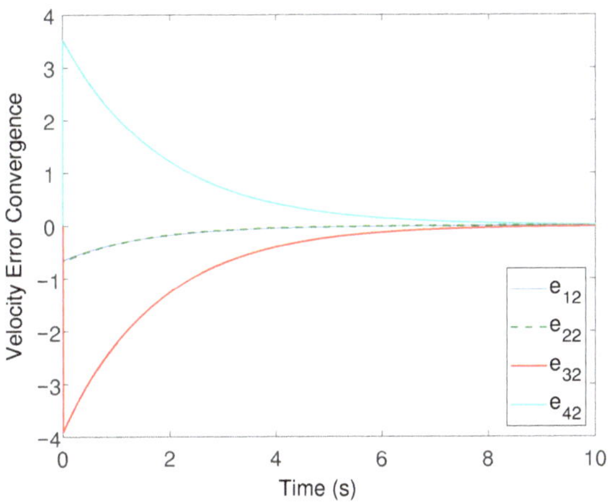

Figure 6. Velocity errors' convergence.

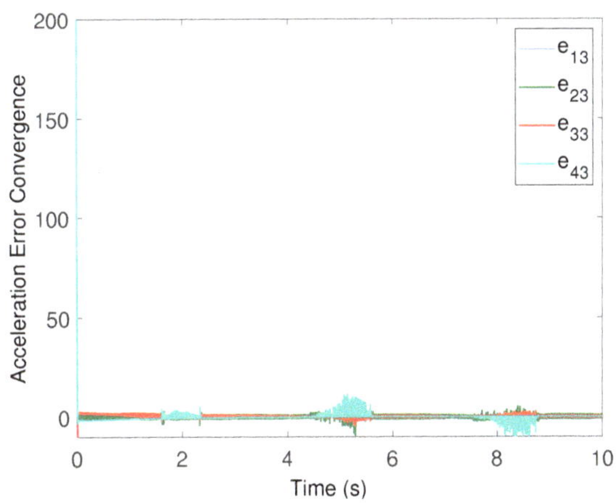

Figure 7. Acceleration errors' convergence.

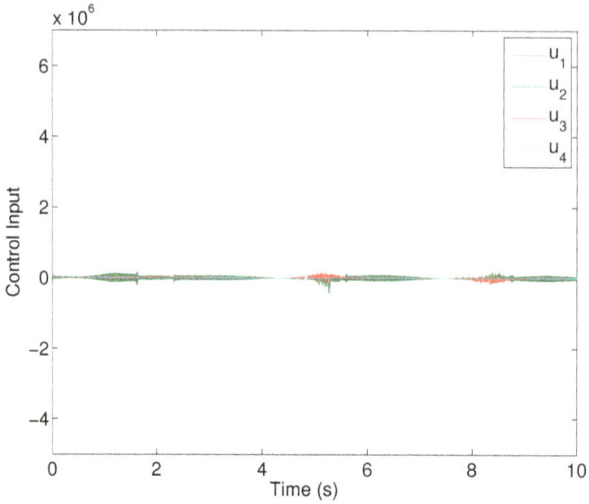

Figure 8. Control inputs' history.

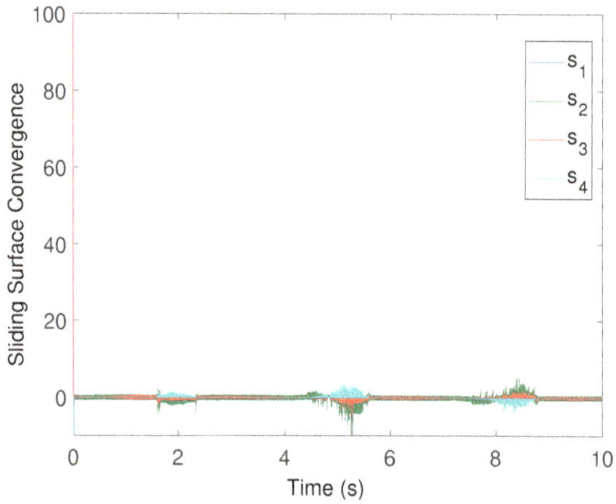

Figure 9. The sliding manifolds convergence from the very start time.

6. Conclusions

In this paper, a network of higher-order nonlinear uncertain agents was considered. The network topology was fixed and was based on a directed graph. The main task was to meet consensus among the leader and n followers. For this purpose, consensus error dynamics were developed, and a novel sliding surface, analogous to proportional-integral type, was considered. The designed control protocol was capable enough to establish sliding mode along the designed sliding surface from the very beginning. In sliding mode, the error dynamics evolved with full states, which were governed by terminal attractors [27]. This confirmed the finite-time consensus errors convergence to equilibrium. This finite time convergence generally results in high precision. In addition, robustness was enhanced from the very beginning because of the reaching phase elimination. Rigorous mathematical stability analysis is presented, and the simulation results are presented to illustrate the benefits of the newly designed distributed control protocols. The results confirmed that the newly designed law is an interesting candidate for higher-order uncertain systems.

Author Contributions: Conceptualization, M.M. and Q.K.; methodology, M.M., Q.K. and S.U.; software, M.M., Q.K.; validation, M.M. and S.U.; formal analysis, M.M. and S.U.; investigation, T.M.S. and A.A.A.; writing—original draft preparation, M.M. and Q.K.; writing—review and editing, Q.K., A.A.A. and S.U.; supervision, Q.K., S.U. and T.M.S.; project administration, Q.K. and S.U. All authors have read and agreed to the published version of the manuscript.

Funding: The APC was funded by A.A.A.

Data Availability Statement: Not applicable.

Conflicts of Interest: The authors declare no conflict of interest.

References

1. Ren, W.; Beard, R.W. *Distributed Consensus in Multi-Vehicle Cooperative Control*; Springer: London, UK, 2008; Volume 27.
2. Bliman, P.A.; Ferrari-Trecate, G. Average consensus problems in networks of agents with delayed communications. *Automatica* **2008**, *44*, 1985–1995. [CrossRef]
3. Fax, J.A.; Murray, R.M. Information flow and cooperative control of vehicle formations. *IFAC Proc. Vol.* **2002**, *35*, 115–120. [CrossRef]
4. Cucker, F.; Smale, S. Emergent behavior in flocks. *IEEE Trans. Autom. Control* **2007**, *52*, 852–862. [CrossRef]
5. Kar, S.; Moura, J.M.; Ramanan, K. Distributed parameter estimation in sensor networks: Nonlinear observation models and imperfect communication. *IEEE Trans. Inf. Theory* **2012**, *58*, 3575–3605. [CrossRef]
6. Li, L.; Fu, M.; Zhang, H. Consensus control for high order continuous-time agents with communication delays. In Proceedings of the 2016 American Control Conference (ACC), Boston, MA, USA, 6–8 July 2016; pp. 4458–4463.
7. Dimarogonas, D.V.; Kyriakopoulos, K.J. On the rendezvous problem for multiple nonholonomic agents. *IEEE Trans. Autom. Control* **2007**, *52*, 916–922. [CrossRef]
8. Huang, J.; Farritor, S.M.; Qadi, A.; Goddard, S. Localization and follow-the-leader control of a heterogeneous group of mobile robots. *IEEE/ASME Trans. Mechatron.* **2006**, *11*, 205–215. [CrossRef]
9. Hou, Z.G.; Cheng, L.; Tan, M. Decentralized robust adaptive control for the multiagent system consensus problem using neural networks. *IEEE Trans. Syst. Man Cybern. Part B (Cybern.)* **2009**, *39*, 636–647.
10. Bai, H.; Arcak, M.; Wen, J.T. Adaptive design for reference velocity recovery in motion coordination. *Syst. Control Lett.* **2008**, *57*, 602–610. [CrossRef]
11. Khan, Q.; Akmeliawati, R. Robust cooperative tracking protocol design for networked higher order nonlinear systems via adaptive second order sliding mode. In Proceedings of the 2017 11th Asian Control Conference (ASCC), Gold Coast, Australia, 17–20 December 2017; pp. 2405–2410.
12. Cheng, L.; Hou, Z.G.; Tan, M.; Lin, Y.; Zhang, W. Neural-network-based adaptive leader-following control for multiagent systems with uncertainties. *IEEE Trans. Neural Netw.* **2010**, *21*, 1351–1358. [CrossRef]
13. Khoo, S.; Xie, L.; Man, Z. Robust finite-time consensus tracking algorithm for multirobot systems. *IEEE/ASME Trans. Mechatron.* **2009**, *14*, 219–228. [CrossRef]
14. Das, A.; Lewis, F.L. Distributed adaptive control for synchronization of unknown nonlinear networked systems. *Automatica* **2010**, *46*, 2014–2021. [CrossRef]
15. Das, A.; Lewis, F.L. Cooperative adaptive control for synchronization of second-order systems with unknown nonlinearities. *Int. J. Robust Nonlinear Control* **2011**, *21*, 1509–1524. [CrossRef]
16. Yang, Z.J.; Takei, D. Robust event-triggered consensus tracking control of high-order uncertain nonlinear systems. *Int. J. Robust Nonlinear Control* **2022**, *32*, 2273–2299. [CrossRef]
17. Yong, K.; Chen, M.; Wu, Q. Finite-Time Performance Recovery Strategy-based NCE Adaptive Neural Control for Networked Nonlinear Systems against DoS Attack. In Proceedings of the 2021 4th IEEE International Conference on Industrial Cyber-Physical Systems (ICPS), Victoria, BC, Canada, 10–12 May 2021; pp. 403–410.
18. Basheer, A.; Rehan, M.; Tufail, M.; Razaq, M.A. A novel approach for adaptive $H\infty$ leader-following consensus of higher-order locally Lipschitz multi-agent systems. *Appl. Math. Comput.* **2021**, *395*, 125749. [CrossRef]
19. Cheng, H.; Xu, L.; Song, R.; Zhu, Y.; Fang, Y. Intelligent $L2 - L\infty$ Consensus of Multiagent Systems under Switching Topologies via Fuzzy Deep Q Learning. *Comput. Intell. Neurosci.* **2022**, *2022*, 4105546. [CrossRef]
20. Ma, X.; Sun, F.; Li, H.; He, B. Neural-network-based integral sliding-mode tracking control of second-order multi-agent systems with unmatched disturbances and completely unknown dynamics. *Int. J. Control. Autom. Syst.* **2017**, *15*, 1925–1935. [CrossRef]
21. Kamal, S.; Sachan, A.; Kumar, D.K.; Singh, D. Robust finite time cooperative control of second order agents: A multi-input multi-output higher order super-twisting based approach. *ISA Trans.* **2019**, *86*, 1–8. [CrossRef]
22. Khan, Q.; Akmeliawati, R.; Khan, M.A. An integral sliding mode-based robust consensus control protocol design for electro-mechanical systems. *Stud. Inform. Control* **2018**, *27*, 147–154. [CrossRef]
23. Wang, W.; Huang, J.; Wen, C.; Fan, H. Distributed adaptive control for consensus tracking with application to formation control of nonholonomic mobile robots. *Automatica* **2014**, *50*, 1254–1263. [CrossRef]

24. Ullah, S.; Khan, Q.; Mehmood, A.; Kirmani, S.A.M.; Mechali, O. Neuro-adaptive fast integral terminal sliding mode control design with variable gain robust exact differentiator for under-actuated quadcopter UAV. *ISA Trans.* **2021**, *120*, 293–304. [CrossRef]
25. Ullah, S.; Khan, Q.; Mehmood, A. Neuro-adaptive Fixed-time Non-singular Fast Terminal Sliding Mode Control Design for a Class of Under-actuated Nonlinear Systems. *Int. J. Control* **2022**. [CrossRef]
26. Zou, A.M.; Kumar, K.D.; Hou, Z.G. Distributed consensus control for multi-agent systems using terminal sliding mode and Chebyshev neural networks. *Int. J. Robust Nonlinear Control* **2013**, *23*, 334–357. [CrossRef]
27. Sarand, H.G.; Karimi, B. Synchronisation of high-order MIMO nonlinear systems using distributed neuro-adaptive control. *Int. J. Syst. Sci.* **2016**, *47*, 2214–2224. [CrossRef]
28. Zhang, H.; Lewis, F.L. Adaptive cooperative tracking control of higher-order nonlinear systems with unknown dynamics. *Automatica* **2012**, *48*, 1432–1439. [CrossRef]
29. El-Ferik, S.; Qureshi, A.; Lewis, F.L. Neuro-adaptive cooperative tracking control of unknown higher-order affine nonlinear systems. *Automatica* **2014**, *50*, 798–808. [CrossRef]
30. Zuo, Z. non-singular fixed-time consensus tracking for second-order multi-agent networks. *Automatica* **2015**, *54*, 305–309. [CrossRef]
31. Mishra, J.P.; Yu, X.; Jalili, M. Arbitrary-order continuous finite-time sliding mode controller for fixed-time convergence. *IEEE Trans. Circuits Syst. II Express Briefs* **2018**, *65*, 1988–1992. [CrossRef]
32. Fillipov, A. Differential equations with discontinuous right-hand sides. *Am. Math. Soc. Trans.* **1988**, *62*, 199–231.
33. Edwards, C.; Spurgeon, S. *Sliding Mode Control: Theory and Applications*; CRC Press: Boca Raton, FL, USA, 1998.

sensors

MDPI

Article

Intelligent Tracking of Mechanically Thrown Objects by Industrial Catching Robot for Automated In-Plant Logistics 4.0

Nauman Qadeer [1,2], Jamal Hussain Shah [1,*], Muhammad Sharif [1], Muhammad Attique Khan [3], Ghulam Muhammad [4,*] and Yu-Dong Zhang [5]

1 Department of Computer Science, Wah Campus, COMSATS University Islamabad, Wah Cantonment 47040, Pakistan; nauman.qadeer@fuuast.edu.pk (N.Q.); sharif@ciitwah.edu.pk (M.S.)
2 Department of Computer Science, Federal Urdu University of Arts, Science & Technology, Islamabad 45570, Pakistan
3 Department of Computer Science, HITEC University Taxila, Taxila 47080, Pakistan; attique.khan@hitecuni.edu.pk
4 Department of Computer Engineering, College of Computer and Information Sciences, King Saud University, Riyadh 11543, Saudi Arabia
5 Department of Informatics, University of Leicester, Leicester LE1 7RH, UK; yudong.zhang@leicester.ac.uk
* Correspondence: jhshah@ciitwah.edu.pk (J.H.S.); ghulam@ksu.edu.sa (G.M.)

Abstract: Industry 4.0 smart manufacturing systems are equipped with sensors, smart machines, and intelligent robots. The automated in-plant transportation of manufacturing parts through throwing and catching robots is an attempt to accelerate the transportation process and increase productivity by the optimized utilization of in-plant facilities. Such an approach requires intelligent tracking and prediction of the final 3D catching position of thrown objects, while observing their initial flight trajectory in real-time, by catching robot in order to grasp them accurately. Due to non-deterministic nature of such mechanically thrown objects' flight, accurate prediction of their complete trajectory is only possible if we accurately observe initial trajectory as well as intelligently predict remaining trajectory. The thrown objects in industry can be of any shape but detecting and accurately predicting interception positions of any shape object is an extremely challenging problem that needs to be solved step by step. In this research work, we only considered spherical shape objects as their3D central position can be easily determined. Our work comprised of development of a 3D simulated environment which enabled us to throw object of any mass, diameter, or surface air friction properties in a controlled internal logistics environment. It also enabled us to throw object with any initial velocity and observe its trajectory by placing a simulated pinhole camera at any place within 3D vicinity of internal logistics. We also employed multi-view geometry among simulated cameras in order to observe trajectories more accurately. Hence, it provided us an ample opportunity of precise experimentation in order to create enormous dataset of thrown object trajectories to train an encoder-decoder bidirectional LSTM deep neural network. The trained neural network has given the best results for accurately predicting trajectory of thrown objects in real time.

Keywords: real-time trajectory prediction; mechanically thrown objects; internal logistics; smart manufacturing systems; multi-camera simulation; many-to-many time series forecasting; encoder-decoder bidirectional LSTM deep neural networks

Citation: Qadeer, N.; Shah, J.H.; Sharif, M.; Khan, M.A.; Muhammad, G.; Zhang, Y.-D. Intelligent Tracking of Mechanically Thrown Objects by Industrial Catching Robot for Automated In-Plant Logistics 4.0. *Sensors* **2022**, *22*, 2113. https://doi.org/10.3390/s22062113

Academic Editors: Luige Vladareanu, Hongnian Yu, Hongbo Wang and Yongfei Feng

Received: 17 January 2022
Accepted: 7 March 2022
Published: 9 March 2022

1. Introduction

Smart manufacturing system is a modern form of production system which consists of industrial robots, numerically controlled machines, sensors, and standalone systems such as inspection machines. It uses semi-dependent workstations and material handling systems designed to efficiently manufacture more than one type of part ranging from low to medium volume [1]. The use of computer-controlled machines and robots in the production segment of manufacturing industries promises a variety of benefits ranging from high utilization to high productivity volume [2]. Replacing people with industrial robots is the long lasting demand of production systems. In order to cope up with this demand, industrial robots are going to be common in factories day by day, and a lot of work has been carried out in this dimension. However, still there is big horizon to explore in the domain of intelligent industrial robots. There is no single definition of intelligence, but the main features that characterize intellectual ability are judgment and adaptation of environment as well as on-the-spot solving of newly occurring problems. The work at hand is a step towards this dimension. Realizing the importance of manufacturing systems especially internal logistics (transportation of parts during manufacturing within the plant), it investigates a new approach for material transport within flexible manufacturing systems by a throw and catch technique implemented by intelligent industrial robots sensing through multiple cameras.

The aim of this research work is to explore the fastest way of transportation of parts as well as the optimum usage of the workspace of manufacturing plants, which can ultimately reduce manufacturing costs. Being the most direct connection between two places, the approach of throw and catch should be the fastest possibility for transportations. The basic principle of this transport approach is that a work piece in manufacturing plant is thrown by a robot to the subsequent workstation where it has to be caught by another robot. The catching is performed with a gripper so that the work piece can be handled variably in further production process steps. This approach is shown in Figure 1.

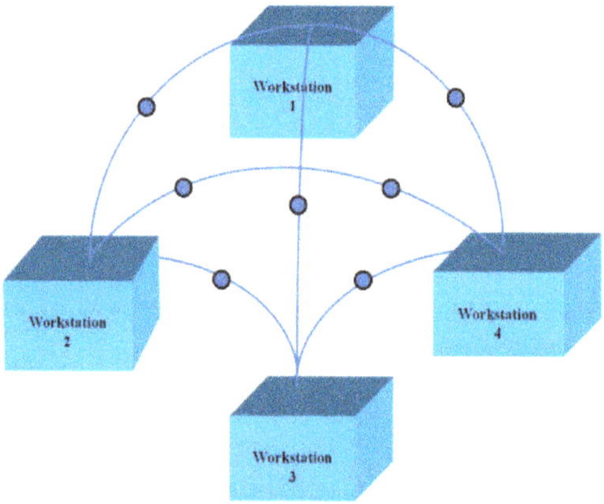

Figure 1. Automated in-plant logistics in industry 4.0 by intelligent throwing-catching robots at different workstations (using different altitude routes).

By applying throw-catch approach for transportation of objects in production systems, the fully automation can be achieved in flexible manufacturing systems which lead to the following advantages:

- Fast transportation
- Productivity increase
- Flexibility
- Optimized utilization of facilities
- Improved safety

The hurdle to implement this approach in industries so far is lack of intelligence in catching robot, as in industrial applications there are many kinds of unsymmetrical objects that can be thrown. Also, the exact position, angle and acceleration of thrown objects is not always known. Furthermore, air resistance and gravitational force are additional factors that influence the flight trajectory of such thrown objects. Due to these non-deterministic parameters, it is not possible to exactly determine the catching location of such thrown objects.

The flight trajectory of a mechanically thrown object can be observed by using optical sensors (i.e., cameras). However, there can be observational errors depending upon the number and positioning of the cameras. We can minimize this observational error if we have multi-camera view by appropriate number of cameras placed at optimum positions in internal logistics settings. Furthermore, enough experimentation of throws is required in order to gain a large dataset to train a supervised machine learning algorithm. In order to gain such dataset, we developed a 3D simulated environment in which a spherical object of any properties (such as mass, diameter, surface air friction, etc.) can be thrown with any initial parameters (initial position, acceleration, throwing angle, etc.) and its trajectory can be captured by a simple pinhole camera placed anywhere within the simulated 3D environment. We used a pinhole camera model for our simulation since perspective projection of most of the modern cameras can be described well by the pinhole camera model [3]. We also employed multi-view geometry among simulated cameras in order to observe trajectories more accurately. Hence it provided us an ample experimentation opportunity in order to create enormous dataset of thrown object trajectories to train any machine learning algorithm.

LSTM deep neural networks provided best results in forecasting time series data [4–7] such as the flight trajectory data in our research problem. However, this algorithm had never been applied in this particular problem of predicting mechanically thrown objects' trajectories. The reason is that such algorithms are data hungry and they need an enormous training in order to have good learning (this is not always possible physically due to limitations of practical settings). However, our simulation made it possible to have enough experimentation of throwing objects with multiple variations as well as having sufficiently captured images within very short time period of thrown object's flight. Moreover, during experimentation, the observed trajectory's intercepting positions are more accurate by applying multi-view geometry.

Our trained encoder-decoder bidirectional LSTM deep neural network has given the best results for predicting trajectory of thrown objects in real time. During testing of our model, the actual intercepting positions of the trajectory are compared with predicted intercepting positions. The next section presents the research work carried out in both academia and industries in this particular problem. Then, in Section 3, our proposed methodology is explained in detail. Afterwards, Section 4 gives testing results to assess successfulness of our work. Finally, Section 5 concludes this research work and gives some future directions.

2. Related Work

The first attempt to apply throwing and catching robots for internal logistics was made in 2006 [8] as a collective attempt by department of Electrical Engineering of Reinhold Würth University Germany and the PMD technologies Germany. This approach has advantages of high flexibility and few resources requirement [9]. Since the acceptance of approach is still not very high for real applications today, certain challenges have to be solved to make it applicable. Such challenges, as summarized in [8], are as follows:

- Mechanically throwing or shooting of objects;
- Tracking of the catching device;
- Catching mechanically thrown objects;
- Detecting thrown object on its trajectory

Work already conducted in production systems with respect to each challenge is described below.

2.1. Mechanically Throwing or Shooting of Objects

Heinz Frank and his team developed a prototype [10] of a mechanical throwing device responsible for throwing circular objects in production systems. Through this device, the characteristics for the acceleration of the objects can be modified only by mechanical settings. With this device, circular objects with masses up to 70 g are thrown with speeds up to 10 m/s over distances up to 3 m. The spring of this throwing device can be compressed with a hydraulic jack and it can be released with a solenoid. Different accelerations of circular object can be set by variation in compression strength and that can be made by changing the distance between the bearing and solenoid.

In [11], Smith, C. and Christensen, H.I. have demonstrated a mechanical ball launcher which was used to throw soft juggling type ball with nearly 6 m/s velocity and they used it in their ball catching experiments where it was placed at the distance of approximately 4 m from the catching robot. Heinz Frank continued this work with cylindrical objects and, in [12], he along with his team introduced another throwing device that could throw cylindrical shaped objects over distances of about 3 m. In this throwing device, a pneumatic cylinder drives over an arm with leverage which can accelerate the object. The speed of throwing can be controlled with the pressure for the cylinder. It is able to throw cylinders with masses up to 100 g and of diameters up to 100 mm. Moreover, the cylinders thrown through this device maintain stable orientation and high targeted precision.

2.2. Tracking of the Catching Device

In [8], Objects to be transported are thrown in x-direction towards catching device. So, in order to catch objects, the capturing device only needs to move in two motion axes (y-axis and z-axis). 3D video camera is attached on capturing device. It can detect thrown object within its field of observation in intervals of 20 ms so with a flight time of 300 ms, 15 positions can be collected with this camera within the range of 3 m. It means, position is measured by camera after nearly 200 mm distance in x-axis (Δx). The accuracy in measurement of position can be judged by distance to the camera. As the distance of object from camera reduces, there is more precision in camera measured position of object. These factors are considered to track catching device. In [13], Cartesian robot is proposed as capturing device. This robot can move in y and z-axis. The vision is made is through a single camera mounted at top of robot. As the ball comes nearer to robot, its more precise capturing position can be predicted. Hence, the robot is moved accordingly to capture the object.

2.3. Catching Mechanically Thrown Objects

To catch fast flying objects in production systems, grippers are required which should have the closing time of less than 10 ms [13]. These grippers can have one or many jaws so that objects of many shapes can be captured. In [14], two types of grippers are proposed to capture flying objects in production systems. First type of grippers is that which use kinetic energy of the flying object to close the gripper. When the flying object enters into the jaw of gripper, it impacts a ram which pushes the lever and the lever closes the gripper without any reaction-delay. After that, object can be released by a linear drive in slow movement through the slope. The second type of grippers is mechanical in nature. With such grippers, the jaw is closed by a pre-stressed rotary spring. The closing movement is released by a ram. When flying object enters into jaw of gripper, the ram is pushed that pulls lever and rotary spring catches the flying object. This gripper is better for light weight objects. It is the kind of gripper that is used as a capturing device for a Cartesian robot in [13].

2.4. Detecting Mechanically Thrown Object on Its Trajectory

There are several challenges for tracking of thrown objects such as continuously changing background, aerodynamic stability and dynamic appearance throughout flight [15]. In order to meet these challenges, a lot of work had already been carried out. Most of the work is in sports domain such as soccer [16,17], cricket [18,19], basketball [7,20], tennis [21], and ping-pong playing robots [22–25]. Some work is also carried out for catching robots such as the work in [26] for a ball catching robot where a ball 8.5 cm in diameter was wrapped in retro-reflective foil and its flight trajectory was observed through stereo triangulation by two cameras mounted as the eyes of a catching humanoid robot. The reflective foil made ball more fluorescent, and hence it was easily detectable by humanoid robot. The

EKF (extended Kalman filter) was used for prediction based upon the flight interception positions judged 0.16 to 0.2 s before catch. That humanoid robot caught 80% successful catches, whereas a successful catch was made whenever the prediction was within range of 15 mm error. However, the total numbers of test trajectories were not specified in that article. A similar work was also conducted in [27] where the article claim 98% successful catches by robot capable of catching tennis ball within error range of approximately 10 cm (i.e., 100 mm).

Except for ping-pong playing robots, all of the other above-mentioned work involves non-mechanical throws. The work of ping-pong playing robots such as [22–25] involves mechanical throw of ball as ping-pong ball is served mechanically by robotic arm. Mechanically thrown objects in production systems are unsymmetrical and not absolutely identical. So, their trajectories are influenced by different factors such as different conditions during the acceleration, the influence of the gravitation and aerodynamic resistance. Therefore, for catching such objects, the trajectory of objects must be observed online during the flight [8]. Some efforts have already employed in this regard. The work in [28] used 3D video range camera to observe flight trajectory. Such a camera employs PMD (photonic mixer device) principle which uses 3D optical detection to measure time-of-flight and it was developed by PMD Technologies. Such high-speed 3D camera was based on 64 × 48 pixel photonic mixer device (PMD) sensor array and enables 3D distance measurements to be made with 50 fps speed. Using PMD, the distance data is acquired using time-of-flight principle with invisible near-infra-red light.

There is very limited work that is specifically carried out for tracking mechanically thrown objects regarding robotic throw catch approach. Those works involve object throws through a mechanical launcher. For example, the work in [29–31] used single camera on the catching side and trajectory of thrown objects was predicted by combination of two methodologies for determination of 3D positions of a thrown object during its trajectory. The first methodology was applied in early phase of trajectory and used measurement of the initial parameters (angles, position and velocity) of the thrown object. The speed of the object was measured by six photoelectric sensors placed at 40 mm vertical distance on an aluminum frame. While calculating the velocity along the approaching axis, aerodynamic resistance had also taken into account. Hence by simply applying model of flight kinematics, 3D positions of object are predicted at specific time intervals in the initial phase of flight. In the next phase of flight trajectory, back-projection of 2D image object position to 3D real world position was made. This back-projection methodology was not used in earlier phase of flight trajectory since good accuracy (in determination of 3D position of ball) cannot be achieved when the object is far from the camera.

The work in [32,33] used stereo vision to collect samples of mechanically thrown tennis ball trajectories. However, they enabled researchers to measure positions of ball in camera-related coordinate system with millimeters of accuracy (even outliers in some measurements). They used KNN regression approach for forecasting on 2D points of camera coordinates. In their experiments they achieved nearly 30 mm precision in predicting future position of ball. Work in [34] used a simple neural network containing only one hidden layer. This NN was trained using 15 simulated trajectory training sets whereas each set had 10 sample trajectories obtained in nearly 2.5 m long flight of tennis balls that was mechanically thrown. The training was made using MATLAB Neural Networks Toolbox. The mean error was nearly 24 to 26 mm between measured values and prediction results in simulated environment.

Other mechanically thrown object's flight prediction experiments were made by [35–38] using stereo vision based observational data as input to a forecasting algorithm responsible for generating trajectory using deterministic motion model further governed by genetic programming algorithm. Their algorithm was tested through MSE (mean square error) in chosen frames 60 to 80 and in only 20 test trajectories. The average MSE in 20 trajectories was 5.4 mm. Although this average MSE was good, it was based upon just 20 testing trajectories. As well, the error was calculated within selected frames and does not reflect the error of whole flight trajectory. The work carried out regarding mechanically thrown object's trajectory tracking is summarized in the next section.

2.5. Limitations in Existing Work of Mechanically Thrown Objects Tracking

The limitations in existing work of mechanically thrown objects tracking are summarized in Table 1.

Table 1. Limitations in existing work of mechanically thrown objects tracking.

Ref.	Year	Trajectory Type	Prediction Algorithm	Results (Accuracy)	Limitation(s)
[22]	2020	Mechanical ball throws using ping-pong playing robot. Observe its flight through 3 cameras (right, left and auxiliary) of speed 169 FPS	Dual Neural Network	300 trajectories for the training set and 30 trajectories for the test set. The test results in absolute mean error of 36.6 mm and standard deviation of 18.8 mm	Limited training and testing
[23] [24] [25]	2020 2019 2020	Mechanical ball throw using ping-pong playing robot and observe its flight (0.8 to 1.2 s) through 4 RGB cameras of speed 180 FPS (Frames Per Second) attached at ceiling	Variational auto-encoder deep NN	614 trajectories for the training set (90% training and 10% for validation) and 35 trajectories for the test set. Prediction's absolute mean error converges to nearly 40–60 mm based upon observations in first 40–50 frames of flight trajectory.	Error is high but could be improved with more training trajectories
[29] [30] [31]	2010 2009 2008	Ball throws using mechanical device. Observe its actual positions in flight with the help of photoelectric sensors. Flight is also captured by single camera of 87 FPS speed.	Observations of ball positions through photoelectric sensors and Size based Tracking of ball through 2D coordinates in image plane are further passed to EKF for prediction of final 2D impact point on DST-Touch screen	The accuracy was measured in 17 test throws only and for final 2D impact position (on a DST-Touch kit) only. The average error deviation of final impact position was 1.20 mm to 3.98 mm.	(1) It is assumed that the line of sight is perpendicular to the camera's measuring plane (2) Photoelectric sensors were used to get actual interception position of ball whereas in practical industrial scenarios such sensors are not easily implementable
[32] [33]	2016 2015	Ball throws using mechanical device. Observe its flight trajectory through stereo vision of 2 cameras (left and right) of spatial resolution 2048 × 2048 and speed was not specified in their articles.	kNN (k-Nearest Neighbor) Regression	2048 real-world trajectories were saved in the database and then testing were performed on 150 trajectories. First 40 frames ball positions were used during testing and after applying KNN the prediction was within 30 mm for 92% of trajectories.	Error is high but could be improved with: (1) More training and better pattern recognizer (such as deep neural networks) (2) Increasing the number of observations (i.e., frames) for prediction
[34]	2013	The mechanical throws were simulated using physical motion model. Each sample trajectory was obtained in nearly 2.5 m long flight of tennis ball.	Neural Network with one hidden layer was used to train 15 simulated trajectory sets whereas each set had 10 sample trajectories	The mean error was nearly 24 to 26 mm between measured values and prediction results in simulated environment.	Being results in simulated environment, this error is high. Also very limited training and testing
[35] [36] [37] [38]	2017 2018 2019 2017	Ball throws using mechanical device. Observe its flight trajectory through stereo vision of 2 cameras (left and right) of spatial resolution 2048 × 2048 and speed was not specified in their articles.	Deterministic motion model further governed by genetic programming algorithm	Their algorithm was tested through MSE (Mean Square Error) in chosen frames 60 to 80 only and in only 20 test trajectories. The average mean square error (MSE) in 20 trajectories was 5.4 mm	Average MSE was good but it was based upon just 20 testing trajectories as well as the error was calculated within selected frames (60 to 80) and it does not reflect the error of whole flight trajectory

3. Proposed Methodology

As described in previous section, the majority of existing work for mechanically thrown object tracking, had chosen a tennis ball as the thrown object for development and validation of proposed ideas in order to implement robotic throw catch transportation approach in industry for small sized objects. This is due to the well-known aerodynamic properties of this object as there is already a number of scientific literature available that explored the aerodynamic properties of the tennis ball; a review of such exploration is given in [39]. Another reason is that detecting and accurately predicting interception positions of any shape object, during its flight, is an extremely challenging problem that needs a step-by-step solution. So, following this tradition, this research work also used tennis ball as mechanically thrown object.

This work consists of four sequential stages. In the first stage, a novel simulating environment is prepared that facilitates to throw any spherical object, in controlled logistics environment, and observe its trajectory by placing a simulated camera at any place within that 3D vicinity. It helped us to capture thrown object's trajectory by placing camera at any place and finally the best camera positions are derived based upon the captured trajectory's error. In the second stage, the best multi-camera setup is derived in a real world environment by placing cameras at optimum positions (derived in last stage) and also applying multi-view geometry among them. Then, in next stage, best derived multi-camera setup is used for thousands of experiments to prepare a comprehensive dataset of trajectories and in final stage an encoder-decoder Bi-LSTM deep neural network is trained. The overall proposed methodology is visually illustrated in Figure 2 and explained in detail in following subsections.

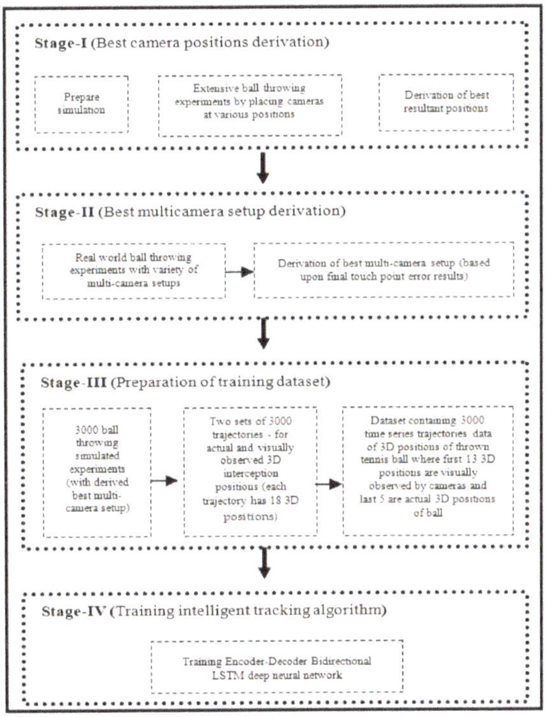

Figure 2. Proposed methodology.

3.1. Simulation

The 3D vicinity of internal logistics environment is simulated in MATLAB as a cube with both positive and negative axis in all three dimensions. This simulation facilitates to throw spherical objects of any mass, diameter or surface air friction in a controlled environment. It also enabled us to throw object with any motion model and observe its trajectory by placing simulated pinhole camera anywhere within 3D vicinity of internal logistics in flexible manufacturing systems which is usually 3 to 5 m [8].

In fact, the perspective projection of most of the modern cameras can be described well by the pinhole camera model [5] and that is the reason for choosing pinhole camera model for implementation of virtual cameras in this simulation. It is to be noted that, in our simulation, virtual camera can capture trajectory with any frame rate but we used the frame rate of 60 fps in order to give it compatibility with real world experimental camera's frame rate. Other properties of virtual camera (such as focal length, pixel pitch which is per pixel area on camera's sensor, resolution of captured image etc.) are set as real world used camera (i.e., IDS UI-1220RE-M-GL) properties.

All simulation used parameters are taken from our real-world experiments. In those experiments, the tennis ball is mechanically thrown towards Y-axis (towards catching robot) and the distance between throwing and final catching point is about 3 m. The initial position of ball is assumed at $(0,0,0)$ in simulation. The ball's radius is set as 32.2 mm (as in real world) and its coloris green in order to give the appearance of a real-world scene. Few visually captured trajectories, in our simulated throwing experiments are shown in Figure 3.

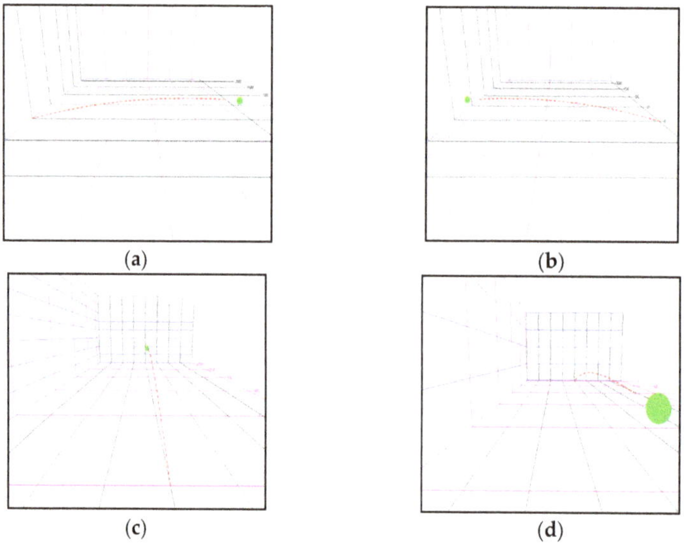

Figure 3. Last frame of trajectory (along with previous trajectory trace) when captured through four different simulated cameras. (**a**) One side camera view. (**b**) Other side camera view. (**c**) Throwing side camera view. (**d**) Catching side camera view.

3.2. Experimental Setup and Simulation Testing

We used a self-developed mechanical device for throwing tennis ball. This device throws ball by using kinetic energy that is produced by stretching a spring. The launching device is shown in Figure 4a. The launching speed of thrown ball is 23 m/h (i.e., 10.282 m/s) which is measured with the help of a radar gun shown in Figure 4b.

(a) (b) (c) (d)

Figure 4. Real world experimental setup. (**a**) Ball throwing device. (**b**) Radar gun to measure launching speed. (**c**) Used camera (UI-1220RE-M-GL). (**d**) Trajectory captured through throw side camera.

The used cameras are "UI-1220RE-M-GL" by IDS imaging development systems. This camera has sensor size of 1/3 inch, sensor area of 4.512 × 2.880 mm, focal length of 6 mm and per pixel area of 0.006 mm. It has the maximum capturing speed of 87 fps and its captured image has resolution of 752 × 480.

Before starting exhaustive simulated experiments for deriving best camera positions, the authenticity of our simulation was checked through a comparison experiment with exactly same parameters in real and simulated setups. There is always some distortion or deviation from ideal projection whenever a scene is captured by real world camera. It is due to several reasons but the prominent ones are lens quality and perspective projection effects such as an infinitely wide real-world plane is mapped onto the finite image area of lens. However, in spite of the deviational margin of results from ideal projection, the results from real and simulated experiments should be similar which authenticates the simulation.

The flight trajectory of thrown tennis ball was captured by placing a single camera at catching side in real world experiment. The exact measurements of camera and ball's starting positions were (−262 mm, 2964 mm, 678 mm) and (0, 0, 0), respectively. The camera was oriented towards starting position of ball and exact measurements of orientation parameters are as follows: roll or tilt (orientation around x-axis) was measured as 23.40° degrees (clockwise), pitch or pan (orientation around z-axis) was measured as 25.13° degrees (anti-clockwise) and the yaw i.e., rotation around y-axis (the rotation of camera plane with respect to real world plane) was measured at 1.06° degrees (anti-clockwise). The same parameters were set in simulation experiment.

The tennis ball is mechanically thrown and the distance between throwing and final catching point is about 3 m. As mentioned earlier, the launching speed of thrown ball (measured through radar gun) was 23 m/h (i.e., 10.282 m/s). The launching angles of thrown ball can be named as alpha (left/right angle along x-axis) and beta (up/down angle along z-axis). The ball is thrown straight so ideally the alpha should be zero but in real world experiments the real value of alpha with precise measurement is 0.5 degrees. Similarly, the launching position makes the beta angle as 17 degrees. Knowing initial speed of ball and its throwing angles (alpha and beta), we can estimate the spherical coordinates (v, θ, φ) of initial velocity; where v is the initial speed of ball, θ is the azimuth angle (angle from the positive x-axis in xy plane) and φ is the inclination angle (angle from the positive y-axis in the yz plane). These spherical coordinates of initial velocity of ball (i.e., v, θ, φ) can be calculated as given in Equations (1)–(3).

$$\text{Launching speed (v)} = 23 \text{ miles/h}$$

$$\text{i.e.,} \quad V = 23 \times 0.44704 \text{ m/s} = 10.282 \text{ m/s} \tag{1}$$

$$\text{Azimuth angle } (\theta) = 90 - \text{alpha} = 90 - 0.5 = 89.5^\circ \tag{2}$$

$$\text{Inclination angle } (\varphi) = 90 - \text{beta} = 90 - 17 = 73^\circ \tag{3}$$

The cartesian coordinates of the initial velocity i.e., (V_x, V_y, V_z) of thrown ball can be calculated using trignometric laws as given in Equations (4)–(6).

$$V_x = V \cdot \sin(\varphi) \cdot \cos(\theta) = 0.088 \text{ m/s} \tag{4}$$

$$V_y = V \cdot \sin(\varphi) \cdot \sin(\theta) = 9.830 \text{ m/s} \quad (5)$$

$$V_z = V \cdot \cos(\varphi) = 3.002 \text{ m/s} \quad (6)$$

In simulation, a tennis ball is launched with above initial parameters and its 3D trajectory is generated using standard ballistic motion model which also considers air density and spin of the ball under room temperature [40]. In our case, we used air density of 1.294 kg/m^3 which is at 20 degree centigrade (similar to our lab temperature). The mass of ball, assumed in simulation, is the exact mass of our used tennis ball and that is 56 g. Similarly, the simulation used radius of tennis ball is 32.2 mm which is its real world radius. At starting point of ball, the time t = 0, so we can represent initial velocity by $V(0)$ and if we ignore all forces (except gravity and drag) influencing the flight then the velocity (in any dimension) of ball at a particular time t (i.e., $V(t)$) and can be calculated by Equation (7) and the future velocities of ball can be derived by simple ballistic motion equation as shown by Equation (9).

$$V(t) = V(0) + g \times t - \int_{T=0}^{t} k \times v^2 \, dT \quad (7)$$

$$\text{where} \quad g = [0,\ 0,\ 9.8] \quad (8)$$

$$\text{i.e.,} \quad V(t + \Delta t) = V(t) + (a(t) + g) \times \Delta t \quad (9)$$

If the starting position of ball, i.e., at time t = 0, is assumed at $(0,\ 0,\ 0)$ then every next position of ball (in any direction) can be calculated from current position (at time t) by using the following formula given in Equation (10).

$$Pos(t + \Delta t) = Pos(t) + V(t) \times \Delta t. \quad (10)$$

When the trajectory is captured by real world camera, the total flight of moving ball is captured in 17 frames of movie which is captured at the speed of 60 fps. If we also consider the launching position of ball (i.e., 0,0,0) then the total 3D interception positions of flight trajectory are 18. The same parameters were used for simulation and hence the total flight time is 283.33 ms. The tennis ball is mechanically thrown and its 3D trajectory is captured through real camera whereas in simulation the trajectory is generated through ballistic motion model and it is captured by simulated camera working under pinhole camera model principles. In both real and simulated experiments, the tennis ball is thrown with the same initial velocities as mentioned by Equations (4)–(6). Both simulated and real cameras capture the full trajectory of thrown ball in 17 frames under the same capturing frame rate of 60 fps. The exact differences at each interception position (along X, Y and Z axes) are shown through graphs in Figure 5a–c, respectively.

The comparison of results (illustrated in Figure 5) has shown the close resemblance of real and virtual camera's reconstructed trajectories as there are few millimeters differences between the three measured axis' values for corresponding interception positions of flight trajectory. It is also observed that reconstructed trajectories (by both real and simulated cameras) had wider difference (from corresponding actual position values) in early stages of flight and the error reduces in later stages of flight; that is, as the thrown object gets closer to camera (which is mounted at catching side).

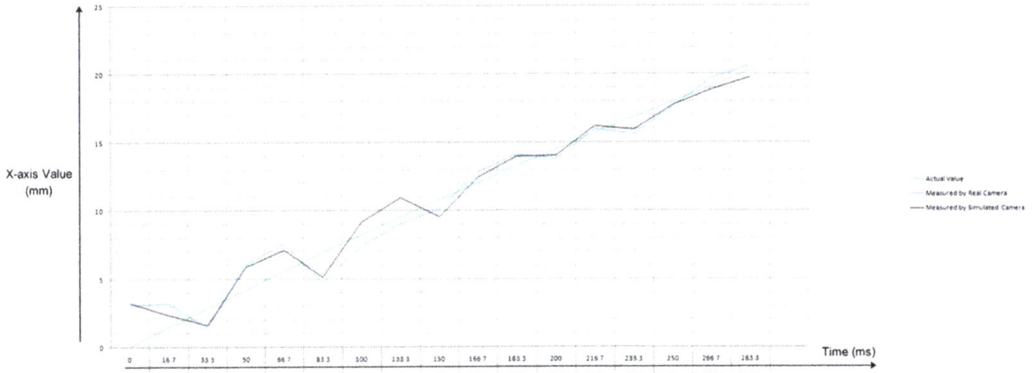

Time (ms)	0	16.7	33.3	50	66.7	83.3	100	133.3	150	166.7	183.3	200	216.7	233.3	250	266.7	283.3
Actual Value	0	1.44	2.85	4.23	5.59	6.93	8.24	9.53	10.8	12.05	13.28	14.49	15.68	16.85	18	19.13	20.26
Measured by Real Camera	3.1	3.17	1.43	6.03	7.57	4.73	7.44	9.08	10.1	12.87	14.13	13.84	15.98	15.63	17.64	19.71	20.69
Measured by Simulated Camera	3.23	2.36	1.62	5.87	7.09	5.13	9.19	10.91	9.5	12.45	13.97	14.06	16.18	15.95	17.72	18.89	19.75

(a)

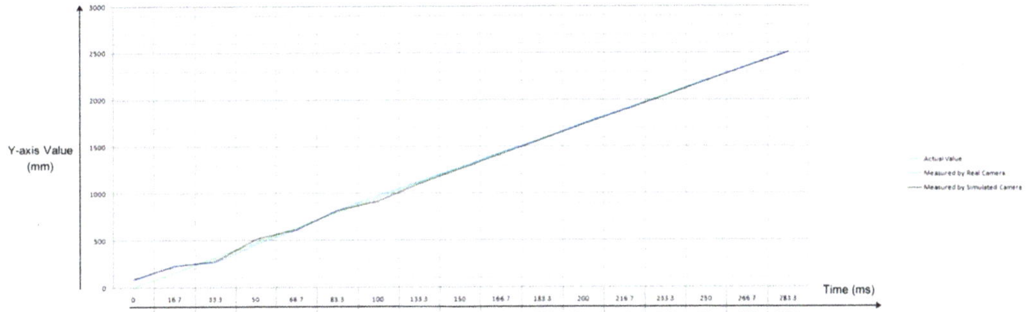

Time (ms)	0	16.7	33.3	50	66.7	83.3	100	133.3	150	166.7	183.3	200	216.7	233.3	250	266.7	283.3
Actual Value	0	157.6	313.8	475.6	636.6	796.9	958.5	1114.7	1272.3	1429.2	1585.5	1741.1	1896	2050.3	2204	2357	2509.4
Measured by Real Camera	73.5	231.1	262.8	452.1	609.1	820.4	980	1128.2	1281.2	1436.7	1576.4	1753.6	1899.5	2040.8	2207.5	2360.5	2512.9
Measured by Simulated Camera	85.7	223.3	278.1	511.3	614.9	815.6	920.8	1102	1263.6	1420.5	1578.8	1735.4	1888.3	2045.6	2199.3	2353.6	2506.7

(b)

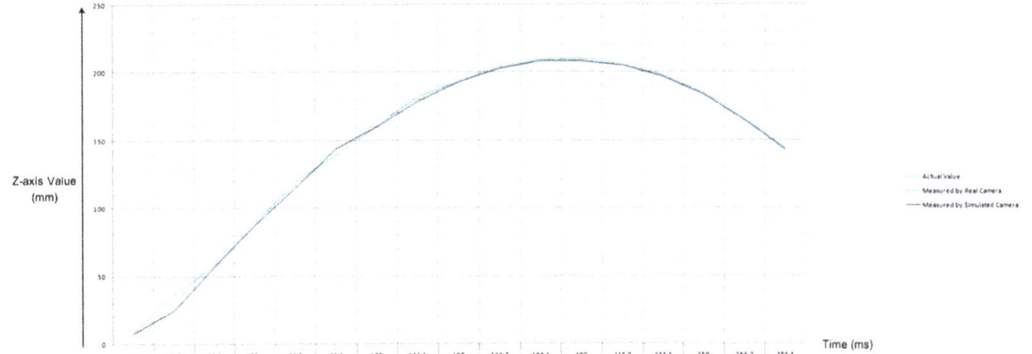

Time (ms)	0	16.7	33.3	50	66.7	83.3	100	133.3	150	166.7	183.3	200	216.7	233.3	250	266.7	283.3
Actual Value	0	31.2	61.4	90.1	116.9	141.3	162.9	180.9	194.9	204.7	210.1	210.9	207	198.4	185	166.8	143.8
Measured by Real Camera	8.5	36.7	57.9	87.6	120	138.9	160.4	182.4	192.6	202.6	207.5	207.3	204.7	196.1	182.9	165.3	142.2
Measured by Simulated Camera	7.3	24.7	56.9	86.8	114.4	143.8	160.2	178.4	193	203	208.6	208.4	205	196.8	183.5	164.3	142.9

(c)

Figure 5. (**a**) Comparison of X-axis values (in actual and reconstructed trajectories by real & simulated camera). (**b**) Comparison of Y-axis values (in actual and reconstructed trajectories by real and simulated camera. (**c**) Comparison of Z-axis values (in actual and reconstructed trajectories by real and simulated camera).

3.3. Best Multicamera Setup Derivation

After testing simulation, we can trust its trajectory results obtained by throwing same object (i.e., tennis ball) and employing simulated camera at any position and orientation within the simulated 3D vicinity of smart manufacturing plants. The process of deriving best multi-camera setup is divided into three phases. The first phase is to guess the areas where the best results can be found.

Assuming the starting position of ball as (0,0,0) and moving towards +ve Y-axis, it covers nearly the distance of 2.5 m (i.e., 2500 mm). So, seeing this, we set the initial 3D experimentation range for simulated camera placement. This initial range is -500 mm to 3500 mm for Y-axis, -500 to 1500 mm for Z-axis and -1500 mm to 1500 mm for X-axis. In order to guess best resultant areas, the simulated experimentation should be performed by placing camera at every 500 mm apart position within the selected 3D initial range. It is to be noted that these limits are chosen as the reasonable limits and can be changed (based upon initial experimentation results). For example, the Z-axis limit is chosen as -500 to 1500. But if the best results are obtained at Z-axis value of -500 then it shows a possibility to get better results beyond this value which ultimately extend the experimentation range so that Y-axis value of -1000 should also be considered (and even this process can be continued further). It gives the justification for choosing the above-mentioned axis limits in initial experimentation.

As the object is thrown straight and moves within a small X-axis value range (i.e., 0 to 25.3 mm), so the trajectories captured by placing the camera at particular (X, Y, Z) position and $(-X, Y, Z)$ position are nearly symmetrical which implies that results obtained at these positions have minute difference. As only guess has to be made within this first phase that which area is better to do refined experimentation, so such minute difference can be neglected for initial experimentation and only positive X-values can be considered. The initial experimentation results have shown that minimum error was obtained at throwing and catching side cameras. So, further experimentation is carried outby placing cameras at 250 mm apart distances from initially guessed area. The results of these further experimentation eventually give us best resultant area which require refined experimentation to find out best capturing camera positions.

As we have to carry out refined experiments in the initially guessed area so we also include earlier neglected negative x-axis area also and now within this area, we performed refined experiments by placing camera at each 100 mm apart camera position. Finally, we got four best capturing cameras positions based upon the minimum trajectory error between actual and observed trajectory. We named those four best camera positions as C1, C2, C3 and C4 and they are precisely shown in Figure 6.

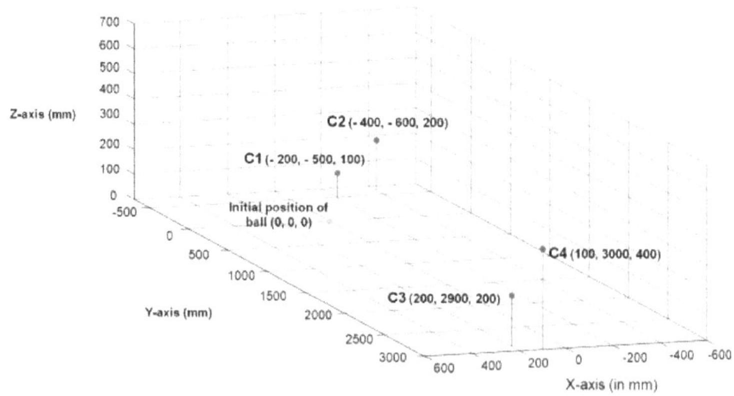

Figure 6. Identified best capturing cameras positions.

It should be noted that the minimum trajectory error is observed when the thrown object trajectory is captured from throwing and catching side cameras at reasonable distances. This is due to the fact that the size of the thrown ball changes significantly in videos when captured from those positions, and this significant change helps in proper identification of distance of ball from camera. Furthermore, reconstructed X-coordinate and Z-coordinates of ball are derived from the distance between camera and ball, so significant change in size of ball are required for proper reconstruction of all three coordinates of the real position of the ball.

Finally, in the last phase, different combinations of these best positioned cameras are employed in real world settings in order to derive best multi-camera setups in terms of maximum accuracy of final touch point 3D position error. It is the last position of ball which is measured on DST (dispersive signal technology) touch screen placed on catching side. Two-camera combinations are made in a way that they must contain both throw and catch side cameras in order to get more accurate results. Since it is necessary to include throw and catch side cameras so there are only four possible combinations of these cameras for two cameras setups. Similarly, there are four possible combinations to make three cameras setup. All of these two and three camera setups are shown in Table 2 along with their obtained experimental results which are given as average value of 50 ball throwing experiments.

Table 2. Final touch point accuracy by different multi-camera setups (results based upon average of 50 real world experiments).

Multicamera Setups	Final 3D Interception Position Error (Average Error—in mm)		
	X-Axis	*Y*-Axis	*Z*-Axis
C2 + C4	2.5	1.7	5.4
C1 + C4	1.9	5.2	2.0
C2 + C3	2.5	6.5	3.1
C1 + C3	2.8	4.5	1.5
C1 + C2 + C4	1.5	5.0	1.9
C1 + C2 + C3	2.3	4.5	1.7
C2 + C3 + C4	1.1	2.0	1.4
C1 + C3 + C4	**0.9**	**1.8**	**1.6**

The results shown in last row, by three cameras setup (i.e., C1 + C3 + C4), are the best ones. So, this setup is considered as best derived multicamera setup which is used in simulation for preparing training dataset of throws.

3.4. *Preparing Throws Datasets and Training Intelligent Tracking Models*

The best derived three cameras setup is employed in simulated environment and 3000 throwing experiments were performed (with very minute variation in throwing parameters). For each throwing experiment, two time series are recorded. The first one consists of actual 3D interception positions of thrown ball and second consists of 3D interception positions of balls as perceived by observing cameras. There are 17 moving 3D interception positions of ball in its trajectory when cameras captured 283 ms of flight trajectory of ball at capturing speed of 60 frames per second. So, there are total 18 captured video frames (including first frame when ball is placed at starting position (i.e., 0,0,0). We need to prepare a training dataset of throws where, in each dataset throw, first few 3D interception positions are cameras observed interception positions and last ones are actual 3D interception positions. So, considering this point, we used first 13 interception positions as perceived by cameras (it captured approximately first 200 ms of flight trajectory) and last five interception positions are actual 3D positions of ball (covering around 83 ms of last part of flight trajectory). We need to train an intelligent tracking model that gets input as camera perceived 3D interception positions of first 200 ms of thrown ball flight trajectory and predict next 83 ms of flight trajectory consisting of last five actual interception positions of the thrown ball. It provides enough time to instruct motor of modern catching robot to place catching gripper at predicted final 3D interception position. A sample throw of training dataset is shown in Figure 7.

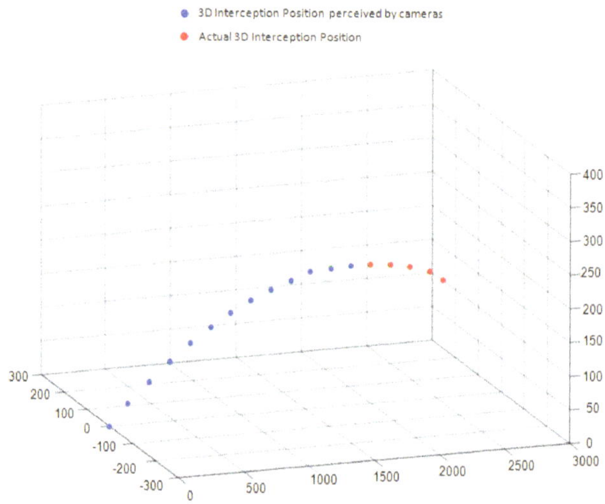

Figure 7. Sample dataset throw.

The main contribution of this work is to propose an enhanced intelligent tracking algorithm that can predict remaining 3D interception positions of thrown object by seeing its initial flight trajectory. It is a pure time series prediction problem and LSTM deep neural networks work best for such problems. In particular, this is a many-to-many time series prediction problem where both input and output vectors consists of multiple time-step data values and each value further consists of three values (*X*, *Y*, and *Z* axis coordinate). The encoder-decoder LSTM is usually used for such many-to-many time series prediction problem. We have particularly used encoder-decoder bidirectional LSTM deep neural networks for this problem and they proved to be so much accurate as depicted by prediction results. The bidirectional LSTM preserves timeseries information both from forward and backward sequential contexts.

The encoder bidirectional LSTM creates an internal representation of the input sequence whereas the decoder bidirectional LSTM interpret this internal representation and responsible for predicting corresponding outputting sequence. The training is performed on 90% of throws dataset and model is validated on remaining 10% of dataset. The initial learning rate is set as 0.005. The model learned best with 'Adam' optimizer. We trained model (in Keras) using different number of epochs and neurons. For example, one of the training codes which we coded in Keras (Python deep learning API) is shown in Figure 8.

```
#optimizer learning rate
opt = keras.optimizers.Adam(learning_rate=0.005)

# define model
model = Sequential()
model.add(Bidirectional(LSTM(100, activation='relu', input_shape=(13,3))))
model.add(RepeatVector(5))
model.add(Bidirectional(LSTM(100, activation='relu', return_sequences=True)))
model.add(TimeDistributed(Dense(3)))
model.compile(loss='mse', optimizer='adam')

# Fit network
history = model.fit(X, Y, epochs=80, verbose=1, validation_data=(test_X, test_Y), batch_size=13)
```

Figure 8. Coding (carried out in Keras) for training one of our encoder-decoder BiLSTM.

This code used the input shape as (13.3), it is due to the fact that each of our training dataset throw has 18 three dimensional points and first 13 points of observed flight trajectory are given as input to encoder BiLSTM which consists of 100 neurons as input to each of its LSTM (i.e., forward and backward LSTMs). This encoder BiLSTM returns output as five points (i.e., the remaining five points of flight trajectory) that are received by RepeatVector which feeds them repeatedly as input to decoder BiLSTM which further has 100 neurons as input to both of its forward and backward LSTMs. The code also depicts that the output is of five time steps distributed where each time step value has three features (i.e., *X*, *Y*, and *Z* coordinates). The decoder BiLSTM in fact uses the value from RepeatVector, the hidden state from previous output and the current input. The return sequence of decoder BiLSTM is set as "true" since the output is in the form of time steps. The RepeatVector is used for only repeating the encoder LSTM output and it has no parameter to train. For example, see the summary of above-mentioned model in Figure 9.

```
_________________________________________________________________
Layer (type)                 Output Shape              Param #
=================================================================
bidirectional_16 (Bidirecti  (None, 200)               83200
onal)

repeat_vector_8 (RepeatVect  (None, 5, 200)            0
or)

bidirectional_17 (Bidirecti  (None, 5, 200)            240800
onal)

time_distributed_8 (TimeDis  (None, 5, 3)              603
tributed)

=================================================================
Total params: 324,603
Trainable params: 324,603
Non-trainable params: 0
```

Figure 9. Summary of trained model (whose coding given in Figure 8).

The Figure 9 shows that RepeatVector has no parameter to train and it can also be seen, from summary, that each of the encoder and decoder bidirectional LSTM (BiLSTM) has 200 input neurons which is due to the fact that BiLSTM has two LSTMs and we have given 100 neurons as input to each LSTM.

The experimentation of training and testing such models is carried out at different volumes of training dataset throws. Also, we trained and tested multiple encoder-decoder BiLSTM deep neural networks (with different number of neurons and epochs) in order to check their accuracy. We gradually increased the volume of training dataset which consists of simulation throws. Initially a model is trained using only 200 training throws dataset. It used 100 epochs (during training) and 100 neurons as input. In Figure 10, the loss along epochs is shown during its training. The prediction results, in root mean square error (RMSE) and mean absolute error (MAE), in 50 tested throws are also shown in this figure.

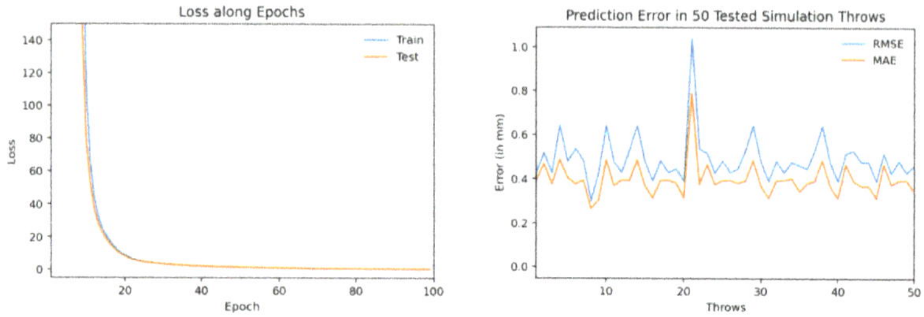

Figure 10. Training and testing results by encoder-decoder bidirectional LSTM deep NN (trained through 200 throws with 100 epochs and 100 neurons).

Then, we trained similar models using 1000 throws dataset. As mentioned earlier, for every model training we used 90% dataset for training and 10% for validation. Figures 11–13 show the training and testing (on 50 tested throws) performance results when encoder-decoder Bidirectional LSTM models are trained on 1000 throws datasets with varying number of epochs and neurons. The comparative analysis of all three of these models shows that over fitting can occur when we cross certain epoch limit and, in this particular case, we got the best results with 50 epochs.

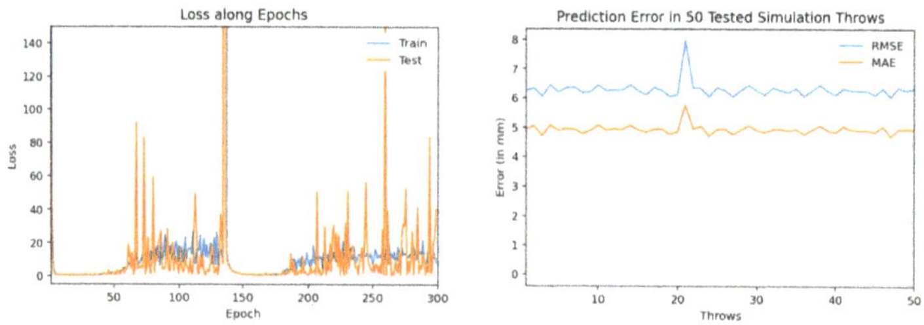

Figure 11. Training and testing results by encoder-decoder bidirectional LSTM deep NN (trained through 1000 throws with 300 epochs and 200 neurons).

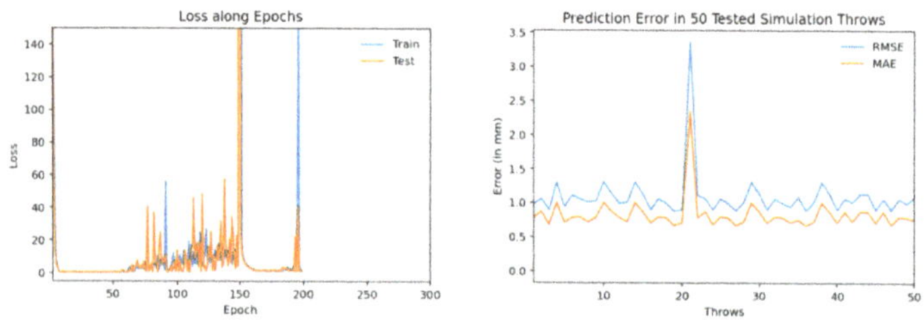

Figure 12. Training and testing results by encoder-decoder bidirectional LSTM deep NN. (trained through 1000 throws with 200 epochs and 100 neurons).

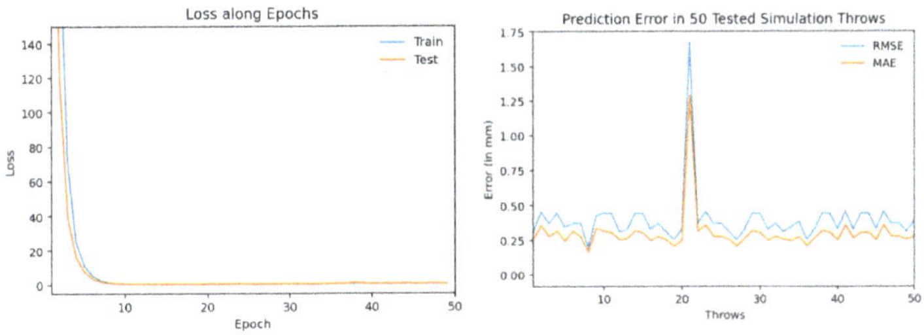

Figure 13. Training and testing results by encoder-decoder bidirectional LSTM deep NN (trained through 1000 throws with 50 epochs and 100 neurons).

Finally, we trained the complete dataset of 3000 throws. Figures 14–16 show the training and testing (on 50 tested throws) performance results when encoder-decoder Bidirectional LSTM models are trained on complete dataset of 3000 throws with varying number of epochs and neurons. The comparative analysis of testing graphs of all of these three models shows that we get best results when model is trained using 80 epochs and with an input of 100 neurons to each LSTM in encoder-decoder bidirectional LSTM. This model is the best intelligent model (with maximum prediction accuracy) in our case. In next section, the testing results of this model are presented with a greater number of tested throws.

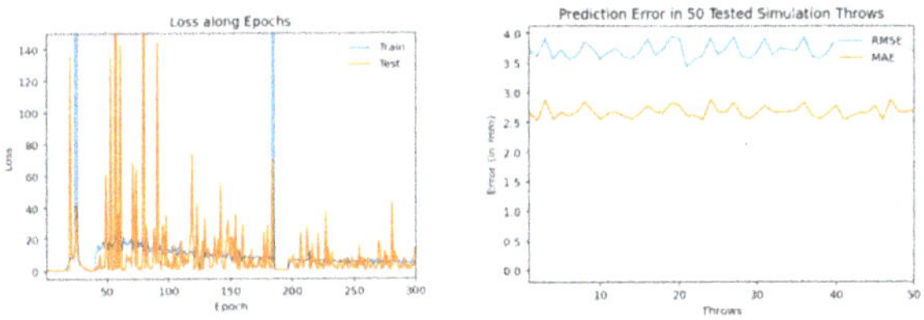

Figure 14. Training and testing results by encoder-decoder bidirectional LSTM deep NN (trained through 3000 throws with 300 epochs and 200 neurons).

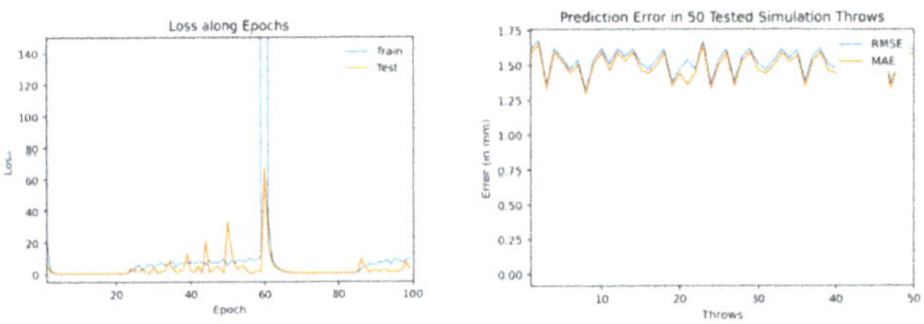

Figure 15. Training and testing results by encoder-decoder bidirectional LSTM deep NN (trained through 3000 throws with 100 epochs and 100 neurons).

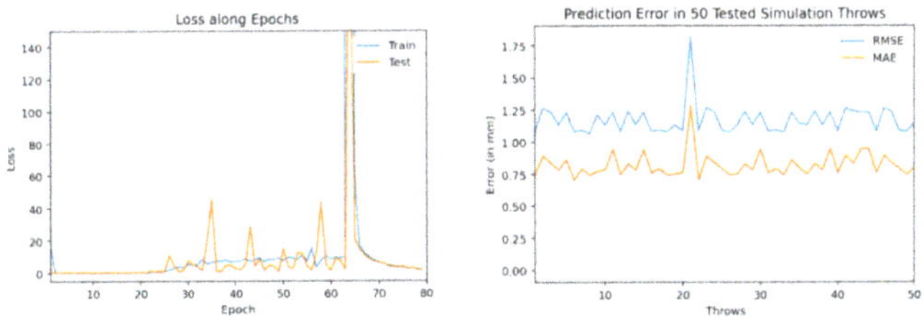

Figure 16. Training and testing results by encoder-decoder bidirectional LSTM deep NN (trained through 3000 throws with 80 epochs and 100 neurons).

4. Results and Discussion

The encoder-decoder BiLSTM deep neural network trained on complete dataset of 3000 throws, with 100 neurons and trained through 80 epochs has presented best results and hence considered as our proposed intelligent tracking model for automated industrial catching robots responsible for in-plant logistics through throwing an catching manufacturing parts. Hence, we further test this trained intelligent tracking model on different throws datasets. Figure 17a–c shows prediction error graphs for three test datasets of 50, 100, and 200 throws, respectively.

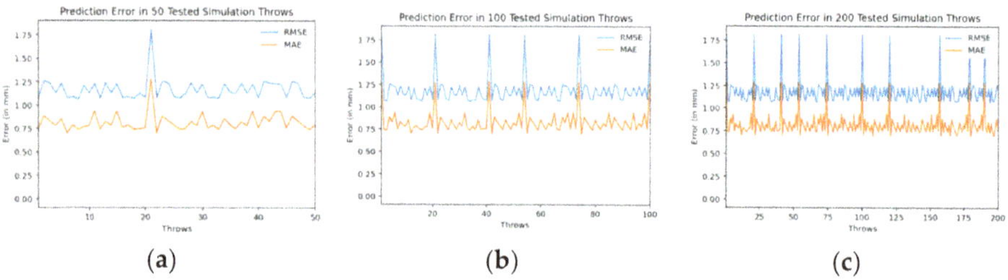

Figure 17. Prediction error results by applying proposed model for different datasets of test throws.

These graphs show the accuracy of predicted values through our intelligent model. The obtained results are within the range of 2 mm error. In Figure 18, the graphs are shown, against each axis value, for 3D interception positions of a tested throw.

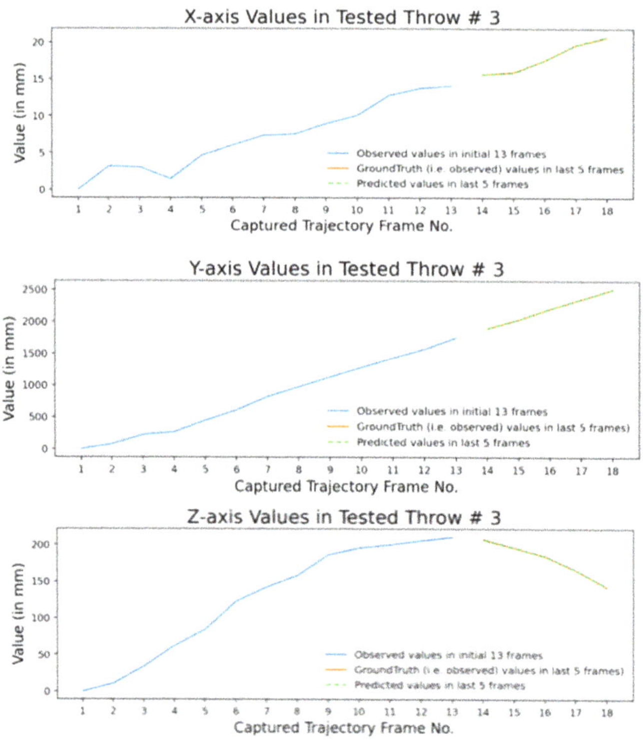

Figure 18. Comparison among predicted and ground truth values in a tested simulated throw.

The first 13 are cameras observed values. The last five are actual (i.e., ground truth) values and predicted values (obtained through our trained intelligent model). The good overlap between predicted values and ground truth again represents the accuracy of our intelligent tracking model.

5. Conclusions and Future Work

The automated in-plant logistics for smart manufacturing systems of Industry 4.0 can be implemented through throwing and catching robots for fast transportation of small sized materials, containers, or packages. However, it needs to enhance the intelligence of existing catching robots by more accurate tracking of mechanically thrown objects. This work includes the development of a 3D simulated environment which enabled one to throw object of any mass, diameter, or surface air friction in a controlled internal logistics environment. It also enabled us to throw objects with any initial velocity and observe their trajectory by placing simulated pinhole camera at any place within a 3D vicinity of the internal logistics space. Moreover, the multi-view geometry can also be employed among simulated cameras in order to observe trajectories more accurately. The simulation further enabled us to derive the best multicamera setup and, after that, a dataset of 3000 throws was prepared using that setup in simulated environment. An intelligent tracking model is proposed using encoder-decoder bidirectional LSTM approach. The model predicts final part of thrown object flight trajectory by observing its initial flight through cameras and in real-time. This model is trained using prepared dataset and its prediction results are compared with ground truth values in simulated test throws. The trained neural network has given best results for accurately predicting the final part of mechanically thrown object trajectory in real time.

This research work only considered tracking of spherical shaped mechanically thrown objects as their 3D central position can be easily determined in video frames. In future, we have planned to extend this work for other regular shaped objects in order to implement it practically in industry for automated in-plant fast transportation of small sized materials such as containers, food, or pharmaceutical products.

Author Contributions: Conceptualization, N.Q., J.H.S.; methodology, N.Q., J.H.S., M.S.; validation, N.Q., J.H.S., M.A.K.; formal analysis, N.Q., J.H.S., M.S.; investigation, N.Q., J.H.S., M.S.; data curation, N.Q., M.A.K., Y.-D.Z. and G.M.; writing—original draft preparation, N.Q. and J.H.S.; writing—review and editing, N.Q., J.H.S., M.A.K. and G.M.; supervision, J.H.S.; project administration, J.H.S.; funding acquisition, G.M. and Y.-D.Z. All authors have read and agreed to the published version of the manuscript.

Funding: This work is funded by Researchers Supporting Project number (RSP-2021/34), King Saud University, Riyadh, Saudi Arabia.

Institutional Review Board Statement: Not applicable.

Informed Consent Statement: Not applicable.

Data Availability Statement: Our dataset is not publicly available yet. However, in future, we will make it publically available along with code on GitHub.

Conflicts of Interest: The authors declare no conflict of interest.

References

1. Black, J.T.; Kohser, R.A. *DeGarmo's Materials and Processes in Manufacturing*; John Wiley & Sons: Hoboken, NJ, USA, 2020.
2. Groover, M.P. *Fundamentals of Modern Manufacturing: Materials, Processes and Systems*; John Wiley & Sons: Hoboken, NJ, USA, 2020.
3. Shirai, Y. *Three-Dimensional Computer Vision*; Springer Science & Business Media: Berlin/Heidelberg, Germany, 2012.
4. Ghazal, R.; Malik, A.K.; Qadeer, N.; Raza, B.; Shahid, A.R.; Alquhayz, H. Intelligent Role-Based Access Control and Framework Using Semantic Business Roles in Multi-Domain Environments. *IEEE Access* **2020**, *8*, 12253–12267. [CrossRef]
5. Ghazal, R.; Malik, A.K.; Raza, B.; Qadeer, N.; Qamar, N.; Bhatia, S. Agent-Based Semantic Role Mining for Intelligent Access Control in Multi-Domain Collaborative Applications of Smart Cities. *Sensors* **2021**, *21*, 4253. [CrossRef] [PubMed]

6. Shi, Z.; Xu, M.; Pan, Q.; Yan, B.; Zhang, H. LSTM-Based Flight Trajectory Prediction. In Proceedings of the 2018 International Joint Conference on Neural Networks (IJCNN), Rio de Janeiro, Brazil, 8–13 July 2018; pp. 1–8.
7. Zhao, Y.; Yang, R.; Chevalier, G.; Shah, R.C.; Romijnders, R. Applying Deep Bidirectional LSTM and Mixture Density Network for Basketball Trajectory Prediction. *Optik* **2018**, *158*, 266–272. [CrossRef]
8. Frank, H.; Wellerdick-Wojtasik, N.; Hagebeuker, B.; Novak, G.; Mahlknecht, S. Throwing Objects—A Bio-Inspired Approach for the Transportation of Parts. In Proceedings of the 2006 IEEE International Conference on Robotics and Biomimetics, Kunming, China, 17–20 December 2006; pp. 91–96.
9. Frank, H.; Barteit, D.; Kupzog, F. Throwing or Shooting-a New Technology for Logistic Chains within Production System. In Proceedings of the 2008 IEEE International Conference on Technologies for Practical Robot Applications, Woburn, MA, USA, 10–11 November 2008; pp. 62–67.
10. Frank, H. Design and Simulation of a Numerical Controlled Throwing Devic. In Proceedings of the 2008 Second Asia International Conference on Modelling & Simulation (AMS), Kuala Lumpur, Malaysia, 13–15 May 2008; pp. 777–782.
11. Smith, C.; Christensen, H.I. Using COTS to Construct a High Performance Robot Arm. In Proceedings of the Proceedings 2007 IEEE International Conference on Robotics and Automation, Rome, Italy, 10–14 April 2007; pp. 4056–4063.
12. Frank, H.; Mittnacht, A.; Scheiermann, J. Throwing of Cylinder-Shaped Objects. In Proceedings of the 2009 IEEE/ASME International Conference on Advanced Intelligent Mechatronics, Singapore, 14–17 July 2009; pp. 59–64.
13. Frank, H.; Barteit, D.; Meyer, M.; Mittnacht, A.; Novak, G.; Mahlknecht, S. Optimized Control Methods for Capturing Flying Objects with a Cartesian Robo. In Proceedings of the 2008 IEEE Conference on Robotics, Automation and Mechatronics, Chengdu, China, 21–24 September 2008; pp. 160–165.
14. Frank, H.; Barteit, D.; Wellerdick-Wojtasik, N.; Frank, T.; Novak, G.; Mahlknecht, S. Autonomous Mechanical Controlled Grippers for Capturing Flying Object. In Proceedings of the 2007 5th IEEE International Conference on Industrial Informatics, Vienna, Austria, 23–27 June 2007; pp. 431–436.
15. Kim, S.; Shukla, A.; Billard, A. Catching Objects in Flight. *IEEE Trans. Robot.* **2014**, *30*, 1049–1065. [CrossRef]
16. Kamble, P.; Keskar, A.; Bhurchandi, K. A Deep Learning Ball Tracking System in Soccer Videos. *Opto-Electron. Rev.* **2019**, *27*, 58–69. [CrossRef]
17. Najeeb, H.D.; Ghani, R.F. Tracking Ball in Soccer Game Video Using Extended KalmanFilte. In Proceedings of the 2020 International Conference on Computer Science and Software Engineering (CSASE), Duhok, Iraq, 16–18 April 2020; pp. 78–82.
18. Desai, U.B.; Merchant, S.N.; Zaveri, M.; Ajishna, G.; Purohit, M.; Phanish, H. Small Object Detection and Tracking: Algorithm, Analysis and Applicatio. In *Lecture Notes in Computer Science*; Springer: Berlin/Heidelberg, Germany, 2005; pp. 108–117.
19. Velammal, B.; Kumar, P.A. An Efficient Ball Detection Framework for Cricket. *Int. J. Comput. Sci. Issues* **2010**, *7*, 30.
20. Chen, H.-T.; Tien, M.-C.; Chen, Y.-W.; Tsai, W.-J.; Lee, S.-Y. Physics-Based Ball Tracking and 3D Trajectory Reconstruction with Applications to Shooting Location Estimation in Basketball Video. *J. Vis. Commun. Image Represent.* **2009**, *20*, 204–216. [CrossRef]
21. Zhou, X.; Xie, L.; Huang, Q.; Cox, S.J.; Zhang, Y. Tennis Ball Tracking Using a Two-Layered Data Association Approach. *IEEE Trans. Multimed.* **2014**, *17*, 145–156. [CrossRef]
22. Lin, H.-I.; Yu, Z.; Huang, Y.-C. Ball Tracking and Trajectory Prediction for Table-Tennis Robots. *Sensors* **2020**, *20*, 333. [CrossRef] [PubMed]
23. Gomez Gonzalez, S. Real Time Probabilistic Models for Robot Trajectories. Ph.D. Thesis, Technische Universität Darmstadt, Darmstadt, Germany, 2020.
24. Gomez-Gonzalez, S.; Prokudin, S.; Schölkopf, B.; Peters, J. Real Time Trajectory Prediction Using Deep Conditional Generative Models. *IEEE Robot. Autom. Lett.* **2020**, *5*, 970–976. [CrossRef]
25. Gomez-Gonzalez, S.; Nemmour, Y.; Schölkopf, B.; Peters, J. Reliable Real-Time Ball Tracking for Robot Table Tennis. *Robotics* **2019**, *8*, 90. [CrossRef]
26. Birbach, O.; Frese, U.; Bäuml, B. Realtime Perception for Catching a Flying Ball with a Mobile Humanoid. In Proceedings of the 2011 IEEE International Conference on Robotics and Automation, Shanghai, China, 9–13 May 2011; pp. 5955–5962.
27. Cigliano, P.; Lippiello, V.; Ruggiero, F.; Siciliano, B. Robotic Ball Catching with an Eye-in-Hand Single-Camera System. *IEEE Trans. Control Syst. Technol.* **2015**, *23*, 1657–1671. [CrossRef]
28. Möller, T.; Kraft, H.; Frey, J.; Albrecht, M.; Lange, R. Robust 3D Measurement with PMD Sensors. *Range Imaging Day* **2005**, *7*, 8.
29. Barteit, D.; Frank, H.; Kupzog, F. Accurate Prediction of Interception Positions for Catching Thrown Objects in Production Systems. In Proceedings of the 2008 6th IEEE International Conference on Industrial Informatics, Daejeon, Korea, 13–16 July 2008; pp. 893–898.
30. Barteit, D.; Frank, H.; Pongratz, M.; Kupzog, F. Measuring the Intersection of a Thrown Object with a Vertical Plane. In Proceedings of the 2009 7th IEEE International Conference on Industrial Informatics, Cardiff, UK, 23–26 June 2009; pp. 680–685.
31. Barteit, D.F. Tracking of Thrown Objects: Catching of Mechanically Thrown Parts for Transport in Manufacturing. Ph.D. Thesis, Technische Universität Wien, Vienna, Austria, 2010.
32. Mironov, K.; Pongratz, M. Fast kNN-Based Prediction for the Trajectory of a Thrown Body. In Proceedings of the 2016 24th Mediterranean Conference on Control and Automation (MED), Athens, Greece, 21–26 June 2016; pp. 512–517.
33. Mironov, K.; Vladimirova, I.; Pongratz, M. Processing and Forecasting the Trajectory of a Thrown Object Measured by the Stereo Vision System. *IFAC-PapersOnLine* **2015**, *48*, 28–35. [CrossRef]

34. Mironov, K.; Pongratz, M. Applying Neural Networks for Prediction of Flying Objects Trajectory. *Bull. Ufa State Aviat. Tech. Univ.* **2013**, *17*, 33–37.
35. Gayanov, R.; Mironov, K.; Kurennov, D. Estimating the Trajectory of a Thrown Object from Video Signal with Use of Genetic Programmin. In Proceedings of the 2017 IEEE International Symposium on Signal Processing and Information Technology (ISSPIT), Bilbao, Spain, 18–20 December 2017; pp. 134–138.
36. Gayanov, R.; Mironov, K.; Mukhametshin, R.; Vokhmintsev, A.; Kurennov, D. Transportation of Small Objects by Robotic Throwing and Catching: Applying Genetic Programming for Trajectory Estimation. *IFAC-PapersOnLine* **2018**, *51*, 533–537. [CrossRef]
37. Mironov, K.; Gayanov, R.; Kurennov, D. Observing and Forecasting the Trajectory of the Thrown Body with Use of Genetic Programming. *Adv. Sci. Technol. Eng. Syst.* **2019**, *1*, 248–257. [CrossRef]
38. Mironov, K. Transport by Robotic Throwing and Catching: Accurate Stereo Tracking of the Spherical Object. In Proceedings of the 2017 International Conference on Industrial Engineering, Applications and Manufacturing (ICIEAM), St. Petersburg, Russia, 16–19 May 2017; pp. 1–6.
39. Mehta, R.; Alam, F.; Subic, A. Review of Tennis Ball Aerodynamics. *Sports Technol.* **2008**, *1*, 7–16. [CrossRef]
40. Alam, F.; Tio, W.; Watkins, S.; Subic, A.; Naser, J. Effects of Spin on Tennis Ball Aerodynamics: An Experimental and Computational Study. In Proceedings of the 16th Australasian Fluid Mechanics Conference Crown Plaza, Gold Coast, Australia, 2–7 December 2007.

sensors

MDPI

Article

Indirect-Neural-Approximation-Based Fault-Tolerant Integrated Attitude and Position Control of Spacecraft Proximity Operations

Fawaz W. Alsaade [1], Qijia Yao [2,*], Mohammed S. Al-zahrani [3], Ali S. Alzahrani [4] and Hadi Jahanshahi [5]

1 Department of Computer Science, College of Computer Sciences and Information Technology, King Faisal University, Al-Ahsa 31982, Saudi Arabia; falsaade@kfu.edu.sa
2 School of Aerospace Engineering, Beijing Institute of Technology, Beijing 100081, China
3 Department of Computer Networks and Communications, College of Computer Sciences and Information Technology, King Faisal University, Al-Ahsa 31982, Saudi Arabia; malzahrani@kfu.edu.sa
4 Department of Computer Engineering, College of Computer Sciences and Information Technology, King Faisal University, Al-Ahsa 31982, Saudi Arabia; aalzahrani@kfu.edu.sa
5 Department of Mechanical Engineering, University of Manitoba, Winnipeg, MB R3T 5V6, Canada; jahanshahi.hadi90@gmail.com
* Correspondence: qijia_yao@126.com

Citation: Alsaade, F.W.; Yao, Q.; Al-zahrani, M.S.; Alzahrani, A.S.; Jahanshahi, H. Indirect-Neural-Approximation-Based Fault-Tolerant Integrated Attitude and Position Control of Spacecraft Proximity Operations. *Sensors* **2022**, *22*, 1726. https://doi.org/10.3390/s22051726

Academic Editors: Luige Vladareanu, Hongnian Yu, Hongbo Wang and Yongfei Feng

Received: 4 January 2022
Accepted: 18 February 2022
Published: 23 February 2022

Abstract: In this paper, a neural adaptive fault-tolerant control scheme is proposed for the integrated attitude and position control of spacecraft proximity operations in the presence of unknown parameters, disturbances, and actuator faults. The proposed controller is made up of a relative attitude control law and a relative position control law. Both the relative attitude control law and relative position control law are designed by adopting the neural networks (NNs) to approximate the upper bound of the lumped unknowns. Benefiting from the indirect neural approximation, the proposed controller does not need any model information for feedback. In addition, only two adaptive parameters are required for the indirect neural approximation, and the online calculation burden of the proposed controller is therefore significantly reduced. Lyapunov analysis shows that the overall closed-loop system is ultimately uniformly bounded. The proposed controller can ensure the relative attitude, angular velocity, position, and velocity stabilize into the small neighborhoods around the origin. Lastly, the effectiveness and superior performance of the proposed control scheme are confirmed by a simulated example.

Keywords: neural adaptive control; fault-tolerant control; integrated attitude and position control; spacecraft proximity operations; indirect neural approximation; Lyapunov analysis

1. Introduction

Nowadays, with the rapid development of sensing and control technologies, space missions have become increasingly complicated. The spacecraft proximity operation plays an important role in various space missions, such as rendezvous and docking, active debris removal, and on-orbit servicing. The relative attitude and position control is a critical technique for spacecraft proximity operations. During the proximity operations, the chaser and target are inevitably affected by uncertain parameters and disturbances. Even worse, the parameters of the target may be fully unknown for noncooperative proximity operations. In addition, the chaser also frequently suffers from actuator faults due to the harsh space environment. The presence of unknown parameters, disturbances, and actuator faults bring great difficulty to the relative attitude and position control of spacecraft proximity operations. Traditionally, the spacecraft relative attitude and position control systems are often designed independently. However, the inherent couplings between the relative attitude and position are neglected in this way and these controllers cannot be directly applied to the spacecraft proximity operations, especially when high control accuracy is required. The integrated attitude and position control based on the six-degree-of-freedom (6-DOF) dynamic model of spacecraft proximity operations is an effective solution to this problem.

Until recently, many relevant results have been reported for the integrated attitude and position control of spacecraft proximity operations. Singla et al. [1] designed a model reference adaptive output feedback control law for the spacecraft rendezvous and docking under measurement uncertainties. Kristiansen et al. [2] presented three nonlinear control solutions for the 6-DOF spacecraft coordination control based on the integrator backstepping and passivity-based control, respectively. In [3,4], an integrated nonlinear optimal control approach was developed for the spacecraft proximity operations. Zhang and Duan [5] proposed a robust adaptive backstepping control scheme for the integrated translational and rotational motion of spacecraft with actuator misalignment. In [6,7], several robust optimal sliding mode control methods were carried out for the coupled attitude and position maneuvers of spacecraft. Sun and Huo [8] designed a 6-DOF integrated adaptive backstepping controller for the spacecraft proximity operations under uncertainties. In [9,10], integrated robust adaptive control approaches were developed for the relative position tracking and attitude synchronization for spacecraft rendezvous. In [11,12], disturbance observer-based robust control approaches were proposed for the spacecraft proximity and docking with input saturation. Hu et al. [13] presented a robust fault-tolerant tracking control scheme for the spacecraft proximity operations by utilizing the adaptive sliding mode control technique. Wang and Ji [14] designed two backstepping control schemes for the relative motion control of spacecraft rendezvous based on the input-to-state stable property and finite-time control technique, respectively. In [15], an adaptive nonlinear state feedback control method was proposed for the fault-tolerant constrained pose control of cooperative spacecraft rendezvous and docking. Zhou et al. [16] developed an adaptive sliding mode method for the robust attitude and position tracking of spacecraft proximity operations by integrating with an unscented Kalman filter. In [17–19], several adaptive nonsingular terminal sliding mode control laws were designed for the fixed-time, 6-DOF tracking control of noncooperative spacecraft fly-around missions. In addition, there have been also some research studies concerned with 6-DOF integrated controls in spacecraft based on the dual quaternion representation [20–27].

It should be noted that most of the above controllers require prior knowledge of nominal model information for feedback. Nevertheless, the physical parameters of the chaser and the target may be fully unknown in some extreme cases. The intelligent approximation is an efficient tool to construct the model-free controllers, owing to the powerful learning capability of the neural network (NN) and fuzzy logic system. By adopting the NNs or fuzzy logic systems to approximate the lumped unknowns, the intelligent control does not need any model information for feedback. In [28,29], robust adaptive backstepping NN control strategies were presented for the spacecraft rendezvous and docking with input saturation. Sun et al. [30] developed an adaptive fuzzy backstepping controller for the pose tracking of spacecraft rendezvous and proximity maneuvers under uncertainties. However, all of the above intelligent controllers involve a large number of adaptive parameters, which restricts their applications in practical engineering, especially considering the onboard computer has limited online calculation capability.

Motivated by the above discussions, this paper proposes a neural adaptive fault-tolerant control scheme for the integrated attitude and position control of spacecraft proximity operations in the presence of unknown parameters, disturbances, and actuator faults. The proposed controller is made up of a relative attitude control law and a relative position control law. In comparison with most of the existing investigations, the main contributions of this research are summarized as follows:

- Both the relative attitude control law and relative position control law are designed by integrating with the neural approximation. Benefiting from this design, the proposed controller is model-free and strongly robust against the lumped unknowns in 6-DOF dynamics;

- Rather than the conventional intelligent approximation [28–30], in which the NNs and fuzzy logic systems are introduced to directly approximate the lumped unknowns, the indirect neural approximation is exploited in this paper by adopting the NNs to approximate the upper bound of the lumped unknowns. In this way, only two adaptive parameters are required for the indirect neural approximation, and the online calculation burden of the proposed controller is therefore significantly reduced;
- Lyapunov analysis shows that the overall closed-loop system is ultimately uniformly bounded. The proposed controller can ensure that the relative attitude, angular velocity, position, and velocity stabilize into the small neighborhoods around the origin.

The remainder of this paper is arranged as follows: Section 2 describes the problem and gives some preliminaries. Section 3 introduces the control methodology and provides the Lyapunov analysis. Section 4 performs a simulated example. Lastly, Section 5 presents the main conclusions of this study.

2. Problem Statement and Preliminaries

2.1. The 6-DOF Dynamics of Spacecraft Proximity Operations

Consider the spacecraft proximity operation system depicted in Figure 1, in which a chaser is approaching a freely tumbling target. P denotes the desired docking point, which is fixed with respect to the target. Three coordinate frames are introduced to describe the 6-DOF dynamics of the spacecraft proximity operation. They are the earth-centered inertial frame F_I, the chaser's body-fixed frame F_c, and the target's body-fixed frame F_t, respectively.

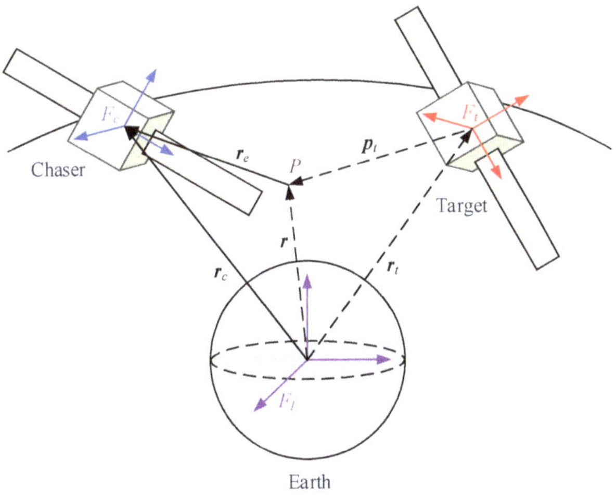

Figure 1. Diagram of the spacecraft proximity operation system.

The modified Rodrigues parameters (MRPs) are utilized to represent the attitude orientation of the chaser. Then, the attitude and position dynamics of the chaser can be expressed in frame F_c as

$$\begin{cases} \dot{\boldsymbol{\sigma}} = \boldsymbol{G}(\boldsymbol{\sigma})\boldsymbol{\omega}, \\ \boldsymbol{J}\dot{\boldsymbol{\omega}} + \boldsymbol{S}(\boldsymbol{\omega})\boldsymbol{J}\boldsymbol{\omega} = \boldsymbol{\Gamma}_{\tau}\boldsymbol{u}_{\tau} + \boldsymbol{d}_{\tau}, \\ \dot{\boldsymbol{r}} = \boldsymbol{v} - \boldsymbol{S}(\boldsymbol{\omega})\boldsymbol{r}, \\ m\dot{\boldsymbol{v}} + m\boldsymbol{S}(\boldsymbol{\omega})\boldsymbol{v} = \boldsymbol{\Gamma}_f\boldsymbol{u}_f + \boldsymbol{d}_f, \end{cases} \tag{1}$$

where $\boldsymbol{G}(\boldsymbol{\sigma}) = \frac{1}{2}\left(\frac{1-\boldsymbol{\sigma}^{\mathrm{T}}\boldsymbol{\sigma}}{2}\mathbf{I}_3 + \boldsymbol{S}(\boldsymbol{\sigma}) + \boldsymbol{\sigma}\boldsymbol{\sigma}^{\mathrm{T}}\right) \in \mathbb{R}^{3\times 3}$. $\boldsymbol{\sigma} \in \mathbb{R}^3$, $\boldsymbol{\omega} \in \mathbb{R}^3$, $\boldsymbol{r} \in \mathbb{R}^3$, and $\boldsymbol{v} \in \mathbb{R}^3$ are the attitude, angular velocity, position, and velocity of the chaser with respect to the earth center in frame F_c. $\boldsymbol{u}_{\tau} \in \mathbb{R}^3$ and $\boldsymbol{u}_f \in \mathbb{R}^3$ are the control torques and forces produced by the actuators. $d_\tau \in \mathbb{R}^3$ and $d_f \in \mathbb{R}^3$ are the disturbance torques and forces acting on the chaser. $J \in \mathbb{R}^{3\times 3}$ and $m \in \mathbb{R}$ denote the inertia matrix and mass of the chaser. The notation $S(\omega)$ stands for the skew-symmetric matrix of ω, denoted as

$$S(\omega) = \begin{bmatrix} 0 & -\omega_3 & \omega_2 \\ \omega_3 & 0 & -\omega_1 \\ -\omega_2 & \omega_1 & 0 \end{bmatrix}. \tag{2}$$

where $\Gamma_\tau = \text{diag}\{\gamma_{\tau 1}, \gamma_{\tau 2}, \gamma_{\tau 3}\}$ and $\Gamma_f = \text{diag}\left\{\gamma_{f1}, \gamma_{f2}, \gamma_{f3}\right\}$ are the actuator health factor matrices, with $0 \le \gamma_{\tau i} \le 1$ and $0 \le \gamma_{fi} \le 1$ $(i = 1,2,3)$. The case $\gamma_{\tau i} = 1$ and $\gamma_{fi} = 1$ means the corresponding control torque and force are healthy. The case $0 < \gamma_{\tau i} < 1$ and $0 < \gamma_{fi} < 1$ means the corresponding control torque and force are partially faulty. The case $\gamma_{\tau i} = 0$ and $\gamma_{fi} = 0$ means the corresponding control torque and force are completely failed. In this paper, the chaser is assumed to be fully actuated with $0 < \gamma_{\tau i} \le 1$ and $0 < \gamma_{fi} \le 1$ $(i = 1,2,3)$.

Similarly, the attitude and position dynamics of the target can be expressed in frame F_t as

$$\begin{cases} \dot{\sigma}_t = G(\sigma_t)\omega_t, \\ J_t\dot{\omega}_t + S(\omega_t)J_t\omega_t = h_\tau, \\ \dot{r}_t = v_t - S(\omega_t)r_t, \\ m_t\dot{v}_t + m_tS(\omega_t)v_t = h_f, \end{cases} \tag{3}$$

where $\sigma_t \in \mathbb{R}^3$, $\omega_t \in \mathbb{R}^3$, $r_t \in \mathbb{R}^3$, and $v_t \in \mathbb{R}^3$ are the attitude, angular velocity, position, and velocity of the target with respect to the earth center in frame F_t. $h_\tau \in \mathbb{R}^3$ and $h_f \in \mathbb{R}^3$ are the disturbance torques and forces acted on the target. $J_t \in \mathbb{R}^{3\times 3}$ and $m_t \in \mathbb{R}$ denote the inertia matrix and mass of the target.

According to the geometric relationship in Figure 1, the position and velocity of the point P with respect to the earth center in frame F_t can be expressed as

$$\begin{cases} r_p = r_t + p_t, \\ v_p = v_t + S(\omega_t)p_t, \end{cases} \tag{4}$$

where p_t is the constant position vector of the point P with respect to the target in frame F_t. The relative attitude, angular velocity, position, and velocity of the target with respect to the chaser can be defined in frame F_p as

$$\begin{cases} \sigma_e = \sigma \otimes \sigma_t^{-1} = \frac{(1-\sigma_t^{\mathrm{T}}\sigma_t)\sigma - (1-\sigma^{\mathrm{T}}\sigma)\sigma_t - 2S(\sigma_t)\sigma}{1+\sigma_t^{\mathrm{T}}\sigma_t\sigma^{\mathrm{T}}\sigma + 2\sigma_t^{\mathrm{T}}\sigma}, \\ \omega_e = \omega - R(\sigma_e)\omega_t, \\ r_e = r - R(\sigma_e)r_p, \\ v_e = v - R(\sigma_e)v_p, \end{cases} \tag{5}$$

where $R(\sigma_e) = \mathbf{I}_3 + \frac{8S^2(\sigma_e) - 4(1-\sigma_e^{\mathrm{T}}\sigma_e)S(\sigma_e)}{(1+\sigma_e^{\mathrm{T}}\sigma_e)^2} \in \mathbb{R}^{3\times 3}$ is the rotation matrix from frame F_t to frame F_p. The matrix $R(\sigma_e)$ has the property $\dot{R}(\sigma_e) = -S(\omega_e)R(\sigma_e)$.

Note that $\dot{r}_p = v_p - S(\omega_t)r_p$ and $\dot{\omega}_t = -J_t^{-1}S(R^{\mathrm{T}}(\omega - \omega_e))J_tR^{\mathrm{T}}(\omega - \omega_e) + J_t^{-1}\omega_t$. Substituting (1), (3), and (4) into (5), the relative attitude and position dynamics of the target with respect to the chaser can be obtained in frame F_p as

$$\dot{\sigma}_e = G(\sigma_e)\omega_e, \tag{6}$$

$$J\dot{\omega}_e = \Gamma_\tau u_\tau + \zeta_\tau, \tag{7}$$

$$\dot{r}_e = v_e - S(\omega)r_e, \tag{8}$$

$$m\dot{v}_e = \Gamma_f u_f + \zeta_f, \tag{9}$$

where ζ_τ and ζ_f are the lumped unknowns in the relative attitude and position dynamics, given as

$$\zeta_\tau = -S(\omega)J\omega + S(\omega)J\omega_e - JR(\sigma_e)J_t^{-1}S\Big(R^{\mathrm{T}}(\sigma_e)(\omega - \omega_e)\Big)J_tR^{\mathrm{T}}(\sigma_e)(\omega - \omega_e) - d_\tau + JR(\sigma_e)J_t^{-1}h_\tau, \tag{10}$$

$$\begin{aligned}\zeta_f = &-mS(\omega)v_e - mS^2(\omega - \omega_e)R(\sigma_e)p_t - mR(\sigma_e)S(p_t)J_t^{-1}S(R^{\mathrm{T}}(\sigma_e)(\omega - \omega_e))J_tR^{\mathrm{T}}(\sigma_e)(\omega - \omega_e)\\ &+d_f - \tfrac{mR(\sigma_e)h_f}{m_t} + mR(\sigma_e)S(p_t)J_t^{-1}h_\tau.\end{aligned} \tag{11}$$

Remark 1. *From the 6-DOF dynamic model of spacecraft proximity operations (8) and (9), the relative translational motion of the target with respect to the chaser is heavily affected by the relative rotational motion due to the inherent coupling between the relative attitude and position.*

2.2. Purpose

The purpose of this research is to design a controller for the spacecraft proximity operation system such that relative attitude σ_e, angular velocity ω_e, position r_e, and velocity v_e can stabilize into the small neighborhoods around the origin, even in the presence of unknown parameters, disturbances, and actuator faults.

2.3. Neural Approximation

Lemma 1. Ref. [31] *For any continuous nonlinear function $f(\mathbf{Z})$, $\mathbf{Z} \in \mathbb{R}^n$, it can be approximated by a radial basis function NN (RBFNN) as*

$$f(\mathbf{Z}) = \mathbf{W}^{*\mathrm{T}}\mathbf{\Phi}(\mathbf{Z}) + \varepsilon(\mathbf{Z}), \tag{12}$$

where $\mathbf{W}^* \in \mathbb{R}^N$ is the ideal RBFNN weight, $\mathbf{\Phi}(\mathbf{Z}) = [\phi_1(\mathbf{Z}), \phi_2(\mathbf{Z}), \ldots, \phi_N(\mathbf{Z})]^{\mathrm{T}}$ is the basis function vector, $\varepsilon(\mathbf{Z})$ is the identification error satisfying $|\varepsilon(\mathbf{Z})| \le \bar{\varepsilon}$, $\bar{\varepsilon}$ is a positive constant, and N is the number of RBFNN nodes. Moreover, $\varphi_i(\mathbf{Z})$ is commonly chosen as the Gaussian function

$$\varphi_i(\mathbf{Z}) = \exp\Big(-\|\mathbf{Z} - \mathbf{c}_i\|^2 / w_i^2\Big),\ i = 1, 2, \ldots, N, \tag{13}$$

where $\mathbf{c}_i = [c_{i1}, c_{i2}, \ldots, c_{in}]^{\mathrm{T}} \in \mathbb{R}^n$, and w_i are the center and width of the Gaussian function, respectively.

3. Control Design Methodology

3.1. Architecture of the Whole Control Design

The structure of the proposed neural adaptive fault-tolerant control scheme is shown in Figure 2. Specifically, the proposed controller is made up of a relative position control law and a relative attitude control law. Both the relative position control law and relative attitude control law are designed by adopting the NNs to approximate the upper bound of the lumped unknowns. The ultimate uniform boundedness of the overall closed-loop system is achieved through Lyapunov analysis.

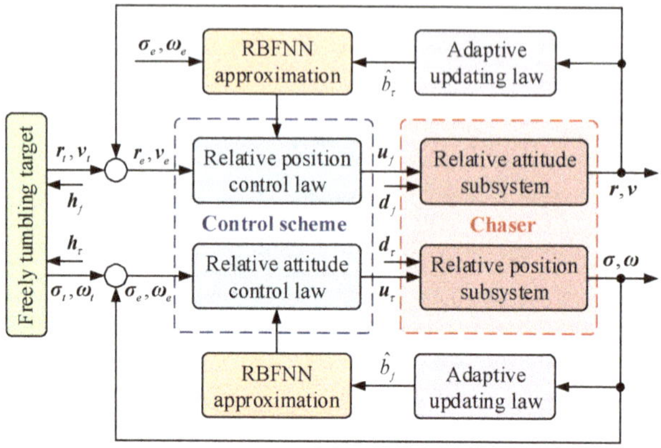

Figure 2. Architecture of the whole control design.

3.2. Relative Attitude Control Design

First, consider the relative attitude subsystem described as (6) and (7). Introduce the following filtered error:

$$s_1 = \omega_e + \alpha_1 \sigma_e, \tag{14}$$

where $\alpha_1 > 0$. Evaluating the time differentiation of s_1 yields

$$J\dot{s}_1 = \Gamma_\tau u_\tau + \xi_\tau, \tag{15}$$

where $\xi_\tau = \zeta_\tau + \alpha_1 G(\sigma_e)\omega_e$. Define the input variable $Z_\tau = \left[\sigma_e^{\mathrm{T}}, \omega_e^{\mathrm{T}}\right]^{\mathrm{T}}$. By Lemma 1, the lumped uncertainty can be expressed as

$$\xi_\tau = W_\tau^{*\mathrm{T}} \Phi_\tau(Z_\tau) + \varepsilon_\tau(Z_\tau), \tag{16}$$

where $W_\tau^* \in \mathbb{R}^{N\times 3}$ is the ideal RBFNN weight, $\Phi_\tau(Z_\tau) \in \mathbb{R}^N$ is the Gaussian basis function vector, $\varepsilon_\tau(Z_\tau) \in \mathbb{R}^3$ is the approximation error satisfying $\|\varepsilon_\tau(Z_\tau)\| \le \bar{\varepsilon}_\tau$, $\bar{\varepsilon}_\tau$ is a positive constant, and N is the number of RBFNN nodes. Note that $\|W_\tau^*\| \le \overline{W}_\tau$. Substituting it into (16) yields

$$\begin{aligned} \|\xi_\tau\| &\le \|W_\tau^*\|\|\Phi_\tau(Z_\tau)\| + \|\varepsilon_\tau(Z_\tau)\| \\ &\le b_\tau \Phi_\tau, \end{aligned} \tag{17}$$

where $b_\tau = \max\{\overline{W}_\tau, \bar{\varepsilon}_\tau\}$ is an unknown constant, and $\Phi_\tau = \|\Phi_\tau(Z_\tau)\| + 1$ is a known function. Then, the relative attitude control law is designed as

$$u_\tau = -k_1 s_1 - \eta_1 \hat{b}_\tau \Phi_\tau^2 s_1, \tag{18}$$

where $k_1 > 0$, $\eta_1 > 0$, and $\hat{b}_\tau$ is the estimation of b_τ. Moreover, the adaptive updating law is designed as

$$\dot{\hat{b}}_\tau = -\mu_1 \hat{b}_\tau + \eta_1 \Phi_\tau^2 \|s_\tau\|^2, \tag{19}$$

where $\mu_1 > 0$.

Theorem 1. *When the relative attitude control law (18) and the adaptive updating law (19) are employed to the relative attitude subsystem described as (6) and (7), the overall closed-loop system is ultimately uniformly bounded and the relative attitude* σ_e, and angular velocity ω_e *can stabilize into the small neighborhoods around the origin.*

Proof. Introduce the following Lyapunov function:

$$V_1 = \frac{1}{2}s_1^{\mathrm{T}} J s_1 + \frac{1}{2\gamma_{\tau \min}} \widetilde{b}_\tau^2, \tag{20}$$

where $\gamma_{\tau\min} = \min\{\gamma_{\tau 1}, \gamma_{\tau 2}, \gamma_{\tau 3}\}$, and $\widetilde{b}_\tau = b_\tau - \gamma_{\tau\min}\hat{b}_\tau$ denotes the estimation error of b_τ. Evaluating the time differentiation of V_1 yields

$$\begin{aligned} \dot{V}_1 &= s_1^{\mathrm{T}} J \dot{s}_1 - \widetilde{b}_\tau \dot{\hat{b}}_\tau \\ &= s_1^{\mathrm{T}}(\Gamma_\tau u_\tau + \xi_\tau) - \widetilde{b}_\tau \dot{\hat{b}}_\tau. \end{aligned} \tag{21}$$

Substituting the relative attitude control law (18) and the adaptive updating law (19), we have

$$\begin{aligned} \dot{V}_1 &= s_1^{\mathrm{T}}\left(\Gamma_\tau\left(-k_1 s_1 - \eta_1 \hat{b}_\tau \Phi_\tau^2 s_1\right) + \xi_\tau\right) - \widetilde{b}_\tau\left(-\mu_1 \hat{b}_\tau + \eta_1 \Phi_\tau^2 \|s_\tau\|^2\right) \\ &= -\gamma_{\tau\min} k_1 \|s_1\|^2 - \eta_1 b_\tau \Phi_\tau^2 \|s_1\|^2 + s_1^{\mathrm{T}} \xi_\tau + \mu_1 \widetilde{b}_\tau \hat{b}_\tau. \end{aligned} \tag{22}$$

Consider the following inequalities:

$$s_1^{\mathrm{T}} \xi_\tau \le b_\tau \Phi_\tau \|s_1\|^2 \le \eta_1 b_\tau \Phi_\tau^2 \|s_1\|^2 + \frac{1}{4\eta_1}, \tag{23}$$

$$\mu_1 \widetilde{b}_\tau \hat{b}_\tau = \frac{\mu_1}{\gamma_{\tau\min}} \widetilde{b}_\tau\left(b_\tau - \widetilde{b}_\tau\right) \le \frac{\mu_1}{2\gamma_{\tau\min}}\left(b_\tau^2 - \widetilde{b}_\tau^2\right). \tag{24}$$

Substituting (23) and (24) into (22) yields

$$\begin{aligned} \dot{V}_1 &\le -\gamma_{\tau\min} k_1 \|s_1\|^2 - \tfrac{\mu_1}{2\gamma_{\tau\min}} \widetilde{b}_\tau^2 + \tfrac{1}{4\eta_1} + \tfrac{\mu_1}{2\gamma_{\tau\min}} b_\tau^2 \\ &\le -\kappa_1 V_1 + \vartheta_1, \end{aligned} \tag{25}$$

where $\kappa_1 = \min\left\{\frac{2\gamma_{\tau\min} k_1}{\lambda_{\max}(J)}, \mu_1\right\}$, and $\vartheta_1 = \frac{1}{4\eta_1} + \frac{\mu_1}{2\gamma_{\tau\min}} b_\tau^2$. Solving inequality (25), we further have

$$V_1 \le \left(V_1(0) - \frac{\vartheta_1}{\kappa_1}\right) e^{-\kappa_1 t} + \frac{\vartheta_1}{\kappa_1}. \tag{26}$$

Combining with the definition of V_1, it follows that the overall closed-loop system is ultimately uniformly bounded, and the error signals s_1 and $\widetilde{b}_\tau$ can stabilize into the small neighborhoods around the origin. Considering the definition of s_1, this further implies that the relative attitude σ_e and angular velocity ω_e can stabilize into the small neighborhoods around the origin. The proof of Theorem 1 is thus finished. □

3.3. *Relative Position Control Design*

Then, consider the relative position subsystem described as (8) and (9). Introduce the following filtered error:

$$s_2 = v_e + \alpha_2 r_e, \tag{27}$$

where $\alpha_2 > 0$. Evaluating the time differentiation of s_2 yields

$$m\dot{s}_2 = \Gamma_f u_f + \xi_f, \tag{28}$$

where $\xi_\tau = \zeta_\tau + \alpha_2(v_e - S(\omega) r_e)$. Define the input variable $Z_f = \left[\sigma_e^{\mathrm{T}}, \omega_e^{\mathrm{T}} p_e^{\mathrm{T}}, v_e^{\mathrm{T}}\right]^{\mathrm{T}}$. By Lemma 1, the lumped uncertainty can be expressed as

$$\xi_f = W_f^{*\mathrm{T}} \Phi_f\left(Z_f\right) + \varepsilon_f\left(Z_f\right), \tag{29}$$

where $W_f^* \in \mathbb{R}^{N\times 3}$ is the ideal RBFNN weight, $\Phi_f\left(Z_f\right) \in \mathbb{R}^N$ is the Gaussian basis function vector, $\varepsilon_f\left(Z_f\right) \in \mathbb{R}^3$ is the approximation error satisfying $\|\varepsilon_f\left(Z_f\right)\| \le \bar{\varepsilon}_f$, $\bar{\varepsilon}_f$

is a positive constant, and N is the number of RBFNN nodes. Note that $\|\mathbf{W}_f^*\| \leq \overline{W}_f$. Substituting it into (29) yields

$$\begin{aligned} \|\boldsymbol{\xi}_f\| &\leq \|\mathbf{W}_f^*\|\|\mathbf{\Phi}_f\left(\mathbf{Z}_f\right)\| + \|\varepsilon_f\left(\mathbf{Z}_f\right)\| \\ &\leq b_f \mathbf{\Phi}_f, \end{aligned} \tag{30}$$

where $b_f = \max\left\{\overline{W}_f, \overline{\varepsilon}_f\right\}$ is an unknown constant, and $\mathbf{\Phi}_f = \|\mathbf{\Phi}_f\left(\mathbf{Z}_f\right)\| + 1$ is a known function. Then, the relative position control law is designed as

$$\boldsymbol{u}_f = -k_2 \boldsymbol{s}_2 - \eta_2 \hat{b}_f \mathbf{\Phi}_f^2 \boldsymbol{s}_2, \tag{31}$$

where $k_2 > 0$, $\eta_2 > 0$, and $\hat{b}_f$ is the estimation of b_f. Moreover, the adaptive updating law is designed as

$$\dot{\hat{b}}_f = -\mu_2 \hat{b}_f + \eta_2 \mathbf{\Phi}_f^2 \|\boldsymbol{s}_f\|^2, \tag{32}$$

where $\mu_2 > 0$.

Theorem 2. *When the relative position control law (31) and the adaptive updating law (32) are employed to the relative position subsystem described as (8) and (9), the overall closed-loop system is ultimately uniformly bounded and the relative position $\boldsymbol{r}_e$,* and velocity $\boldsymbol{v}_e$ *can stabilize into the small neighborhoods around the origin.*

Proof. Introduce the following Lyapunov function:

$$V_2 = \frac{1}{2} m \boldsymbol{s}_2^{\mathrm{T}} \boldsymbol{s}_2 + \frac{1}{2\gamma_{f\min}} \widetilde{b}_f^2, \tag{33}$$

where $\gamma_{f\min} = \min\left\{\gamma_{f1}, \gamma_{f2}, \gamma_{f3}\right\}$, and $\widetilde{b}_f = b_f - \gamma_{f\min} \hat{b}_f$ denotes the estimation error of b_f. Evaluating the time differentiation of V_2 yields

$$\begin{aligned} \dot{V}_2 &= m \boldsymbol{s}_2^{\mathrm{T}} \dot{\boldsymbol{s}}_2 - \widetilde{b}_f \dot{\hat{b}}_f \\ &= \boldsymbol{s}_2^{\mathrm{T}} \left(\mathbf{\Gamma}_f \boldsymbol{u}_f + \boldsymbol{\xi}_f\right) - \widetilde{b}_f \dot{\hat{b}}_f. \end{aligned} \tag{34}$$

Substituting the relative position control law (31) and the adaptive updating law (32), we have

$$\begin{aligned} \dot{V}_2 &= \boldsymbol{s}_2^{\mathrm{T}} \left(\mathbf{\Gamma}_f \left(-k_2 \boldsymbol{s}_2 - \eta_2 \hat{b}_f \mathbf{\Phi}_f^2 \boldsymbol{s}_2\right) + \boldsymbol{\xi}_f\right) - \widetilde{b}_f \left(-\mu_2 \hat{b}_f + \eta_2 \mathbf{\Phi}_f^2 \|\boldsymbol{s}_f\|^2\right) \\ &= -\gamma_{f\min} k_2 \|\boldsymbol{s}_2\|^2 - \eta_2 b_f \mathbf{\Phi}_f^2 \|\boldsymbol{s}_2\|^2 + \boldsymbol{s}_2^{\mathrm{T}} \boldsymbol{\xi}_f + \mu_2 \widetilde{b}_f \hat{b}_f. \end{aligned} \tag{35}$$

Consider the following inequalities:

$$\boldsymbol{s}_2^{\mathrm{T}} \boldsymbol{\xi}_f \leq b_f \mathbf{\Phi}_f \|\boldsymbol{s}_2\|^2 \leq \eta_2 b_f \mathbf{\Phi}_f^2 \|\boldsymbol{s}_2\|^2 + \frac{1}{4\eta_2}, \tag{36}$$

$$\mu_2 \widetilde{b}_f \hat{b}_f = \frac{\mu_2}{\gamma_{f\min}} \widetilde{b}_f \left(b_f - \widetilde{b}_f\right) \leq \frac{\mu_2}{2\gamma_{f\min}} \left(b_f^2 - \widetilde{b}_f^2\right). \tag{37}$$

Substituting (36) and (37) into (35) yields

$$\begin{aligned} \dot{V}_2 &\leq -\gamma_{f\min} k_2 \|\boldsymbol{s}_2\|^2 - \tfrac{\mu_2}{2\gamma_{f\min}} \widetilde{b}_f^2 + \tfrac{1}{4\eta_2} + \tfrac{\mu_2}{2\gamma_{f\min}} b_f^2 \\ &\leq -\kappa_2 V_2 + \vartheta_2, \end{aligned} \tag{38}$$

where $\kappa_2 = \min\left\{\frac{2\gamma_{f\min} k_2}{m}, \mu_2\right\}$ and $\vartheta_2 = \frac{1}{4\eta_2} + \frac{\mu_2}{2\gamma_{f\min}} b_f^2$. Solving inequality (38), we further have

$$V_2 \leq \left(V_2(0) - \frac{\vartheta_2}{\kappa_2}\right)e^{-\kappa_2 t} + \frac{\vartheta_2}{\kappa_2}. \quad (39)$$

Combined with the definition of V_2, it follows that the overall closed-loop system is ultimately uniformly bounded, and error signals s_2 and $\tilde{b}_f$ can stabilize into the small neighborhoods around the origin. Considering the definition of s_2, this further implies that the relative position $\boldsymbol{r}_e$ and velocity $\boldsymbol{v}_e$ can stabilize into the small neighborhoods around the origin. The proof of Theorem 2 is thus finished. □

Remark 2. *In the conventional intelligent approximation [28–30], the NNs and fuzzy logic systems are introduced to directly approximate the lumped unknowns, and the number of the adaptive parameters is* $2 \times 3N$. *Alternatively, the indirect neural approximation is exploited in this paper by adopting NNs to approximate the upper bound of the lumped unknowns. In this way, only two adaptive parameters,* $\hat{b}_\tau$ and $\hat{b}_f$, *are required for the indirect neural approximation, and the online calculation burden of the proposed controller is therefore significantly reduced. Actually, the indirect neural approximation makes the proposed controller more suitable for practical engineering, especially considering the onboard computer has limited online calculation capability.*

Remark 3. *According to Theorems 1 and 2, the proposed controller can ensure the relative attitude, angular velocity, position, and velocity stabilize into the small neighborhoods around the origin. From (26) and (39), it follows that the small neighborhoods around the origin are adjustable. If we set the parameters* α_1, α_2, k_1, and k_2 *as large as required, the small neighborhoods can be made sufficiently small.*

Remark 4. *It is noteworthy that the RBFNN utilized for intelligent control in this paper can also be replaced by some other approximation tools, such as recurrent NNs, wavelet NNs, and fuzzy logic systems. Moreover, adaptive dynamic programming is an effective methodology for the optimal control of unknown nonlinear systems with the help of critic NNs [32–35]. Future investigation building on this research will focus on extending the present results by embedding them with an adaptive dynamic programming approach.*

4. Simulated Example

A simulated example is performed to illustrate the proposed control scheme. The sampling frequency for feedback is set as $f_s = 20\,\mathrm{Hz}$. The initial attitude, angular velocity, position, and velocity of the chaser are given as $\boldsymbol{\sigma}(0) = [0,0,0]^{\mathrm{T}}$, $\boldsymbol{\omega}(0) = [0,0,0]^{\mathrm{T}}\,\mathrm{rad/s}$, $\boldsymbol{r}(0) = [1,1,1]^{\mathrm{T}} \times 7.078 \times 10^6\,\mathrm{m}$, and $\boldsymbol{v}(0) = [2,3,-2]^{\mathrm{T}}\,\mathrm{m/s}$. The initial relative attitude, angular velocity, position, and velocity of the target with respect to the chaser are given as $\boldsymbol{\sigma}_e(0) = [0.2,-0.4,0.3]^{\mathrm{T}}$, $\boldsymbol{\omega}_e(0) = [0.02,-0.02,0.02]^{\mathrm{T}}\,\mathrm{rad/s}$, $\boldsymbol{r}_e(0) = \left[50\sqrt{2},0,-50\sqrt{2}\right]^{\mathrm{T}}\,\mathrm{m}$, and $\boldsymbol{v}_e(0) = [0.5,-0.5,0.5]^{\mathrm{T}}\,\mathrm{m/s}$. Moreover, the constant position vector of the desired docking point with respect to the target in frame F_t is given as $\boldsymbol{p}_t = [0,5,0]^{\mathrm{T}}\,\mathrm{m}$. The inertia matrices of the chaser and the target are chosen as

$$J = \begin{bmatrix} 38 & -2.5 & -5.5 \\ -2.5 & 44 & -2.7 \\ -5.5 & -2.7 & 36 \end{bmatrix} \mathrm{kg}\cdot\mathrm{m}^2, \quad (40)$$

$$J_t = \begin{bmatrix} 3336 & -135.4 & -154.2 \\ -135.4 & 3184 & -148.5 \\ -154.2 & -148.5 & 2423 \end{bmatrix} \mathrm{kg}\cdot\mathrm{m}^2. \quad (41)$$

The masses of the chaser and the target are chosen as $m = 58.2$ kg, and $m_t = 5425.6$ kg. The inertia matrices and the masses are assumed to be fully unknown for the control design. The disturbance torques and forces acted on the chaser and the target are chosen as

$$d_\tau = h_\tau = \begin{bmatrix} 1+\sin(\pi t/125)+\sin(\pi t/200) \\ 1+\sin(\pi t/125)+\sin(\pi t/250) \\ 1+\cos(\pi t/125)+\cos(\pi t/250) \end{bmatrix} \times 10^{-5}\,\text{Nm}, \tag{42}$$

$$d_f = h_f = \begin{bmatrix} 1+\sin(\pi t/125)+\sin(\pi t/200) \\ 1+\sin(\pi t/125)+\sin(\pi t/250) \\ 1+\cos(\pi t/125)+\cos(\pi t/250) \end{bmatrix} \times 10^{-4}\,\text{N}. \tag{43}$$

Due to the actuator saturation, the acceptable maximum control torques and forces are set as

$$|u_{\tau i}| \leq 2\,\text{Nm}, \; \left|u_{fi}\right| \leq 200\,\text{N}, \; i = 1,2,3. \tag{44}$$

In addition, the actuator faults are also considered. The actuator health factor matrices are given as

$$\Gamma_\tau = \text{diag}\{0.8+0.1\sin(0.1t), 0.8-0.1\cos(0.3t), 0.7-0.2\sin(0.2t)\}, \tag{45}$$

$$\Gamma_f = \text{diag}\{0.7+0.1\sin(0.2t), 0.6+0.2\cos(0.1t), 0.8+0.2\cos(0.1t)\}. \tag{46}$$

The commonly used proportional-derivative (PD) controller is employed for performance comparisons. The compared PD controller is also made up of a relative attitude control law and a relative position control law. The relative attitude control law is designed as

$$u_\tau = -k_{p1}\sigma_e - k_{d1}\omega_e, \tag{47}$$

where $k_{p1} > 0$ and $k_{d1} > 0$. Moreover, the relative position control law is designed as

$$u_f = -k_{p2}r_e - k_{d2}v_e, \tag{48}$$

where $k_{p2} > 0$ and $k_{d2} > 0$.

The parameters of the proposed neural adaptive fault-tolerant controller are given as $\alpha_1 = 0.5$, $\alpha_2 = 0.5$, $k_1 = 20$, $k_2 = 20$, $\mu_1 = 1$, $\mu_2 = 1$, $\eta_1 = 0.1$, and $\eta_2 = 0.1$. Seven nodes are selected for the hidden layer of the RBFNN. The parameters of the RBFNN are selected as $c_i = [-3,-2,-1,0,1,2,3]^T$, and $w_i = 6$. The initial values of the adaptive parameters are set as $\hat{b}_\tau = 0$ and $\hat{b}_f = 0$. Additionally, the parameters of the compared PD controller are given as $k_{p1} = 12$, $k_{p2} = 16$, $k_{d1} = 12$, and $k_{d2} = 16$.

The translational motion of the chaser and the target for proximity operation is provided in Figure 3. It is clearly seen that the chaser, under both the proposed neural adaptive fault-tolerant controller and the compared PD controller, can quickly approach the target, and the spacecraft proximity operation can be well accomplished. Specifically, the simulation results of the proposed neural adaptive fault-tolerant controller are given in Figures 4–7. Figure 4 shows the time profiles of the relative attitude and angular velocity under the proposed controller. The time profiles of the relative position and velocity under the proposed controller are presented in Figure 5. Figure 6 gives the time profiles of the control torques and forces of the chaser under the proposed controller. The changing curves of two adaptive parameters under the proposed controller are depicted in Figure 7. Moreover, the simulation results of the compared PD controller are given in Figures 8–10.

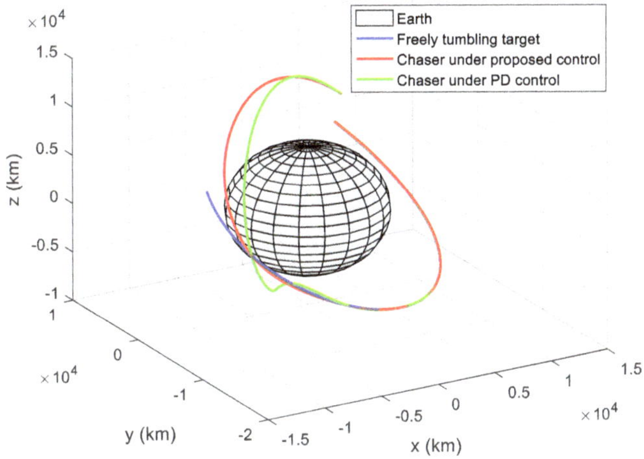

Figure 3. Translational motion of the chaser and the target for proximity operation.

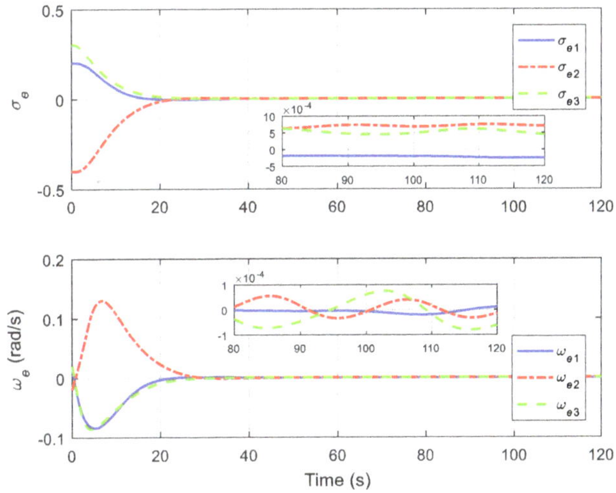

Figure 4. Relative attitude and angular velocity under the proposed controller.

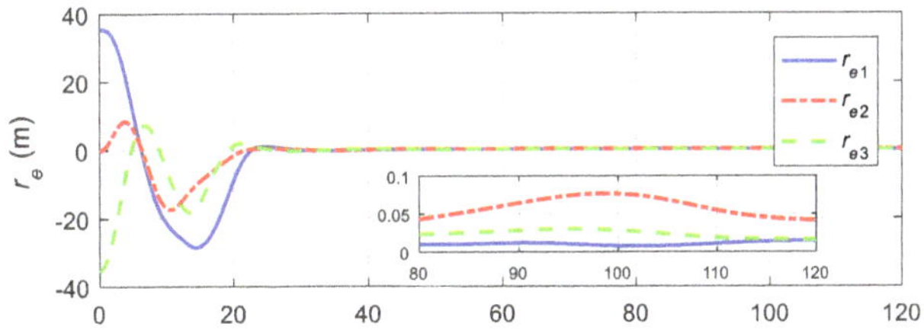

Figure 5. *Cont.*

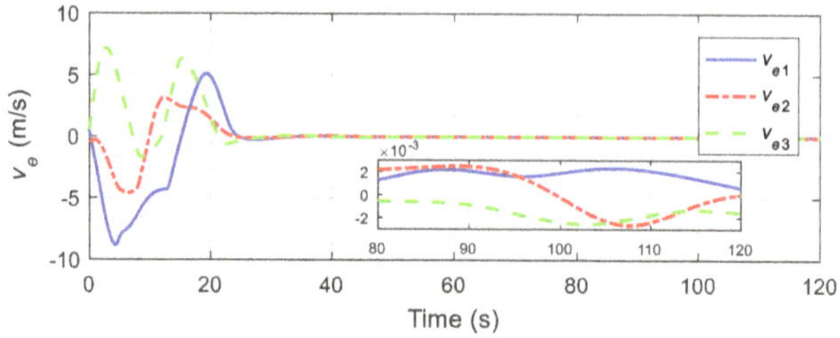

Figure 5. Relative position and velocity under the proposed controller.

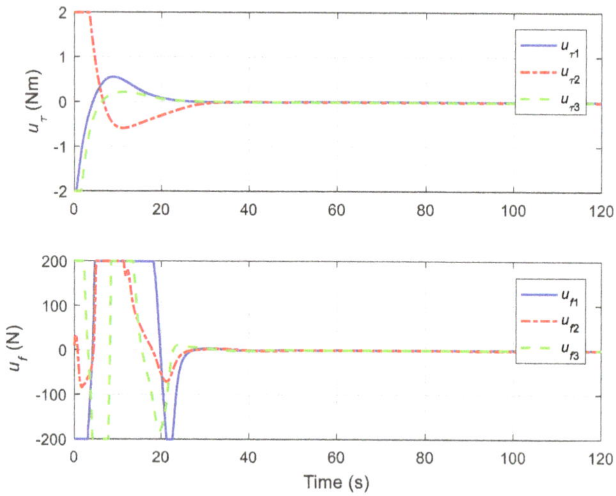

Figure 6. Control torques and forces of the chaser under the proposed controller.

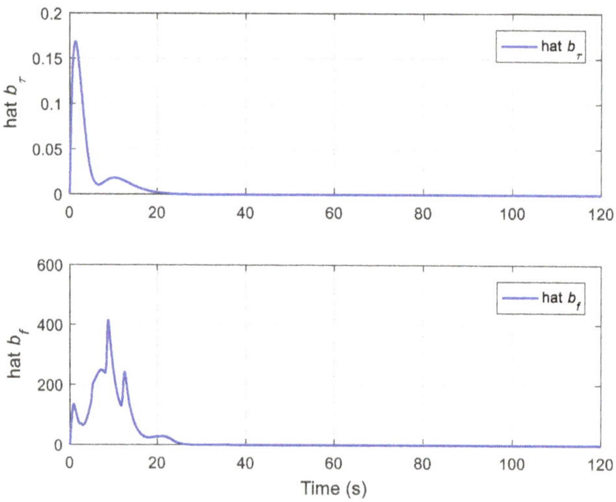

Figure 7. Two adaptive parameters under the proposed controller.

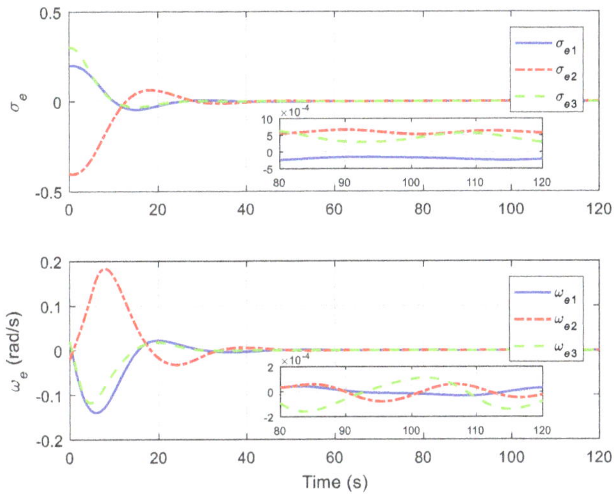

Figure 8. Relative attitude and angular velocity under the PD controller.

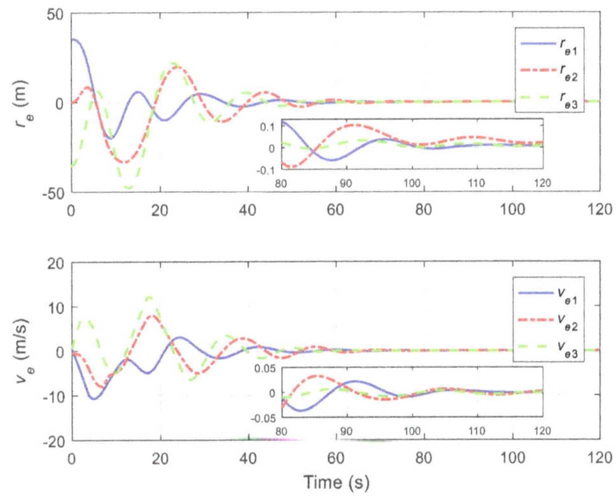

Figure 9. Relative position and velocity under the PD controller.

From Figures 4, 5, 8 and 9, it is revealed that the steady-state relative errors under the PD controller are much larger than those under the proposed controller. Meanwhile, the PD controller has the obvious unexpected overshooting problem, which the proposed controller does not have. The proposed controller can achieve superior performance, even in the presence of unknown parameters, disturbances, and actuator faults. Nevertheless, the performance of the PD controller is relatively poor, due to the existence of lumped unknowns in 6-DOF dynamics. Benefiting from the indirect neural approximation, the proposed controller is robust against unknown parameters and disturbances and is also insensitive to actuator faults. Figures 6 and 10 reveal that the control torques and forces of the chaser can always satisfy the actuator saturation constraints during the spacecraft proximity operation. From Figure 7, it can be inferred that the two adaptive parameters are bounded and change with time smoothly.

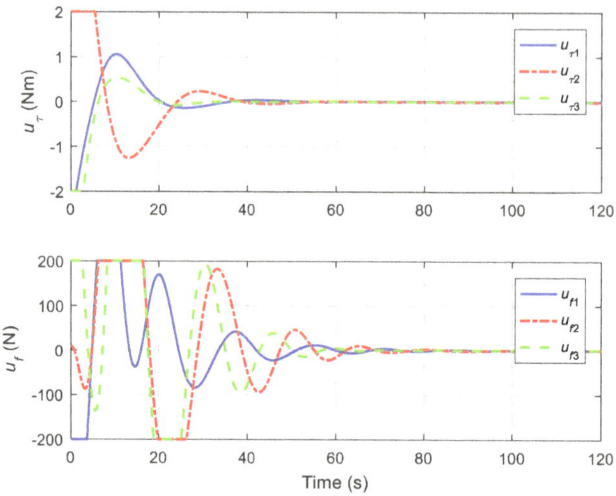

Figure 10. Control torques and forces of the chaser under the PD controller.

Furthermore, some crucial indexes are introduced to quantitatively compare the performance between the proposed controller and the PD controller. Specifically, the integrated absolute errors (IAEs) are defined as $IAE_\sigma = \sum_{i=1}^{3} \int_0^t |\sigma_{ei}(\tau_s)|\mathrm{d}\tau_s$, $IAE_\omega = \sum_{i=1}^{3} \int_0^t |\omega_{ei}(\tau_s)|\mathrm{d}\tau_s$, $IAE_r = \sum_{i=1}^{3} \int_0^t |r_{ei}(\tau_s)|\mathrm{d}\tau_s$, and $IAE_v = \sum_{i=1}^{3} \int_0^t |v_{ei}(\tau_s)|\mathrm{d}\tau_s$, which evaluates the steady-state response performance of the controller. Moreover, the integrated time absolute errors (ITAEs) are defined as $ITAE_\sigma = \sum_{i=1}^{3} \int_0^t \tau_s|\sigma_{ei}(\tau_s)|\mathrm{d}\tau_s$, $ITAE_\omega = \sum_{i=1}^{3} \int_0^t \tau_s|\omega_{ei}(\tau_s)|\mathrm{d}\tau_s$, $ITAE_r = \sum_{i=1}^{3} \int_0^t \tau_s|r_{ei}(\tau_s)|\mathrm{d}\tau_s$, and $ITAE_v = \sum_{i=1}^{3} \int_0^t \tau_s|v_{ei}(\tau_s)|\mathrm{d}\tau_s$, which evaluates the transient response performance of the controller. The total time for performance comparison is set as $t = 120\,\mathrm{s}$. The IAEs and ITAEs under the proposed controller are $IAE_\sigma = 3.64$, $IAE_\omega = 1.70$, $IAE_r = 424.95$, $IAE_v = 116.73$, $ITAE_\sigma = 28.16$, $ITAE_\omega = 15.83$, $ITAE_r = 4480.8$, and $ITAE_v = 1265.6$. By contrast, the IAEs and ITAEs under the PD controller are $IAE_\sigma = 3.75$, $IAE_\omega = 2.33$, $IAE_r = 797.86$, $IAE_v = 243.22$, $ITAE_\sigma = 30.55$, $ITAE_\omega = 25.12$, $ITAE_r = 13900$, and $ITAE_v = 4695.2$. It is not difficult to find that the IAEs and ITAEs under the PD controller are much larger than those under the proposed controller. This means that the proposed controller can achieve better steady-state and transient responses than the PD controller.

In summary, the simulation results indicate that the proposed neural adaptive fault-tolerant controller can realize superior performance and good uncertainty rejection capability, which guarantees the successful implementation of the spacecraft proximity operation.

5. Conclusions

This paper aimed to propose a neural, adaptive, fault-tolerant control scheme for the integrated attitude and position control of spacecraft proximity operations in the presence of unknown parameters, disturbances, and actuator faults. The proposed controller is made up of a relative attitude control law and a relative position control law. Both the relative attitude control law and relative position control law were designed by adopting the NNs to approximate the upper bound of the lumped unknowns. By introducing the indirect neural approximation, the proposed controller is more suitable for practical engineering, especially considering the onboard computer has limited online calculation capability. The ultimate uniform boundedness of the overall closed-loop system can be achieved through Lyapunov analysis. The proposed controller can ensure the relative attitude, angular velocity, position, and velocity stabilize into the small neighborhoods around the origin. Lastly, simulation results indicate the effectiveness and superior performance of the proposed control scheme.

Author Contributions: Conceptualization, F.W.A., M.S.A.-z. and A.S.A.; methodology, Q.Y. and H.J.; formal analysis, F.W.A., M.S.A.-z. and A.S.A.; writing—original draft preparation, Q.Y.; writing—review and editing, F.W.A. and H.J.; supervision, F.W.A. and H.J.; funding acquisition, F.W.A. All authors have read and agreed to the published version of the manuscript.

Funding: This study is supported by the Deanship of Scientific Research at King Faisal University under Grant No. 17122015.

Institutional Review Board Statement: Not applicable.

Informed Consent Statement: Not applicable.

Data Availability Statement: Not applicable.

Conflicts of Interest: The authors declare no conflict of interest.

References

1. Singla, P.; Subbarao, K.; Junkins, J.L. Adaptive output feedback control for spacecraft rendezvous and docking under measurement uncertainty. *J. Guid. Control Dyn.* **2006**, *29*, 892–902. [CrossRef]
2. Kristiansen, R.; Nicklasson, P.J.; Gravdahl, J.T. Spacecraft coordination control in 6DOF: Integrator backstepping vs passivity-based control. *Automatica* **2008**, *44*, 2896–2901. [CrossRef]
3. Xin, M.; Pan, H. Integrated nonlinear optimal control of spacecraft in proximity operations. *Int. J. Control* **2010**, *83*, 347–363. [CrossRef]
4. Xin, M.; Pan, H. Indirect robust control of spacecraft via optimal control solution. *IEEE Trans. Aerosp. Electron. Syst.* **2012**, *48*, 1798–1809. [CrossRef]
5. Zhang, F.; Duan, G. Robust adaptive integrated translation and rotation control of a rigid spacecraft with control saturation and actuator misalignment. *Acta Astronaut.* **2013**, *86*, 167–187. [CrossRef]
6. Pukdeboon, C. Inverse optimal sliding mode control of spacecraft with coupled translation and attitude dynamics. *Int. J. Syst. Sci.* **2015**, *46*, 2421–2438. [CrossRef]
7. Pukdeboon, C.; Kumam, P. Robust optimal sliding mode control for spacecraft position and attitude maneuvers. *Aerosp. Sci. Technol.* **2015**, *43*, 329–342. [CrossRef]
8. Sun, L.; Huo, W. 6-DOF integrated adaptive backstepping control for spacecraft proximity operations. *IEEE Trans. Aerosp. Electron. Syst.* **2015**, *51*, 2433–2443. [CrossRef]
9. Sun, L.; Huo, W. Robust adaptive relative position tracking and attitude synchronization for spacecraft rendezvous. *Aerosp. Sci. Technol.* **2015**, *41*, 28–35. [CrossRef]
10. Sun, L.; Zheng, Z. Adaptive relative pose control of spacecraft with model couplings and uncertainties. *Acta Astronaut.* **2018**, *143*, 29–36. [CrossRef]
11. Sun, L.; Zheng, Z. Disturbance observer-based robust saturated control for spacecraft proximity maneuvers. *IEEE Trans. Control Syst. Technol.* **2018**, *26*, 684–692. [CrossRef]
12. Sun, L.; Huo, W.; Jiao, Z. Disturbance observer-based robust relative pose control for spacecraft rendezvous and proximity operations under input saturation. *IEEE Trans. Aerosp. Electron. Syst.* **2018**, *54*, 1605–1617. [CrossRef]
13. Hu, Q.; Shao, X.; Chen, W.-H. Robust fault-tolerant tracking control for spacecraft proximity operations using time-varying sliding mode. *IEEE Trans. Aerosp. Electron. Syst.* **2018**, *54*, 2–17. [CrossRef]
14. Wang, Y.; Ji, H. Integrated relative position and attitude control for spacecraft rendezvous with ISS and finite-time convergence. *Aerosp. Sci. Technol.* **2019**, *85*, 234–245. [CrossRef]
15. Sun, L. Adaptive fault-tolerant constrained control of cooperative spacecraft rendezvous and docking. *IEEE Trans. Ind. Electron.* **2020**, *67*, 3107–3115. [CrossRef]
16. Zhou, B.-Z.; Liu, X.-F.; Cai, G.-P. Robust adaptive position and attitude-tracking controller for satellite proximity operations. *Acta Astronaut.* **2020**, *167*, 135–145. [CrossRef]
17. Huang, Y.; Jia, Y. Adaptive fixed-time relative position tracking and attitude synchronization control for non-cooperative target spacecraft fly-around mission. *J. Frankl. Inst.* **2017**, *354*, 8461–8489. [CrossRef]
18. Huang, Y.; Jia, Y. Robust adaptive fixed-time tracking control of 6-DOF spacecraft fly-around mission for noncooperative target. *Int. J. Robust Nonlinear Control* **2018**, *28*, 2598–2618. [CrossRef]
19. Huang, Y.; Jia, Y. Adaptive fixed-time six-DOF tracking control for noncooperative spacecraft fly-around mission. *IEEE Trans. Control Syst. Technol.* **2019**, *27*, 1796–1804. [CrossRef]

20. Wang, J.; Liang, H.; Sun, Z.; Zhang, S.; Liu, M. Finite-time control for spacecraft formation with dual-number-based description. *J. Guid. Control Dyn.* **2012**, *35*, 950–962. [CrossRef]
21. Filipe, N.; Tsiotras, P. Adaptive position and attitude-tracking controller for satellite proximity operations using dual quaternions. *J. Guid. Control Dyn.* **2015**, *38*, 566–577. [CrossRef]
22. Filipe, N.; Valverde, A.; Tsiotras, P. Pose tracking without linear- and angular-velocity feedback using dual quaternions. *IEEE Trans. Aerosp. Electron. Syst.* **2016**, *52*, 411–422. [CrossRef]
23. Gui, H.; Vukovich, G. Dual-quaternion-based adaptive motion tracking of spacecraft with reduced control effort. *Nonlinear Dyn.* **2016**, *83*, 597–614. [CrossRef]
24. Gui, H.; Vukovich, G. Finite-time output-feedback position and attitude tracking of a rigid body. *Automatica* **2016**, *74*, 270–278. [CrossRef]
25. Vukovich, G.; Gui, H. Robust adaptive tracking of rigid-body motion with applications to asteroid proximity operations. *IEEE Trans. Aerosp. Electron. Syst.* **2017**, *53*, 419–430. [CrossRef]
26. Tsiotras, P.; Valverde, A. Dual quaternions as a tool for modeling, control, and estimation for spacecraft robotic servicing missions. *J. Astronaut. Sci.* **2020**, *67*, 595–629. [CrossRef]
27. Stanfield, K.; Younes, A.B. Dual-quaternion analytic LQR control design for spacecraft proximity operations. *Sensors* **2020**, *21*, 3597. [CrossRef]
28. Xia, K.; Huo, W. Robust adaptive backstepping neural networks control for spacecraft rendezvous and docking with uncertainties. *Nonlinear Dyn.* **2016**, *84*, 1683–1695. [CrossRef]
29. Xia, K.; Huo, W. Robust adaptive backstepping neural networks control for spacecraft rendezvous and docking with input saturation. *ISA Trans.* **2016**, *62*, 249–257. [CrossRef]
30. Sun, L.; He, W.; Sun, C. Adaptive fuzzy relative pose control of spacecraft during rendezvous and proximity maneuvers. *IEEE Trans. Fuzzy Syst.* **2018**, *26*, 3440–3451. [CrossRef]
31. Sanner, R.M.; Slotine, J.-J.E. Gaussian networks for direct adaptive control. *IEEE Trans. Neural Netw.* **1992**, *3*, 837–863. [CrossRef] [PubMed]
32. Zhao, J.; Na, J.; Gao, G. Adaptive dynamic programming based robust control of nonlinear systems with unmatched uncertainties. *Neurocomputing* **2020**, *395*, 56–65. [CrossRef]
33. Liu, X.; Zhao, B.; Liu, D. Fault tolerant tracking control for nonlinear systems with actuator failures through particle swarm optimization-based adaptive dynamic programming. *Appl. Soft Comput.* **2020**, *97*, 106766. [CrossRef]
34. Liu, D.; Xue, S.; Zhao, B.; Luo, B.; Wei, Q. Adaptive dynamic programming for control: A survey and recent advances. *IEEE Trans. Syst. Man Cybern. Syst.* **2021**, *51*, 142–160. [CrossRef]
35. Na, J.; Lv, F.; Zhang, K.; Zhao, J. Adaptive identifier-critic-based optimal tracking control for nonlinear systems with experimental validation. *IEEE Trans. Syst. Man Cybern. Syst.* **2022**, *52*, 459–472. [CrossRef]

sensors

MDPI

Article

Rethinking Sampled-Data Control for Unmanned Aircraft Systems

Xinkai Zhang [1,*] and Justin Bradley [2]

1 Artificial Intelligence, Volvo Cars Technology USA, Sunnyvale, CA 94085, USA
2 School of Computing, University of Nebraska-Lincoln, Lincoln, NE 68588, USA; justin.bradley@unl.edu
* Correspondence: xinkai.zhang@huskers.unl.edu

Abstract: Unmanned aircraft systems are expected to provide both increasingly varied functionalities and outstanding application performances, utilizing the available resources. In this paper, we explore the recent advances and challenges at the intersection of real-time computing and control and show how rethinking sampling strategies can improve performance and resource utilization. We showcase a novel design framework, cyber-physical co-regulation, which can efficiently link together computational and physical characteristics of the system, increasing robust performance and avoiding pitfalls of event-triggered sampling strategies. A comparison experiment of different sampling and control strategies was conducted and analyzed. We demonstrate that co-regulation has resource savings similar to event-triggered sampling, but maintains the robustness of traditional fixed-periodic sampling forming a compelling alternative to traditional vehicle control design.

Keywords: resource-aware control; co-regulation; feedback scheduling; time-varying system

Citation: Zhang, X.; Bradley, J. Rethinking Sampled-Data Control for Unmanned Aircraft Systems. *Sensors* **2022**, *22*, 1525. https://doi.org/10.3390/s22041525

Academic Editors: Luige Vladareanu, Hongnian Yu, Hongbo Wang and Yongfei Feng

Received: 20 January 2022
Accepted: 14 February 2022
Published: 16 February 2022

1. Introduction

The design of efficient, intelligent, and safe unmanned aircraft systems (UASs) is challenging, especially as onboard resources are stretched to maximize performance [1]. Emerging UASs are equipped with complex suites of computing (cyber) and mechatronics (physical) systems. They are expected to provide both highly varied functionalities, outstanding application performances, and remain safe, all within the available resources [2]. Computing and timing are key factors determining holistic system behavior [3,4] and, hence, must be first-class design parameters in such intelligent control systems. To optimize the use of computing resources—autonomy and control algorithms and associated resource requirements need to be considered simultaneously, or "co-designed" [5].

In this article, we focus on comparing the control performance of a multicopter UAS under different sampling strategies varying in the level of a "co-design" of computing resources (sampling rate) and holistic system performance. Specifically, we examine traditional fixed-periodic control [6], event-triggered control [7], self-triggered control [8], and a new hybrid sampling strategy we developed—"cyber-physical co-regulation" [9]. Cyber-physical co-regulation incorporates computational resource allocation alongside traditional control performance in a single model [9]. Cyber and physical controllers can then be co-designed to meet holistic performance requirements. The computational effector, sampling rate, is adjusted in response to off-nominal conditions in the controlled system, and the physical effector adjusts control outputs corresponding to the current (changing) sampling rate. To analyze the influences from computing and timing, the controllers are all designed based on a unified optimal control strategy—linear quadratic regulator (LQR). Our previous work focused on co-regulation design methodologies [10], co-regulated system stability analysis [11], co-regulated controller design [12], and proof-of-concept demonstrations of control and computing features of co-regulation design on a simple inverted pendulum system [13]. In this work, we focus on a detailed analysis of control and computing for UASs. We conducted a thorough comparison of control performances and computational efficiencies among different sampling strategies on an UAS to demonstrate how computing and timing can affect control. We highlight the unique benefits of our proposed co-regulation strategy on control performance, computational efficiency, and system robustness over the traditional fixed-periodic, event-triggered, and self-triggered controllers. We propose new evaluation metrics for analyzing UAS control and computing performances. We discuss the implementation of a co-regulation strategy to provide insight to control engineers on how to design co-regulated systems. Moreover, a more thorough discussion on the pitfalls of event-triggered and self-triggered sampling strategies on UAS is presented. Quantitative evaluations for all of these strategies were conducted based on evaluation metrics that could reflect both control performance and computing costs.

2. Motivating Example

In a traditional fixed-periodic, computer controlled system, the control laws and their associated sampling or execution rates are intrinsically linked [6]. The sampling rate is typically overdesigned—selected to account for the worst-case anticipated noise and response characteristics, giving the system a safety margin [14]. The behavior of the control loops, and the relation between the control performance and controller execution rate, such as the results in [15], suggest that static resource allocation may not be optimal for system performance when computing resources are limited. Intuitively, a controller of a plant operating close to its equilibrium may only require a much lower sampling rate than a plant operating far from its equilibrium point [16]. In size, weight, and power constrained vehicle systems running control tasks and a myriad of other tasks, such as perception, learning, planning, and data processing—redistributing these computing resources at runtime is key to maximize the overall system performance [15,16].

Figure 1 illustrates three possible resource allocation strategies for a simplified surveillance multicopter in which a flight control task and a perception task are executed concurrently and share a fixed amount of computing resources. The plots depict an example response from the simulation for illustration purposes. The flight control task in this example is for the UAS to track a series of waypoints and the control system response in each subfigure depicts the cross tracking error with respect to the reference waypoint in meters. Assume that the processor has a limited amount of resources that can allow only one task to run at a higher rate and the other at a lower rate during runtime. The lower rate and higher rate tasks respectively correspond to lower and higher resource consumption. In typical priority-driven scheduling, the highest priority task is given system resources—CPU cycles [17]. A task's priority, in most safety-critical systems, is dependent on the task's period, particularly for hard real-time tasks, such as control and perception [17].

Figure 1a,b show two static (fixed-rate) resource allocation strategies; Figure 1c shows a simple dynamic (variable-rate) resource allocation policy. In Figure 1a, the control task is consistently executed at a high rate, while the perception task is executed at a low rate because of the limited computing resources. This leads to a good control task performance, but potentially poor perception performance. In contrast, in Figure 1b, the control system performance deteriorates because a major portion of the computing resources are allocated to the perception task. The control task has to be executed at a low rate; thus, the system response becomes slow. In Figure 1c, the resources are dynamically allocated, in a closed-loop fashion, according to plant dynamics and performance to the control and perception tasks. The benefits of this dynamic resource allocation are that it has good control performance *and* efficient and effective resource usage. Thus, the system computational resources are efficiently allocated to different tasks in a closed-loop fashion, which can increase the holistic system performance.

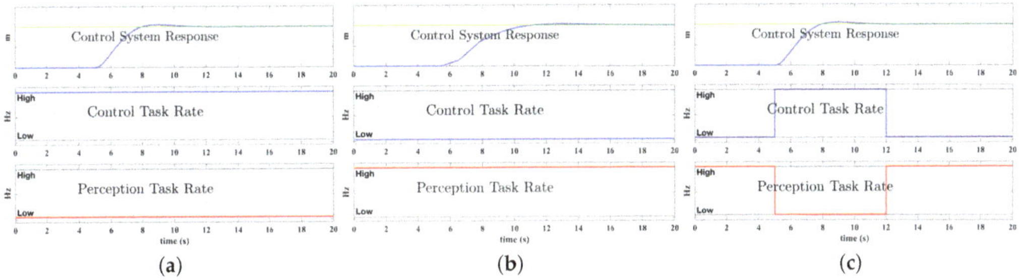

Figure 1. Different resource allocation strategies for UAS (example response for illustration purposes). (**a**) static high-rate control with low-rate perception; (**b**) static low-rate control with high-rate perception; (**c**) dynamic resource allocation for control and perception tasks.

Figure 2 provides an example of this dynamic resource allocation design on a UAS. When flying from an initial position to waypoint 1, in a dynamically quiescent environment, the planning and control task should consume fewer resources as the UAS moves closer to its target (less trajectory tracking error). The resources are more efficiently applied to improve perception, reasoning, or data collection activities. In contrast, when flying from waypoint 1 to waypoint 2, the UAS should "pay more attention" (i.e., reallocate resources) to the planning and control task to navigate itself to the target while avoiding obstacles in the congested environment. During this time, higher level reasoning and perception tasks can wait, while resources are reallocated to control, planning to improve tracking performance.

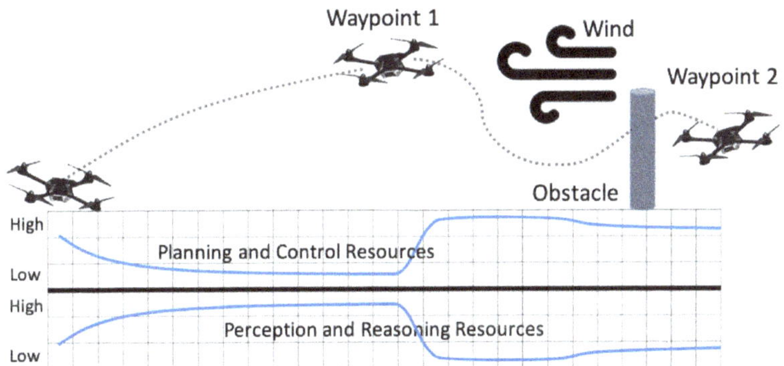

Figure 2. Dynamic resource reallocation of a UAS.

To enable a resource-aware controller capable of adjusting performance and resources as needed, we developed a feedback control-based model for controller tasks, in which computing resources and control performances are jointly considered. The co-regulated systems are capable of dynamically reallocating resources to control tasks based on system states in a closed-loop fashion, while the control task could provide an adjustable performance depending on the dynamically reallocated resources at runtime. In this paper, we conduct a comparative experiment based on a multicopter UAS to analyze the computational and physical control performances of co-regulation and the conventional fixed-periodic, event-triggered, and self-triggered sampling and control strategies. Results show that the co-regulated UAS preserves the resource savings similar to event- and self-triggered control strategies, but maintains the high-quality control performance and system robustness as a fixed-periodic control strategy.

3. Background

Here, we provide a brief overview of dynamic resource allocation and its relationship to intelligent control. We then narrow down to resource allocation in control systems, focusing on how computational resources, in the form of a sampling rate, have traditionally been allocated.

3.1. Dynamic Resource Allocation

Although dynamic physical resource allocation in the form of mutable or reconfigurable structures has been studied, we focus on dynamic cyber resource allocation (i.e., CPU time, memory). This approach offers system adaptability to available resources when performance requirements of a running application are changed, or the current allocation is not sufficiently close to optimal [18]. Strategies, such as voltage and frequency scaling CPUs [19], dynamically adjust CPU clock rates, thereby adjusting the actual physical CPU time any task gets. A side-effect of these strategies is a corresponding change in power consumption. Rate-adaptive and rhythmic tasks [20] adjust the CPU schedule to obtain a similar result leaving remaining CPU cycles to be reallocated elsewhere, thereby forfeiting power savings. A framework called "time bands", in contrast, reallocates tasks to different levels of time granularity [21]. To know when, and how much to adjust resources, the above must be connected to a measure of "quality of service" and other performance metrics [22]. This was addressed most recently by applying reinforcement learning to design an optimal resource allocation system [23].

These methods have largely remained divorced from the specifics of control and UAS, or otherwise do not incorporate such systems into their models. In contrast, most recently, attention has been given to building formal resource architectures and controllers for computer systems utilizing knowledge gained in the control community, specifically for robust control [24]. Our work complements and enhances this work, but takes the approach of directly integrating computational resources into control-specific models, allowing for the co-design of both computational and physical controllers.

3.2. Overview of Sampling Strategies

Controllers are designed to meet performance specifications for the system and are executed on a digital computer. In this paradigm, allocating CPU cycle/time takes the form of different sampling strategies resulting in the sampled-data control class of systems [14]. If we consider the sampling period as a control variable, the predominant design amounts to open-loop control of periodic execution, or fixed-periodic sampling. The period is typically chosen according to worst-case conditions, leading to inefficient implementations in terms of processor usage, communication bandwidth, energy, etc. As in the UAS example, executing the control tasks are under a fixed period, when states and the environment are quiescent waste computational resources that could be used for reasoning, decision-making, or adaptation.

The inefficient allocation of resources in fixed-periodic sampling motivates research in aperiodic sampling strategies [13]. Aperiodic sampling in the control is exemplified by event-triggered control where control actuation instances are performed when needed [13]. In event-triggered control, a control cycle is only executed when the triggering condition is violated [8]. These aperiodic sampling strategies can greatly conserve computational resources, but suffer from the disadvantages of event-triggered systems. The triggering condition needs to be continuously monitored and, thus, more sampling instances may be required. Moreover, the cases where trigger conditions are not met cannot be distinguished from failure in detecting/communicating the event [13,17]. This reduces the robustness of event-triggered control strategies in dynamical environment and network conditions, and makes developing a mathematical foundation for this class of controllers challenging [13,25].

The research in self-triggered control provide a new type of sampling strategy, time-varying periodic sampling [13]. Time-varying periodic sampling achieves the benefits of periodic methods in terms of design, but because the sampling period changes, it conserves computational resources similar to aperiodic control strategies [13]. In self-triggered control, the time for next sampling and control instance is precomputed during the current control cycle using previously received data and knowledge of system dynamics [8]. In [9], we introduced a new hybrid time-varying periodic sampling strategy that can dynamically vary the sampling period at runtime, depending on computing demands and system state feedback. This allows computational and physical resources to be dynamically reallocated as needed. Therefore, going beyond the traditional classification of Riemann and Lebesgue sampling approaches in [25], we reclassify computer control systems into three categories: fixed-periodic sampling, aperiodic sampling, and time-varying periodic sampling, as shown in Figure 3.

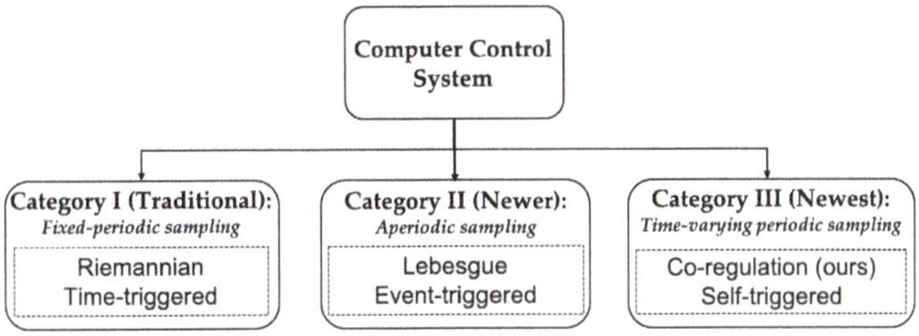

Figure 3. Three categories of control systems.

4. Control under Different Sampling Strategies

Consider a linear control system model in a general form,

$$\dot{x} = Ax + Bu. \tag{1}$$

where $x \in \mathbb{R}^n$ is the state and $u \in \mathbb{R}^m$ is the control input. We introduced the control design for each of the sampling categories in Figure 3 based on this general model. To analyze the performance of different sampling strategies, we employed a unified discrete linear quadratic regulator (DLQR) algorithm for fixed-periodic, event-triggered, self-triggered, and a co-regulated controller design.

4.1. Category I—Fixed-Periodic, or Time-Triggered Control

For a fixed sampling interval T_d, we can discretize the system model (1) as

$$x[k+1] = \Phi x[k] + \Gamma u[k]. \tag{2}$$

For the common state-feedback control [14], the control input can be denoted as $u[k] = -Kx[k]$, where the control gain K can be designed to meet the performance criteria. For the DLQR algorithm, the control gain, K, can then be decided by choosing appropriate Q and R matrices.

4.2. Category II—Event-Triggered Control

Event-triggered control consists of two elements—a feedback controller that computes the control input and a triggering mechanism that determines when the control input has to be updated again [8]. To implement event-triggered control in a computer, the controller needs to sample the system at a fixed base-period T_d (internal sampling interval) to decide if a new control update is needed [26]. Generally, a triggering parameter needs to be designed to execute a control instance to guarantee system stability. This triggering parameter should be designed depending on the system model. In this paper, we have adapted the event-triggered controller in [27] to our multicopter UAS and used it as the basis for results comparison. This algorithm updates the control signal once the UAS states deviate more than a certain threshold from a desired value.

4.3. Category III—Self-Triggered Control

Event-triggered is reactive; it requires constant monitoring of a triggering condition. Self-triggered control, on the other hand, is proactive and computes the next sampling and control instance ahead of time [8]. At each sampling instant, the control signal values, as well as the next sampling instance time, are both calculated based on the current state. To implement self-triggered control in a computer, an inter-execution time T_d is required to work as the time span unit that, when combined with the calculated next control time step k^*, the exact time for the next sampling and control instance can be achieved as $k^* T_d$. Similar to event-triggered control, a triggering parameter is needed to decide the appropriate next control instant to guarantee system stability. In our comparison test, we leverage the self-triggered control algorithm in [27]. This algorithm determines the subsequent control updates based on the prior ones, obviating the necessity for continual measurement error monitoring [13].

4.4. Cyber-Physical Co-Regulation

Cyber-physical co-regulation is a time-varying periodic sampling and control strategy, it can adjust system performance by simultaneously co-regulating the control input and its required computing resources. We augmented a traditional state space control model as in Equation (1) with a model of the computational control task. This resulted in an augmented, stacked state-space system model

$$\begin{aligned} \dot{x} &= Ax + Bu \\ \dot{x}_c &= u_c \end{aligned} \tag{3}$$

where c denotes "computational". The term "computational" refers to the state of the resource, and in this case, x_c refers to the physical system's control task execution rate, which is regulated by the computational control input u_c.

Figure 4 shows the co-regulation method developed for the multicopter UAS control in our previous work [10]. The computational system monitors the physical state error at runtime and dynamically reallocates computational resources (i.e., sampling rate) in reaction to physical performance. When the physical state error increases, the computational controller increases the sampling rate; when error decreases, the sampling rate decreases [13]. The physical system then executes the control task and adjusts the physical system performance according to the time-varying sampling rate. The physical controller is designed to provide performance guarantees for the UAS when working under the time-varying sampling rate.

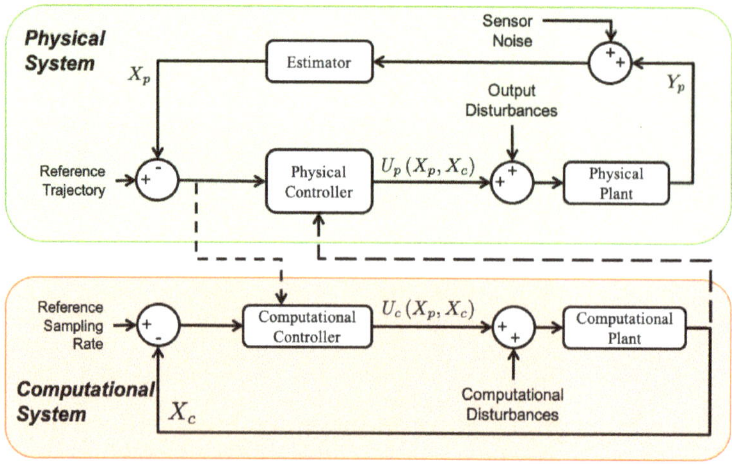

Figure 4. Co-regulation block diagram [10].

Because of the dynamically changing sampling rate at discrete intervals, the discrete system matrices Φ and Γ are not static and need to be recalculated at each time step k. The resulting discrete-time-varying system model is then [13],

$$x[k+1] = \Phi[k]x[k] + \Gamma[k]u[k] \tag{4}$$

and the control input is

$$u[k] = -K[k]x[k] \tag{5}$$

The controller is designed using a sequence of DLQR control gains for a sequence of sampling rates [14]. The control gains are mapped with different sampling rate values, and are then deployed corresponding to the current sampling rate [13]. This control design is referred to as a "gain-scheduled DLQR (GSDLQR)" and is described in Table 1 [10,12], with stability results demonstrated in [11]. In this work, we primarily focused on a comparative analysis of the control and computing features among different sampling strategies. Although advanced methods for UAS nonlinear control [28] exist, we leveraged a unified linear DLQR control algorithm for different sampling strategies to simplify the control design and highlight the performance differences brought by different sampling strategies.

Table 1. Scheduled Gains at different sampling rates [10].

Rate x_c	**Gain $K[k]$**
$x_c = x_{c,\min}$ Hz	$K[k]$ = DLQR @$x_{c,\min}$ Hz
x_c = 10 Hz	$K[k]$ = DLQR @10 Hz
x_c = 11 Hz	$K[k]$ = DLQR @11 Hz
$\vdots$	$\vdots$
$x_c = x_{c,\max}$ Hz	$K[k]$ = DLQR @$x_{c,\max}$ Hz

Co-regulation, as with event- and self-triggered strategies, needs to know when to take the next sample [13]. We structured this as a feedback computational controller that calculates the coupled control input u_c, which dynamically modifies the sampling rate in response to the system's dynamics. In prior work [10], we defined a control law for computational systems as

$$u_c[k] = K_{cp}\Big(x[k] - x_{ref}[k]\Big) - K_c\Big(x_c[k] - x_{c,ref}[k]\Big). \tag{6}$$

In response to physical state error, the coupling gain K_{cp} was employed to increase the sampling rate of the system. The gain K_c, conversely, directs x_c in the direction of the desired reference sampling rate $x_{c,ref}$. We applied an optimization approach introduced in [10] to determine values for the gain values K_{cp} and K_c. As a result, the discrete-time computational system model for the current sampling instance k can be denoted as [13]

$$x_c[k+1] = x_c[k] + \frac{1}{x_c[k]}u_c[k]. \tag{7}$$

Thus, based on the current state of the plant, the next sample instance time can be determined using Equations (6) and (7).

To implement the co-regulation strategy in the software, we needed to add constraints to the computational system model (7) to limit the sampling rate values, x_c, to a set Σ that contained a finite number of possible values. $\Sigma = \{f_1, f_2, \ldots, f_N\}$ is a pre-defined finite set that contains stable sampling rate values as prescribed operating points. This limits the sampling rate of the co-regulated system to a finite number to simplify the analysis. The bounds and the resolution of the values in Σ can be customized depending on the application. The general rule to generate Σ is to:

1. Set the upper bound based on the system computational bandwidth given all other computing tasks;
2. Set the lower bound to the rate where system performance degrades beyond acceptable limits, or otherwise is unstable;
3. Set the resolution based on the system dynamics and application scenarios, which can guarantee system stability and accommodate performance requirements, such as disturbance rejection, dynamic response, etc.

In the software implementation, the GSDLQR gain matrices are saved as a look-up table. In each control cycle, the appropriate DLQR gain matrix that maps with the current sampling rate is leveraged to compute the control signal. Then the next sampling rate value is calculated by the computational control model based on the current state feedback. The control task execution rate is decided by the computational controller based the the real-time state feedback. The software implementation of the co-regulation algorithm is summarized in Algorithm 1.

Algorithm 1: Cyber-physical co-regulation.

Result: Physical control input $u[k]$
Control task rate $x_c[k+1]$
Input: $x[k], x_{ref}[k], x_c[k], x_{c,ref}[k], K_{cp}, K_c, \Sigma$
Output: $u[k], x_c[k+1]$
while *Algorithm is running* **do**
  if $t = t_{last} + 1/x_c[k+1]$ **then**
    //Update the control instance time
    $t_{last} = t;$
    //Calculate the physical control input
    $K[k] = DLQR \,@\, x_c[k] Hz;$
    $u[k] = -K[k](x[k] - x_{ref}[k]);$
    //Calculate the computational control input
    $u_c[k] = K_{cp}\left(x[k] - x_{ref}[k]\right) - K_c\left(x_c[k] - x_{c,ref}[k]\right);$
    //Calculate the following tasks execution rates
    $x_c[k+1] = x_c[k] + \left(\frac{1}{x_c[k]}\right) u_c[k];$
    $x_c[k+1] = closest\ value\ in\ \Sigma;$
  Return: $u[k], x_c[k+1];$

The novelty of the co-regulation approach is in its coupling of computational and physical systems via equations of motion rather than incorporating the delays of motion into the models used for task scheduling. That is, at the feedback control level, computational and physical resources are balanced dynamically rather than at a higher planning level [9]. Co-regulation does not replace traditional planning, but supplements it by reactive reallocation of resources within the reference trajectories commanded by the planner [9].

Co-regulation, conceptually, can be applied to a wide variety of control problems, including nonlinear controllers, and there are currently two main approaches to designing them. The most widely applicable are methods such as the presented gain scheduling framework that are generalizable to virtually any control strategy as long as multiple sampling-rate-targeted controllers can be designed. In this paradigm, co-regulation becomes a switched system with associated performance guarantees [12]. More generally, however, smoother, more robust controllers can be developed as long as a single control law that works for a wide range of sampling rates can be found. As an example, for attitude control of a CubeSat, we introduced a control strategy based on propagating the Riccati equations forward in time (rather than the traditional "backward in time") [9]. In that paradigm, the controller evolves alongside the sampling rate and discrete-time-varying dynamics. Such strategies are more difficult to design since they rely on discrete-time-varying dynamics (due to the time-varying sampling rate) and developing such control laws is an active area of research. Minimum sampling rates to ensure good performance are highly dependent upon the speed of the system dynamics, and experimentally, we observed that single co-regulated control laws tend to evolve more slowly without an associated sampling rate prediction mechanism or trajectory. As a result, our existing controllers of this type are applied to systems with slower dynamics (e.g., CubeSat). In contrast, the presented gain scheduling paradigm, due to its switching nature, is better applied in systems with faster dynamics. Eventually, we envision an all-encompassing framework for designing co-regulated controllers dependent upon the speed of the system dynamics, expected computational capabilities, expected computing task sets, and resource requirements.

5. Evaluation Metrics

We intend to quantify both physical and computational characteristics of the system in order to more holistically evaluate system performance. Physical evaluation metrics primarily assess performance of the plant's response to references and the actuation effort required to achieve it. Computational evaluation metrics primarily assess the computational resources allocation for control task, which include the number of sampling and control instances during the test cycle.

5.1. Physical Evaluation Metrics

Our first metric is the time averaged square of physical state error (PSE),

$$\text{PSE} = \frac{1}{t_{tot}} \sum_{i=0}^{n} \left(x_i - x_{ref} \right)^2 t_i. \tag{8}$$

This metric provides an all-encompassing look into how well all states are being regulated. Because average error does not address control inputs that may saturate actuators, we introduce an additional metric, maximum state error (MSE), which evaluates the maximum deviation of the plant states from the reference,

$$\text{MSE} = \max \left(x_i - x_{ref} \right)^2. \tag{9}$$

For control effort, we introduced a metric capturing the time weighted average of the square of the control input (i.e., control effort (CE)),

$$\text{CE} = \frac{1}{t_{tot}} \sum_{i=0}^{n} u_i^2 \, t_i \tag{10}$$

where t_{tot} is the total simulation time (in seconds), t_i is the length of time for the ith simulation step, n is the total number of simulation steps, $u_i = u[k] = const.$ on $kT_d \leq t < (k+1)T_d$. This metric provides an indicator of energy and power usage. We also introduced a metric to quantify the energy cost W for the UAS in one entire flight test process. The power required to produce a given thrust is $P = \sqrt{\frac{T^3}{2\rho A}}$, where T is the rotor thrust, A is the area of the spinning propeller, and ρ is the air fluid density [10]. Then the energy cost W in the whole process can be denoted as

$$\text{W} = \frac{1}{t_{tot}} \sum_{i=0}^{n} P \, t_i, \tag{11}$$

as an additional way to evaluate the controller efficiency.

5.2. Computational Evaluation Metrics

On the computational side, we evaluated the sampling and control task resource utilization by counting the number of sampling instances and control instances, respectively, during the test time. Let k_{sample} represent the execution cycle (time index) of the sampling task, incrementing each time the sampling task runs. We introduce the sampling computational time (SCT) metric as

$$\text{SCT} = k_{sample}. \tag{12}$$

Similarly, we define the control computational time (CCT) metric as

$$\text{CCT} = k_{control}, \tag{13}$$

where $k_{control}$ represents the execution cycle (time index) of the control task.

6. Results

In this section, we deploy different sampling strategies on a multicopter UAS nonlinear simulation and compare the resulting flight control performances and resource consumption. The UAS state consists of the vehicle's position $(x, y, z)^T$, velocity in $\mathbb{R}^3$, orientation in roll (ϕ), pitch (θ) and yaw (ψ) angles, and angular rate of change in yaw [12]

$$x_p = (x, y, z, \phi, \theta, \psi, \dot{x}, \dot{y}, \dot{z}, \dot{\psi})^T.$$

A lower-level attitude controller was integrated with the UAS, which accepts the desired thrust (T), roll angle (ϕ), pitch angle (θ), and body yaw rate (r) as inputs [12]. Thus the control input for the UAS is $u_p = (\phi, \theta, r, T)^T$. The equations of motion of the UAS model are

$$\begin{bmatrix} \ddot{p}_n \\ \ddot{p}_e \\ \ddot{p}_d \end{bmatrix} = -\frac{T}{m} \begin{bmatrix} \cos\phi \sin\theta \cos\psi + \sin\phi \sin\psi \\ \cos\phi \sin\theta \sin\psi - \sin\phi \cos\psi \\ \cos\phi \cos\theta \end{bmatrix} + \begin{bmatrix} 0 \\ 0 \\ g \end{bmatrix}$$

where m is the total mass of the UAS, and g is gravity [12]. These nonlinear equations of motion were employed to build the high-fidelity UAS flight simulation. The controllers were designed using a linearized state-space system model, such as (1), by linearizing the model at a stable hover equilibrium point. To compare and analyze the control performances and resource consumption among different sampling strategies, we developed fixed-periodic, event-triggered, self-triggered, and co-regulated controllers for this UAS and conducted the tests in unified environments. We leveraged the nonlinear equations of motion of the UAS to build this high-fidelity test environment to simulate the UAS performances when operated under different strategies.

6.1. Simulation Setup

The comparison test was conducted in a simulation environment that was built in *Matlab* R2017a on a 2.3 GHz Intel i5 processor computer. The control and computational performances of the UAS were recorded and quantified using the evaluation metrics in Section 5. The UAS parameters are specific to the "Ascending Technologies Hummingbird" and are listed in Table 2. More detailed specs of the UAS can be found in [29]. To study the effects of computing and timing, the fixed-periodic, event-triggered, self-triggered, and co-regulated controllers were all designed based on a unified optimal DLQR control algorithm with unified parameters. The controller parameters Q and R were manually tuned, and are shown in Table 2. The selection of computational gain K_{cp} and k_c parameters for co-regulation are based on the optimization scheme in [10] that targets minimizing a cost function composed of terms measuring resource usage, control performance, and energy consumption.

Table 2. System constants.

Parameter	Value	Parameter	Value
g	9.80665 m/s^2	m	0.515 kg
Q	$\mathbb{I}_{10\times10}\boldsymbol{q}$	R	$\mathbb{I}_{4\times4}\boldsymbol{r}$
$\boldsymbol{q} = [130\ 130\ 130\ 150\ 150\ 150\ 2\ 2\ 2\ 1]^T$		$\boldsymbol{r} = [180\ 180\ 180\ 3]^T$	
$K_{cp} = [1\ 1\ 1\ 1\ 1\ 1\ 1\ 1\ 1\ 1]$	$K_c = 1$		

The sampling rate of the fixed-periodic control was set to 10 Hz as it could provide a sufficient control performance for this multicopter UAS. The internal sampling interval T_d for event- and self-triggered control was set to 10 Hz, the resulting discrete system model and control gain matrix were the same as the fixed-periodic control. The triggering parameters for this multicopter UAS model were manually tuned as $\sigma = 0.9$ (event-triggered control) and $\mu = 0.6$ (self-triggered control) based on the system response to perform the "best" trade-off among resource utilization and control performance. The selected triggering parameters were located in the range where the system stability for the multicopter UAS model could be guaranteed [27]. For co-regulation, the reference sampling rate $x_{c1,ref}$ was set to 1 Hz as the minimum resource we allocated to the control task. The time-varying control gain $K[k]$ was calculated at runtime to provide performance guaranteed control.

6.2. Test Results

We compared the system performances of fixed-periodic control, event-triggered control, self-triggered control, and co-regulation in a UAS waypoint in the following scenario. In the first test, we set a single reference waypoint for the UAS to test the step response. The initial state of the UAS was set to a stable hover at one meter above the origin of the inertial frame, the single reference waypoint was set to two meters away in the x direction. Each test was timed for a total of 15 s, and we manually added a wind disturbance of 0.2 N in the positive x direction from 7 to 9 s.

In this work, we assumed the magnitude and direction of the wind disturbance was constant to simplify the analysis. In an extended trajectory with varying disturbances, the system will adapt as "error" from the controller increases. The results are depicted in Figure 5, and quantified by evaluation metrics in Table 3. The "Position (x)" in Figure 5 depicts the UAS moving trajectory in the x direction in meters, which reflects the UAS flight control performance. Those transient responses in "Position (x)" that have smaller deviations from the reference (2 m) exhibited better performances. The controllers were designed as waypoint followers, which took position information as references. Waypoint following is the most ubiquitous type of multicopter control strategy in deployment.

The system performances from different sampling and control strategies are compared and depicted in Figure 5. In general, fixed-periodic control provides the "gold standard" of control performance but also utilizes the most computing resources [13]. Thus, a performance that is closer to the fixed-periodic controller generally indicates better control. The number of sampling and control instances reflects the resource consumption. Higher computational efficiency is exemplified by sparser instances. When compared with fixed-periodic control (Figure 5a), event-triggered control (Figure 5b) can save computational resources at the cost of significantly degraded control performance. The event-triggered controlled UAS has a 20% longer settling time and a 60% higher overshoot than when being controlled by the fixed-periodic controller. For the self-triggered control performance (Figure 5c), more computational resources can be saved since both sampling instances and control instances are reduced. In terms of physical control performance, self-triggered control has a similar settling time to event-triggered control, but has a 10% lower overshoot.

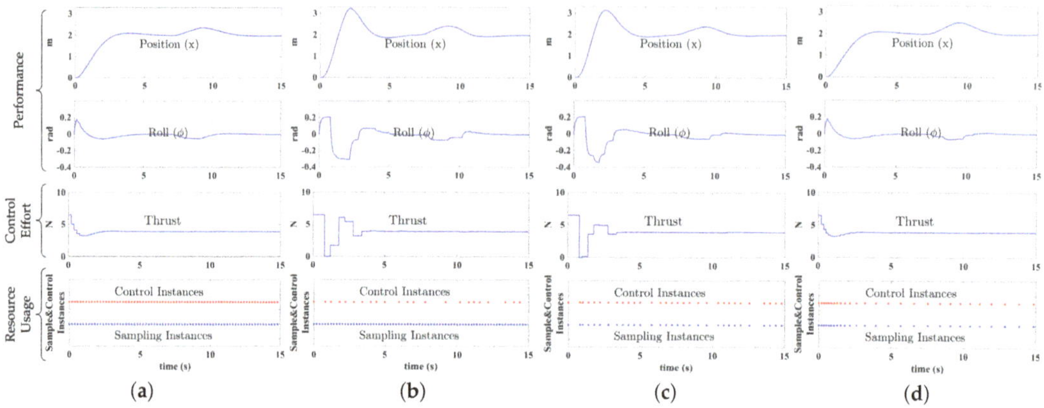

Figure 5. Performance comparison of fixed-periodic, event-triggered, self-triggered control, and co-regulation. (**a**) fixed-periodic DLQR; (**b**) event-triggered control; (**c**) self-triggered control; (**d**) co-regulation.

The co-regulated controller (Figure 5d) provided the best balance of control and computational performances among all sampling strategies. On the control side, co-regulation could achieve a nearly identical physical control performance compared with the fixed-periodic control, which retained significant advantages over event- and self-triggered controllers. On the computational side, co-regulated control required the fewest sampling instances, providing the greatest computational efficiency. In this test, the fixed-periodic, event-triggered, self-triggered, and co-regulated controllers all responded similarly to disturbances. Uniquely, however, when a disturbance occurred, the sample rate of the co-regulated controller quickly increased, allowing the system to promptly respond to the state deviation induced by the disturbance and maintain robust performance.

In Table 3, we show quantified results for the comparison test based on evaluation metrics. The results are normalized to provide a more straightforward comparison. The physical control performances best illustrate the PSE and MSE metrics; fixed-periodic control and co-regulation can provide approximately the same level of control performances, significantly better than event-triggered and self-triggered strategies. The control performances in the fixed-periodic control and co-regulation also lead to better energy efficiency presented by lower CE and lower W. The computational system performances are best illustrated by the SCT and CCT metrics. In all cases, the decrease of SCT and CCT metrics denoting less computational resources were allocated to the sampling and control task. The fixed-periodic DLQR controller consumed the most computational resources among all strategies. The event-triggered and self-triggered controllers could perform considerable savings in computing resources as a trade-off for degraded physical control performances. Event-triggered control consumed the least control instances during this test process. However, since it required consistently monitoring of the system states, the computational resource consumption for state sampling was the highest. Co-regulation consumed the least resource in sampling, and the physical control performance was far better than event-triggered and self-triggered strategies. From the results, co-regulation provided the most significant computing resources savings with minimal loss of physical performance. That is, the co-regulated system could achieve an (approximately) identical physical system performance as the fixed-rate controllers while saving significant computational resources similar to event-triggered and self-triggered controllers.

Table 3. Evaluation metrics of different sampling and control strategies (the lower value denotes better performance).

Control Strategy	Physical				Computational	
	MSE	PSE	CE	W	CCT	SCT
Fixed-periodic	1.0000	1.0000	1.0000	1.0000	3.2609	2.7778
Event-triggered	2.1752	2.4783	1.0917	1.0426	1.0000	2.7778
Self-triggered	1.7726	2.3041	1.0778	1.0376	1.3478	1.1481
Co-regulation	1.0031	1.0270	1.0002	1.0001	1.1739	1.0000

PSE : physical state error; **MSE:** maximum state error; **CE:** control effort; **W:** energy cost; **SCT:** sampling computational time; **CCT:** control computational time.

Figure 6 demonstrates a top view of the UAS waypoint following performance under disturbances. This can provide a more straightforward comparison of how the UAS responds to disturbance under different sampling strategies. Two consecutive reference waypoints are set to 1 m away in the x direction, then 2 m away in the y direction. A disturbance of 0.3 N is set in the positive x direction when the UAS moves towards the second waypoint. The results show that all four sampling strategies can provide robust performances against the disturbance. However, fixed-periodic control and co-regulation show better robustness to disturbances as the trajectory deviation caused by disturbances are smaller than event-triggered and self-triggered controllers.

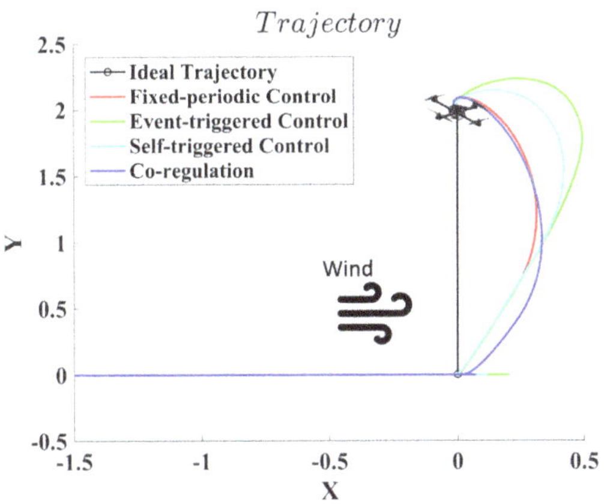

Figure 6. Waypoint following performance under disturbances.

7. Discussion

The primary benefits of the co-regulation strategy in computing resource saving and physical control performance were discussed, based on the comparison test results. Moreover, the proposed co-regulation design has some unique advantages, from the design prospective, when compared with event-triggered and self-triggered control strategies. It can overcome the disadvantages of not being able to distinguish lack of new information from detection/communication failures in an event-triggered control. For self-triggered systems, the only information provided at each time step is the next sampling instance. Co-regulation has the advantage of knowing precisely when the next sampling instant will be unless it is changed. That is, in the absence of a computational control law, it reverts to a fixed-rate control—a strong robustness characteristic.

Event-triggered and self-triggered control algorithms add additional tuning and triggering parameters, which can bring extra uncertainties in the control performance. Thus, the system robustness can be reduced when compared with fixed-periodic and co-regulated controllers. During the test process, we found event-triggered and self-triggered control algorithms are very sensitive to parameter changes; that is, a tiny change in the triggering parameter can lead to huge changes in system performance. The UAS step responses under different triggering parameter values are recorded. Figure 7a,b, shows the UAS performance difference when the triggering parameter (σ) value is changed from 0.7 to 0.9, the resulting number of control instances decreases from 27 to 22, but the control performance is dramatically changed.

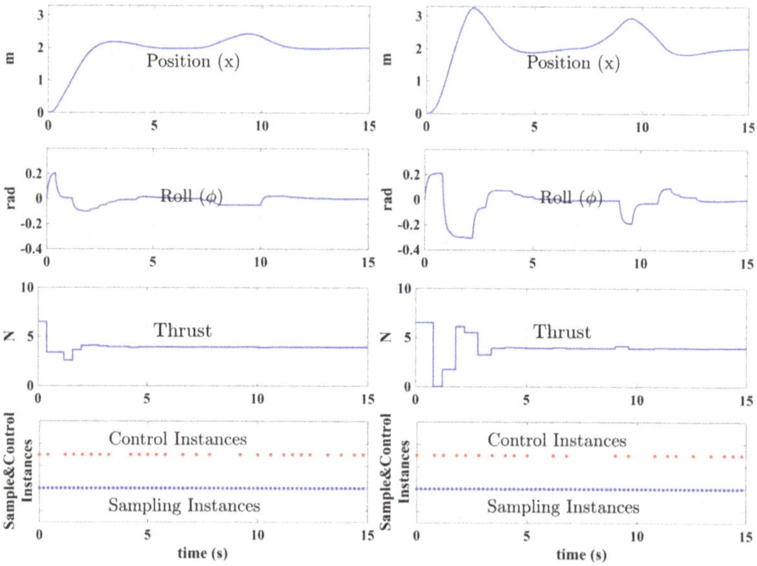

(a) $\sigma = 0.66$ **(b)** $\sigma = 0.77$

Figure 7. Event-triggered control performances with different σ values.

In self-triggered control, the system performance is even more sensitive to triggering parameter changes. Figure 8a,b shows the UAS performance difference when the triggering parameter μ value changes from 0.7 to 0.9, the resulting number of control instances decreases from 30 to 26, and the control performance is greatly affected.

The performances of event/self-triggered controllers can become more robust when we select more conservative triggering parameters. However, the sampling and control instances will increase to approximately the same level as a high-rate fixed-periodic controller, which will lose the advantages in conserving computing resources. On the other hand, less conservative triggering parameters of event-triggered and self-triggered controls can lead to more savings of resources at the cost of decreased system robustness. Co-regulation, as opposed to event/self-triggered control strategies, can provide much more robust and consistent system performances when we change either Q and R parameters for the physical system controller or K_{cp} and K_c parameters for the computational system controller.

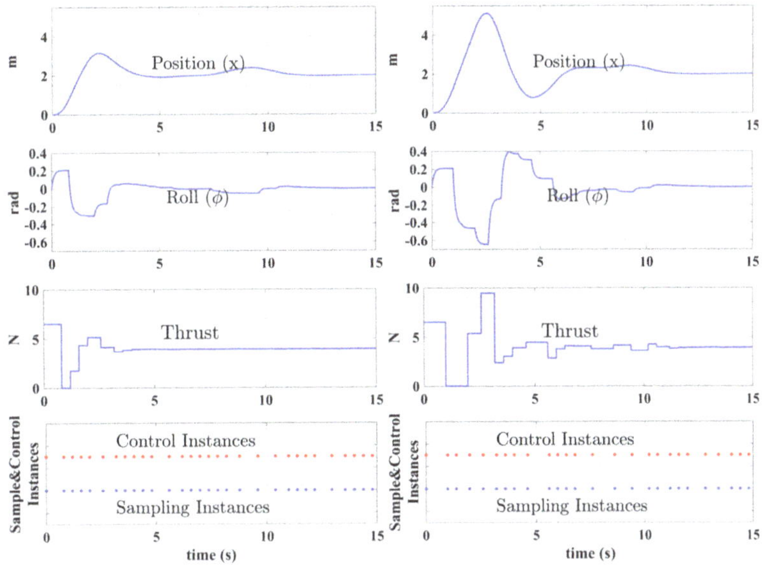

(a) $\mu = 0.7$

(b) $\mu = 0.9$

Figure 8. Self-triggered control performances with different μ values.

Recent research studies have provided more advanced designs for event-triggered and self-triggered controls, where better trade-offs among resources and performances could be achieved. An important issue surrounding event-triggered and self-triggered controls is the complexity of the algorithms used for the online implementation that decides the sampling interval [30]. Such complex calculations can be challenging to real-time implementations, especially for applications where fast system dynamics are required. However, the co-regulation scheme calculates the sampling rate trajectory by a separate computational controller that can be executed extremely fast (complexity $\mathcal{O}(1)$) with negligible resource consumption, such as a PID controller [9]. The physical controller can also be customized depending on different application requirements. The proposed GSDLQR algorithm for co-regulated systems can be implemented as a lookup table, which can be executed fast enough to meet real-time requirements in highly dynamic applications [10]. By detaching the computational and physical system, co-regulation can provide a higher degree of freedom for system design, as well as a highly robust framework that can provide performance guarantees for different application scenarios. Though discussed in the context of UAS in this work, co-regulation design is broadly applicable to cyber-physical vehicle and robotics systems, particularly those where careful allocation of resources is desirable (e.g., size, weight, and power constrained vehicles). More detailed information of a co-regulated control algorithm [10,12] and co-regulated system stability analysis [11] can be found in our previous work. Our future work will focus on extending the co-regulation design to different vehicle and robotic systems.

8. Conclusions

In this paper, we analyzed the trade-offs between computing resource utilizations, represented by sampling rate and control performance, to further explore an opportunity for more intelligent design strategies for UAS, to accomplish more with fewer resources. We conducted a comparison test of different sampling strategies to demonstrate how computing and timing can affect control performance. We highlighted the benefits of our proposed cyber-physical co-regulation strategy in overcoming the drawbacks of event-triggered and self-triggered controllers, while saving far more resources compared with traditional fixed-periodic strategies.

To make UAS more intelligent, they need the ability to adjust behavior (performance) *and* resources to meet increasing demands in uncertain environments. This type of rethinking of the foundations of autonomy is required to build the next generation of autonomous robotic systems. Co-regulation does exactly this, and can form the core of a new intelligent control system to meet this challenge. We anticipate this will make autonomous robotic systems more efficient, robust, and capable of adapting to changes.

Author Contributions: Conceptualization, X.Z. and J.B.; methodology, X.Z.; software, X.Z.; validation, X.Z. and J.B.; resources, J.B.; writing—original draft preparation, X.Z.; writing—review and editing, J.B.; supervision, J.B.; project administration, J.B.; funding acquisition, J.B. All authors have read and agreed to the published version of the manuscript.

Funding: This work was supported in part by NSF CNS-2047971.

Institutional Review Board Statement: Not applicable.

Informed Consent Statement: Not applicable.

Data Availability Statement: Not applicable.

Conflicts of Interest: The authors declare no conflict of interest. The funders had no role in the design of the study; in the collection, analyses, or interpretation of data; in the writing of the manuscript, or in the decision to publish the results.

References

1. Bradley, J.M.; Atkins, E.M. Optimization and control of cyber-physical vehicle systems. *Sensors* **2015**, *15*, 23020–23049. [CrossRef] [PubMed]
2. Salhaoui, M.; Guerrero-González, A.; Arioua, M.; Ortiz, F.J.; El Oualkadi, A.; Torregrosa, C.L. Smart industrial iot monitoring and control system based on UAV and cloud computing applied to a concrete plant. *Sensors* **2019**, *19*, 3316. [CrossRef] [PubMed]
3. Wolf, M. Computing in the real world is the grandest of challenges. *Computer* **2018**, *51*, 90–91. [CrossRef]
4. Wang, H.; Huang, Y.; Khajepour, A. Cyber-physical control for energy management of off-road vehicles with hybrid energy storage systems. *IEEE/ASME Trans. Mechatron.* **2018**, *23*, 2609–2618. [CrossRef]
5. Lee, D.H.; Joo, Y.H. A note on sampled-data stabilization of LTI systems with aperiodic sampling. *IEEE Trans. Autom. Control* **2015**, *60*, 2746–2751. [CrossRef]
6. Nise, N.S. *Control Systems Engineering*; Wiley: Hoboken, NJ, USA , 2015.
7. Heemels, W.; Donkers, M. Model-based periodic event-triggered control for linear systems. *Automatica* **2013**, *49*, 698–711. [CrossRef]
8. Heemels, W.; Johansson, K.H.; Tabuada, P. An introduction to event-triggered and self-triggered control. In Proceedings of the 2012 IEEE 51st IEEE Conference on Decision and Control (CDC), Wailea, HI, USA, 10–13 December 2012; IEEE: Piscataway, NJ, USA, 2012; pp. 3270–3285.
9. Bradley, J.M.; Atkins, E.M. Coupled Cyber-Physical System Modeling and Coregulation of a CubeSat. *IEEE Trans. Robot.* **2015**, *31*, 443–456. [CrossRef]
10. Zhang, X.; Doebbeling, S.; Bradley, J. Co-regulation of computational and physical effectors in a quadrotor unmanned aircraft system. In Proceedings of the 9th ACM/IEEE International Conference on Cyber-Physical Systems, Porto, Portugal, 11–13 April 2018; IEEE Press: Piscataway, NJ, USA, 2018; pp. 119–129.
11. Zhang, X.; Bradley, J. Stability Analysis for a Class of Resource-Aware, Co-Regulated Systems. In Proceedings of the 2019 IEEE Conference on Decision and Control (CDC), Nice, France, 11–13 December 2019; IEEE: Piscataway, NJ, USA, 2019; pp. 193–200.
12. Zhang, X.; Bradley, J. Controller Design for Time-Varying Sampling, Co-Regulated Systems. *IEEE Control Syst. Lett.* **2020**, *5*, 2132–2137. [CrossRef]
13. Zhang, X.; Bradley, J. Computing for Control and Control for Computing. In Proceedings of the 2021 Design, Automation & Test in Europe Conference & Exhibition (DATE), Grenoble, France, 1–5 February 2021; IEEE: Piscataway, NJ, USA, 2021; pp. 469–474.
14. Åström, K.J.; Wittenmark, B. *Computer-Controlled Systems: Theory and Design*; Courier Corporation : North Chelmsford, MA, USA, 2013.
15. Shankar, A.; Doebbeling, S.; Bradley, J. Toward a cyber-physical quadrotor: Characterizing trajectory following performance. In Proceedings of the 2017 International Conference on Unmanned Aircraft Systems (ICUAS), Miami, FL, USA, 13–16 June 2017; IEEE: Piscataway, NJ, USA, 2017; pp. 133–142.
16. Martı, P.; Lin, C.; Brandt, S.A.; Velasco, M.; Fuertes, J.M. Draco: Efficient resource management for resource-constrained control tasks. *IEEE Trans. Comput.* **2009**, *58*, 90–105. [CrossRef]

17. Kopetz, H. *Real-Time Systems: Design Principles for Distributed Embedded Applications;* Springer Science & Business Media: Berlin/Heidelberg, Germany, 2011.
18. Singh, A.K.; Dziurzanski, P.; Mendis, H.R.; Indrusiak, L.S. A survey and comparative study of hard and soft real-time dynamic resource allocation strategies for multi-/many-core systems. *ACM Comput. Surv. (CSUR)* **2017**, *50*, 1–40. [CrossRef]
19. Nowka, K.J.; Carpenter, G.D.; MacDonald, E.W.; Ngo, H.C.; Brock, B.C.; Ishii, K.I.; Nguyen, T.Y.; Burns, J.L. A 32-bit PowerPC system-on-a-chip with support for dynamic voltage scaling and dynamic frequency scaling. *IEEE J. Solid-State Circuits* **2002**, *37*, 1441–1447. [CrossRef]
20. Kim, J.; Lakshmanan, K.; Rajkumar, R.R. Rhythmic tasks: A new task model with continually varying periods for cyber-physical systems. In Proceedings of the 2012 IEEE/ACM Third International Conference on Cyber-Physical Systems, Washington, DC, USA, 17–19 April 2012; IEEE Computer Society: Washington, DC, USA, 2012; pp. 55–64.
21. Burns, A.; Hayes, I.J. A timeband framework for modelling real-time systems. *Real-Time Syst.* **2010**, *45*, 106–142. [CrossRef]
22. Lee, C.; Lehoezky, J.; Rajkumar, R.; Siewiorek, D. On quality of service optimization with discrete QoS options. In Proceedings of the Fifth IEEE Real-Time Technology and Applications Symposium, Vancouver, BC, Canada, 2–4 June 1999; IEEE: Piscataway, NJ, USA, 1999; pp. 276–286.
23. Gai, K.; Qiu, M. Optimal resource allocation using reinforcement learning for IoT content-centric services. *Appl. Soft Comput.* **2018**, *70*, 12–21. [CrossRef]
24. Pothukuchi, R.P.; Pothukuchi, S.Y.; Voulgaris, P.G.; Torrellas, J. Control Systems for Computing Systems: Making computers efficient with modular, coordinated, and robust control. *IEEE Control Syst. Mag.* **2020**, *40*, 30–55. [CrossRef]
25. Åström, K.J.; Bernhardsson, B.M. Comparison of Riemann and Lebesgue sampling for first order stochastic systems. In Proceedings of the Decision and Control, 41st IEEE Conference, Las Vegas, NV, USA, 10–13 December 2002; IEEE: Piscataway, NJ, USA, 2002; Volume 2, pp. 2011–2016.
26. Heemels, W.H.; Donkers, M.; Teel, A.R. Periodic event-triggered control for linear systems. *IEEE Trans. Autom. Control* **2012**, *58*, 847–861. [CrossRef]
27. Eqtami, A.; Dimarogonas, D.V.; Kyriakopoulos, K.J. Event-triggered control for discrete-time systems. In Proceedings of the 2010 American Control Conference, Baltimore, MD, USA, 30 June–2 July 2010; IEEE: Piscataway, NJ, USA, 2010; pp. 4719–4724.
28. Sabatino, F. *Quadrotor Control: Modeling, Nonlinearcontrol Design, and Simulation*; KTH: Stockholm, Sweden, 2015 .
29. AscTec Research UAVs. Available online: http://www.asctec.de (accessed on 19 January 2022).
30. Hetel, L.; Fiter, C.; Omran, H.; Seuret, A.; Fridman, E.; Richard, J.P.; Niculescu, S.I. Recent developments on the stability of systems with aperiodic sampling: An overview. *Automatica* **2017**, *76*, 309–335. [CrossRef]

sensors

Article

Nonlinear Intelligent Control of Two Link Robot Arm by Considering Human Voluntary Components

Mingcong Deng *, Shotaro Kubota and Yuanhong Xu

Department of Electrical and Electronic Engineering (The Graduate School of Engineering), Tokyo University of Agriculture and Technology, 2-24-16 Nakacho, Tokyo 184-8588, Japan; 1212kubota@gmail.com (S.K.); xuyuanhongdp@gmail.com (Y.X.)
* Correspondence: deng@cc.tuat.ac.jp

Abstract: This paper proposes a nonlinear intelligent control of a two link robot arm by considering human voluntary components. In general, human arm viscoelastic properties are regulated in different manners according to various task requirements. The viscoelasticity consists of joint stiffness and viscosity. The research of the viscoelasticity can improve the development of industrial robots, rehabilitation and sports etc. So far, some results have been shown using filtered human arm viscoelasticity measurements. That is, human motor command is removed. As a result, the dynamics of human voluntary component during movements is omitted. In this paper, based on the feedforward characteristics of human multi joint arm, a model is obtained by considering human voluntary components using a support vector regression technique. By employing the learned model, a nonlinear intelligent control of two link robot arm is proposed. Experimental results confirm the effectiveness of this proposal.

Keywords: nonlinear intelligent control; support vector regression; feedforward control; human arm viscoelastic

Citation: Deng, M.; Kubota, S.; Xu, Y. Nonlinear Intelligent Control of Two Link Robot Arm by Considering Human Voluntary Components. *Sensors* **2022**, *22*, 1424. https://doi.org/10.3390/s22041424

Academic Editors: Andrey V. Savkin and Shafiqul Islam

Received: 6 January 2022
Accepted: 9 February 2022
Published: 12 February 2022

1. Introduction

In recent years, in the medical and welfare fields, human resources with appropriate skills are required for treatment/surgical support for patients and long-term care for the elderly. However, the shortage of human resources due to the declining birthrate and aging population has become a problem. As one of the solutions to the above problems, it is conceivable to adopt robots as a labor force. In the future, the places where robots will be active in society will increase not only in factories, but also in facilities and general households where they have contact with humans, so it is necessary to operate robots in cooperation with humans. Therefore, it is desirable that the robot has an excellent man-machine interface, has an affinity with humans, and has the same kinetic characteristics as humans.

Multi-joint viscoelastic properties are attracting attention as an elucidation of human motion control principles. Human arm multi-joint viscoelasticity is the characteristic of the arm joint when the human arm comes into contact with the outside world. The torque that moves a human skeletal joint is generated by the difference in tension between the leading and competing muscle groups. The above tension difference is caused by the activity of muscles controlled by commands from the central nervous system. Muscle control is used not only to generate the joint torque required for exercise, but also to change the stiffness of joints during exercise and at rest. The hardness of the joints mentioned above plays an important role in stabilizing posture and interacting with the outside world [1]. For example, when a person performs a movement to move a cup, the target is mediated by the arm. In addition to interacting with objects, it is also affected by the multi-joint viscoelasticity of this arm. In other words, it is thought that humans perform the desired movement by adjusting the multi-joint viscoelasticity so that the operating environment interacts with the arm and the object. Therefore, learning the work is not only learning the work procedure, but also learning how to control the viscoelastic properties of the above-mentioned musculoskeletal system and contact with the outside world. Exploring the mechanism of adjusting the joint mechanical impedance of the musculoskeletal system is to elucidate the motor control principle of the brain that controls complex multi-joint movements, quantitatively understands the deterioration of movements caused by nerve and muscle disorders, and has human-friendly mechanical interfaces. It can be said that it is an important issue in the development of [2].

Based on the above, many studies on human arm multi-joint viscoelasticity have been conducted [3–11]. In 1998, Gomi et al. proposed a method for estimating the viscoelasticity of the human arm during exercise using a Kalman filter [12]. Furthermore, Deng et al. focused on the numerical instability caused by the Kalman filter's digit loss, and he proposed the adaptation of the UD decomposition method as a solution. Based on these previous studies, Wang proposed motion control of a robot arm considering human arm multi-joint viscoelasticity, and its effectiveness was confirmed by simulation [13]. On the other hand, there is no example of applying human arm multi-joint viscoelasticity to the control of an actual robot arm. The problem in applying it to robot arm motion control is the reproduction of voluntary motion components. The voluntary movement component is a feedforward (FF) component output from a model based on experience in the brain when exercising. In the research to actually estimate the multi-joint viscoelasticity of the human arm, the estimation is performed after removing the above voluntary movement components with a filter. Therefore, in order to apply the multi-joint viscoelasticity of the human arm to the robot arm, it is necessary to reproduce the voluntary movement component with a feedforward controller.

In this study, we focus on the reproduction of the above voluntary movement components. Specifically, we aim to design a feedforward controller that has high control performance in the control of the robot arm. Since the feedforward controller proposed in the previous research is designed based on a mechanical model, there is a concern that the control performance will deteriorate due to modeling errors when conducting actual machine experiments. Therefore, in this research, we use Support Vector Regression (SVR) [14–18], which is a kind of machine learning methods, to design the feedforward controller to reduce the modeling error and improve the tracking performance. The control system is designed based on operator theory [19–24] to compensate for the interference and uncertainty inside the controlled object that exist when controlling the robot arm. Finally, in order to confirm the effectiveness of the proposed control system, we conduct an actual machine experiment and verify its effectiveness.

In summary, the contributions of this paper are as follows: the viscoelastic properties of the multi-joint arm are measured and analyzed through experiments. Based on the characteristic of multi-joint arm viscoelastic, a controller to simulate the human body is designed, and support vector regression is used for feedforward control.

In what follows, in Section 2, as a mathematical preparation to avoid complicating this paper, Lagrange's equation of motion used for modeling and SVR theorems used in the design of feedforward control are explained. In Section 3, as a preparation for setting the problem, we introduce the human arm multi-joint viscoelasticity, robot arm modeling and the configuration of the experimental equipment used, and then raise the problem. Section 4 explains the proposed control system, where we explain the design method for the feedback controller using multi-joint viscoelasticity of the human arm, the feedforward controller based on SVR, and the stabilization controller based on the operator theory. Section 5 first describes the experimental conditions and the SVR parameter determination method based on actual machine experiments. After that, experiment is conducted to confirm the effectiveness of the feedforward controller based on SVR. In the absence of a feedforward controller, the experimental results of using a feedforward controller based on a mechanical model and the experimental results of a feedforward controller based on SVR are compared. Section 6 describes the conclusions of this study.

2. Mathematical Preparation

In this section, Lagrange's motion equation, which is necessary when deriving a mechanical model of a robot arm, is explained.

2.1. Lagrange's Equation of Motion

When deriving the equation of motion of an object, Newton's equation of motion is generally used, but in the case of a complicated mechanical system, it is often difficult to derive it by Newton's equation. Lagrange's Equations are often used in the analysis of mechanical systems because they can solve the equations of motion of complex mechanical systems more efficiently than Newton's equations of motion. However, note that the derived solution does not change from Newton's equation because it is essentially based on the same physical law as Newton's equation of motion. In this section, we derive Lagrange's equation of motion. It is divided into three sections.

2.1.1. Generalized Coordinates and Nonholonomic Constraints

In order to show the dynamic behavior of mass system and rigid system, it is necessary to select physical variables appropriately. In this section, we discuss the mass point system for simplicity, but the same idea is possible for systems including rigid systems. Generally, positions are expressed using plaque points in orthogonal coordinate systems, cylindrical coordinate systems and spherical coordinate systems, but here we consider coordinates that are convenient for expressing the position (arrangement) of the entire plaque point system and defined it as generalized coordinates. A set of generalized coordinates may include parts of a Cartesian or spherical coordinate system, but may also use angles, lengths, distances, and so on.

Now, considering any geometrical arrangement that a given mass system can take, a generalized coordinate system is said to be perfect when any of these arrangements can be represented by giving coordinates. Also, the set of generalized coordinates corresponds to continuous fluctuations in some of the coordinates, whether one of them is removed and all the rest are fixed, or all but some of them are fixed. It is said to be independent when a continuous change in its geometrical arrangement can remain. Taking some generalized coordinates for a very wide class of mass and rigid systems, including robot manipulators such as akrobot, which is the subject of this study. The number of independent coordinates in it is often constant despite changes in the permissible arrangement, which is then called the degree of freedom of the system.

A mass system has less degrees of freedom when it receives a geometric constraint. If the geometric constraint can be expressed analytically by generalized coordinates and an equation that depends only on time, the constraint is nonholonomic. Now, suppose choosing $(x_1, x_2, \ldots, x_m)$ as the complete generalized coordinate system for a mass system, the coordinate system is not independent, there are p holonomic constraints such as:

$$\begin{cases} h_1(x_1, x_2, \ldots, x_m, t) = 0 \\ h_2(x_1, x_2, \ldots, x_m, t) = 0 \\ \cdots\cdots\cdots\cdots \\ h_p(x_1, x_2, \ldots, x_m, t) = 0 \end{cases}. \quad (1)$$

When these constraints are independent, there are $n = m - p$ independent coordinates out of m coordinates. The mass system has n degrees of freedom. Therefore, suppose that a generalized coordinate system $(q_1, q_2, \ldots, q_n)$ that is completely and independent from the beginning is selected for the mass system of n degrees of freedom. In addition, if part of a complete generalized coordinate system $(x_1, x_2, \ldots, x_m)$ is $(q_1, q_2, \ldots, q_n)$, then the remaining p of the former are determined by Equation (1). Assuming that the mass system consists of N mass points, it is expressed that the position vector $\boldsymbol{r}_i$ of any mass point m_i is determined by the generalized coordinate system $(q_1, q_2, \ldots, q_n)$.

$$\boldsymbol{r}_i = \boldsymbol{r}_i(q_1, q_2, \ldots, q_n, t) = \boldsymbol{r}_i(\boldsymbol{q}, t) \quad (2)$$

The velocity v_i of this mass point is

$$v_i = \frac{d}{dt}r_i = \sum_{j=1}^{n} \frac{\partial r_i}{\partial q_j}\dot{q}_j + \frac{\partial r_i}{\partial t}. \quad (3)$$

This time derivative $\dot{q} = (\dot{q}_1, \dot{q}_2, \ldots, \dot{q}_n)$ is called general acceleration.

Since the generalized position coordinate system $(q_1, q_2, \ldots, q_n)$ is complete and independent, the set of infinitesimal variations of coordinates $(\delta q_1, \delta q_2, \ldots, \delta q_n)$ is also complete and independent. Therefore, the variation of the position r_i of the quality point m_i is represented by the variation δq_1 of the generalized coordinates.

$$\delta r_i = \sum_{j=1}^{n} \frac{\partial r_i}{\partial q_j}\delta q_j \quad (4)$$

Next, assuming that the force f_i is acting on each mass point m_i, the increment of all the work done by f_i is calculated under the variational δr_i of the arrangement of the mass system.

$$\sum_{i=1}^{N} f_i^T \delta r_i = \sum_{i=1}^{N}\sum_{j=1}^{n} f_i^T \frac{\partial r_i}{\partial q_j}\delta q_j = \sum_{i=1}^{N}\left(\sum_{j=1}^{n} f_i^T \frac{\partial r_i}{\partial q_j}\right)\delta q_j \quad (5)$$

The jth on the right side represents the force component in that direction obtained from the infinitesimal variation δq_i of one of the generalized coordinates q_j, and this force is called the generalized force.

$$F_j = \sum_{j=1}^{N} f_i^T \frac{\partial r_i}{\partial q_j} \quad (6)$$

Using the generalization force, (5) is expressed as,

$$\sum_{i=1}^{N} f_i^T \delta r_i = \sum_{j=1}^{n} F_j \delta q_j. \quad (7)$$

2.1.2. Hamilton's Principle

If the momentum vector of the mass point m_i is set as p_i, the equation of motion of the mass point system is expressed as

$$f_i - \frac{d}{dt}p_i = 0 \quad (8)$$

Note that with the nonholonomic constraint, this equation is redundant and can be expressed for any variation δr_i.

$$\sum_{i=1}^{N}\left(f_i - \frac{d}{dt}p_i\right)^T \delta r_i = 0. \quad (9)$$

However, since δr_i is generally not independent, (8) is (9). Therefore, we derive Hamilton's principle from (9) and derive n independent equations of motion equal to n degrees of freedom.

$$\sum_{i=1}^{N} f_i^T \delta r_i \quad (10)$$

In general, the equation represents the sum of the work done by the forces acting on all mass points in the mass system, but it is divided into a part due to conservative force and a part due to non-conservative external force. That is, the potential energy corresponding to the conservative force is $V(\boldsymbol{q})$, the generalized force is F_j, and (10) is expressed as the following equation.

$$\sum_{i=1}^{N} \boldsymbol{f}_i^T \delta \boldsymbol{r}_i = -\delta V + \sum_{j=1}^{n} F_i \delta q_j \tag{11}$$

The first term on the right side is the decrease in potential energy, and the second term is the work done by the external force. Substituting (11) into (9) gives the following equation.

$$-\delta V + \sum_{j=1}^{n} F_i \delta q_j - \sum_{i=1}^{N} \boldsymbol{f}_i - \frac{d\boldsymbol{p}_i^T}{dt} \delta \boldsymbol{r}_i = 0 \tag{12}$$

Here, the third term on the left side can be rewritten as

$$-\frac{d\boldsymbol{p}_i^T}{dt} \delta \boldsymbol{r}_i = -\sum_{i=1}^{N} \frac{d}{dt}\left(\boldsymbol{p}_i^T \delta \boldsymbol{r}_i\right) + \sum_{i=1}^{N} \boldsymbol{p}_i^T \frac{d}{dt} \delta \boldsymbol{r}_i. \tag{13}$$

Also, assuming that the mass fluctuation of each mass point of the target mass point system does not occur in the time interval considered, the variation of the total kinetic energy is

$$\delta K = \sum_{i=1}^{N} \boldsymbol{p}_i^T \frac{d}{dt} \delta \boldsymbol{r}_i. \tag{14}$$

Substituting (14) into the right side of (14) palce yields

$$-\frac{d\boldsymbol{p}_i^T}{dt} \delta \boldsymbol{r}_i = -\sum_{i=1}^{N} \frac{d}{dt}\left(\boldsymbol{p}_i^T \delta \boldsymbol{r}_i\right) + \delta K. \tag{15}$$

Substituting (15) into (12) yields,

$$\delta K - \delta V + \sum_{j=1}^{n} F_i \delta q_j - \sum_{i=1}^{N} \frac{d}{dt}\left(\boldsymbol{p}_i^T \delta \boldsymbol{r}_i\right) = 0. \tag{16}$$

This equation holds for any time interval $[t_1, t_2]$ we are thinking of, so that the variation of position $\delta \mathbf{r}_i(t_1) = 0$ and $\delta \mathbf{r}_i(t_2) = 0$. This is possible because the generalized coordinate system is perfect, and when (16) is integrated over the interval $[t_1, t_2]$, the fourth term on the right side disappears and the following equation holds.

$$\int_{t_1}^{t_2} \left(\delta(K - V) + \sum_{j=1}^{n} F_i \delta q_j \right) dt = 0 \tag{17}$$

Equation (17) is called Hamilton's principle for a nonholonomic mass system with n degrees of freedom.

2.1.3. Lagrange's Equation of Motion

In order to derive an independent equation of motion equal to n degrees of freedom from Hamilton's theorem, we introduce a physical quantity called Lagrangian as in the following equation.

$$L = K - V \tag{18}$$

where K is the kinetic energy and V is the potential energy. Since V is the potential energy, it is a function of only the generalized coordinate $\dot{q}_j$, but K is a function of $\dot{q}_j$, q_j and time t. Lagradian L can be written as,

$$L = L(\dot{q}, q, t). \tag{19}$$

The variation is

$$\delta L = \sum_{j=1}^{n} \left(\frac{\partial L}{\partial \dot{q}_j} \delta \dot{q}_j + \frac{\partial L}{\partial q_j} \delta q_j \right). \tag{20}$$

Substituting this into (17) yields,

$$\int_{t_1}^{t_2} \sum_{j=1}^{n} \left(\frac{\partial L}{\partial \dot{q}_j} \left(\frac{d}{dt} \right) \delta \dot{q}_j + \frac{\partial L}{\partial q_j} \delta q_j + F_i \delta q_j \right) dt = 0. \tag{21}$$

Here, if the first term on the left side is integrated by parts, it can be seen that (21) becomes,

$$\int_{t_1}^{t_2} \sum_{j=1}^{n} \left(-\frac{d}{dt} \left(\frac{\partial L}{\partial \dot{q}_j} \right) + \frac{\partial L}{\partial q_j} + F_i \right) \delta q_j dt = 0. \tag{22}$$

Since (22) must hold for any variation δq_j, the following n equations must hold for the time interval $t \in [t_1, t_2]$. This is the equation of motion of the mass system described in generalized coordinates $\mathbf{q} = (q_1, \ldots, q_n)$, and is called the equation of motion of Lagrange.

$$\frac{d}{dt} \left(\frac{\partial L}{\partial \dot{q}_j} \right) - \frac{\partial L}{\partial q_j} = F_j \tag{23}$$

Many of the equations of motion of mass and rigid systems with nonholonomic constraints can be derived by using Lagrange's equation of motion with the following steps.

- Select a complete and independent generalized coordinate system.
- Identify non-conservative generalization forces.
- Find the kinetic energy and potential energy to construct the Lagrangian.
- Substitute Lagrangian into Lagrange's equation of motion and write down the equation of motion concretely.

2.2. *Support Vector Regression*

Support vector regression is an application of a support vector machine to a regression problem [14–18]. Support vector regression is called SVR and support vector machine is called SVM. SVM is a typical method of binary classification and has a high prediction for unknown data. It has been reported that it is possible to construct a classifier (function) with measurement accuracy. SVM uses methods such as margin maximization and kernel tricks for identification hyperplane design, and SVR is an adaptation of these methods to regression problems. Therefore, SVR has features such as high generalization performance and effectiveness even for those with non-linear input/output relationships. This section describes the procedure for deriving the regression function and the kernel function used for the regression function.

2.2.1. Derivation of Regression Function

This section describes the procedure for deriving the regression function based on SVR. The regression function of SVR is expressed by the following equation.

$$f(x) = \omega^T \phi(x) + b \tag{24}$$

Let $f(x)$ be the regression function, x be the input vector, ω be the regression coefficient of the feature space, ϕ be the feature function of SVR, and b be the bias term. The regression function is determined from the training data using an SVM-based method. In order to determine the regression function, it is necessary to derive the regression coefficient ϕ

and the bias term b. Let (x_i, y_i) be the input/output training data used to determine the function of (24). Here, the slack variable is introduced as follows. ϵ is a setting parameter.

$$\begin{aligned} \xi_i^+ &= \begin{cases} 0 & (y_i - f(\boldsymbol{x}_i) \le \epsilon) \\ y_i - f(\boldsymbol{x}_i) - \epsilon & (y_i - f(\boldsymbol{x}_i) > \epsilon) \end{cases} \\ \xi_i^- &= \begin{cases} 0 & (y_i - f(\boldsymbol{x}_i) \ge -\epsilon) \\ -\epsilon - y_i + f(\boldsymbol{x}_i) & (y_i - f(\boldsymbol{x}_i) < -\epsilon) \end{cases} \end{aligned} \tag{25}$$

By using the slack variables ξ_i^+ and ξ_i^-, SVR is formulated as follows.

$$\min_{\omega,b,\xi} \left[\frac{1}{2}\omega^T\omega + C\sum_{i=1}^{n}(\xi_i^+ + \xi_i^-) \right] \tag{26}$$

It is assumed that the constraint condition

$$\begin{cases} y_i - \omega^T\phi(\boldsymbol{x}_i) - b & \le \epsilon + \xi_i^+, \quad i = 1, \ldots, n \\ \omega^T\phi(\boldsymbol{x}_i) + b - y_i & \le \epsilon + \xi_i^-, \quad i = 1, \ldots, n \\ \xi_i^+, \xi_i^- & \ge 0, \qquad\quad i = 1, \ldots, n \end{cases} \tag{27}$$

is satisfied. Here, C is the setting parameter and n is the number of training data. (26) maximizes the following objective function by introducing the Lagrange multiplier $\lambda_i^+, \lambda_i^-, \mu_i^+, \mu_i^-$.

$$\begin{aligned} L_p = {} & \frac{1}{2}\omega^T\omega + C\sum_{i=1}^{n}(\xi_i^+ + \xi_i^-) \\ & - \sum_{i=1}^{n}(\mu_i^+\xi_i^+ + \mu_i^-\xi_i^-) \\ & - \sum_{i=1}^{n}\lambda_i^+\left(\epsilon + \xi_i^+ - y_i + \omega^T\phi(\boldsymbol{x}_i) + b\right) \\ & - \sum_{i=1}^{n}\lambda_i^-\left(\epsilon + \xi_i^- + y_i - \omega^T\phi(\boldsymbol{x}_i) - b\right) \end{aligned} \tag{28}$$

Since the optimal solution is the point where the partial derivative of L_p with respect to ω, b, ξ_i^+, and ξ_i^- becomes 0, the following equation holds for the optimal solution.

$$\frac{\partial L_p}{\partial \omega} = \omega - \sum_{i=1}^{n}(\lambda_i^+ - \lambda_i^-)\phi(\boldsymbol{x}_i) = 0 \tag{29}$$

$$\frac{\partial L_p}{\partial b} = \sum_{i=1}^{n}(\lambda_i^- - \lambda_i^+) = 0 \tag{30}$$

$$\frac{\partial L_p}{\partial \xi_i^+} = C - \lambda_i^+ - \mu_i^+ = 0 \tag{31}$$

$$\frac{\partial L_p}{\partial \xi_i^-} = C - \lambda_i^- - \mu_i^- = 0 \tag{32}$$

from (29), ω is

$$\omega = \sum_{i=1}^{n}(\lambda_i^+ - \lambda_i^-)\phi(\boldsymbol{x}_i) \tag{33}$$

Therefore, (24) is rewritten as

$$f(\boldsymbol{x}) = \sum_{i=1}^{n}(\lambda_i^+ - \lambda_i^-)\phi(\boldsymbol{x}_i)^T\phi(\boldsymbol{x}) + b \tag{34}$$

Substituting (29), (31) and (32) into (28) results in the following dual problem.

$$\max_{\lambda_i^-,\lambda_i^+} L_p = \max_{\lambda_i^-,\lambda_i^+}\left[-\frac{1}{2}\sum_{i=1}^{n}\sum_{j=1}^{n}(\lambda_i^+-\lambda_i^-)\left(\lambda_j^+-\lambda_j^-\right)\phi^T(\boldsymbol{x}_i)\phi(\boldsymbol{x}_j)\right.$$
$$\left.+\sum_{i=1}^{n} y_i(\lambda_i^+-\lambda_i^-)-\sum_{i=1}^{n}\epsilon(\lambda_i^++\lambda_i^-)\right] \tag{35}$$

λ_i^+ and λ_i^- are

$$\sum_{i=1}^{n}(\lambda_i^+-\lambda_i^-)=0,\quad 0\le\lambda_i^+,\quad \lambda_i^-\le C \tag{36}$$

Using the kernel function,

$$K(\boldsymbol{x}_i,\boldsymbol{x}_j)=\phi(\boldsymbol{x}_i)^T\phi(\boldsymbol{x}_j) \tag{37}$$

(35) becomes

$$\max_{\lambda_i^-,\lambda_i^+}\left[-\tfrac{1}{2}\textstyle\sum_{i=1}^{n}\sum_{j=1}^{n}(\lambda_i^+-\lambda_i^-)\left(\lambda_j^+-\lambda_j^-\right)K(\boldsymbol{x}_i,\boldsymbol{x}_j)\right.$$
$$\left.+\textstyle\sum_{i=1}^{n} y_i(\lambda_i^+-\lambda_i^-)-\sum_{i=1}^{n}\epsilon(\lambda_i^++\lambda_i^-)\right] \tag{38}$$

The regression function is obtained from (39) using the kernel function.

$$f(\boldsymbol{x})=\sum_{i=1}^{n}(\lambda_i^--\lambda_i^+)K(\boldsymbol{x}_i,\boldsymbol{x})+b \tag{39}$$

2.2.2. Kernel Function

This section introduces the kernel function used for the regression function. As mentioned above, by using the kernel function, a complicated model can be realized without explicitly calculating $\phi(\boldsymbol{x})$. However, not all functions can be used as kernel functions, and it is generally necessary to satisfy Mercer's theorem. The necessary and sufficient condition for a continuous object and square-integrable function $K(\boldsymbol{x},\boldsymbol{x}')$ to have the following expansion for the eigen $\lambda_i\ge 0$ and the eigenfunction ϕ_i is an arbitrary square-integrable function.

$$K(\boldsymbol{x},\boldsymbol{x}')=\sum_{i=1}^{\infty}\lambda_i\phi_i(\boldsymbol{x})^T\phi_i(\boldsymbol{x}') \tag{40}$$

The following conditions are satisfied for g.

$$\int_{\mathcal{X}\times\mathcal{X}} K(\boldsymbol{x},\boldsymbol{x}')g(\boldsymbol{x})g(\boldsymbol{x}')d\boldsymbol{x}d\boldsymbol{x}'\ge 0 \tag{41}$$

Any function that satisfies the above theorem can be used as a kernel function. In addition, there are many kernel functions that satisfy Mercer's theorem, and the model learned by changing the kernel function is completely different. Various kernel functions have been proposed according to the application, but this section introduces the basic kernel functions that are used very frequently. There are three basic kernel functions:

$$K(\boldsymbol{x}_i,\boldsymbol{x})=\boldsymbol{x}_i^T\boldsymbol{x} \tag{42}$$

$$K(\boldsymbol{x}_i,\boldsymbol{x})=\left(\boldsymbol{x}_i^T\boldsymbol{x}\right)^d \tag{43}$$

$$K(\boldsymbol{x}_i,\boldsymbol{x})=\exp\left(-\frac{\|\boldsymbol{x}_i-\boldsymbol{x}\|^2}{2\sigma^2}\right) \tag{44}$$

The above equations represent a linear kernel, a polynomial kernel and an RBF kernel, respectively. The parameter σ in the RBF function in (44) is expressed as y_i as the output data, N as the total number of data, and $\overline{y}$ as the average value of the output data.

$$\sigma^2 = \frac{1}{N}\sum_{i=1}^{N}(y_i - \overline{y})^2 \tag{45}$$

A linear kernel is a simple kernel function derived when $\phi(\mathbf{x}_i) = \mathbf{x}_i$, but it is often used when a simple model is desired. Both the polynomial kernel and the RBF kernel are capable of implementing non-linear models. Since the above two kernel functions can further adjust the complexity of the model by parameters, in many cases, they are adaptively determined for the data by using cross-validation methods or the like.

3. Problem Setup

In this section, the problem setup will be described after explaining the human arm multi-joint viscoelasticity required and the robot arm used in this study.

3.1. Human Arm Multi-Joint Viscoelasticity

Human arm multi-joint viscoelasticity is a characteristic that determines the "hardness" of a person's arm joint. The torque that moves a human skeletal joint is generated by the difference in tension between the leading and competing muscle groups. The above tension difference is caused by the activity of muscles controlled by commands from the central nervous system. On the other hand, muscle control is used not only to generate the joint torque required for exercise, but also to change the "hardness" of joints during exercise and at rest. When both muscle groups between the joints have high tension, the human arm joint becomes "hard". However, when the tensions of both muscle groups are small, the human arm joint becomes easy to move. The above-mentioned "hardness" of joints has an important role in interaction with the outside world in work and stabilization in posture maintenance.

The behavior of the human musculoskeletal system is often modeled as a spring-damper mass system, including the inherent characteristics of individual muscles and the characteristics of the reflex system. Since the human musculoskeletal system actually has complicated characteristics, the expression method is not unified, but in general, the coefficient of the spring characteristic is the elasticity (stiffness) and damper characteristic of the musculoskeletal system. The coefficient is called viscosity. The coefficient of change in force with respect to change in acceleration is almost determined by the inertia of the musculoskeletal system, so it is called inertia (mass). These three coefficients are collectively called the mechanical impedance parameter of the musculoskeletal system. Among the mechanical impedance parameters, the stiffness is mainly caused by the elastic properties of the muscle, which changes according to the activity level of the muscle. In the "equilibrium position control hypothesis" [25,26], there are models of the musculoskeletal motor system, utilizing the servo system composed of its elastic characteristics and reflection. It is thought that motion and external force are generated by giving the equilibrium position as a motor command. It can also be said that "learning work" is not only learning the work procedure, but also learning how to control the viscoelastic properties of the above-mentioned musculoskeletal system and come into contact with the outside world. Therefore, exploring the adjustment mechanism of the joint mechanical impedance of the musculoskeletal system is to elucidate the movement control principle of the brain that controls complicated multi-joint movements. It can be said that it is an important issue for quantitative understanding of deterioration of movement caused by nerve and muscle disorders and development of human-friendly mechanical interface.

3.2. Robot Arm

In this section, we will introduce the robot arm, which is the experimental device handled in this study, and then explain the derivation of the dynamic model. Finally, we will introduce the hardware configuration of the experimental equipment.

3.2.1. Experimental Device

In this research, we conduct an experiment using the two-degree-of-freedom horizontal robot arm that imitates a human arm. Figure 1 shows the horizontal multi-joint robot. It is characterized by using lightweight aluminum for each link and driving each link by a direct drive method.

Figure 1. Robot arm used in this research (Mechanical part).

The self-made buffer circuit used in the experimental equipment of the robot arm is shown in Figure 2. This circuit consists of two boards, the first stage has an input connector for a rotary encoder and an output connector for connecting to a PCI board. The motor controller for the Link 2 motor is also screwed to his first stage, but the power system is separate. In the second stage, the width of the input/output voltage differs between the PCI board and the motor controller, so an amplifier circuit composed of operational amplifiers is built.

Figure 2. Robot arm used in this research (Electric part).

3.2.2. Mechanics Modeling

The dynamic model of the two-link robot arm that is the control target is shown in Figure 3. Lagrange's equation of motion is used to derive the dynamic model. The equations of motion of Lagrangian and Lagrange are shown below.

$$L = K - V \tag{46}$$

$$\frac{d}{dt}\left(\frac{\partial L}{\partial \dot{x}}\right) - \frac{\partial L}{\partial x} = F \tag{47}$$

K is kinetic energy, V is potential energy, x is generalized coordinates and F is generalized force. The mechanical model derived from Lagrange's equation of motion shown in (47) is expressed as the following equation [27]. (48) represents link 1 and (49) represents link 2.

$$m_{11}\ddot{\theta}_1 + m_{12}\ddot{\theta}_2 + \sum_{j=1}^{\infty}\{m_{14}(j)\ddot{v}_{2j}\} + f_1 + B_1\dot{\theta}_1 = \tau_1 \tag{48}$$

$$m_{12}\ddot{\theta}_1 + m_{22}\ddot{\theta}_2 + \sum_{j=1}^{\infty}\{m_{24}(j)\ddot{v}_{2j}\} + f_2 + B_2\dot{\theta}_2 = \tau_2 \tag{49}$$

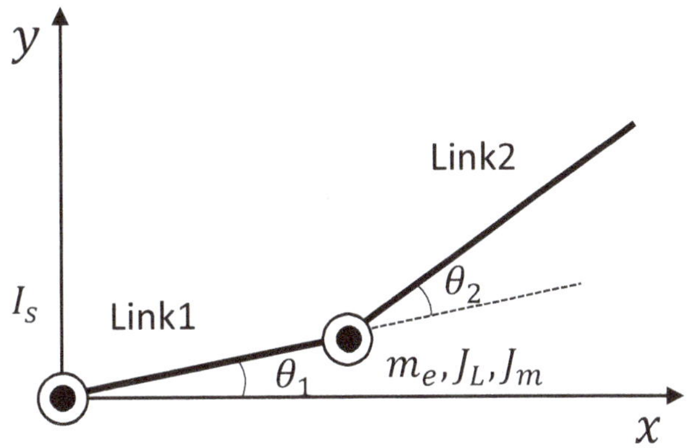

Figure 3. Robot arm used in this research (Conceptual diagram).

The parameters used in (48) and (49) are shown in the following equations and Table 1.

Table 1. Parameters of each link.

ρ_1	Link1 density	[kg/m^3]
ρ_2	Link2 density	[kg/m^3]
L_1	Link1 length	[m]
L_1	Link2 length	[m]
A_1	Link1 cross-sectional area	[m^2]
A_2	Link2 cross-sectional area	[m^2]
I_s	Moment of inertia of rotor	[kg/m^2]
J_L	Moment of inertia of set collar	[kg/m^2]
J_m	Moment of inertia of rotor	[kg/m^2]
τ_1	Torque applied to Link1	[N·m]
τ_2	Torque applied to Link1	[N·m]

$$
\begin{aligned}
m_{11} &= I_s + I_{me} + I_e + m_e L_1^2 + \int_0^{L_1} \rho_1 A_1 x_1^2 dx_1 + \int_0^{L_2} \rho_2 A_2 \left\{ L_1^2 + x_2^2 + \left(\sum_{j=1}^{\infty} \phi_{2j}(x_2) v_{2j} \right)^2 \right. \\
&\quad \left. + 2L_1 x_2 \cos(\theta_2) - 2L_1 \sum_{j=1}^{\infty} \phi_{2j}(L_2) v_{2j} \cos(\theta_2) \right\} dx_2 \\
m_{12} &= I_e + \frac{\rho_2 A_2 L_2^3}{3} + \int_0^{L_2} \rho_2 \left\{ x_2^2 + \left(\sum_{j=1}^{\infty} \phi_{2j}(x_2) v_{2j} \right)^2 \right. \\
&\quad \left. + L_1 x_2 \cos(\theta_2) - L_1 \cos(\theta_2) \left(\sum_{j=1}^{\infty} \phi_{2j}(x_2) v_{2j} \right) \right\} dx_2 \\
m_{14}(j) &= I_e + \int_0^{L_2} \rho_2 A_2 \{ x_2 \phi_{2j}(x_2) + L_1 \phi_{2j}(x_2) \cos(\theta_2) \} dx_2 \\
m_{22} &= \int_0^{L_2} \rho_2 A_2 \left\{ x_2^2 + \left(\sum_{j=1}^{\infty} \phi_{2j}(x_2) v_{2j} \right)^2 \right\} dx_2 \\
m_{24}(j) &= \int_0^{L_2} \rho_2 A_2 x_2 \phi_{2j}(x_2) dx_2 \\
f_1 &= 2\rho_2 A_2 (\dot{\theta}_1 + \dot{\theta}_2) \sum_{j=0}^{\infty} v_{2j} \dot{v}_{2j} + L_1 (2\dot{\theta}_1 + \dot{\theta}_2) \dot{\theta}_2 \cos(\theta_2) \sum_{j=0}^{\infty} \rho_2 A_2 \int_0^{L_2} \phi_{2j}(x_2) dx_2 v_{2j} \\
&\quad + 2L_1 (\dot{\theta}_1 + \dot{\theta}_2) \sin(\theta_2) \sum_{j=0}^{\infty} \rho_2 A_2 \int_0^{L_2} \phi_{2j}(x_2) dx_2 \dot{v}_{2j} - \left(\frac{\rho_2 A_2 L_1 L_2^2}{2} + m_e L_1 L_2 \right) \dot{\theta}_2 \sin(\theta_2) \\
f_2 &= 2\rho_2 A_2 (\dot{\theta}_1 + \dot{\theta}_2) \sum_{j=0}^{\infty} v_{2j} \dot{v}_{2j} + L_1 \dot{\theta}_1^2 \cos(\theta_2) \sum_{j=0}^{\infty} \rho_2 A_2 \int_0^{L_2} \phi_{2j}(x_2) dx_2 v_{2j} \\
&\quad + \left(\frac{\rho_2 A_2 L_1 L_2^2}{2} + m_e L_1 L_2^2 + m_e L_1 L_2 \right) \dot{\theta}_1^2 \sin(\theta_2)
\end{aligned}
\tag{50}
$$

3.2.3. Hardware Configuration

Figure 4 shows a schematic diagram of the experimental equipment. Motor 1 is TOYO TECHINICA DM-008D25F, motor 2 is maxon RE25 series 118752, encoder 1 is NEMICON 38H-4096-2MC and encoder 2 is NEMICON 18M-1024-2MC. The control program is written in C#. The command value calculated by the PC is DA-converted by PCI3521, then amplified twice by the buffer circuit and input to the servo amplifier. The voltage value is converted into a current value by the servo amplifier, and the current drives the motor to operate each link. The angle of each link is measured by capturing the number of pulses obtained from the encoder into a PC using the pulse counter board PCI6204.

3.2.4. Problem Setup

Human arm multi-joint viscoelasticity is,

- Elucidation of the motor control principle of the brain that controls complex multi-joint movements,
- Quantitative understanding of motor deterioration caused by nerve and muscle disorders,
- It is considered to be an important factor in the development of human-friendly mechanical interfaces, and many studies have been conducted up to now.

Among them, there are many studies on the estimation of human arm multi-joint viscoelasticity and there are few examples of application to mechanical interfaces as in the third entry. The challenge in applying it to machine interfaces is the reproduction of voluntary movement components. The voluntary movement component is a feed-forward component output from a model based on experience in the brain when exercising.

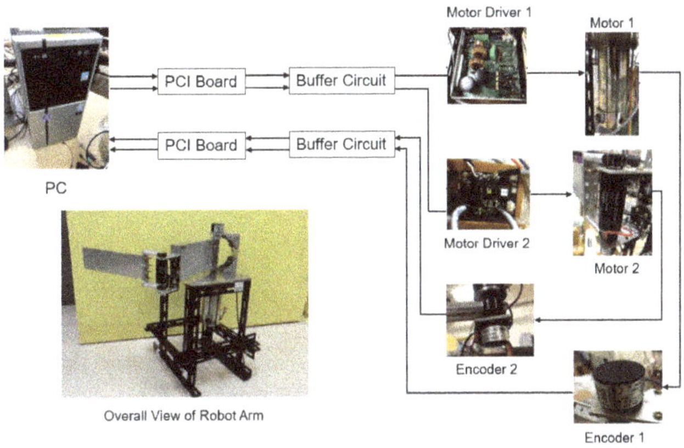

Figure 4. Proposed control system.

Humans suppress disturbances with feedforward controls composed of the cerebellum. It is believed that the body is controlled by a feedback controller. The voluntary movement component represents the above feedforward component, and the human arm multi-joint viscoelasticity represents the feedback component. In the research to actually estimate the multi-joint viscoelasticity of the human arm, the estimation is performed after removing the above voluntary movement components with a filter. Therefore, when applying the multi-joint viscoelasticity of the human arm to the motion control of the robot arm, it is indispensable to reproduce the voluntary motion component. In the previous research, the motion control of the robot arm by the two-degree-of-freedom control system has been introduced using multi-joint viscoelasticity. A feedforward controller based on a mechanical model has the advantage that it is easy to design if the modeling of the system is completed, but it is easily affected by modeling errors. It may cause deterioration of control performance when conducting an actual machine experiment. In fact, in this study as well, when a control experiment using a feedforward controller based on a mechanical model was conducted, good control results can not be obtained due to things that are not taken into consideration during modeling, such as the influence of the dead zone of the motor driver. Therefore, in this research, we propose a feedforward controller based on SVR, which is one of machine learning methods. SVR is an application of SVM to a regression problem, and has features such as high generalization performance and effectiveness for non-linear input/output relationships. In addition, by learning the input/output relationships of the entire system including the motor driver as training data, it is possible to create a model that includes modeling errors and parts that were not considered during modeling. In this research, we design a feedforward controller using SVR and confirm its effectiveness in actual machine experiments.

4. Control System Design

This section shows the proposed control system design method. Figure 5 shows the proposed control system. We design a two-degree-of-freedom control system by simulating the control system of the human body introduced in Section 3. The multi-joint viscoelasticity measured from humans is applied to the feedback controller C. The feedforward controller F based on SVR is also designed. In addition, in order to eliminate the influence and uncertainty due to interference inside the controlled object, the control system is designed based on the operator theory.

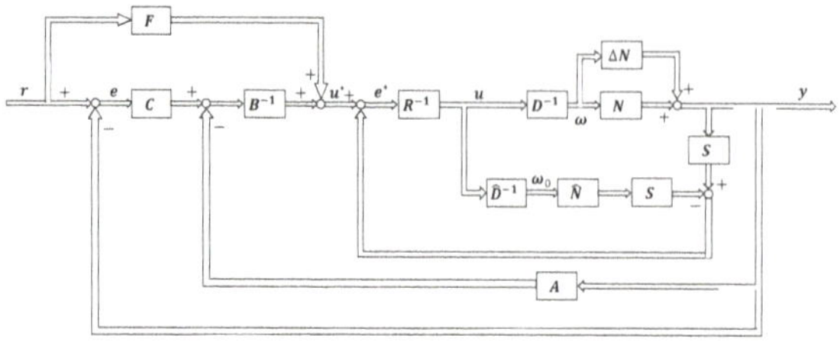

Figure 5. Block diagram of the proposed control system.

4.1. Controller Design Based on Multi-Joint Viscoelasticity

The follow-up controller C based on multi-joint viscoelasticity is shown by the following equation.

$$C(\mathbf{e}) = D\dot{\mathbf{e}} + \mathbf{Re} \tag{51}$$

R represents an elastic matrix and D represents a viscoelastic matrix. By applying this multi-joint viscoelastic matrix to a feedback controller, we aim to reproduce the same motion as humans. The elastic matrix and the viscosity matrix are 2-by-2 matrices and can be expressed as follows.

$$\begin{aligned} \mathbf{R} &= \begin{pmatrix} R_{11} & R_{12} \\ R_{21} & R_{22} \end{pmatrix} \\ \mathbf{D} &= \begin{pmatrix} D_{11} & D_{12} \\ D_{21} & D_{22} \end{pmatrix} \end{aligned} \tag{52}$$

The multi-joint human arm viscoelasticity used in this paper is shown in Figure 6. The combined movement of Link1 and Link2 produces translational movement, as shown in Figure 7.

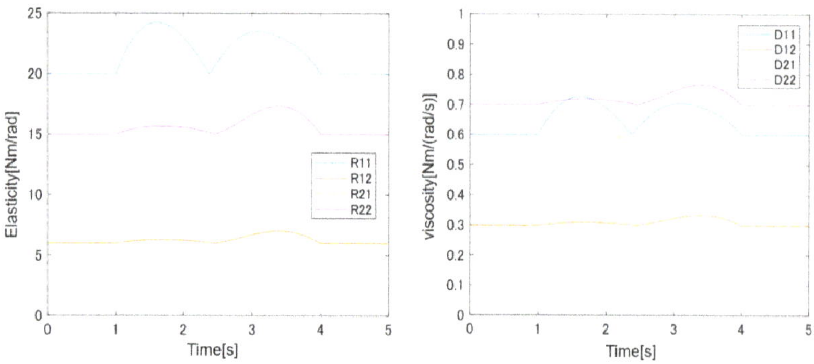

(**a**) Multi-joint human arm elasticity. (**b**) Multi-joint human arm viscosity.

Figure 6. Multi-joint human arm elasticity and viscosity.

4.2. Feedforward Controller Design Based on SVR

This section describes the design method of the feedforward controller based on SVR. Since SVR is one of the regression analysis methods, it is necessary to select training data. PD control is performed for the target trajectory used in the experiment in this study, and the input voltage applied to the motor driver of each link, the angle of each link and the angular velocity of each link at that time are measured as training data. The training data is shown in Figure 8.

SVR learning is performed based on the results shown in Figure 8. Since the angular velocity of link 2 was greatly affected by the measurement noise, the data filtered by the

RC filter was trained as training data. In addition, the controller to be designed calculates an appropriate input voltage for the target angle and angular velocity. Therefore, the input/output relationship of the data to be learned by the SVR is the angle and angular velocity at the input and the voltage at the output. Note that it is the opposite of the normal input/output relationship.

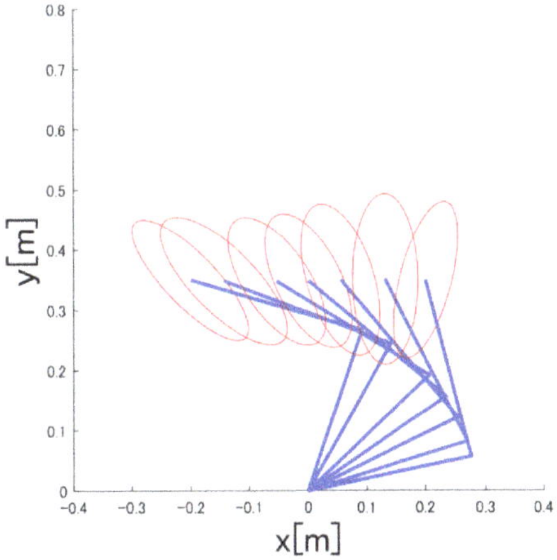

Figure 7. Multi-joint viscoelasticity.

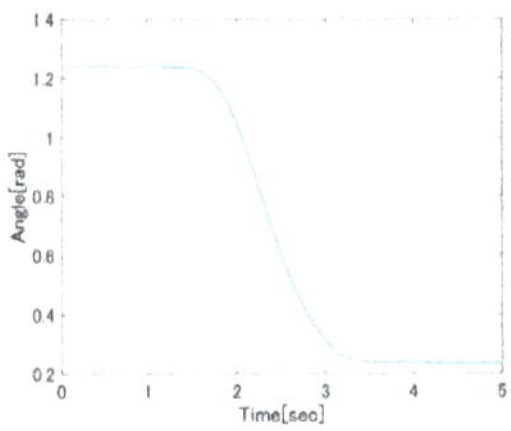

(**a**) Angle of link 1.

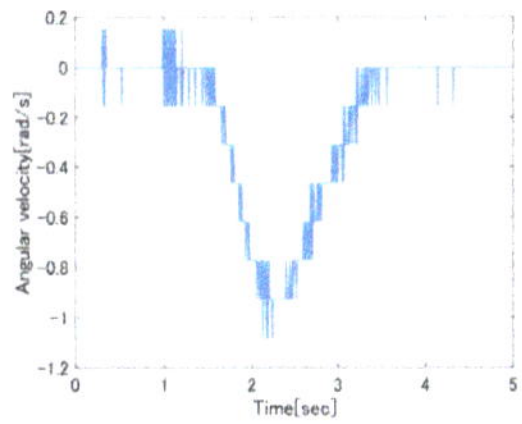

(**b**) Angular velocity of link 1.

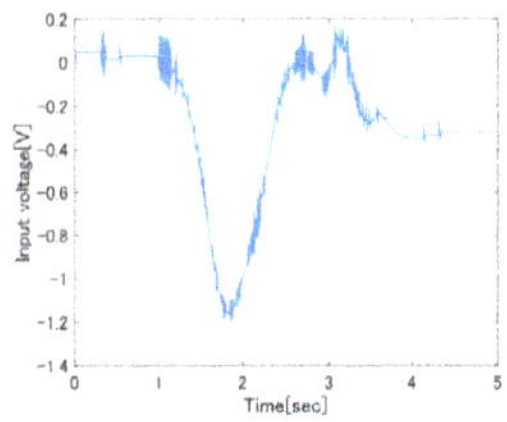

(**c**) Input voltage of link 1.

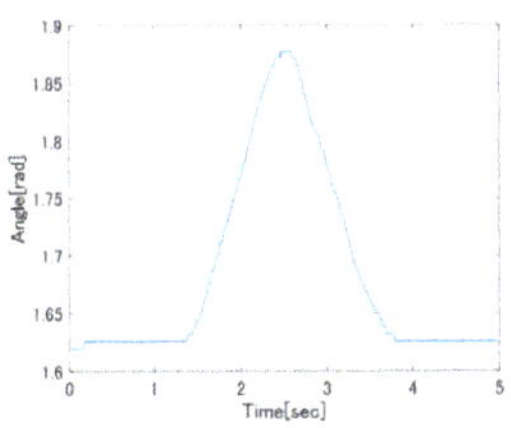

(**d**) Angle of link 2.

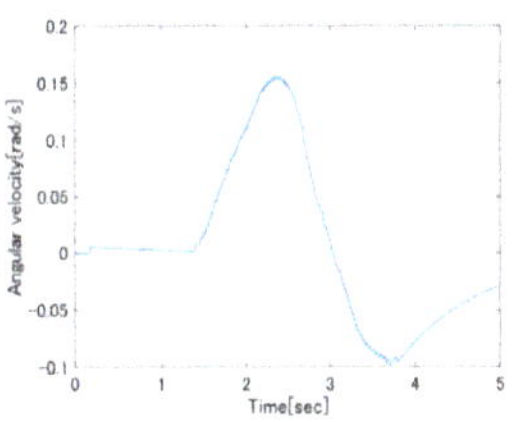

(**e**) Angular velocity of link 2.

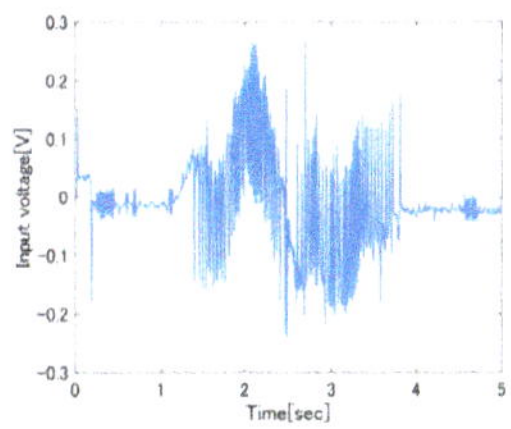

(**f**) Input voltage of link 2.

Figure 8. Training data of Link 1 and Link 2.

4.3. Control System Design Based on Operator Theory

4.3.1. Elimination of Uncertainty and Interference

The nominal model $\hat{P}$, which eliminates uncertainty and interference from other variables, can be expressed by the following equation.

$$\hat{P} = \begin{cases} \hat{m}_{11}\ddot{\theta}_1 + B_1\dot{\theta}_1 = \tau_1 \\ \hat{m}_{22}\ddot{\theta}_2 + B_2\dot{\theta}_2 = \tau_2 \end{cases} \quad (53)$$

Using this nominal model, the operators S and R are designed to eliminate the effects and uncertainties caused by interference inside the controlled object [13]. By designing the controllers S and R as $S\hat{P} = I$, $R = I$, the uncertainty of the model and the influence of interference inside the controlled object can be eliminated, where I is an identity map. The following equation holds from the nonlinear feedback system shown in Figure 5.

$$\begin{aligned} u^*(t) - S(y)(t) + S\hat{N}\hat{D}^{-1}(u)(t) &= R(u)(t) \\ u^*(t) &= S(y)(t) - S\hat{P}(u)(t) + R(u)(t) \\ &= \hat{P}^{-1}(y) \end{aligned} \tag{54}$$

At this time, $y(t) = \hat{P}(u)(t)$, which shows that the uncertainty of the model and the influence of interference inside the controlled object can be eliminated. Equivalent feedback loops before and after removing uncertainty and interference are shown in Figure 9.

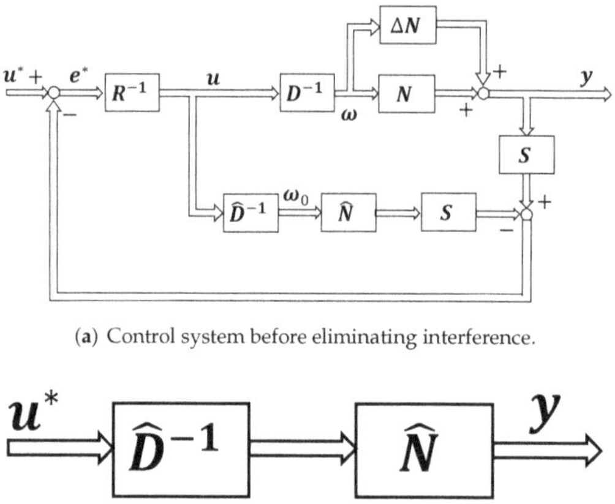

(**a**) Control system before eliminating interference.

(**b**) Control system after eliminating interference.

Figure 9. Control system before and after eliminating interference .

4.3.2. Guarantee of Stability

In this section, the control system is designed based on operator theory, and the stability of the proposed control system is guaranteed. Specifically, based on operator theory, we design stabilization controllers A and B^{-1} that satisfy the Bezout equation $A\hat{N} + B\hat{D} = I$. The right decomposition of the nominal plant $\hat{P}$ from which interference and uncertainty have been removed gives the following equation.

$$\hat{N} = \begin{cases} \hat{m}_{11}\ddot{y}_1 + B_1\dot{y}_1 = \omega_1 \\ \hat{m}_{22}\ddot{y}_2 + B_2\dot{y}_2 = \omega_2 \\ \theta_1 = y_1, \theta_2 = y_2 \end{cases} \tag{55}$$

$$\hat{D}^{-1} = \begin{cases} \omega_1 = \tau_1 \\ \omega_2 = \tau_2 \end{cases} \tag{56}$$

The parameters used are shown below.

$$\begin{aligned} \hat{m}_{11} &= I_s + I_{me} + I_e + m_e L_1^2 + \int_0^{L_1} \rho_1 A_1 x_1^2 dx_1 \\ &+ \int_0^{L_2} \rho_2 A_2 \left\{ L_1^2 + x_2^2 + 2L_1 x_2 \right\} dx_2 \\ \hat{m}_{22} &= \int_0^{L_2} \rho_2 A_2 x_2^2 dx_2 \end{aligned} \tag{57}$$

Operator A is designed as follows:

$$A\hat{N} = kI \tag{58}$$

From the Bezout equation, B can be expressed as follows.

$$B = (1-k)\hat{D}^{-1} \tag{59}$$

k is a design parameter. By constructing a nonlinear feedback system as shown in Figure 9b using operators A and B, the BIBO stability of the control system can be guaranteed.

5. Experiment

In this section, in order to confirm the effectiveness of the proposed control system, we verify it with an experimental device.

5.1. Experimental Conditions

Table 2 shows the parameters of the experimental equipment. The initial angle and target angle are the same as the angles used when the multi-joint viscoelasticity estimation was performed. Also, the sampling time was set to 0.01 s.

Table 2. Laboratory equipment parameters.

ρ_1	Link1 density	8030 kg/m^3
ρ_2	Link2 density	8030 kg/m^3
L_1	Link1 length	0.2 m
L_1	Link2 length	0.2 m
A_1	Link1 cross-sectional area	127.5 mm^2
A_2	Link2 cross-sectional area	25 mm^2
I_s	Moment of inertia of rotor	7.33×10^{-6} kg·m^2
J_L	Moment of inertia of set collar	8.71×10^{-9} kg·m^2
J_m	Moment of inertia of rotor	1.08×10^{-6} kg·m^2
$E_2 I_2$	Flexural rigidity of the arm	359 N·m^2
C_1	Attenuation coefficient	1.88×10^{-5}
B	Viscous friction coefficient	2.1×10^{-3} N·s/m
K_{t1}	Torque constant of motor 1	0.38 N·m/A
K_{t2}	Torque constant of motor 2	0.0234 N·m/A

5.2. Selection of Hyperparameters of SVR

In this section, we select the hyperparameter c of SVR. There are three hyperparameters in SVR, and it is known that the regression model changes depending on the parameters. In this research, we focus on c among hyperparameters, experiment by changing the value of c step by step, and select the parameter with the best result. As the content of the experiment, for the proposed control system, only the hyperparameter c of the feedforward controller based on SVR is changed to 0.01, 0.05, 0.1, 1, 7, 10, and 100, and the experiment is performed. After that, the error between the experimental result and the target value is derived and evaluated by RMSE (root mean squared error). RMSE is expressed by the following equation.

$$\mathrm{RMSE} = \sqrt{\frac{1}{n}\sum_{i=1}^{n}(f_i - y_i)^2} \tag{60}$$

Since the closer the RMSE is to 0, the smaller the error is, we select the hyperparameter c that minimizes the RMSE. The RMSE changes with different values of c, shown as Table 3. The experimental results are shown in Figure 10. Looking at the result of link 2, we can see that the control result changes depending on the value of hyperparameter c. When $c = 100$, it can be seen from Figure 10 that a large overshoot occurs. If c is set to a large value, SVR is closer to the hard margin. While it is possible to create an accurate regression model that reflects most of the training data, it has the characteristic that noise during training data measurement is easily reflected in the regression model. Therefore, when a large value such as $c = 100$ is set, a regression model that reflects the measurement noise contained in the training data is created, and it is considered that the overshoot shown in Figure 10a occurred. On the other hand, it can be confirmed that when c is made smaller, the above overshoot decreases and almost disappears at the time of $c = 0.1$. It can be seen that when c is set to 0.1 or less, a slight delay occurs at the time of 3s to 4s due to the effect of the output from the SVR controller becoming smaller. Since the value of $c = 0.1$ is also the minimum in the evaluation of RMSE, the c of link 2 is set to 0.1 in this study. For link 1, c is selected as 0.1 in the same way as link 2.

Table 3. RMSE results with different value of c.

The Value of c	RMSE (Link 1)	RMSE (Link 2)
100	0.0263	0.0263
10	0.0214	0.0166
7	0.206	0.0131
1	0.0200	0.0108
0.1	0.0188	0.0065
0.05	0.0226	0.0069
0.01	0.0250	0.0085

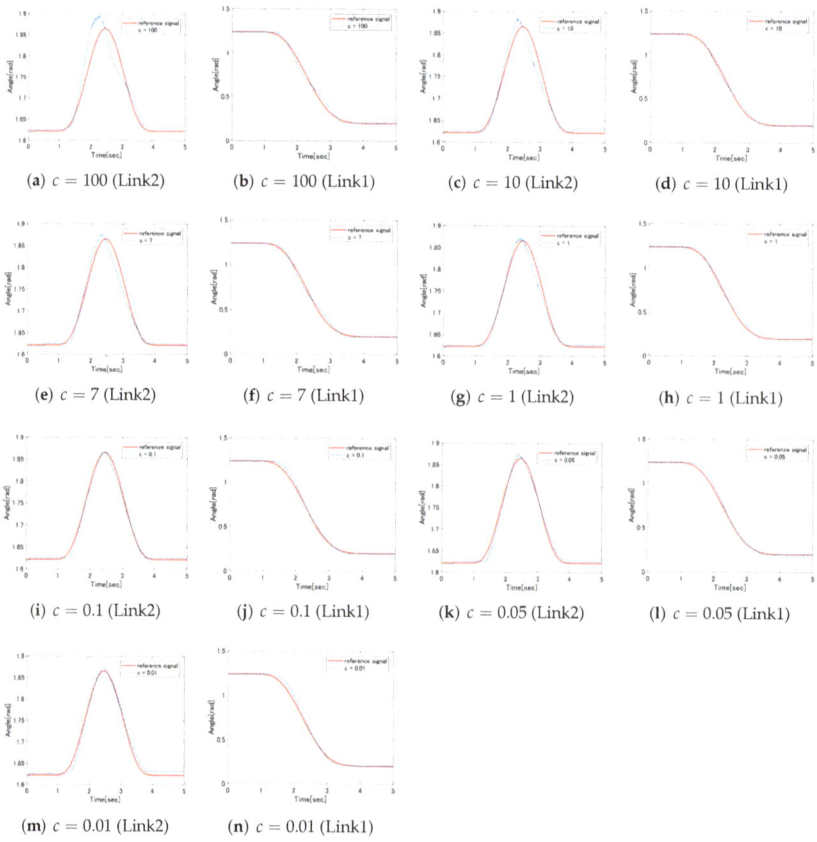

(**a**) $c = 100$ (Link2) (**b**) $c = 100$ (Link1) (**c**) $c = 10$ (Link2) (**d**) $c = 10$ (Link1)

(**e**) $c = 7$ (Link2) (**f**) $c = 7$ (Link1) (**g**) $c = 1$ (Link2) (**h**) $c = 1$ (Link1)

(**i**) $c = 0.1$ (Link2) (**j**) $c = 0.1$ (Link1) (**k**) $c = 0.05$ (Link2) (**l**) $c = 0.05$ (Link1)

(**m**) $c = 0.01$ (Link2) (**n**) $c = 0.01$ (Link1)

Figure 10. The experimental results.

5.3. Experimental Results

In this section, we conduct experiments to confirm the effectiveness of the proposed control system and introduce the results. Specifically, in order to confirm the effectiveness of the proposed SVR-based feedforward controller, it is effective to compare the experimental results of the feedforward controller based on the dynamic model without the feedforward controller with the experimental results of the proposed method. In addition, the control systems other than the feedforward controller are the same, and the performance of the feedforward controller is compared. Figure 7 shows the elastic ellipsoid of the hand calculated from the multi-joint viscoelasticity used in the feedback controller. As in the previous section, RMSE is used for comparison of experimental results, and the best result is the experimental result with the smallest RMSE. Table 4 shows the RMSE results.

Table 4. RMSE results.

FF Controller	RMSE (Link 1)	RMSE (Link 2)
None	0.0271	0.0142
Mechanical model	0.0273	0.0136
SVR	0.206	0.0174

Figure 11 shows a comparison of the control results between the feedforward controller without the feedforward controller and the feedforward controller based on the dynamic model. In the result of link 2, it can be confirmed that the tracking performance is improved from 2.5 s to 3 s . The result of RMSE is also smaller in the feedforward controller based on the dynamic model than in the case without the feedforward controller, and the effectiveness of the feedforward controller can be confirmed. On the other hand, for Link 1, no significant improvement is seen in the control results, and the analysis results by RMSE did not change much. The cause is thought to be the error that occurred during modeling.

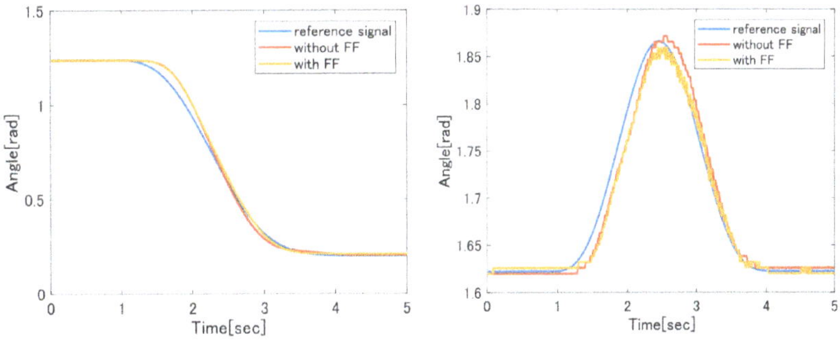

(**a**) link 1. (**b**) link 2.

Figure 11. Comparison of FF without controller and dynamic model with FF controller.

Figure 12 shows a comparison of the control results between the feedforward controller without the feedforward controller and the feedforward controller based on SVR. It can be confirmed that the tracking performance is improved for both link 1 and link 2. The analysis result by RMSE is also smaller in the feedforward controller based on SVR than in the case without the feedforward controller, and the effectiveness of the feedforward controller can be confirmed.

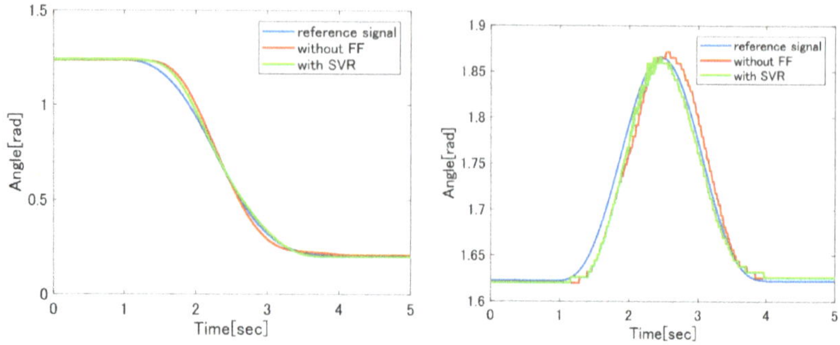

(**a**) link 1. (**b**) link 2.

Figure 12. Comparison of FF without controller and SVR FF with controller.

Figure 13 shows a comparison of the control results of the feedforward controller without the feedforward controller, the feedforward controller based on the dynamic model and the feedforward controller based on the SVR. Comparing the control results of the feedforward controller based on the dynamic model and the feedforward controller based on SVR, it is confirmed that the feedforward controller based on SVR follows the target value more for both link 1 and link 2. The RMSE value is also lower in the feedforward controller based on SVR, and it can be seen that the feedforward controller based on SVR has better tracking performance numerically. It is considered that this is because it was possible to create a model closer to the experimental equipment by creating a model from the training data of the actual machine experiment using SVR.

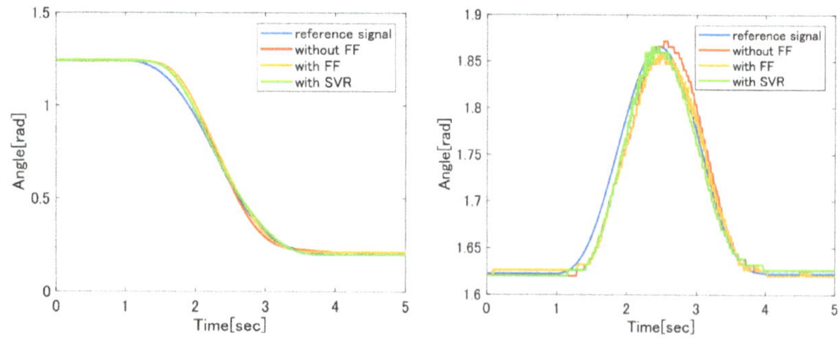

(**a**) link 1. (**b**) link 2.

Figure 13. Comparison of all control results.

Figure 14 shows the target value of the hand position coordinates and the actual output. With the proposed control system, we are able to confirm the follow-up of the hand. From the above, we are able to verify the effectiveness of the feedforward controller based on the proposed SVR method in actual machine experiments.

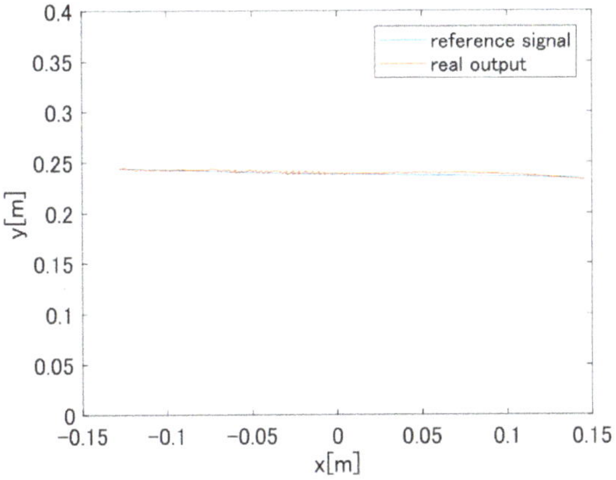

Figure 14. Multi-joint arm movement trajectory.

6. Conclusions

In this study, we propose a two-degree-of-freedom control system using multi-joint viscoelasticity, and conduct a motion control experiment of a two-link robot arm. Focusing on the feedforward controller in the two-degree-of-freedom control system, we propose a feedforward controller based on SVR, which is one of machine learning methods. Finally, the effectiveness of the proposed method is verified by an actual machine experiment. The controller is designed as a multi-joint arm like one and it is based on the characteristic of the human arm multi-joint viscoelasticity. The characteristic is analyzed from the experiment.

In the future, some intelligent control as well as adaptive control methods [28–30] can be considered to further improve the current work.

Author Contributions: Data curation, S.K.; Investigation, S.K.; Methodology, M.D.; Software, S.K.; Supervision, M.D.; Validation, S.K.; Writing, original draft, Y.X. All authors have read and agreed to the published version of the manuscript.

Funding: This research received no external funding.

Institutional Review Board Statement: Not applicable.

Informed Consent Statement: Not applicable.

Data Availability Statement: Data are not publicly available due to privacy considerations.

Conflicts of Interest: The authors declare no conflict of interest.

References

1. Hogan, N. Impedance Control: An approach to manipulation. *J. Dyn. Syst. Meas. Control* **1985**, *107*, 1–24. [CrossRef]
2. Kearney, R.E.; Hunter, I.W. Dynamics of human ankle stiffness: Variation with displacement amplitude. *J. Biomech.* **1982**, *15*, 753–756 . [CrossRef]
3. Gomi, H.; Kawato, M. Equilibrium-point control hypothesis examined by mesured arm-stiffness during multijoint movement. *Science* **1996**, *272*, 117–120. [CrossRef] [PubMed]
4. Deng, M.; Teramura, Y.; Wang, A.; Yanou, A. Particle filter-based viscoelasticity estimation of human multi-joint arm. In Proceedings of the 18th World Congress of IFAC, Milano, Italy, 28 August–2 September 2011.
5. Deng, M.; Inoue, A.; Zhu, Q. An integrated study procedure on real time estimation of time varying multijoint human arm viscoelasticity. *Trans. Inst. Meas. Control* **2011**, *33*, 919–941. [CrossRef]
6. Deng, M.; Saijo, N.; Gomi, H.; Inoue, A. A robust real time method for estimating human multijoint arm viscoelasticity. *Int. J. Innov. Comput. Inf. Control* **2006**, *2*, 705–721.
7. Deng, M.; Inoue, A.; Gomi, H.; Hirashima, Y. Recursive filter design for estimating time varying multijoint arm viscoelasticity. *Int. J. Comput. Syst. Signal* **2006**, *7*, 2–18.

8. Deng, M.; Bu, N.; Yanou, A. Framework of an estimation algorithm of time varying multijoint human arm viscoelasticity. In Proceedings of the 3rd International Conference on Bio-inpsired Systems and Signal Processing, Valencia, Spain, 20–23 January 2010.
9. Gomi, H.; Kawato, M. Human arm stiffness and equilibrium-point trajectory during multi-joint movement. *Biol. Cybern.* **1997**, *76*, 163–171. [CrossRef] [PubMed]
10. Kataguchi, T.; Deng, M.; Noge, Y. Online Human Multi-joint Arm's Viscoelasticity Estimation during Movement. In Proceedings of the 2019 International Conference on Advanced Mechatronic Systems, Kusatsu, Japan, 26–28 August 2019.
11. Wang, A.; Deng, M. Operator-based robust nonlinear tracking control for a human multi-joint arm-like manipulator with unknown time-varying delays. *Appl. Math. Inf. Sci.* **2012**, *6*, 459–468.
12. Gomi, H.; Konno, T. Real time estimation of time-varaying human multijoint arm viscoelasticity during movement. In Proceedings of the 20th Annual International Conference of the IEEE Engineering in Medicine and Biology Society, Hong Kong, China, 29 October–1 November 1998.
13. Wang, A.; Deng, M. Robust nonlinear multivariable tracking control design to a manipulator with unknown uncertainties using operator-based robust right coprime factorization. *Trans. Inst. Meas. Control* **2013**, *35*, 788–797. [CrossRef]
14. Vladimir, N.V. *Statistical Learning Theory*; John Wiley Sons: Hoboken, NJ, USA, 1998.
15. Jiang, L.; Deng, M.; Inoue, A. Obstacle Avoidance and Motion Control of a Two Wheeled Mobile Robot Using SVR Technique. *Int. J. Innov. Comput. Inf. Control* **2009**, *5*, 253–262.
16. Cristianini, N.; Shawe-Taylor, J. *An Introduction to Support Vector Machines and Other Kernel-Based Learning Methods*; Cambridge University Press: Cambridge, UK, 2000.
17. Cherkassky, V.; Mulier, F. *Learning from Data: Concepts, Theory, and Methods*; Wiley-IEEE Press: Hoboken, NJ, USA, 1998.
18. LIBSVM—A Library for Support Vector Machines. Available online: http://www.csie.ntu.edu.tw/cjlin/libsvm/ (accessed on 12 April 2011).
19. Deng, M. *Operator-Based Nonliner Control Systems Design and Applications*; Wiliy-IEEE Press: Hoboken, NJ, USA, 2014.
20. Deng, M.; Inoue, A.; Ishikawa, K. Operator-based nonlinear feedback control design using robust right coprime factorization. *IEEE Trans. Autom. Control* **2006**, *51*, 645–648. [CrossRef]
21. Furukawa, K.; Deng, M. Operator based Fault Detection and Compensation Design of an Unknown Multivariable Tank Process. In Proceedings of the 2013 International Conference on Advanced Mechatronic Systems, Luoyang, China, 25–27 September 2013.
22. Umemoto, K.; Matsuno, F.; Deng, M. Control system design for nonlinear uncertain plants using robust right coprime factorization. In Proceedings of the 12th Society of Instrument and Control Engineers, Control Department Competition, Akita, Japan, 20–23 August 2012.
23. Chen, G.; Han, Z. Robust right coprime factorization and robust stabilization of nonlinear feedback control systems. *IEEE Trans. Autom. Control* **1998**, *43*, 1505–1510. [CrossRef]
24. Bi, S.; Deng, M.; Xiao, Y. Robust Stability and Tracking for Operator-based Nonlinear Uncertain Systems. *IEEE Trans. Autom. Sci. Eng.* **2015**, *12*, 1059–1066. [CrossRef]
25. Feldman, A. Functional tuning of nervous system with control of movement or maintenance of a steady posture, II. Controllable parameters of the muscles. *Biophysics* **1966**, *11*, 565–578.
26. Feldman, A.G. Functional tuning of nervous system with control of movement or maintenance of a steady posture, II. Mechanographic analysis of execution by man of the simplest motor task. *Biophysics* **1966**, *11*, 766–775.
27. Cheol, H.; Choi, S. Position control of a two-link flexible manipulator featuring piezoelectric and sensors. *Mechatronics* **2001**, *11*, 707–729.
28. Tavoosi, J.; Shirkhani, M.; Abdali, A.; Mohammadzadeh, A.; Nazari, M.; Mobayen, S.; Bartoszewicz, A. A New General Type-2 Fuzzy Predictive Scheme for PID Tuning. *Appl. Sci.* **2021**, *11*, 10392. [CrossRef]
29. Tavoosi, J. Intelligent Model Predictive Control for Boiler Temperature. *Autom. Control Comput. Sci.* **2021**, *55*, 16–25. [CrossRef]
30. Mo, H.; Farid, G. Nonlinear and adaptive intelligent control techniques for quadrotor uav—A survey. *Asian. J. Control* **2019**, *21*, 989–1008. [CrossRef]

MDPI
St. Alban-Anlage 66
4052 Basel
Switzerland
Tel. +41 61 683 77 34
Fax +41 61 302 89 18
www.mdpi.com

Sensors Editorial Office
E-mail: sensors@mdpi.com
www.mdpi.com/journal/sensors

www.ingramcontent.com/pod-product-compliance
Lightning Source LLC
Chambersburg PA
CBHW041937260926
51850CB00018B/214
9783036581484